"Dedicated to all Italian vintners"

THE MODERN HISTORY OF ITALIAN WINE

edited by Walter Filiputti

Design
Marcello Francone

Editorial Coordination
Eva Vanzella

Editing
Emily Ligniti

Layout
Serena Parini

Iconographical Research
Massimo Zanella

Translations
Elizabeth Burke, Johanna Kreiner,
Jeremy Carden on behalf of NTL,
Florence

First published in Italy in 2016 by
Skira editore S.p.A.
Palazzo Casati Stampa
via Torino 61
20123 Milano
Italy
www.skira.net

Printed and bound in Italy. First edition

ISBN: 978-88-572-2623-1

Distributed in USA, Canada, Central &
South America by Rizzoli International
Publications, Inc., 300 Park Avenue
South, New York, NY 10010, USA.
Distributed elsewhere in the world
by Thames and Hudson Ltd., 181A
High Holborn, London WC1V 7QX,
United Kingdom.

Editorial Committee

Mario Busso
Walter Filiputti
Davide Rampello
Attilio Scienza
Angelo Solci

Texts by

Paolo Benvenuti *P.B.*
Rita Biasi *R.B.*
Mario Busso *M.B.*
Antonio Calò *A.C.*
Angela De Marco *A.D.M.*
Maurizio Di Robilant *M.D.R.*
Walter Filiputti *W.F.*
Michele Mannelli *M.M.*
Stefano Micelli *S.M.*
Michele Morgante *M.Mo.*
Luca Pedrotti *L.P.*
Cesare Pillon *C.P.*
Davide Rampello *D.R.*
Attilio Scienza *A.S.*
Roger Sesto *R.S.*
Angelo Solci *A.So.*
Raffaele Testolin *R.T.*
Diego Tomasi *D.T.*

With contributions by

Magda Antonioli
Gilberto Arru
Daniele Bartolozzi
Nicolas Belfrage
Ampelio Bucci
Angelo Carrillo
Tania Di Bernardo
Umberto Gambino
Piera Genta
Paolo Ianna
Alberto Mattiacci
Riccardo Modesti
Bernardo Pasquali
Jens Priewe
Guido Ricciarelli
Franco Santini
Alma Torretta

We also thank
Rosita, Angela and Luca Missoni

Contents

PART THREE

**The Geography
of Italian Wine**

Luigi Veronelli:
"The Philosopher of Italian Wine"

Walter Filiputti

What can truly remain for us as people depends on our ideas, on the contribution that our thoughts can make to the world. In Phaedo, *when his students invited him not to drink the hemlock or to drink it slowly to delay death, Socrates – convicted for impiety, in other words, for not believing in the gods – refused, explaining that death would not prevent his soul from surviving anyway. And for Socrates, the soul is represented by his ideas, which are immortal and in fact have come all the way down to us.*

From an interview with Umberto Veronesi, in *Corriere della Sera*, 30 December 2012, insert in "La Lettura"

L uigi Veronelli was the philosopher of the "renaissance of Italian wine", the man who designed the architecture of thought and popularized it. He was a philosopher, scholar, journalist and author of about 200 works on wine and food, some of which are fundamental (his Bolaffi wine catalogues; the still unsurpassed *Guide Veronelli all'Italia piacevole*, published by Garzanti in 1968). He created a new language of wine, as Gianni Brera did for sports (in fact, they were very good friends). It was a dry, sometimes scathing, language – basic, but exciting.

I met him when I was a boy, the day he left the house on Via degli Alerami in Milan to move to upper Bergamo and the extraordinary residence that once belonged to Gustavo Testa, Cardinal and Apostolic Nuncio of Pope John XXIII. He greeted me with the dregs of a very old (and delicious) bottle of port and two small pieces of bread. "This is all that was left in this house," he said apologetically. I was first won over by the fact that he put off the move for an hour while waiting for me, and then by his ability to give and engage. From that day forward, we had a partnership that turned into a close friendship that continued until his death. Anywhere in Italy, he had a way of surrounding himself with hosts of winemakers – friends who adored him. Vintners whom he defended and exalted and with whom he shared his thoughts, his vision of the future of Italian wine. He not only showed them how to sell and later how to market them, he also made a significant contribution to giving the right economic value to wines (one should pay for quality) while at the same time enhancing the concept of the vineyard to distinguish itself in a market that would become increasingly jaded. One of his memorable battles was against Law 930 of 12 July 1963 that established the DOC (Denomination of Controlled Origin) in Italy, and whose speaker was Senator Desana, with whom Veronelli had fierce verbal confrontations. The truth was that Gino (as his friends called him) immediately understood the limits of the new law and denounced them forcefully. One of his broad criticisms was published in the opening pages of the first *Catalogo Bolaffi dei vini del mondo* in 1968. He soon proved to be right. In the early 1970s – in opposition to that platform of newborn DOCs that Gino called "myopic" – the "table wines" were born, wines that on national and foreign markets were soon placed above those same DOCs. He was inspired by his thought that, at the time, names of wines that identified with the vineyard, and the territory, were beginning to appear on labels.

His struggle to achieve wine-territory identification was prescient: he sensed its strategic power – both in the market and communications and what we call sustainability today – even in the late 1960s.

He became the de facto spokesman for winemakers, small vintners in particular, with whom he had a sort of exchange: he gave them ideas and visions for the future and from them he drew the spiritual lifeblood that exalted his free-fighting spirit.

What is described above is an oversimplification of the many reasons that led us to begin this work with Luigi Veronelli (his name will appear numerous times); of course, Italian winemakers were the material authors of the renaissance, inasmuch as the miracle of Italian wine is the result of the intuitions, the courage, the huge sacrifices and economic risk-taking of their healthy ambitions.

Here it seemed sacrosanct to us, especially for those who never had the privilege of knowing Gino, to open this publication with the person to whom all Italian wine owes so very, very much.

His ideas have given him the gift of immortality.

The Reason behind the Work

Walter Filiputti

The idea of writing a modern history of Italian wine materialized while I was holding the "Linguaggio e comunicazione sul vino" (Wine Language and Communication) course for oenology students at the School of Agriculture in Milan.

Almost fearfully, I told a small group of friends that, like me, they had been living this history right from their beginnings, albeit from other perspectives: Angelo Solci, an oenologist and owner with his brother Piero of one of the most important wine shops in Milan; Mario Busso, writer and editor of texts on oenogastronomy who, in recent years, created the first guide to autochthonous Italian wines; Davide Rampello, historian of material culture; and Attilio Scienza, professor of viticulture at the School of Agriculture in Milan. Besides myself who came to wine as a sommelier in the earliest days, then a winemaker, oenological consultant and scholar of what the world of wine, food and agriculture has been able to produce.

We liked the idea. We agreed that there was a historical and cultural gap to fill. Then came the meeting with the publisher Skira, whose President, Massimo Vitta Zelman, was immediately enthusiastic about the project. With Busso, Rampello, Scienza and Solci we created the editorial committee, which completed the initial idea.

The modern history of Italian wine, which began to take shape in the late 1960s and early 1970s, is the finest page ever written by our agriculture.

It gave birth to the most important agrarian revolution of modern times, in a few years turning poor farmers into entrepreneurs whose bottles are now found worldwide. "Contadino" (peasant/farmer) was a derogatory term, sometimes used offensively. Until the 1970s, it was very difficult for a farm/peasant boy in the Friuli countryside, for example, to marry outside of his social class. They were considered labourers more than anything. Now, instead, that word has been re-

evaluated to such an extent that it can be used with pride, even privilege. And if the language reflects the changes, we can say that these were put in place by those farmers who Veronelli would have defined as winemakers at the time.

These aspects are well known, but would not have been enough to write this history.

What led us to write this work was our observation of how the wine sector has been able to create innovative models in every branch of the industry.

In communication, language and marketing strategies, a school of thought has been established that has gradually been adopted by other sectors, such as spirits, oil, cheese, coffee, chocolate, plus craft beer which is inspired by wine in both production (beer in *barriques*) and marketing techniques. This school of thought finds its true masterpiece in the management model: the family business, so derided by many, by too many influential economists also on the international level. It is no coincidence then that the history opens with the enlightening chapter by an economist, Stefano Micelli, presenting the history of Italian wine: "The Lesson of Wine".

Its capacity for innovation was momentous, as was its capacity to believe in science and research, with a fervour that could be defined as an Enlightenment. In fact, oenology's conquest – combined with entrepreneurial courage – was the key to success. In the late 1960s, bad oenology reigned, and easily and without investment it managed production processes aided by chemistry, without worrying about consumer health. As early as the mid-1970s, the arrival of cold technology, supported by a new awareness of respect for public health, laid the groundwork for *mechanical oenology or knowledge*, which produced and continues to produce wines that have never been so healthy or of such quality. That was the moment in which the seed of sustainability was germinated, contributing, among other things, to the growth of an industry of winemaking machines, which today is a world leader.

Another gem is the conquest of international markets, particularly the American one, which brought us up against a hitherto unknown way of doing business, and Robert Mondavi was a master at it. He was a model for us. He taught us that we had to be open and fearless. We had to take chances. We had to open our cellars to the consumer: there was noth-ing to hide, and everything to show. Mondavi taught us that it would be the market comparisons, sometimes very harsh, that would make us grow. And that is exactly what happened, and in this we were also helped by the fact that many of them were those immigrants who had opened restaurants: they proved to be strategic for our successes.

Before the DOC law in 1963, the production of Italian wine was in the hands of a few dealers. They mocked the "peasant-farmers", those who insisted on investing in the vineyard. Those dealers were defeated.

But another reason for writing this history was that of giving young people entering the fascinating world of wine a starting point. To tell them about the foundations on which the fortune of a sector was built; it is now a driving sector, but one that up until 1970 did not count for much. We wrote it to help people understand how those insights, that courage, those visions need to be constantly nurtured. Italian wine needs young people to rejuvenate the dream.

Finally, we are more than convinced that wine can become the model for a possible economic, cultural and commercial rebirth in agriculture. The entrepreneurship of wine – which witnessed many very brave farmers take huge risks alongside the very first visionaries – represents a continuum of the spirit that drove the economic boom of post-war Italy.

The following is a history of labour and creativity that is all Italian, something to be proud of.

PART ONE **The Renaissance
of Italian Wine**

The Lesson of Wine

Stefano Micelli

In vino veritas

The world of economics has long considered agriculture to be a lesser topic of study – marginal, entrusted to the attention of few specialists. The production and consumption models that over the last century have contributed to transforming Western society have taken shape in very diverse sectors. We often talk about the paradigm of mass production through the expression "Fordism", because the automobile industry has transformed production logic, as well as ways of consuming, to organize communication through such media as TV, radio and national newspapers, up to policies and social representation. We speak of Fordism because few things like the assembly line in the automobile production system have marked a sea change in the very idea of labour.

Over the last thirty years, the emergence of new technologies has emphasized a major break with the logic of production inherited from the second industrial revolution. Computers and networks have allowed for acceleration in globalization of the economy and society, shifting the focus onto knowledge as a key resource for economic development. In a relatively short time, manufacturing has also been quickly relegated to the area of marginal activities. Production has become a trivial activity, because emerging economies have inevitably begun to bear the brunt of this task, taking charge of managing low-cost manufacturing, perhaps not necessarily of the best quality, but certainly competitive in terms of price. Not only the agriculture sector appeared to more obsolete, but also manufacturing as a whole was little more than a cumbersome legacy of the past. It certainly was not from these two sectors – this was the common feeling – that we would have drawn inspiration and impetus to look to the future.

After the great crisis of 2008, the effects of which lasted for five years in countries like Italy, we now have a different view of the changes underway. The world has changed. Emerging economies have rapidly become superpowers. International trade has shifted its centre of gravity, moving quickly to the east. The demographic profile of the European coun-

Wine production worldwide
(hl/millions)
Source: www.inumeridelvino.it
OIV (Organismo Italiano di
Valutazione) data

	2006	2007	2008	2009	2010	2011	2012 E	2013 E	2014 E
France	52.1	45.7	42.7	46.3	44.4	50.8	41.5	42.0	46.2
Italy	52.0	46.0	47.0	47.3	48.5	42.8	45.6	54.0	44.4
Spain	38.1	34.8	35.9	36.1	35.4	33.4	31.1	45.7	41.6
Germany	8.9	10.3	10.0	9.2	6.9	9.1	9.0	8.4	9.3
Portugal	7.5	6.1	5.7	5.9	7.1	5.6	6.3	6.3	6.2
Romania	5.0	5.3	5.2	6.7	3.3	4.1	3.3	5.1	4.1
United States	19.4	19.9	19.3	22	20.9	19.1	21.7	23.6	21.1
Australia	14.3	9.6	12.4	11.8	11.4	11.2	12.3	12.5	12.0
Argentina	15.4	15.0	14.7	12.1	16.3	15.5	11.8	15.0	15.2
Chile	8.4	8.3	8.7	10.1	8.8	10.5	12.6	12.8	10.5
South Africa	9.4	9.8	10.2	10.0	9.3	9.7	10.6	11.0	11.3
Others	52.6	55.2	58.0	54.7	52.1	55.5	52.1	55.5	56.9
Total	**283.1**	**266.0**	**269.8**	**272.2**	**264.4**	**267.3**	**257.9**	**291.9**	**278.8**

tries does not seem to give a chance to the economies of societies that are too old and anchored to the past to take on the challenges of the future. What we called *crisis* has quickly become a depressing *new normal*, without there being visible references for a different quality of growth.

It is precisely in this context that considering one of the most typical products of Italian culture takes on a different meaning. In recent years, the wine industry has given some major and very satisfying results for the nation's economy, showing great vitality despite the country's general crisis. It is not a case of today recognizing the vindication of a sector that has long been poorly treated: what is at stake is more important than that. What happened in the wine industry in recent years, especially in Italy, was something profound and meaningful. Various factors have contributed to these transformations: growth strategies developed by our vintners, a competent demand that helps to increase the quality of the product, substantially effective regulations that have created certification of provenance and reliable quality, a thriving relationship between production and territory, an original and never trivial bond with tourist hospitality and an architecture that has been able to make the most of the places of work. Today, all these aspects are not merely the features of great economic success, but, more generally, a lesson to learn from in order to tackle the challenge of the *new normal* which is forcing us into the deeply transformed international context. It is

well worth studying this lesson carefully, as well as its protagonists, to conceive of wine as one of the cornerstones of a truly innovated idea of economics.

More Value, Smaller Quantities (Finally A Happy Decrease)

Looking at wine figures, especially if you look at the Italian market, you will be astonished. Over the last decade, the volumes of production and consumption have declined steadily.

In absolute terms, Italian production (in quantity) has experienced a substantial decrease, as happened in other European countries. In 2006, Italy produced more than 50 million hectolitres per year (about the same as France, 25% more than Spain); in 2011, the production volume dropped to fewer than 45 million hectolitres.

In the European scenario, this decline was not an isolated case. A similar trend was seen in France and Portugal. Spain, by contrast, was able to expand its production base, reaching the threshold of 40 million hectolitres. With respect to the international scenario, the decline is something of an exception: all the major non-European producers increased their production capacity, exceeding the threshold of 10 million hectolitres in the case of Chile and South Africa.

As for consumption, Italy experienced a similar decline. For different reasons, ranging from a significant change in lifestyle to a change in regulations with regard to alcohol con-

Per capita consumption
Source: www.inumeridelvino.it

Wine consumption, production,
exportation, importation in Italy
(hl/thousands)
Source: ISTAT data

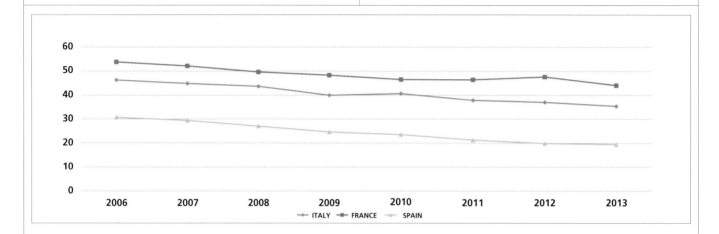

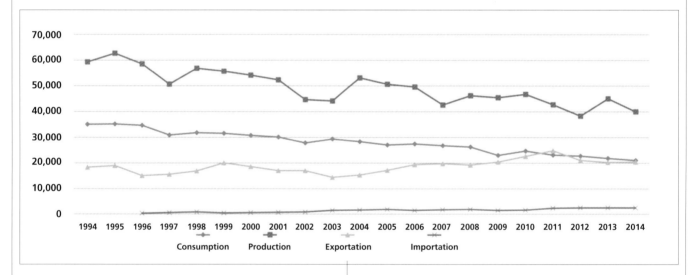

sumption when driving, over a decade the consumption of
wine went from more than 45 litres per capita to just over 35.
The same negative trend was seen in two other Mediterranean
countries in Europe, namely France and Spain.

In the face of declining numbers in terms of quantity,
substantial growth was recorded in the value generated by
the sector, particularly in the area of exports. Italian wine
continues to grow on the international markets, demonstrating an increasingly greater quality and appreciation. It
is true that we produce less, but we produce better wine. And
the world recognizes this fact by assigning a significant *premium price* to our wines, and this coincides with a significant growth of average unit values in exports. Ten years ago,
a litre of wine cost 20% less than the average bottle that we

now offer to the international market. In the case of *spumanti* or sparkling wines, this growth and this capacity to impose
a new value for the international consumer are even greater.
In this sector, which is quickly expanding, the growth can
be seen in the annual statistics. In this case, they tell us that
for a bottle of Italian sparkling wine, the international consumer gives it a value that is 20% higher than the previous
year.

In short, we produce less in terms of quantity, but we produce greater value. This improves its international competitiveness, opening it up to an international community that
appreciates the quality of the product. The winemaking sector represents a truly successful example of decreasing production, one of the few cases where a country with a very spe

2014 sales rank
Source: Mediobanca study
March 2015

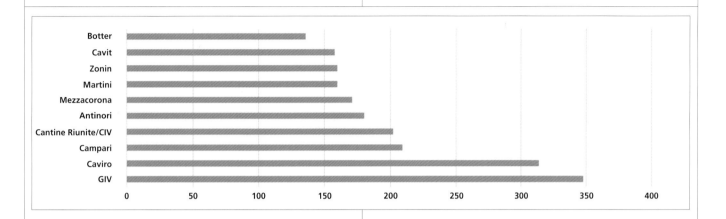

cific demographic and cultural profile faces a decline in volumes without sacrificing the compensation of this reduction with a quality production that safeguards the overall quality of the sector.

How did we arrive at this? From a chronological point of view, the scandal of methanol-spiked wine in the mid-1980s certainly marked a watershed in the culture of wine production. The scandal brought out all the limitations of a productive model aimed at efficiency and systematic reduction of costs: the story of Ciravegna, the main protagonists in the scandal, and the many victims of adulterated wine, showed the most pathological dimension of a growth trajectory that did not deserve to be travelled any further. The scandal of those years made it possible to change course quickly, because the sector had already developed its internal stirrings of a new culture on the supply side as well as on the demand side. This ferment evolved rapidly into successful experiments and initiatives that have won international visibility.

In the last thirty years, the evolution of the wine sector in Italy has reserved many surprises. It is truly worth closely exploring this world to understand what is really behind this success and the lesson of a sector which is in no way secondary.

Variety and Globalization

A look at the ranking of companies that drive the Italian wine sector, carefully prepared each year by Mediobanca, has two surprising aspects. On the one hand, a coexistence of different management models: in our country, cooperatives and privately held companies exist side by side. If we look at the growth trend that has marked the sector consolidation process in recent years, we see that there is no single winning model. Cooperatives, primarily IRP and Caviro, have shown over the years that they are able to keep up with private business models.

The industry appears to be characterized by a fragmentation that reflects a typical feature of the domestic industry, in other words, its limited size. It is certainly true that in the wine sector, as in other fields of the Italian economic sector, a platoon of medium-sized enterprises led by a capable management and projected onto the international market have been able to consolidate their position on a global scale, benefiting from the economic recovery that has characterized the American and Asian economies from 2010. In general, however, the average size of the businesses operating in the sector is contained: the sector proves to be competitive with a great variety of businesses that operate even below the 50 million euro mark. It is important to be able to count on leading businesses capable of growing internationally and promoting Italian products throughout the world. It is equally true, however, that Italian wine owes its success to a wide variety of growers whose turnover is more contained, from 10 to 50 million Euros, or growers that have shown themselves capable of holding to a perspective of international development by using original approaches to growth.

The great variety of Italian wines is mainly linked to the variety of the territories where the wines are produced. The discovery of local specificity has been an important differentiation factor over the years, and it is proving to be a strong

point in the marketplace. An international demand that is growing in terms of acculturation and spending capacity give value to this variety of supply also because it perceives its most authentic dimension. Italy is varied, and so are its wines.

Compared to other typical sectors of the Italian economy linked to the territory, wine has shown that the theme of local specificity does not imply "localism". The wine experience has highlighted how defending the *autochthonous* vine does not mean international closure, but rather international extroversion, dialogue with other cultures, the quest for legitimacy and comparison with other territories. It is important to emphasize that the enhancement of local specificity has always been accompanied by an experimentation and innovation that have maintained strong roots in the culture of belonging.

Moreover, the Italian wine producer has been able to use his abilities for innovating and refining the product, which is a deeply artisan product in the best sense of the term. He has taken a holistic view in the production process, preserving ancient techniques and blending them with innovative winemaking tools, and has constantly maintained a dialogue in

terms of demand (especially with restaurants) to have motivation and advice in return. This leaning toward continuous improvement has shaped a very wide audience of growers who know how to make unique products that are difficult to imitate, consolidating a variety that is unequalled in other countries.

The idea of territories and cultures that can speak to the world through the enhancement of their specificity underlies the process of preservation of economic values in the face of a decline in the quantity produced and consumed in the country. Behind – or rather, in – the bottles of Italian wines, we find a blend of tangible and intangible economy, a territorial culture of action-taking, which offers an idea of variety that other parts of the agri-food sector, and not only, are learning to experiment with.

The spread of the network as a means of consumer acculturation, dialogue and international trade could, already in the short term, be an element that strengthens this trend. In fact, the network makes it possible to construct a sophisticated story, through multimedia tools, based on dialogue and interaction, capable of transmitting the values and specificity of smaller vintners.

Workspaces as New Places of Communication

Some experts in business marketing have explained the concept of a brand with the idea of the stage curtain. The brand – this is the metaphor – serves to create a theatrical separation between public and stage. It divides the market in two: on the one side is the demand, and on the other, the production. The curtain serves to divert attention from the production process in the strictest sense, a process that in most cases neither reassures nor encourages the purchase by the end consumer. Modern factories have never been inviting places: working conditions, processes for transforming materials, the overall architecture of the spaces are all factors that have never provided the inspiration to open their doors to visitors and curious folk. Better to create an alternative ideal for consumers by designing images and slogans for them that could reassure and drive them to make the purchase.

Today, the factories that marked the beginnings of economic development, for the most part, no longer exist, at least in Europe. Curiosity surrounding the way that even the simplest goods are manufactured has grown enormously: it is no coincidence that there are even television shows that explain production processes of all kinds, from sports cars to leather handbags. And yet we are just at the beginning. It is difficult for production spaces to open up, because they were not designed as meeting places. Changing trajectory is hard work and requires a vision.

Surprisingly, one of the first sectors to open up and tell its story by way of the workplace and architecture was actually the world of wine. The project "Cantine Aperte" (Open Cellars) was a decade ahead of its time in terms of the trend of opening up work and production spaces for visits, and use by conferences and/or events. Opening up cellars meant removing the curtain that separates the time of consumption from that of production and betting on its capacity to tell of its identity and working methods to justify the product's value.

After more than twenty years since the launch of the days dedicated to "Open Cellars", it is easy to grasp how advanced this form of communication was. While manufacturing companies, which have relocated their production facilities en masse, come up against growing problems of legitimacy and, therefore, adopt codes for protecting the company's social responsibility, the cellars have actually opened up their spaces and are talking about who they are and how they operate. Now it is possible to travel around Italy getting to know the wineries, and often meeting families who open their homes to visitors, both experts and newcomers to the sector.

The success of the event has generated an important spin-off that has turned many of these wineries into true tourist attractions, helping to transform the way visitors get to know Italy. Today, there is an astonishing number of portals that contribute to directing visitors, indicating the destinations and ways to have access to these places. The wineries, in turn, have equipped themselves with inns and restaurants that give a more enriching and original flavour to the hospitality experience.

It is not surprising that the architecture of production spaces has been experiencing a significant development in this particular sector. The Italian pavilion at the Venice Architecture Biennale in 2012 proposed an entire range of amazing projects that have made wineries more or less famous places of special interest from the point of view of art and architecture. Of the 180 projects presented by the curator Luca Zevi, almost half were related to the wine sector, with a homogeneous distribution throughout the nation. And it is not simply a philological recovery of villas and castles offering the specificity of the territory from a historical point of view: if ever there were a sector that has effectively welcomed the idiom of contemporary architecture, it is certainly that of winemaking. An outstanding example is the extraordinary design of the Antinori cellars and offices which left the centrally located Via de' Tornabuoni in Florence to occupy a wonderful space between Siena and Florence. All in the name of contemporary design and environmental sustainability.

Creating a New Language to Tell the Story of Wine

On the YouTube portal there is a variety of available clips of television broadcasts that Veronelli launched to talk about the culture of food and wine in Italy. His duets with Ave Ninchi are still very pertinent and entertaining today, despite the fact that television has evolved dramatically. As early as the broadcasts of the 1970s there was a visible tendency toward the folktale approach that was, at the same time, far from trivial when it came to talking about the variety of flavours and their bond with regional cultures. The pleasure of cuisine was not simply a matter of taste, but rather, the point of access to many local cultures that had condensed lifestyles and values into recipes that deserved to be communicated to the public.

In the field of wine, Veronelli's effort was crucial: through his reviews, courses for sommeliers, television broadcasts and guides, Veronelli paved the way to making the variety of flavours the thing that would explicitly refer to cultural values. The determination with which Veronelli defended territorial specificity went hand in hand with the need to go far beyond the production of brands with certified provenance. Primarily, his effort produced a language. His polished terminology, and his passion for original, almost idiosyncratic Italian, made it possible to reveal the differences in aroma and taste that distinguish wines and vineyards.

One of Veronelli's great merits was that of having constructed a way to spread his idioms following concentric circles. By starting up sommelier courses, he provided the opportunity to create a new generation of experts who were able to convincingly describe the wine to customers in the restaurant business. Newspaper columns helped to spread a new language to a wider audience, a curious and attentive one, though not necessarily connoisseurs. This new language made it possible to describe increasingly complex and sophisticated wines, to focus on the differences in aroma and taste that had previously been left in the background. In economic terms, it gave value to a variety of products and territories that were otherwise difficult to understand.

Veronelli's lesson of thirty years ago can be read in the effort made by many wineries to develop through the network and new technologies. In fact, the network makes it possible to quickly retrace all the stages of wine through new tools. Virtual communities of consumers that bring together enthusiasts of all types, from sports fans to those with cultural interests, from the passion for travel to that for good food, make it possible to socialize in specific languages and spread knowledge related to specific topics. Television is no longer the only broadcaster available: videos, which can be easily uploaded, are replacing the broadcasts of yesteryear; blogs are an effective alternative to print media to keep fans informed on a spe-

cific theme; chat forums are a great way to start comparisons and debates.

The challenge for the wineries, as well as for many cultural institutions, is the same one as that launched by Veronelli: to build a language that gives meaning and value to variety. Without the right words, it is impossible to account for the differences. Without a suitable language, it is difficult to sustain the variety and especially the economic value that it produces.

Thanks to his extraordinary communication effort, Veronelli created the basis for a large community of consumers before the arrival of the Internet. His skill was that of giving a language not only to a new generation of winemakers and competent professionals, but also – and especially – to a large audience of enthusiasts who, for various reasons, over time became the new authorities of an increasingly careful and sophisticated consumer culture. Thanks to this initial effort, the work of organizations like Slow Food have been able to count on an intangible infrastructure that have proven especially valuable in consolidating a community at the international level and institutionalizing an increasingly ambitious economic and cultural movement for the future.

It is worth mentioning that Veronelli had a cultural background in the humanities. It was precisely his studies that allowed him to promote a new interpretation of the wine sector. His professional origins made it possible for him to relate to otherwise distant worlds: that of production and that of culture. This lesson is still as relevant as ever. The "Made in Italy" that imposed itself on the international markets is increasingly a product that combines manufacturing quality with clear cultural origins. Wine broadly anticipated this trend by making manifest the need for a sophisticated, but still accessible, language, shared by a growing demand that is increasingly attentive and aware. Veronelli's lesson, in particular, seems more timely than ever for all those who want to build their own Web marketing investment to assert their specificity.

Scientific Research, Tradition and Respect for Taste: A Unique Combination

In May 2013, Angelo Gaja, one of the most famous Italian winemakers, gave a keynote speech at Turin's Politecnico. The title of the lecture was surprising: "Engineering and Wine: Wi-fi for the Sustainability of Vineyards". The audience also had little to do with the agri-food sector. They were students of telecommunications engineering. In fact, Angelo Gaja was one of the forerunners of the use of digital technologies for the management of vineyards. Using a widespread network of sensors, he keeps track of the main parameters that characterize the life of the vineyard, providing valuable guidance for those who must optimize the crops: an example of "smart" agriculture that passes through an innovative use of the network.

However, Gaja's example is not a rarity. The wine sector in Italy has been developing cutting-edge technologies for years. Those who attend the SIMEI (International Oenological and Bottling Trade Fair) know the technological quality and the capacity for innovation that is typical of producers in this sector. From crushers to autoclaves, centrifugal bottling machines, wooden vats and bottles, SIMEI hosts all the products that are used to manage the supply chain for wine. Today, Italian operators are leaders in various key technologies in the production process, confirming that excellence is not only the product, but also the process.

As mentioned earlier, the initial push to this path of innovation brought on the crisis of methanol, a passage that marked the start of a new season of Italian wine. Methanol-spiked wine represented the final chapter of an excessive use of chemistry at the service of wine production. Innovation in winemaking machinery, in particular the management of the cold chain, was the real antidote to the abuse of chemicals in stabilizing wine fermentation processes. Italian technology producers have met the demands of winemakers and have initiated a process that allows for a considerable reduction in the use of chemicals in wine production, at the same time releasing a variety of scents and flavours that would otherwise be unthinkable.

The path taken by the wine sector has anticipated what happened in other Italian fields. In many sectors of so-called "Made in Italy", the manufacture of machinery has stayed abreast of the successes of products for the end consumer: Italy is now a leading country, after Germany, in mechanical engineering, thanks to a formidable ability for innovation in the upstream part of the supply chains that characterize our

industry. We were world leaders in the production of tiles, and today we are leaders in kilns for firing ceramics. We sold Venetian and Tuscan marble slabs, and today we are the world leaders in the production of machines for cutting marble. We produced jewellery in different districts, such as Vicenza or Valenza Po, and today we are leaders in machines that produce gold chains.

In the wine sector, to be honest, we have been able to do something that has proved to be more problematic in other areas. While in some cases the export of machinery coincided with a relative decline in the production of finished products for final consumption, with wine this cannibalism phenomenon has not happened. Thanks to the bond with culture and the territory, wine has maintained its specificity, which is independent of the technology that is now increasingly available on a global scale. We can also imagine more and more vineyards and wineries being wired and computerized. Today, wine is still a surprising combination of technology and passion, of analogue and digital, of science and experimentation by talented winemakers.

This two-fold excellence, linked to the ability to manage the market for capital goods and that of final consumption in a differentiated way, deserves to be explored and studied more thoroughly. In many sectors, the example of wine can become a useful indication in understanding how to keep different

processing methods competitive. The technology and culture of the product are ingredients that should be doled out in careful doses.

Another Idea of Entrepreneurship

The history of the Antinori family is inexorably linked to the history of Italian wine. The origins of this prestigious producer date to the late fourteenth century. Over the last century, Piero Antinori and his heirs have continuously experimented and innovated, bringing to market wines that have made the history of the sector. This vintner is all about the obsession with excellence and passion. The birth of Tignanello, in particular, was a key moment in the recent events of Italian wine. The wine made for the first time in 1971 by Piero Antinori entailed the exclusion of white grapes of Chianti Classico with the addition of Cabernet Sauvignon and ageing in *barriques*, thus leaving behind the historic regulation for Chianti DOC wines. For this reason, Tignanello lost the DOC and retained only the generic table wine indication until 1994 when it began to use the IGT designation (Typical Geographical Indication).

The history of Tignanello, like that of the other Super Tuscans and prestigious Italian "table wines", is the story of an ongoing process of experimentation and transformation that vies, also dialectically, with tradition and opens itself to the market. It is an emblematic story that recounts the efforts of so many entrepreneurs who were able to rethink the acquired rules and facts, betting on excellence and launching the Italian product onto the world.

You might say: "What's new about this? Successful entrepreneurs innovate. That's how you stay competitive on the international market." In fact, the lessons of the great entrepreneurs of Italian wine from Antinori to Gaja, from Masi to Jermann is different from a rhetoric of innovation by some proponents of the new digital economy. The way in which the world of wine has been able to shape and transform itself has characteristics that deserve to be carefully examined because today they are more relevant than ever.

Passion: a key ingredient in the history of Italian wine. You become an entrepreneur because you want to profit from your business ventures – this much is certain. But the wine sector, first and foremost, teaches us that excellence does not simply pass through the desire to conquer new market shares with low-cost products. The excellence of wine passes through the dedication and enthusiasm of entrepreneurs who are often obsessed with the idea of doing something important. Entrepreneurs who have deeply loved the area where they have lived. In their work, they found a source of satisfaction and commitment that goes far beyond the economic gain that they could derive from their businesses.

Time. The peculiarity of entrepreneurship in winemaking is also in the dimension of time. In winemaking, it is hard to think of rapid successes, and even more difficult to imagine a financial way out a few years from the launch of a product. Like Antinori, other Italian winemaking entrepreneurs sought excellence in their product, regardless of the goal of achieving short-term results. Wine is patience. To make good wine requires skill, luck and time. A lot of time. And sometimes the results arrive.

There is also another difference that is tied to the passion of doing. There are no *a priori* recipes for making the perfect wine. Of course, oenology studies and field experience are very useful. Scientific and technical research have made amazing strides, providing information that is particularly useful to those who work in the field. That said, to make a good wine one has to try and get their hands dirty. One must accept the challenge of a raw material that changes, which is affected by the seasons and the air. By processes that, to the extent that is known, have secrets that can only be revealed through practice and experimentation in the field.

Today, international journals talk incessantly about the third industrial revolution and a revival of the manufacturing sector. New technologies that link the digital production processes and a new generation of intelligent products, according to the *Economist*, suggest epochal changes produced primarily by a new generation of entrepreneurs. In an era of great change like the one we are experiencing, signs emerging from the wine industry can be very useful. After seeing the work of platoons of digital entrepreneurs aimed at observing business plans tailored to financial institutions, we rediscover the need for a new way of being on the market. In many people's opinion, the future of these technologies will be the prerogative of those who are not afraid to get their hands dirty, putting passion and creativity into their work. Dealing with these major technological changes requires courage and the desire to experiment. It takes passion and ambition. It is necessary to embrace the medium term, disconnected from short-term results. Once again, wine and its successful entrepreneurs represent an important anticipation of the journey that successful entrepreneurs will take in the coming years.

The Renaissance of Italian Wine: The People Who Changed History

Walter Filiputti with Alberto Mattiacci and Guido Ricciarelli

Precursors

Premonitory signs of the "renaissance of Italian wine" came many years before it fully blossomed, though they were unrelated and not able to create the "mass movement" that resulted in Piero Antinori's Tignanello, the first vintage year of which – 1971 – has been chosen as marking the start of the new history of Italian wine.

The signs of the reawakening stemmed from the acquisition of knowledge. It is no accident that the success of Brunello – and its extraordinary vintage years – was the work of an oenologist, Tancredi Biondi Santi, who consulted on another great wine of the time, Boncompagni Ludovisi's Fiorano.

"The Tuscan experiences of the time," observes Attilio Scienza, "had a different inspiration to those in Trentino. In Lazio and Tuscany, they emulated wines produced in Bordeaux by noble families [*Rothschild*], and were experiences of Italian nobles [*Mario Incisa della Rocchetta*]. They were, then, elitist, perhaps even a bit snobbish, though the Tignanello project was prompted by the crisis facing Chianti, and the presence of Peynaud as the estate's consultant was what made the difference. In Trentino, the spark came from within the alumni association of the Istituto Agrario di San Michele, which organized a study trip abroad each year."

One of these trips – to Bordeaux in 1957 – gave rise to two reds: Castel San Michele, made by the homonymous oenology school, and the Fojaneghe of Bossi Fedrigotti, whose winery was run by Leonello Letrari.

It should be noted that the estates of such visionaries, apart from Biondi Santi, had the same oenological goal in breaking with the past: the Bordeaux Blend.

Brunello and Biondi Santi

To guarantee the conservation of the aged bottles of wine he had inherited and continued to collect, **Tancredi Biondi Santi** adopted the top-up technique.

That invention – at once useful and spectacular – was the work of Tancredi Biondi Santi, born in 1893. He did his last topping up operation in March 1970, of his old bottles of Riserva 1888, 1891, 1925 and 1945. The "celebration" was held in the Greppo winery in the presence of Mario Soldati, Luigi Veronelli and Paolo Maccherini.

Tancredi Biondi Santi was one of the most important Italian winemakers of the age (he got his diploma with Dalmasso in Conegliano), and he was frequently asked to supervise estates in many parts of Italy, including the Fiorano estate of Boncompagni Ludovisi.

From the 1920s onwards, thanks to technical improvements he introduced in the winery, he enhanced even further the quality of the Brunello made by his father Ferruccio, effectively becoming the ambassador of Montalcino and its wines. It was one of his ancestors, Clemente Santi, who had obtained, in 1865, the first recognition of the "selected red wine" (brunello), and whose daughter married Jacopo Biondi. The son, Ferruccio, inherited the passion for wine and combined the two surnames. But above all, at the end of the nineteenth century, he intuited the potential of Sangiovese, perfecting the individual selection by identifying the particular clone that would give rise to the history of this wine. He regarded himself, and ultimately he was, a mere custodian of that legacy.

The task would then be completed by Franco Biondi Santi, who selected the BBS-11 clone, that is, the Brunello Biondi Santi 11. It is the only approved clone bearing the name of a producer, and has its own characteristics, which are different from those of a normal Sangiovese (a truncated cone-shaped bunch without wings and with thicker skins).

Franco Biondi Santi – *"il Dottore"* – also an oenologist, after earning a degree in agriculture, learnt from his father the subtle art of winemaking, and took over the Tenuta Greppo. Inherited with four hectares of vineyards, he built it up to

twenty-five. He held on to the precious collection of bottles, including those from 1888 and 1891. Great years: the first because it is the one in which the history of Brunello Biondi Santi started, the second because Franco always sustained it was the best in his cellar. Without forgetting the 1955 vintage, for which the magazine *The Wine Spectator* included Brunello – the only Italian wine – among the top twelve wines of the twentieth century, and likewise his subsequent vintages, the first of which was the 1970. The 1988 vintage was also excellent, coinciding with the centenary of the family's first Brunello.

Franco Biondi Santi died on 7 April 2013, during Vinitaly, and on the day of his funeral the Tuscany pavilion emptied.

The Brunello del Greppo is, then, a precious gem of history, capable of an unparalleled aristocratic longevity and remaining within the furrow of tradition. Like the Brunello Riserva 1971 and 1983 ("Riserva" is obtained from vineyards over twenty-five years old and in particularly favourable years); and 1985, 1997 and 2001 – wines for which the passing years seem not to count.

Today it is Franco's son, Jacopo, who is continuing the family tradition.

Fiorano

Fiorano – made on the outskirts of Rome, between the Appia Antica and the Ardeatina – was almost contemporary to Sassicaia. It shares with it the Bordeaux blend, though with the presence of Merlot, which Sassicaia does not have. Veronelli discovered it in 1972, tasting the white at Angelo Paracucchi's restaurant at the Motel Agip of Sarzana in Liguria, while he wrote about the red in *Panorama* on 29 November 1977.

Boncompagni Ludovisi bottled the wine, but did not sell it. The bottle bore, on a strip above the label, the words "wine from vines not chemically manured". In a letter to Luigi Veronelli, replying to his questions, Boncompagni Ludovisi wrote: "Wine began to be produced at Fiorano around 1930, but from local grape varieties. It was in 1946, when I received the Fiorano farm property from my father, that I judged its production to be poor and consulted the oenologist Giuseppe Palieri . . . who proposed grafting Cabernet and Merlot onto the Fiorano vines, in 50% proportions, and similarly Malvasia di Candia and Semillion, respectively for the red and the white. That's what I did, and I used Palieri's services as long as he lived. He was succeeded by the winemaker Tancredi Biondi Santi, he too as long as he lived."

Biondi Santi brought with him a young cellar assistant, Giulio Gambelli, who would later become the most appreciated Chianti taster.

Boncompagni Ludovisi added: "I uprooted almost all the vineyards due to my poor age and health" (he died in 2005). Then, to the question as to whether his grandchildren's passion for wine derived from him, he said to Veronelli: "My Antinori grandchildren did not inherit their interest in wine from me, but from their father Piero, an eminent maker of superior wines."

Fiorano stopped being produced in 1995. Veronelli saved a selection of bottles, and had them sold in the United States. Following years of abandonment, part of the estate now belongs to Boncompagni Ludovisi's three grandchildren. They are tended by one of them, Alessia, who managed to revive the small portion of vineyard – eight rows – that had survived years of neglect, and to plant fourteen hectares with the same grape varieties as those of her grandfather.

The Fojaneghe "of" Leonello Letrari,
Italy's First Great *Barrique*-aged Red

Fojaneghe anticipated Sassicaia (1968) by as much as seven years. Though nothing can detract from the greatness of Gia-

como Tachis, the first person to use *barriques* in a professional way and with a commercial plan was Leonello Letrari, who at the time was a young oenologist running Bossi Fedrigotti in Rovereto, Trentino. Let's listen to Leonello, who, born in 1931, has sixty-four harvests under his belt, having done his first in 1950.

"The club of former pupils at the San Michele all'Adige school of oenology used to organize study trips. In 1957, we went to Bordeaux, and visited the top châteaux. Their wines impressed us greatly. On the way back we kept saying we had to do something to escape from the situation of inferiority we were in. I was director of Bossi Fedrigotti. With the next harvest – 1958 – both the oenology school and I myself for what would become Fojaneghe decided on a radically different and strongly innovative vinification technique. For many years we had both Bordeaux grape varieties. At Bossi Fedrigotti we had Carmenere and Merlot, which were used in Fojaneghe in respective proportions of 40% and 60%. We adopted prolonged maceration at controlled temperatures, and malolactic fermentation – the real secret that the French kept carefully hidden, but which we intuited – began the following spring. The first Slovenian-oak *barriques* were made for me by Damian, later Italbotti, in Conegliano. The wine remained in them for fourteen months, followed by another ten in 25-hectolitre barrels. We released – Castel San Michele and Fojaneghe – in 1961, just a few months from each other." "How did the market respond"? "For Fojaneghe it was an immediate and unexpected success. The market was ready, but not the vast majority of oenologists and producers. In less than ten years we reached 200,000 bottles out of a total of 450,000 at Bossi Fedrigotti. A box of Fojaneghe – sold at 990 Lire a bottle – was equivalent

in price to ten other wines, which cost 120–130 a bottle. Some years later, on 25 April 1971, a gentleman came to pay us a visit: his name was Robert Mondavi. He had tasted our wine in America, and he told me it was incredible that in Italy there could be a better wine than in Bordeaux. We became good friends." "What was your last Fojaneghe vintage?" "1975" (as from 2007, the Bossi Fedrigotti family began to work together with the Masi of Sandro Boscaini. The current composition of Fojaneghe is 45% Merlot, 40% Cabernet Franc and 15% Teroldego).

Sassicaia

It was some time since I had last met **Nicolò Incisa della Rocchetta**, who greeted me on 6 December 2013 with news that made me want to shout with joy. "Sassicaia has become a DOC." "What do you mean, a DOC?" "Yes, they informed us yesterday, and now we are waiting for the official documentation." He invited to our meeting the estate's director, Carlo Paoli, who was aglow at this magnificent achievement. "The first DOC Bolgheri of 1994 bore two names: DOC Bolgheri and DOC Sassicaia, which, according to the new community norms of 2011, could not coexist. The decision was up to the regional and municipal authorities." Nicolò Incisa expressed his pride and satisfaction: "The wonderful thing is that it was the local author-

ities and the winemakers of DOC Bolgheri who wanted Sassicaia to be granted separate DOC status, the first in Italy", a demonstration of their far-sightedness, intelligence and grateful recognition, the latter being a very rare virtue.

In a letter to Luigi Veronelli on 11 June 1974, Mario Incisa revealed to him when he began to imagine his winemaking project: "The experimentation originated in the years between 1912 and 1925, when, as a student at Pisa and often a guest of the Salviati dukes of Migliarino, I had drunk a wine produced in one of their vineyards that had the same unmistakeable bouquet of an old Bordeaux." It was in 1944 that Incisa planted the first thousand Cabernet Sauvignon vines on a 2000 metre plot, given to him by his Salviati friends. "The vinification was done in a rough and ready way," noted Mario Incisa. It was aged in 225-litre barrels "that leaked all over the place". From 1948 to 1967 this wine was consumed in the family and offered to guests. Mario Incisa was the godfather of Lodovico Antinori, who remembers his uncle with raptures and deep fondness.

"He taught me respect for nature. At a certain point he gave up hunting and established, in 1958, the first wildlife reserve in Italy, 513 hectares of paradise. This was the reason why Prince Philip of England came to see him in the early 1960s. When he tasted the red, he began asking specific questions: What grapes it was produced from, where they came from, how it was vinified and aged. He was amazed. That, in my view, was the crowning moment that led my uncle to think the time had come to increase production in order to release it onto the market. In 1964, in fact, he planted over ten hectares at Sassicaia, 200 metres lower – with the same grapes. It should be remembered that my uncle was the owner of the 'strongest horse in the world', the legendary Ribot of the 1950s, born in his Dormello Olgiata stables. Uncle was a great dreamer."

Piero, the other Antinori nephew, recalls:

"My uncle began to take seriously the production of what would become Italy's most famous wine. 'I am not a market man,' he used to say, 'in this field you are the experts.' That is how he came to ask me to take care of the distribution of Sassicaia and to help him modernize the production structures. We went to Bordeaux together in the early 1970s. He came

back satisfied from that trip, because he had had full confirmation of his far-sighted theories. The high density, the low height of the cordon, the usefulness of 'hedge' pruning, the skilful and pondered use of new *barriques*. I think it is right to remember and stress that if this happened, we owe it in large part to the far-sightedness of Mario Incisa della Rocchetta. The agreement with my uncle began with the 1968 harvest, which was the year of birth of Sassicaia. We went to Florence together, to Pineider, to have the label done."

In the meantime, Antinori sent him his oenologist, Giacomo Tachis, along with Émile Peynaud, who was still the Antinori's consultant, and therefore of Sassicaia as well. Tachis then supervised all the harvests, up until 2008, after which Graziana Grassini, his pupil, took over.

The first world-level performance of Sassicaia was in London in 1978, in a contest organized by *Decanter Magazine* between thirty-three top Cabernet Sauvignon wines from eleven different countries, including Bordeaux grand crus. The Sassicaia 1972, to the great surprise of the tasters, trounced all the opposition. From then on its fame grew exponentially, which Piero Antinori managed in an impeccable manner, prompting Nicolò Incisa to say: "We owe a great deal to Piero Antinori. He positioned the wine very well."

The agreement with the Incisa della Rocchetta family ended with the 1982 vintage.

When Mario Incisa died on 4 September 1983, his brother-in-law Nicolò Antinori paid tribute to him with these words: "Having invented Sassicaia justifies a life, it explains everything." He could not have put it better. Robert Parker awarded 100 points to the 1985 vintage and proclaimed it the "wine of the century".

Below
Ampelio Bucci

The First Hotbeds of the New Italian Wine Style

The Renaissance, the artistic and cultural period that began in Florence in the second half of the fourteenth century, was viewed by the majority of its protagonists as an age of change. A new way of conceiving the world and oneself took shape, influencing also the mentality of the time. Its point of reference was the "classical", understood in its original meaning: excellence. That is why, in the Renaissance, each individual sought to turn their own life into a masterpiece, a unique work, in short, a classic.

"The renaissance of Italian wine," says Ampelio Bucci, a winemaker from the Marches, "developed gradually in the final decades of the last century, and moved in step with the birth and success of those products that we associate with the term 'Made in Italy'. The most significant phenomena is social and cultural, and has involved a silent revolution in consumerism in all the industrialized nations: the birth, that is, of what is called 'postmodern consumerism', with the advent of aesthetic and sensory culture, which has brought Italy into the international limelight in the fields of fashion, design, food and wine. Consumer choices are now segmented and dif-

ferentiated, and do not just respond to needs, but also to new desires, aesthetic cues and considerations relating to taste, curiosity, experience and so on."

In retrospect. The difficulty lay in reading the first signs of change. In grasping the changes and implementing the entrepreneurial choices they entailed; this involved, and let's not forget, an often drastic break with the past, which had been guarded by an invisible army that did not want those transformations. Besides vision, there was a need for lots, really lots, of courage.

The renaissance of Italian wine, as we have seen, even though the first signs of it came at the beginning of the 1960s, would have, in Piero Antinori's Tignanello, the wine that broke definitively with the past, and which in a short space of time managed to interest the whole of Italy in what was coming into being in the heart of Chianti Classico, one of Italy's main DOCs.

An attentive agronomic and oenological reading is offered by Maurizio Castelli, Milanese by birth and later a "naturalized" Tuscan. From 1973 to 1979, before embarking on a career as an agronomical and oenological consultant, he was an inspector for the Consorzio del Chianti Gallo Nero, when it was presided over by Bettino Ricasoli. "Qualitatively, the early 1970s were the worst, both in Tuscany and the rest of Italy. Chianti, what's more, was stifled by the formula envisaging the use of 30% of white grapes, which, note, produced 50–60% of the total. That's where the revolt started."

Tuscany

Tignanello, the Wine that Changed Chianti and Italy

Niccolò Antinori gave his son Piero the responsibility for the family business in 1966, when he was twenty-eight years old. He said to him: "It's your turn, from now on the Antinori are taking first-hand responsibility. Do what you think best, and if you need advice, I am always available." It was 1966, recalls **Piero Antinori**, "the year that ended with the flood in Florence. Thousands of young people from all over Europe came to shovel mud and dry out books and paintings in the sun. For Tuscany there began, in many respects, a new era. And I was there, the twenty-fifth head of the Antinori family."

Tignanello was the result of a very complex situation. "When I found myself running the family business," continues Piero, "those were the years in which direct management of the fields and vineyards by the owners was taking the place of sharecropping [*abolished by law in 1964*]." An age was ending, and another one, clumsily, was beginning. In the space of a few years, millions of vines appeared in every free corner of space, describes Piero Antinori in his book *Il Profumo del Chianti* (Mondadori, Milan 2011). The grape rush soon became uncontrolled, and, to some extent, improvised.

These were the results of the European Agricultural Guidance and Guarantee Fund (EAGGF), set up in 1962:

"The second natural consequence of the collapse of the sharecropping system," continues Piero Antinori, "was a drop in the quality of wine. It was a thin, watery and unstructured Chianti. Incapable of ageing. Everything fell apart, both image and quality, leading to the fall in prices and in exports. It was a general crisis of Tuscany's whole rural system. I saw that it was necessary to re-establish the relationship between the wine and its habitat, starting from the magnificent lands put together by my family over the years. At the same time, there was a need for 'a wine invention', which had perhaps never been attempted before in Tuscany. A further leap was required, we used to say, discussing it for days and nights with Giacomo Tachis [*the oenologist from Piedmont who would support him in this courageous journey*]. It was thanks to him that I had the fortune to meet Professor Émile Peynaud, one of the few great figures of wine in the last half century. He was the one who taught us all how to start and control malolactic fermentation. He helped us to formulate a different philosophy for wine. His teachings were, above all, a list of things not to do. To make a fine red you cannot use large proportions of white grapes. Nor can it be closed up for three to four years in excessively large chestnut barrels. Nor can you always use the same large barrels. Effectively, it was necessary to revise, and drastically, the customary formula for Chianti.

Where could a great wine be made if not on the estate where our best Sangiovese had always ripened? Now occupied by two vineyards, Tignanello and Solaia. The place was born for wine, with a southwest aspect and lying between 350 and 450 metres above sea level. Tignanello has an ideal rocky terrain and a perfect microclimate.

We produced a first, experimental Tignanello – just twenty thousand bottles – back in 1970. It was a Chianti Classico made from Sangiovese with small dollops of white grapes. An excellent Chianti Classico, I must say, but still in some way linked to tradition. It was the following year that we really burnt the bridges with the past [*the 1971 harvest*]. After the alcoholic fermentation, the wine was subjected, under Peynaud's supervision, to malolactic fermentation, and put into small, new 225-litre oak barrels for a couple of years. But this was only the beginning of the revolution. Already at that time the plan was to perfect the 'sacrilege' by mixing Sangiovese with Cabernet, which my father had already experimented with in his own time in the precise same place. Then came 1974, the year in which the first Tignanello faced its test in the *enoteca*."

Here Piero Antinori takes a step back, which is also fundamental to understanding the situation that had arisen with the DOC appellations:

"The DOC Chianti had been introduced in 1967. What happened is that many producers deluded themselves that innovation automatically meant commercial success. A method

crystallized precisely when it showed its full age and all its inadequacies. Without any scope for experimentation and personal initiative. It was soon clear that the new regulations and my Tignanello were speaking different languages. The moral of the story was that one of the most ambitious wines to have been produced by my family in six hundred years of history, born and bred in the heart of Tuscany, would have to be released, on the basis of the new rules, without the wording Chianti Classico, but as *vino da tavola*. From my point of view that legislation certified mediocrity."

Let's return to the future Tignanello. During the conference of sommeliers at Orvieto (1973), Piero Antinori invited Veronelli to dinner at the Castello della Sala. He got him to taste the 1971 Anonymous. "Excellent, what is it?" asked Veronelli. "That evening he assured me that with a wine like that, the problem of the appellation became a negligible detail. He explained that the right name was the simplest one: Tignanello. The best thing to do was to link this wine directly with its vineyard, its *terroir*, without lots of embellishment. That would be its 'controlled origin'. And so we baptized the new creature with an ancient name." It was once again Veronelli who suggested a designer for the label: Silvio Coppola. The next evening it was presented to a large group of sommeliers in Orvieto: it had an extraordinary reception.

"Tignanello had a name, a form and a growing fame," Piero Antinori continues. "This is what led us to create, in 1975,

with the second vintage, the 'definitive' Tignanello [*the ones from 1972 to 1974 were not declared, because they were not considered good enough*]. The Sangiovese was perfect, the Cabernet as well . . . the result was 25,000 unforgettable bottles. With Sassicaia improving year by year, and the addition of Solaia in 1978, it was clear that we had given rise to a new generation, to a movement that would change the image of Chianti itself. Twenty years later, on the day the announcement was made that Solaia had won first place in the rankings of *The Wine Spectator*, the one in which the Super Tuscans [*the term was coined by Frank Prial, for many years a wine columnist with* The New York Times, *to provide a 'placement' for those wines, headed by Tignanello, that departed from the conventional mould*] officially ended up in history books and on television news reports, summed up what had happened in Tuscany like this: 'We wanted to match France. But it was wrong to produce simple imitations of Bordeaux. And so we made wines with the so-called international grapes, but with a Tuscan style and a character of their own. This was the key to the future.' Exactly one year after, Solaia topped the international wine rankings drawn up by *The Wine Spectator*, the same place went to an Ornellaia, the 1998 vintage, of my brother Lodovico."

When Piero Antinori lifted the business onto his shoulders he had 50 hectares of vineyards. That figure is now 2,000. He had two wineries, now about fifteen, "also because we try to preserve a specific identity for each of them," he says. Turnover? "At present, 150 million Euro, and 20 million bottles. When I began, around 200–300 million of the old Lire. The real strategic decision, which took shape gradually, was to work only with grapes of our own production."

For thirty-five years Piero Antinori has had, in Renzo Cotarella, a right-hand man who, "besides being an excellent oenologist, has also become a first-rate manager [*he is the managing director of Antinori*]. I have retained the last word on the style of all the Antinori wines: it's a task I want to continue to perform."

Piero Antinori led the profound and radical innovations in the family business, taking it to extraordinary turnover figures, but proceeding with an Italian craft culture. Each of his wines remains, and is, a unique work, and, as such, a craft

product. This is what is perceived by his customers around the world. This is his true masterpiece.

Those smallholdings, run with the passion and meticulousness put into them by the small winegrower, have yielded wines that have distinguished and mapped out the modern history of Italian wine, often anticipating it.

Following on the heels of the Sassicaia of Mario Incisa della Rocchetta – whose intuition was transformed by his nephew Piero Antinori into a wine of worldwide value – and Tignanello came a series of wines of extraordinary value, in terms both of quality and prestige, which contributed massively to enhancing the good name of Italian wine around the world.

Solaia – the first vintage was in 1978 – is only produced when harvests are excellent. Its 20 hectares, planted with Cabernet Sauvignon, Cabernet Franc and Sangiovese, form part of the 77 hectares of the Tenuta Tignanello, with 57 being given over to the wine of that name. Then there is Guado al Tassi, whose Bolgheri Superiore was released in 1990. Pian delle Vigne is 6 km from Montalcino: 184 hectares, 65 of them under vine. Another very evocative estate is Badia a Passignano, in the heart of Chianti Classico, a fortified abbey dating to the eleventh century and belonging to the Vallombrosan monks, from whom, in 1987, Piero Antinori bought the 325 hectares of vineyard surrounding the castle, continuing to use the ancient cellars.

If Tignanello was the great modern red that looked to the future, Cervaro della Sala was its wood-matured white equivalent, the first vintage of which dates to 1985.

The Tignanello Effect

Tignanello enabled us to describe an Italian red wine with previously unused adjectives. This wine expressed itself elegantly and softly. It was a big wine, but at the same time could be drunk with joy. Its fruity aromas were enveloping, the colour intense, bright and deep. Well-structured tannins, but not overpowering.

It was obvious, then, that it would also influence Tuscan winemakers. A crucial factor in triggering this new movement of innovation in the style of Chianti wine was the immediate success it had on the market. In short, thanks to this wine, the Chianti Classico area became a hotbed from which an amazing series of great red table wines would come. In a single stroke, Tignanello had made all the Chiantis obsolete.

From then on the red wines also began to change, and the bitter, arid and unpleasant tastes they often had gradually disappeared. Tuscany attracted many entrepreneurs from outside the wine world, who brought in a further innovative capacity, turning to top-quality consultants for assistance. Professionals like Maurizio Castelli and Vittorio Fiore, for example, would design many Super Tuscans, alongside great local masters who, in turn, proved able to adapt.

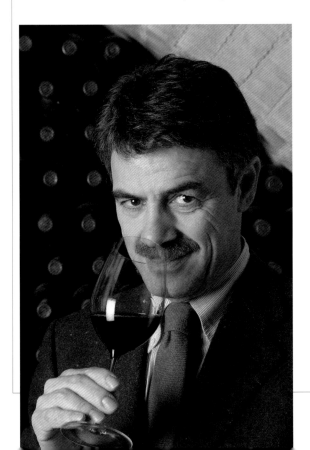

One of them was the unforgettable Giulio Gambelli, a very fine taster who assisted **Sergio Manetti**, in 1977, in creating another legendary "table wine", Le Pergole Torte di Montevertine. Manetti remained loyal to Sangiovese, though he allowed himself to be influenced by the new style. He bought the holding in an auction in 1967 – 40 hectares of woodland and vineyards – for less than 6 million Lire. A successful track record in the steel business (born in Poggibonsi, he studied in Milan and ran a company in Castellina Scalo) gradually made way for the dream of a great wine. A man with a strong character, little inclined to mediation, he planted new vineyards and waited for the results to be good enough. He soon clashed with the protocols of the denomination, leaving the Consorzio del Chianti Classico in 1980 and self-classifying his own output to simple table wines. The sound advice of the master taster Giulio Gambelli and the unseen work of the historic cellarman Bruno Bini rapidly elevated the signature wine, Le Pergole Torte, to among the labels leading the Italian renaissance. The formula was 100% Sangiovese, with low yields, and no particular oenological "interventionism". His son **Martino**, who is at his side, dropped out of university in 1990 and began, as a simple worker, to thoroughly learn the winemaking trade. The magic vintage of Le Pergole Torte was 1990, which followed the legendary 1988: acidity admirably worked into the structure to produce a perfectly balanced effect. Martino no longer has these figures to turn to, but he continues to make wine as before, and, above all, as he likes it. Castello di Monsanto, dated mid-eighteenth century, is situated in a commanding position above the Elsa Valley and was one of the first in Tuscany to apply the cru concept to Chianti Classico. **Aldo Bianchi** bought the estate at end 1961, but it was his son **Fabrizio**, with his passion for viticulture, who created the winery and then received it as a gift in 1964. As early as 1962, Fabrizio already had the idea to create the first cru of Chianti Classico by vinifying the grapes of a single vineyard: Il Poggio. The decision to modify the Chianti Classico mix of varieties, keeping only Sangiovese, Canaiolo and Colorino, matured in 1968. Over the years, Fabrizio has passed much of his expertise on to his daughter, **Laura**, who has been working with him since 1989 and has introduced important innovations in the winery: temperature-controlled steel fermentation tanks and Slavonian oak casks have replaced those of chestnut wood. The technique of a second fermentation, known as "governo alla Toscana" has been abandoned while maceration on the grape skins has been extended. The *barriques* arrived in the mid-1990s, later replaced by *tonneaux*. Il Poggio 1995, one of the best ever, is a splendid champion of that decade. Today the estate covers 206 hectares, of which 72 are vineyards. The 300-metre long underground tunnel, where about 1200 *tonneaux* and small casks are stored, is of considerable architectural interest.

Brunello di Montalcino

Alberto Mattiacci, professor of economics and business administration at the University of Rome La Sapienza, introduces the Brunello area like this:

In these brief thoughts, then, we will undertake to mention a few of the steps that might outline an economic history of Montalcino. Let's follow, in ideal terms, the four cardinal points on an imaginary geographic map, in order to mark out this path.

One cannot but begin from the South, from where, 10,000 years ago, the story of humankind began. A description of the Montalcino scene would speak of a poor area of Tuscany [it is no accident that Maremma is, in local slang, still more often

than not, "piggish"], *sparsely inhabited and not yet aware of the riches upon which the town and its territory rest. A series of people and events intertwined to bring about the start of Montalcino's great adventure: a chemist who invented a vinification formula, a dialect name for a grape, which was already – unknowingly – the euphonic brand name, an Aretine politician who "imported" that wine to the capital, some visionary and innovative "wine merchants".*

Our journey then takes us towards the North, in the direction of lands where structure needs to be given to things in order to stand comparison with an increasingly harsher nature. The history of Montalcino, here, speaks of a territory which, an innocent victim of the "methanol" scandal, changed gear and got behind the steering wheel of the resurgence in Italian wine. "The Americans arrived", and with the help of the top Italian oenologist of the period, they sat down and created an enterprise already conceived on a large scale. Capital and people began to arrive from outside to invest in Montalcino: the wave of interest in Tuscan wines was fuelled and ridden, the town began to change and to prepare itself to adequately welcome the visitors who began to arrive in ever-increasing numbers.

The passage towards the West marked the area's first, great international success. Brunello discovered America, and America, Brunello. The production structure was consolidated with the arrival of important new players and the definitive maturing of the plants of the great historic Tuscan producers. The number of producers with their own brands rose to over two hundred; the appearance of the town, on the other hand, had by now been completed: the demography had changed, with a growing population and greater variety of origin [with over forty nationalities being recorded]; *the number of guest beds – in hotels and other structures – increased ten-fold, and restaurants and wine shops became a constant presence in the streets of Montalcino.*

The future looks East. The Eastern markets are now among the most frequently visited destinations of Montalcino's wine producers, who look in that direction with a combination of hope and perplexity. The East is a state of the spirit for Western culture, at once attractive and frightening: it is a new challenge with which every producer and the system as a whole is dealing, backed by the solidity of Brunello, of a forward-looking consortium and of a local population that is facing this new challenge with a positive attitude. China, Russia, South America, Thailand and India are starting to feature in bar conversations, interwoven with talk about football and political rows.

Montalcino is a history, not just a place; it is a history in which families and surnames blend with brands and wineries; it is a history in which new ideas have swept through vineyards and rows of vines, wineries and large wooden barrels, houses and derelict ruins, individuals and families; it is a three-hundred-and-sixty-degree history which can, and must, still act as a model and as a positive lesson for all of us who love Montalcino.

Ezio Rivella, the First Oenologist-Manager

Ezio Rivella is an atypical oenologist, outside the conventional mould of his time. He became an idol of the **Mariani brothers** – **John Jr.** was the family visionary, while **Harry** was the practical one – in that he solved the stability and oxidation problems of the Frascati wines of Gotto d'Oro in Marino (where Rivella was consultant and manager) that they imported into the US. From then on they turned to him for advice. Rivella says: "At the Milan trade fair in 1967, John Mariani Jr. asked me if I knew a producer of Lambrusco: he was looking for a fresh, fizzy red. I advised him not to concern himself too much with this wine, which I considered to be too acidic for American palates. The stand of the Cantine Riunite of Reggio Emilia was in front of mine. He ordered 100 cases, which arrived a few weeks later in the US. John called me: 'You were right, it's too acidic and lacks colour. The product needs making. Please make contact with the company's oenologist and give him the necessary instructions.' That is how we came to invent the beverage wine."

It should be said that prior to Lambrusco, Banfi was a small importer with a 300-square-metre store on the Avenue of the Americas in New York. By 1970, Banfi had already reached the point of placing a million cases onto the market. Over 150 million bottles were drunk each year. It was the first Italian wine born from marketing, and the best known in the States.

"The Marianis found themselves wallowing in the money Lambrusco made for them. Towards the middle of January 1977, John Mariani, Jr came to Italy, as usual, and we met. Amongst other things, during dinner at Grottaferrata, he told me that perhaps it would be best if Banfi became a producer as well. That is when the Montalcino project came to me. I knew there were lots of parcels of land on sale at trifling prices: 3.5 million Lire a hectare, houses included. I put the idea to him. He said: 'Alright, let's do it. I'll send you the money. How much is needed?' I was dazed: 'I don't know, I would imagine at least 50 million Dollars.' It was a colossal sum. John said to me: 'Give me five years, I'll send you a bit at a time. On one condition: that you give up all your other consultancies and work on this project alone.' We said goodbye, and the more the days passed the more I thought John had allowed himself to be carried away by enthusiasm. It wasn't the case. A week later I received a call from the manager of the Credito Italiano bank in Rome: 'Dr Rivella, look, four billion Lire have arrived here for you.' 'For me? And who sent them?' 'Banfi.' I called John: it was true. He gave me a free hand."

The Birth of Castello Banfi

"When I invited him to visit Montalcino to see with his own eyes where I would spend his money, he gave me a reply that committed me totally to the cause: 'Ezio, I could come, but I don't know anything about it. You're the expert. What we'll do is this: you make it all happen, and I'll fund you, or rather, we Banfi will fund you.'" At the time Rivella was forty-five years old.

What was Rivella's great idea? Think big: he wanted to produce at least 500,000 bottles of Brunello. Under vine in Montalcino at the time, and recorded in the land use registry, there were 293 hectares given over to specialized cultivation and 73 to the promiscuous kind (in 1967, there were 76). Now there are 2,300. The number of bottles produced used to be 300,000, compared to over 10 million today.

Let's get back to the project.

"The buying campaign," the Cavalier recounts, "began in 1977 and continued until the autumn of 1983. I drew a schedule that envisaged 50 hectares for the first three years, and then 100–150 a year. In total, we arrived at 2,830 hectares, all grouped together. The number of hectares under vine became 850, out of the total 3,300 in the whole Montalcino area. The final investment exceeded 100 million Dollars, including the restoration of the castle [*the first harvest was in 1982*]. The curious thing is that my American friends didn't place great hope in Brunello, which they regarded as a 'super niche' product, capable of no more than 100,000 bottles [*production reached 600,000 bottles in the 1980s, and a million in the 1990s!*]."

The New Style of Brunello

Banfi's Brunello Poggio all'Oro Riserva is far removed from the model developed by Ferruccio Biondi Santi at the end of the nineteenth century. Two different schools of thought, which, in truth, find their *raison d'être* in the area of origin. The historic one for the production of the Brunello of Biondi Santi was concentrated entirely on the northeast slope of the town, high up and cool. Castello Banfi's land, on the other hand, all faces southwest, lying on the hot hills sloping down toward the plain.

The wines, inevitably, are very different, and, in departing from the original model, have attracted many consumers to the Brunello label, previously viewed with awe for its "austerity".

Castello Banfi's Brunello "with a smile" took off on the international markets and established itself as a symbol of Italian quality in the world.

The 1990 vintage was excellent. Released onto the market in 1995, just 3 million bottles were made, which were all immediately sold, but this laid the foundations for placing the output of the new vineyards entering into production.

"At Villa Banfi – that was its name at the time, then it became Castello Banfi," affirms Rivella, "we were leaders in the area. Fortune had it that the young **James Mariani** arrived in the company, fresh out of business school. James put the firm back on the market: from importer-distributor to the top producer of Brunello di Montalcino. A programme was therefore drawn up which involved me going to the United States to do tastings and presentations in fifteen cities in a like number of days. A twelve-seater Falcon was rented, which took off each morning for a different city. It was an incredible operation, which enabled us to meet thousands of people, and set in chain that virtuous cycle which then thrust Brunello into the firmament of the world's great reds."

Besides enhancing the knowledge and image of Italian wine. What Ezio Rivella says is true: "Banfi set a pattern with regard to policy, visitor hospitality and promotion of the business with wine tourism, and, we can quite justifiably affirm that it is the company which has contributed in a determinant way to the establishment of Brunello at an international level."

Bolgheri

In Tuscany, besides Brunello and Tignanello, there was, as we have seen, another wine of world stature, the Sassicaia of Bolgheri, which for decades remained without any followers.

Piermario Meletti Cavallari was the first person, after Mario Incisa, to perceive the area's great potential. Born in Ferrara, and after having then lived between Bergamo and Milan, where he taught management training, he pursued the dream of a great wine, "infected" by his friend Veronelli. In 1977, he bought 6 hectares of vines at Grattamacco.

"With the 1982 harvest I knew I had taken the right path," recalls Piermario, who in the meantime became the councillor for agriculture of Castagneto Carducci, of which Bolgheri is part. "At the time Sassicaia was 'table wine'. Absurd!"

Meletti Cavallari devoted a lot of hard work to preparing the denomination, succeeding in bringing together the different orientations, leading, in 1994, to the establishment of the DOC Bolgheri Rosso. "We were the first in Italy to present an application for a DOC linked to the zoning, which would prove to be a very important choice – carried out by Attilio Scienza."

There is a significant photo that immortalizes the informal birth certificate of the DOC, taken by Stefano Hunyady underneath the holm-oak of Grattamacco: it features the Marquis Nicolò Incisa, Piero and Lodovico Antinori, then Michele

Satta and Piermario Meletti Cavallari. "Bolgheri did not have an oenological tradition, so we felt free to imagine a wine in tune with the times we were living in. Market growth was very rapid: the locomotive was the Sassicaia of the Incisa family, but much of the credit must also go to Lodovico Antinori, who, with his Ornellaia, launched the name of Bolgheri around the world."

In 2002, he rented and then sold vineyards and cellars to Maria Iris and Claudio Tipa (then also the owners of Castello ColleMassari in the Upper Maremma, and subsequently of Fattoria Poggio di Sotto in Montalcino), keeping for himself the house of Grattamacco. It was a lightning agreement, propitiated by the contact created by the oenological consultant they had in common, Maurizio Castelli.

In 2003, Meletti Cavallari joined the Tenuta delle Ripalte on the island of Elba, where he planted and now runs the 15 hectares of vineyard, together with the winery designed by Tobia Scarpa.

In 1966, **Lodovico Antinori**, then twenty-three years old, was sent by his father to get to know the American market. Antinori recounts:

"I went on a nine-month tour around the States, covering a distance of 36,000 miles. I came back from it depressed about how Italian wine was viewed, but with a knowledge of the market that no Italian had. A market that was dominated by the French and Germans. Italian wines? Besides our own, Fazi Battaglia, Soave Bolla, Ruffino, Cirò and Chianti Nozzole. I had meetings there which impressed me, like the key one with André Tchelistcheff, the oenologist of Russian origin who, together with Robert Mondavi, engineered the lift-off of Californian oenology, and is considered one of the finest palates of all time."

Lodovico met him in 1978. His dream of producing a wine outside the family umbrella was taking root in his mind. The first idea was to buy land at Paso Roble in California. He confided his plans to Tchelistcheff, with whom, in the meantime, a solid friendship had formed.

In 1980, he invited him to Bolgheri. Tchelistcheff said: "El Dorado is here!" He was right. Ludovico took the cue immediately and asked his mother not to sell the Ornellaia parcel of land, then valued at 18 million Lire. Part of the land was given to him by his godfather, Mario Incisa della Rocchetta. In total, he put together around 50 hectares, including woodland. He started with 18 hectares, planted in 1982. The first harvest of Ornellaia was in 1985.

"I wanted to give that wine an international voice. Made in Bolgheri, yes, but which spoke many other languages as well, apart from Italian." His friend Tchelistcheff – who had the intuition to select the Merlot that then led to the creation of Masseto (first vintage: 1988) – consulted for him until 1990, but continued to visit him in Bolgheri after that. We believe Lodovico saw in him his godfather, Mario Incisa. Lodovico set about searching for someone to replace his friend, and the choice fell on Michel Rolland, who had not yet become the celebrated Bordeaux consultant. He began his work in 1991, and for two harvests worked only on the Masseto. "It was a terrible year for Cabernet," recalls Lodovico, "which suffered from the rain, while the Merlot matured perfectly and was truly fine. Undoubtedly, Masseto was one of the great successes of Michel Rolland . . . The 1997 harvest was what I consider to be my best. The 1998 one allowed me to win, in 2001, the title of the world's best wine from *The Wine Spectator*. The previous year, Piero had won it with Solaia 1997: two brothers with different companies who, for two years in a row, were the world's best. Immense satisfaction! My last harvest at Ornellaia was in 2001, and 110,000 bottles were made, an excellent year. In 2002, Mondavi, after having initially bought a 50% stake, acquired 100% of Ornellaia, but then – in a totally unexpected way that surprised the international wine world – sold 50% to Frescobaldi [*at the beginning of 2005, Frescobaldi bought the remaining 50% of Luce and Ornellaia*]."

In his record book as a winegrower, Lodovico Antinori skipped a harvest, in 2002. He resumed in 2003 with renewed energy and vision, again with the assistance of Michel Rolland. "Together we created the greatness of Masseto. He is able, like

few others, the interpret the places where he intervenes." As Nelson Mandela said, "You must be able to dream": Lodovico set a new and very innovative project in motion, as is his wont, together with his brother Piero. It is called Tenuta di Biserno, extending 50 hectares, which makes two wines: Tenuta di Biserno and Il Pino. The latter was an immediate success, less demanding than the leading wine, but very agreeable. The estate is once again in Upper Maremma, near Bibbona, the municipality adjoining Bolgheri, and was taken on a ninety-year lease. A place of rare beauty, also natural. A *relais* from the small eighteenth-century palazzo stands out among the vineyards on the upper part of the estate, from where there is a glimpse of the sea.

The new challenge is Cabernet Franc. The style of the wines is different, and the first vintage was 2003. Besides the Tenuta di Biserno, there is Bibbona Campo di Sasso, covering 32 hectares, which produces Insoglio. And finally, the Tenuta dei Pianali, in the DOC Bolgheri zone (35 hectares). In total Lodovico and Piero Antinori have 117 hectares of vineyards.

Why is Cabernet Franc the leading light? "Cabernet Franc ripens well here, and produces excellent results, which have been somewhat underestimated to date. It is no accident that the wine spearheading the whole project, called Lodovico – from the Vigna Nord at Bellaria, around 4 hectares in size – is made from 90% Cabernet Franc, with the rest consisting of Petit Verdot, which is the second surprise. Grapes which in the Bordeaux Blend result in overly hard and powerful wines, ripen very well here, and have an exotic range of aromas, including discernible notes of rhubarb and liquorice, and are clearly distinguishable from the wines of the Bolgheri DOC. It is what we were looking for, and is the real challenge of our new adventure. The most important wine in the project is Biserno, whose real point of departure came with the 2011 harvest, after previous years developing and fine-tuning the whole programme. The 2011 vintage permitted us to say that a new style of wine had come into being in the Upper Maremma: that of Bibbona."

The change in the ownership of Ornellaia brings us to the Marchesi de' Frescobaldi. Guido Ricciarelli writes: "Summarizing 700 years of history, 30 generations and 1200 hectares of vineyard in a few words is an impossible task. Choosing a

flagship wine would mean doing an injustice to all the others. Frescobaldi now comprises seven different estates, each of which is independent, with dedicated agronomists and oenologists. They have a far from simple mission: to yoke together the Frescobaldi style with the exaltation of the specific character of each area. Perhaps the element of greatest characterization is offered by Castello di Nipozzano, which, with its duo of Mormoreto and Montesodi [*the latter is a Chianti Rufina Riserva*], manages to find that extra and evermore precious touch of specificity. Rufina, however, also means Pomino, with another Castello and other wines such as a Vin Santo to discover. Frescobaldi is, however, also Colli Fiorentini, Maremma, and – a new phase – a concern for social issues. In fact, the latest arrival in the Frescobaldi household is Gorgona, the offspring of a project arising out of collaboration with the local prison, the aim being to give inmates the possibility to learn the viticultural trade under the supervision of experts from Frescobaldi, enabling them to get back into the job market with greater ease. An initial hectare of vineyard, on the island since 1999, to which another is in the process of being added, formed the foundations for the first 2700 bottles of Gorgona, a white based on Vermentino and Ansonica. A wild brew, stemming from uncontaminated terrain."

Giovanni Geddes da Filicaja has been the managing director of the Gruppo Marchesi de' Frescobaldi since 1997. In 1995, he was the consultant for the joint venture between Fres-

cobaldi and Mondavi on the project for the "Luce della vite" wine, the first vintage of which was in 1993. Previously, Geddes had worked in the Remy Cointreau group until 1982. Between 1983 and 1994 he had been managing director of Antinori. In that period, he made Italy, for more than ten years, the top world market for Krug champagne, distributed by Antinori.

In short, Geddes is one of the most skilled and all-round experts in luxury as applied to the wine sector. I met him at the Florence base in Palazzo Frescobaldi. I found in him an unusual ability to picture markets and build strategies capable of increasing their value. One might be inclined to think that buying a very strong brand like Ornellaia leaves no space for new ideas, and that it just needs to be run on automatic pilot. But not Giovanni Geddes. He always sets himself the goal of raising the benchmark, not just of the quality, but of the image, the market position, the style of communication. First of all, the Ornellaia brand must remain independent of the Frescobaldi one. In other words, you will not find "Frescobaldi" written on the Ornellaia label. It is not always easy to propose such an idea to an owner, and get their agreement, but it is completely shared by the Frescobaldi family, to whom the idea of the value and independence of brands is quite clear, maintained also on Attems and Luce.

In 2006, came the first "Artist's harvest". The technical staff was asked to sum it up with a single adjective. The chosen artist was then invited to create a work inspired by that word. In 2006, it was Exuberance, in 2007, Harmony, in 2008, Energy and in 2009, Balance. For 2010, Ornellaia's twenty-fifth, it was Celebration – and the chosen artist was Michelangelo Pistoletto.

Each year has a limited edition, normally 111 magnums that bear the artist's work and are sold at auctions in the world's most important cities. All proceeds go to a different charity

foundation that supports art. Between 2006 and 2013, over 1,200,000 Euro were donated.

What's more, Masseto and Ornellaia must be, in order not to overshadow each other, two separate brands and never tasted together. In short: separated under the same roof. Masseto – for which the company Masseto s.r.l. was set up – is also distributed through *négociants* on the Place de Bordeaux. Nor will they have the same winery any more. In fact, the design project for a winery under the old hilltop farmhouse of the 7.7 hectares that produce this inimitable wine is in the process of completion. The design is by the Japanese architect Hikaru Mori.

"In Italy," observes Geddes, "we historically viewed wine as a food commodity like bread or milk, and as such it had to be cheap. Piero Antinori with his Tignanello, in splitting away, in 1971, from the Chianti Classico DOC, which dragged prices down, and Mario Incisa della Rocchetta, with Sassicaia, created the first high-value table wines. They were followed by many other excellent winegrowers. If we look at the Liv-ex index, which measures the great wines, we can find five Super Tuscans: Masseto, Sassicaia, Ornellaia, Tignanello, Solaia; all five increased in value from June 2008 to June 2013 [*also present in the Liv-ex index are the Piedmontese Gaja, Bruno Giacosa and Giacomo Conterno*].

The companies must claw back value on the wine they produce. Our wine must have an international outlook and we must employ strategies appropriate to the goal. Ornellaia was born with Tchelistcheff. Then Michel Rolland arrived in 1991. The internal organizational structure of Ornellaia and Masseto s.r.l. is very streamlined: as of 1 January 2015 we have two function directors: Axel Heinz, the estate director [*German father, French mother, trained at the University of Bordeaux*] and Alex Belson, responsible for marketing and sales."

In 1995, the Luce della Vite project got under way, thanks to the vision of two great figures in the wine world: Vittorio Frescobaldi and Robert Mondavi. They decided to combine their cultures and passions, applying them to the great area of Montalcino. Today, Lamberto Frescobaldi is continuing, independently, to pursue the values of the founders.

Situated at Montalcino, it extends over 192 hectares, of which 55 are under vine. The terrain comprises two main zones: low, clay-rich areas, particularly suited to Merlot, and areas rich in *galestro*, a clayey schist, which sets off the characteristics and qualities of Sangiovese. Luce is the first wine ever produced in Montalcino that combines the elegance and structure of Sangiovese with the roundness and softness of Merlot (around 50%).

Luce is a shining sun with a crown of twelve flames. The label is inspired by the designs of the Main Altar of the Church of Santo Spirito, Brunelleschi's masterpiece of the late fifteenth century, built on land donated by the Frescobaldi.

Luce Brunello was born with the 2003 harvest, and represents the bond the Luce della Vite estate has with the prestigious Montalcino area, of which Brunello is a symbol.

Lucente is the second wine of Luce, the fruit of a selection of the same vineyards. Grapes are chosen that are capable of producing a wine with a contemporary profile.

Friuli Venezia Giulia

At the same time as Tuscany – between the end of the 1960s and the early 1970s – but on the white wine front, there came into the limelight a small Italian region, Friuli Venezia Giulia, where the viticultural situation was very different.

Properties there are highly segmented, with the output of the majority of estates not exceeding 100,000 bottles. The whole sector produces circa 3% of Italy's wine. For the first time in history, however, this region – afflicted by wars, foreign domination and which, for fifty years, bordered onto the Iron Curtain – would find itself, with a strong spirit of resurgence, at the right place at the right time.

The profound renewal was possible thanks to a series of favourable convergences which, almost by magic, came together to pay off the credit the Friulians had built up with history.

In 1963, the autonomous region was established. It introduced a programme to support new vineyards, transforming a strictly "promiscuous" form of viticulture into a specialized one. By 1979, the latter covered 22,235 hectares, 95% of the total.

Part of the secret to the success should also be attributed to the plant nursery industry that began here at the end of the nineteenth century. The Austrians were looking for a solution to the dramatic problem of phylloxera, and in Friuli they found the ideal climatic and soil conditions for producing cuttings grafted onto American root stock. Friuli Venezia Giulia still produces 25% of the world's rooted cuttings. So, at the time, the region already had excellent quality genetic material.

That is not all: the high concentration of oenologists – almost all from Veneto, at least in the first phase, thanks to the Conegliano Institute of Oenology – were carriers of applied innovation. In the 1990s, there were as many as 250 working oenologists in the region, while now there are 290, which means, with output of around 1,400,000 hectolitres, an oenologist every 4,800 hectolitres against an Italian average of 1 oenologist every 11,000 hectolitres.

Mario Schiopetto, an Udine innkeeper, whose first own-label bottle dates to 1965 (it bore the name "Mensa arcivescovile di Gorizia"), was the first to sound the charge. His oenology was of German inspiration. Luigi Soini – the oenologist who played a crucial technical role, in that he helped Mario to make wines of great stature – offers this reflection: "If Mario had been born a producer, he would not have had the same mental liberty, because producers were bound to tradition and mistrusted progress." Mario brought about an epochal change in the style of white wines, effectively inventing modern Italian white wine, and not just that. With him there was a shift from heavy, alcoholic, flat whites lacking in aroma to graceful, fresh, easy-drinking wines with distinct varietal notes, which fitted well with the rejuvenation of Italian cuisine. Particularly memorable are the white-label Tocai (now called Friuliano) of 1971 and 1972: one of the greatest I have ever drunk. It is a pity that Mario did not produce anymore of that selection.

The surprising thing was that, in the space of just a few years, almost all the growers followed suit and shed their past. In short, he set a trend. In 2014, the firm was bought by **Emilio Rotolo**, already owner of Volpe Pasini. A long-time rival of Schiopetto was **Vittorio Puiatti**, a very capable oenologist, the advocate of an even more modern wine than that of Mario, whose lead-

ership overshadowed him. In his views, white wines had to be fine, elegant, fruity, mineraly and with lots of aroma. Pale in colour, with a greenish hue. He was also one of the greatest tasting teachers. In 1970, together with Francesco Gottardo and Zuppichini, he founded Enojulia, a brand that Stock – which produced Grappa Julia – obliged to be changed to Enofriulia. Vittorio rigorously followed the path of the *négociant*: he bought all his grapes. He was, for young sommeliers of the time, a fundamental and formidable wine-tasting teacher. In 2010, his children Giovanni and Elisabetta, after having expanded the business to 70 hectares of vineyard, what with DOC Collio and DOC Isonzo – 650,000 bottles produced in a super-modern winery built in 2008 – sold out to Bertani Domains, a company belonging to the Gruppo Angelini.

Livio Felluga bought his first 30 hectares – abandoned land – at Rosazzo from Count Trento. This was between the end of the 1950s and the beginning of the 1960s. Then, with the arrival of his children, the number of hectares owned rose to 146. His first-born, Maurizio, joined the firm in 1971. In 1974, he began dealing with the American market, against the view of his father.

"It was a crucial turning point. I understood the importance of marketing, communication and company relations. We signed a deal with Mediterranean Import of the Di Belardino family. At the time I was the only Friulian viticulturalist – we began with Pinot Grigio – in the USA. I had realized that on the world markets our whites had a problem of longevi-

ty. We needed to renew. I prepared 25 hectolitres: 1/3 Tocai, 1/3 Sauvignon and 1/3 Pinot Grigio. My father didn't want to know. Fortune had it though that it was tasted by Willsberger, the German journalist who had set up *Grand Gourmet*, a magazine which was very influential in Italy as well. He wrote about it enthusiastically. My father had to give way. That's how the table wine Terre Alte came into being."

This wine is now worth 40,000 bottles a year, and stands at the top of Livio Felluga's pyramid of products. The fortunes of the business then developed thanks to Pinot Grigio, which still represents around 500,000 bottles, about half the entire production. It has gradually been joined by demanding – and successful – wines like the Sossò reds and one of Friuli's best pure varietal Refoscos. The wines of Livo Felluga – who, on 1

September 2014, turned 100, to mark which the family dedicated to him a limited edition wine called "100" – are on the market around the world. The firm has for a long time now been run by his children: besides Maurizio, Elda, Andrea and Filippo.

Marco Felluga – at the beginning of the 1960s – created a business management model that would become standard practice: he made agreements with many Collio growers, who supplied him with grapes, while he implemented a programme of continual viticultural assistance designed to improve quality and offered guaranteed minimum prices. In this way, he formed a group of 45 grape producers, which was unthinkable at the time. In 1966, he took on Gianni Bignucolo – an oenologist from Conegliano, who remained with him for twenty-three

years – who oversaw the winery's steady growth in quality. A supporter of the Consorzio Collio from the very outset, he soon saw that the future would belong to those who owned the vines. In 1967, he bought and restored the historic Russiz Superiore estate; first he went to work on the hillside vineyards – 50 hectares all together – and then built the winery at the foot of the hill. The first Russiz Superiore appeared in 1971. His dream was completed in 1988, with the construction of a vaulted-roof ageing cellar. It was designed by the Udine-based architect Aldo Bernardis, and, at Marco's specific instructions, built partly under the owner's house (linked to the cellar with stairs and a lift), and partly beneath the front garden of the house, now lived in by his son Roberto – a work that is entirely respectful of the environment.

In 1975, he revamped the image, and to do it he turned, for the label, to Silvio Coppola. The result was a graphic design as innovative as the one for Tignanello, but profoundly different. While the Antinori label conveyed the information that it was a *vino da tavola*, and the name of the vineyard coincided with that of the wine, Marco's, by his own choice, had to feature the DOC. So there were three things to indicate: the cru (Russiz Superiore), the DOC (Collio) and the name of the wine, which was the same as that of the vine. It was another profoundly modern label, which set a trend on a par with the Tuscan one. Marco was a volcano of ideas, which he pursued with determination and decision. In 1977, he went to see Luigi Veronelli, and asked him to point out at least twenty high-quality businesses, one for each region, in order to create a group which, together, could do promotional work. This led to the foundation, in 1978, of VIDE (Vini Italiani di Eccellenza/Italian Wines of Excellence). For many years it was a point of reference for the quality of Italian wine, and its stand at Vinitaly became a symbol of how it is possible to collaborate to promote the image of Italian wines and, at the same time, the commercial relations of the individual firms.

After Russiz, he acquired three further estates: La Poggiona in Tuscany, and, in Friuli Venezia Giulia, Castello di Buttrio and Zuani in San Floriano del Collio.

In 1999, he became president of the Consorzio Collio (now *ad honorem*). During his two terms in office he addressed various crucial themes, such as how to strengthen and boost the image of "Collio Bianco" and "Collio Rosso", interpreted, from then on, as the flagship wines of companies, the aim being to reinforce the territory by yoking together the wine with the name of the DOC. He solved, as was his character, one of the problems that was creating divisions among growers: to modify the production regulations so that wines with a rich gold colour, the Gravner-style ones, could also be admitted. Marco recalls: "The purists said amber-coloured wines would falsify the wine concept recognized as Collio. How did I convince them? By saying to them that our heritage is diversity: that we grew out of diversity."

In 2000, Marco handed the firm over to his son Roberto, who had worked with his father since 1980. Roberto has piloted the take-off of Marco Felluga on the world market, increasing from twenty to forty the countries where the firm has a presence; in 2014, the foreign market represented 40% of turnover. He has also given a well-defined style to his simultaneously elegant and complex wines, enhancing the minerality typical of these hills. He has also worked hard to offer the market a demanding, well-developed Pinot Grigio capable of improving with age: Mongris. This work was rewarded when it was listed among the 100 world wines of *Wine Enthusiast* in 2014.

Now, following the division with his sisters, Roberto can count, including the Russiz Superiore cru, on 150 hectares of vineyard – all in the DOC Collio – of which 80 are owned and the rest are rented.

But producers in Grave del Friuli also rose to the quality challenge. The innovators, in fact, were not just in the hills. A Pordenone-based family working in the haulage business, the **Fratelli Pighin**, invested in Risano in 1964, planting their first 30 hectares of vineyard. That figure rose to 120 in 1970, besides 72 of fruit orchards. In 1967, they also acquired the Spessa di Capriva estate in the Collio Goriziano with 30 hectares of vineyards resembling an amphitheatre with annexed winemaking cellar. In Risano, they had a winery built by the most celebrated Friulian architect of the time, Gino Valle, who designed the first example of an Italian insulated winery with prefabricated materials (temperature-regulated vats had not yet appeared, and this work can still be found in architecture books). The terrace roof was irrigated with well water, which contributed to cooling down the spaces. No water was wasted as it went back to where it had come from.

As regards their viticultural choices, they were amongst the first to place faith – already in 1975 – in a modern Sauvignon, thanks to a selection of Rauscedo, the R 3. It broke with the standards of the time, and immediately made an impact on the market, a success due in particular to land suited to this clone. The year 1982 saw the arrival of Paolo Valdesolo, an oenologist who would perfectly interpret the new style of these wines. Cold technology arrived in 1983, and the cement vats were replaced by stainless steel. Pighin was one of the very first, if not the first, market-oriented wine businesses. In turn it was a profound systemic innovation, which enabled the business to plan its production development in the vineyards and on the markets.

In 2003, part of the family pulled out of the business and turned their share over to Fernando Pighin, assisted by his wife Danila and children Raffaela and Roberto.

Exports were the prime goal of **Manlio Collavini**, who took over the family firm at the beginning of the 1960s. In 1970, he sent his first cases of Tocai (now Friuliano) to Montreal in Canada. Soon after, he would be present on various other markets. Collavini has an uncommon capacity to discern the evolution of markets. One of the very first Friulian winemakers to intuit the future of the white-wine vinification of Pinot Grigio, and he anticipated by far a sector that would not open up for a long time, that of "easy" spumantis like the current Prosecco style. In 1972, he created Il Grigio, still in vogue over forty years later. He went to work, then, assisted by *dottor* Paronetto, on modifying the Charmat method. After years of experimentation, the Collavini Method saw the light of day: it consisted of leaving the wine on yeast lees for at least 24 months in 200 hectolitre tanks laid on their sides so a large surface of yeasts come into contact with the wine. This is followed by a further 12 months of bottle-ageing. What's more, he chose Ribolla Gialla, an indigenous variety, as the base. The first vintage would be 1987. For the 2009, released in 2014, he resumed production of a classic method spumante based on Pinot Nero and Chardonnay, called Applause, which remains on the lees for at least four years.

The winery is in the ancient castle (1560) of the Zuccus di Cuccanea counts, situated in Gramogliano, Corno di Rosazzo, and purchased in 1966. The structure has been tastefully restored, and Collavini also has his home there. On the ground floor is the most beautiful ancient kitchen in Friuli.

It was an idea of his, in 1989, that led to "the streets of wine from around the world", whose godfather was Ugo Tognazzi.

Still today, beneath each white sign of the historic streets, there is a yellow one with the name of a wine: from Via della Ribolla Gialla to Via del Porto. For years he has been assisted by his sons Giovanni, Luigi and Eugenio.

Silvio Jermann was the *enfant prodige* of Friulian oenology. He joined the family business in 1971, at the age of seventeen, when he was still an oenology student. He considers "his" first year to be that of 1974, when he presented the new label and began to move into markets outside Friuli. In 1975 – after two trial harvests – he picked ripe grapes from an old hill vineyard planted with Chardonnay, Sauvignon, Malvasia, Ribolla Gialla and Picolit. In so doing, he abandoned a trend that had in just a few years become dominant: early harvesting to emphasize the acidity. He also revived a local custom, picking the grapes together and vinifying them together, and has done so ever since. This marked the birth of Vintage Tunina, a watershed wine in the history of whites, which has and continues to influence many producers from Friuli and beyond. With his Tunina, he anticipated by twenty years a now consolidated tendency, namely, to emphasize pleasantness of taste, roundness, persistence in the mouth, and enveloping, fruity notes.

He invented the first Italian auteur white, in that it was a distinctly recognizable, perfect combination of old and new. It did not, however, fit into the regulatory code for Collio, and so had to be classified as a *vino da tavola*. The wine was an immediate success. Veronelli described it as "the Mennea of wines".

"The wines of Collio have always combined structure with elegance, and I tried to preserve this. To them I added tech-nology and careful control over the fermentation and bottling phases, so it could last in the bottle," he affirms.

Silvio Jermann's style? "Wines should be fine, have body and balance, and be drinkable. They must always, especially whites, be 'feminine': conscious of their ability to seduce, but in a tasteful, never invasive way. Instead wines nowadays have to amaze, and God only knows what damage they have done to the market, distracting consumers from the canons of true beauty. Wines are to be drunk, not tasted and then abandoned. They must fascinate."

In November 2003, the magazine *Gambero Rosso* published a classification of the wines that had had the most "3 glasses" from the guide since 1988. Four wines head the list: the Lunelli's Giulio Ferrari, Piero Antinori's Cervaro della Sala, Nicolò Incisa della Rocchetta's Sassicaia and the Vintage Tunina of Silvio Jermann.

Sustainability is another key notion for Silvio, and, moreover, not one used for marketing purposes.

"It is necessary to be balanced and tell things as they are: an apple, if it's not looked after, rots, even if it's natural. We can't make out that drinking bitter, unbalanced, clumsy wines is a

pleasure just because they are described as 'natural'. I have a vineyard, Pignolo, which is effectively biodynamic, but I don't turn it into a media operation. We have got down – with oenological choices and the introduction of the screw top – to 80–100 mg/l of SO$_2$, well below that of organic wines. We have not used grass- and weed-killers for years. I have always had a high vine per hectare density, as my father taught me: from 5,000 to 8,000 vines. I do not shout it from the rooftops, and have no intention of doing so. When I chose to use the screw top also for fine wines – the first was Dreams – I did not lose any customers. Not one! Which means that people pay attention to the work we do, that consumers have faith in our name."

In 2002, work began to build the winery among the vineyards of Ruttars, so as to handle the company's great wines in an optimum manner: besides Vintage Tunina, the other whites are Capo Martino and Dreams, and there are three reds: two made with Pignolo, Pignacolusse and Vigna Truss – the latter is a four-year Riserva, obtained from a vineyard worked by horses – and a Pinot Nero. It is here, at Ruttars, that "the Jermann philosophy" reaches its fullest expression, combining tradition with the most advanced innovation. The Capo Martino vineyard has just one row of vines per terrace, because it is positioned right in the centre so as to give the vines the best possible conditions. "The Vigna Truss, planted with Pignolo, which we work with horses, reflects the choice of holding on to the old. Ground worked in this way is ideal, only it is not possible to do it for the whole estate, given the costs. But it is a firm principle." Temperatures in the winery are regulated with geothermal energy. The firm is managed by Edi Clementin, who is also responsible for the market, aided by Michele, Silvio's young son.

Silvio Jermann is the Armani of Friuli: he has turned innovation into a classic – in that it is based on good taste – giving rise to a new tradition.

In 1976, a young oenologist named **Giuseppe Lipari** opened a mobile bottling centre (today Centro di Riferimento Enologico), a truck on which he set up a complete bottling line to offer a home service. It was a brilliant intuition, which helped many small winegrowers, who accounted for the majority of production, to release perfect wines onto the market, enabling Friulian whites to become better known.

This was one of the keys to the success and the widespread diffusion of the wines of this region.

One of the patriarchs of Friulian wine, Marco Felluga, observed: "Our small producers of the time, the ones who made 30–40,000 bottles, were a disaster for Collio. Their bottling was poor, and after a couple of months the wines had gone off. Lipari made it possible to raise the average quality of the region's wine." Angelo Solci writes:

"In 1978, **Walter Filiputti** began to restore the historic vineyards of the Abbazia di Rosazzo [*twelfth century*], owned by the Archdiocese of Udine, which for many years had been abandoned. The company looked to the future, and distinguished itself both for the revival of indigenous grape varieties – such as Ribolla Gialla and Pignolo – and for its communication, language and marketing, a true hotbed that foreran many things today. Without forgetting the major revolution wrought by what would be the first dry white Italian wine fermented in *barriques*, the Ronco delle Acacie 1981 [*made only from Tocai grapes*]. We tasted a magnum of the 1984 vintage on 11 October 2014 – so, exactly thirty years old. Rarely have I drunk such a superbly uplifting wine. It reminded me of the very great Montrachet wines.

Walter's work of great historical, viticultural and oenological value was undoubtedly his recovery of the Pignolo in the abbey vineyards, their place of origin [*the first document dates to 1398*], starting from the last two surviving vines. From the very first harvest he interpreted it as a red for ageing. The result was an extraordinarily potent wine, which soon found its way onto the wine lists of the world's most celebrated restaurants. For the 1999 vintage I personally organized the auction for its sale *en primeur*. Those bottles are still today – in 2014 – of sublime youth and fascination. On the occasion Walter held a memorable vertical tasting, starting from 1984, its first year of production. Present at the event were Gino Veronelli and other renowned journalists, including the German Jens Priewe. The best wine was the 1985! It was fantastic, and still young. Walter Filiputti's insight had proved a happy one: Pignolo really was a long-lived wine with an inimitable personality."

The idea of the Vino della Pace ("Wine of Peace"), which rightly had a great deal of resonance in the media and among

consumers, came from **Luigi Soini**, the-then director of the Cantina sociale di Cormòns, a post he handed over, in 2014, to the oenologist Rodolfo Rizzi, in the firm since 1978 and the current president of the oenologists of Friuli Venezia Giulia. In April 1983, Soini planted what would become the "vineyard of the world", comprising 540 different grape varieties (80% of which are white); the figure has now risen to 855, and they are from the five continents, including 12 vines taken from the slopes of Mount Ararat, planted on 2 hectares alongside the winery. The first harvest was in 1985. It yielded a unique white wine (with white-wine vinification of red grapes). About 10,000 bottles are produced each year, and they are sent in three-bottle packs to every civil and religious head of state, as a message of peace and brotherhood. Each year is illustrated with three labels by a like number of artists, who, it should be stressed, ask nothing for their services. The labels are produced, with great skill, by Grafiche Tonutti in Fagagna, Friuli, one of the leading companies in this field in Europe.

The artists are highly celebrated: the first Vino della Pace was recounted by Baj, Pomodoro and Music; in 1986, by Dietman, Minguzzi and Dova; then, in 1987, by Arman, Spoerri and Fiume. In 1988, it was the turn of Santomaso, Dorazio and Consagra; in 1989, of Manzù, Knížák and Paik.

Josko Gravner has devoted much of his life as a winegrower to the search for the ideal wine. His path has been troubled.

A trip to California in the mid-1980s made him reflect. He refused the standardization of taste. A morally rigorous figure, in 1996 a hailstorm destroyed his grapes: he harvested just 18 quintals from 15 hectares. He sent a letter to all his clients, informing them that he would be skipping a year. His decision conferred on him an aura of professional seriousness. He allowed those 18 quintals of white grapes to macerate in wooden vats without adding yeast or temperature control. "Finally," he affirmed, "I have rediscovered the grapes in the wine."

In 1998, he did his first trial in macerating in amphorae. He became the head of a school, and was more than satisfied. In 2001 he began using amphorae, and in 2005 he completed his new winery, where he buried 46 of them, all from Georgia.

The white grapes were left to macerate in them for a whole six months, then the wine was racked off and put back into the amphorae until before the next harvest, after which it went into wood, followed by very long bottle ageing, to the extent that the last white from blends – the Breg amphora 2012 – will be released in 2020. The whites made with grapes from subsequent harvests will be 100% Ribolla Gialla.

In 2003, finally, he vinified Pignolo. "It will only go onto the market when it's ready," he said. It would be released ten years later, in 2013, under the name Rosso Breg.

Now back in the family fold is his daughter Mateja, a woman of strong inner allure. She has the task of recounting the wines of the family. She does so by describing her father:

"We are convinced there are two elements you cannot get back again in life," says Mateja, weighing her words, while her gaze grows serious, "time and health. We can do nothing to control the former, but when it comes to health we certainly can. We have no possibility of replacing it with another asset. Our wine is the result of this creed.

For the most part we eat what we produce. Papà does not use chemicals either in the country or in the cellar. Only the necessary SO₂ prior to bottling. Even though our viticulture is more than organic, he says it serves no purpose to exhibit your choices with certificates. The seriousness of the producer speaks for itself and is the real guarantee."

Josko has an instinctive feel for marking, which enables him to grasp future consumer trends. "Yes, I believe that is the case. He is an anticipator. His strength is the belief he transmits, a kind of unshakable faith in what he does."

We ask Mateja about Marco Simonit, the vine dresser. "My father listens to Marco a great deal. He introduced modified *al-berello* pruning, transferring it onto the Ribolla. They have a frank relationship and understand each other in a flash. On some agronomic choice or other, my father will say: 'Marco told me. And that is that'".

How much do you produce now? "From our 15 hectares under vine we obtain between 22 and 30,000 bottles a year, 85% of which is Ribolla. The rest is Pignolo."

Piedmont

The culture of wine, in Piedmont as in many other Italian regions, has propelled the promotion of a model for the territory to perceive and express its potential for development, while protecting and developing it.

This is the philosophy that has spread so rapidly even in Piedmont, thanks to the renaissance of Italian wine.

The consecrated success of Langhe-Roero and Monferrato, today a part of the UNESCO World Heritage, is without a doubt the accomplishment of the local winegrowers, and the value of Italian style. Great wine is a product of the most beautiful places, and Italy is well endowed with many such places. The Italian cult of beauty has not only conserved them but also improved them.

Ermete Realacci wrote: "These productive and territorial communities continue to exhibit enviable vitality and capacity to grasp and interpret the trends of global markets in a convincing way . . . We are among only five countries in the world – together with China, Germany, Japan and South Korea – to have a foreign exchange balance of more than 100 billion Dollars. The extra power of our enterprises stems precisely from their territorial roots. This is the primordial 'soup' that nourishes their know-how, creativity and initiative . . . Their culture generates entrepreneurship, innovation, originality, adaptability and resistance. The beauty we breathe is, in the words of Carlo M. Cipolla, the main ingredient in making things the whole world wants, in our very own surroundings. The place to find quality in Italy is the territory itself". In the Italian oenological renaissance, Piedmont has done its part with figures like Gaja and Giacomo Bologna. However, the number of those who played key roles in renewing and building a new image is infinite. The image, born of history, has made the difference and lent an identity to the

territory. This resourcefulness born on the farm was successfully transformed into entrepreneurship, while maintaining the typical reserve of local culture in work and communications.

Here, the family business – typical of almost all Italian wine
growers – created the conditions that led to them to respect
their own territory while making its cultural assets and property values clear to onlookers.

*If you love Italian wine, you owe a debt of gratitude
to Angelo Gaja.*
Marvin Scanken (*The Wine Spectator*, editor and publisher)

In Piedmont, the new ideas from Tuscany and Friuli Venezia
Giulia were greeted with less enthusiasm, at least in the first
years of the renaissance, excluding **Angelo Gaja**.

When Angelo joined the company in 1961, Gaja was the
most important winery for Barbaresco. His father sent him off
straight away to gain experience in the vineyards, under the
guidance of Gino Cavallo, then responsible for the agricultural side.

"I stayed there for 7 years, and for me it was a very con-
structive experience. Only in 1968 did I begin to get my nose
into the winery. In March 1970, I entrusted it to Guido Rivel-

GAJA

la, who had full responsibility for forty-three years. The experimentation with *barriques* began in 1966, and continued
[*exclusively with Barbera*] until 1977. The first year *barriques*
were used for Barbaresco was 1978."

In 1972, Angelo Gaja made his first trip to the United
States. "At that time in the USA, Italian wines had a cheap and
cheerful image. That is why I had to come up with a marketing strategy to sustain them." During that trip he met Robert
Mondavi:

"He made an immediate impression on me. I met him again
in 1974. Every time I went to see him I told myself that we had
to change as well. We became friends. He was an insuperable visionary. He would involve you totally. I admired him. In 1978,
he visited me with his staff. Then he returned alone. I took him
to the Belvedere of La Morra, to admire the magic view of the
vineyards. He kept saying: 'Do you hear the sound of the air?' 'I
can't hear any sound,' I replied. 'Listen more carefully.' 'I can't
hear anything,' I insisted. Finally, looking me in the eyes: 'I can
hear a sound coming from the houses. I can hear snoring. It's
you *langaroli* sleeping. With land like this you should be the masters of the world.' I was speechless. Thunderstruck. His belief
was to produce great wines in great volumes. Some years later
everyone began copying him. He invented wine tourism. The
Napa winery was designed also to receive large numbers of people. The open cellars started there: at that time we closed them
and they opened them – no secrets!"

Besides battling in the marketplace, Angelo also had to deal
with local "guerrilla warfare". The innovators first divided and
then constrained the incredulous, suspicious and fearful to accept their ideas. In Piedmont at that time, the traditionalists
were an almost plebiscitary majority. The struggle had become
ideological.

In the end, there was a kind of osmosis, and the heated feel-
ings died down. The final result, in any case, was that the style
launched by Gaja set a trend and, in the end, his wines con-

The Gaja family: Giovanni, Lucia, Rossana, Angelo and Gaia

quered the world. He is at pains to stress that the merit for the quality of Gaja wines belongs to Guido Rivella. "Aren't 50 Three Glasses in the Gambero guide enough? It was much more difficult to obtain them in Italy than abroad."

Angelo played the trump card of uniqueness, of diversity, with great intelligence. In short, his Sorì were to be modern in style without losing the identity of the local territory. It was one of his masterpieces. He immediately saw the force of market penetration that the American press could give him, and he kept a careful and constant eye on it. He presented himself at the world's most important Italian restaurants with his wines. "The first migratory wave," he observes, "had made its fortune in the restaurant trade. They thus became great promoters of our products and wines. Now the second and third generations come to Italy to improve and then go back, and in this way they raise even further the quality of our cuisine, with great benefits for everyone. We will never be able to thank them enough."

Angelo proved to be an unparalleled master in public relations. He remembers his grandmother Rey (to whom he dedicated the white Gaia & Rey): "She always used to say there were four steps to take to have success: doing, knowing how to, knowing how to get others to do, and getting others to know."

Angelo is engaging, pro-active, frank, spell-binding. He knows how to sharp-sightedly use the Piedmontese rigour of his Barbaresco wines, together with the modernity of interpretation that he brings to them.

His marketing policy is precise, incisive and unhesitating. While he raised his Sorì Tildin, San Lorenzo and Costa Russi to their peak, he planned new international-style wines, such as Darmagi (from Cabernet Sauvignon) and Gaia & Rey with Chardonnay.

In 1977, he had a further great idea: he founded Gaja Distribuzione, thanks to which he built up a selection of world-level wines. In the same year, he distributed Romanée-Conti, and in 1985, Mondavi. He entrusted the task to his wife, Lucia, who is excellent, besides being of rare sensitivity and intelligence.

Another strategic move would be to start distributing the glasses of Georg Riedel.

"At the end of the 1980s I began to believe I could do it. *The Wine Spectator* had judged the Sorì Tildin 1985 as 'a wine of incredible depth, suppleness, and elegance', perhaps 'the finest Italian red ever made'. In the middle of the 1990s, thanks also to some excellent harvests, the impression that my project was heading in the right direction became concrete.

Success also arrived – Angelo emphasizes – because a new change was taking place in American consumers: they were understanding our fine, clean wines. Those tannins, which in the meantime we had further shaped, became a plus point, like the vintages."

After returning, in 1988, to Barolo, where he would produce Sperss, he decided that in the future he would invest in Tuscany: in 1994, at Montalcino and in 1996, at Bolgheri, the new winery of which reflects his own character: rigorous, perfectionist, essential. Designed by his architect friend Giovanni Bo from Asti, it is minimalist, with some concessions being made in the furnishings. Functional, but no less fascinating for that. Far from it: it needs to be explored, lived in, walked through. A visit begins with the vineyards, which has always been his passion.

"In 1973 we had 21 hectares of vineyards," declares Gaja, "and we produced 60–65,000 bottles. Now in Piedmont, we have 100 hectares and make 350,000 bottles. At the Pieve di Santa Restituta, Montalcino, we about around 100,000 bottles from 27 hectares, while at Ca' Marcanda, Bolgheri, we have 110 hectares which currently give us about 500,000 bottles."

For Italian winegrowers, Angelo Gaja also represents a form of sweet historic revenge over more celebrated French cousins. He teaches that moral rigour in production – like ascribing credit where it is due, hard work on the international markets, marketing, image, putting yourself on the line and communication – are an integral part of the product.

It was inevitable that the success of Angelo Gaja would spread from Barbaresco to nearby Barolo, which, until his arrival on the market, had been the older brother.

Always on the side of the innovators, Angelo Gaja involuntarily stimulated a reaction from the "traditionalists", creating, in this way, a very positive effect – a widening of the offer on the market, especially in terms of the spontaneous marketing that has made Italian wine so great.

Winemakers such as Bruno Giacosa and Bartolo Mascarello greatly defended tradition. The latter, almost right till the end of his days, said: "No to the *barrique*!" but, even more: "The only way is not to follow a frivolous fashion, but to open our minds to a high-quality oenological culture, with a critical revival of local culture and acquired experience."

"Loyal to the line" could then be the motto of **Bartolo Mascarello**, champion of the most authentic viticultural and winemaking tradition of the Langhe. Founded in 1918 by Giulio – the father of Bartolo, who entered the business in 1945, taking over the reins in the 1960s – the winery owned 5 hectares of vines, and that is still the figure now. From the start, the production of its Barolo involved ageing in large wooden barrels, which have never been abandoned for *barriques*, with grapes from different vineyards. That is still the case today. "First my grandfather, then my father [*who died in 2005*]," recounts Maria Teresa, "immediately chose a *modus operandi* that we have never thought should be changed. We conserved the practice of using a blend for the production of Barolo, our emblematic wine, in order to maintain a stylistic constancy impossible with cru wines. Certainly, we could earn a lot more by vinifying a vineyard like Cannubi separately, but it is a question – also of marketing – that does not interest us." And the famous "aversion" toward *barriques*? "Same thing. Barolo started out in large casks and then, in an effort to chase the market, many turned to small wood barrels, only to then retrace their steps, at least in part." Over the long term, not changing has proved paradoxically to be a revolutionary and spot-on choice. Also commercially – 60% of the wine is exported to North America and "Old Europe" – nothing has changed. A direct relationship is cultivated with the clientele, without sales networks: everything leads back to the winery, the sole centre of gravity and an obligatory port of call for anyone interested in learning about the company's wines. Time has told with Mascarello.

Bruno Giacosa is a visionary *vigneron* who has managed to interpret the territory with unique wines. His knowledge of the Langhe vineyards made him a highly refined *négociant* even before he was a producer, enabling him, when his Falletto estate had not yet been set up, to produce, using bought grapes, some of the best ever Barolos and Barbarescos.

Le Rocche del Falletto at Serralunga d'Alba, Asili at Barbaresco and Santo Stefano at Neive are the most important owned vineyards: three crus that he bought and which immediately yielded stylish wines, never too material, of sober elegance and deep complexity.

"I started as a young man," recounts Bruno, "with a passion for wine in my blood. I had no mentor, and I made my

own way: I gained my experience by going to vineyards, discovering the best crus in the area, but above all by loving this work." He continues with the ardour of a young boy: "I consider myself a cellarman; I have created great wines and, even now that I am eighty-four and am starting to have some health problems, with the help of my assistants I still manage to stir great emotions in those who drink my nectars."

When he started his business, at the end of the 1940s, wine was for the most part sold by bulk. In 1961, he began to bottle it: an anticipation of the times that enabled him to establish himself, before other colleagues, on the Italian market and then internationally. As regards the promotional and trading activities, Giacosa is clear-cut: "I have never done anything to promote my wines, I have never travelled the world to present them, the world has come to me to buy them!"

Piedmont has a long wine tradition thanks both to the reign of the Savoy and to strong ties with French nobility. The story of the Giacomo Borgogno, one of the oldest wineries in Piedmont (founded in 1761 by **Bartolomeo Borgogno**) is emblem-

atic. In 1861, their wines accompanied the official dinner in celebration of the union of Italy. In 1920, **Cesare Borgogno** took over the winery. He is remembered for the dispute with French authorities (who wanted him to remove the name Borgogno from the label, too similar to Borgogna), but even more so for the fact that every year thereafter a part of Barolo production was forgotten and the bottles were jealously conserved in the wine cellar. The best years (today there are twenty thousand bottles conserved) represent the historical memory of Langa. This reserve is practically unique and is a real gem for the wine collection market (US and UK above all). The memory of vertical wine tastings from the 1940s to the 1980s is still vivid, with participants moved by reliving so much history in a glass.

After World War II, it was Ida's time (Cesare's granddaughter) with her husband Franco Boschis. Their sons, Cesare and Giorgio, ran the estate until a few years ago. After almost 250 years, in 2008 the Borgogno-Boschi transferred the estate to the Farinetti family. This introduced another young fellow, Andrea Farinetti, into the story. He has already created a stir with the provocation of his No Name, a Barolo 2008 downgraded by the winery itself to Langhe Nebbiolo as a protest against bureaucracy.

It was the influence of France that led to identifying the name of the wine with the main towns, like Barolo and Barbaresco, within which the various crus were identified. One of the first was that of **Aldo Conterno**, a country gentleman born in 1931 who conquered the world of oenology with Riserva Granbussia, created in 1970 and produced only in the best

years. Like Cicala, Romirasco and Colonello, it is named for splendid vineyards (28 hectares) situated in Bussia di Monforte d'Alba, today entrusted to the care of his sons Stefano, Franco and Giacomo.

In 1969, he separated from his brother Giovanni to follow his own personal path toward his own style in producing Barolo. True to tradition, he also prepared his wine to satisfy the modern expectations of easy drinking by reducing fermentations, using stainless steel with continuous pumping over, limited contact with tannins and ageing for at least two years only in large casks of Slavonian oak. When his sons entered the business, some labels began to make use of small wood, just for ageing.

Another banner of Barolo and Italian oenology in the world is **Giacomo Conterno**'s Monfortino, one of the best known and most expensive wines, awarded the highest ranking by many Italian and foreign guide books. Giacomo created it in the 1920s, later his son Giovanni produced it and now, after his death, it is produced by Roberto Conterno, son of Giovanni and grandson of Giacomo.

Roberto is not an oenologist or an agricultural scientist, but a champion of tradition and opponent of *barriques*. With Nebbiolo Lampia grapes, he produces wine with long macerations, which can last more than one month in large casks using methods learned from his father and grandfather. His Barolo goes on the market after seven to eight years of ageing and the wines continue to evolve in the bottle for decades.

Giovanni was one of the protagonists of the creation of Barolo as it is known today. A proud opponent of conferring Neb-

biolo to the cooperative wineries, he urged his fellow townsmen to bottle their own, attempting to make them understand the full potential of those grapes.

The caption Monfortino appeared for the first time on a Barolo Extra of 1924. However, it is not a cru but a name conceived to emphasize the town where the winery is located and where some of the grapes to produce it are grown. In 1974, Giacomo acquired the Cascina Francia farm in Serralunga. Since 1978, Monfortino is born here and produced exclusively with the grapes of these vineyards.

In the duel between traditionalists and modernists, the latter earned points thanks to the group of *Barolo Boys* and to the Ceretto brothers.

It was the 1980s, and the Langhe were not what we now know today: they were "the places of rack and ruin" of Beppe Fenoglio, of Barolo that cost just a few Lire more than Dolcetto and which some producers handed over as part payment for goods. Some young producers decided to react to the state of affairs, to make their area a second Burgundy, to change the way the Nebbiolo grape was interpreted. That was the beginning of the story of what *The New York Times*, in 1990, would call the Barolo Boys: Elio Altare, Luciano Sandrone, Domenico Clerico, Enrico Scavino, Roberto Voerzio, Bruno Rocca, Chiara Boschis and Giorgio Rivetti of La Spinetta.

Defined as modernists, they introduced some important innovations such as thinning out in the vineyard, a drastic reduction in yields, separate vinification of crus, the use of new technology in the winery and the introduction of small French oak barrels in place of the traditional large casks. A season of change, in which it was necessary to overcome familiar aversions made up of deep-rooted traditions and a fear of the new.

Their courage in innovating was related in a documentary shot in the Langhe, and which came out in spring 2014. The work of writer Tiziano Gaia and director Paolo Casalis, both born in the Alba area, it is titled *Barolo Boys. Storia di una rivoluzione*, a story that began precisely in 1986, a couple of months after the methanol wine scandal. The film brings together the testimony of winemakers, critics and opinion leaders, importers – in particular the Italian-American Marc de Grazia, who launched them in the United States – restaurateurs and coopers.

Elio Altare, acknowledged to have inspired the movement, is a winemaker at La Morra, in the hamlet of Annunziata, with 10 hectares, only half of which are owned. He anticipated everyone in 1983, when he decided to get rid of the old casks. "Nature had much more good sense than man, who ruined those wines with rotting casks." He changed over to *barriques*. Two months later his father went to a notary and disinherited him. "Not even two years later," Elio recalls, "he died convinced that I was mad." His Barolo wines broke with the past and responded to the need for change: 60,000 bottles a year, including Barolo DOCG, Langhe Rosso DOC, Dolcetto d'Alba DOC and Barbera d'Alba DOC. Now, as a real master of the vineyard, Elio Altare has set himself a fresh challenge: to farm two hectares of vineyard on his small Campogrande estate at Riomaggiore in the Cinque Terre.

What immediately springs to mind when thinking of **Luciano Sandrone** is his Cannubi Boschis, the winery's only cru, sold since 1985. He was the cellarman of the Marchesi di Barolo until 1978, the year in which he began to make wine for himself after having bought a parcel of land.

Domenico Clerico, completely self-taught, became a winemaker in 1976, when he decided to throw in his job as a commercial agent to dedicate himself full-time to the family farm. His most representative label is Ciabot Mentin Ginestra, a vineyard in the municipality of Monforte d'Alba. In 2003, he was awarded the Cangrande Medal, given each year to figures who have distinguished themselves in viticulture and winemaking.

The winery of **Enrico Scavino** bears the name of its founder, Paolo. It is situated in the municipality of Castiglione Falletto. The first Barolo Bric del Fiasc – which made him known around the world – dates to 1978. In their Rocche dell'Annunziata vineyard, there are vines dating to 1942.

Roberto Voerzio started out, in 1986, with just two hectares. Now he owns 12, amongst the most beautiful in the municipality of La Morra. A small number of bottles, but of extraordinary quality.

Bruno Rocca, who is famous for the Rabajà cru of Barbaresco, set out in the trade at the end of the 1970s, driven by a strong passion and motivation. He is now accompanied in this adventure by his children Luisa and Francesco, who share with him strong ties to the local area, combined with a great desire for innovation.

Below
Bruno and Marcello Ceretto

Facing page
Giacomo Bologna

Below, on right
Chiara, Giorgio and Luisa Soldati

Chiara Boschis, the only woman in the midst of so many men, was, in the 1990s, the first woman to run a historic wine estate in Barolo, E. Pira e Figli, bought by the Boschis family in 1981.

Giorgio Rivetti was another important player in the Barolo Boys grouping, who was to lead the family business, La Spinetta, to great success.

The Barolo Boys disbanded long ago. But their story lives on in their businesses and in their wines, known and sold around the world.

Bruno and **Marcello Ceretto** played a very important role in the innovation of the Barolo style and of Piedmontese wine in general, but above all in the field of marketing. They developed a project that anticipated by decades the concept of forging a territorial system, linking wine to other local products of excellence. The name Ceretto is associated not only with fine wines, magnificent vineyards and modern wineries, but also hazelnuts, *torrone*, cheeses and top-quality dining, with the purchase of the Piazza Duomo restaurant in Alba (now with 3 Michelin stars under chef Enrico Crippa), their objective being to attract foreigners to come and visit the Langhe.

If Marcello Ceretto, of the two brothers, is the reflective, technical one, Bruno complements him: dynamic, creative, market-oriented, one of the first to "tread the sidewalks of the world, otherwise no one will bother coming to look for you".

"The land, the land, the land, and once again the land," wrote Luigi Veronelli: the same philosophy that the two brothers pursued right from the 1960s, when they entered the business alongside their father Riccardo. They selected and acquired top vineyards – they now own over 160 hectares – in an area that knew nothing about the cru concept. To create labels able to communicate effectively, they turned also to Silvio Coppola, who designed some of their most celebrated ones. "That way, anyone drinking the wine have the vineyard of origin in front of their eyes, with the possibility of then being able to visit it. The vineyard is history, and the names of the hills remain: that reinforces the quality and credibility of the nectars produced there."

Today, the company has four independent production estates, each with its own winery and bearing the name of its specific geographic location: Bricco Rocche in Castiglione Falletto, which makes Bricco Asili at Barbaresco (1973); the Vignaioli di Santo Stefano at Santo Stefano Belbo (1973), together with brothers Gianpiero and Andrea Scavino, given over to the production of Moscato d'Asti and Asti Spumante; the Barolo crus (1982), famous for the glass cube, a work of art and monument to Barolo; the Tenuta Monsordo Bernardina at Alba (1987), devoted to the production of Langa and Roero wines. Emblematic of the Cerettos production are, from a sentimental point of view, the Barolo Bricco Rocche, and in terms of commercial success, the Blangé. The family's winemaking history is being continued by the brothers' children, who have been in the business since 1999: Lisa, Roberta, Alessandro and Federico.

The renewal spread to overly berated Barbera as well. In the early 1980s, it was **Giacomo Bologna** who took on the task of taking it back to the top position it deserved. His work would influence all of Italian oenology. After losing his father at a very early age, in 1953, he helped his mother Caterina run the *trat-*

toria Braida, which soon set standards in Monferrato, and was frequented by gourmets and celebrated figures. Wine was already his passion.

A crucial year was 1971, when he met Luigi Veronelli. From then on news spread about the fine Barbera Braida of Rocchetta Tanaro. In 1980, Giacomo closed the *trattoria* and devoted himself entirely to wine, together with his delightful wife, Anna, who fully shared the winemaking adventure with him. Also dating to the same year were the experiments with maturing Barbera in *barriques*, which soon led to the revolution in quality of this wine and its worldwide success.

At the end of the 1980s, Giacomo, who died on 25 December 1990, was joined in the business by his children Raffaella and Giuseppe, both oenologists. They pursued the visionary philosophy of their parents, leading them, amongst other things, to purchase 17 hectares of fine vineyards in the Montebruna area, Bricco and Bricco Limonte. "The quality of my father that fascinated me most was his inexhaustible curiosity," Raffaella remembers. "If he liked a wine, he did everything he could to study it, understand its secrets. He saw himself as an impassioned peasant, keen to share in friendship his boundless love of the land."

The estate's flagship wine is undoubtedly Bricco dell'Uccellone, created in 1982 from the strong desire of "Braida" to produce a Barbera d'Asti of great quality, power, complexity, elegance and longevity. A dream come true.

To disprove those who believe that Piedmont only produces big reds, along came the "peasant with a degree" **Giorgio Soldati**, of La Scolca, the emblem of Gavi.

The business was founded in 1919 in a farmhouse belonging to Soldati's grandfather. After graduating in economics and buisness at the Bocconi in 1971, Giorgio decided to become a *vigneron*. He went to Épernay to take a microbiology course on the life of yeasts: a key step. Upon his return to Italy he devoted himself full time to the company, producing "wine for a trade and spumante for passion".

La Scolca has a rigorous agronomic approach: the grapes of each vineyard are vinified separately, leading to the production of the famous Gavi dei Gavi, the fruit of the best bases. The discovery of the longevity of La Scolca's wines came about by chance. With the commencement of spumanti production, reserves were set aside for the liqueur. When tasted again years later, their extraordinary minerality came to light: and so, in 1981, it was decided to create the "past times" line, the fruit of the bottling of small unblended quantities of this wine, released onto the market many years after the harvest. These efforts were repaid with excellent commercial success, especially abroad, thanks also to the exceptional communication work done by Chiara Soldati, Giorgio's daughter. Amongst the various labels that are produced, the one that is still recalled

with greatest affection is the Etichetta Nera, the progenitor of the company's output, which has been made since 1969.

Another challenge in the white wine category came from Roero, with Arneis: a genuine phenomenon for the exponential growth of a rare variety (indigenous since 1400), which rapidly became the cutting edge of Piedmontese whites.

Roero was granted DOC status in 1989, and became a DOCG in 2004.

A technological and economic neo-Enlightenment was born in wild Roero; it was a revolution that started from the bottom up, with the pupil exceeding the master. Arneis, in fact was planted among other rows of vines because its early ripening grapes attracted the starlings, who sated themselves on these, thereby preserving the precious red grapes. The classic nemesis of history.

In the early 1970s there were a dozen or so hectares, while now there are almost a thousand.

The great protagonists in Roero are Roberto Damonte (Malvirà), Matteo Correggia, Piero Bovone (Cornarea), Bruno Ceretto, Domenico Almondo, Antonio Deltetto and Giovanni Negro. The first experiments were carried out in the Castello di Neive of Count Riccardi, who then sold the estate to the Stupino brothers. "In 1978," confirms Angelo Solci, who witnessed that innovative process at close hand, "Italo Stupino, the owner of the Castello di Neive with his brothers, began, in conjunction with professors Eynard and Gandini from the School of Agriculture in Turin, the planting and clonal selection of Arneis, in the rediscovery of which it played a central role."

Even the choice of a traditional name (from *vinum Renexii*, mispronounced and transformed by the local idiom into *arneis*) worked in its favour: a fun name well suited to this versatile product. Arneis, in fact, denotes *arnese*, "tool, instrument", but when used to describe character, it means "mischievous, impish".

Piedmont also has a sweet side to it, in the form of Moscato naturale d'Asti. Its definitive consecration arrived thanks to an English wine writer, Tom Stevenson, who included it among the spumantis with a very high score – 96 points – obtained by the "star of Moscato d'Asti", as it was described by Romano Dogliotti (*Christie's World Encyclopedia of Champagne & Sparkling Wine*, Absolute Press, 2013).

Let's say that it was high time, given the absolute greatness of this wine, undoubtedly the most pleasing, easy-drinking, perfect and enchanting dessert wine in the world, which, unlike Asti, is largely produced by small and medium-sized wineries.

Romano Dogliotti (La Caudrina), Paolo Saracco, Walter Bera and I Vignaioli di Santo Stefano spearheaded an innovation that had its followers.

The work done in the vineyard and the winery by these pioneers resulted in a wine with a very white, soft froth; a fine-grain perlage; a lively and pure array of aromas; a supple sweetness of structure; and intricately wrought and tailored persistence. It is a wine, as Francesco Falcone says, that you can addresses without formality, avoiding superfluous preliminaries: it is the propensity for enjoyment that reigns supreme here. And the wine responds with equal frankness, as a true champion of liveliness, frothiness and fragrance.

Veneto

During the six grape harvests – 2009 to 2014 – the Veneto region has confirmed its leadership as the most productive among the regions of Italy, with a mean harvest of 7,780,000 hectolitres.

What inspires consideration is the capacity to unite quantity with quality. Both are growing. This turning point does honour to the producers in Veneto, who have taken a stance that puts them in the best possible conditions to face market challenges. An example for others.

But there is more to the story. Their capacity to revive and strengthen wines such as Soave, Valpolicella and Bardolino is amazing. After the splendour of the first post-World War II decades, they seemed tarnished and on the slide to decadence.

To the contrary, these wines have recovered quality, image and markets, taking their position among the most important Italian export wines. Soave made a leap of 30% in production and its quality is surprising, to say the very least. Lugana is growing steadily, especially in Germany. Valpolicella – with Amarone – and Bardolino guarantee fine return on investment and good performance on the market.

Last, but not least, Prosecco: the greatest international phenomenon among spumante wines, discussed in great detail in the chapter dedicated to it. It suffices to say that the two DOC protocols – Prosecco and Conegliano-Valdobbiadene – account

for 54% of DOC production in the Veneto region. Soave follows with 12%, then Valpolicella (8%) and Bardolino (6%).

The middle of the 1960s saw the rise to celebrity of the Riserva Capo di Stato created by **Count Loredan Gasparini**. This wine owes its name to the fact that it was often used during visits to Venice by heads of state, who greatly admired it. The newspapers of the time – not just Italian, but English, French and, later, American ones as well – included it among the world greats. It was the result of a selection of grapes, especially those from an old 1946 vineyard called "Le 100 Piante" ("The 100 Plants"), located at Venegazzù del Montello, 40 km north of Venice. It comprises Cabernet Sauvignon, Merlot, Cabernet Franc and Malbec from old clones.

Veneto is also home to a fine, highly rated wine, which, for over fifty years, has enjoyed uninterrupted success around the world: the Pinot Grigio of Santa Margherita. A worldwide success that was born at the dawn of the renaissance, and perhaps even anticipated it: we are in 1960, and at that time it took courage to radically modify the style of a wine. It could only come about from within a family business whose DNA contained a capacity for vision like that of the counts Marzotto di Valdagno.

Count Gaetano was a far-sighted entrepreneur, with assets in the textile industry, who rose to the challenge of agriculture with the purchase, in 1930, of the 1,000-hectare Stucky property. Thus began one of the most fascinating adventures in twentieth-century Italian oenological history. The Count called his estate Santa Margherita, a tribute to his wife, and on the label he put the Venetian villa he owned at Villanova di Fossalta di Portogruaro, where he lived with his eight children, and where the business was based. A new town sprang up around it, which Count Gaetano wanted to become a model town for the high quality of life of the workers and peasant farmers.

The history of Santa Margherita is bound to a particular wine: Pinot Grigio, one of the most important Italian brands in the world. The wine that marked a turning point came in 1961.

It was a watershed wine that obliged everyone, in the span of a decade, to follow suit. It was not just the fortune of Santa Margherita, but also of thousands of wineries and farms, especially in the Triveneto, where, as the Friulian Marco Felluga says, it ought to be called "Saint Pinot Grigio".

The managing director at the time was Arrigo Marcer, while the winery was run by the oenologist Giorgio Mascarin.

The capacity of the company's own vineyards was not nearly sufficient, so it was necessary to bring together a very large group of winegrowers – today, what with cooperatives and individual grape producers, there are around a hundred – and di-

rect them toward the production of high-quality grapes in compliance with a well-defined protocol. The area envisaged for production was Alto Adige, which then, in view of the success, was also extended to the Val d'Adige in Trentino.

It was a case of building a chain based on trust with the historically mistrustful world of smallholders. The surprising aspect of the story is that, besides having formed this group, still active today – there are not a few families that have been growing Pinot Grigio grapes for Santa Margherita for fifty-two years! – the company also convinced members to follow it in a development strategy designed to avoid price speculation.

The Marzottos, in fact, proposed to maintain price levels without excessive oscillations, by adopting a sales policy that guaranteed, over time, a greater than average remuneration, thus providing protection from dangerous collapses. Making the growers understand that the company would distribute a share of the earnings to the whole chain was indubitably a work of great value, in human and not just in business terms.

Ettore Nicoletto, the current managing director of Santa Margherita, observes: "The company's policy has never been to stimulate the market, but to follow it. To never compromise on quality. To invest heavily on the positioning of the brand, especially on the American market, where Pinot Grigio arrived in 1979 thanks to an agreement with Anthony Terlato's Paterno."

From the outset, Santa Margherita positioned its wine at the top, with a sale price to restaurants of 6–7 Dollars. In 2013, it had sales of 620,000 cases (that is, 7,440,000 bottles), making it into the top three in the Most Popular Italian Wines ranking drawn up by the American magazine *Wine & Spirits* in April 2013: Antinori with Tignanello and Chianti Classico Peppoli, Santa Margherita with Pinot Grigio dell'Alto Adige and Gaja with Sorì Tildin Barbaresco and Promis Ca' Marcanda from Bolgheri.

And that is not all: it is the only wine in the United States sold in quantities exceeding 500,000 cases at a restaurant price of 21.5 Dollars a bottle. Today the company is present in 85 countries, with a total of 14 million bottles, of which 10 are Pinot Grigio.

The Veneto was also able to display, besides wines of world-level importance, some authentic gems that opened up the way for small but great winemakers who raised to the highest level the reputation of the nation's wines: one of these is **Bepi Quintarelli**, the spiritual father of Amarone, the person who made it an icon, but at the same time part of the world heritage. A simple man, in love with life, but not the bright lights and fanfare of success. His relationship with nature was poetic and spiritual.

Bepi was the youngest son of Silvio, and from his father he acquired a love for the vineyard and a passion for wine. He started out in the business on the hill of Cerè, in the municipality of Negrar, when he took over the firm at the beginning of the 1950s. He immediately began searching for a valid method of producing a great "dry" wine that could make the sweet Recioto more readily adaptable to international dining tables. The result was his Amarone, which found admirers

everywhere. The celebrated Veronese chef, Giorgio Gioco, designed the unmistakeable label, which has always remained the same. Between 1955 and 1960 he received due tribute, for that great dry red Valpolicella wine obtained from dried grapes, from the likes of Mario Soldati, Ernest Hemingway and Luigi Veronelli, an admirer of his.

Robert Chadderdon, who has imported and distributed the wine in the United States since the 1970s, played an important role. He was an emblematic figure in the development of the greatest Italian wines in America. For Bepi, Amarone had to encapsulate the supreme excellence of its territory, and as of 1999 he decided that it would not be produced except in exceptionally good years: "When the Amarone doesn't turn out as I want, I don't sell it as such, but as Rosso del Bepi. It's still an Amarone, but not with the qualities I want from it!" A man of times past, he brought modernity to Valpolicella and was both far-sighted and enlightened for his modern style. His wines were states of mind, a feverish search for beauty, balance, elegance. His life was an extraordinary adventure that finished ordinarily, as he wanted: at home with his beloved family, the aroma of must and the gentle stirring of leaves caressed by the breeze of Valpolicella (he died on 15 January 2012). "One must be content in life. For us everything comes from Providence", he used to say.

"His vineyard," recalls Angelo Solci, whose Enoteca Bepi supplied, "consisted of old stock producing indigenous grape varieties. He left just a small number of bunches to ripen; he oversaw the running of the vineyard and the production of wines with maximum attention, using only natural products and materials, in full respect of nature and its tempo: a forerunner of natural-organic precision viticulture and oenology. The per hectare grape yield was, and still is today, 30–40 quintals. The drying was carried out with the methods of a consolidated local tradition: once the Corvina grape bunches had been harvested, he removed the wings, the so-called *recie* [*'ears'*], hence Recioto. He then placed them on racks to dry, a method still used today by Bepi's heirs. The wines were matured at length in large oak barrels [*8–10 years*] and then bottle-aged for a further 5–6 years."

The resulting wines were incomparable, and fortunately the story continues today.

"It seemed like the vineyard had become an optional for the wine companies. The industrialists of wine smiled, dismissing us as 'peasants', but time proved us right. When the law on DOC appellations was passed in 1963, the wine industry dominated the market, but it was unable to respond to the emerging concept of quality associated with the territory that new consumers were demanding." This is how **Sandro Boscaini** effectively summed up of the situation in the Italian wine world before the renaissance.

If Quintarelli was the man who made Amarone a must, Sandro Boscaini – the owner, with his family, of Masi – made it an international phenomenon. But without budging an inch on quality. Indeed, he innovated constantly. "My father," recalls Boscaini, "judged Valpolicella to be too simple, albeit successful. From 1958 he kept thinking about how to modernize it. In 1967, the idea took concrete form when Masi refermented the

Grape withering in a traditional
fruit-drying room for Amarone
production

wine on Amarone skins, releasing onto the market a new style of Valpolicella: it was the Campofiorin Ripasso 1964."

The term "Ripasso" was registered as a trademark. Burton Anderson wrote in *Decanter*: "Masi has created a new class of Veronese wines". On the market it received growing international success, which subsequently led to lots of emulation, including an improper use of the "Ripasso" trademark. But Sandro, instead of taking legal steps, made it freely available, donating it to the Verona Chamber of Commerce.

Campofiorin was the archetype of a whole series of wines inspired by it. Amarone was described as "a modern wine with an ancient heart".

At Vinitaly in 1987, Masi presented his 1983 vintage Amarone, while other producers were offering the 1977 or 1978. There was surprise, almost outrage, amongst the Veronese producers, while the press and national and international customers appreciated the wine's new style.

"It was," reflects Sandro, "the first example of Amarone created to satisfy a more highly evolved consumer", the result of a long-term programme of renewal, which unfolded in various phases. The technical team – the oenologist then was Nino Franceschetti – identified the first problem as lying in an erratic management of the fermentation and the subsequent lengthy ageing in large wooden barrels, where the wines oxidized. The arrival in the company's technical team of Lanfranco Paronetto, the leading Italian expert on yeasts, marked the beginning of a process of renewal which also involved the rediscovery of the *fusto veronese* (a 660- to 700-litre barrel made from top-quality wood). The elegance of the wine increased, without distorting the broad complexity. All this happened with the 1983 harvest.

Another critical area were the drying premises. The "NASA" system (Natural Appassimento Super Assisted) was devised to manage, with digital technologies, the long phase of *appassimento*, so as to avoid harmful moulds. In ideal climatic conditions, grapes are left in the hands of benign nature; in the event of this not being so, windows are opened or closed, and humidity and ventilation controlled.

The third innovation took place when Attilio Scienza began to work with the technical team. Traditional varieties were studied and revived, also through the planting of an experimental company vineyard, from which Oseleta was selected, which would then be added to Molinara, Corvina and Rondinella to create innovative Amaroni.

Scienza and his team conducted rigorously scientific research on the best vineyards in Valpolicella classica, which led to the identification of three Amarone crus, Campolongo di Torbe, Mazzano and Vaio Armaron, to which two further Amaroni were added: Costasera and Riserva di Costasera. These five Amaronis made Masi the most important producer of this appellation.

Masi brought about changes not just in his wines, but also in terms of image creation and communication, thanks to the Premio Masi. The credit for conceiving of this award must go to three Veronese friends: Sandro Boscaini, the writer Cesare Marchi and the journalist Giovanni Vicentini. The Premio Masi Civiltà Veneta got off the ground in 1981, and is awarded to personalities originating from the Venezie who have distinguished themselves in the fields of literature, art, journalism, science, the performing arts and show business, and economics.

An apt synthesis of Masi's immense commitment came from Andrea Rea, professor of marketing at the Bocconi: "Masi is a cultural cru."

Sandro Boscaini found it hard to bear that Amarone was ignored by part of the international press. He therefore contacted *The Wine Spectator* in 1995, and proposed holding a tasting in their New York offices, consisting of various vintages of the Mazzano cru dating from 1941 to 1990. The tasters were amazed at the complexity of this wine, its capacity for ageing and its originality, due not only to the grapes and the method

of production, but also to the organoleptic spectrum it embraced. The magazine's editor, Bruce Sanderson, in an article entitled "Meeting Italy's Gentle Giant", stated, among other things: "It was a wonderful occasion to understand the complex and mysterious nature of this gentle giant."

The Veneto can boast of having the largest private Italian wine producer, both in terms of hectares under vine – 2,000, on a par in this with Piero Antinori – and number of bottles (40 million): the man in question is **Gianni Zonin**, who has an amazing lucidity and vision of the wine world: "Estates are like men: each different from each other insofar as they are born in different climes and lands, and with different histories. We now own nine winemaking companies in seven Italian regions, which individually are small- to medium-sized with around 140–180 hectares under vine, with the exception of Ca' Bolani [*in the DOC Aquileia zone of Friuli*], which has 600. Nine estates that we manage – and look after – as if they were a like number of family businesses, flexible and reactive to markets. Our offer consists of around 65 different types of wine, mostly indigenous, which enable us to go onto the market and to always find a product that attracts and interests customers. Each of our estates, moreover, is geared in to providing hospitality, and offers the same informal style, but with the characteristics, tastes and typical food and wine products of the individual areas.

Betting on indigenous varieties was my most important wine production insight, and the facts are proving me right. As a representative example I might mention Prosecco, whose name we made a decisive contribution to saving with the extension of the DOC to Friuli Venezia Giulia, the region where the place of origin is actually found – Prosecco, near Trieste. It is now the largest DOC in the world, capable of yielding 300 million bottles."

Gianni Zonin often mentions his uncle Domenico, whose wise sayings he gathered together into a booklet entitled *Va piano e fa presto. I proverbi dello zio Domenico* (Bassano del Grappa, 2000) – "Go slow, go quick. The proverbs of Uncle Domenico". "It is a saying that expresses, more than any other, his philosophy of life: always reflect at length about things before deciding, but then, once having decided, act quickly. My uncle lived to 102 years of age, straddling three centuries; having

been born in 1899, he had a truly uncommon wisdom. In 1921, he turned around the smallholding family [*which had worked a few own-property vineyards since 1821*]. Not having any children, he saw me as the one to keep the business going. He lived opposite the offices. He always helped me, from every point of view."

In 1976, as the leading Italian producer, Zonin invested in Virginia in the United States. What were the reasons for this? And why not California? "I felt the wines of that area to be too different to the Italian style, which I did not want either to compromise or alter. Virginia, in terms of climate and terrain, guar-

anteed me wines as I imagined them: sophisticated, elegant, pleasing and easy. Plus, and this is a very important aspect, it was on the East Coast, where the major markets were for the consumption of wine in the States."

The decisive change for Italian wines came in 1986. Zonin continues: "Our winemaking history was one associated with poverty, with absurd distortions in production. In the middle of the 1960s we used to distil 32 million hectolitres of wine!

There were firms that were set up just for this purpose. The traders took advantage. Then there was the methanol scandal, which convinced consumers to choose quality wines, paying an appropriate price for it, while until then it had been a kind of food commodity. From then on, importers came to see us at the winery, and the first thing they asked was where the vineyards were, so they could go and visit them. Italy's entry into the WTO in 1996 was crucial: it opened up lots of markets for us.

We found ourselves faced with a constant fall in domestic consumption, offset by an increase in exports. As I have said, we had to optimize the farm estates, which we proceeded to do with a clear method and far-sightedness. Uncle Domenico's philosophy is pertinent here as well. He used to say: 'So little does so much'. He was referring to money, and this maxim contains a nugget of ancient wisdom that we now tend to forget: even modest earnings, provided they are repeated, can build a considerable capital over time. That is how our 2000 hectares came into being, divided between nine small estates, besides the one in Virginia."

In March 2016, Gianni Zonin completed the generational transition by giving the company to his three sons: Domenico became president, with Francesco and Michele as vice-presidents.

Trentino-Alto Adige: The Phenomenon of Cooperative Wineries

The majority of Italy's cooperative wineries, or *cantine sociali*, struggled to include the word "quality" in their vocabulary. In Trentino-Alto Adige, on the other hand, the best wines were being produced precisely by these *cantine* – we are talking about the very early 1970s – which innovated with a vision

that might be described as privatistic. It is no accident, then, that the cooperative wineries still account for the vast majority of local wine production today.

Trentino

In Trentino, over 80% of wine production is in the hands of the *cantine sociali*, which turn out wines of excellent quality and have a strong export orientation. Certainly, Trentino can also boast a fine school of *spumante classico*, thanks to the work of the Istituto Agrario di San Michele all'Adige, and the leadership, in the business field, of Ferrari in Trento.

Cavit is the most important of the cooperative wineries and just a few data suffice to back up such an affirmation. Founded in 1950, it is a consortium bringing together thirteen of the fifteen *cantine sociali* in Trentino, and accounting for 70% of the provincial oenological production. It has 5,400 winegrowing members, and around 7,000 hectares under vine. Its headquarters, at Ravina di Trento, is around 50,000 square metres, and it produces 62 million bottles, 75% of which go abroad. It is the pilot plant of Trentino's oenology, but also one of the leading ones at a national level. The operational base, boosted in 1977, is at Ravina, on the outskirts of Trento, where the prestigious Cantina dello Spumante is also situated.

The technical staff directly checks the vineyards, date of harvest and the choice of the grapes before they are transported to the consortium's wineries for vinification, once again carried out under the supervision of oenologists. Directed by **Enrico Zanoni**, amongst the projects realized by Cavit is one called Masi. Begun in 1988, in collaboration with the Istituto Agrario di San Michele, it involves a plan for production revolving around the ancient mountain farm (*masi*) environment, with studies being carried out on "high-potential microzones" to enhance to the full the vine-environment relationship. Since 2010 Cavit has been developing the PICA project (Piattaforma Integrata Cartografica Agriviticola), a study conducted in conjunction with MPA Solutions, the Edmund Mach Foundation and the Bruno Kessler Foundation. The goal is to orient winemakers and the management of the environment-cum-landscape-cum-local territory towards a perspective of total sustainability, which gives due consideration to ecological, social and economic aspects.

Kellerei Cantina **Terlan**

Alto Adige Terlaner

DENOMINAZIONE DI ORIGINE CONTROLLATA

Classico

Following pages
Vineyard in Trentino

Alto Adige

The Cantina di Terlano, founded in 1893, is one of the oldest cooperatives in Alto Adige. One hundred and forty-three members contribute to it, with 16 hectares of vineyard, of which 70% is given over to white varieties. Production amounts to 1.2 million bottles. As the winery's current, and very capable *Kellermeister*, **Rudi Kofler**, observes, "from the most ancient times, particular areas such as the strip of hillside wedged between the San Pietro mountain stream and Rio Meltina were known for the quality and longevity of their wines, as is the case of the Pinot Bianco Vorberg, from steep, well-exposed vineyards lying between an altitude of 250 and 900 metres". The same can be said of Terlaner – a blend of Pinot Bianco, Chardonnay and Sauvignon – which has been going since the establishment of the winery. Returning to the longevity of these wines: while it is due to the natural combination of terrain and microclimate, it is also in large part due to the intuitions of **Sebastian Stocker**, the brilliant winemaker who, for almost forty years (until 1993), crafted these miracles. It was he who devised a personal maturation method that bears his name – the "Stocker method", subsequently borne out by scientific research – which involved ageing the whites in large wooden 75-hectolitre vats for around a year, and then on the lees in stainless steel vats for up to ten years! It is our good fortune that Stocker "hid away" 500 hundred bottles of each vintage to test the worth of his theory. There are now twenty thousand bottles stored 13 metres below ground level in the winery's oenological archive, starting with the 1955 vintage. There are still bottles dating to 1893, the year the cooperative was founded. This is the technical observation of the oenologist Angelo Solci:

"Stocker understood, with his experience and sensibility as a winemaker/oenologist, the importance of vinifying white wines delicately and keeping them on the fine lees. He anticipated by twenty years the university research findings demonstrating the importance of glutathione, a powerful reducing substance comprising three amino acids, present in grapes and yeasts, capable of substituting sulphur dioxide and avoiding the precocious browning of wines. Glutathione transfers from the grape to the must, and decays strongly with the oxidation caused by crushing and pressing. It returns in appreciable quantities with the autolysis of yeast, remaining at good levels with the fine lees that have to be periodically remixed. This is *battonage*, which is now widely applied. Stocker worked with meticulous care, demanding perfectly healthy, ripe, hand-harvested grapes. He personally supervised the pressing, which had to be light [*low pressure*] and with little mashing. He did not yet have membrane presses, but knew from experience that the must should come out a pale green colour and not brown. At the end of the fermentation phase, he accumulated the yeast lees to the utmost, without adding sulphur dioxide, and remixing every week.

Stocker's shrewd and skilful management of the yeast lees, carried out not only in stainless steel vats, but also in large wooden barrels, triggered spontaneous malolactic fermentation with the heat of early spring. This important bacterial action not only reduced the acidity of the wines, transforming bitter malic acid into a soft, 'sweet' lactic acid, but also favoured an important enzymatic process which released aromas and scents consisting of glycoside precursors. The long autolysis of the yeasts liberates large quantities of mannoprotein, substances able to produce proteinic and tartaric stability with their molecular support, enhancing the quality of the wines in terms of structure and softness. The surprise of tasting white wines three, four or even more years old, fresh, perfect, rich in taste and well-structured, amazed everyone, but not him, who observed his interlocutors with amusement, without fully revealing his secrets."

It is not that private operators have not participated in the renaissance in Alto Adige. Far from it. The symbol of winemakers is Hofstätter, of the **Foradori family**, in Mazzon (Termeno). The founder was **Josef Hofstätter**, at the beginning of the last century, but it was only after the marriage of one of his descendants to Paolo Foradori that the business found great success, which was the story of a number of fundamental insights. The most significant one was having understood in advance – and in this the precursor was Josef Hofstätter's grandson, Konrad Oberhofer – the value and importance of crus. Indeed it was the first estate in Alto Adige to do its vinification vineyard by vineyard. Two of this are now considered historic: the Gewürztraminer Kolbenhof and the Pinot Nero Barthenau

Below
Lageder winery of Magrè

Facing page
Casimiro Maule

Below
Vineyard in Valtellina

from the Sant'Urbano vineyard. The winery has passed into the hands of Paolo's son, Martin. Despite his young age, he has proved able to continue the family tradition and also to establish himself as a promoter of the image of Alto Adige's wines.

The Barthenau estate takes its name from Ludwig Barth von Barthenau, born in 1939 in Rovereto. An erudite and chemist, he fell in love with Pinot Nero, and was the first to introduce it to Alto Adige. The area of Mazzon is now called *Blauburgunder-Himmel,* the paradise of Pinot Nero, now re-

garded as the best Italian habitat for this vine. The archive documents of the Kolbenhof estate date back to 1722, when it was the property of the Jesuit Fathers of Innsbruck. It is now completely devoted to the cultivation of the most classic of Termeno's wines: Gewürztraminer. On the premises of the business, in the centre of the town, is an excellent restaurant.

Alois Lageder has made a key contribution, with his sophisticated and innovative winery of Magrè (Margreid), to the recent success of Alto Adige's wines. The son of a carriage builder, his great grandfather founded the wine company in 1855, in Bolzano. In 1934 the family purchased the Löwengang estate at Magrè. In the decades that followed, the property expanded further, including smallholdings sited in the best viticultural areas of Alto Adige. In the middle of the 1970s, the reins of the business were handed over to Alois Lageder, born in 1950, who introduced new ideas and strategies. He was responsible for in-

ALOIS LAGEDER
1823

troducing organic cultivation methods and for the creation of one of the first energy-saving wineries. Earlier still, he established his brand of quality wines abroad, especially in Germany, at a time when Alto Adige was still associated with low-quality, widely distributed wines, a trend he reversed. The business is divided into two branches: Alois Lageder, which produces wines from grapes pooled by growers working under the close supervision of the company's experts; and the Tenuta Lageder, comprising 52 hectares, cultivated under a certified biodynamic regime adopted in the early 1990s, which is under the technical direction of the oenologist Georg Meissner. Production totals around 250,000 bottles. The clearly distinguishable wines are characterized by a style oriented entirely towards the quest for elegance and total respect of the typicality of the grape varieties.

The Tenuta is also a cultural attraction due to Alois Lageder's interest in modern art.

Lombardy

Founded in 1897 as a small family-run winery, in the 1960s the Casa vinicola Nino Negri in Valtellina greatly extended its market presence under the skilful direction of **Carlo Negri**, thanks also to a series of excellent harvests. On the back of current output of around 900,000 bottles, Nino Negri is an enterprise which, over recent decades, has successfully combined tradition with innovation, weathering the stormy patch experienced by Valtellina's winemaking world in the 1970s. In 1986, the Gruppo Italiano Vini took over from the Swiss company Winefood,

which had previously bought out the Negri family. Investment increased sharply, both in the vineyards and the winery, and success was not long in coming. The man responsible for the turnaround was undoubtedly the Trentino-born Casimiro Maule, who, first as the company's oenologist and then as director, achieved the results that are now before everyone's eyes. It was one of his intuitions, in fact, that gave rise, at the beginning of the 1980s, to Sfursat 5 Stelle, indisputably the best-known wine of the entire Valtellina, and of international repute.

Nebbiolo grapes are harvested and left to dry on lattices in airing sheds for around three months, then vinified with lengthy maceration and aged in new *barriques* for 18 months. The result is a complex, long-lived wine of great class. Nino Negri also produces a range of products to satisfy those searching for all the different tones offered by the wines of Valtellina. A further, very interesting development was the reconversion of the historic 7-hectare Fracia cru, subzone Valgella, from the traditional vertical to contour ploughing, in order to permit mechanization.

Emilia-Romagna

Lambrusco has found a place in the modern history of Italian wine because it acted as the *passepartout* of Italian wine in the United States from 1970 onwards, with 300 million bottles be-

ing consumed there each year at that time. No other wine would achieve such a quantity in a single market.

It entered history insofar as it was a "multiplier of Dollars" that served to help Brunello become the best-known Italian wine in the world. As Ezio Rivella said: "The popularity of Riunite's Lambrusco [*created in the 1970s by Rivella himself for Banfi in the US*] was such that other producers immediately followed suit". The result was two-fold: overall exports rose to 25 million cases (equivalent to the entire production of Champagne or of Prosecco nowadays), reviving the fortunes of Riunite and making the fortunes of other producers. Success then generated excess: Lambrusco also began being sold in cans.

It also entered history due to a capacity for profound renewal, to the extent that, in the twenty-first century, it is still one of Italy's most exported wines. A genuine resurrection that is drawing toward wine millions of potential clients willing to taste our grand crus as well. The first to catch on, as always, were the restaurants, who put it back on the wine lists and offered it with conviction.

In the last decade, Lambrusco has significantly raised the level of quality. Slowly but surely. And take note: we are not talking about a production microcosm, but of over 50 million bottles sold as DOP and more than 100 million as IGT, with exports accounting for 60% of production. It is also one of the Italian

wines that is being promoted most extensively on the markets of the future, such as Russian, China and Brazil. What brought about this success with consumers and critics? The recognition, on the part of the wineries, including cooperative ones, that only quality reaped dividends. First of all, vineyards were reconverted according to quality standards, and then modern, sustainable oenological methods were adopted in the winery.

The zone is in full "ferment", with the large wineries (many with artisanal features, despite producing millions of bottles) being constantly stimulated by small emerging ones. The classic method, the ancestral method and yeasts in the bottle are some of the more recent reinterpretations of a wine so agreeable that it knows no hostile palate. Lambrusco has occupied a strategic band of the market with enormous scope: that of customers who want a simple, but not banal wine that is good, unique and friendly. Its strengths are that it is very recognizable and incredibly pleasing. A real song of praise to drinking, to joy.

Umbria

Besides being one of the cradles of Italian art, Umbria can boast a family of winemakers that are among the founding fathers of the Italian renaissance: the **Lungarotti**.

Giorgio Lungarotti, who possessed an entrepreneurial vision rare to the 1950s, started a project that led Torgiano, a

Facing page
Lambrusco vineyards

Above
Lungarotti vineyards, Torgiano, Perugia

medieval village a little south of Perugia, to become one of the first Italian wine producing districts. The messenger of this territory was Vigna Monticchio, a wine made exclusively with local grapes (Sangiovese and Canaiolo) from a single parcel of land situated on the hills around the village. The law establishing the DOC appellation represented an occasion to be grasped at once, and Giorgio Lungarotti had the opportunity to shape its own production regulations (the DOC was introduced in 1968, the DOCG in 1991). Lungarotti's project foresaw, alongside wine, also culture and hospitality.

In 1974, together with his wife Maria Grazia Marchetti – an art historian who, at almost ninety, still gave brilliant lectures – founded a wine museum, and, soon after, the resort Le Tre Vaselle, again in Torgiano, "where there didn't use to be anything, not even a *trattoria*".

Their daughter Teresa recalls: "He [*Giorgio*] and my mother were an exceptional couple, so different, so together, and utterly complementary: one soared, the other acted."

Angelo Valentini, an agronomist but above all a man of great and refined culture, worked with them for many years.

Lungarotti is still a forward-looking business, and the other daughter, Chiara, affirms:

"Never stop. Never presume you have reached the maximum, because striving for continual improvement is the driving intent of any successful initiative. Operate against the grain of standardization. This is what we were taught, and what

we have done over these years. Research and innovation have been the path whereby my sister Teresa and I have managed to give fresh input to the Gruppo Lungarotti estates. Extremely rigorous vine selection, zoning, boosting of the five computerized weather stations at the heart of our sustainable viticulture. In the winery, we have built up a young and dynamic team of experts. In 2000, we embarked upon a new adventure at Montefalco, where we bought new land, built a winery and planted vines for the production of the second Umbrian DOCG, Sagrantino. Here, from the 2014 vintage, the grapes are certified as organic. We have been supported in this wide-ranging project by the consultancy of Lorenzo Landi and Denis Dubourdieu. We have created new wines: the L'U project with a coupled white and red, the Sagrantino reds, Rosso di Montefalco and Sagrantino Passito at Montefalco, Vin Santo at Torgiano and much more. The winery's *Enoteca* has been built up, and the available farm accommodation extended, with two more *agriturismi*, in addition to the first – Poggio alle Vigne – active since 1994. A great deal has also been done to bring the Tre Vaselle resort up to the new 5-star standards and to refine the restaurant offer. A wine therapy spa [*BellaUve*] has been opened, specializing in wine and grape treatments. We like to conceive Lungarotti according to the slogan 'Wine, Culture, Hospitality'. In the field of culture, the latest creation was the olive and oil museum, opened in May 2000."

Cervaro della Sala is the most glorious Italian wood-aged white wine, and it is Umbrian. It bears the signature of the **Antinori family**. The first vintage was 1985, and, by the admission of the man who created it, came about by chance. The natural process of malolactic fermentation made Renzo Cotarella, who at the time ran the Umbrian estate under the supervision of Giacomo Tachis, all the potential of a Chardonnay with, however, the imprinting of the region of provenance, plus a dollop of local grapes (in this case, Grechetto). At any rate, wines that go the distance, generally sharing an initial buttery and "tropicalizing *plénitude*", which, when they absorb the fining oak, tend to make way to more intriguing notes of officinal herbs, resin, hazelnut, flintstone, truffle and camphor.

The other icon of Umbrian wine is the Sagrantino of **Marco Caprai**, that is, its redeemer. In the difference between these numbers, 14 and 140, there perhaps lies the whole path trav-

elled by Marco in less than thirty years. In 1986, then in his twenties, he was entrusted with the business by his father Armando, who could count on 14 hectares under vine. Sagrantino did not then enjoy a great reputation. Marco was the artificer of a radical change. The following year he met Leonardo Valenti, professor of viticulture at the University of Milan. A collaboration began which engaged the university and the estate, dozens of researchers and the whole Sagrantino area, for years. The priorities were to identify the best clones, to try out the most appropriate cultivation methods and the winery techniques best suited to enhancing its worth (drawing on the talents of Attilio Pagli for this purpose). Sagrantino today is nothing like the rough version of former times. Now it is a potent, deep-structured, complex, long-lived wine The key moment for this estate came in 1993, when Marco, to celebrate a quarter of a century of activity, launched the Sagrantino 25 Anni, which immediately became the flagship wine for the whole appellation. Marco effectively became its ambassador. He continued with his research laboratories, his experimental vineyards and a range of wines with few equals in Italy. In 2008, he set up a project called *Montefalco 2015, The New Green Revolution*, bringing together some ten Umbrian estates with a view to adopting innovative and ecologically sustainable production methods – because, since 1995, Arnaldo Caprai, now ten times the size it once was – there are now 140 hectares under vine – has worked to defend biodiversity.

The Marches

The modernization of Italian wine has, in the Marches, a winery which in some ways anticipated the great renaissance: Fazi Battaglia.

The story of Fazi Battaglia, founded by Signor **Fazi** and Signor **Battaglia**, began at Cupramontana in 1949. Bound up with it is the image of the region's quintessential wine, Verdicchio dei Castelli di Jesi DOC Classico. The entrepreneur **Francesco Angelini** took the business over soon after, and in 1953 launched a competition for a bottle that would make his Verdicchio unique and instantly recognizable around the world. The design of the architect Antonio Maiocchi gave rise to the "amphora" bottle, inspired by the ancient Etruscan wine recipients. It was a decisive communication choice, even

though, unfortunately, the bottle was often imitated. In 1960, the company, which had already moved to new headquarters at Castelplanio, began to purchase other land, for a current total of 210 hectares under vine. Verdicchio's first cru, Le Moie, arrived in 1988. In 1990, Maria Luisa Sparaco, Francesco Angelini's granddaughter, took over the helm.

In March 2015, the business was taken over by Bertani Domains, a company which also includes a number of other estates: Val di Suga at Montalcino, Tre Rose at Montepulciano, San Leonino at Castellina in Chianti, Puiatti in Collio and Isonzo, and Collepaglia in the Castelli di Jesi area. Now, with the acquisition of Fazi Battaglia, the group has 400 hectares of vineyards, with overall production exceeding 4 million bottles.

To **Ampelio Bucci** must go the merit for having seen in Verdicchio, thanks to the brilliance of Giorgio Grai, who has worked for him for thirty years, the potential of the quality grape variety at a time when the prevailing tendency was to style this wine for easy drinking.

A professor at the IULM in Milan, Bucci's Verdicchio dei Castelli di Jesi Riserva Villa Bucci constantly ranks at the top in the crisscross of awards made by Italian wine guides. Notoriously little inclined to compromise, a refined man now almost Milanese by adoption, he came to wine by way of the family farm property, in which he has always taken an interest. His Verdicchio is emblematic of the peculiarity of a grape that is amongst the most interesting in our ampelographic

heritage. One might almost say that the wine resembles him. It expresses itself in a "low voice", but with propriety and authoritativeness. It matures in large wooden barrels and ages extremely well, to the extent that the versions produced in the 1980s (it was launched with the 1983 vintage) still make for satisfying drinking. A "red dressed up as a white" which makes it even more fascinating and sensitive to climatic variables, and indeed it is only produced in the most favourable years. It offers intense aromas, with floral notes that, with time, achieve a supple, elegant, minerally verve.

Verdicchio Classico Bucci, on the other hand, is produced every year. It is less complex than the Villa Bucci, but is likewise of great elegance.

Abruzzo

Though production in Abruzzo is modest, the region can boast some first-rate winemakers.

Edoardo Valentini was the spiritual father of Abruzzo's oenology and a standard-setting producer on the whole national scene. Rigorous, unassuming but not shy, he was a charismatic personality. After Valentini's death, his son Francesco Paolo took over the helm of the enterprise, continuing the work of his father and achieving, with his whites, high peaks of expressiveness and elegance. Legend has it that no journalist has ever stepped foot in the Valentini winery, a bunker of who knows what vinification secret.

"My father taught me that the vineyard is our winery," says Francesco. "It is there that I must invest my money, my labours and also my worries. In the winery, I must intervene as little as possible, because I firmly believe in the principle of

Socratic maieutics: everything already exists in nature. If the final wine is not up to my standard, I don't bottle it and I sell it by bulk. It's painful, but also wonderful, because it demonstrates that, at the end of the day, the only universally valid rules are those of Mother Nature."

The grape variety with which the Valentinis have really marked out a clear-cut distinction for themselves compared to all the others is Trebbiano d'Abruzzo. Their clone is very different from the more widespread Trebbiano toscano, in that it can boast a century's-old adaptation to the area. The training system used is *pergola abruzzese*, more suited to protecting the bunches from strong sunlight.

In the 1990s, **Gianni Masciarelli** redefined the modern canons of excellence of Abruzzo's wines, convinced as he was that he lived in a special land capable of special wines.

The Masciarelli business is now an international giant, with over 230 hectares under vine, from which more than 3 million bottles of wine are obtained. The company also produces extra virgin olive oil and is active in the field of wine tourism.

Following the sad death of Gianni, the business is now run by Marina Cvetic , who, with her effective mixture of practicality and humour, always offset the boisterous, dreamy character of her husband.

She says of him: "Gianni was, as someone described him, a peasant citizen of the world, with boundless horizons, who was happy amidst the four houses of San Martino, as he was in the chaos of American or Japanese metropolises."

An extremely open-minded businessman, with an uncommon ability to translate thought into action, Masciarelli had analysed and thoroughly grasped the dynamics of international markets. "I refuse to think of the Europeans as the Chinese of wine", he would say, "as the small-time manufacturers of the agricultural world, who go door to door in the United States offering a discount of a few cents per bottle, just to hold on to their positions. I don't think that's the way. We are not reps with cardboard or fake leather suitcases selling unknown, low-quality brands. We are the best of Italian production and European production."

His Montepulciano Villa Gemma, a full-bodied red of rare elegance, is the synthesis of such a philosophy.

Molise

Di Majo Norante is the standard bearer of Molise in the world. Based in Campomarino, just a few kilometres from Termoli, it is in fact the only wine producer in this tiny region that has managed to make a name for its wines throughout Italy and on the main international markets.

"Ours is an ancient history," recounts Alessio. "We have been producing wine with our own grapes since 1800. A hereditary dedication. All our grapes come from the approximately 120-hectare property, which we farm organically. The oenological philosophy is based on a traditional approach to vine cultivation and winemaking, in an effort to preserve the qualities of Mediterranean grape varieties.

At the origin of all our wines is clonal selection of indigenous varieties, effected by studying their adaptability to south-

ern parts. We try to preserve the peculiar qualities of each with rigorous selections when harvesting, and in the winery, with a view to the constant improvement of the quality and salubriousness of the wine.

Without doubt the turning point was the year 2000, when the new clones of Montepulciano and Aglianico entered production, with lower per-vine yields in order to obtain more structured and elegant wines. In addition to expressing the local area to a greater degree."

The estate's champion act is undoubtedly Don Luigi, which over the years has bagged many awards and received great acclaim in the chief trade publications. It is a blend of Montepulciano and Aglianico, elegant and characterful, rich in sour black cherry and spices on the nose, and with a rich, full taste.

Campania

A land with an extremely long winemaking tradition, home to indigenous varieties left in legacy by the Romans, Campania was one of the first southern regions to embark upon renewal, starting from its most difficult area in terms of climate and territory, Irpinia, and giving rise to estates of world repute.

One of these belongs to the **Mastroberardino** family, which, with now a century of activity under its belt, has greatly helped Campanian oenology to emerge on the markets.

The first traces of the Mastroberardinos' presence in Irpinia date to the time of the House of Bourbon, in the mid-eighteenth century, at Atripalda, where they still are today. Since then, ten generations of winemakers have succeeded each other. Their pioneering role in defending and valuing indigenous varieties such as Fiano, Greco and Aglianico has proved crucial.

Mastroberardino thus opened up a path that is now followed by many of the region's viticulturalists. As Piero Mastroberardino who, in addition to being chairman of the family business, is also professor of economics and business management at the University of Foggia, says: "The *Antiche Cantine* project is a synthesis of the most advanced technological and technical knowledge. However, the purpose of the project is not to change the nature or fundamental char-

acteristics of our ancient wines, but to preserve their existence and value, making them compatible with the evolution of the schemes that distinguish wine tasting. These are the principles that have always inspired our family philosophy".

The company's best-known wine is undoubtedly Radici. It is the result of an idea developed at the beginning of the 1980s as a project designed to react to the earthquake that hit Irpinia in 1980, and to defend and lend value to ancient Greek and Roman viticulture. The "Radici project" was conceived and promoted by Antonio Mastroberardino (who died recently), Piero's father and the acknowledged "father" of Campanian wine.

Since the first, 1986, vintage resulting from this project, Radici has represented a new frontier for the production of Aglianico and Taurasi.

"Our winery has innovation in its DNA, starting with the vineyards," affirms **Antonio Capaldo**, president since 2009 of Feudi di San Gregorio, founded in 1986 and committed to opening up new markets, in addition to redesigning the business plan.

"We set ourselves the goal of involving the many local grape growers, around 250 in all for a total of 300 hectares, to which we must add our 150. A unique human and professional asset, watched over with the viticultural guidance of Pierpaolo Sirch, who is now the managing director. In our communication we also emphasize that the growers are part of Feudi." Pierpaolo oversees almost a thousand vineyards, ranging from 350 to 700 metres above sea level, dotted around the area.

The viticultural project has gradually been extended to Manduria in Puglia and Vulture in Basilicata, where an extraordinary vineyard, the Vigna di mezzo, has been preserved; over fifty years old, it is an authentic living museum where the ancient methods of cultivation have been retained. Likewise, the *tennecchie* (of the Patriarchs) training system is still in use in the vineyard at Taurasi. The ancient indigenous va-

rieties yield noble wines such as Piano di Montevergine, a Taurasi Riserva made with Aglianico grapes. "We decided to take the difficult path of indigenous varieties – crowned by success – for the production of *spumante classico* as well," says Antonio. Greco di Tufo and Falanghina are used for the white base wine, and Aglianico for the rosé. Amongst the reds suited to ageing, the leading label has always been Serpico, made with Aglianico grapes from the oldest vines (over a hundred years old) of the Dal Re vineyard in the Taurasi area.

After the vineyards comes the hyper-modern winery, designed by the Japanese architect Hikaru Mori, completed in 2004. Inside is the Marennà restaurant, for which the great graphic artist Massimo Vignelli (who died in New York on 27 May 2014) designed all the furnishings and much else besides: from the kitchens to the forks, the tables to the chairs. Vignelli was also behind the stamp-shaped label, which set a trend.

"Today, Feudi di San Gregorio," reflects Antonio Capaldo, "wants to be more and more a place for coming together, interaction, knowledge, meditation – a hotbed of ideas and culture."

Basilicata

"True, living witnesses of the culture of Vulture" is how **Anselmo**, **Sergio** and **Vito Paternoster** like to describe themselves

today, having inherited the legacy of their father Pino and, before him, their grandfather Anselmo. "We have a sole mission, long, hard and ambitious" Vito Paternoster points out: "To continue to convey to the world, and over time, the force of the Paternoster family, and likewise that of its *terroir*, the Vulture."

The business was founded in 1925 by granddad Anselmo, who was the first to decide to put the first bottles of Aglianico up for sale.

"For us," Vito explains, "rigour remains unchanged in the vineyard, cellar and in every subsequent process, just like the artisanal spirit of over 80 harvests ago."

After Anselmo, the second generation made the quality leap with Pino, probably the first oenologist in the whole Vulture, a technical expert and manager all in one. He was responsible for many innovative steps in the 1980s: the first fine oak barrels; the purchase of land under vine, including Villa Rotondo; and the first big merits of promoting Aglianico del Vulture on the market.

It is now the turn of the third generation, with Anselmo and Sergio Paternoster, both oenologists: the former works in the lab, controlling the quality of the grapes and wines; the latter is the winemaker, the real interpreter of the noble primary material of the Vulture. Then there is Vito, the PR and spokesperson for the company brand in Italy and abroad; Rosalba, who manages the winery and offices; and Anna, lawyer and administrator.

The company has five Aglianico labels, first and foremost the cru Don Anselmo, dedicated to their grandfather and produced only in the best years.

Puglia

Castel del Monte is an icon of tourism in the south. In the lands surrounding its celebrated octagonal castle, Emperor Frederick II used to go hunting with falcons. The same area is now home to Cantina Rivera, owned for the last three generations by the **De Corato** family. Il Falcone, an "ancient" blend of indigenous red grapes, has been their flagship wine for over forty years.

"In the 1950s and 1960s Rivera was already a very well-known brand," explains Sebastiano De Corato, the current owner, who bears the same name as the founder, "and my grandfather immediately started with the idea of producing exclusively bottled wine. He began with the typical grape varieties of the Castel del Monte area, first Bombino Nero, now DOCG, used to make lighter rosés than those from Salento. Commercial success was not long coming. The form of cultivation back then was *misto andriese*, consisting of Nero di Troia and Montepulciano. The former was undoubtedly the most characteristic, the only thing was that it yielded 'difficult' wines, big in structure and with rasping tannins. To 'soften' it a bit, peasant farmers used to plant a row of Montepulciano every two of Nero, and vinified them together. In 1971, as a tribute to Frederick II, my grandfather chose the name Il Falcone,

maintaining unvaried the ratio of *misto andriese*, but vinifying the two varieties separately. It is still our flagship wine."

Il Falcone is one of the great wines of the south, thanks to a particular microclimate, with the Murgia to the rear and the Adriatic just opposite; cold winds from the Balkans, alternating with hot Mediterranean ones, ensure optimal ripening of the grapes and confer both elegance and complexity on the wine.

Puglia is one of the few regions in Italy where rosé wines were traditionally produced, especially in the Salento, their ideal zone.

Mino Calò, from Puglia but based in Albizzate in Brianza, chose rosé as his company's iconic wine. He changed its style and promoted it on the new markets that were opening up. The winery is now managed by his son **Damiano**, proud of the fact that Rosa del Golfo is considered the best-known rosé in the south. This is also thanks to the brilliant contributions of two of Mino's friends: Antonio Piccinardi, whose label design perfectly conveyed Mino's business message, and, above all, **Angelo Solci**, who still handles the oenological side of operations, giving the wines character and refinement.

"The watershed decade was the 1970s," recounts the owner Damiano Calò. "My father, a curious observer of oenologi-

C A N T I N E
ROSA DEL GOLFO
S A L E N T O

cal technique and meticulous in the search for modern equipment, attempted to bring the principal innovations to bear precisely on rosé wine. Employing temperature-control techniques, already well known in the North, but which had never been used in our parts, he managed to obtain a fresh, supple, easy-drinking wine, which was a big novelty at the time."

Add in a territory with qualities like few others, and a spot-on name – "rosa" like the coral colour of the wine and "golfo" to evoke Gallipoli and its splendid sea – and you will understand its immediate success! Today the company produces around 250,000 bottles. Amongst its other most successful wines there are Vigna Mazzi, Primito, Portulano, the rosé brut spumante Rosa del Golfo, and a white wine, Bolina, made with Verdeca, an indigenous variety that had almost disappeared and which Mino Calò again contributed to reviving, obtaining a fresh, easy-drinking wine with intense aromas of fruit.

Cosimo Taurino was the pioneer of Negroamaro. In the 1970s and 1980s, in a period of major change, Cosimo Taurino, together with the oenologist Severino Garofano, one of the great protagonists in the rebirth of viticulture in the South, demonstrated that Puglia was not just a "cistern land", but that its reds could compete on all the markets. In the 1980s, when he began exporting wine to the US, no one had ever heard about Guagnano, Lecce and the Salento.

The Taurinos were affluent and owned extensive lands and vineyards, from which they obtained blending wines. The family scion, Cosimo, was sent north to get a degree in pharmacy. He graduated from university in Pavia, where he met his wife, Rita. He returned to Guagnano, outside Lecce, and after five years of activity, he sold the pharmacy almost against his father's wishes. He told his father: "If our wine is good enough for others and they bottle it, why don't we bottle it ourselves?" So, in 1970, when his daughter Rosanna was born, he bottled his first wine, the Notarpanaro, a traditional blend of Negroamaro and Malvasia Nera. The "miracle" took place shortly afterwards, when his path crossed that of Garofano: from the collaboration of two minds capable of anticipating the times there sprang Patriglione, a wine that is a legend in the whole of Southern oenology. As Rosanna, who now runs the company with her husband and general manager Fernando Antonio Bello, recounts: "My father and *dottor* Garofano drew inspiration from Amarone, only that round here, 30 kilometres from the Adriatic and 20 from the Ionian Sea, a hot breeze blows constantly, drying the grapes with any need for a drying chamber. It's enough just to leave them on the vine. We still follow the same protocols today, drying 30% of the grapes and obtaining just 40 quintals per hectare." Patriglione is now made with 100% Negroamaro, and, with its strong, elegant character, has the confident poise of one who is not bothered about pleasing everyone. Taurino makes about 900,000 bottles each year, with 80% destined for abroad (US, Canada, Japan and Europe).

Calabria

Say the name **Librandi** and you think immediately of Calabrian wine. The company is based at Cirò Marina, in the heart of the DOC Cirò zone, and has always been run by the family: the brothers Antonio (who died in 2012) and Nicodemo Librandi, the latter's sons, Raffaele and Paolo, and Antonio's children, Francesco and Teresa.

The history of the winery began in the 1950s with Antonio, a second-generation viticulturalist (his father Raffaele already produced wine). At the beginning of the 1970s he was joined by Nicodemo. Very rapid commercial development enabled the Librandis to purchase various holdings. The company now owns 232 hectares of vineyards, and in addition can count on a further 100 hectares of selected vineyards belonging to members of the Associazione I Vignaioli del Cirò. Li-

brandi's now exports to around forty different countries. The company can boast the services of Donato Lanati for the technical side of operations.

The red Magno Megonio represents the winery: a modern and highly complex interpretation, made entirely with Magliocco grapes. This wine is the result – together with the Efeso Bianco made from Mantonico grapes – of considerable research by the firm over the last twenty years. "In our experimental spiral vineyard, we have collected around 200 indigenous varieties," confirms Nicodemo Librandi. "Some of

them, including Magliocco and Mantonico, immediately gave us very great oenological satisfaction."

New and original wines, starting from an extremely ancient historic base – something which makes Librandi wines very "territorial" and authentic.

Sicily

Giuseppe Tasca d'Almerita wanted to demonstrate that the island's indigenous varieties could also produce elegant, long-lived wines, on a par with the greatest Italian wines. He succeeded. In 1957, he took over the family's farm estate at Regaleali, and focused decisively on viticulture. A new vineyard, San Lucio, was planted in 1959. After more than ten years of experimentation in the vineyard and the winery, conducted in collaboration with the then young oenologist Ezio Rivella, the Regaleali Riserva del Conte saw the light of day, made from Nero d'Avola from San Lucio, with a small dollop of Perricone. It would then become famous as Rosso del Conte. The first vintage was in 1970.

In 1984, the count produced another of the estate's great classics, this time a white: Nozze d'Oro, based on Insolia and Sauvignon Tasca, created to celebrate fifty years of marriage.

In the meantime, experiments began at Regaleali with some international varieties, watched over also by Lucio, Count Giuseppe's son. Cabernet Sauvignon had been planted in 1979, resulting in the first pure varietal in Sicily. The following year it was the turn of Chardonnay. The 1991 harvest would prove

legendary, rendered unique by *Botrytis Cinerea*. Tasca d'Almerita also paved the way in the production of spumanti: in 1990, Almerita came out "for friends", and it is still one of the best Italian sparkling wines made with the classic method. Count Giuseppe died in 1998.

In the last few decades, Lucio's children have also joined the firm: Giuseppe in production, and Alberto, who is responsible for marketing. Other properties have been purchased or leased: the Tenuta Tascante on Etna; Tenuta Capofaro on the island of Salina, including vineyards planted with Malvasia and a luxury resort; an ancient vineyard of Grillo on the island of Mozia, in collaboration with the Fondazione Giuseppe Whitaker; the property of the Sallier de la Tour cousins, between Monreale and San Giuseppe Jato, where an excellent Syrah is produced.

A fascinating story that continues to unfold, played out along the guiding threads of innovation and respect for the environment.

Settesoli – comprising 2,000 members and which was presided over by **Diego Planeta** for forty years – is Sicily's largest wine-producing business, with the biggest vineyard in Europe: 6,000 hectares in the province of Agrigento, between Menfi, Montevago and Santa Margherita Belice. Some 70% of the families in the district, 3 out of 4, work directly for the co-operative or allied activities. It all began on 21 December 1958, when about sixty members set up the cooperative winery of Menfi, which then became Settesoli. Diego Planeta, then little more than thirty years old, was appointed president in 1973. He abandoned the production of bulk wine in order to bottle his output and earn more for the member growers, who he oriented toward the market with international varieties as well. And that is not all. In 1987–1988, with Attilio Scienza of the Istituto Agrario di San Michele, he commenced an intense zoning project, making available as many as fifty experimental fields with a programme of microvinification. It was a full-blown revolution, which would transform southern viticulture.

His work acted as a dynamo for the whole Menfi district, where other wineries were also set up, including that of the Planeta family itself, oriented towards the middle and upper range of the market. In 2012, after serving as president for forty years, Diego Planeta left a company that produces 22 million bottles a year, with turnover of almost 50 million Euro a year.

The helm was taken by **Vito Varvaro**, the descendant of one of the founding families of the cooperative and with thirty years' experience in the American multinational Procter & Gamble. Varvaro set a goal as visionary as that of Planeta: to increase the income of the members, also to encourage young people not to leave their native land, with an integrated and

sustainable model of agricultural and tourist development. In 2008, the cooperative inaugurated the largest Italian photovoltaic plant in the wine production sector. Initiatives are also being developed, along the line begun by Planeta, to combine wine, the local area, tourism and cuisine.

Malvasia delle Lipari risked dying out, and might have done so if **Carlo Hauner**, born in Brescia in 1927 into a family of Bohemian origin, had not arrived on the island of Salina in 1963 as the result of a casual invitation. He fell so totally in love with the place that he decided to move and live there. He discovered Malvasia, that local sweet grape that peasant farmers dry on racks in the sun to obtain a veritable nectar of the gods. When he arrived, he was already a painter and designer of international fame. With great determination, he bought tiny abandoned parcels of land on Salina, about 20 hectares in all. On the hills of Malfa he established his agricultural business, which would enable the world to discover the joys of Malvasia delle Lipari. The arrival of DOC status in 1973 was thanks to him. Since then, other winemakers have also successfully resumed production. His bottles, whose labels reproduce his Aeolian paintings, would find their way onto the wine lists of the most prestigious restaurants. In the 1980s a new, larger winery, built in a local style, would be erected at Lingua, another hamlet on

Salina. Still in ferment, he even started experimentation and production of dry wines like Salina, in both white and red versions, and Antonello, aged in *barriques*. He relaunched the cultivation and commercialization of the island's excellent capers. He died in 1996, on his beloved Salina, and the reins of the company passed to his son, Carlo, Jr who, in collaboration with his friend Gianfranco Sabbatino, continued his father's work, to the extent that he is contributing to the revival of viticulture on the almost completely abandoned island of Vulcano, where he produces the red wine Hierà.

Modern Marsala was the work of **Marco De Bartoli** who, with his Vecchio Samperi, which made its market debut in 1976, sent a strong signal for the rebirth of this centuries old wine.

Marco was an extraordinary and unusual character, who showed great courage in defending his opinions. Linked to tradition, he was at the same time an extreme experimenter. In the early 1970s he devoted more time behind the wheel of a racing car than on the family estate in *contrada* Samperi, until his mother inherited the business from her mother Josephine. Marco put the same passion into running it that he felt for cars. He decided to take inspiration from the ancient production method called *il perpetuo*, which had been used before the arrival of the English, who had begun to produce fortified Marsala by adding alcohol. To that end, the grapes had to be capable of over 15 per cent natural alcohol, and the Grillo variety permitted it, provided the yield per vine was reduced. The wine was then subject to a maturation similar to Soleras, adding new wine to older wine. A particularly complex product was obtained thanks to the old wine, which at the same time had a good level of acidity conferred on it by the younger wine. The Vecchio Samperi could not however be called Marsala. Other Marsalas were also made according to his personal interpretation, but Marco showed above all how Grillo (Grappoli del Grillo, 1990) and Zibibbo di Pantelleria (the Pietra Nera label, first vintage 1989) could, if worked properly, also produce excellent dry wines. His Vecchio Samperi, and other of his creations, were an immediate and great success with enthusiasts. In 1996, he was accused of adulteration, and production at the winery was blocked for the duration of the trial, which ended with a full acquittal. He was greatly embittered, and profoundly hurt. His son Renato, who had created the Terzavia brand with him, continues his work.

Sardinia

The 1970s were the years of the large-scale production of bulk wines that went off to France, but also those in which a radical change got under way in both viticulture and oenology, thanks, first of all, to Sella & Mosca, founded in 1899 by the Piedmontese **Erminio Sella**, nephew of Quintino, and the Sardinian **Edgardo Mosca**. The 1960s saw the employment of Mario Consorte, a young oenologist from the Veneto, who envisaged being on the island for a short period and ended up staying there for over fifty years! Consorte began from the vineyard to obtain fresher, lighter wines. "They were tough years," he recounted, "and we had to work quite hard to make small producers, but above all, the managers of the cooperative wineries, understand that it was not possible to carry on producing bulk wines of little personality." In the second half of the 1970s, Vermentino di Alghero arrived on the market, signalling the new course of the island's oenology. The symbol of this revolution was the abandoning of Torbato *passito,* an extraordinary dessert wine on a par with the great Ports, for a more supple and modern wine that was not to the liking of Vittorio Sella, the last descendent of the founders. The success was immediate, favouring excellent financial statements. Many cooperative wineries

began to glimpse new market prospects, especially abroad, and followed the example, not all with the same result. Sardinian wines, thanks to Sella & Mosca – now part of the Campari Group – began to be viewed with less scepticism: they were no longer heavy and often unharmonious due to high alcohol content, but more balanced, fruity and agreeable. To Sella & Mosca must also go the merit for having made people understand the importance of good and coherent communication, which has contributed to enhancing the image not just of the company's wines, but of Sardinia as a whole.

"100 Antonio Argiolas" is the wine that was dedicated to **Antonio Argiolas** for his one-hundredth birthday. Small in stature, tenacious and determined by character, independent and enterprising until a late age – that was Antonio Argiolas, who died a few years ago. He took over his father's business in 1938. In the 1970s and 1980s, his sons Franco and Giuseppe (Peppetto) grasped the changes. The real and big turnaround came with Giacomo Tachis (after 1985), when a new production philosophy emerged: modern, fresh, elegant wines that accentuated varietal characteristics, in addition to the valorization of indigenous grape varieties. The first wines arrived on the market at the end of the 1980s: Vermentino, Nuragus, Monica and Cannonau. "The first years were difficult. They got to know us abroad first and then in Italy," Franco Argiolas explains. The precious collaboration with Tachis gave rise, in 1988, to Turriga, a big red made from Cannonau, Carignano, Bovale Sardo and Malvasia Nera: a new wine in a viticultural scene that was not yet clearly defined in Sardinia.

The great good fortune of this firm was having followed the advice of the patriarch Antonio, who wanted a business that was modern and dynamic, but respectful of the viticultural legacy whose value he had helped to enhance. We are

now at the third generation, with Valentina and her husband Elia, Francesca and Antonio. "They are our strength and our fortune," continues Franco, "without them it would have been difficult to continue such important work". Argiolas wines are now sold in over fifty countries round the world, and the shape of the business has changed thanks to the young, dynamic and competent young faces who occupy important sectors like communication, marketing and hospitality, at the same time continuing research into the old clones of indigenous varieties.

The **Ragnedda** brothers from the Cantina Capichera have always struck a maverick note in the island's viticultural and winemaking world. In a short time, they changed both appearance and production philosophy. The foreign markets are increasingly interested in Sardinian wines and the guides greatly help those wineries that stress quality. Medals, glasses and stars aside, with Capichera there began to be talk of big-bodied, structured wines, of full, enveloping wines, but also of different price ranges. It was a difficult choice, which, sustained by quality, ultimately rewarded the courage of the young Ragnedda brothers. Their greatest satisfaction was seeing their wines being compared with the rest of the world in the best *enoteche* and in top restaurants outside Italy. Vermentino was the standard-bearer of those years, and it still is today, though the range has become wider and more diversified, with big reds based on indigenous varieties like Carignano.

Italian history is the sum of many regional histories, of different phases of domination and historical, political and cultural influences. Moreover, Italy is, let's not forget it, a boot entering into the Mediterranean, so the variables of climate and terrain are boundless.

Though spumante is produced in many regions, there are four more important ones, and for reasons of climate and cultural influence (especially French and Habsburg) they are all in the North: from Piedmont to Veneto-Friuli Venezia Giulia, passing by way of Lombardy and Trentino.

The two wings have made their fortunes with supple, immediate, "fun-loving" sparkling wines, even though they are diametrically opposite: Asti Spumante from the Moscato grape in Piedmont; and Prosecco, from the Glera grape, in Veneto-Friuli Venezia Giulia. At the centre of the East-West line are the spumante centres that have opted for the *metodo classico* (the champagne method): Franciacorta, Oltrepò Pavese in Lombardy and Trentodoc in Trentino. The stories are different and equally singular, besides being fascinating.

Italian Spumante Pops the Cork

In 2013, Tom Stevenson – the English journalist regarded as the leading world expert on champagne and sparkling wine, and never tender with Italian wines – brought out the third edition of his 528-page *World Encyclopedia of Champagne & Sparkling Wine*, published by Christie's auctioneers (the first edition appeared in 1998, and Italian sparkling wines did not even get a look in, the second in 2003). For the first time Italy occupied a major role, the country with the most pages devoted to it after France. Stevenson placed Franciacorta in the top flight (61 reviews), with Cuvée Annamaria Clementi scoring 90 points, followed by Bellavista Franciacorta Riserva Vittorio Moretti (86) and Barone Pizzini, Franciacorta Satèn (84). Then there were Oltrepò Pavese and Trentodoc, at the top of which he placed the Riserva del Fondatore Giulio Ferrari, with 86 points. Then came the Alta Langa, with the "star Moscato d'Asti", as Romano Dogliotti was described, which obtained 96 points. While in Veneto the Prosecco di Valdobbiadene received just glory with 83 points for the Cartizze of Bisol.

It marked, finally, due recognition of the quality of Italian sparkling wines, the history of which stretches far back, as is also confirmed by ancient texts. In this regard we will cite two. The first, printed in 1570, was written by the Brescian physician Girolamo Conforti and significantly entitled *Libellus de vino mordaci*, the intent being to inform readers about wines in the Franciacorta area. The author emphasizes the remarkable diffusion and widespread consumption of bubbly wines in that age, describing them as *mordaci*, that is, lively and frothy. The second, *De salubri potu dissertatio*, was printed in Rome in 1622 and written by Francesco Scacchi. There are just five copies in the world, one of which is held by the Cantine Ferrari.

Without in any way detracting from the ability of the French, who created the legendary champagne, Italy can claim to be the cultural first-born. Both texts precede, in fact, the arrival on the scene of Dom Pérignon, the French Benedictine monk who lived between 1639 and 1715, and to whom legend attributes the invention of sparkling wine.

Jumping centuries forward, we would like to recall a book written by Antonio Piccinardi and Gianni Sassi in 1988: *Champagne & Spumanti. 100 Champenois scelti per la gola* (Arnoldo Mondadori): a book of rare graphic beauty, and a collector's item. It tells the story of forty-one champagnes, fifty-seven Italian and two Spanish sparkling wines.

Canelli, the Capital of Asti Spumante

History takes us back in time, to 1850, well before the Unification of Italy. It was **Carlo Gancia** who had the idea of applying the champagne method, which he had learnt during a stay in Rheims, to the Moscato of Canelli. In 1865, the Cantine Gancia were the birthplace of Moscato Champagne, the first Italian spumante produced with the classic method. Carlo Gancia was soon joined by other Moscato producers such as Contratto, Martini & Rossi, Cinzano, Cora, Bosca and Fontanafredda, which became celebrated brands. By the end

of the nineteeenth century, over forty-eight wine companies were concentrated in Canelli, on a surface area of around three square kilometres, while in nearby Santo Stefano there were another ten or so.

The turning point in the production of spumante was the invention, in 1895, "of the device and procedure for the continual production of sparkling wines"; it was the work of the Casale-born **Federico Martinotti**, director of the Regia Stazione Enologica of Asti. In the 1920s, this became the controlled method of refermentation in large recipients and tanks, then patented, in 1907, by the French oenologist Eugenie Charmat.

The Martinotti-Charmat method has become very widespread because it is better suited to the production of sparkling wines based on aromatic or fruity grape varieties, for which prolonged lees contact, a characteristic of *champenoise*, would be negative. It also involves considerably lower production costs, with the length of lees contacts being regulated in tanks according to the market goals. It is no coincidence that the vast majority of the world's sparkling wine is obtained with this method.

It should be said however that the Martinotti-Charmat technique can also produce great sparkling wines, like the one styled and shaped by Manlio Collavini in Friuli to produce his Ribolla Gialla brut.

Italy's two most widespread sparkling wines, Asti and Prosecco, are produced using the Martinotti-Charmat method.

Returning to Asti (the consortium of which was recognized in 1934), we must mention the extraordinary cellars of Canelli, authentic cathedrals of wine beneath the historic centre, now listed as a UNESCO site. These spectacular cellars originated as smaller rooms carved out in the tufa rock during the Late Middle Ages as storerooms for goods destined for Ligurian ports. Some twenty kilometres of tunnels stretch out at a depth of more than 30 metres, with vaulted or dome cap red-brick ceilings, sometimes with several aisles. Highly atmospheric, they are still used for the maturation of spumante.

Contratto was founded in 1876 by **Giuseppe Contratto**, and sold in 1993 to Carlo Bocchino, a well-known producer of grappa, who was responsible for renovating the cellars and

the company headquarters, one of Italy's most beautiful art nouveau buildings. In 2011, ownership of the famous brand passed into the hands of the Rivetti brothers.

Cantine Gancia is a business with impressive statistics. In 2011, Russian Standard, one of the largest integrated liquor and wine producing groups, purchased a 70% stake, increasing it to 94.1% in 2013. The cellars stretch over about one kilometre, and one of them is 100 metres long. Also of interest is the museum with a historic collection of advertising posters by leading twentieth-century poster designers.

Bosca makes wine and spumante since 1831. It is one of the few companies still owned by the founders, now in their sixth generation. From the start much importance has been given to new market and product studies. Even today it ex-

ports the majority of its production, focussing on everyday innovation and confident in its bicentennial traditions.

As of 2014, over 4,000 businesses are cultivating Moscato grapes on 9,700 hectares in 52 municipalities of the DOCG zone. Production is currently around 100 million bottles, of which 75% is Asti and 25% Moscato naturale. The *New York Times* described the enthusiasm for this sparking wine in the United States as "Moscatomania". In 2006, in fact, 2 million bottles were sold in the States.

That figure has now risen to 12 million, and counting. The work on improving quality among the small producers is bearing fruit.

Franciacorta

Franciacorta is the youngest of the areas given over to the production of classic Italian spumante.

Right before the DOC (1967), there were 11 producers in the area, with 29 hectares under vine and production totalling 2,000 hectolitres.

Its climb to the heights of the market is text-book stuff, the result of a far-sighted project whose goal from the start was total quality. But how did the name Franciacorta come into being?

In an interview given to Jessica Bordoni for *Civiltà del bere*, the journalist and TV presenter Bruno Vespa declared: "Do you know why we talk about Franciacorta today? One day Zanella came to me in search of advice about how to launch the classic method in Lombardy. The first thing I suggested was to avoid calling it spumante, but Franciacorta instead [francae curtes, *area not subject to duty*]. In a word, the idea for the name came from me. And for free as well."

This is confirmed by the current president of the consortium, Maurizio Zanella: "It was Vespa himself who gave us that advice about the communication."

As already stated, DOC status was granted in 1967, while the first Italian brut to obtain the DOCG was in 1995. In the same year, the Franciacorta production method was officially recognized, enabling the expression "vino spumante" to be dropped. Since then, labels have just borne the word "Franciacorta", a single term to define the territory, the production method and the wine. In the whole of Europe, there are just ten appellations that enjoy such a privilege, and of these only three produce sparkling wines with bottle refermentation: Cava, Champagne and Franciacorta.

A total of 3,200,000 bottles were produced in 1998; in 2013 – with 111 producers now belonging to the Consorzio founded in 1990, when 724 hectares were under vine – that figure rose to 14,070,552, with 2,800 hectares given over to Franciacorta DOCG (82% Chardonnay, 14% Pinot Nero and 4% Pinot Bianco). When the 350 hectares of the Curtefranca DOC are added, the figure is 3,150 hectares.

Today Franciacorta is the second most important zone, after Champagne, for the production of top-quality, classic-method sparkling wine. While producers initially chose to draw inspiration from champagne, a distinct Franciacorta style has been around for many years now, with an elegance and vitality that makes it truly unique.

Besides Berlucchi – unanimously considered to be the winery that established Franciacorta – mention should be made of two other producers who have contributed to raising the quality and knowledge of sparkling wines to the heights of excellence: Ca' del Bosco, founded by Maurizio Zanella in 1968, and Bellavista, created by Vittorio Moretti in 1977.

Franco Ziliani's love affair with bubbly goes back to a Christmas of many years ago. The family around the dining table and his father calling for glasses to be raised for a toast. He tasted the champagne, and was bowled over. It made such an impression on him that he enrolled in the Oenological School of Alba, in the conviction that only with the best possible training would he manage to produce a spumante capable of competing with the noble French bubbles. The goal he set himself was to produce a classic-method sparkling wine that was excellent value for money, capable of spreading the pleasure of celebrating, but also accompanying a meal, with an Italian brand.

"There grew in me the curiosity to try out techniques that might contribute to the quality of the product, independently from the *terroir*. That's why I preferred to start with the wine and not the vine, trying to solve the winery problems, from the pressing to the bottling. After the early death of my father, a friend of his recommended me to a Brescian nobleman, **Guido Berlucchi**, owner of Palazzo Lana in Borgonato di Corte Franca, who was looking for assistance to solve the bottling problems of batches of dry white wine of his production."

At the end of their meeting, with youthful courage, Franco greeted Guido Berlucchi with this question: "And if we were also to make a spumante in the French manner?" It was the beginning of an incredible partnership that would lead the company to produce 5 million bottles. The first vintage was 1961.

Over the course of half a century, Franco Ziliani perfected his trail-blazing role in the Franciacorta area, helping to create the conditions for the latter's emergence and establishing his winery as a market leader. After the death of Guido and of Giorgio Lanciani, co-founders of Guido Berlucchi

& C., and now alone in the position of president, he effectively handed over the company to his children Cristina, Arturo and Paolo, who now pursue and introduce new guidelines that never fall short of expectations. And so the dream of a young oenologist contributed to changing the destiny of an area, starting in the 1960s.

Maurizio Zanella was a key figure in the rise of Franciacorta and in the start of the Italian wine renaissance. Eclectic and visionary, Zanella took his first steps in the wine world in 1968, when, despite his young age – he was just fifteen – he focused his energies on something that transformed the former house in the woods, with its half hectare of vineyard, into today's universally acknowledged symbol of excellence. Zanella did not follow a rational, planned project, but instead listened to his own intense aspiration toward excellence. He searched for a way shaped neither by family tradition nor local tradition. Over the course of the years, this gave rise to ideas and trail-blazing wines that lay at the foundations of the company's fortunes, where extreme attention to detail made the difference. Details with quite precise connotations. To mention just a few: the precursory collaboration with the French *chef de cave* André Dubois; the pioneering approach to the denseness of vine layout; the introduction of technology to eliminate contact with oxygen in the production process; the use of gravity for the moving of grapes and must in the winery; the washing, and consequent drying, of just-harvested grapes prior to vinification. The sum of all this is well represented by the firm's standard-bearing wine, Cuvée Annamaria Clementi, dedicated to Maurizio's mother: a very balanced, elegant Franciacorta, obtained from a very rigorous selection of Chardonnay, Pinot Nero and Pinot Bianco, vinified in wood and aged on yeast lees for seven and a half years. The house in the woods still exists today, but everything has changed around it: the hectares under vine are now 184.5 in all, with around 90 employees and output of 1,500,000 bottles, while the main company building exudes elegance, refinement and the quest for beauty right from the entrance, where visitors are greeted by Arnaldo Pomodoro's *Cancello solare*, a signal that at Ca' del Bosco wine, art, culture and nature blend together into a magical harmony.

Vittorio Moretti, the founder of Bellavista, is an entrepreneur who turns dreams into reality. "I am, and remain, a builder, a businessman who horizons are always moving, but my roots are in Franciacorta. Above all I think I'm a dreamer with my eyes wide open, with the will and tenacity to give life to them."

Vittorio Moretti was born in Florence to a Franciacorta family. After moving to Milan, in the 70s, after having spent his youth on his father's building sites, he devoted himself to the production of pre-fabricated industrial units – a challenge that would remain at the core of his business activities. But for Moretti, always strongly tied to his land of origin, that was not enough. He believed in the potential of the Franciacorta *terroir*, and wanted to contribute to its establishment as a viticultural and winemaking area. "In my many travels I have always closely observed the characteristics that made an area, a place or a product unique and extraordinary. I have therefore always looked for the best people and instruments for exploring new paths. In those years I found myself thinking strategically about the future of

Franciacorta, and decided to give voice to the area." Bellavista was founded in 1977, and in 1979 came the first Gran Cuvée Brut and Pas Operé. In 1984, with Mattia Vezzola, he created an entirely new typology, which would then spread with success: Satèn. In the same year, the first Riserva was also made: "It is difficult for a producer to choose from amongst his wines, but I believe that our Cuvée represents for all of us the spirit and primary root of Bellavista: in it can be found the synthesis of Franciacorta according to our philosophy. A philosophy that receives its final seal in the Riserva Vittorio Moretti, the supreme expression of our constant search for characterful, complex and long-lived wines, and at the same time representative of a territory and of Italian production."

Today Bellavista – thanks also to the invaluable contribution of the oenologist Mattia Vezzola, who has overseen vineyards and winery from the start, proving to be one of Italy's best *chefs de cave* for the classic method – has the honour and duty to represent Italian style and quality around the world. Its clients are regarded as key ambassadors: it is also thanks to them that the wines of Casa di Erbusco and other wineries in the group are present in fifty nations.

Oltrepò Pavese, the *Terroir* of Italian Pinot Nero

Angelo Solci, the Milanese *enoteca* owner and oenologist, has a deep knowledge of Oltrepò Pavese, a very important area for the production of Italian sparkling wines made with the classic method:

"Pinot Nero [*spumante base clone*]," he affirms, "finds its ideal habitat in Oltrepò, thanks also to the initiative of Agostino Depretis back in the nineteenth century. In 1865, Carlo Gancia and Count Carlo Giorgi di Vistarino joined forces to produce and promote 'Italian champagne', and in 1870, the engineer Domenico Mazza di Codevilla took on an oenologist from Reims to perfect his Montelio spumante. At the beginning of the twentieth century, Pietro Riccadonna, Raffaello Sernagiotto, Angelo Ballabio and Mario Odero, with the Società Vinicola Italiana di Casteggio, obtained international success with their Gran Spumante SVIC. After World War II, the cooperative winery of Santa Maria della Versa, under the management of Duke Antonio Denari [*the first pres-*

ident of the Istituto Italiano dello Spumante Classico], led the new season of great successes. At present, around three-quarters of the Pinot Nero [*base spumante*] produced in Italy comes from the Oltrepò, even though the zone has lost the leadership of the classic method spumante."

Trentodoc

The Istituto Trentodoc was set up in 1984 to safeguard and oversee the sparkling wines of Trento, and in 1993 became the first, after champagne, to receive DOC appellation status for "classic" bubbles. The year 2007 saw the creation of the collective Trentodoc brand, which now brings together 39 of the 43 sparkling wine businesses in the area, with sales of around 7 million bottles over 5 years (2007–2012). The majority is made by the top 4 wineries, namely Ferrari, Rotari, Altemasi and Cesarini Sforza, which together account for 80% of production.

Eight hundred hectares are under vine with base spumante grapes (above all, Chardonnay, plus Pinot Nero, Pinot Bianco and Pinot Meunier).

At Trento in 1902 (there were still the Hapsburgs at that time), Giulio Ferrari (born in 1879) began to write his way into the history books of Italian classic method spumante production. Exactly half a century later, in 1952, he sold his winery (it produced 8,000–10,000 bottles) to Bruno Lunelli, owner of the best-known wine shop in Trento.

The story is summed up by Mauro Lunelli, one of the three brothers – the others are Gino and Franco – who built the

Gino, Bruno and Mauro Lunelli

Marcello, Camilla, Matteo
and Alessandro Lunelli

fortunes of Cantine Ferrari. "Giulio remained the technical manager until he died in 1965. I stepped foot in the winery as a boy, and was at his side almost every day. He was my first teacher, and I inherited his knowledge."

Mauro obtained his diploma in oenology at San Michele in 1968.

In the same year, Bruno handed over the company to his son, who divided up the responsibilities. He died five years later. Mauro became the chief winemaker, while Gino and Franco dealt, together, with sales and administration. They used to produce 80,000, then came an incredible progression: a million in 1980, three million in 1990 and four million in 2000. The five million mark was passed in 2007. The winery now extends over 30,000 square metres, and there are always 20 million bottles in the cellars.

But to return to Mauro: having obtained his diploma, and after a year in the laboratory to study the effects of oxidation on white wines, he went to Champagne and made friends with Rémi Krug, who let him taste many different vintages with very prolonged maturing in contact with the lees.

"A world opened up for me. In 1972, I started putting aside 5,000 bottles a year of the best Chardonnay, without saying anything to my brothers. In 1980, I got them to taste an anonymous bottle. They appreciated it greatly. It was one of the 5,000 'hidden' ones of 1972. When I revealed my secret, they almost hit me. I had 'removed' 40,000 bottles from the market over eight years, and we always used to run out. Their anger faded before the bottle was finished. We decided that it would be the Riserva del Fondatore Giulio Ferrari. A Riserva which initially spent eight years on the lees, then ten, and now eleven, for around thirty to forty thousand bottles a year."

It was the first noble Italian spumante. As Mauro succinctly puts it: "The Giulio Ferrari is the synthesis between oenology and viticulture." While for his daughter Camilla, Perlé – five hundred thousand bottles with six years of lees contact, 100% Chardonnay – "is the icon of the Ferrari style".

The sourcing of the grapes is a story within a story. The Lunellis are the owners, in Trentino, of 120 hectares of vineyards, and they also have around 500 grape suppliers. Since the 1960s they have had a pact with their suppliers that they describe as "sale on honour". "There are families with us who have supplied us with grapes for fifty years. We have eight agronomists in our employ, who supervise all the suppliers' vineyards. We have never signed a contract with the grape producers. Never! We pay more than the average market price for the grapes. The price is determined in relation to the quality. We have a procession of producers coming to ask to supply us with grapes."

Since 2011 the enterprise has been run by the third generation, who, to enter the business, had to respect of a series of rules agreed upon by the whole family.

"We signed a family pact together with our children," says Mauro.

First: you must have a degree.

Second: you must have worked for at least three years outside the company.

Third: you must speak at least two foreign languages.

Fourth: you cannot hold a post formerly held in the company.

And so, wives, husbands, children and relatives that do not respect this pact cannot enter the company.

The president of the company now is Matteo, Giorgio's son. Then there is Marcello, Franco's son, an oenologist, who assists his uncle Mauro in the cellar. And Mauro's children, Camilla, responsible for communication, and Alessandro, an electronic engineer, who deals with programming and controls.

The new generation is moving with a sure foot and looking to foreign markets, confirmed by the acquisition of shares in Oscar Farinetti's Eataly and 50% of Bisol in Prosecco.

Why Prosecco? Camilla is in no doubt: "It is the most important Charmat-method sparkling wine in the world, and Bisol is one of the top wineries, which will continue to be run by brothers Gianluca and Desiderio. Prosecco is one of Italy's oenological and territorial riches."

It goes without saying that Ferrari set a trend, effectively creating the Trentino spumante style, in addition to stimulating research at the Istituto Agrario di San Michele and the establishment of various classic method sparkling wine companies, including small-scale ones like Equipe 5, founded by **Leonello Letrari** in 1961 together with four school friends. When it was sold in 1988, it was producing 490,000 bottles. This "brut band" consisted, besides Letrari, of Giuseppe Andreas, a fruit grower, and the oenologists Pietro Tura, Riccardo Zanetti and Ferdinando Tonon, now ninety-four years old. The first bottle was released on the market in 1967. Letrari then poured his experience into the family business at Rovereto, run by his daughter Lucia, an oenologist. The Trentodoc Riserva del Fondatore 976, with ninety-six months of lees contact, is of noble lineage, and regularly receives awards from guides.

PROSECCO SUPERIORE
DAL 1876

Leonello Letrari was among the founders, in 1975, of the Istituto Italiano Spumanti, which first met, recalls Anna Pesenti, who then headed the institute, at Riva del Garda in 1974. With Letrari were Piero Antinori, Gino Lunelli from Ferrari, Alberto Contratto, Antonio Carpenè and Duke Denari di La Versa, who was elected president.

Prosecco, All-Italian Casual Style

The history of Prosecco dates to very remote times, and there are innumerable historic references. Ever since antiquity the original rootstock of the *Puxinum* (Puccino-Prosecco, a place in the municipality of Trieste) variety attracted a good deal of attention even before it was selected and cultivated for what we know today. Pliny the Elder wrote about it in 77 AD in his *Naturalis Historia*: "Nec aliud aptius medicamentis indicatur" (No other wine is more suited for medicinal purposes).

If the ancient cradle of Prosecco is the eponymous village in the province of Trieste, its success and legendary fame are associated with the Conegliano-Valdobbiadene area, where there is an abundance of documents relating to economic transactions, and, consequently, of pleas to the authorities, who, in turn, inevitably imposed duties. This one, dating to 1318, was imposed by the City of Treviso: ". . . free trade of mountain wines beyond the Alps is hereby granted to Conegliano [*who claims it*], subject to Trevigiano duties".

Prosecco was first produced in the second-half of the 1800s, using bottle refermentation. Only subsequently were innovative solutions adopted that led to the Martinotti method, that is to say, with tank fermentation, which later, thanks also to the local school of oenology and the Istituto Sperimentale di Conegliano, would be interpreted in an original manner. Indeed, it can now be defined as the Conegliano Valdobbiadene method, designed to obtain a fruity sparkling wine that is elegant to the nose and balanced in the mouth.

The modern history of Prosecco began on the hills of Conegliano and Valdobbiadene, with the granting of DOC status in 1969. The first year of production of the appellation dates to 1970, when there were about 1,500 hectares, with a potential for almost 15 million bottles, though only half was bottled. In 2014, the DOCG reached 79 million bottles.

Prosecco is undoubtedly the most trendy sparkling wine in the world. A youthful, jeans-wearing wine, suited to every moment, easy and agreeable, fun and alluring, it has reached a vast market. In many countries, Italy included, it has become synonymous with "spumante".

The key qualities of the "Prosecco phenomenon" of the DOCG Conegliano and Valdobbiadene area are:

– the rare beauty of its hills, a candidate for inclusion in UNESCO's World Heritage List;

– the Conegliano School of Viticulture and Oenology, founded in 1876, the first in Italy;

– the ability to integrate all the players in the area, to the point of obtaining recognition, in 2003, as Italy's sparkling wine district, one of the major strong points of which is the high quality of its human capital;

– the 6,861 hectares under vine are managed by 3,214 viticulturalists, an average of around 2 hectares per person: a limit but also a quality that has been grasped by producers as an opportunity for an economic-social revival;

– in 2009, with a demonstration of far-sightedness and pragmatism, the Prosecco world was revamped: the historic DOC of Conegliano Valdobbiadene and the small one of Asolo became DOCG, while the areas of Prosecco IGT – which, besides Treviso, extends over 8 provinces in Friuli Venezia Giulia and Veneto (Vicenza, Padua, Venice, Belluno, Pordenone, Udine, Gorizia and Trieste) – became one large new DOC. So, from being associated with the variety, Prosecco became identified with the historical denomination of Conegliano-Valdobbiadene, Asolo and the splendid village of Prosecco, situated at the top of the Trieste coastline, that gave rise to the name and where, for centuries, a grape variety

called Glera has been grown. The safeguarding from imitations, in fact, had become increasingly difficult as Prosecco gradually grew from a local into an international phenomenon;

– around the wine – and this issue is dealt with well by Stefano Micelli – a number of businesses have developed which are world leaders in terms of oenological equipment (from vats to winery plants), services, laboratory testing, logistics and even trade regulation support.

The Consorzio di Tutela di Conegliano Valdobbiadene can count on 183 sparkling wine producers, 430 vinification wineries and over 3,000 winemakers, who together have skilfully built in a little more than a century one of Italy's most vital production models.

From the start of the 1990s, all the wine would be sold in the bottle. Some 3,000 hectares of land were under vine, and the number of bottles produced reached 23 million. Ten years later, in 2000, the figures had risen respectively to 4,000 hectares and 36 million bottles. Today, years later, the hectares are almost 7,000 with a production of 69 million bottles. The DOCG is a "closed" area, as Giancarlo Vettorello, the Consorzio's director, calls it, in so far as the historic hills of Prosecco have almost completely reached their pro-

duction potential. The DOC area, recognized in 2009, has a surface of almost 20,000 hectares of vineyards with 307 spumante companies, which in 2014 produced 306 million bottles. Overall, both DOCG and DOC areas have together produced in 2015 over 400 million bottles, thus constituting the first denomination in the world of spumante, preceding Champagne and Cava.

In 1868, **Antonio Carpenè** and **Angelo Malvolti** opened the Carpenè Malvolti winery, "with annexed vapour distillery", as a late nineteenth-century sign reads. They made the first Prosecco. Thus Antonio, Sr was able to fulfill his mission: to open a company and provide customers high-quality wines of the Marca Trevigiana. The Carpenè Malvolti was the first in Italy to make spumante with scientifically controlled systems against the widespread superficial empiricism of the age. Since 1873 he began his campaign to open an Oenology School in Conegliano, of which he was president. His son Etile, Sr relaunched the Carpenè Malvolti after the destruction of World War I and was the first to call Prosecco with the vine variety name.

Etile, Sr was followed by Antonio, Jr who, while a student at university in Bologna, in 1934–1938 perfected Prosecco production methods and was engaged in legally safeguarding it. He restored the company after World War II, during which time it had been used as a base for Allied troops. The company's current size is due to him. Etile Carpenè, Jr, with a degree in chemistry from university in Ferrara and a very learned man, followed in the footsteps of his family and has been constantly involved in research and innovation to enhance Prosecco across the world. His daughter Rosanna, the fifth-generation Carpenè, has been working in the company for years and represents the youth of a world with local roots, from which she draws her energy as she looks upon the brilliant future of this wine, born from a dream of her great-grandfather, Antonio, Sr, and today a symbol of *Italian Lifestyle*.

Cooperative Wineries
From Vineyard Safeguarding to Winemaking Excellence

There are around 600 cooperative wineries operating in Italy, and amongst them are some genuine peaks of excellence. De-

spite this, they are still not talked about much, with the result that one of the most dynamic and innovative sectors of Italian oenology gets left in the shadows.

There might be a number of reasons for this apparent forgetfulness, and one at least is worth highlighting: cooperative wineries cannot be associated with the name and face of a producer. By their very nature, in short, they do not lend themselves to being recounted through the story of individual people. It is a pity, because in reality the cooperative winery model appears extremely modern, even though the ideals of cooperativism date to the beginning of the nineteenth century.

Their modernity today rests above all on the fact that they control thousands of hectares of vineyards in Italy's best vine-growing areas, with an amazing variety of soil and climatic conditions and historic and social traditions. By its very definition, in fact, the cooperative winery is a vertically integrated structure: a kind of bridge linking viticulture to the vinification phase and to bottling and market distribution. Consequently, in a world that tends ever more frequently to forget its agricultural and rural roots, they remain firmly anchored to their land of origin. It may sound paradoxical, but in this historic phase, true modernity is yoked together more and more frequently with an intelligent recovery of the past, with the rediscovering and valuing of a given territory, and with the desire to look at tradition with new eyes. Many cooperative wineries today seem to have responded in an exemplary manner to these issues, with the result that they find themselves fully in tune with the spirit that animates our complex historic age.

In recent years, once again in order to ensure stricter control over the production process, some of them have even begun to farm some hectares of vineyard, for instance parcels of land belonging to older members no longer able to work. Furthermore, ever more often they have decided to purchase vineyards. They have done so in order to start producing top-range wines, controlling the complete chain, which has obliged them to equip themselves with the most modern winery technology, besides vinifying separately grapes from the most favourable areas. In so doing, they have begun to acquire the skills and know-how that once belonged to private compa-

nies alone. Consequently, they have managed, in many cases, to compete on equal footing with the top names in national and international oenology. In the last few years, they have even begun to buy vineyards in areas other than those where their members have always operated.

In the cooperative wine-producing world, we are therefore witnessing a series of profound changes, from which there is emerging an increasingly felt need to bring cooperative thinking up to date with the characteristics of the age. If the cooperative wineries came into being with a defensive role – to preserve the interests of viticulturalists – they now seem focused above all on providing guarantees to their consumers.

With regard to the latter, in fact, they can play at least two key trump cards: first of all, an attractive value for money ratio, and secondly, the ability to directly control vast expanses of vineyard which, even with less than ideal harvests, ensures good levels of quality.

Without forgetting their attention toward issues such as health and food safety, which they became receptive to very early on; they set themselves the objective of producing wine in as compatible a way possible with the surrounding environment, so as to safeguard not only the health of consumers, but also the long-term survival of the ecosystem. It is precisely these values, together with others, that over the coming years will be able to form the basis for a new chapter in the history of Italian wine cooperatives, all to the advantage of those who love and drink wine, perhaps daily. Admittedly, in a future that has already begun, the cooperative wineries will probably end up resembling private ones more and more . . . their average size could in fact easily increase, and some may even decide to finance their development by being listed on the Stock Exchange.

The fact remains, however, that the pillar of these wineries will always be the viticulturalists and the respective wine-growing areas. In the coming years, then, the cooperative movement could also play a very important role in keeping Italy's rural fabric alive, helping to preserve the memory of the country's farming roots, and at the same time fuelling that love of the land which, in these years as never before, has found a place in our collective sensibility.

Methanol
The Dramatic Episode Had Nothing To Do
with the World of Winemakers

It was a terrible fact that led to fear the Italian wine renaissance would be forced back into the Dark Ages.

As Angelo Gaja said: "To reach paradise, Italian wine had to pass through hell".

"The most important reason for definitively putting the lid on the ugly methanol story," says Ampelio Bucci, "is that this dramatic episode had nothing to do with the world of winemakers, the people who grow the grapes in the vineyards, transform them into wine in the cellar, and then bottle and sell it with their own name. It related instead to sordid dealings between unscrupulous dealers and distributors interested only in making money. We winemakers had nothing to do with it."

What happened? A small network of criminals increased the alcoholic strength of wine by adding massive doses of methyl alcohol which an outrageous law had detaxed not long before, to the point that it cost less than sugar and ethylic alcohol. It was a golden opportunity for crooks, who could not believe it was so simple to line their pockets with money. But let's be clear: it is not as if Italian winemakers suddenly began, after 1986, to make quality wines, with everything that this entails. The history of the renaissance had begun almost twenty years earlier. The risk was that this tragedy might compromise its path. That did not happen.

But the dreadful episode had various effects:

First: it weeded out the few rotten apples, and at the same time tightened the mesh of controls, which since then have been exemplary;

Second: the scandal did not change the path that Italian winegrowers had embarked upon some time earlier. If anything, it prompted a composed, but decisive reaction to reaffirm our seriousness, moral conduct, values and work. Put under pressure, we became a team;

The third and perhaps most significant effect was on consumers. The methanol-tainted wine was an effective, albeit terrible, advertising campaign on behalf of quality, which consumers grasped immediately. Guaranteed quality was something that had to be paid for. And the symbol of that guarantee were the winegrowers, as individuals, their past and present, their projects, their vineyards and wineries open to the public, their ability and energy in travelling the world. Everybody understood this lesson. In fact, the "presidentialism" of the winegrower became necessity, and continues to be so. No law, no edict, no regulation can be more of a guarantee than the winegrower who tastes and drinks with you;

The fourth, and perhaps the most important, effect involved the importers, for some of whom only price mattered. All of a sudden they began turning to producers who could guarantee quality. It really was the end of an epoch. Since then the search for a wine producer necessarily entailed a real history, a project, an identity, an ethical approach to work. They discovered that Italy was made up of people of this kind;

The fifth effect was on the manner of communicating, which took a step forward. It became integrated with marketing. It was understood that it no longer sufficed to talk of quality in generic terms, but that this quality had to be recounted. It was necessary to initiate it and then support it with a philosophy, and that this could help to make the diversity of a product with respect to a competitor's. The press also assisted in this evolution, and understood that quality was essentially linked to the ethics of the person who conceived and then realized this quality. It was a project. A vision. From then on, this spontaneous reaction took form, which was then in some way codified. We began to believe in the value of the history we had, and which many of our competitors around the world, excluding France, do not possess.

The reaction was choral. Certain initiatives taken by the Ministry of Agriculture both on the communicative level – above all, on the foreign markets – and as regards control – with the reorganization of the Anti-Food Adulteration Service and the introduction of Nuclear Magnetic Resonance, equipment which was installed for the first time at the Istituto Agrario di San Michele all'Adige – had an immediate impact in restoring faith in Italian wines. But in particular it made producers understand the importance that the intrinsic quality of wine had on its consumption, and the role played by the vineyard and its management in determining its organoleptic qualities.

The Challenge of International Markets

Walter Filiputti with Ampelio Bucci, Nicolas Belfrage and Jens Priewe

The markets have been the testing ground for the visionary momentum of the people involved in the "renaissance of Italian wine". The challenge would have been shattering had it not been sustained by that alchemy that underlies the act of doing business: a combination of courage and temerity that has no formulas. It is the "pleasure" of risk.

From an economic point of view, this has been the real driving force of the renaissance: never before had farmers become entrepreneurs in the span of just a few years. Nor had small and large producers ventured – with the same energy – into new markets, often in countries that were unknown to them, carried away by magic that is positive involvement in a project that everyone felt was feasible.

The encounter with the markets, in particular, the American market, also helped to develop the corporate culture, creating the conditions to look at globalization as an opportunity.

Time and again the world of Italian wine has faced battles – because this is what they indeed are – in the marketplace. It was not easy to go up against, for example, the arrival of the New World wines whose production costs for us were unthinkable, combined with good quality.

It was a crucial moment in which we learned to draw from our great heritage: first, the natural one – Italy produces wines from the Valle d'Aosta to Pantelleria with a variety of offerings that is unique in the world – and then the cultural one, which is the basis of "Made in Italy", our artisan interpretation of labour, despite its modernity.

Three hundred and sixty-one autochthonous varieties; myriad of recipes from our regional cuisine; the many, many artisans of taste who make unparalleled foods; the fifty UNESCO sites, the landmark goal achieved with the recognition of the vineyards – the first ones in the world – of the Langhe-Roero, Monferrato and Pantelleria areas, producing what the German journalist Jens Priewe calls "a spontaneous marketing, though less scientific and pragmatic than in the US, it proved more effective".

We agree that there is a great deal to be done. It would be trouble if this were not the case, because life would be meaningless.

As well as being an eminent winemaker with his Verdicchio di Villa Bucci from the Marches, Ampelio Bucci is a professor at IULM in Milan where, a decade ago, he designed the first master's programme on "Made in Italy". The course put together all the important strategic sectors of artisan Italy. This master's programme is as ingenious as it is successful. Here are his thoughts:

"Looking back on the short history of quality Italian wine – short, because it starts in the 1970s, and is not yet forty-five years old – perhaps the most interesting thing is not so much the worldwide success of the large winemakers from known areas like Piedmont and Tuscany, with renowned brands, millions of bottles produced and a sales organization and marketing that has always been cutting-edge. Instead, the miraculous thing is what the thousands of medium and small producers managed to do, producers from areas that are not traditionally winegrowing ones: planting the vines, making wine and exporting it worldwide. Even in the secondary cities of the US or Japan as well as Europe, in fact, one often finds Italian wines from wineries that are little-known even at home, from small wineries that have developed over the last years of the past century.

This aspect is of the utmost importance and we could almost call it a 'non-marketing' Italian style, based on entrepreneurial/artisan intuition and initiative and not the canonical rules of management. There is something peculiar in this typically Italian story, because it can be found in other sectors of Made in Italy, for example, food, clothing and interior decor. In Italy, these sectors took off almost simultaneously, in the 1970s, and offer products in which the coexistence of the good and the beautiful is a fundamental element.

It happened this way with wine as well. The beginnings were often simple peasant beginnings, no marketing, no Bocconi, no strategy, no Philip Kotler [*one of the gurus of international marketing*]. Just a desire to make and sell. We could then add 'no knowledge' as a spontaneously strategic factor, because then intuition takes over, the capacity for entrepreneurial risk and, above all, the capacity to look around and see what others are doing. In the countryside, word of mouth and watching what the others are doing is a way of working that has always been known and used. The grass is always greener.

And so, in short, besides wine, those Italian industrial sectors were established [*more than a hundred!*], sectors that involve everyone, absolutely everyone, the sectors of beauty and goodness [*clothes, shoes, furniture, sofas, textiles, kitchens, glass, wool mills, food . . .*].

In wine, intuition led many to focus on what they knew, in other words, the vintners in one's own area who knew how to manage and 'distil' the best, hopefully with the help of an oenologist [*a profession that no one had practiced and until then had never been heard of*].

Others chose the international vine varieties, in one way more certain, because they were better known abroad. At any rate, on different terrains, they became something else: a Sicilian Chardonnay will never be the same as one from Borgognotto or South Tyrol.

And so, even the large industrial wine producers began to plant and sell autochthonous varieties. Again in retrospect, it is easy to say that the most cutting-edge principle of strategic marketing was applied, one that can be summarized in the slogan 'Be different or die', in an increasingly global, increasingly complex and increasingly saturated world, increasingly crossed again and again by goods and by people. And the 'Be different or die' slogan, in wine, has an advantage over other sectors. Because the vineyard and the terrain cannot be moved. For this reason, the territory must be defended [*more than the vine, which can travel*]. Barolo is a place before it is a wine. In the Marches, now, the DOCG has become Castelli di Jesi.

Wine artisans and wine industrialists: two parallel worlds are emerging.

The wine industry of non-European countries, new producers, should gear up to be as modern as possible, in the new, wonderful wine cellars of the world, with the use of machines and technologies that can improve the quality of the wine, which must be, above all, constant.

On the other hand, there is the artisan aspect to wine [*and not just wine*] where – as Richard Sennett [The Craftsman, *Yale U Press, 2008*] and Stefano Micelli [Futuro artigiano, *Marsilio, 2011*] state – the primary objective is to make the most of one's own work and one's own product. So, for example, not producing wine in the less perfect vintages is a

choice, not of classical marketing, but one which strengthens credibility.

This Italian 'craftsmanship' in wine seems to contradict a principle on which everyone agrees today in light of global markets: think global and act local.

Well, the basic principle on which Italy's excellences in the world of wine are working is exactly the reverse: think local and act global [*Ampelio Bucci*, L'impresa guidata dalle idee, *Domus Academy, 1992*]. Think, try as much as possible to be local because this – the place – cannot be exported. This world is becoming more and more monochromatic and increasingly seeks authentic, original and unique products. Our cultural roots, like those of our vines, must be cultivated, disclosed, communicated, transmitted because they are and will be the most modern thing in the coming years."

The United States

The success achieved on the American market launched Italian wine in the world. Several factors, in addition to courage, capacity for innovation and the entrepreneurial determination of our producers, contributed to this:

- the US's very great influence all over the planet. New York is the real capital of the world – what Rome was during the imperial age. Styles, trends and fads blossom in New York and then conquer the rest of the world: art, culture, music, economics, socio-political aspects and finally cuisine and wines;

- a very important presence of Italian restaurateurs who, as immigrants, were able to reach the top, making our cuisine a model to follow: worth mentioning are Sirio Maccioni, Tony May, Lidia Bastianich and Piero Selvaggio;

- it was precisely the Americans who discovered the values of the Mediterranean diet, thanks to studies initiated by

Ancel Keys in 1969. He published the research work *Seven Countries Study* and then *Eat Well and Stay Well, the Mediterranean Way* (Doubleday, 1975), making our lifestyle a model suited to everyone. Keys decided, not surprisingly, to settle in Italy, in Pioppi in Cilento, where he continued to live for another forty years, proof of the soundness of his theory. In fact, he lived to be one hundred years old. Since 2010, at the request of Italy, UNESCO included the Mediterranean diet in the intangible heritage of humanity;

- importers of wine were also crucial and many of them are Italian or children of Italians: Anthony Terlato – formerly of Paterno – in Nocerino, Leonardo LoCascio, Di Belardino and Fabrizio Pedrolli who, together with Louis Iacucci, founded Vias Imports. Without forgetting the valuable work, in the early 1980s, done by Gelasio Lovatelli and Andrea Franchetti with their River Wine;

- the press, which saw in the emerging Italian wine a means to counter the monopoly of French wine and the domination of the Anglo-Saxon world in the media. It is no coincidence that *The Wine Spectator* began writing only about Italian and Californian wines. Also worth noting is the great contribution made to the Bel Paese by the many American and Italian-American writers with their Italian cookbooks;

- the American market made us face a way of doing business that was unknown to many of us, masterfully pioneered by the Italian-American Robert Mondavi. He was a constant point of reference for us, a model (he also invested in Italy). He taught us that we had to open ourselves fearlessly to the markets. We had to be daring. We had to open our cellars, on the model of what he did in Napa Valley, to attract visitors, as well as producing wine. It was the market comparison – sometimes very hard – that made us grow. Contact with the American mind-set led us to understand the importance of marketing. It was an open, democratic and courageous marketing, capable of enhancing all our enormous potential. At the time, however, we did not have the right way of seeing them. That way was given to us by them;

- fashion that, like wine and cuisine, found its consecration in the United States, also involving design;

- cinema: in the first post-war period, we were awarded eight Oscars – four with Federico Fellini and four with Vitto-

rio De Sica – to which five more were added (we are the nation that has won the most Oscars after the United States: thirteen, against twelve in France). Many Italian-American names in the star system own an Italian restaurant: Francis Ford Coppola, Lady Gaga, Sylvester Stallone, Robert De Niro, Danny De Vito and Hulk Hogan.

Lucio Caputo and the Role of the ICE in New York
Lucio Caputo arrived in New York in 1972, in charge of opening the ICE (Italian Institute for Foreign Commerce) headquarters, becoming its head, with the task of reorganizing the Italian sales network in the Atlantic coast states. The man was able to make unconventional decisions, and revolutionized promotion.

He understood that you had to focus on the finest products, the only ones capable of driving the entire sector.

In 1981, with the reorganization of the great Park Avenue branch in New York, he opened a wine shop, stocked with all the best Italian wines, including some very old vintages. He was available to the press. It opened with an event that made history. It was attended by many celebrities from the fields of entertainment, culture, politics and business, as well as a large group of wine producers which, with Pino Khail's initiative with the magazine *Civiltà del Bere*, offering 94,539,970 Lire, managed to buy the famous painting by Giorgio de Chirico *The Disquieting Muses* so that it could be exhibited in the wine shop.

It was a sign of great importance inasmuch as, for the first time, an unparalleled number of quality companies were united in a communication project in the United States market, and were able to pass the new style of our wines to American opinion leaders. Pino Khail was, to some extent, the soul of that operation. He was responsible for creating the group and it was his idea to donate the painting. For many of these companies, also through his magazine, he was a highly professional communicator.

In 1982, Lucio Caputo left the ICE, and in 1984 became president of the Italian Wine & Food Institute, an organization that, under the auspices and with the financial support of the Ministry of Agriculture, organized several promotional campaigns in favour of Italian wines and food products, with major events such as the "Gala Italia", still considered one of the most successful Italian promotional initiatives in the United States. In fact, Lucio Caputo was thirty years ahead of everyone with his system, combining the best of our manufacturing excellence and expertly joining music, culture, design, fashion and cuisine.

The Best Ambassador of Our Wine Is American: Burton Anderson

In 1965, Maynard Amerine published *Wine* (University of California, Davis), followed by the second edition in 1975, revised and expanded with Vernon L. Singleton. The image of Italian wines was disastrous. Here is a passage from the 1975 edition: "Vines are grown on or between trees and in competition with tomatoes, olives, and other crops in the fields . . . Winemaking procedures have frequently been rather primitive. The small size of the vineyards makes it difficult for the winemaker to receive proper training . . . Many of the traditional Italian production practices are outmoded."

In 1971, *The World Atlas of Wine* (Mitchell Beazley) by Hugh Johnson dedicated a seventy-two-page section to France, while Italy was limited to a miscellaneous chapter: "Southern and Eastern Europe and Mediterranean".

In 1983, Michael Broadbent, English historian and authoritative taster, wrote an important book titled *The Great Vintage Wine Book*, for the publisher Knopf in New York. In its 432 pages, the wine sector in Italy does not exist, while many far less important countries than ours at this time are discussed, reserving, for example, up to thirty-nine pages for Germany, two for Tokay in Hungary and three for Australia.

Again in 1983, *The Wine Roads of Europe* by Marc and Kim Millon (Nicholson) came out in New York. Italy is represented by only four wine regions: Piedmont, Tuscany, Veneto and Colli Albani. Friuli Venezia Giulia is given only a few lines in the chapter on the Veneto.

This is how our wines were seen at the time. It was an American journalist who solved the problem of image. In the early 1970s, he was managing editor of the *Herald Tribune* in Paris: **Burton Anderson**. He moved to Cortona, in Tuscany, in 1969. His first article, in 1972, was dedicated to Brunello di Biondi Santi.

His project was to write a book that talked about the new reality of Italian wine. It came out in 1980: *Vino. The Wines and Winemakers of Italy* in English. Finally, there were 579 pages, all dedicated to our wines!

With a modern, engaging and no-frills journalistic style, Anderson talks about his journey through Italy where he discovered, along with the wine, the people that produce it and the land that nourishes it. The work was presented by Johnson, who wrote: "The first publication of Burton Anderson's *Vino* introduced the world to Italian wine and winemakers in a wholly new way. It sets on record the pride of a generation with higher ambition than any of its predecessors".

Since then, Anderson also began to collaborate on guides with Johnson, handling the section on Italian wine, thereby contributing to further strengthening our image in the world.

Anderson's book immediately became the new Bible of Italian wine. For Angelo Gaja, "*Vino* shed light on our wines in the United States, opening the curtains on the darkness into which they had been forced".

"As soon as the book was published [*40,000 copies sold*], they began to call me," Anderson confesses with his delicate shyness, "importers, journalists, wine bars, restaurants. They were surprised by the abundant supply of premium wines and at the same time were asking for more information and contacts".

For Anderson, showing these people the goodness of our wines became a pleasant challenge. Like when he convinced the critic of *The New York Times*, Frank J. Prial, to taste an Italian wine and "started" with a stupendous Barbaresco Santo Stefano 1971 by Bruno Giacosa. You know what Prial said? That it was not possible an Italian wine could be so good. The Englishman Steven Spurrier – who worked in the wine trade with Christopher & Co., the oldest wine merchant in London – had opened the Cave de la Madeleine in Paris in 1970. It quickly became one of the most renowned spots for quality wines. Well, to convince Spurrier that ours were of a very high level (at the time, he did not have them in his wine shop), in 1976, Anderson showed up at his place with an Antinori Tignanello and a Barbaresco from Angelo Gaja. It goes without saying that there was no match.

In 1982, Anderson published *The Mitchell Beazley Pocket Guide to Italian Wines* in English, then had it published in German and Italian. In the following years, he had as many as forty editions in various languages, including Japanese. The guide, which is updated every two years, came to sell over 450,000 copies.

In 1990, Anderson presented his most challenging work, *The Wine Atlas of Italy*, published in Italian, English and German, which sold 70,000 copies. In the work, not only does he describe Italian winemaking, DOC after DOC with related maps, but also the most innovative winemakers. But it did not stop there. At the end of each chapter on the different regions, there is tourist information with restaurants, hotels, wine bars, markets and places to visit.

In 2001, he published another excellent book, *Burton Anderson's Best Italian Wines* (Little, Brown and Company), in which the reporter selects and presents more than 200 vintners.

Joe Bastianich, Wine and Food Tycoon
Joseph, aka Joe, Bastianich was born in New York in 1968 into an Italian family from Pula, Istria, from which they were forced to flee because of the system introduced by Tito in the former Yugoslavia.

His parents Felice and Lidia, who arrived in the US in 1958, opened up a small trattoria called Buonavia in 1971 in Forest Hills, Queens. In 1979, they bought a second restaurant, Villa Seconda, also in Queens. In 1981, they sold both restaurants to open their most important venue, Felidia, on the East side of Manhattan. It was immediately successful.

From the early 1990s onward, Joe would prove to be a formidable entrepreneur and promoter of our wine, with a clear vision of the market and convinced of the enormous yet hitherto unexpressed potential of our wines and food.

His idea was clear: wine, cuisine and products must go hand in hand. Joe's way of thinking began to take shape before the influence exerted by Oscar Farinetti who, together with his mother Lidia and Mario Batali, has been a partner, since 2009, in the development of Eataly North, Central and South America.

"The spread of Italian products, combined with the culture of our table, allows our wines to travel the world. The products arrived before wine, and before wine there was – and is – the Italian restaurant, now of the highest world level. Americans love *Italian Style*, but getting it to them requires organization."

According to Bastianich, the work of the renaissance of Italian wine was completed in the American market, with the 1989 and 1990 harvests. "Those vintages – joined with an intelligent refinement of style – have permanently changed the image of our wine, which takes top place in the American market".

In his story, loaded with intensity and enthusiasm, he mentions his tasting teachers, who were two importers. They are Louis Iacucci, who had a wine shop in Queens, not far from his parents' first restaurant, and Robert Chadderdon, who already in the early 1970s imported the unrivalled Amarone di Quintarelli, in addition to Forteto della Luja Rocche dei Manzoni, Bartolo and Gianfranco Bovio. "I was weaned on the incredible Amarone of '69 and '71 in tastings with Robert, perhaps the greatest wines I have ever drunk". Wine fascinates him. A long trip he took in Italy in 1990, from Friuli to Pantelleria, through all the most important Italian regions, made him fall even more in love with it.

In October 1993, Joe convinced his parents to invest with him in his first restaurant – Becco in Manhattan – also funded by his grandmother Erminia, who lent him $ 60,000. "With

Joe Bastianich

my mother – with whom we do a lot of things – I couldn't have shared a restaurant. If I put a bottle in one place, she arrives and moves it. Just as I do. And I am the kind of person who wants no masters. In '93, New York was in crisis. Wine did not sell. Becco had a list with 200 Italian wines, all priced under 15 Dollars a bottle". It was the first success.

In June 1998, Bastianich opened Babbo Ristorante Enoteca, with chef Mario Batali, and changed the model of Italian restaurants in New York. Wine became the main player. "Our increased turnover was because of the wine," he says with satisfaction. "We had six sommeliers". Sure, the cuisine was top-notch, rigorous in its research of regional Italian dishes and quality basic ingredients. It was also not an Italian-American cuisine, but true Italian, albeit interpreted by Batali. In the following years, Joe and Mario opened another seven restaurants, including Del Posto that, in 2010, became the first Italian restaurant with a four-star review by *The New York Times* after thirty-six years. Later, Batali and Bastianich opened a place in Los Angeles and Las Vegas. In August 2013, Bastianich opened, with his mother, the Orsone in Cividale del Friuli, next to the company cellars acquired in 1997.

And we come to the meeting that would change his life. In 2007, Bastianich was invited by Oscar Farinetti to visit the newly born Eataly in the former factory of Carpano, in Turin. He went with his mother. They saw, ate extremely well in Langa and it all began there.

Driving back, his mother said, "Today you met your first boss."

"She was right. Even in 2012, I did not imagine that we would have opened an Eataly in New York and that I really would have a 'boss'. She had understood that Oscar's proposal could coincide with my idea of combining wine, products and food". Joe sums it up: "Eataly is changing Americans' perception of Italian food. Until then, they had never been able to separate or to understand the difference between the Italian-American products – born thanks to the first emigrants and that inevitably were hybridized with the local style – and the 100% Italian products. Eataly, before being a vast range of products of sublime quality, is a formidable communication machine for the 'Made in Italy' artisans of taste. A strat-

egy that, through perfect organization, manages to reach – for the first time – a vast market that did not even know about Italy's incredible wealth of products."

Thanks to *MasterChef USA*, with Gordon Ramsay and Graham Elliot, and *MasterChef Italia* on Sky1, together with Bruno Barbieri and Carlo Cracco, Joe became a TV star.

Fabrizio Pedrolli, between Business and Culture
Fabrizio Pedrolli was part of the group that launched Italian sommeliers. For many years he was the trustee of the sommeliers of Trentino. In 1975, he was appointed to present the wines of his land in New York. He spoke about it to Franco Colombani, *patron* of the magnificent restaurant Del Sole in Maleo and president of the Sommelier Association, who urged him to invite his very dear customer who, every time he came to Italy, went to eat at his restaurant either on the day of his arrival or the day of departure: his name is Louis Iacucci. Which is just what Fabrizio did as soon as he met Lucio Caputo, then director of the ICE on Park Avenue, who told him, "If we don't invite Iacucci, it will be trouble. He's the true ambassador of Italian wines in the US".

Then Fabrizio learned that in his wine shop, Goldstar, "he had 1,700 Italian wine labels. Of Barolo alone there were 60–70". That knowledge was crucial for Fabrizio. They became friends. Pedrolli is a fine wine *connoisseur*, and has the didactic art of the sommelier in his DNA. Between one trip and another came the idea of "doing something together". In 1983, VIAS (Italian Wines Selected Foods) was founded, and the first delivery was organized.

In 1988, on one of the many trips to Italy – during which Piero Antinori gave him an award for the best ambassador of Italian wine in the US – Iacucci died in a car accident.

After a period of corporate turmoil, VIAS became Viaswine and resumed its path in 1991, with Pedrolli at the helm and a renewed commitment.

Fabrizio Pedrolli

Today the company has a 36-million Dollar turnover. In its thirty-year history, it has launched on the American market a very long series of small and prestigious winemakers: Castello dei Rampolla, Dal Forno, Josko Gravner, Aldo Conterno, Produttori del Barbareso. And then Abbazia di Novacella, Maso Poli, Foradori, Guerrieri Gonzaga (Tenuta San Leonardo), Suavia in Soave, Salvioni and Argiano in Brunello, Principe Pallavicini in Lazio, Planeta, Walter Mastroberardino's Terredora in Campania, Cantele in Puglia, Cottanera on Etna, Capichera in Sardinia, Damilano (Barolo), Peccchenino and Ca'Viola.

Certainly atypical among importers: in fact, he puts the absolute goodness of the wines before market fashions.

Italian wine is also committed to education through a series of concrete actions. In 1991, he convinced the then director of the ICE in New York, Giorgio Lulli, to do twelve broadcasts on our wine culture on RAI International, widely followed in New York. From there he invented an operation that looked far into the future, again supported by the ICE: organizing meetings in sixty American cities that included a seminar on Italian wine which was followed, in the evening, by a wine tasting for which all importers of Italian wines were asked to provide their wines.

From 100 to 150 people participated in the seminar, including waiters, restauranteurs and wine shops, while in the evening, as many as 500 people came. In the end, 6,000 people attended! The teachers were twelve American journalists selected by Burton Anderson, who gave them a series of lessons on Italian wines, in order to put them in a position to manage the seminars.

In 1994, in fact, with his friend and partner Pino Sola – he, too, was part of the historical group of sommeliers – he published an English version of *Vias Wines* (Alvin Service). In it they taught the basic aspects of wine tasting, as well as managing the cellar, serving and pairing wine with food. It was the school of Italian sommeliers. He gave away 30,000 copies of the book to his American customers, waiters and sommeliers.

American Journalism

While Burton Anderson was the man who, more than any other, helped to introduce our wines in the US, Europe and the world, the American press, in particular, was able to grasp the value of their change and the huge choice in offer.

In 1976, in San Diego, **Bob Morrisey** founded a magazine that, more than any other, made the fortune of our wines: *The Wine Spectator*. **James Suckling**, who for twenty-nine years was a correspondent from Europe and Italy (where he settled), reminds us that they began by talking about California and Italian wines and that their headquarters was in a garage. In 1979, it was taken over by the current editor and publisher, **Marvin R. Shanken**, who turned it into the most important wine magazine in the world. Together with **Robert Parker**, he influenced consumers around the globe. At the beginning, the communication strategy of the American wine world – and the press from it that was supported by advertising – was subtle and far-sighted. By talking about us and the French, the Americans accredited their wines. Angelo Gaja notes that "the American design was to identify leaders in other countries, like Italy, for example, to build a group of producers who could counter the power of the French".

Robert Parker, in 1978, with his first newsletter *The Baltimore-Washington Wine Advocate* – which a year later became *The Wine Advocate* – revolutionized the style for talking about wine. Frank Prial called him "the most influential wine critic in the world". His nose and his palate are insured for a million Dollars!

The leadership was taken away from the British, who were caught off guard by his modern and essential vocabulary. Rough controversy rained down on him. His great innovation was the scale of the quality judgments expressed in hundredths, accompanied by a brief text, followed only by *The Wine Spectator*. Some of the first Italian wines examined were the Piedmonts by Bruno Giacosa and Angelo Gaja. Robert Parker met the latter in 1981 in Washington, DC, thanks to his importer in the United States, Ms Segre (originally from Turin) owner of the AL.SE.CA. Corporation. "It was my lucky moment," says Angelo today.

In his *Wine Buyer's Guide* of 1987 (Simon & Schuster), Italian wines are given considerable space and all the more important producers are included. It resulted in a major shift in the style of the wines, especially the reds.

According to Lodovico Antinori, "Parker got customs clearance for the wines in a geographic band – that of the outskirts, as he calls them, or a good part of the United States – which did not drink wine. At the time there were few snobs who drank it, but the rest loved beer and spirits. Parker managed to bring wine to the small American town".

According to Joe Bastianich, Parker's most important collaborator in Italy was **Antonio Galliano**. "He was able to make American collectors appreciate the great Italian wines, collectors who own million-Dollar wineries, where they collect the best wines in the world. There are about two hundred opinion leaders, of strategic importance to a wine's image. Galliano knew how to fit into this exclusive club of *connoisseurs*, putting the world's top wines in competition with Italian wines, which appeared frequently at the top of the tastings, to the amazement of enthusiasts. In the face of a Monfortino 1978." Joe concludes, "there is very little to say: it can stand alongside the top reds in the world as an equal."

Frank J. Prial, an American from Newark, New Jersey, died at eighty-two in 2012. For thirty years he was the wine critic for *The New York Times*, for which he edited the column *$25 and Under*. Given the importance of the newspaper, his notes on Italian wine are very important.

Eric Asimov, of Bethpage, New York, has been the wine critic for *The New York Times* since 2004, when he took over from Frank Prial. From 2000 to 2004 he was co-author of the annual *The New York Times Guide to Restaurants*, with Ruth Reichl and William Grimes.

There is another important work by **Sheldon** and **Pauline Wasserman**, who in 1987 published *Italy's Noble Red Wines* (Sun Designs), then reissued in 1991 with an impressive 762 pages, two-times the number of the first edition. Many wines were tasted, and each one is described with a plethora of thoughts, information and news.

Edward Steinberg, an American who lived in Rome for many years, was the founder of the Forum School of Rome, an international high school. In 1992, he published *The Vines of San Lorenzo. The Making of a Great Wine in the New Tradition* (Ecco Press). It is primarily a book on the production of a great wine, one that stands on the sidelines, and addresses a number of related topics, first and foremost, the great revolution in Italian wine. "At the time, I had not even met Angelo Gaja". Angelo Gaja confirms: "He was looking for me, to ask about writing a book that told the millennial story of wine. To tell that story, he needed a vineyard, and a wine, and so he said that he would choose Sorì San Lorenzo. He did not ask to be paid for the work he was going to do, only that we host him during his travels in Barbaresco and that we would have no secrets when talking about our way of working in the vineyard and cellar."

Alexis Bespaloff was born in Bucharest in 1934 and died in 2006. He was the wine columnist for *New York Magazine* for twenty-four years. His book *The Signet Book of Wine* (New American Library), whose first edition is from 1971, sold over a million copies in all subsequent editions. There remains that memorable message he recorded on his answering machine, which responded to the many calls: "I cannot take your call right now, but if it's an emergency, white with fish and red with meat." He is considered legendary.

Matt Kramer is a columnist for *The Wine Spectator*. He loves autochthonous Italian wines, and states that they possess integrity that comes from time and local tradition. He is the author of the excellent *Making Sense of Italian Wine* (Running Press, 2006).

Thomas Matthews, executive editor for *The Wine Spectator*, has always given a lot of attention and been very drawn to "Made in Italy", and in his work always speaks of it in positive terms.

In 2002, **Joe Bastianich** and **David Lynch** published (Clarkson Potter) a book that became highly successful, surpassing the 100,000 copies sold, titled *Vino italiano. The Regional Wines of Italy*. The book, in its 528 pages, examines the wines by region and contains the recipes of his mother Lidia, and his friend, chef and partner, Mario Batali. There is no lack of wine routes, as well as a comprehensive glossary of terms and list of Italian importers of Italian wine in the United States. In short, it is a wine Bible that Robert Parker called "a terrific and candid guide to the wines of Italy that should be on the bookshelves of all wine lovers".

Authors of Books on Italian Cuisine in the US

The authors of books on Italian cuisine have also made an important contribution to the dissemination of our wines throughout the world.

Of those who, starting with cuisine, elevated our image in the United States, we wish to remember **Marcella Hazan** – who passed away on 29 September 2013 – and her husband, Victor. She was originally from Cesenatico in Emilia-Romagna. Victor, however, is an Italian born in New York, a famous writer of books on wine and translator of his wife's writings. When they married, in 1955, Marcella had never cooked before. She began to take her first cooking classes in New York. Her recipes, traditional and not contaminated with English or American influences, were simple and could be easily made at home. She anticipated seasonal cuisine by decades.

She wrote many books. The first was *The Classic Italian Cook Book: The Art of Italian Cooking and Italian Art of Eating*, 1973 (Harper's Magazine Press), which was followed by seven others, including *Marcella Cucina* in 1997 (Harper-Collins) which won the James Beard Best Mediterranean Cookbook and Julia Child Cookbook Awards in the category of international cuisine. Her son Julian is a known cuisine writer and teaches as his Mamma did.

Anna Del Conte, author, was born in 1925 near Milan but lived for many years in London, returning regularly to Milan and Venice. She edited, among other things, the version for the UK market of *The Classic Italian Cook Book* by Marcella Hazan. The volume published in 1987, *Gastronomy of Italy* (Prentice Hall), is very fine, well done and complete.

Fred Plotkin lives in New York. He has published several works on Italian cuisine. *The Authentic Pasta Book* (Simon & Schuster, 1985) is the first cookbook written directly in English (and not translated from Italian) that explained Italian cuisine and the twenty regions, with their geographical,

agricultural, political and cultural differences. *Italy Today: The Beautiful Cookbook* (HarperCollins, 1997), written with **Lorenza de' Medici**, was one of the first books to describe the ways and methods of contemporary Italian cuisine rather than focusing on the historical and traditional aspects.

Italy for the Gourmet Traveller (Little, Brown and Company, 1996), also by Plotkin, is the most complete and detailed guide for the reader-traveller in search of traditions, products, classic recipes, food and wine in more than five hundred cities in all Italian regions. *Recipes from Paradise: Life and Food on the Italian Riviera*, cited by *The New York Times* as the best cookbook published in 1997 (Little, Brown and Company), is a portrait of Liguria through recipes, stories, photos and literature. In *La Terra Fortunata. The Splendid Food and Wine of Friuli-Venezia Giulia* (Broadway Books, 2001), Plotkin explains why Friuli is a kind of hidden treasure of the Italian regions.

He writes for *The New York Times*, the *Guardian* and *Bon Appétit*.

John F. Mariani is the author of *How Italian Food Conquered the World* (Palgrave Macmillan) and, for over thirty years, critic for *Esquire Magazine*.

Faith Willinger is American, but lives in Florence and was a spokesperson for "Made in Italy" in the United States. "In Tuscany," she said sympathetically, "I began my renaissance. Here I met my husband, the love of my life. They are literally crazy about Italian regional cuisine. Italian cuisine is very different from Italian-American cuisine. When Americans start to try Italian cuisine, they become more passionate than before". She has written numerous books on our cuisine.

Giuliano Bugialli is considered to be one of the most influential writers in the English language on Italian food. His first book, *The Fine Art of Italian Cooking* (Times Books Co), dates back to 1977. Among those published later, we wish to remember the *Ricettario nazionale delle cucine regionali italiane* published from 1992 to 1998 by the Italian Academy of Cuisine in fifty-two instalments. It is a valuable work that restores and safeguards national cuisine. Bugialli was one of the first to use TV as a medium for his culinary courses.

Carol Field is a very serious connoisseur of Italian cuisine. Her *The Italian Baker* (HarperCollins), dedicated to breads and pastries, is so popular that it is used in many Italian bakeries and pastry shops as a reference point. *In Nonna's Kitchen* (William Morrow Cookbooks, 1997) collects recipes and suggestions based on extensive research for which Field toured the country, visiting the homes and kitchens of many grandmothers, to learn and pass on their stories and their secrets.

Nancy Harmon Jenkins is an American who has lived in Cortona, in Tuscany, for over forty years. She is the author of cookbooks of Tuscan cuisine and the cuisine of Puglia. Moreover, she is a great olive oil expert.

Lynne Rossetto Kasper is the author of *The Splendid Table* (William Morrow Cookbooks, 1992), a text that is still appreciated, and which explains in detail the rich, complex and elegant cuisine of Emilia-Romagna. She hosts a radio program on a national station in the United States, in which she presents and teaches the recipes of many cuisines, including Italian.

Arthur Schwartz is a well-known author of books about the cuisine of Southern Italy. His most important work is *Naples at Table* (HarperCollins, 1998) on the cuisine of Campania.

Lidia Bastianich, *last but not least*, is the great lady chef of Italian cuisine in the United States. From an Italian family (originally from Pula, Istria), she arrived in the United States in 1958, but only met with success in 1981, when, with her husband Felice Bastianich, she opened the restaurant Felidia in New York. In 1998, she began to talk about Italian cuisine on TV: she is now a star of American television. In 2014, she was also on television with *Junior MasterChef Italia*, together with Bruno Barbieri and Alessandro Borghese. On the show, children between eight and twelve compete in the kitchen. "The young competitors are like my grandchildren [*Lidia has five*]. I would like to explain to them the beauty of food. How many gifts nature gives us".

One of the most interesting books is *La cucina di Lidia. Distinctive Regional Cuisine from the North of Italy* written in 1990 (Doubleday), but only one of the many.

She herself states: "When it was published, in 2001, *Lidia's Italian-American Kitchen* [*Alfred A. Knopf*] was enormously successful. The volume takes into account the culinary traditions that Italians brought with them to America, but were forced to change because of the limited availability of some products. Some of the books that I enjoyed writing the most were *Lidia's Italy* and *Lidia Cooks from the Heart of Italy* [*Alfred A. Knopf*], because during the research I had the opportunity to travel through the most beautiful regions of Italy, discovering their great products, stories, recipes and traditions. In fact, every one of my books has a different angle, although they are all united by the great attention that I dedicate to the ingredients: I think that everything should start from a deep understanding of the ingredients. My job was knowing how to include more useful tips and techniques for preparing the recipes that came from my memories or were my favourite dishes. You do not always have access to the ideal ingredients. In Italy, it is easier. In the United States, it is not always possible. In Italian-American cuisine, the base is provided by traditional Italian recipes, but then you have to find ways to adapt, depending on how much is available, not distorting them and achieving a great result all the same. Even if it is not actually 100% Italian."

The Great Italian Restaurants in the United States
As previously mentioned, the Italian restaurants in the US were a formidable ally as well as a springboard for our winemakers.

Historically speaking, **Sirio Maccioni** remains unparalleled. A Tuscan from Montecatini, in 1974 he opened the New York restaurant Le Cirque in the Mayfair Regent Hotel, where he stayed until 1997. It became a starting point for many Italian winemakers.

In 1995, Le Cirque was recognized as the best restaurant in the United States by the James Beard Foundation (US awards from this association are regarded as the Oscars of food and

SIRIO

wine). No one has ever managed to stay on top of dining in New York for so long, in a city that burns and devours. In his forty years of business, Le Cirque remains the one most visited by *The New York Times*, winning the most visits *(reviews)* in history from critics of this newspaper and receiving the maximum four stars on three occasions. In May 2014, the James Beard Foundation awarded Sirio the Lifetime Achievement Award for having kept Le Cirque at an unmatched level of excellence over a period spanning six decades.

You arrived at his place and met the world. This was the reason he was so important to all us wine producers. His wine list was a necessary step to get your wines known and accredited in New York. His ability to manage the customer was histrionic. "I had all the Tignanello 1971, the first Super Tuscans that *The Wine Spectator* journalists came to order from me for their articles," said Sirio. "Piero Antinori often reminds me how important Le Cirque was for the affirmation of Italian wine in high dining".

"Although it is a restaurant with a French name," says his son Marco, "the only French thing was the name, while the heart, craft and spirit were all Italian. Made in Italy! My father Sirio was not only proud to serve typical Italian culinary products and dishes, but also all the wines from the best producers of Italy that made him look good".

We can confirm that it has always been a restaurant where the products – oil, pasta, rice, truffles, radicchio, coffee (Illy) – were and are Italian. And from which came many Italian dishes. Sirio tells us: "The first time Bocuse came to Le Cirque was with Roger Vergé and Pierre Troisgros. He said, 'We heard you have good pasta.' So I prepared pasta primavera at the table. When my partner, a French chef, came

out and said, 'And now we come to serious matters: What can I make for you?' Bocuse said, 'I'm sorry, but we'd like to have more pasta.'"

"For me, the way Italian Food is cooked, put on the plate, seasoned and prepared is the best," he writes in his incomparable *Sirio: The Story of My Life and Le Cirque* (written with P. Elliott, Houghton Mifflin Harcourt, 2004), a book that every restaurateur and chef should study. Today the Maccioni family – his wife Egidina and children Mario, Marco and Mauro – has twelve restaurants (three in New York, three in Las Vegas, two in the Dominican Republic, two in India and two in the Emirates). It has a fifty-million Euro turnover, and one thousand employees. And the great Sirio's indomitable desire to give his best to everyone.

Another key figure is **Tony May** (actually, Antonio Magliulo), who arrived in New York in 1963. In 1968, Tony opened one of the most exciting restaurants in the world, the Rainbow Room, on top of the Rockefeller Center, where you can see all of New York, an immense space enclosed only by windows. He ran it until 1986. Tony has managed fourteen restaurants, including the Palio (1986), another restaurant of rare beauty, which was then taken over by Andrea di Merano. In 1988, Tony reached another milestone for Italian restaurants in New York: in front of Central Park and not far from the Metropolitan, he opened the San Domenico. I attended that opening: it really was the triumph of great Italian cuisine, officiated by Marcattilii, the chef of the Italian San Domenico. On the top floor of the building was the home of Luciano Pavarotti, and it was Tony May alone who spoiled him with his dishes. With his daughter Marisa, Tony has opened the SD26 in Madison Square Park, a restaurant with an open kitchen where chefs and customers can talk, entirely designed by Massimo Vignelli, who is recognized as one of the greatest masters of design. Milanese by birth, he lived in New York for a long time, and died there on 27 May 2014.

We would also like to discuss what Tony has done and is doing for the good name of Italian cuisine in the US. Tony May, who in 2013 celebrated his fiftieth year in the United States, is a true ambassador of Italian cuisine.

"When I arrived in America in 1963, I found a kind of cuisine I didn't recognize, and sometimes a language I didn't un-

derstand. I promised myself I would do something in this regard. So in 1979, I founded the Leading Italian Restaurants in America [GRI], over which I still preside today. In 1984, with the GRI, I established the Caterina De' Medici Restaurant at the Culinary Institute of America, and in 1991, I founded the Italian Culinary Institute for Foreigners in Piedmont. During my time on the board of the Culinary Institute of America in Hyde Park, New York, the school founded the Colavita Center for Italian Food and Wine, in 2001. Finally, in 2004, I founded the Italian Culinary Foundation to create educational programs in the culinary institutions across America. I think the best way to change the old perception of Italian cuisine is education. Every year we organize a trip to an Italian region to educate our members and the American press about a different regional Italian cuisine, its products and culture that guarantees tradition and taste. We have created and support the study program on Italian cuisine at the Culinary Institute of America. We have also testified before Congress on behalf of the Italian pasta manufacturers in the fight against customs duties on imports of the product to the United States."

On 30 March 2015 the restaurant SD26 closed. Tony May sold the business to John Doherty, the former executive chef at the Waldorf Astoria in New York, for 1,125,000 million Dollars. May states: "I'm seventy-seven. I can't do business the way I like anymore, that is, spending time with my customers.

I've become an administrator and am forced to play by the rules of a government that doesn't understand this business." What can we say: people are the same the world over!

Another important voice for the success of Italian wine and cuisine in the United States is **Piero Selvaggio**, a Sicilian from Modica, who in 1972 opened the restaurant Valentino in Santa Monica, California. It became a sort of "house of Italian wine" with a spectacular wine cellar and the highest level of cuisine. Irreplaceable. Piero, a very intelligent man, opened other restaurants in the Los Angeles area. He is truly a legend of Italian style, and not only in food and wine.

In the United States, it is worth mentioning other talented chef-restaurateurs, such as **Odette Fada**. This extraordinary woman from Brescia came to Los Angeles in 1988. She was supposed to stay there for just a month, and instead that stay changed her life. She started at the restaurant Pazzia in West Hollywood. In 1996, she made the leap to New York, to the San Domenico with Tony May, who stood out as one of the great interpreters of modern Italian cuisine. Today she lives in New York. She is a consultant for entrepreneurs who want to open Italian restaurants in the United States, but also for major brands such as Giovanni Rana and Barilla, who opened premises in the Big Apple.

Finally we would like to remember **Mauro Vincenti** of Rex's restaurant in Los Angeles. In New York, **Pino Luongo** at Cantinori, Le Madri and Coco Pazzo. In addition, **Aldo Bozzi**

Jens Priewe

at Mezzaluna, **Mario Tucci** at Delmonico's on Wall Street, where Sirio Maccioni began his career. Finally, **Cipriani**, **Cesare Casella** and, in Houston, **Tony Vallone** who promoted the Italian "dolce vita", the sweet life, in Texas.

On 31 March 1997 *The Wine Spectator* dedicated its cover to our restaurants in the US: *America's 10 Best Italian Restaurants*. These are listed on the basis of the quality of the food and the wines. Here they are: *Top 10 by Food Rating*: Valentino, Acquarello, Campanile, Felidia, Galileo, Oliveto, Vivere, Palio, Il Tulipano, San Domenico. *Top 10 by Wine Rating*: Valentino – which is the first in both rankings – Felidia, Vivere, Galileo, Campanile, San Domenico, Acquarello, Palio, Oliveto, Il Tulipano.

Germany

Jens Priewe, German Chronicler of Italian Wine

Jens Priewe, a journalist of economics and politics, in 1977 was sent by his director to Tuscany to write about our wines. He is certainly the most important journalist of German wines, as well as the leading expert of Italian wines.

"Then I knew nothing of wines," Priewe confesses, "but I had a journalist's curiosity. I could find no books, no brochures or anything else to give me an idea of where I should go. So I lived day to day and this was fortunate, because I had the opportunity to discover a world that fascinated me so much that, on my return, I said to myself that I would write the book that I had not found." From those thoughts came *Italiens grosse Weine* which came out after ten years of meticulous research, in 1987 (Busse Seewald). It sold 50,000 copies. With great emotional involvement, it discusses three hundred winemakers known throughout Italy with a view that also extends to the territory. A journey worthy of Goethe. A work that made the fortune of modern Italian wine in Germany, inasmuch as it changed the German perception of us. It also changed Priewe's professional life when he became the most important German wine journalist.

Jens states, smiling: "The Germans had rediscovered Italy at the end of the 1960s. Tuscany, in particular, had become the destination of many intellectuals, many of whom bought farms, but continued to make traditional wines, undrinkable wines. It was a good thing we journalists grasped the new thing

that was coming. On that trip I found out that Italy did not have a history of an industrial country, but one with agricultural roots. Many of the successful entrepreneurs were homesick for their origins, and as soon as they could, they invested in wineries, knowing full well that it would be a long time before that earned anything. This injection of new forces that were foreign to wine created a very interesting mix that spurred the whole industry to innovate faster thanks to, it must be said, Piero Antinori, the heir of a historic Florentine family. Antinori was certainly the most important protagonist of those years. They sent out a strong message indicating the way forward, while Sergio Manetti represented everyone who went into the winemaking business with the enthusiasm of neophytes, but well aware of their roots and who created, in turn, memorable wines. Already in the 1980s, however, the new generation of Italian wine was beginning to find its space in Germany. Our market was dominated by Bordeaux, although it had declined because of the bad vintages in the early 1970s [*1972 and 1973*]. They resumed with the 1982, also magnified by Parker. It is interesting to note that people bought Bordeaux, and while waiting for it to age [*at the time, no one opened it before ten years had passed*], they drank the great innovative Italian reds that, at that time, began to come on the market. Especially the Tuscans, followed by Piedmonts, led by Gaja, not to mention the Friulian whites. The Italian wines were less austere than the French, more modern, pleasant and easily satisfied the tastes of most consumers. They were also in tune with a cuisine that in turn was rapidly evolving. While Witzigmann was the chef who opened the way for modern cuisine in Germany, an important role was played by the many Italian restaurants, trattorias and pizzerias, to the point of changing the cuisine styles of many Germans. Since then, the path to becoming more Mediterranean, fresher, lighter, has opened up. Italian-style restaurants, it must be said, played a key role: they were a determining factor in your success. I would also say that wine and food support each other. It is a formidable combination on the markets and not only on the German market. Cuisine was, and still is, the 'great accomplice' of Italian wine's success."

"The distribution too," continues Priewe, "has something that is all-German. The big importers of Bremen remained tied to the French and Bordeaux and did not realize that the consumer was changing and that Italians were unleashing their trade offensive with new wines. All of this was done with a marketing that was anything but scientific, which is how the Americans were doing it. No, Italians created a spontaneous communication and market action. They arrived in our country thanks to word of mouth, sympathy, relationships with their countrymen, restaurants and their intellectual flexibility.

Soon, those we would later call 'the garage importers' began to emerge: dozens of small local distributors who went to Italy, selected wines and took them home to their garages, and distributed them there. This phenomenon arose spontaneously, also favoured by the EU which eliminated the trade barriers. Of these distributors – both Italian and German – there were at least fifty important ones, scattered throughout Germany. Think of the Enoteca Garibaldi in Munich, owned by my friend Eberhard Spangenberg, who comes from a family of publishers. In 1983, he opened his first shop of Italian wines. Now he has seven, he is the leader in Munich, and his is a German! . . . The great expansion of Italian wine took place between 1985 and 1995. At that time, exactly in 1986, Italy surpassed France and has since remained at the top. It still holds 22% of the market, compared with 19% in Spain and 14% in France. Another winning combination was Germany's discovering Italy as a great country for tourism, and this helped us get acquainted with wines and products, as well as the cuisine. Once we returned home, we wanted to find those flavours again. Your country was so popular that it was obligatory to say that you had been to Tuscany, for example . . . Although the markets have since changed, Italians have been able to constantly improve, both in restaurants and in wines. The arrival of the native varieties helped them make a further leap forward, highlighting the strong personality of Italian wines and the diversification of the offer. From the point of view of time, the three regions driving the renaissance in the early 1970s follow this order: Tuscany, Piedmont and Friuli, and then the other regions followed. The South was the last to move, for example, but it immediately found space on the markets. It must be that one never finishes discovering Italian wines!"

The "Wertheim Challenge"

On 27 May 1991, the "Wertheim challenge", as Veronelli called it, took place in Germany. It was a challenge between the Italian wines and the great cru French wines, and it had a very strong public inasmuch as it was organized by two leading figures in the industry: Andreas Schmitt, son of Adalbert, founder of the "Schweizer Stuben" in Wertheim – one of the best restaurants in Germany at that time, which served Italian cuisine – and Hardy Rodenstock, a famous wine collector.

The challenge took place to examine wines between 1970 and 1986. Each of the two team captains chose their own: Schmitt chose eighteen Italian wines, and Rodenstock, eighteen French wines.

A notary oversaw the challenge to ensure compliance with the agreed rules. One of these was the blind tasting in Riedel glasses and a ban on talking during the tasting.

The jury was made up of six "French wine enthusiasts" (Hardy Rodenstock, Karl Geisel from the Hotel Königshof of Munich, August F. Winkler, journalist, Helmut Romè, journalist, Ralf Frenzel, importer, and Hans Janssen, journalist) and six "Italian wine enthusiasts" (Andreas Schmitt, August Kesseler, a winemaker from the Rhine, Elisabeth Jusczick, importer, Georg Riedel, journalists Johann Willsberger and Jens Priewe, who personally brought from Tuscany the first vintage of Percarlo, that then came close to being victorious).

The result of the "challenge": of the top ten wines that classified, seven were Italian!

After the winner – Château La Mission Haut Brion 1978 (with 220.5 points) – just half a point away from the Percarlo 1985 with 220 points, then Bruno Rocca 1985 with 216.5 points, Ornellaia 1986 with 214.5 points, Château Petrus 1970 with 212 points, Sassicaia 1985 with 211.5, Barbaresco Santo Stefano di Neive 1971 with 210. With the same number – 208 points – were Château Mouton Rothschild 1986 and Tignanello 1985. In tenth place, were Château Pichon Lalande 1978 and Sammarco 1985, both with 207.5 points.

It was the confirmation of a trend of improving quality in Italian wines, which was being established in Germany and other countries.

Willi Breuer, Falling in Love with Italy, Twice

Willi Breuer fell in love with Italy, twice. The first time because he married a woman from Trieste, Serena. The second because, although he was of the French school, as we shall see, he started importing wines, focusing exclusively on Italian wines. In 1984, in fact, with his wife he founded Vinissimo in Munich, the company run by his nephew, Thomas Zeller.

Willi Breuer is an authentic, fine connoisseur: after having been in charge of French wines for Bols in Germany, in 1976, he moved to the sales department of Moët & Chandon in Germany, where he remained until 2003.

Vinissimo led several new winemakers to success, such as Brunello di Caparzo, Vecchie Terre di Montefili and Bruno Rocca in Tuscany, the Abbazia di Rosazzo in Friuli in the 1980s and now Vistorta, Prunotto in Piedmont, Adami in Prosecco, and Ca' dei Frati in Lugana. From being a distributor for Munich alone, he now manages a large portfolio of companies nationwide.

Breuer's many years of work in the area of high-end restaurants allow him a thorough and detailed interpretation of the evolution of Italian wines in Germany: "Initially there was very good value for money compared to French wines. The modernity of your wines was also confirmed, wines that bravely broke away from those old ones of the flask years, and the very vast supply was due to the Italian soil and climate. But if we go beyond the mere value for money aspect, we find that in the 1960s, Germans began to have a genuine 'desire for Italy'. Quality wine arrived later and found fertile ground. A movement that spread like wildfire and that led many Germans to buy homes, after Tuscany and Piedmont, in Friuli Venezia Giulia, on Lake Garda, in the Marches, Abruzzo and Umbria . . . A role that I would define as silent, but decisive, was that of the Italian restaurants in Germany, which was growing at the same pace as that of wine. The second generation of Italian restaurateurs was innovative, and the cuisine of a high technical level and quality. Also, we must not forget that many of the most valuable regional wine distributors began as Italian food wholesalers. They can also be credited with having paved the way for German restaurants as well, which gave greater credibility to our wines."

Munich is the most important German city for the positioning and guarantee effect that it then gives the rest of the system.

Breuer also remembers: "A key figure in the city was a Sardinian sommelier who worked at Witzigmann, then the best German restaurant until the opening of the Aubergine, in 1978. It earned three Michelin stars for innovative cuisine and a strong Italian influence. The sommelier's name was Gesumino Pireddu. He ran the dining room, as well as being responsible for the wine list, which had a good number of Italian wines. The fact that the best German restaurant had opened up toward high-end Italian wines turned out to be, at the time, a very effective message."

An event of great importance for Italian gastronomy was the opening, in Munich in 1974, of El Toulà, by the supreme **Alfredo Beltrame**. The restaurant was run by Bruno Benussi, a statuesque man from Trieste, and one of great poise and class. He introduced the elegance of Italian *savoir faire* and not only in the kitchen, but also in the decor and hospitality. The cost of a plate of pasta caused a "scandal" in the newspapers: 20 German Marks.

Again in Munich, the restaurant Tantris, in its contemporary setting, was a kind of school. It was run by the brilliant chef **Heinz Winkler** from South Tyrol and, in 1981, it earned three Michelin stars. He was thirty-one years old and was the youngest chef in Germany to earn them. In 1991, Winkler opened "his" Residenz Heinz Winkler, in a former fifteenth-century convent at Aschau, south of Munich. On the opening

Below
Egidio Sommavilla and Prisco
De Stefano in front of the Osteria
Italiana in Munich

night, with its perfect dinner, there were, among others, my wines, along with Maurizio Zanella's Ca' del Bosco. His cellar also has a wealth of our wines, particularly since he has employed Italian sommeliers.

In the university area of Munich, Katzlmacher was also successful for many years. The restaurant was very welcoming and usually very busy: traditional but high quality cuisine and service in perfect Italian style. The owner, Claudio Zanuttigh from Cividale del Friuli, was whimsical but capable, and had a wonderful list of Italian wines, in which, for a winemaker, it was very important to be included.

That which was to become the Osteria Italiana in Munich was opened on 23 May 1890 by Josef Deutelmoser, a German gastronome who had travelled the world working on ships, in love with Italian cuisine and our concept of conviviality. He wanted to recreate it in what he called the Osteria Bavaria, in Schellingerstraße 62, where it is now. In fact, it was the first Italian restaurant in Germany.

After World War II, Clotilde Salvatori, an experienced gastronome, took it over and renamed it Osteria Italiana, retaining the initial spirit that still gives life to the restaurant. From 12 October 1997, the owners have been Egidio Sommavilla and Prisco De Stefano, who wanted and knew how to preserve both the original decor and the Italian cuisine, in addition to the style of service, made up of sympathy and simplicity, capable of making all types of customers

feel comfortable. No beer or soft drinks are served, only water and Italian wines. It continues to be one of the hot spots in the city, with a high-level clientele. It is necessary to book early.

Again in Munich, the work of **Lorenzo Cattaneo** (Friuli in Spilimbergo) was very important. For many years, he was the director of the Hotel Königshof, with a famous restaurant with a Michelin star and the wine cellar of one's dreams. Owned by the Geisel family (Karl was part of the jury for the "French side" at the "Wertheim challenge"), they invested a great deal in wine, opening an Italian-style tavern nearby, the Vinotek Geisel, whose sommelier, Italian, was Ireneo Tucci.

"Other great learning experiences," Willi remembers, "were the restaurant Pippo, run by **Giuseppe Culoso**, who then sold it to Mario Gamba, who renamed it Acquarello and which in turn became one of the most fashionable spots in town. So Giuseppe opened another, calling it Pippo as well. **Hans-Peter Wodarz** also created his first restaurant in Munich. A brilliant chef, he then moved to Wiesbaden, and kept the same name: Die Ente vom Lehel in Nassauer Hof, with a wine list of first-class Italians . . . A determining factor in spreading the new message of Italian food and wine similarly to the Aubergine were two restaurants in the centre of Germany, owned by Germans with German chefs, but with Italian cuisine and wines: Da Gianni in Mannheim and the aforementioned Schweizer Stuben in Wertheim, owned by the Schmitt family. The founder, Adalbert, was an industrialist who manufactured plastics and loved Italy. Next to the hotel, he built two major restaurants: the Schweizer Stuben and La Vigna, the latter serving only Italian cuisine, and at the time deemed the best Italian restaurant in Germany, run by a German chef, Stefan Marquard. The Schweizer Stuben constantly had two Michelin stars, and deserved them all. He had great chefs like the Müller brothers, Jörg from 1973 to 1981, and Dieter from 1981 to 1990. In both of the restaurants, the cellar of Italian wines was extraordinary."

In Hamburg, the restaurant Anna and Sebastiano had great influence. Then the couple broke up and Anna opened a place by herself and called it Anna Sgroi, again in Hamburg; in Düsseldorf, there was the restaurant of the Saitta brothers; while in Cologne, **Rino Casati** was providing an experience.

Johann Willsberger

In Berlin, I experienced a truly unique period, which has left an indelible mark on my life. Just three weeks after the unification of Germany, which took place on 3 October 1990, we organized the first-ever presentation of Italian wines, in the case of Friuli, in a restaurant in East Berlin. We had heard of a restaurant that served Italian cuisine and was also frequented by the staff of the embassies. We invited the press, which understood the situation as never before. We asked Georg Riedel to send his glasses to us. Doris, the owner and chef, was gracious, smiling and very nervous. We soon discovered that she had only one round of dishes and cutlery and was very slow in preparing food. After all, then, the differences were really abysmal, but the void was quickly filled thanks to the tenacity and skill of the Germans. So we went into the kitchen to wash dishes and to cook. In short: we took the situation in hand. It was a wonderful evening, under the banner of collaboration and conviviality, in pure Italian style and where everyone breathed an air of real enthusiasm (from the media point of view, it was one of the best presentations I did in Germany).

That success also helped Doris, who for a time came to Italy to learn more about our cuisine. Now she has her own restaurant in Prenzlauer Berg, also in Berlin, the Trattoria Paparazzi, where she still makes Italian cuisine.

The German Press

In Germany, the renaissance of Italian wine gained the sympathy of many journalists and writers.

Among these, in addition to Priewe, there was **Johann Willsberger**, a German photographer of the highest calibre, who for many years lived in Switzerland. In 1976, he invented that magnificent magazine that was *Gourmet* which many gourmets collected. His photo shoots on cuisine changed the way food was represented, as well as being a valuable record of the revolution that the most important European cuisines underwent, starting with French and followed by Italian. He then followed very closely the evolution of the modern history of our wine.

The magazine continued publication until 2001.

"We printed 101 editions," says the founder-editor Willsberger, "the idea was to present food at its best. Which means first of all: fresh ingredients with no artificial additives [*such as colorants . . .*]. For each issue roughly 20,000 copies were sold. We had subscribers in more than fifty countries around the world."

What is the secret to the pictures?

"There is no secret. But one thing was important: I always took the photos in their original place, or in the restaurant. Never in a studio. In this way, I obtained the best result by prominent chefs from around the world."

What was the situation with Italian food and wine?

"At the time, there was a big influence from France, the Nouvelle Cuisine. It was a kind of new wave in the kitchen and the restaurant. The knowledge of wines and Italian products abroad was very limited, but we must not forget one thing: Italy had excellent products. I met Gualtiero Marchesi, at the beginning of his *nuova cucina*, in Bordighera. It was really fascinating to see what was going on at that time. Of the wines, I have a very strong memory of tasting the first vintages of Bruno Giacosa's Barolo and Barbaresco. Exceptional."

Gourmet was printed in Italian starting in the spring of 1983, on a quarterly basis, taking the name of *Grand Gourmet*.

The publisher was Electa, owned by Giorgio Fantoni and Massimo Vitta Zelman, who in 1996 took over Skira, the publisher of this book.

The first director was a personal friend of Fantoni and Vitta Zelman and an ingenious restaurateur: Alfredo Beltrame, who created El Toulà, was joined as director of operations by Giuseppe Maffioli, then replaced in the role, in the spring of 1984, by Antonio Piccinardi. Alfredo died that same year and Piccinardi became sole director until 1988, when he was succeeded by Enrico Guagnini. In 1992, Davide Rampello came on board as managing editor of the prestigious magazine and the area that also included the magazine *Il Vino di Grand Gourmet*, which was then closed some time after Giorgio Fantoni and Massimo Vitta Zelman left Electa, which took place in late 1994.

Of the important journalists in Germany, worth mentioning are **August F. Winkler**, Austrian, **Hanspeter O. Breuer**, Steinhart, **Dr Supp** and **Madeleine Jakits**, competent and with an extensive knowledge of Italy, the director of the monthly food and wine magazine, *Der Feinschmeker*, in Hamburg. One of the best Italian food photographers, Stefano Scatà, often worked for her newspaper. So there were **Dr Braatz**, **Christian Eder**, **Guy Bonnefoit**, **Klauke und Eberle**, **Rudolf Knoll**, **Martin Kilchmann** for his books on Chianti. And there was **Horst Dohm**, a columnist for the *Frankfurter Allgemeinen Zeitung*, who wrote, in 1988, the great *Flaschenpost aus Italien* then published in Italian under the name *L'Italia in bottiglia*. He collected the stories of sixty great Italian winemakers, from north to south. Finally, there were **Helga Baumgärtel**, **Paula Bosch** and **Rudolf Steurer**.

Adalbert Schmitt, of the restaurant Schweizer Stuben – who spoke not only of our wines, but of our culture, landscapes and cuisine – an eclectic, industrialist, photographer, gourmet, first-class restaurateur, father of seven with three wives – published several books on Italy. In addition to *Nero Cipresso* about Tuscany, with recipes of Dieter Müller, he wrote *Re delle Langhe*, also with recipes by Dieter, *Ti Saluto Liguria* and *Cucinare come Cesare, i miei piatti italiani preferiti*.

Switzerland

Fourth Italian Wine Market

Switzerland is the fourth import market in the world for Italian wines. Our wine exports amounted to more than 350 million Francs that make Italy the second largest supplier, behind France (over 400), and by far the first in terms of quantity.

The Swiss consumer is knowledgeable and careful about quality, and uses the high purchasing power to buy well-known and niche wines. Italian products are fashionable and successful, among all age groups; it is consumed in restaurants and homes, but also in bars and venues for the young and affluent.

Switzerland is a rich and dynamic market, and can absorb large volumes, despite the reduced population size.

Global consumption of wine is 2.8 million hectolitres for a per capita datum of 38 litres per year, much like the Italian one, just over 40 litres. Switzerland is also a major importer, as domestic production covers only one-third of the market.

German-speaking Switzerland is the wealthiest and most coveted market: the Italian-speaking Switzerland is oriented toward wines from Valtellina and Graubünden, the French-speaking toward French labels.

The historic agency of representatives for Switzerland is that of **Dr Stopper**, but the distribution is carried out by wholesalers/distributors who are local and of the canton. Some of the most important are: Weibel, Vini D'Amato, Bonvini, Caratello, Bindella, Zanini Sulmoni, Giardino del Vino.

It should not be forgotten that up to fifteen to twenty years ago, with the favourable exchange rate, merchants on the border, including Milan, benefited from strong sales to Swiss consumers who paid without asking for discounts and bought all the great Italian wines, promoting the Piedmont wines.

Of the importers, the one who deserves special recognition is Bindella in Zurich, a house founded in 1909. It is headed by **Rudi Bindella**, who bears the name of his father, who, in 1965, opened the first pizzeria with an Italian pizza oven in Zurich. This insight into the importance that Italian cuisine would eventually have is equal to that of believing in our wine's evolution toward modernity. An invaluable collaborator for Casa Bindella is Bruno Orlandi, the talent scout of Italian wines. He is no longer working in the market, although

he is still on the Board of Bindella, whose staff he joined in 1984.

In 1971, Rudi, who was studying economics at the University of St Gallen, decided to go to Perugia for six months to perfect his Italian: he fell in love with our country and decided that in Italy, and with Italy, he would have to do something.

Working with Bindella means sharing market strategies and investing together in the long term.

"The example is the relationship that we have with Antinori, whose importers we've been since 1953. Piero is certainly the one who turned modern Italian wine around. The most important. I discovered his Tignanello 1971 and Sassicaia of Incisa," confesses Rudi, "by accident on my honeymoon in Italy, in 1976. We asked Piero why he had never offered them to us, they were so good. 'We're still experimenting with them,' he said humbly. We purchased 1,200 bottles of Tignanello in 1976 and the sales price reached almost 20 Swiss Francs. My father asked me how I thought I was going to sell it. We presented it at the Expovina in Zurich. I ran out in three days". It's just one of many stories. Bruno Orlandi: "One of our great successes were the wines of Giacomo Bologna, with which we began to work in 1986–1987. We established a very strong relationship that led us to selling a great deal of his wine. The relationship has continued, intact, with his children. The same is true with Sandro Boscaini of Masi. His Campofiorin is the Tignanello of Veneto: innovative and fantastic. Or what we created with Giovanni Geddes and his team for Ornellaia, with whom we are doing wonderful projects. Looking back at our history, we realize that we really experienced the new interpretation of the tradition of Italian wine. The wines reflect the beauty of the landscape. It is no accident that Tuscany has had such success, then followed by Bruno Giacosa's Piedmont and Veneto, Alto Adige with Alois Lageder, Manlio Collavini in Friuli, and the extraordinary area of Bolgheri, from which we import various wines: Sassicaia, Guado al Tasso, Ornellaia, the Biserno by Lodovico Antinori, not counting the area of Brunello with – among others – Castello Banfi. Then there is Umani Ronchi in the Marche, Rivera in Puglia, Antonio Mastroberardino in Campania, Tasca d'Almerita and their Regaleali in Sicily. Then there is Punica – Sassicaia & Santadi – Sardinia, in addition to the historical Sella & Mosca."

Bindella, in the end, has over fifty Italian companies in its portfolio, including the queen of grappa, Nonino.

In 1984, more and more in love with Italy, Rudi decided to invest directly in wine, Montepulciano DOCG, in Vallocaia: "The choice of having the company in Tuscany brought us only advantages. In addition to helping us better understand the problems of the producers, we also gained a higher profile, thanks to what we believe was a kind of mutual sharing of the work."

The foresight of papa Rudi in throwing himself into Italian cuisine has also influenced his son, who now owns forty restaurants in Switzerland, of which twelve are restaurants with wood-burning pizza ovens.

"Italian cuisine," Rudi effectively summarizes, "speaks through products with which one does not play hide and seek. Everywhere, you read, you see, you understand what you eat, and added to that you have a sensibility toward style and your products – meats, cheeses, fruits and vegetables – are unique. And the tomato! Just think that thirty years ago here in Zurich French cuisine dominated, and no one wanted to hear talk of Italian wine, but now there are more Italian labels than French! When people said they were going to have Italian food, it was almost a non-compliment. Today, Italian cuisine has become part of our food culture. It certainly was and still is a formidable vehicle for the sale of your wines. Of our forty restaurants, thirty have Italian wines only."

The Swiss Press

"As in other countries," says Bruno Orlandi, "in Switzerland, too, the interest in Italian food and wine has conquered entire pages of the press, in newspapers, magazines and books." Certainly the most important publication is *Vinum*, founded in 1980 by **Rolf Kriesi**. Currently, the chief editor is **Thomas Vaterlaus**.

A love story for Italy is that of **Andreas März**, a Swiss journalist who crowned his dream of being a farmer in Lamporecchio, in Tuscany, where he lives with his family since 1981 on a farm with 3,600 olive trees and produces a superlative extra virgin olive oil. In 1994, together with a group of friends, he founded the magazine *Merum*, of which he is editor-in-chief. It is published six times a year and is aimed at professionals and lovers of Italian wine and olive oil. Made entirely in Italy, it is published in German and deals exclusively with Italian products. The editorial staff, in addition to Andreas, is made up of **Markus Blaser**, **Raffaella Usai** and **Jobst von Volckamer**. Through the independent voice of *Merum*, Andreas has become one of the most determined defenders of Italian oil, to the point of being called "the advocate of extra virgin oil".

Also worth mentioning are the magazines *Schweizerische Weinzeitung* and *Gastronomie & Tourisme* in Ticino, by the well-known **Alberto dell'Acqua**, and among journalists dedicated to wine are **Andreas Keller**, at first chief editor of *Vinum* and now a freelancer, and **Martin Kilchmann**, also author of several books on Piedmont and South Tyrol.

"You have to say," Orlandi specifies, "that much more than the books, there has been a strong influence from the guide *Gambero rosso*, thanks to the edition in German by Hallwag. Then there are the articles on Italian wines by two important American magazines: *The Wine Advocate* of Robert Parker and *The Wine Spectator*."

Some of the authors who have contributed to the success of Italian cuisine include **Marcella Hazan**, who became famous in the United States with her *Die klassische italienische Küche* (2010) and **Marianne Kaltenbach** who published *Aus Italiens Küchen* (2011), both very popular in Switzerland.

For the food/restaurant sector the Slow Food Editore guide, *Osteria d'Italia*, is increasingly popular, with a German version by the publisher Hallwag.

Italian Restaurants in Switzerland
Among the forty Italian restaurants of Bindella, we should point out the Bindella and Cantinetta Antinori in Zurich, which was modelled on the historic cellar of Palazzo Antinori in Florence where, before moving to Bargino, there was also the winery headquarters.

So, again in Zurich, there is the restaurant Conti, while in Lucerne, there is the restaurant Barbatti.
Other restaurants of Italian cuisine are Casa Ferlin in Zurich, Chez Donati in Basel, Roberto in Geneva and Villa Principe Leopoldo in Lugano.

Great Britain
Giovanni Geddes da Filicaja is the CEO of Frescobaldi and has thorough knowledge of the UK market and beyond. Here's his analysis: "More than 50% of the wine consumed in Great Britain has an importer's brand name or that of the British chain that sells it . . . This is historical: England is an island and it was the richest country in the world during the empire. Its inhabitants have always been great sailors and great merchants. They are the ones who honoured French wines – Bordeaux and Champagne, in particular – and Port. British consumers have always had faith in the choice made by the wine merchant, who knew the foreign producer, something almost impossible for the end consumer. This confidence has continued with the British retail chains . . . Some 82% of these volumes [*data from 2014*] is sold at take-away prices, with a large prevalence of the few chains [*Sainsbury's, Tesco, Waitrose*] that have accustomed consumers to very low prices, but also to a modest choice. This channel represents only 59% in value, confirming the low supply. The segment, therefore, is dominated by cooperatives and mass producers . . . More interesting is the independent winemakers segment, which have grown in number after the split of the chain Oddbins, which was taken over by private interests. The department stores are not particularly important for the volumes, due to the extra charges, but very important for the image. Of the chains, the most successful business model is the Majestic, which in its 180 stores sells good products by the carton [*and now also in the bottle, at a higher price*] . . . Important, finally, for quality wines, is the wine club segment and the various online players. The HORECA [*hotels/restaurants/ cafes*] sector provides a better product mix, up to 18% in volume, but 41% in value of the total market. In this segment, Italy is in second place after France, with nearly 5 million cases, and a similar average price [£16.93 *a bottle against* 18.42 *from beyond the Alps, data from 2014*]."

From several interviews with British importers, we can see a clear trend toward wines with less woodiness, more variety and more territories. This was the evolution of the consumer palate that triggered the success of our wines in the UK – a market where mainly the premium groups are growing, from 7 to 10 pounds per bottle (shelf price), where

there is more space for interesting wines and good value for money.

Twenty years ago Italian wine of quality was very difficult to sell. Now it has the same opportunities as those from more qualified countries. In those years, the diversity of Italian wine, also for the many autochthonous wines, was seen as a weakness, but now is one of the features that attracts more consumers, always looking for original things, both on the plate and in the glass.

Nicolas Belfrage: Master of Wine Who Loves Italy and Italian Wines

Nicolas Belfrage, an American from Los Angeles, moved as a young man to Britain, where he obtained a Master of Wine. He published his first book in 1985, on Italian wines, *Life beyond Lambrusco. Understanding Italian Fine Wine* (Sidgwick & Jackson), commissioned by Jancis Robinson, dedicated to the person who more than any other had helped him in the quest for quality Italian wines: Renato Trestini.

Nicolas Belfrage's interest in Italian wine began in the early 1970s thanks to several visits he made to the Bel Paese. Even at that time he quickly realized our great potential.

In the following years, he created a selection of Italian wines that earned him, in 1985, the recognition of Wine Merchant of the Year. In 1994, he moved with his family to Tuscany, where he conducted research and wrote his following two books: *Barolo to Valpolicella - The Wines of Northern Italy* (1999) and *Brunello to Zibibbo - The Wines of Tuscany, Central and Southern Italy* (2001), published by Faber & Faber. He also continued to frequently write articles on Italian wine for *Wine & Spirit*, *Decanter* and other publications in the industry. His latest book, *The Finest Wines of Tuscany and Central Italy*, came out in 2009 (Aurum Press and University of California Press).

It was during his years in Tuscany that he founded his Italian wine agency, Vinexus Ltd, which for nearly two decades was an intermediary between sector operators. Vinexus is currently run by Nick Bielak.

Nicolas Belfrage, then, is a distinguished ambassador of our wines in the UK.

You dedicated your first book to Renato Trestini. Why?

"Renato's main importance consisted in challenging the prevailing notion among wine merchants and experts of the UK that fine wine was the preserve of France and perhaps Germany and Portugal [*Port, Madeira*] but certainly not Italy. The function of Italy, in the 1960s and '70s, was to produce large volumes of mediocre plonk, wine which supermarkets could 'pile high and sell cheap'. Renato simply refused to accept this view and was determined to bring to the attention of UK wine drinkers that Italy also made special wines in interesting terroirs. He organised tastings and recruited allies amongst influential people in the trade, like Brian Barnet of Augustus Barnet [*later Bottoms Up*] and Dennis Ing and Nick Baile who succeeded the genius Ahmed Pochee, founder of Oddbins and later the Great Wapping Wine Co."

Who were the most important writers and journalists for modern Italian wine?

"Renato was indeed a leading and creative luminary of *Forum Vinorum*, which brought together a small group of people passionate about Italian wine like Richard Hobson MW, Maureen Ashley MW, Paul Merritt, Michael Garner, Luciana Lynch and various others. I, influenced by Renato, was also quite active in *Forum Vinorum* . . . A peculiarity of the British wine scene is that there is a long and honourable tradition of wine writers doubling as wine traders. This is true of myself and David Gleave, as well as Michael Garnet and Paul Merritt, authors of *Barolo: Tar & Roses*, Rosemary George MW [*Chianti*] and, later, Michael Palij. Non-trade writers influential in the early days included Maureen Ashley and Richard Baudains [*Decanter*]. More latterly Stephen Brook [*freelance*], Tim Atkin MW [*freelance*] and Walter Speller [*Jancis Robinson*] have made valuable contributions."

What were the reasons for the success of our wines?

"There could be several answers to this question . . . The wine-drinking public are getting a bit tired of always being presented with Cabernet, Merlot, Syrah, Chardonnay, Sauvignon, especially since they became international. They want a change, a challenge. Italy offers greater diversity than any other wine-producing country. Of course, the universal popularity of Italian cuisine has helped enormously, too . . . There are still, and increasingly, people in the UK who take Italian wines very seriously, like Philip Contini of Valvona & Crolla in Edinburgh, whose enoteca boasts one of the finest Italian wine collections in the world. In my trade capacity I do a lot of work with the 'Wine Society', one of the most important stockists of Bordeaux and other top French and international wines, and thanks to their foresightful Italy buyer, Sebastian Payne MW, a veritable *appassionato*, they have built up a list of wines from all over the Italian peninsula and islands which, every year in June, attracts hundreds of other *appassionati* to their annual exclusively Italian tastings. Anyone who experiences the buzz of these tastings, as of the annual 'Definitive Italian' tasting also in June, can appreciate how much the British have become enamoured of Italian wine, to the extent that they have grown around 50% in the last three years."

Renato Trestini, First Ambassador of Italian Wine to Britain
Renato Trestini, to whom Belfrage dedicated his first book, is a key figure in the first stage of knowledge of the new Italian wines in Britain.

He was born in Chamonix in 1935 to a farming family of Venetian origin – his father was *chef de rang* and *maître* at the legendary restaurant Savini, in the Galleria in Milan. In 1953, to learn English, he arrived on the island of Jersey. Then back in London in 1969 and the following year he founded the R. Trestini Ltd Italian Wines of Distinction. Among those first wines was Masi by Sandro Boscaini, with whom he forged a deep friendship that enabled us to get in touch with Trestini, who we talk about here: "In the beginning, I came up against a lot of difficulty with wine tasters. Their parameters at the time were dictated by the wines of France and Germany. They could not conceive of the complexity of Barolo, Amarone, Recioto, Campofiorin, etc. The important brands [*Bolla, Bertani and Ricasoli*] on the market at the time of my debut were mainly distributed in the restaurants by Italian agents who handled almost exclusively this ethnic market, probably wines along with Italian foods. The secret was to deal with the na-

tional clientele, hitherto convinced that only wine with a French label could make the grade . . . For my part I focused on planning tastings with leading journalists and with the Masters of Wine. The first success was with the prestigious Harrods. The support from James Burgis [*wine buyer*] was decisive, and our selection had been proposed to him: Masi was in the forefront with the complete selection, followed by Ceretto, Collavini, Colli di Catone, Ferrando, Cantina di Sizzano and Ghemme. The second success sprang from Mark Harrison's decision, a former employee of Dolamore, for whom I organized a visit to important Italian wineries. His enthusiasm was so great that he declared his intention to devote himself entirely to the sale of Italian wines and came to work with me. Nick Baile, owner of the retail chain Oddbins, declared that he had never had the opportunity to try so many Italian wines of high quality. Therefore, he asked to meet him. He introduced the full range in all their stores. This event was a great opportunity to put Italian quality on display. Oddbins was run by intelligent, capable, enthusiastic and usually young people. I organized bonus trips to Italy for those who distinguished themselves with the best sales, and many of them later became important ambassadors of Italian wine. Among the many were Michael Garner, Paul Merritt, Michael Benson and Richard Hobson. The last became part of the group Trust House Forte heading the new department of 'Italian Wine Agencies'. With the help of these ambassadors, the agency gained a wealth of additional major labels, such as Tedeschi, Ferrari Spumante, Enofriulia by Vittorio Puiatti . . . During the 1970s, Hugh Johnson asked my opinion about producers and wines. Many of these have been included in his famous *Pocket Wine Book* . . . Another historical journalist was Pamela Vandyke Price who, convinced for many decades of the primacy of French wines, was not sympathetic to Italian wines. I arranged a tasting of my range for her. She was surprised and excited. She wrote: 'Dear Renato, I confirm that this experience led me to change my mind and in a positive way.' But the most important breakthrough came with Nicolas Belfrage and his first book *Life beyond Lambrusco*. It was one thing to promote Italian wine through Italians, but it was more important to have the opportunity to receive rave reviews by a local writer's renowned reliability. Nicolas provided the opportunity to look again at Italian wines under a new guise and through the appropriate lenses, while generating greater trust and respect."

Gianni Segatta began working with Trestini in 1977, ten years after he had come to London thanks to an employment contract through the Istituto Agrario di San Michele, where he graduated in oenology in 1967.

"At the time," Gianni recalls, "there were very few Italian wines: Valpolicella, Chianti, Soave, Barolo. The vast majority were not very good and sold at low prices. We were dominated by French, German and Spanish wines. The market was virgin territory, because instead of battling against the price, we managed to introduce great Barolo, Barbaresco, Brunello, Carema and Amarone at much higher prices and representing the new Italian wines. I think I was the first to introduce the Pinot Grigio and Prosecco".

The story of Gianni Segatta is amazing for two reasons: the first is the Italian ability to invent the marketing spontaneously and with few resources. The second is the impressive number of great Italian wines that were launched on the British market by Alivini Trestini. Practically speaking, the Gotha of Italian wine.

The British Press

Among British authors as well there is no lack of friends of Italian wine, such as **Steven Spurrier**, who was "converted" to Italian wine by Anderson, and then wrote several books and wine guides. He is director of "Christie's Wine Course".

Hugh Johnson is considered the most important wine author in the world. His books have sold more than anyone. Of great value is his *The World Atlas of Wine* (first edition in 1971 and later ones). His work of 2004 with Jancis Robinson, the monumental *The Story of Wine* (1989), and his annual *Pocket Wine Book* are very popular.

Jancis Robinson studied mathematics and philosophy at Oxford University. She started writing about wine in 1975. In 1984, she was the first Master of Wine who was not from the world of wine. Her encyclopaedia, *The Oxford Companion to Wine*, is considered a seminal text the world over. In addition to having written with Hugh Johnson *The World Atlas of Wine*, very important and with excellent graphics and text, there is

Vines, Grapes and Wines from 1986, where we find – often referring to the work of Burton Anderson – a lot of native varieties of the Italian regions.

Kate Singleton, who has lived in Tuscany since 1988, is the author of the 2011 *Mister Amarone*, the book on the history of Sandro Boscaini of Masi fame (English edition from 2012, Bench Publishing). She contributed to *Il Giornale* and has written many books about Italian wines: *Learning from the Landscape in Sassicaia* (2000), *Montalcino and Montepulciano: Val d'Orcia and Surroundings* (2004), *Flavors of Liguria* (2010) and *Flavors of Umbria* (2010).

Tom Stevenson has written twenty-three books on wine, many of which have been translated into over twenty-five languages. Considered the leading expert in the world of Champagne and sparkling wines and never soft on Italian wines, at the end of 2013 he came out with the third edition of his *World Encyclopedia of Champagne & Sparkling Wine*, 528 pages, published by the auction house Christie's (the first edition was in 1998, when Italian sparkling wines were not present, and the second in 2003). In the 2013 edition, there is finally an awareness of the reality of Italian sparkling wine, ranking it second after Champagne. One of his most important works is the *Sotheby's World Wine Encyclopedia*. In the first edition (1988), while devoting fewer pages to Italian wines than German ones (twenty-six versus forty!), he begins to discover the first winemakers who then went on to make the history of modern Italian wine.

David Gleave, Canadian resident in the United Kingdom and a Master of Wine, published *The Wines of Italy* in 1989, followed by *Wines of Tuscany* and *Wine Renaissance in Tuscany* in 1999.

One of the most important magazines in the sector is certainly *Decanter*, which played an important role in spreading knowledge of new Italian wines.

Japan
The Rising Sun "Roots For" Italian Products

Italian restaurants in Japan are one of the strengths of this market. Suffice it to say that in Tokyo alone there are over 1,500 Italian restaurants, plus the fact that young and emerging Japanese chefs are among the most frequent visitors to our

Below, on left
Enoteca Pinchiorri in Tokyo

Below, on right
Annie Féolde, owner with her
husband Giorgio Pinchiorri of the
enoteca in Florence by the same
name

cooking schools. They stay in Italy for at times as much as two years after completing their studies to learn more about – as interns – the many variants of our cuisine, from north to south. Then, once they have acquired a wealth of knowledge, they return home, where they open Italian restaurants, using high-quality basic ingredients from our country.

Data from executives of the Monte Bussan and Suntory, the two most important importers and distributors of wines in Japan, tells us that consumer trends are directed toward an increase in consumption of wine linked to the territory, made from indigenous grapes that are identified with the place of origin. Even the Aglianico, Nero d'Avola, Primitivo, Negro Amaro and Barbera, etc. are beginning to see success, with a broadening of the choice and therefore an increase in consumption.

Another positive fact is that Italian wines are not consumed only in Italian restaurants, but also in those with Japanese cuisine and other ethnic cuisines. These trends are very interesting, and a new phenomenon has been added in recent years, the *popularization and daily* consumption of wine, thanks to products with affordable prices and easy to drink like Prosecco and Lambrusco. If people begin to consume wine daily, a certain percentage will then move on to higher quality wines. This is a positive phenomenon that occurred in the US market in the 1980s and gives us hope.

In the market of the Rising Sun, a growing interest in wines with great value for money has been observed. The Japanese consumer is very curious, and wants to know everything about wine: where it grows, who produces it, its history. It is not enough that the wine is good. It must have something to tell.

These requirements, therefore, promote our wines, which are not lacking in history and tradition.

Finally, we must not forget that Italy is the country most loved by the Japanese, and therefore we must cultivate and respond to this love for Italy by presenting Italian wine as a key part of the Italian lifestyle, for example by launching cooking classes that can interact with the wines themselves, by talking about the individual territories and at the same time approaching the Japanese with our way of life at the table, with aperitifs or after-meal drinks.

*Those Million High-ranking Bottles at the Enoteca
Pinchiorri in Japan*

If we want to find an exemplary story about how Italian wines and cuisine of the highest level can become part of the system and raise image and business on the markets, this story can be told by **Annie Féolde** and **Giorgio Pinchiorri**, with the Enoteca Pinchiorri in Florence. It is a world-famous venue, and here is a little information to give an idea of its size: the cellar has 100,000 bottles, of stratospheric value, with unimaginable collections. *The Wine Spectator* has awarded it the "Grand Award" every year since 1984. Its cellar is among the top five in the world. Annie was the first woman chef, outside France, to receive three Michelin stars in 1993 for Italian cuisine. The kitchen has eighteen chefs, of which two are executive chefs. They have, in total, forty-two employees. This masterpiece in Florence is located on Via Ghibellina, number 87.

Their second masterpiece, however, is in Japan: on 15 March 1993, they opened in Tokyo, where they brought the

Italian food, wines, style and charm of the Florentine Enoteca.

"It all started in Hong Kong in 1986," remembers Giorgio, "when we opened the restaurant Capriccio at the Ramada Renaissance Hotel. We also created the wine list. Shortly after, the Japanese company Matsuya proposed opening in Tokyo – in Ginza, the best neighbourhood in the centre – where it owned the famous Department Store and had expanded the company to various satellite activities. The gestation was long and laborious. Until, on 15 March 1993, we found ourselves with a restaurant of 1,000 square meters and 150 covers. We were in Japan for four months for the opening, with our staff, including chefs and sommeliers. It was the year in which we earned the first three Michelin stars. Just think that the first shipment of 28,000 bottles of wine, of which 40% were Italian and the remaining French, all were from the cellar in Florence. The great transalpine cru served to attract a gourmet clientele that still did not know the great, new Italian wines. Soon the roles were reversed. Now we are at 65% of Italian wines with everyone, indeed, our highest quality wines, including those of small producers. We are very happy about this."

"We were the precursors because, in the early 1990s, Japan knew little of Italian wines, but now our culture is very well recognized," Annie adds, with unconcealed satisfaction. "With Matsuya, we also opened La Cantinetta, in Odaiba, in front of Tokyo, while in the city we opened a small chain called I Primi."

"We had twenty-five vintages of Sassicaia," says Giorgio, with his usual enthusiasm, "twenty of Sorì Tildin di Gaja, not counting the Monfortino, ten vintages of Amarone Dal Forno, collections of Solaia and Tignanello and I could go on with many Brunelli and other great Tuscan wines. We had a huge success with the Vintage Tunina di Jermann and we had collectors' bottles of Nonino grappa. We organized cooking and wine courses at a cost of 500 Euro a head. There were countless tastings of our great crus. Not to mention the weddings, sumptuous, Italian-style. Then they began to celebrate them according to Japanese custom, but eating and drinking Italian. It was fantastic. Well, now I can tell you [*the interview with Giorgio Pinchiorri is from 31 October 2014*]: I just received information that tells me that from 1993 to 2013 in Japan we sold over a million bottles, mostly Italian! Now the building where the restaurant was is under renovation, so we are planning to re-open in Tokyo in 2015. Meanwhile, the same company wanted us to open in Nagoya, on the 82nd floor of the skyscraper where the Toyota headquarters is located, with which Matsuya has an excellent relationship. We are more than five hundred kilometres south of Tokyo, on the Bay of Ise. From there the view is unforgettable. We can accommodate no more than fifty people, with a cellar of 'only' 12,000 bottles, mostly Italian. The menu is the same as the one in Florence. The staff is all Japanese, and has worked extensively with us in Florence. The general manager is H. Sakama, the first chef, Koshidakaf, the pastry chef Shima, and the chef sommelier is Okamura. Periodically we update things in Florence and also by going to Nagoya ourselves."

This beautiful page of Italian history that Annie and Giorgio have written is the confirmation of how important wine and food can be if integrated into the delicate global market systems with great Italian professionalism and *savoir faire*.

Ampelio Bucci, in the introduction to this chapter on markets, wrote, "Think local and act global". The fact of Annie and Giorgio's business in the Land of the Rising Sun moves in that direction: what we create at home we can export to the world, because they like what we do and the way we do it. The story of the Japanese who marry according to local ceremonies, but who eat and drink Italian, is a measure of the respect and consideration that we enjoy in the world.

China

In China – the future market – Italian cuisine has had its outposts for many years, particularly in Hong Kong, where the story of an immigrant from Bergamo, Umberto Bombana, stands out. His restaurant, 8½, has pinned three Michelin stars to his chef's jacket, and is firmly established among the fifty best restaurants in the world. From Italy, he has also brought his yeast starter – it was in 2002 – which he still regenerates to make bread every day. "And we do it the way we did fifty years ago."

The style – as Guido Santevecchi writes in *Style* (April 2014) – is proudly Italian, with Eastern influence in some ingredients. "They come from all over the Republic of China, and from outside, because the palate is the palate everywhere." Translated: everybody likes good food, which is the gospel truth! "Bombana first worked in Los Angeles, New York, then Paris. He arrived in Hong Kong, to run the Toscana, the famous restaurant at the Ritz Carlton, which was later demolished." So Bombana decided to start his own business and in 2010, opened 8½. In 2012, he received the three Michelin stars, continually reconfirmed. Then he opened a sophisticated pizzeria in Shanghai and Beijing.

There are many people in the world like Bombana, and Italian wine owes them a lot. Cuisine and wine form a combination that has an exceptional power for penetration, in addition to having the advantage of reinforcing the image of Italian style.

The Project of the Comitato Grandi Cru d'Italia
A few years ago, the ambassador in Rome for the People's Republic of China said that if every Chinese person in the future drank only half a glass of wine, the world production would be insufficient.

In China, Italy is behind with respect to other competitor countries, to the point of having (data from 2014) only 7% of the market share; but it is moving on the right track, with concrete and effective projects that also capture the great sympathy that the new Chinese middle class has toward our country. One of the programmes to be launched is the Comitato Grandi Cru. Paolo Panerai, a founder of the Committee and its executive president, summarizes it for us: "The Chinese billionaires, almost all of them having grown rich with real estate thanks to the hundreds of millions of buildings constructed in the last twenty years, have also discovered the status symbol of wine. The Italian ambassador in Beijing, Alberto Bradanini, proposed a television campaign on the main channel of CCTV simply to say that history teaches us that wine is Italian, that Italy was called Enotria [*from the Greek* enos, *meaning wine*] and that the king of Enotri was called Italus, who gave the name to Italy. In coordination with Ambassador Bradanini, the Comitato Grandi Cru d'Italia, which represents the excellence of Italian wine with its 101 members, has launched an educational programme on Italian wine,

to train Chinese professionals in all the provinces who will in turn train thousands of sommeliers. The Committee is facilitated in this task by the wisdom of the Chinese government, which, when it decided that wine could replace distilled rice with its 65% to 70% alcohol, responsible for millions of tumours, drew up a precise plan, by setting up Committees in every province to educate the Chinese about wine. The project of the Comitato Grandi Cru is open to all Italian public and private resources, such is the need to create a system. The first to join immediately were the University of Milan, led by Professor Attilio Scienza, and the AIS. Training is planned for China and Italy, again in partnership with the Chinese Committees on wine education, with the coordination of the Committee's ambassador of honour in Hong Kong, Marco Iodice. In Italy, the educational sessions were also planned as part of the Expo. With the support of the Italian Pavilion, the Committee has scheduled two sessions for monthly training in the classroom and on the field, with visits to the 101 wineries of the grand crus, for sixty Chinese super trainers.

With actions like this, Italian wine is in recovery, because, finally, in China the truth has begun to circulate, that the value for money of Italian wine is unbeatable. The 'word of mouth' message is also making its way around China."

Italian Cuisine throughout the World

Walter Filiputti, Davide Rampello

In drafting this work, there has been much analysis, many testimonials and reflections indicating the fundamental role our cuisine plays in the world, and that we could define as strategic. Here are just a few.

"The spread of Italian products, combined with the culture of our table, allows our wines to travel the world. The products arrive before the wine, and before wine there was – and is – the Italian restaurant, now a planetary leader." (Joe Bastianich)

"The way to make wine and the artisans of taste popular throughout the world is to promote cooking schools." (Angelo Gaja, *le roi* of Italian vintners throughout the world)

"We are less trenchant on the markets where Italian restaurants are not a forceful presence." (Roberto Felluga, Friulian winemaker)

The Virtual Group of Italian Chefs in the World, Great Allies of Winegrowers

There are some 72,000 Italian restaurants in the world, while other estimates go as high as 100,000. They are invaluable and irreplaceable champions of Italian wines and food resources.

Recently, a significant number of them have succeeded in organizing themselves into a virtual association, chaired by Rosario Scarpato, originally from Naples, a long-term resident in Melbourne, Australia and now resident in Dubai.

The name of the association is Itchefs-GVCI, the operational branch (communications and events) of this network of chefs and culinary professionals working in the Italian cuisine sector in 70 nations of the world. The chefs participate in an on-line forum – **GVCI, the Virtual Group of Italian Chefs** – formed in late 2000 by Scarpato himself and Mario Caramella, today the chef-owner of the inItaly restaurant in Singapore. At the start, they numbered only 50. In 2015, they are more than 2,500 (www.itchefs-gvci.com).

They promote many initiatives to diffuse information about excellent Italian agricultural and food products, Italian cuisine and the chefs in the world, with attention to quality and authenticity. They also offer, guided by the expertise of Chef Aira Piva, on-site assistance to restaurants that need help.

Italian and/or Italian-sounding restaurants are in great shape around the world. It is a functional business model, regardless of the size of the space. Italian emigrants first carried it to the corners of the earth, demonstrating that a restaurant could be successful with limited investments and a menu that did not require hundreds of perishable, costly preparations like French cuisine. They created first true globalization of food. Pizza and pasta, but also rice dishes and desserts like tiramisù became as popular as the symbols of contemporary American fast food. There were various eras of the spread of Italian cuisine in the world: the wave of emigrants, self-made chefs and restauranteurs, followed by the diffusion of professional chefs trained in Italy, who went to work mainly in emerging nations (primarily in Asia and the Middle East), often in 5-star hotels. Finally, we have the phase of non-Italian chefs who prepare a truly authentic Italian cuisine.

On the marketplace, it has the advantage of being the best-loved cuisine in the world and is regularly among the favourites after the national cuisines. This is true in China, for example, but also in Russia. In Australia, surveys report that the most popular dish is pasta. New Yorkers believe that some classics of the Italian cuisine are part of American history. There are over 1,500 Italian restaurants in the metropolitan area of Tokyo-Yokohama. There are 500 Italian restaurants in Hong Kong. In Asmara, some women roll out their lasagna pasta with the same naturalness as when they make *zighnì*. Not to mention South America. In Asia, interest developed in the large hotels, at the start. It was Il Grissini (with the name suggested by Angelo Gaja) inside the Grand Hyatt of Hong Kong 25 years ago that inaugurated this model, which was then reproduced at will.

There is, however, an anomaly: there are very, very few star chefs in the world and the only one with three stars is Umberto Bombana, chef-owner of the 8½ restaurant in Hong Kong. This situation is quickly explained. Michelin assigns the stars and Michelin strongly favours the French. This is not so much because it favours French restaurants (not many), but rather because it has a powerful distribution and supports the system that promotes distribution of French ingredients and, above all, wines (read Sopexa) in the restaurants of various cities. Italian restaurants are the only ones who do not

make use of these ingredients. For better or worse, they believe in the Italy system. A San Daniele ham, a piece of aged Grana Padana, extra virgin olive oil from Liguria: these are not merely ingredients, but banners that Italian restaurants use to distinguish themselves. We don't mean to doubt the honesty of the Michelin inspectors, but to understand how it is possible that only one or two Italian restaurants deserve a single star, while dozens of restaurants of the most unexpected cuisines collect a great number. Despite this, the fame of Italian cooking keeps growing in the world, continues to satisfy customers and, consequently, to fill the restaurants.

Italian restaurants in the world could be a big opportunity for Italian wine producers.

It is important to note that there are many mid- to high-level Italian restaurants that are searching for small producers. They want to have the exclusive for an artisan product that their competitors cannot offer. This is an enormous opportunity for our winegrowers and artisans of taste. Who better than a chef can suggest the name of a serious and interested importer? Isn't that how it was done in the United States and Germany? It was the on-site Italian restauranteur to whom producers turned for information about importers and to ask to be introduced. That is why this virtual organization of Rosario Scarpato can become a strategic bridgehead into new markets. *W.F.*

The Ambrosian Refectory

The spirit that fuels Italian cuisine is wonderfully summarized in the project conceived by Massimo Bottura – with his Osteria Francescana in Modena, which has 3 Michelin stars, and for four years has been one of the fifty best restaurants in the world – and Davide Rampello, curator of the Pavilion Zero at Expo Milano 2015.

This is a story where human and ethical values are joined with culinary and artistic values. A story that could only thrive in Italy and which is entitled "Refettorio Ambrosiano" or "Ambrosian Refectory".

Massimo Bottura tells us (*Corriere della Sera*, 17 April 2014) that "as I listened to the *buongiorno* [*the good-mornings*] and *buon pranzo* [*have a good lunch*] from Pope Francesco, I thought something momentous was happening

and somehow had to be part of it . . . When the third Michelin star came along, I remembered thinking that I had reached that milestone by cooking boiled Parmesan rinds." It was during the launch of Andrea Berton's restaurant in Milan that Bottura decided to confess his idea to Davide Rampello. "That evening," Rampello recalls, "shut in Berton's office in front of the kitchens, we began to flesh out the idea of creating a new space in which the Greek concept of καλοκαγαθία

[*kalokagathia, a crasis or blend of* καλός καί άγαθός, *kalòs kai agathòs, in other words, 'the beautiful and the good'*] – an ideal combination of ethics and aesthetics – could achieve its most authentic expression: a refectory of art and solidarity." Rampello then thought of involving Luca Bressan, President of Caritas Ambrosiana, and the Episcopal Vicar of the Diocese of Milan, so that the initiative would also receive the support of the church community. The proposal was immediately accepted. A new inspiration. Why, they wondered, don't we combine the practise of solidarity – recovering the excess from the Expo kitchens to create a charitable soup kitchen for the poor – with that of artistic creativity? A beautiful and good place, in short, just like any gourmet meal or work of art. This is how the Refettorio Ambrosiano went from being an idea to becoming a project.

The Refettorio Ambrosiano, created inside a theatre dating back to the 1930s and annexed to the parish of the Greek district in Milan, is a space where the beauty of the act of offering food and comfort is reflected in an atmosphere that celebrates the best Italian contemporary art and design. The renovation project was provided by the Milan Politecnico and has led to the creation of a large dining room with twelve large tables, each with eight seats, designed by leading designers – Aldo Cibic, Pierluigi Cerri, Fabio Novembre, Giulio Iacchetti, Michele De Lucchi, Mario Bellini, Piero Lissoni, Alessandro Mendini, Franco Origoni, Italo Rota, Gaetano Pesce, Patricia Urquiola, Matteo Thun, Dwan Terry – and made entirely of oak by the Riva 1920 company in Cantù. There are also other design pieces such as the chairs, provided by Kartell, and lighting fixtures manufactured by Artemide, as well as tableware accessories by Alessi. On the walls are works created for the occasion by leading Italian contemporary artists, thanks to the collaboration and sponsorship of the ANGAMC (National Association of Modern and Contemporary Art Galleries). The initiative is also supported by Lavazza, Sanpellegrino, KME Group and Eataly. The International MBA students of the Food and Wine of Bologna Business School at the University of Bologna manage the communication.

The main source of creativity for the project, however, is the cuisine. Rampello writes: "We want to ensure that this feeling of great sensitivity toward beauty is transmitted through the form of expression that, more than any other in this age, is making itself felt in terms of inspiration, culture, identity, art and tradition. It is signature cuisine, a cuisine that in recent years has brought Italy to the centre of the world stage, thanks to the capabilities of its formidable chefs. The combination of food and social responsibility is also one of the most important and urgent core themes at the Expo Milano 2015."

A signature cuisine that involves the great masters of our time. "Our colleagues, when they received the phone call with the proposal to cook at the Refettorio Ambrosiano, almost didn't believe it. But more than the yes's," says a surprised Bottura, "I was amazed by the few no's." After the Expo ended, the soup kitchen continues to provide community service through collaboration with the Caritas Ambrosiana. *W.F.*

Italian Cuisine: The Etymology of a Country

Your home is what you know and understand.
Luigi Veronelli

"What should we do, should we eat?" "Yes, yes, let's eat and then we'll go." It is this exchange that ends the famous scene of the outcome of the referendum of 1948 in the film by Dino Risi, *A Difficult Life*. In the scene, Alberto Sordi and Lea Massari find themselves toasting to the victory of the Republic in front of a sumptuous monarchists' table, now cleared, while in the background, the sounds of the anthem of the new Italy reach a crescendo.

History is set out like this then, in front of a full plate of pasta, the paradigm of a longed-for abundance, dreamed of, and finally won. The rebirth of the country, in fact, also necessarily passes through the recovery of lost food rituals that expand and renew with the joyful and light spirit of a whole nation to rebuild. The table, configured as a "place of survival", is finally set. The table is then configured as an emblematic *locus* for the narration of the Italian culture and tradition that was still very fragmented in that era. And Italian cuisine starts from here: from an artisan fresco of villages and natural ravines where every dish had a fragrance that was

primitive, perhaps elementary, yet complete. The urban version of this culinary theatre, marked by the slow ringing of the town bells, was certainly that of the local markets and shops.

In these vestries of flavours and fragrances, there was all the beauty of courtesy and trust, of the intimate knowledge of special treatment: in those grottos everything, from the confession of a secret ingredient to an expert opinion on the packaging, was a kind of schooling.

The atmosphere changed as soon as the Italians understood that food could stop being an event to become, instead, an appointment. To understand Italian cuisine and its history it is necessary to look at its communication. We are mainly talking about communication via road, linked to that great capillary nerve system of highways and going along the mythical Aurelias, the marine drives, in the Cinquecento automobile, where meals began to become synonymous with day trips, escape and getting out of the house. Throughout the peninsula, Italians were discovering the aesthetic (and not just ecstatic) pleasure of cuisine: the industry and advertising created new concentrations of knowledge and flavours around which Italy came together as if it were a new cultural wave, only made up of evolving flavours and fragrances.

In 1956, just two years after the birth of Italian television, the writer and director Mario Soldati invented "food and wine reportage" with the creation of *Viaggio lungo la Valle del Po alla ricerca dei cibi genuini* – investigative television, something new and absolutely innovative for its time, dedicated to exploring and narrating culinary specialties and local traditions.

"What is travel? Traveling is about getting to know places, peoples and countries. And what is the easiest way, the most basic way to travel? Through eating, enjoying the cuisine of a place you are traveling through. Because if you really think about it, everything is in the cuisine: there is the nature of the place, the weather, then the agriculture, the pastoralism, the hunting and the fishing. And in the cooking method is the tradition of a people, the history and the culture of this people."

In those years, moreover, the way of recounting cuisine and its socio-cultural context of reference began to undergo a major revolution in the world of publishing and communication. After the first great, historical guides to restaurants of the early twentieth century (Michelin, Touring Club), the first women's magazines appeared with recipes and some volumes that, for their form and style, invented a whole new genre: food critics. The most authoritative and intellectually profound voice in this field is undoubtedly that of Luigi Veronelli. His *Ristoranti di Veronelli*, published in 1978 by Rizzoli, changed food and wine criticism, passing from the purely analytical-descriptive approach used in the already existing guides to a more hedonistic evaluation.

In a review of the turning points and the revolutions in the history of our cuisine it would be impossible not to include the "post-musical" moment, as it was defined by Gualtiero Marchesi, who changed it forever. Marchesi contributed with a desire for reviving Italian food and wine culture that aimed to construct a total cuisine, the sum of various artistic experiences: an aesthetic cuisine, but primarily intellectual, full of reasoning and the fine arts. The son of wealthy Milanese hoteliers – his parents were the owners of the hotel-restaurant Al Mercato on Via Bezzecca, in Milan – the chef of Porta Vittoria began to take his first steps into the world of catering by attending a hotel school in Switzerland. On his return to Italy he officially entered the kitchens of the family hotel, where he began to profess the first dictates of what would later become *haute cuisine*. In the 1960s, he made a courageous decision. At thirty years old, with a wife and two daughters, he left Italy to take part in the excitement and transformations that were affecting what until then had been the culinary school *par excellence*. Marchesi moved to Roanne, in the south of France, where he spent two years at the famous restaurant of the Troisgros brothers, the true precursors of the French *nouvelle cuisine* revolution.

"At that time only a few French chefs, including my brother and I, were fraught with trying to find the best way to simplify the recipes, so as to release the natural flavour of foods: like the two of us, Gualtiero wanted to completely renovate the traditional cuisine of his country, still firmly dictated by its strict rules," writes Pierre Troisgros in his introduction to the book *Oltre il fornello* (Rizzoli) by Marchesi. And, indeed,

Gualtiero Marchesi

what the Milanese chef did was carry out an investigation that translated into the complex and long-running dispute between linguistic form and content, signifier and signified, *langue* and *parole* on gastronomic terrain. "Form *is* material," said Marchesi, also rediscovering in the virtues of contrast ("From contrast flows a beautiful harmony," said Heraclitus) and lightness (the aesthetics of "subtraction of weight" of Calvino) the keystones of his new code. Once the lesson of the master Escoffier had been assimilated – "instead of simply copying these admirable works [*recipes*], we ourselves must tread new ground, leading to new ways of working, according to ways of living in this day and age" – Marchesi returned to the Lombard capital where, in 1977, he opened the historic Gualtiero Marchesi on Via Bonvesin de la Riva. The restaurant, in an almost unstoppable way, notched up a series of memorable successes: winning his first Michelin star the following year at the inauguration, and the first three stars in Italy in 1985. Then came the turning point, the momentous step, the radical and irreversible transformation of what until then had been the traditional and codified canon of Italian gastronomy. Marchesi's was the revolution that opened the door to a renewed conception of cuisine, of tradition and history, local products and territoriality, but also of style and art, aesthetics and inspiration – in short, *material* and *form*. The place of food created by Marchesi in the 1970s tended to be increasingly like the space of an artistic factory, a reference point for the varied community of the cream of Italian intellectual life at the time – painters, filmmakers, designers – who, through using the new gastronomic code, were honing and matching their languages. For Marchesi, who had always loved art and music, the act of inventing flavours was nothing other than artistic composition in its most natural combination of technique and genius. On the staves of his creations the peasant *stracotture* were interpreted with new essential and sophisticated approaches, melodic, just like the sweet piano sonatas shared with his wife. From his forge came talents who then populated the firmament of global celebrities, transforming the craft of cooking into a catalysing art garnering international fame and attention. Just think of the fame acquired in recent years by names like Andrea Berton, Carlo Cracco, Enrico Crippa,

Davide Oldani, Pietro Leemann, Ernst Knam, former students of his who have become real stars of world gastronomy. The founder of the New Italian cuisine can then be said to be "the head" of a real media revolution in the cuisine of our country, even though he, paradoxically, prefers to be called simply *cook* instead of *chef* (literally "boss", in French), emphasizing the humility and substance of his role as creator in a constant quest to find the perfect balance rather than empty but fashionable names. Thanks to Marchesi, in short, the cultural dignity of Italian cuisine has been restored, its academic value – in the sense of both research and expressive quality – but also glamor and visual seduction, and this break is a true starting moment in a regeneration of its now more conscious narratives.

Cuisine is everything that surrounds it, in its being, in its appearance, in its making. It is the experience of gastronomy "everywhere", our departure point, and the point where we hope to be able to finish. Or maybe not, because the final word has not yet been written in the history of our gastronomy that, in fact, continues to change and evolve. And then, perhaps, the real story of Italian cuisine lies in its never ending, in this continuous watching us eat. There, where everything flows, and nothing is forgotten. *D.R.*

PART TWO   **Italian Wine.
Innovation**

Milan: Wine Intellectuals

Mario Busso, Walter Filiputti, Cesare Pillon,
Davide Rampello, Angelo Solci

Milan Comes into Its Own in the Modern History of Italian Wine

The Lombard capital is the target market for Italian wine production. Milanese distribution and consumption models, in fact, anticipated what would happen, a few years later, in the rest of Italy and, a mirror of developed foreign markets, prepare to face foreign customers in an increasingly globalized and standardized world.

The economic capital of Italy has a solid foundation for deserving and maintaining this role, with its capacity for exhibiting products and services in an ongoing Expo Fair, products brought from abroad to Italian consumers. It also exhibits the precious nature of our country to the foreign consumer. It is a continuous media event, like those found in few other cities in the world: London, Paris, New York and Hong Kong.

The first trade fair in Milan, the Fiera Campionaria di Milano, *Campionaria* meaning "sample", was inaugurated on 12 April 1920 in Porta Venezia. It was called this because, unlike the ancient trade fairs, it exhibited mass-produced goods that could be traded by showing a simple sample, while in traditional exhibitions, it was essential that all the goods be there on site, and these were sold at the time.

Milan then became the point of arrival for foreign penetration of the national economy, the financial hub and capital of Italian wholesale trading, with the largest fruit and vegetable market in Europe.

It was a city in perpetual intellectual ferment, in which the socio-economic fabric drew its lifeblood from all the major professional associations related to wine: the Italian Sommelier Association (AIS), which was established in 1965 in the prestigious Savini restaurant, in the centre of the Galleria Vittorio Emanuele II, the throughway between Piazza Duomo and Piazza della Scala, one of the most respected and renowned throughout the world; the AEI (Association of Italian Oenologists and Oenotechnicians); the UIV (Italian Wine Union); the AMIRA (Italian Restaurants and Hotels Maître Association); the AIBES (Italian Association of Barmen and Supporters); and Vinarius (Italian Wine Shop Association). All of these were in the economic capital for its high national and international profile, with the one exception of ONAV (National Organization of Wine Tasters), founded in 1951 in Asti, where it still has its headquarters.

Milan is also in the lead for the latest research in viticulture: in fact in 2014, the DISAA (Department of Agricultural and Environmental Sciences) in the School of Viticulture and Oenology at the University, after years of research, implemented the visionary project for selecting new grapevine rootstocks classified under the symbol "M", which stands for Milan.

Even Luigi Veronelli, the undisputed prophet of the "renaissance of Italian wine", worked in Milan, where he found the ideal coordinates for promoting and distributing his books, and working on a famous television broadcast. It was also where he met – at the Enoteca Solci – Giannola Nonino, with whom he created the literary prize linked to rural culture, the "Nonino Risit d'Âur", still one of the most important in Italy.

It was natural in those times of enthusiasm to present wines and production areas. I remember those of Collio Goriziano, Friuli, Brunello di Montalcino, Barolo, Sassicaia, just to mention some of the most famous labels.

Milan, finally, became a major Italian centre for publishing, matrix of the new language of wine, which would also influence the agri-food system. *A.So.*

Italian Oenologists, the Banners of the New Science of Wine

The modern history of Italian wine would not have been possible without the contribution of oenologists, the banners of knowledge and themselves an integral part of the research and technological innovation. It would not have been possible – along with the ideas and the entrepreneurial courage of winemakers – to so rapidly express the enormous potential that was hidden in every Italian region.

Oenologists have been – and continue to be – the banners of qualitative growth, not only in their field, but also in complementary fields, such as that of winery equipment or the applied research in many laboratories.

In the mid-1960s, my father's friend and oenologist Gigi Valle came to look at the wines that my father produced for the restaurant. He arrived in secret, as was happening almost

Solci enoteca interior,
opened in Milan in 1938
and closed in 2007

Following pages
Milan's new skyline

everywhere. Oenologists were seen as alchemists, not to be introduced to anyone, and vintners were very careful about saying that they had a technician working with their winery.

After the war in Friuli Venezia Giulia, oenologists at the time were called oenotechnicians; there were seven graduates of the Institute of Conegliano Veneto: in 1946 Marcellino Pillon and Italo Gottardo graduated, the year after that, Orfeo Salvador, in 1948 Vittorio Puiatti, and in 1950, Gigi Valle, Giorgio Zucchiatti and Marco Felluga. When Mauro Lunelli (Ferrari) completed his studies at San Michele, in 1968, there were eight students in his course and in the previous one, there had been three. And no one, back then, wanted to be an oenologist.

There were three very important technical institutes that produced the graduates who "colonized" Italy, bringing knowledge and accompanying Italian wine into the modern era: Alba in Piedmont, San Michele in Adige in Trentino and Conegliano in Veneto.

In 2014, there were four thousand oenologists working in Italy, an army of worthy technicians who contribute to the production of quality wines.

In 1876, in Conegliano (Treviso), the first school of viticulture and oenology in Europe was established.

In 1891, Arturo Marescalchi, an oenotechnician who had graduated from the Conegliano school, with forty-six colleagues, founded the Society of Italian Oenotechnicians; after two years, in 1893, with his colleague Antonio Carpenè, he published the first issue of the magazine *L'Enotecnico*, today, *L'Enologo*. In 1916, the Society of Italian Oenotechnicians moved its headquarters from Conegliano to Milan. At that time the association had a hundred members, almost half of all oenotechnicians then employed in the sector – today, as has been said, there are nearly four thousand of them, equal to 90%.

With the advent of fascism, the association was dissolved in 1946 to be reconstituted by the oenotechnician Giuseppe Asnaghi, with the new wording Associazione Enotecnici Italiani (Association of Italian Oenotechnicians). In 1959, Antonio Carpenè was called again to be chairman. He was witty and humorous, and there is a wonderful photograph of him where, with a hoe on his shoulder, he declares himself the Cincinnatus of the oenologists. In 1965, Emilio Sernagiotto was elected, flanked by the first secretary-director Giuseppe Pietro Dossi, with whom he began a series of training and improvement courses for the sector. I remember them with great affection and esteem. At the time, being an oenologist took a lot of courage.

From 1967 to 1970, I, a young oenotechnician, worked with them in the analysis laboratory and in organizing conferences and meetings. From 1978, Giuseppe Martelli was appointed director of the association, the first full-time director, the driving force and main protagonist of the development of the AEI. In April 1991 – the centenary of the association – the approval of Law no. 129 was celebrated, for the official recognition of the title of "oenologist", which opened the European professional doors to Italian viticulture technicians.

The title of oenologist, therefore, is nothing other than the logical evolution of the qualification of oenotechnician, just as university preparation is the right evolution of the already valid training guaranteed for more than one hundred years by the six-year course in viticulture and oenology.

Currently, oenology schools no longer have the sixth year and, therefore, theoretically there are more oenotechnicians (of the old style). There is only the three-year degree in Viticulture and Oenology.

But let us take a step back in history. Why were we in those conditions? The answer can be found in the letter published by Arturo Marescalchi in *L'Enotecnico* (no. 7, 30 September 1893):

"Jaquemin and Marx, which runs La Claire Institute for the preparation of yeasts grown, sent agents to Italy to buy our best grapes in order to separate their enzymes, study them, grow the best ones and sell them this year in our country. It's painful to see that here, too, Italians are letting foreign industries take business away from them; it is painful to always see Italians as others' slaves, and not because we lack the talent, the resources, raw materials, but only because of a deplorable laziness, a stubborn aversion to all that is new, for an unjustified lack of confidence in our strengths, in our businesses; we Italians first want to witness the experiences of others, and only when we see that new industries are flourishing and lucrative, only then will we begin to gather the leftovers or be left there chomping on our fingers for not having understood in time!"

The article continues with suggestions, technical advice and a list of the improvements resulting from innovations. The current association, therefore, is the result of a hundred and twenty years of history and commitment to the sector's progress. In 1920, there were one hundred members, six hundred in 1950, one thousand six hundred in 1980, while today there are nearly four thousand, representing approximately 90% of the viticulture technicians.

The goals are to protect the profession ethically, legally and economically, protect its unions, and to represent the category at all levels. Another important role is technical updating, with publications, conferences and seminars that are integrated with events for the improvement and protection of the national production, promotion and distribution of our wines in Italy and abroad. *A.So.*

The District Oenotechnician

It was one of Luigi Veronelli's countless ideas. He repeatedly urged the Association of Italian Oenotechnicians to create structures capable of providing technical assistance to small growers with the same spirit as that of the local health authority doctor. There was only one district oenotechnician who left a mark in the history of contemporary Italian wine, although very few remember him.

It happened in the early 1980s, in Carema, a small mountain village in Alto Piedmont, because of three coinciding factors: the resourcefulness of an enlightened Councillor for Agriculture, Gianni Fabiole Nicoletto, the generous availability of Gaspare Buscemi, oenotechnician originally from Sicily, but Friulian by adoption, with the vocation of a wine missionary, and the interest of a wine shop in Milan that was sensitive and prepared, Luigi Gaviglio, who provided an outlet for that experience. In 1967, when the Carema area was bounded by DOC, there were 33 hectares of vineyards, divided among two hundred owners. It was unthinkable to pay for the advice of a technician. It was the municipality that took care of that, in the period when Fabiole was Councillor, from 1980 to 1985, intervening on the part of the winery co-

operative, whose growers Buscemi met with. Inaugurated by Veronelli himself, the district oenologist helped Carema make an exciting quality leap, giving birth to Carema di Carema, which since then has been the winery's flagship. The experiment of a district oenologist proved unfortunately not to be exportable, despite Buscemi's enthusiasm and the personal commitment of Giuseppe Martelli, secretary of the Association of Italian Oenotechnicians (in reality, "oenological" was passed on thanks to the many DOC consortia, which involved both viticultural agronomists and oenologists). The seed that was sown continued, however, to produce results on site. Thanks to the relationship sealed with Luigi Ferrando, the only Carema winemaker that at the time produced all the Canavese wines, Buscemi made consulting agreements with some manufacturers to start the rehabilitation of Erbaluce, showing that from this vine, whose grapes gave a product so acidic that only Passito di Caluso could be made from them, it was instead possible to make one of the most fascinating Piedmont white wines. *C.P.*

Wine Tasters and Promotion of Italian Wine

ONAV, the Italian wine tasters organization, was founded in Asti in 1951. It was an initiative of the local Chamber of Commerce and was supported by eminent figures of the wine sector at the time, particularly those of Piedmont.

The reason for its constitution was the need, considered quite important, to make a corps of trained tasters available.

From the date of its foundation when it was clearly a phenomenon limited to Piedmont, ONAV began to expand to all the other Italian regions. The objective, to spread the pleasure of the art of tasting and to make its importance known, was expressed through many initiatives. The most important of these at the national level is the Douja d'Or, celebrating its 43rd edition in 2015. This oenological competition takes place every year in Asti in the month of September. Every year a national competition is launched. The commission of ONAV experts and technicians, in collaboration with the Asti Chamber of Commerce, assigns the Douja d'Or prize to wines that reach a ranking of 85/100. These labels can then display the Douja d'Or seal. The Douja Oscar, however, is awarded only to wines that surpass 90/100.

From the time of its foundation, ONAV has held specialized courses to investigate the themes of wine tasting at all levels. The goal is to increment and improve the reliability of wine evaluation, to offer continuing updates on tasting methodologies and, above all, to spread awareness about Italian wine assets. *M.B.*

On the Tip of the Tongue

Is it true that *in vino veritas*, as they say, one can also blindly trust the sincerity of one's tongue? In other words, is it possible that the codes of expression with which the "odorous liquid" is presented to us today can actually give us the all-encompassing sensory experience of taste with the same intensity? To tackle a question of this kind it is essential to understand whether there is continuity between the material and its expression, between the content and its form.

Language is a necessary condition to the existence of humans, because it is the basis of exchange and, therefore, the birth and evolution of a civilization, of a people, a culture. In his *XII Scelera Friderici Imperatoris*, an anti-imperialist work, the medieval monk and chronicler Salimbene de Adam da Parma tells of an experiment that gives us food for thought that is very fitting: Emperor Frederick II, intent on discovering what natural language was innate to all people, decided to entrust a group of orphaned children to the care of nurses. The nurses were absolutely forbidden to speak to them. The result, in the absence of an education that used the linguistic medium, was that the children all died in a short space of time. It is, therefore, clear that language, the primary medium of expression, is not only the vehicle for information, but a condition necessary for identity, and thus life.

Today, gastronomy journalists generally have a common and somewhat restricted and immobile vocabulary, made of linguistic conventions that are always the same and unchanging expressive rules that do not do justice to the multi-sensory experience of tasting. The Italian *enolalia* is a generic apparatus of terms, often ambiguous and imprecise, of abused solutions, such as human attributions ("amiable", "robust", "full-bodied") or francophone seductions ("bouquet", "perlage"), placed inside tables and information files where the craze for scores and hundred-point evaluations is replaced

almost definitively by the fascination of taste and interpretation. Veronelli's illuminating glimpses, with his sensory accuracy and great expressive power, are, unfortunately, only a distant memory.

What the language of criticism needs right now, therefore, is a rapprochement, a reconciliation of the object with the expressive medium, the wine with its code, so that its description returns to being an art that will complete the experience, that continues its suggestions, recovering the narrative dimension. On the other hand, it is the etymology of the word "code" that reveals its natural relation of vital synonymy: the term derives from *caudex* that from its original meaning of "stock, tree trunk" began to be used by the Latins in the broadest sense, to indicate the wax tablets on which the first written characters were engraved. From the trunk to the book, then, from life to its story. The chalice, then, is a crystal mirror through which to interpret: thrown together inside it are landscapes and faces, labours and memories, stories of people, and the privilege of being able to give oneself up to the narrative of these frescoes is incomparable – from green horizons to falling in love – without suffering the privations of an utterance without a soul, with emotions suspended on the tip of the tongue. *D.R.*

The Language of Wine according to Veronelli

The father of the new language of wine was Luigi Veronelli. His first *Catalogo Bolaffi dei vini del mondo*, published in 1968, is still a very up-to-date work even today. In it are descriptions that eventually became part of everyone's lexicon. Gian Arturo Rota and Nichi Stefi produced an extremely valuable publication – *Luigi Veronelli. La vita è troppo corta per bere vini cattivi* (Giunti-Slow Food, Florence-Bra, 2012) – in which they use his documents to talk about the commitment to the renaissance of our wine. Rota remembers: "His study had numerous bookcases full of books; one, to his left, was dedicated exclusively to dictionaries and lexicons [*there were about fifty: Italian, Latin, Greek, synonyms and antonyms, dialects; some were shabby-looking due to continuous use*]. This detail surprised me [*why were there so many?*] and also disturbed me [*why did such an erudite man need all of these?*]. So one day I mustered up the courage and I asked him. He

Associazione Italiana Sommelier

took me seriously, understanding that it was a serious question and not just superficial curiosity. Here is his answer: 'Words, like people, wines, all things, have different tones, nuances, sometimes hidden, imperceptible, but waiting to be found; I seek until I'm sure that I'm using the right one.' Wherever worked practically for the modulation of his writing. 'You do the same' – his punch line: most of those dictionaries and vocabularies are in my study." Gian Arturo Rota met Veronelli when he was a student. Having grown up with him as a journalist and publisher, he worked beside him for twenty years. He looks after the immense archive and website Casa Veronelli.

"Veronelli's writing," for Nichi Stefi, "is as rigorous as anything one can find in journalism. It is based on a precise language; for every sensation there is a corresponding single word, and for every word there is a unique sensation: this was his conviction. But what words was he seeking? He sought them in literature, in the tradition that was dialect as well, and used different origins in a fertile mix. Thus *pronta beva - ready drink* recovers the archaic *beva* or *drink* to describe something easy, anything but challenging. The word *nerbo* or *backbone* gives a wine a sleek elegance, the *stoffa* or *stuff* does not only refer to the material that Veronelli always respected, but especially to those high quotes that give a wine unexpected dignity. We then add inventions like 'a wine for meditation' that have no linguistic value if not the sensory transposition, a kind of synaesthesia, in which the wine becomes thought." *W.F.*

The First Intellectuals of Wine: Sommeliers of the AIS

The Italian Sommelier Association (AIS) was founded in Milan on 7 July 1965 by Professor Gianfranco Botti, a biologist. In a few years – particularly since the third Congress in Florence in 1969, when Franco Tommaso Marchi took over all communication and public relations – the AIS became a reference point for involving the consumer in the "renaissance of Italian wine". The far-sighted project was designed by Luigi Marinatto and his friend Antonio Cendali, both high-calibre journalists to whom Botti had entrusted communications. In 1971, the writer became part of the National Council during the V Congress of Bolzano-Trento. The meeting with Mar-

inatto and Cendali was enlightening for me. At dawn, after a night full of tastings in Ivo Cardinali's well-stocked tavern in Udine, the idea of doing my thesis on the figure of the sommelier burgeoned forth (I was a student of Economics in Trieste). It was Marinatto himself who helped me prepare the outline. The title? *Il sommelier e la sua funzione di educazione enologica del consumatore* (*The sommelier and his role as a wine consumer educator*). It included the project of the new profession, which then come true. I graduated on 1 March 1973, and for my research I went to New York to be a sommelier for three months.

The great director of the AIS's fast and vibrant growth, the one who put into practice the philosophy outlined by the founders, was Franco Tommaso Marchi, who had become secretary in the meantime.

A man of great insights, he had the ability to choose people full of enthusiasm in every Italian region. With an exuberant, sometimes difficult personality, he had a deep sense of friendship. He knew all the best Italian wine cellars. The National Congresses, which took place every year from 1969 onwards, thanks to him became a captivating event for the new Italian oenology. The regions scrambled to hold the sommelier Congresses.

One of his masterpieces was managing to bring the world sommelier championship to Italy, held for the first time in Milan in 1971. "Piero Sattanino from Piedmont won it that year," Angelo Solci reflects, "one of the first to become part of the AIS, in addition to inspiring awe in Italian and Euro-

pean oenophiles. He made everyone understand the change that was taking place in our oenology, no longer trivial and for the masses, but serious and of great quality. We took note and became confident of our means, our potential."

Since then the AIS was seen by its foreign counterparts – which thanks to the Italians formed the ASI (Association de la Sommellerie Internationale) – as a reference point that still holds supremacy. In 2014, the AIS boast 35,000 members, with chapters in all the regions and 162 provincial delegations.

During Marchi's time, Antonio Piccinardi also worked with the AIS. A prolific author of books on wine and gastronomy, he has an extraordinary aesthetic sense (he is a great connoisseur of modern art), as well as being a creative event planner. During the courses he gave some very fine lessons, particularly those on tasting.

In 1972, a small group of AIS sommeliers broke off to found the FISAR, the Italian federation of sommeliers, hotel-keepers and restauranteurs, copying the uniforms and courses of the original association. Today, FISAR has its registered office in San Giuliano Terme (Pisa).

On 9 December 2013, the Rome section of AIS headed by Franco Ricci broke away from the Italian Sommeliers Association to create the Italian Sommeliers Foundation. The seat remained at Hotel Cavalieri Hilton, where the association had operated for years.

In addition to carrying on with the professional courses, it has issued a number of publications including the magazine *Bibenda* and *Bibenda. La guida, vini e ristoranti d'Italia*. It also organizes the annual Oscar of wine, an event that is much appreciated by producers, the press and consumers. *W.F.*

Professional Courses

The AIS's great insight were the professional courses, a sort of itinerant professorship with several teachers to whom the association assigned the task of training future sommeliers in every region of Italy. So it was that in a few years we managed to unify the Italy of wine at the table, to some extent as Pellegrino Artusi had done with the publication, in 1891, of the book *La Scienza in cucina e l'Arte di mangiare bene*, which is still one of the most famous texts on our cuisine.

The first course was held fewer than two years after its foundation. It opened in Milan at CAPAC (Centro Addestramento Perfezionamento Addetti al Commercio) on 9 February 1967. Since then the progression of enrollment has been constant and has involved all of the Italian provinces.

The aim was twofold: on the one hand, to seriously deal with restaurant staff's lack of preparation on wine, which was disastrous, and on the other, to enhance the role of the "member sommeliers", or those who, while not working in the restaurant business, took part in the social life out of passion. We had already created *wine lovers*!

In an age when wine was evolving rapidly, sommeliers were the true *liaisons* between producers, still not used to communication, and final customers. The wineries held us in high regard.

The courses transformed, and are still transforming, thousands of fans into conscious consumers, prepared and therefore equipped with an ability to critique. They are capable of understanding the choices of many winemakers and giving a correct value to the quality of wine. In fact, these learned enthusiasts also became precious ambassadors of good, moderate and healthy drinking, whose motivations became pleasure, as well as real material culture.

It was the AIS that made this language more affordable, easier to understand and use. Indeed, it did more than that: it made it universal inasmuch as it managed to make it part of a communication system that involved a wide audience, both professional and amateur. It is no coincidence that all the other agribusiness sectors – coffee, oil, beer, chocolate, cheese, salami – have adopted the same communication style, liberally borrowing the vocabulary coined by wine.

The AIS was really an association of wine intellectuals, the first that managed to have a clear vision on how to proceed. A veritable coterie of avant-garde experts of quality, not only was it instrumental in publicizing wine, but it was also instrumental to the professional growth of our restaurants which, thanks to wine, broke free from the stagnation of the past, beginning a journey that brought our cuisine to be the most loved in the world.

In that period, the 1970s and early 1980s, many of the future greats of our cuisine were part of the AIS, starting with Gualtiero Marchesi and Franco Colombani (the latter president of the association for many years). But there were more. Giorgio Pinchiorri in Florence and Gianfranco Bolognesi of Frasca di Castrocaro; Gianluigi Morini of San Domenico in Imola; Gianni Cosetti, Aldo Morassutti, Giorgio Trentin of Boschetti in Friuli, Alberto Ciarla in Rome, Ezio Santin of Cassinetta di Lugagnano, the Santini family of Dal Pescatore in Canneto. And again Lucio Pompili in the Marches with his Symposium, while in Sardinia there was the Dal Corsaro of Filippo Deidda. In Palermo there was the Charleston of Angelo Ingrao with his maître-sommelier Carlo Hassan, and we could go on.

Wine lists, guided by the AIS, were born at the end of the 1970s, and the shrewder restaurants immediately realized their potential. Two examples: the restaurant Don Alfonso 1890, of the Iaccarino family, in Sant'Agata sui Due Golfi, found fame thanks to the immediate creation of a superb wine cellar, and the most important case, the guiding star, Giorgio Pinchiorri, transformed the simple Chianti wine shop where crostini were served into the largest winery in the world, then flanked by the magical cuisine of Annie Féolde. From there the fortune of many Italian wines began. Pinchiorri made the wineries understand the very important role that the great restaurants would have: they were showcases onto the market, as well as irreplaceable ambassadors of the "new style" of Italian wine.

The imitation effect soon spread to taverns, small restaurants and pizzerias everywhere in Italy, and they entered the gourmet Olympus thanks to their lists of high quality wines, in addition to the wellbeing of Italians. Wine was a multiplier of opportunities and earnings. The cuisine, in the early years of the renaissance, was a kind of complementary element, still closed in on itself. When wine broke with the traditional mould, people began to believe that cuisine, too, could change, to rightly recover its role years later. In fact, this happened when Gualtiero Marchesi arrived on the scene.

Not only did the great restaurants grow thanks to the AIS courses, but also many salespeople and representatives who, in turn, took the message of the new Italian wine abroad and made it known, commercial agents who had an innate ability to choose emerging products and impose them on the market, as well as educating the restaurants.

We encountered many people and established deep friendships with many. Out of all of them, I mention Roberto Tacchella in Versilia, Sergio Mosconi in Mantua, Roberto Scopo in Brescia, Giuseppe Farinasso in Cuneo, Carletto Fagnani in Arma di Taggia in Liguria, Luciano Gheduzzi in Bologna, Vincenzo Tannoia in Puglia and Ciro Cestaro in Naples.

In the role of Italian sales manager for Antinori, as someone who accompanied the birth of two labels that paved the way for the modern history of Italian wine – Sassicaia and Tignanello – there is the very humane and professional figure of Giancarlo Notari. *W.F.*

Claus Riedel and AIS Sommeliers

Riedel stemware, made in Austria, also speaks Italian. Claus Riedel was brilliant: he was the first in the world to realize that the size and shape of the glass affected the perception of the aromas and tastes. It was at this point that his story – and that of the world's first glasses designed for wine – crossed paths with that of the new Italian Sommelier Association, which he asked to work with to see if his hunch was correct. It was 1973. In the same year, in Orvieto, the VII National Congress of the AIS was held. On that occasion, in the city's

crowded theatre, Claus Riedel presented his theory on the glass created for wine. The resulting line of glasses, which included thirteen with different shapes whose inception we of the AIS actively participated in, was called the "Sommelier series" in honour of Italian sommeliers. The revolutionary concept of these stylish glasses, still blown at the historic plant in Kufstein today, was to bring the glass back to its most basic form, a plain and simple style, a smooth thin glass with a long stem.

It was the end of the era in which the chalice was detached from its contents.

While Claus Riedel certainly deserves the credit of brilliant intuition, his son Georg then created the conditions to bring this huge discovery to the rest of the world. The added value of Georg Riedel, as determined as his father to produce something that did not simply contain wine, but ennobled it, was to design a new glass for each type of wine.

In order to first convince the winemakers and then the restaurateurs of the veracity of the discovery, he developed a course on glasses that showed how his father's theory had a solid and unassailable basis. Since July 2013, Georg Riedel has put his son Maximilian – eleventh generation – born in 1977, in charge. He is also a creator of innovative wine glasses and decanters. *W.F.*

The Vinarius Wine Shops

Between the 1960s and 1970s the *enoteca*, or wine shop, was born. It was a natural fact that sprang from the evolution of our wine production, from the transformation of restaurants and following an economic wellbeing resulting from the industrial and commercial boom of the post-War period. We had a sense of mission, but without losing our business sense: the new-born quality wines were in need of communication and culture, of "boutiques", of welcoming environments where we could subliminally teach people how to preserve, order and pair these hedonistic wines, no longer made simply to quench a thirst. And so the form, the "Council of Wine", was born.

It was then that we created Vinarius – the Association of Italian Wine Shops.

The project sprang from an idea of mine shared with wine merchant friends – Gaviglio, Bolis, Meregalli and Trimani –

and with Marco Felluga (producer of Collio) and Antonio Piccinardi (dynamic wine journalist). The motivation was similar to that of the Sommelier Association: we wanted to promote quality wines in the years when confusion was reigning and make it clear to the public that a wine shop was distinguished by its excellence and professionalism. The constitution took place 24 March 1981 at the Hilton in Milan. I was appointed president and Antonio Piccinardi, secretary.

We organized conferences on tasting, marketing as well as numerous study trips to Italian and foreign wine regions, and then transferred our knowledge and excitement to our customers, and in this way bound them to our wine shops.

During its first year of life, the "Vinarius Award" was also created, similar to the "Bancarella Award". The wine shop owners expressed their judgment to elect a wine of the year – a product that contained these characteristics: it had to be of the highest quality, express particular personality, have been elected by *opinion leaders*, have created a fashion and have a special graphic look.

The first prize was awarded in 1982 to the Marchesi Antinori's Tignanello. The prize was awarded during an elegant ceremony at the Press Club of Milan and ended with a dinner at the Savini restaurant, in the Galleria. Sassicaia, the wine of the year in 1987, had a legendary presentation. It was designed by Antonio Piccinardi, who organized, at the Piccolo in Milan, a memorable tasting, which will remain unique in the history of this great vintage wine of 1968 and that of 1984, masterfully led by Giacomo Tachis.

The intelligent work of a few people, including sommeliers, wine shop and restaurant owners, had a huge influence on the promotion of quality wine, when mass consumption was still oriented toward bulk wines, and often not good ones. *A.So.*

The Importance of Wine Auctions

A telling sign of fine wines appeared in London in 1966, when Christie's auctions resumed. This encouraged public interest in the intrinsic value of high-ranking wines. Christie's serious intentions proved to be concrete when they hired one of the most gifted wine merchants and tasters, John Michael Broadbent, bringing together a good working knowledge, skill in critiquing wines, academic preparation and the talent of an art merchant, a combination destined for great success.

In the mid-1970s, Broadbent was at our wine shop in Milan and attended an auction that we had set up at the Casino of Saint-Vincent. On that occasion, we had him taste the great Italian red wines he was unacquainted with (apart from those of Tuscany and Piedmont), arousing his interest and awe. We had added another piece to the big puzzle of the history of Italian wine.

At the beginning of 1972, one of the first auctions for collectible wines was organized at the Press Club of Milan, and it was the auction that had the greatest national resonance.

Many representative wines were offered for tasting, thus allowing gourmets and collectors to assess quality and conservation. It was also a wonderful opportunity, not to be missed, to taste the special flavours and aromas of great bottles, very appreciated by connoisseurs. At the appointed hour the auctioneer, a very stern and righteous character in his black turtleneck sweater, silenced the room, briefly explained the rules of the auction and started with the first lot. His gaze was magnetic. He seemed to understand the intentions of each participant, looking at those who raised their hands to buy the desired lot and assigning to the highest prices, but perhaps, to those he had strategically chosen, changing the pace of the gavel's strike, speeding up or slowing down on purpose to maintain the high tension in the room.

I, too, attracted by this magical atmosphere and interested in some bottles that I wanted to have in my fledgling wine shop, certain to increase the prestige of the assortment, bought some lots. In the evening, we went home, aware of having had a special day, not just because of the unusual sale, unusual in Italy for our sector, but confident that our fine wines had acquired a "metaphysical" aura of importance. Intangible assets that helped develop all of oenology. In later years, I organized many wine auctions for the sale of wines and collectibles and *en primeur* (anticipated sale of wine in casks), gaining considerable experience as an auctioneer in the magnetism, pace, tension, the synthetic but comprehensive descriptions, which transformed the rounds of sales into promotional parties for the overall image of the wines. *A.So.*

The Italian Wine Union and SIMEI

The winemaking machinery industry is one of the flagships of our manufacturing supply chain. *Machines for oil and wine, and exports reaching 2 billion* headlined *Il Sole 24 ore* on 12 November 2013, on the occasion of the XLV SIMEI (International Oenological and Bottling Trade Fair). "We have become world champions of mechanical engineering," writes Franco Vergnano, ". . . not much is said about this, but the sector is valued on the international market, with exports that in the last decade have had double-digit growth rates." At least five hundred companies, of which one hundred and fifty, control 70% of the entire business. Exports reached almost two billion with a +9%, a positive trade balance of over 1.5 billion. In the last ten to fifteen years, the Italian bottling system has reached, and in some niches exceeded, the Germans, our most aggressive competitors.

Since 1963, this high-tech sector has had its own trade fair, SIMEI, which is held every two years in Milan.

An important exhibition run by the Italian Wine Union, it was established thanks to the intuition of four entrepreneurs: Nino Padovan, Aldo Gianazza, Santiago Carletti (Italian Oenological Agency) and Romolo Comini (Seveso Workshop).

The first fair had 170 exhibitors, of which 114 were Italians. It grew to 758, with 578 Italians. Then with mergers between companies, in 2013, there were 438 exhibitors. The exhibition is held at the fair in Rho.

The areas where the most important manufacturing centres are concentrated are Piedmont, Emilia-Romagna, Lombardy and Veneto, which are worth about 80% of production. This sector's contribution to the renaissance of Italian wine was decisive.

The advent of what we call "mechanical oenology" meant the permanent downfall of "chemical oenology", which was dominant until the early 1970s. Knowledge applied to technology allowed us to make that monumental leap which was an integral part of our success in world markets. Innovation and improved technologies bring back our production to the naturalness of a time when everything was done manually, without adjuvants, but with wines that had a low resistance to transport. This was a momentous achievement.

In 2015, the year of Expo Milano, the Italian Wine Union celebrated its one hundred and twentieth anniversary. It was founded in Milan on 2 December 1895, on the initiative of a group of wine merchants, to address the issue of enlarging the city's customs barriers. The late nineteenth-century group was gradually joined by wholesale merchants, bottlers, winemakers, wholesalers, importers, distributors and manufacturers of winemaking machines. New challenges had been launched. Attilio Scienza, on the side-lines of the research and development project for the new "M" series rootstocks, said: "The young people on the Board of Directors, Marcello Lunelli and Domenico Zonin in particular, did some proselytizing among the members to convince them to form the Winegraft company, which guarantees the continuation of the project research. They have never despaired of achieving the goal. The fate of our vines and oenology is in their hands. If they are able to address the problems of this sector with this kind of spirit, our future will be brighter." *W.F.*

Indigenous Wines

Mario Busso, Walter Filiputti, Attilio Scienza

Facing and following pages
Aglianico di Taurasi grown like *tennecchia* or pergolas ("Patriarch" vineyard, Feudi di San Gregorio)

In the words of Attilio Scienza: "The world of wine needs to find new sources of narrative." One possibility, undoubtedly one of the most fascinating, leads to recovery of antique vine varieties, what we call the "patriarchs" of our viticultural history. Many Italian winegrowers have already travelled this route. From Caprai to Montefalco and Feudi di San Gregorio in Irpinia, at Mastroberardino with the vineyard inside the walls of Pompeii, as far as Bisol in Venissa (Venice) with Dorona and, of course, in Friuli where the movement for indigenous varieties first blossomed.

The "Patriarchs" of Italian Wine

The "patriarchs" carry a scent of the Orient. With their moral authority, they have led peoples out of natural and spiritual deserts. The etymological significance of the Greek word *patriarchēs* is "founder of a family (or a clan)".

Vines of eighty to one hundred years of age stimulate surprise and admiration. Prior to the phylloxera era, there were many examples of plants ageing 300 to 400 years. A vine in the province of Novara was claimed, in the 1920s, to be 445 years old. At the time of the French Revolution, vines on the upper part of the Clos de Vougeot vineyard were then 400 to 500 years old. Even today, there is a famous 300-year-old vine at the Jesuit college of Reims. The 30 kg of grapes it produces are used to make wine for mass. The vine of Versolan, a variety that is practically extinct, has been present in the town of Prissiano (Alto Adige) for over 350 years, at least. Along the Amalfi coast and in Irpinia in Campania, it is not difficult to find vines of Tintore, Aglianco and Sirica that are over 250 years of age.

Saint Albertus Magnus had this to say about the importance of old vines: "Older vines produce better grapes that yield better wine, but when young, the vine produces fewer grapes in proportion to its age".

These observations, penned in the thirteenth century, were recently confirmed by the results of a Swiss study. The quality of wine produced by grapes from forty- to fifty-year-old vines was found to be superior to that from vines of seven to eight years. This was especially true for red fruits because of the greater balance they have, resulting in better tolerance of climate change, in particular, of prolonged drought.

It is only natural to wonder what the source of such longevity can be. Just as for humans, this depends on many factors: genetics and diet, lifestyle and sentiments. Similarly, vine longevity is not a casual result, but depends on specific choices of the winegrower. A short survey of the places in Italy where such vines are found reveals that the common denominator linking these examples of longevity in viticulture is the method of dry pruning.

Some ten to twenty years ago, the panorama of Italian viticulture was full of "patriarchs". The economics of vineyard management and the rapid mutation of consumer preferences accelerated their disappearance. Today they are present only in a few marginal vineyards with a very traditional approach.

The forms of cultivation and the pruning techniques that protected and, in a certain sense, led to conservation of these plants are the most archaic (bush vines, extended arbours, vines on trees, etc.). They did not restrict the natural expression of vegetation in its form as climbing vines. In alternative, spur pruning saved the plant from the irreparable damage caused by cutting the old wood.

What should be done with the "patriarchs" that remain? First, the problem of their extinction should be discussed to demonstrate that this would be a grave loss for Italian viticulture, not merely for the aesthetic values offered by the plants, but above all for the information that their genomes can offer.

Not only for the secrets of their longevity, but because they can reveal the mystery of vine formation in European viticulture.

To prevent a rapid erosion of the surviving examples, in addition to onsite conservation activities, offsite collections should be formed to host the offspring of the "patriarchs".

Well then, what is so special about grape vines? A glance at a map of their distribution in Europe immediately reveals that they are present at the sites of the great Mediterranean civilisations. There seems to be a sort of underlying empathy between humans and grape vines. Wherever they have settled, the grape vine has become an essential element of daily life. This is yet another reason to prolong this partnership with the "patriarchs", even in our time. *A.S.*

The Indigenous Vine Movement Thanks to the Nonino Risit d'Âur Prize

How curious it is that grappa enacted the cultural movement in favour of the indigenous Italian varieties in danger of extinction. This is how Giannola Nonino tells the story: "At the end of the 1960s, grappa was considered a coarse form of distilled alcohol and a legacy of poverty, cold and hunger. I read Luigi Veronelli's column in *Panorama* magazine where he urged winegrowers to make their wines cru by cru, vineyard by vineyard, without mixing them together. So it happened that after years of research and tasting, I found the winning idea: to do for grappa what Veronelli suggested for wine. On 1 December 1973 in the Percoto distillery, Benito revolutionised a world that had been following the beaten track for centuries. He created the first grappa called Monovitigna Picolit and registered the name as a trademark. It was distilled exclusively from the pomace of Picolit grapes, the noblest variety in Friuli Venezia Giulia. We dedicated the distillation to Gino Veronelli, who was invited to attend the historic event. When I asked him how much we owed him he replied, 'Madame, it is for me to thank you for having involved me in this historic moment, giving me the possibility to write about it before anyone else.' Years later, Veronelli added, 'What Giannola and Benito accomplished was the start of a revolution that succeeded thanks to the genius and folly of the protagonists and the faithful steadfastness of their magical daughters. They no longer distil only pomace or grapes, they distil the earth, the culture and the ways of life.'"

Monovitigno Picolit rapidly became the favourite of the most demanding consumers. On the one hand, Benito radically transformed the production method: fresh slightly fermented pomace distilled in separate batches for each variety, using artisan stills. On the other hand, Giannola revolutionised the image, the packaging and marketing strategies. In a single season, the Nonino duo transformed the qualitative parameters of grappa. These had seemed to be consolidated and immovable. Instead, grappa became one of the great distilled beverages of the world. Giannola continues: "After Picolit, we decided that separate distillation should continue for the indigenous grape varieties: Schioppettino, Pignolo and Tazzelenghe. To obtain the separate pomace variety by variety, we offered 2,000 Lira per kilo instead of quintal [*100 kg*]. However, aside from Picolit, the names of these vines could not be cited in invoices because officially they no longer existed. The authorities had not included them in the EEC roll of the varieties cultivated in Friuli, thus effectively condemning them to certain death. To save them, or lose our identity if we failed, we offered a prize of one million Lira and the 'golden vine shoot' [*Risit d'Âur in the dialect of Friuli*] to the winegrower who creates the best plantation of one or more of these varieties, while respecting the historic traditions of the vine varieties themselves. There was also a scholarship of 500,000 Lira for the author of the best technical and historic research paper demonstrating that the vine was indigenous and cultivated for centuries in a specific zone. The Nonino Risit d'Âur Prize was announced on 29 November 1975. It was published in an article by *Messaggero Veneto* and in an interview that Isi Benini, director of RAI [*Italian national television*] facilities in Udine at that time, conducted during a very popular radio programme dedicated to 'life in the fields.'"

It was a daring declaration of war against an absurd law and the reaction was immediate. "On the Monday following publication of the competition, several officers of the regional Agriculture Department came to our offices and threatened us with a fine of 300,000 Lira per hectare and uprooting all the shoots of these varieties planted by any winegrowers if we did not annul the competition. They also promised to burn grafts of the same varieties in the plant nurseries. At the same time, Piero Pittaro reported us in *Il Punto* magazine: 'Nonino incites planting forbidden vine varieties.'"

For years, the family was the object of reports and was targeted for tax inspections, but this merely increased Giannola's ardour in the battle. "To overcome the obstacle we included the authorities, who were supposed to punish the participants, on the jury and we obtained authorisation for experimental cultivation of Schioppettino, Pignolo and Tazzelenghe." It was the first protection for the winegrowers who cultivated these varieties and Benito was able to distil the first Schioppettino Grappa with the vine name written on the label. On 5 February 1979, EEC regulation no. 347/79, with effect from 12 March 1978, authorised cultivation in the province of Udine. In December 1983, EEC regulation no. 3582/83 included the three varieties among recommended vine varieties.

This is how the Premio Nonino Risit d'Âur won the battle for which it was created and gave birth to the movement to protect and return numerous indigenous Italian grape vine varieties to production, which now represent the future of Italian oenology on world markets.

On 24 February 1985, Giuseppe Turani wrote in *La Repubblica*: "Nonino products have become something of a legend in the world . . . If you try to understand the workings of this strange company, you will discover that it is a mix of ancient artisan tradition, the art of living, commercial acumen, maniacal attachment to a trade and the most sophisticated and up-to-date marketing". R.W. Apple, Jr. chimed in from *The New York Times* on 31 December 1997: "For decades, grappa was little more than a portable form of heating for the farmers of Northern Italy. Fashionable Italians and most foreigners disdained it. But this was all before the Nonino family of Percoto came to the forefront."

To educate the world about grappa, from 1977 Nonino added the Literature Prize to accompany the Premio Nonino Risit d'Âur. From 1983, the competition became the Inter-

national Nonino Prize to defend farmer civilisation, nature and humans.

Giannola understood the need to link the product to its territory. In the long term, this was one of her clearest visions. At that time no wine producer in Italy, and certainly not in Friuli, knew how to put this link into practice. Today, it has become strategic for the success of a brand.

That is why the wines of Friuli Venezia Giulia owe so much to Nonino grappa. It made a decisive contribution to creating awareness of this fine microcosm. It also guided all of Italy to comprehend the cultural duty, and related economic benefits, of recovering the great Italian indigenous varieties. *W.F.*

Italy: Nation of Diversity

On 3 August 2013 Monica Larner, who lives in Rome and had recently been named the correspondent of *The Wine Advocate* for Italian wines, gave an interview to *Corriere della Sera*. She was enthusiastic about indigenous Italian wines and declared the necessity of "continuing to make Americans more aware of what no other country in the world possesses, an extraordinary wealth of different wines, very distant from standardised tastes . . . The search is completely different now, wine lovers of America now want the least known of the indigenous wines. The great reds of Piedmont and Tuscany are still the banner bearers, but this is the moment to talk up the other wonders of Italy. Parker agrees".

Fantastic news for those (not many to tell the truth) who fought and believed in the recovery of extraordinary vines for modern times. I am honoured to belong to this group of slightly mad visionaries. It was quite unthinkable to propose Ribolla Gialla in New York or Munich in 1982. Pignolo on foreign markets in 1985 was also taboo. And yet, that dream has come true.

Yes, the idea we had then has turned out to be right. Those indigenous wines all over Italy were the true force that no one had. Even many winegrowers had no notion of their possibilities. "Wines that no one else in the world has," as Monica Larner put it. These timeless wines intrigue, charm and are loved by young people, too. They have a touch of diversity that makes the difference. Reading that phrase took me back to the beginning of my career in the mid-1970s. Many producer colleagues derided us back in those days. It is no accident that Luigi Veronelli, a philosopher, and the Nonino family, a family distiller business, inspired the recovery of indigenous varieties. Consumers, however, immediately listened to our ideas. They gave us the energy to go forward.

The reasons? Ancient varieties are, and will continue to be, formidable witnesses to the uniqueness of Italian wine production. Of course, we know that the force of the market can be destructive at times, especially if the reaction is passive, and the dominance of international markets is undeniable. This does not mean that there is no space for these wines. Quite the contrary!

The "patriarchs", as presented by Attilio Scienza, are priceless as far as their genetic and cultural value is concerned (like the writings of Sophocles and Aristotle, still so contemporary today), but also keystones of market strategy. Their status with respect to international wines is like that of couture (the indigenous) with respect to prêt-à-porter.

While it is necessary to follow market trends, it is also wise to know how to navigate along the borderline to find a personal place to shine. These sought-after spaces reinforce the company image and contribute to the image of a prosperous Italy, too, with a dowry of these varieties unlike any other nation. This history and this heritage must produce a return!

A distinguished position on the market, with unique products for niche targets, is a requirement, just as for handmade watches, shoes, bags and clothes, even if the niches are larger thanks to globalization. A chic product is one that more than any other succeeds in telling a story, capturing and pulling along a listener with its message of unique emotions, and even the rest of the production. Markets do not shy away from novelties, but welcome them. The problem is how to present and propose them.

We leave the last word on this subject to the American journalist Matt Kramer, so famous and respected for his seriousness, who wrote in *The Wine Spectator* on 30 June 2013: "Do you think that at this moment the most important word in wine is 'natural'? Or 'authentic'? Or better still 'commercial'? None of these. The most important word in wine today is 'authochthonous' (*indigenous*)." Even though everything that occurs in the vineyard and the cellar is important, nothing is as essential as three key elements: microclimate, terrain and vine. Indigenous wines have an integrity that only time and local tradition have conferred, even before globalized brands invaded the market. The market is full of good wines. But nothing can equal an indigenous wine because it's impossible to reproduce. *W.F.*

Indigenous Wines Have Won the Challenge of Globalization

Biologist Edward O. Wilson, in his book *The Diversity of Life. The New Ethics of Ecology* (W.W. Norton, 1999), sustains that all nations have three kinds of heritage, or legacy: material, cultural and biological. Together with material and cultural wealth, biological diversity is another form of wealth on this planet.

The microcosm of Italy alone has the richest mosaic of indigenous grape vine varieties on the planet: over 1,500 known varieties of which 361 are written in the Roll of Varieties utilised in the production of wine.

The success obtained by indigenous Italian wines does not depend only on the capacity demonstrated in recent years by Italian winegrowers to raise the quality of their productions, but on their valorisation of the immaterial aspects of wine, which interact with its quality and can, if elevated to a systematic approach, also contribute to promotion of a territory.

Much has been done in this sense, but it is not yet sufficient. If the territory factor is accompanied by use of varieties that were born and have evolved together with the men who cultivated them for centuries, if technique is accompanied by history, and history by marketing capable of giving it added value, the result will be even more positive. This is why the techniques of promotion and sales cannot ignore the bond that wine, especially Italian wine, has with its territory and its history. The possibility of associating wine with a territory, its gastronomy, the beauty of its landscape, its archaeological findings, its architecture and the people who live and work in the territory is an element that also heightens the perception of quality in its wines. This happens in Italy. Thus, wine is an important vehicle for making local cultures known. By reflex, promotional activity intended to create a system of synergistic promotion of the various elements composing the culture of a given territory, will augment the degree of preference and loyalty of consumers for the wine itself. Many recent surveys confirm that if at the time of tasting, the mind can recall the knowledge or emotions stimulated by the landscape, that wine will undoubtedly receive a greater level of preference than wine whose origins are unknown.

Claude Lévi-Strauss loved to quip "good thoughts, good eating", alluding to the greater inclination to express a positive evaluation when the consumer recalls a product's place of origin, in this case, that of the wine in the glass. While wine producers have taken giant steps in comprehending the great potential of Italian viticulture in recent years, much remains to be done at the political level to make the uniqueness, rarity and diversity of Italian vines known throughout the world. *M.B.*

From DOC to DOCG: Rules Supporting a Competitive Marketplace

Walter Filiputti

. . . That "930" Law

The DOC protocol, promoted and submitted to Parliament by Paolo Desana (senator from Piedmont), was dated 12 July 1963 and split wine producers into opposing factions right from when it was being compiled.

At the time, the wine community in Italy was in poor shape. Changes were far off. Vittorio Fiore, an oenologist born and raised by his Italian-speaking family in Alto Adige/South Tyrol, later made Tuscany his second home where he began his consulting work in 1972, has observed: "In those years, the leitmotiv in Tuscany was to ensure that wine was available to all at an affordable price. It was an easy concept, because tradesmen controlled the market." At the time, of course, wine was treated as a food, but that was destined to change. The salesmen had no wish to change their habits and were not able to perceive the rapid transformation of the world that was in fact unfolding right before their very eyes. It seems incredible, but many of the great families dedicated to wine commerce were convinced, again in the words of Fiore, that "they should leave it to the French to make good wines, and not only Tuscany. In Piedmont, a vintner chose French wines for his public relations gifts at Christmas time."

"Before the '930'," wrote Andrea Gabbrielli in *Terre del vino* (January–February 2012), "a bottle of Valpolicella could have been produced in Siena, or similarly in Milan or Catania indifferently". The Agricultural Commission of the Senate found that the facts demonstrated "it was possible to produce wines classified with typical geographical denominations in any town of Italy, at no risk and without possessing either rights to the location or even the characteristics that had contributed to the prestige and success of wine consumption" (Parliamentary Acts, Agricultural Commission of the Senate, minutes of the hearing held on 27 June 1952).

Certainly, introduction of the DOC protocols had a profoundly positive effect. Many of them brought refined areas of Italian production to public attention. Unfortunately, the invisible but terribly weighty army opposing any change succeeded in making the new system less potent than it could and should have been. In the words of Vittorio Fiore: "Even bad weather was a factor – in Central and Northern Italy at that time we were fortunate to get three excellent years in a decade (now the opposite is true) – contributing to the practice of blending the production with wines from the South. In any case, the French were doing the same, particularly in Bordeaux, with Sicilian and Sardinian wines." (The revolt of the Midi winegrowers in the port of Sète, France, in 1981 to block tanker ships and lorries carrying Italian wine was also a consequence of this practice. The dispute was not resolved until 1985 in Nice when the wine agreement between France and Italy was signed.)

It is necessary to review some history to comprehend the viticultural situation at that time. Just five years after the EEC was founded on 25 March 1957, the European Agricultural Guarantee Fund (generally abbreviated FEOGA) was enacted in 1962. The purpose was to guarantee earnings for producers of agricultural goods and to orient them to producing mainly what the market requested. This mechanism immediately revealed a defect: the objective of the guarantee prevailed over orientation. As a result, the first and only scope obtained was quantity. As they say in Veneto, "Peso el tacòn del buso" (the patch is worse than the hole).

As mentioned above, the DOC protocol divided, instead of uniting, the viticultural world. The industrialists stood on one side and were much more imposing than their adversaries, the winegrowers led by Luigi Veronelli. The author, from the earliest phase of drafting the law, took a stand against the very structure of it because it did not defend quality and, more importantly, it was not based on a pyramidal quality structure inspired by the Burgundy model.

The "damned" industrialists, as Veronelli called them, won the day, but it was indeed a flimsy victory. The first rumblings of a coming storm were heard when the most sophisticated of the winegrowers began to renew their wines and had to call them "table wines" because they were not included in the protocols. Here are some voices of the protagonists of the "930".

- Piero Antinori reflects on the Chianti Classico DOC in his narration of the creation of his Tignanello: "The Chianti DOC was introduced in Tuscany in 1967. Many producers mistakenly believed that the innovation would automatical-

ly bring commercial success. I was not convinced by this hunt for a DOC just for the sake of having a DOC. In many respects, the protocol revealed a conservative spirit and was already behind the times. It crystallised a method precisely at the time it was revealing its age and inadequacy. It left no space for experimentation and personal initiative".

- **Sandro Boscaini of the Masi group:** "In my undergraduate thesis I had sustained that emanating the DOC protocols would have helped the denominations of the microzones dedicated to quality production to prevail over individual brands. The truth is that the brands open the way and the viticultural microzones follow in their wake. It seemed that the vineyard had become an optional for wine producers. The industrialists of wine smirked and wrote us off as farmers, but time has proven us right. We have represented the territory where they have had to return to stay in the game. At the time, the wine industry dominated the marketplace, but was not able to respond to the emerging demand for quality linked to the territory from the new consumer".

- **Hugh Johnson**, in his *The Story of Wine* of 1989, wrote that a DOC represents the idea that any wine made recently is the best that its region can produce. So all it accomplishes is freezing the status quo. For him, the best producers make many of their best wines outside of protocols. In fact, he believes that today at least half of the best Italian wines are downgraded to table wines.

We had to wait for the "930" reform in Law no. 164 of 1992 to overcome this nonsense. As Piero Antinori would later remark: "The wine generated the law, and not the contrary" because the new Chianti Classico DOC traced the production model of his Tignanello!

- **Vittorio Fiore**: "The misconception of the '930' was in its very scope. The consideration was that the existing situation of wine production in Italy at that precise historical time represented the greatest potential quality that could be attained, so it had no need for improvements, not to mention viticultural or oenological evolution. Practically speaking, each wine aspiring to become a DOC was treated as a sort of archaeological find to be catalogued. This was the origin of the table wines paradox".

"Table Wine", an Italian Paradox

Oenological techniques, together with the demand from new international markets, led, as seen, to the creation of wines that went against the tide of DOCs, which were rigid and born old. Many producers followed the road of innovation – ageing in *barriques*, new mixes of varieties and reduced yield per hectare – to obtain decidedly superior wines that were in step with their times. They saw the DOC protocol like a straitjacket, insensitive to change. They also perceived a negative commercial message that lowered the value of their wines. At the conference held at Castagneto Carducci in 1990 to discuss the DOC, one of the speakers was Luigi Veronelli. He quoted a letter published "Legislazione vinicola" in May 1990, written by a group of winegrowers from Veneto: "Until now, we have refused to sell our wines with DOC or DOCG labels essentially for two reasons. First, our blend of varieties is undoubtedly better than the local DOC, but it does not follow the parameters of the protocol, so we are obliged to call the product a 'table wine'. Second, we refuse to give our wines the same name as the DOC, because it has often been used scandalously by other producers".

Thus, it is no accident that many who would make the history of Italian oenology were united under that same banner.

It is also interesting and curious to note that it was the international press that ranked these wines highest, creating a sort of Italian paradox. This transformed a denomination chosen to define low-quality products into a symbol of taste innovation and absolute quality. These "table wines" opened the way to conquer world markets.

Andrea Gabbrielli helps to focus on subjects of great interest: "The revolution of the Super Tuscans was born of the will to meet the new demands of the market. The introduction of other grape varieties, with respect to the Chianti protocol, was originally a 'necessary choice' to overcome some insufficiencies of the wines such as structure, colour, texture, etc. With the breath of innovation in the vineyards and the wineries, the selection of grape varieties became a matter of company style. Today, recalling that experience serves as an invitation to keep an open and flexible mind with regard to changes on the international scene . Remember-

ing the Super Tuscans is a matter of method rather than merit . . . In light of the rigidity of the DOC protocols, there is always a need for a space, such as the current IGT regulations, where companies and producers can express their creativity while maintaining a link with the Italian system of denominations."

This space must be maintained and expanded because "it is the space where the inventions of tomorrow will grow. The clash in the world is between viticulture of the territory and viticulture of the vine," Gabbrielli continues. "We have a duty to create innovative formulas that can include the positive elements of both models, so that we can try to compete on our adversary's ground [vine] while also relying on the strong points of our territory model."

Vinitaly: A Fair, an International Community and Merano WineFestival

Mario Busso, Walter Filiputti, Cesare Pillon

Verona: Italian Wine Embassy open to the World

Would the "renaissance of Italian wine" have had such a deep impact on the history and economy of Italy without Vinitaly? Surely it would not. This fair, today so central to the Italian viticultural system, was founded without much ado, to fill a gap. At the Agricultural Fair, the most important of the fairs held in Verona, fewer and fewer visitors found their way to the two pavilions dedicated to wine. Instead, they flocked to the stands exhibiting spectacular combine harvesters and tractors. Evidently, very few operators were capable of comprehending that the flop of 1964 was a sign of a turnover and that it would mark the change of an epoch: the end of the farmer tradition as known until then.

The nation was industrialising, lifestyles were changing and wine was no longer a food but a pleasure. One of the few to grasp the importance of the change, and the new opportunities it would offer, was Angelo Betti, the chief of the press office who would become secretary general of the Fair in 1976.

Betti immediately realised that Antonio Niederbacker, director of the Italian Wine Union, was right when, in response to a request for advice from the directors of the Verona fair, he suggested the abolition of those two pavilions and the organisation of an event dedicated entirely to wine. But, how should such a fair be structured? As a journalist, it was clear to Betti that the most urgent task was to talk about wine in a different way. A refurbishing project was needed and Niederbacher claimed he had the right person at hand to unite the ideas and inspirations that would be necessary: a university student writing a thesis about the perspectives of wine marketing.

That student was Sandro Boscaini, who would later play a leading role in the international success of Amarone. At that early date, he already demonstrated his talent for taking advantage of opportunities. When he was hired for a year at the fair, he proceeded to collect material for his thesis at Bocconi University, also for the viticultural show still in the preliminary phase.

With the proposals collected by Boscaini, Angelo Betti had a series of guidelines for revolutionising the methods of presenting wines that had been in use until that time. Such a radical change of course could not be implemented from one day to the next. In 1967, he began to probe interest by organising a two-day event, the "Italian Wine Days" in Palazzo della Gran Guardia on 22–23 September. It was an occasion for many debates, conferences and round tables to discuss the most difficult themes facing viticulture and oenology.

Boscaini's principal suggestion, to endow the "Days" with cultural importance that would, at last, acknowledge the nobility of wine, was so well received and achieved such an unexpected level of participation that Betti was encouraged to proceed in the same direction. Since then, the fair in Verona has continued to expand every year by hosting more companies, occupying more space and examining new themes, but never superficially. The debates and conferences have stimulated interdisciplinary exchanges of ideas that were a novelty in the world of wine and contributed to the qualitative improvement of Italian viticulture.

Paradoxically, Betti encountered the greatest difficulty when, in 1969, he decided that the "Italian Wine Days" should become a full-blown viticultural and oenological fair. It was not easy to convince exhibitors to leave the Agricultural Fair, which drew 600,000–700,000 visitors at the time, to undertake a new adventure with a new fair, the success of which was unknown to all. The ideas elaborated by Boscaini were very important in convincing them: the possibility to taste the wines presented at the show was supported to attract an interested public (today known as "wine lovers"). Scheduling in November, closer to Christmas, was intended to induce visitors to consider bottles of wine as prestigious gifts. These ideas may seem obvious today, but at the time they were brilliant intuitions. In fact, Betti succeeded in obtaining the presence of some 130 wine producers.

It took approximately four years of experience to refine the structure of the fair. During the same years, the appreciation of wine, which until then had been marketed as a bulk product, began to rise with regard to bottled products. In fact, the first DOC wines, instituted by Law no. 930 in 1963, were appearing on the market.

With his foresight, Betti was convinced that Italian viticultural production would have a solid future only if the qual-

ity level was sufficient to achieve success abroad via exportation. This is why he baptised the event with the name Vinitaly when the salon of viticultural and oenological activities was launched in 1971. After achieving the first objective – to make the Fair of Verona the primary showcase of Italian wine and bring in foreign buyers from around the world – in 1998, he sought to achieve the same result by doing the opposite. That was to export Vinitaly and make it the ambassador and representative of its own exhibitors, by creating a network of solid institutional and commercial relationships. At first called Vinitaly in the World, later known as Vinitaly International, for the past fifteen years it has been a travelling show presiding over strategic export markets such as China, United States, Russia, Japan and Hong Kong with hundreds of seminars, tasting sessions and workshops. The winegrower, who can meet the international marketplace here, is at long last represented for the first time with equal dignity to large companies and can react with creativity, having found the stage where such qualities are appreciated. This is the theatre that became a legend in the 1980s when the stand of Giacomo Bologna in pavilion no. 9 "was the place to meet the world to share a generous portion of *salame cotto* and a glass of Barbera La Monella". Angelo Betti claimed that, ironically, Vinitaly had attracted foreign visitors from the start because Verona is the southernmost of German cities and that its success was so explosive, because of the success of Italian wines. However, he did note that Vinitaly had sponsored a multitude of initiatives to trigger that explosion.

From the 130 wine producers that Angelo Betti succeeded in bringing to the fair in 1969, the 2014 edition set a new record of 4,100 exhibitors, occupying an exposition area of 100,000 square meters, with requests exceeding availability. Over 50,000 foreign buyers attended from 120 countries. There were 155,000 visitors of which 56,000 (36%) were foreign professionals. Growing from the previous year, Vinitaly continues to take the pulse of the Italian oenological evolution. In fact, the 48th edition proposed Vinitalybio, organised in collaboration with Federbio (the organic farming federation) to give certified organic wines their own specific visibility. Thus, Vinitaly 2014 transformed organic wines from a niche product to a trend product. *C.P., W.F.*

The Best in Merano

There is another major event that has selected the best Italian wine production over the last twenty years. Founded in 1992, the Merano WineFestival owes its origin to the oenological and gastronomical passions of Helmuth Köcher who, together with two friends, organized the first event in Italy dedicated to the best oenological production, evaluated on the basis of the high level of the products submitted for admission. Each year, ten tasting committees create the "festival of excellence", selecting quality wines and the products of refined gastronomy. In recent years, over 500 wineries from Italy and abroad and over 100 Italian businesses of refined gastronomical products have participated. It all takes place in the splendid Alpine surroundings of Merano, in the art nouveau-style Kurhaus palace. Merano WineFestival now takes place together with Culinaria, the festival of traditional flavours, BeerPassion, dedicated to artisan beers, GourmetArena reserved to the most refined kitchens and bio&dynamica, which celebrates the excellence of organic, biodynamical and natural wine. Merano WineFestival, born from the fact of having embraced the concept of product quality from the first moment, unlike other events has continued to evolve offering space to new trends as they emerged from time to time in the world of wine. Its success has not only been in monitoring quality, but also in its capacity to identify winning trends. An example is the identification of the organic and biodynamical viticultural trend, a segment that has evolved and today is better reflected in the concept of environmental sustainability of the productions. *M.B.*

Oenology and Winegrowing: From Chemistry to Sustainability

*Antonio Calò, Walter Filiputti, Michele Mannelli,
Michele Morgante, Attilio Scienza, Angelo Solci,
Raffaele Testolin, Diego Tomasi*

A Revolution in the Wine Cellar

The early 1960s represented a decisive moment in the modern history of wine, and not only for Italians. A radical new concept emerged at the same time in many different places – from California to Australia, from South Africa to New Zealand. Wine was no longer a mysterious relic of ancient times, or simply a cheap way to get drunk, but an expression of a territory, the end product of technology and experience that had the power to enchant and bring pleasure to anyone. Furthermore, and this was the catch, none of the players wanted to surrender this whole business to the French. This leads to the conclusion that whenever we have witnessed a revolution in taste, the market has opened the way.

Tangible, incontestable and spectacular evidence of this planetary revolution comes from the Napa Valley where, in 1966, an Italian immigrant launched what would become his flagship for the last quarter of the century: the Robert Mondavi winery, which revived the spirit of the missions. His vineyard immediately illustrated the true splendour of new technology: great stainless steel tanks with temperature meticulously controlled by glycol in the external jacket. It was a huge investment, challenging major producers with the combination of quality and quantity that the most advanced technology could provide. He turned out to be right, and many followed his example. Mondavi switched from the empiricism of oenologists, jealous and protective of their trade, to consequential mathematical certainty, later strengthened by the arrival of computers.

His example led the way for all California and beyond, stimulating Italy as well. *A.So.*

The Path to Sustainable Oenology

The "renaissance of Italian wines" thus germinated during the radical transformation of oenology in the late 1960s that evolved into precision oenology, with all the inflections for each step of vinification: grape harvesting, pressing, fermentation, refinement, stabilisation, bottling and conservation of bottled wine. This process calls for cutting-edge cellar instrumentation. A visit to the SIMEI fair reveals the advanced level of all the products required to control the wine production process. Italian enterprises are sector leaders, confirming that excellence depends on the process, in addition to the product and the territory. Innovation for the equipment, particularly temperature management and the cold chain during fermentation and conservation, has drastically reduced the use of chemicals.

Italian oenologists play a key role in the battle to improve quality while respecting health and the environment. Today even less expensive wines are much superior to their counterparts of thirty years ago. They are clean, express the character of their origin and their vineyard and have smooth, balanced tannins. A strictly sustainable process guided by winegrowing technicians (today an oenologist is no longer an all-rounder) that guarantees a harvest of healthy, ripe grapes is an essential condition to initiate vinification protocols for clean, quality wines.

The improvement of harvesting technology, with delicate and precise grape harvesting machines, is approaching the quality of manual collection but at lower costs, shorter harvests and is much more precise in terms of the ideal harvest time for each variety.

Enormous progress in all phases of vinification makes it possible to radically reduce the use of sulphur dioxide (sulphites). The pneumatic presses used for white and rosé wines are a good example: their soft and delicate pressure is very similar to the pressing by foot used so many years ago. The latest generation of wines, rendered inert with nitrogen or carbon dioxide, represent the cutting-edge of vinification without sulphur dioxide: full realisation of all aromatic and flavour components of the grapes. Coordinated use of biotechnology – progressing at the same speed as oenological instruments – makes it possible to achieve significant quality objectives, with the option to select specific types depending on the organoleptic characteristics the oenologist wants to enhance.

For red wines, the delicate grape destemmer crushers detach the whole grape berries from the cluster, thus avoiding the unpleasantly bitter taste of the cluster stems and without breaking the grape skin. The polyphenols, consisting of tannins and anthocyanins, are extracted by controlled maceration in the presence of specialised enzymes. The nutritional requirements of the yeasts and their fermentation cycles are accurately determined so that nitrogen compounds and vitamins can be precisely dosed. Together with temperature management, this allows regular fermentation with low sulphur dioxide dosage and prevents interruption of fermentation. Some years ago, this frequent problem led to unpleasant flavours and products with no market.

The oenologist decides whether to use selected dry yeasts or to launch the spontaneous fermentation of the indigenous yeasts depending on the condition of the grapes. The oenological industry offers an infinity of active dry yeasts selected for diverse oenological properties, extracted from many grape varieties grown around the world. Although it is not possible to obtain all the organoleptic qualities of the new wine in this phase, a significant aspect – its keeping quality – does emerge in these first few days. That is why products of biotechnology and the most costly and expensive technological instruments are employed, even for very short periods during vinification and successive processes.

All tanks, autoclaves, filters, pumps, etc. used for vinification are made of special stainless steels: AISI 304 and AISI 316. The Englishman Harry Brearley of Sheffield discovered the use of this material in 1913. Successive progress in metallurgy between the 1940s and 1960s gave modern oenology an extraordinary instrument for hygiene and temperature control.

Equipped with these instruments, the oenologist determines the type and the duration of fermentation, pumping over, stirring the lees and *delestage* operations, etc., which can be computer controlled to avoid timing and process errors.

The possibility to trigger and control malolactic fermentation at desired intervals is another great step forward for precision, quality oenology. Organoleptic improvement is accompanied by greater food safety. Selection and guaranteed purity of bacteria has effectively eliminated wine disorders that were endemic until the 1960s and 1970s: acescence, ropiness, amertume and oxidation.

Oxygen management, using special diffusion devices to deliver the stoichiometric quantities calculated by oenologist, represents another milestone of progress in winemaking.

For red wines in particular, this technique has achieved chromatic stability and clean flavours while reducing sulphite dosages.

The oenologist considers consumer health even during the final clarification and finishing processes. In addition to mechanical methods such as centrifuging, filtering and refrigeration, the oenologist can also employ allergen-free products that eliminate unstable components and unbalanced taste.

Today, leading wine cellars are the result of architectural projects where functionality must coexist with spaces for public relations at the production site, so dear to wine lovers who want to learn production secrets and know the stories of the personalities and the territory. Modern *barrique* and cask cellars have become meeting places. Extreme cleanliness and attention are dedicated to refinement in wood to obtain the right balance between the flavours of the grape varieties and the delicate vanilla aromas of the wood.

Finally, sophisticated equipment in bottling rooms is worth admiring. The final phase of wine production is similar to the packaging of pharmaceuticals. Hygiene and pollution prevention are primary concerns. Hazard Analysis and Critical Control Point (HACCP) and International Organization for Standardization (ISO) standards are very strict. The packaging process is automatic. Beautiful designs and materials characterise the bottles, which consumers appreciate and enjoy.

Future development of these modern technologies will depend on those who put passion and creativity into their work. Oenological studies and cellar experience will not suffice. Courage and the will to experiment and innovate will be necessary. The oenologist of the future will have to know what to do and what to say. It will not suffice to be just a well-prepared technician. It will require culture, both specific knowledge and broader interests, to take on the technological and environmental mutations.

Without knowledge, quality will be inaccessible. Success will depend on the science of oenology, research, study and experimentation. Our time is favourable because the whole wine-related sector is on the right path to sustainability. Sustainable wine, as mentioned, but also sustainable enterprise management. *A.So.*

Sulphite Additives

Sulphite additives call for further consideration. Oenological research and technologies have made it possible to reduce them to levels that would have been unthinkable in the past. The renaissance of oenology was born with the DNA of sustainability, because it took a stance against cellar processes that relied on the worst aspects of chemistry: the ones that do not require investments, wisdom or preparation. This was the first battle first-generation winegrowers faced, and they won it!

This launched the oenological revolution, and carried Italian wines around the globe.

Now another important and positive process is taking place. The pioneers of organic viticulture are winning over most Italian winegrowers and their pragmatic approach.

The decision of Vinitaly 2014 (which has always expressed the status of the Italian oenological evolution) to dedicate pavilion 11 to organic wines transformed them from niche to trend products and confirmed their rising prospects. A critical aspect is the confirmation of the quality target, one of the most essential but also criticized points regarding these wines from their origin. This is good news for Italian wine in general and is the result of oenologist commitment to sustainability and quality at the same time.

If we consider the differences between organic wines and so-called conventional ones – an ugly term for wines that are the exact opposites of conventional, better just to call them sustainable – the differences are much reduced if not eliminated altogether.

Mauro Lunelli, of the Ferrari cellars, says: "The studies I did on oxidation of white wines enabled me to define vinification techniques with drastically reduced sulphite content. For spumante that meant approximately 50 mg/l when 250 was the norm".

The "vinification techniques" are important. It is a mechanical oenology, not chemical.

Silvio Jermann, one of the best and most honoured white wine producers in Italy says: "The decision to use screw caps was the single factor that allowed for a further 25% reduction of sulphites! Now my wines don't exceed 80–100 mg/l and we'll try to reduce that further as we go forward".

Reduction of sulphites is a common objective for all producers, and many protocols aim for wine production without sulphite "additives". *A.So.*

Another Style of Communication

To be honest, wine is no longer just wine, but also marketing, communication, storytelling, image and positioning. In this case, the game is different, because the patterns do not depend on the laws, but represent the concepts of the enterprise, just like the wine. These strategies must have a solid foundation of ethical conduct, which must always be present. The risk stems from confusing, or cleverly intermingling, the two aspects: production and marketing.

Perhaps a metaphor will make this point clear.

When Gualtiero Marchesi began, Italian cooking changed radically and began a new sort of development that would make it the leading cuisine in the world. At that time, the end of the 1970s, many took a hard position against Gualtiero. The orthodox crowd, led by Franco Colombani, immediately founded the "Linea Italia in Cucina" association to oppose the blasphemous ideas of the newcomer. The author admired both and both offered fine dining. Initially, they had two quite separate substantial and aesthetic viewpoints.

The final result was that both schools "absorbed" from each other just like wine and wood, and that osmosis created true masterpieces. Gualtiero Marchesi transformed old-fashioned Italian cooking into modern cuisine, while the Colombani group incorporated the lessons of the great Marchesi (short cooking, aesthetics of presentation, clean flavours) while still remaining traditionalists. In the end, both Italian cuisine and the consumer were winners.

This sort of stimulating competition is extremely advantageous for consumers, in terms of wine excellence and healthfulness. As it should be. It had never happened before in the history of this millennial product. *W.F.*

A *Barrique* Is Like Bread in the Oven: A Few Minutes Too Long and It Burns

The introduction of *barriques* was overwhelming in Italy. It took place following an intuition of Mario Incisa della

Rocchetta for his Sassicaia. Later, in 1971, the first vintage of Tignanello by Marquis Piero Antinori came from *barriques*.

The vinification model was French because the consultant to Antinori and his oenologist at the time, Giacomo Tachis, was Émile Peynaud. The style does not exalt the wood, which still characterises these wines, especially Sassicaia (one-third new *barriques*, one-third first passage and one-third second passage) unlike the Californian character of Lodovico Antinori's wines (Ornellaia, Masseto and now Biserno) who wanted Tchelistcheff, the head priest of American oenology, next to himself.

In the end, the Italian style was born, too: polite, elegant and modest as in the Sorì by Angelo Gaja, for example. This style sets off the unique qualities of our wines, especially the indigenous vines. The revolution went forward by clicks, then settled and found new balance.

I was among the enthusiastic admirers of the new style.

The role of the *barrique* was analysed, and still is, often losing sight of the numerous innovations it set into motion.

When the *barrique* arrived in cellars, it brought great advantages with it.

Of course, the quality attained by Italian wines did not depend only on the *barrique*. That would have been too simple. The *caratello*, as Veronelli defined it, was only one of the many components of the quality itself. Renzo Cotarella is right when he says "the *barrique* is like a mini skirt that doesn't look well on every woman."

However, its introduction was providential, because it forced the winegrowers to design their wine projects. They had to reconsider their own supply lines. Its use immediately demonstrated to the most observant winegrowers that it was necessary to rethink the whole process, starting from the vineyard. There were fewer returns, grapes were cultivated to perfect ripeness, maceration of the colour and tannins were under observation. That was the moment when we all understood that given the same baggage of knowledge and oenological innovations, the vineyard could make the difference. This monumental achievement raised quality expectations and is now widely followed.

The *barrique* also made a significant contribution to reviving the nobility and second youth of many ancient indigenous vines and launching them successfully on the markets of the world. I am thinking of my Pignolo. From a red wine found only in books it became a wine with international prestige, capable of ageing for more than thirty years! This happened everywhere in Italy: Taurasi and Nero d'Avola, Negroamaro and Sangiovese, Nebbiolo and the list continues.

Of course, use of the small barrels was not limited to the indigenous vines only. It enhanced the potential of all of Oenotria, above all in terms of quantity, for the international vines.

It also influenced the production of classic method spumante, finding a typically Italian style as was only right, compared to that of Krug in Champagne, where wood predominates. For years, our leading classic spumante producers used small kegs with several passages to refine part of their base wines. They expected the wood not to become the dominant note, but to add a silent extension and silkiness to the flavour while retaining freshness. *W.F.*

Italian Viticulture: An Archipelago of Communities, Vibrations and Cultural Islands

Erri De Luca has written that the boot shape of Italy has never served to kick away the peoples who have approached. Instead, given its position in the middle of the Mediterranean, it has always welcomed them and given them the possibility to interact with the original populations while developing commercial, agricultural and cultural activities. This meeting of men, traders and immigrants has created an infinity of interfaces in our country, meaning cultural borderlines where the infinite expressions of the agricultural and alimentary kaleidoscope that the whole world envies us were born.

Whenever a population enters the territory of another, a frontier is created and one of two possible scenarios can follow. There can be opposing forces that maintain the stability of the two separate cultures. Or, alternatively, the two cultures can join at the conditions dictated by the stronger of the two.

Borders are notorious for being the site of crises, ethnic tensions and contrasts, but also exchange, regulation of di-

verse systems and of innovation. Anthropologists call these edge effects of cultural expression. A border is, in fact, a cultural paradox that can be a place of separation (where so-called parallel cultures take form) and, at the same time, a place for meeting and mergers or convergence. Italy, situated as it is between Orient and Occident, along the routes that populations have followed in all eras, is the most convincing evidence of the outcome of so many cultural encounters.

This continuous flux of peoples and goods brought with it specialised productions such as fabrics, vases, amphora, crystal and wines, but above all people, cultivations and vines that have expressed the connotations of alpine, hill and Mediterranean viticulture. In such a mosaic, it is at least audacious to try to pin down exactly what Italian viticulture is. It is certainly not a single thing, but rather a meeting. It is not a single viticulture, but many, with elements of plurality and heterogeneity on one side, of exchange and connection on the other.

The great history of Italian viticulture is, in reality, the outcome of many small histories that still must be told. It is the history of an archipelago of communities, vibrations, cultural islands and distant villages that have taken shape through the stratification of experiences and peoples along the places of great transit and commerce. *A.S.*

New Viticulture Emerges from Zones

In the late 1970s, it became clear that good oenology was not sufficient to bring about a decisive qualitative improvement. The second profound renaissance of wine was on the horizon, the one that would involve viticulture.

This new vision put the vineyard at the centre of the entire process and depended significantly on the results obtained by viticultural zoning. This was the identification, within the DOC territories, of the best interactions between microclimate and vine through the sensory characteristics of the wine.

This approach was an important innovation because, for the first time, the assessment was not limited to the characteristics of the grapes alone, but the vocation of the place was assessed by evaluating the wine produced there. In the late 1970s, we at the Institute of Arboreal Cultivation, School of Agronomy, University of Milan, began to zone the Oltrepò Pavese territory. The method was perfected as work went forward and was subsequently applied to winegrowing areas of the Lavis public wine cellar in Trentino with the collaboration of the Istituto Agrario di San Michele all'Adige (where I was director general at the time). In the long term, the project was fundamental when a new micro vinification wine cellar was built at the Institute in 1987 (the first in Italy) and a sensory analysis group was formed. The group applied tasting methods using non-structured parameter cards. Results were processed with multivariation analysis. It was a true revolution!

Today a total of forty winegrowing areas have been zoned, as well as the areas of many leading wine enterprises, which undertook structural investments and research from the 1970s to 1990s. All these studies, carried out by the University of Milan and the CRA of Conegliano, were recently gathered in the book *Atlante geologico dei vini d'Italia*, published by Giunti in 2015 (Florence).

Zoning is above all a scientific instrument for describing and discovering the relationships between the vines and the microclimates where they are cultivated. This serves, on the one hand, to improve the intrinsic quality of wines. On the other, it permits the insertion of vineyards in environmental contexts where some important natural and landscape qualities must be protected. The synthesis brings beauty and harmony to the wines and their territories. The results make it possible to identify sub zones with recognizable organoleptic profiles, thus contributing to the mapping of crus. These are well-defined areas with their place names that will appear on wine labels in the future. *A.S.*

The *Terroir* Concept: Oenology, Viticulture and Neuromarketing

"Territory" is a word that entered the world of Italian winemaking at the end of the last century and has broader connotations than the analogous French *terroir*. The qualities of the territory and their effect, in terms of media, culture, tourism, institutions, wine quality, etc., on the winegrowing sector are the object of a grand interdisciplinary project to

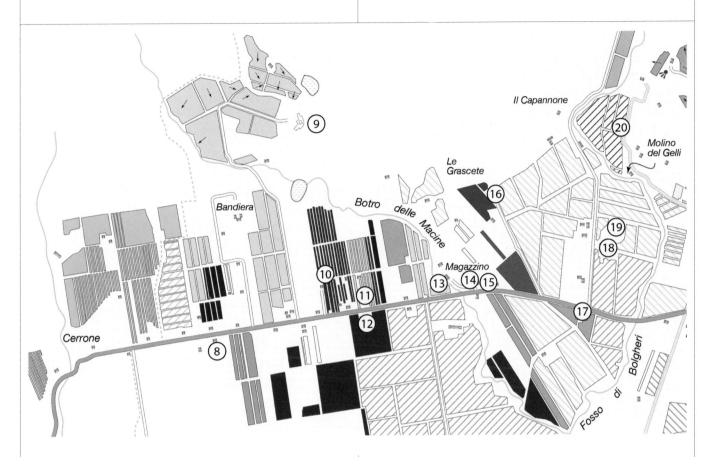

favour viticulture and its ideal synthesis: viticultural zoning. The alliance between producer and consumer, the true protagonist of this change, is actually concluded on the winegrowing territory where the rules of the denomination and the evermore-fragile environmental resources must be protected. This respect and protection, which might be defined as the ethics of the DOC consortium, is the expression of a unique *terroir* and unshakeable faith in the values that have made it possible to retain its structural characteristics and the unequalled quality of its wines. These connotations of the winegrowing landscape constitute an identity that is linked, more and more intimately, with cultural content and social organisation. It is not the *genius loci* that animates the winegrowing territory, but the *genius saeculi*, the spirit of time that allows us to think and tell stories.

Neuromarketing, based on the development of the cognitive sciences, uses a story to stimulate synaesthesia. The process involves a visual stimulus (the landscape with its iconemes) or a cultural evocation that is associated with the sensory perception of the wine and the desire to repeat the tasting experience, and thus the stimulus to think. Iconemes are to the landscape as phonemes are to words. They are associated with the sensorial sensations of wine, the desire to repeat that tasting and, therefore, the stimulus to think.

It is the collective interpretation of a territory and not an action claimed by an occasional hero or a systematic study of its environmental resources that constitutes the necessary project consensus to understand and distinguish the original contents of a wine from the territory, which make it so diverse from globalised wine.

If the quality of a wine is good based on its sensory characteristics, to be excellent it must incorporate additional immaterial values that are not expressed in the wine itself, but in the spirit of its territory, the humanity of the producers and the relationship of the producers' humanity with the drinkers' humanity.

A great artist once affirmed that to become universal one must first be local. Italian wine producers have understood that their wine must not abandon its original and authentic style. Its qualitative imprinting makes it immediately recognisable, even by foreign consumers. That is why they will choose it among another thousand, for its uniqueness.

Some guidelines can be extrapolated to direct production toward more competitive models, not only with regard to vineyard management, but above all to improve the quality of the wines, linking them more and more intimately to their territory:

– improve the interactive relationship between vines and environment to remove that cultural criticality that reduces the efficiency of the plant. Focus on the elements of interaction often linked to genetic choices that add complexity and originality to the wine. As mentioned and also demonstrated, viticultural zoning is a very effective tool in many cases;

– reintroduce some vines to the Italian platform of varieties that for various reasons have been confined to marginal viticulture;

– develop an ecological approach to vineyard landscape for conservation of the significant iconemes of our viticulture (environmental contexts, traditional forms of cultivation, antique vines, local cultivation techniques, etc.);

– endow the wines with greater originality by use of so-called varietal oenology which applies appropriate oenological techniques to exalt the great compositional diversity that characterises our indigenous vines and contrasts the banality introduced by the so-called international varieties;

– associate communications with production to spread the most important aspects of local culture and local gastronomic traditions together with the peculiar characteristics of the wine. *W.F., A.S.*

Precision Viticulture Is Born

Precision viticulture, not to be confused with organic or biodynamic, is implemented by applying greater phenological knowledge of the plant, microclimates and the terrain.

All choices are made as a purpose of the final product to be obtained:

– highly adaptive rootstock in symbiosis with soil constitution, vine and clone, capable of forcing or controlling production;

– vines and clones appropriate for the soil constitution and the climate (first essential concept of quality);

– cultivation and pruning as a function of the final product;

– precision and attention in care and management of foliage;

– precision in tillage and water control;

– root and foliage fertilisation with the meticulousness of a nutritionist;

– harvesting based on grape ripeness, with rapid, delicate collection systems. *A.So.*

The Bilateral Cordon

The "great transformation" of Italian viticulture that occurred in the 1960s as share farming was eliminated began by simplifying the systems of cultivation. These were reduced from several dozen to the two or three now in use, consisting primarily of the bilateral cordon and trained branches, on one or two walls.

The availability of mechanical pre-pruning and cutting facilitators such as pneumatic and electric shears has made large cuts manageable.

These simplifications in instructions to the pruner, often immigrants from countries where grape vines are not present, have revealed that large cuts are associated with precocious ageing of the trunk and potential reduction of liquid transport. When a vine shoot is cut off, a portion of the vascular elements that supplied it dry up and become useless. This desiccation cone, which enters deep into the trunk, is the defence of the plant against the entry of pathogens. Repeated cuts year after year and the relative formation of the desiccation cones cause loss of functionality in a part of the trunk.

Injuries and lesions are the main channels of entry for fungi that cause wood diseases, also for the vine's drop in healing.

There is a relationship between the size of pruning cuts and the occurrence of grapevine measles (also known as *esca*).

In particular, as the size of cuts increases, a larger surface is exposed and this facilitates entry of the fungi that cause the wood diseases.

The experience of recent years suggests that more respectful treatment of the plant would guarantee greater vitality and longer lifetime because respecting the natural inclination to grow (acrotony) would avoid invasive and damaging management. *A.S.*

"Preparatori d'uva": From Friuli to Château d'Yquem

This pruning technique, described as "branched" in Italian (in the words of Attilio Scienza), was perfected and spread by the technicians of the "Preparatori d'uva" company with the following objectives:

– preserve the main sap flows (hydraulic efficiency of the plant);

– give the vine a branched form similar to the natural growth of climbing vines;

– control spatial expansion of the plant;

– facilitate the correct balance of fruit production.

Marco Simonit, for many years the vineyard technician responsible for the Consorzio del Collio, and his friend and school companion Pierpaolo Sirch, are two vineyard technicians from Friuli who felt that the vines were reacting against the invasive technique of mechanical pruning. Their curiosity led them to travel around Europe where they discovered that bush vines did not suffer from *esca* and, even more importantly, reached old age. Their idea, born spontaneously and far from the universities and technical institutes they would later call upon for collaboration, was to transfer that respectful tradition to trellised vines. In 1999, they founded their company, the "Preparatori d'uva". Their message was compelling: "Let's save the vineyards of Italy and Europe".

As of 2003 they began to focus on recovery of the pruning trade, with training and tutoring tools. It is the only accredited and structured group in Europe.

In the words of Marco Simonit: "We have perfected a method for branched pruning that reduces the devastating impact of cuts on the lymphatic system of the plant and can

be adopted to all forms of grape vine cultivation, because the rules of proper pruning are independent of the system of cultivation".

For his part, Denis Dubourdieu, professor of Oenology and director of ISVV (Institut des Sciences de la Vigne et du Vin) at the University of Bordeaux, explains: "Considering that as things stand now, there are no truly effective remedies to contrast wood diseases, it is necessary to change our approach and work on the plant structure with the aim of preventing disease. Prevention begins with proper pruning, which makes the vines less vulnerable." It was Dubourdieu who first called the team from Friuli to France. "We were invited as lecturers to the viticulture course of the National Diploma of Oenology of Bordeaux. We also concluded a convention for research and experimentation with the ISVV. We are working in their vineyards and training their employees." Dubourdieu comments: "We wish to assess the effect of the pruning method on the evolution of vascular diseases of the vine, in particular, *esca*. The point we must clarify is whether less invasive pruning [*that respects the flow of lymph, limits injuries and reduces the proportion of dead wood in the arms*] can better protect the vines from *esca*.

It will also be interesting to see whether the resistance of the vine to hydraulic stress [*and thus the oenological quality of the grapes*] can be improved by non-mutilating pruning."

These "master pruners" are also conducting their training work at several famous Bordeaux chateaux, first and foremost the only *premier grand cru classé*, Château d'Yquem, in addition to the vineyards of the national institute of agrarian research (INRA).

They are also at work in Champagne (Louis Roederer) and in Provence (Domaines Ott).

Their activities are also underway in Austria, Switzerland, Germany, Portugal and Italy. And finally also in the United States and Argentina.

In Italy and abroad, over 130 enterprises have called upon this young and dynamic group. They also founded the Italian school of grapevine pruning, with twelve centres in the main winegrowing areas of Italy. *W.F., A.S.*

Greenhouse Cultivation in Italy

During the 1960s, application in Italy of the EU directives concerning multiplication and sales of nursery materials set the stage for genetic and sanitary improvement of the grafted shoots. Certified material was then offered in the place of "standard" material, which gave no guarantees concerning genetic identity or protection against viral diseases. The new directive also forced many nursery operators to make a choice only a few could undertake: create vineyards where they could gather buds for grafts and collect cloning material for certified materials. Creation of the pre-multiplication nuclei, which were set up in some of the winegrowing areas in Central and Northern Italy, gave the nursery operators valid help, especially the smaller companies, by providing certified buds for multiplication. The competition of large-scale nursery operations, especially cooperatives and those in France, forced many of the smaller, often family-run businesses to wind up their activities due to high costs and limited availability of clones (especially for international varieties). The signal and the organisation solution, followed in good time by the sales solution to take on opening markets, came from Friuli Venezia Giulia.

Greenhouse Cultivation in Friuli Venezia Giulia

Phylloxera appeared in France – in a vineyard of the Cote du Rhone – in 1863. It came from the United States, and for years was hiding in ambush. The County of Gorizia and Gradisca (under the Hapsburgs at that time) had access to an experimental viticulture station of the highest level. It was located in Klosterneuburg near Vienna. Founded in 1860, it was directed by the German Baron August Wilhelm von Babo.

As soon as the first news arrived from France of timid victories over this insect that attacks the roots of the European species with grafts on American rootstock, the central deputation of the Gorizian Agrarian Society requested funding for 2000 Florins from the Austrian government to set up a nursery for phylloxera-resistant American rootstock.

The marshes near the city of Aquileia face the sea and benefit from a very mild climate. The deep and sandy soil is ideal for nurseries, and in 1902, the state nursery for mother plants was established near Monfalcone. It produced 780,000 graft cuttings of *Rupestris Monticola*. Successively, a new plant raised production to 1,500,000 American vines.

Other plants followed the first, leading to the modern expression of "nursery technology".

The Vivai Cooperativi Rauscedo (cooperative nurseries) were founded on 4 September 1936 and this represented a new and important chapter. Rauscedo became a protagonist on the scene in Italy and later on the world (from the 1960s), when they perceived the enormous market that was opening for their cuttings grafted with a multitude of clones.

Today, the production in Friuli Venezia Giulia covers 72% of the nursery material market in Italy and 25% of the world.

Italy is the leading producer of grafted cuttings in the world. *A.S., W.F.*

How Research Has Changed the History of Wine

Roma Caput Vini, written by Giovanni Negri and Elisabetta Petrini, with the contributions of Attilio Scienza, has revised the narration of this history from the right point of view. This history tells of Rome, the protagonist of spreading vines and wines in Europe. DNA research has confirmed this story. There are two key dates in a summary of this history: 232 AD and 1997 in modern times.

Rome conquered Gaul, Pannonia (Hungary), Iberia (Spain) and Dalmatia. Where Rome went, *vinum* also arrived. Aquileia was founded in 181 BC, much earlier than Narbo (which became Narbonne) in 118 BC. Aquileia became the centre of production, storage and distribution of wines, which were then given to the legions guarding the northeastern borders. They also produced casks, which were much safer and more practical for transportation than amphora.

Why did Rome decide to plant grape vines instead of grain, barley, fruit trees, sugar beets or carrots? Considering that Rome gave the centurion a symbol of command in the form of a baton shaped like a vine, the choice was political.

The *Pax Romana* anticipated the American imperial model. In newly conquered lands, Rome built roads and aqueducts. Then it provided entertainment in the form of circuses, stadiums and races. Rome explained to the occupied territories that they would live better under its command. To achieve this objective it needed an agricultural cultivation that would be profitable in the long term. Vines were the answer. Thus, wine became a matter of state, an instrument of mass politics.

Domitian (Titus Flavius Domitianus) was elected emperor in 81 AD, and in the year 92 he issued the first law ever against viticulture and winemaking. He cancelled the policy of Rome to plant vines in every conquered land. It was a sort of prohibition before its time. This was terminated 189 years later by emperor Probus who annulled it in the year 281. Under Probus, Rome planted vineyards in Gaul, Pannonia and Mesia (Hungary, Romania and Bulgaria).

Marcus Aurelius Probus was born in 232 in Sirmio, today known as Sremska Mitrovica, not far from Belgrade. He became emperor in 276. His mother was from Serbia, his wife from Aquitaine (in Gaul). Today we understand why Probus transformed the Roman Empire into a winegrowing empire as well. He did it because it was the only way to repopulate the territories devastated by barbarian invasions. He also did it because he had to provide supplies to the legions in addition to assigning their missions. At the time, the soldiers represented an impressive attack force of at least 450,000 men.

Now we will leap approximately 1,700 years ahead to the 1990s when DNA analysis invaded the ancient ampelography and nothing would ever be the same again. It radically changed the history we all thought we knew.

The Americans ran the first DNA search on the Cabernet Sauvignon vine. The study, published in 1997, concluded that it descended from Cabernet franc and Sauvignon blanc. The next study came out in 1999, and it was fundamental. It revealed that most of our current grape vines are the result of spontaneous DNA combinations. It also presented the first evidence of a combination between an indigenous European vine (Pinot) and a vine from the Orient (Gouais or Heunish) from which many varieties descend, re-

presenting the evolutionary model for the whole platform. To be clear, Chardonnay was not created in France as was thought. It came from a well-defined area of ancient Pannonia (Hungary). The protagonists of these studies were the team of the American researcher Carole Meredith, the team of Attilio Scienza and a group of French and German collaborators.

The boundless curiosity of Scienza was fundamental, because he succeeded in treating anthropology and oenology together, just like chemistry and paleobotany and archaeology with molecular genetics.

Now it is worthwhile to ask how wine became successful across the entire continent. By studying and classifying the genetic characteristics of seventy-eight European grapevines including Chardonnay, Riesling, Gamay, Sauvignon and all the others, the team headed by Meredith discovered that the seventy-eight vines and the hundreds of European wines produced today with their grapes all descend from a single father called Heunisch. In Italian, this is known as *unno*, which means "oriental" in the Germanic tongue.

Where does this "ours" come from? Who spread it? And why?

Heunisch comes from the area defined by Stiria (Austria), Slovenia, Croatia and Hungary. Then there are two maps drawn up by archaeologists. The first traces the fabrication of casks. The second reports all the localities where there are burial stones, memorials or monuments dedicated to cask makers in Roman times. The traces indicate that new containers full of wine left from Andria and from Aquileia for the Danube and the Rhine, the two border rivers where the legions were stationed.

Suddenly, this flow was interrupted. At the same time, the casks and cask makers also disappeared and they were no longer praised on elaborate funeral monuments. Archaeologists explained that the distance between the place of production and that of consumption of the wine had become excessive.

In fact, they realized that ancient sickles, essential for planting vines, began to appear along the Rhine and Danube immediately after the disappearance of the great shipping venture of casks from Aquileia to the north.

With regard to the second question about who actually did the planting of vines between Stiria and Pannonia, historians gave the answer that confirmed the route of Probus. It was he who created European viticulture not, as was imagined, by carrying the grapevines from South to North, but from East to West. For example, it was thought that Ribolla Gialla had arrived from Greece. Actually, it arrived in Friuli from the East.

The exact location where the vines were selected is still a mystery. The ridge where this took place is no longer than 300 kilometres in a territory that encompasses part of contemporary Austria and Hungary. In fact, it passes exactly through Probus's place of birth.

In the words of Attilio Scienza: "The varieties that are still present today in many European viticulture areas are not descendants of vines from Pannonia. Rather, they are the outcome of spontaneous cross fertilisation of Pannonian vines with semi-domesticated wild vines present along the banks of the Rhine. For example, Chardonnay is the outcome of a genetic cross between Heunisch and Pinot, which was a son of the cross between Traminer and an ancestral tomentose Pinot. Traminer and the ancestral vine were semi-domesticated vines crossed with Oriental vines. Today, on the island of Ketch on the Rhine, there are still wild vines with the DNA of Traminer. The selection of the seedbeds was the next result of the inhabitants' action. It is likely they were the offspring of unions between Germans or Gauls and Romans, so they, too, were the expression of a new culture." *W.F.*

Sustainable Viticulture
The Conflict between Science and Society and the Importance of Research

In oenology, the distances between different visions are much limited, but there is still work to be done in viticulture. The eternal fear of science must be overcome, because science is the only way to face problems.

The grapevine is a tired plant, too weary to defend itself from the attacks of parasites.

One fact is clear: those who brought innovation into the cellar to implement clean oenology have fostered production ethics that now allow them to take on the work in the vineyards with the same commitment. Oenology has achieved its objective, because innovation in the cellar began at least fifteen to twenty years before the vineyard.

The truth is that no one has a magic wand. In his comments on the new European directive concerning organic wines applicable to the 2012 harvest, professor Mario Fregoni writes: "There is still need to ensure that the rules are observed . . . For myself, whether wine is organic or not, the label should declare all the substances not strictly pertinent to grapes and their transformation. It is a paradox that neither organic or biodynamic agriculture has impeded the use of a toxic substance such as copper in the soil. Copper is a pollutant.

It is not very toxic for man because it precipitates during fermentation and never exceeds the limits. But it is toxic for the environment: it is a pollutant in the soil, especially in continental Europe where soils are acidic and dangerous because it is absorbed by the plant. In Italy, acid terrain is at 1%–2% at the most, as in France, Spain or Portugal. We have calcareous and alkaline or sodium-rich soils where the copper remains inactive and is not absorbed by the plant. However, copper is toxic for bacteria, fungi and all the living creatures in the soil, and they become intoxicated. Copper was never used in agriculture before the late nineteenth century when we imported oidium and downy mildew from America together with phylloxera" (Gian Luca Mazzella, "Piacere quotidiano", supplement of *Il Fatto Quotidiano*, 10 February 2012).

It is likely that European viticulture will have many resistant grapevines in the coming years that will produce good quality wines, similar to those obtained from vines of European descent. The impact on production and on the consumer will be similar to what happened 150 years ago when phylloxera arrived. We must expect a true cultural revolution, so we must consider leaving prejudices aside to find a convincing response to all our doubts. Clearly, the problems do not stem from research, but, as in the past, from the level of acceptance of genetic renewal by consumers and producers.

At this time research in the field of protecting grape vines is oriented toward:

– reinforcing the natural defences of the vine through application of synthesized products known as elicitors (or synthesized inductors of resistance substances);

– creation of transgenic and cisgenetic varieties that are more disease tolerant or resistant and capable of producing quality grapes. The response from the first tastings by experts and winemakers are of the greatest interest. Raffaele Testolin and Michele Morgante discuss the results below;

– technological innovation concerning the distribution of pesticides to modulate product quantities in relation to plant coverage;

– defining new strategies for the fight based on the risk of attack, using damage forecast models.

In most wine producing enterprises of the world, defence is conducted with awareness, in order to implement strategies that will limit negative environmental effects and prevent the selection of resistant strains of pests.

Agricultural operators and institutions have increased their trend toward integrated production models where the fight against insects is conducted by relying on natural competitors or techniques. For the defence against fungi, very selective products with very low environmental impact are employed. Improved professional preparation and training for agricultural operators and agronomists have been fundamental, and they intervene only when the attack exceeds a certain level.

To reassure consumers, however, it is necessary to sustain analytical data with a holistic approach. This identifies maintenance of biodiversity in the vineyard, in all of its declinations, as the scope of viticulture in the future.

In coming years, the trend toward ethical products will grow, sustained by the values of eco-sustainability and eco-solidarity.

These will constitute strategic elements for the development of production, communication and marketing.

The contribution of precision viticulture will be decisive for an integrated production of grapes and wine in order to balance economic efficiency, environmental protection and respect for consumer health with the quality of the wine.

The results obtained in recent years in numerous experiments conducted in many vineyards demonstrate that by applying elementary valuation techniques (that are consequently inexpensive) to assess the vegetative and productive characteristics of the vineyard, it is possible to reduce the quantity of pesticides and fertilizers by 50% while also improving wine quality.

Antonio Pascale writes in *Pane e pace. Il cibo, il progresso, il sapere nostalgico* (Chiarelettere, Milan 2012) about fear of innovation and scientific research in general: "Would you rather be treated by a dentist of the 1940s with the instruments and anaesthesia of his time or by a contemporary? Who would reply: 'I would prefer the remedies of the old dentist?' Why should a remedy in another field of endeavour be any different? Why is a remedy against insects considered to be natural only because ancient solutions should be healthier? Is it possible that innovation is of no interest? Is it possible that we are so concentrated on our sweet memories and so distracted when it comes to modern tools? In the end, the cultural culprit, nostalgic knowledge, is always responsible."

Il nuovo terrore del progresso is the title of a long essay by Pierluigi Battista, published in *Style* (January–February 2014): "We live in an era in which socially useful innovation has little space for affirmation. It is hindered by prejudice and suffocated by a new wave of superstition. We pay great attention to new smartphone models and the latest novelty in tablets, but we are disinterested by news that can truly improve the life of millions of people . . . The most irrational fears are indulged. We become gullible, we take every alarm seriously, we justify all sorts of prohibitions, we demonise whoever is described as a noxious vandal intent upon destroying the idyllic harmony of nature."

Atul Gawande, in his book *The Checklist Manifesto: How To Get Things Right* (Metropolitan Books 2009), complains about this new "sluggishness of ideas", so out of place in an era when everything seems to move at supersonic speed. *A.S., W.F.*

The Organic Philosophy of Massimiliano Degenhardt, Physician and Winegrower

"Food is one of the main sources of our health. Above all, it is the only one we can completely control on our own. Medicine began to comprehend this in the 1970s [*the same period as the wine renaissance*] when major studies were conducted linking arteriosclerosis to cholesterol; degenerative diseases, cancer, diabetes and senility with various types of dietetic conduct". Massimiliano Degenhardt is a general practitioner. His medical office is in Ronchi dei Legionari (near Gorizia). He approached non-conventional medicine following the example of his uncle, Felice Giacconi, a recognised practitioner of acupuncture and massage therapy.

There in his own city he began a process that would lead to his dedication to non-conventional medicine, from homoeopathy to acupuncture and phytotherapy. He defines it as the medicine "that considers good health to be patients' primary asset, rather than big numbers or speculation at the expense of the ill". Degenhardt has very clear ideas, which he expresses with great conviction. "Just as I don't hesitate to use antibiotics when necessary, I would adopt drastic measures in a vineyard if it was an emergency. The first objective is to save the patient. I'm no fanatic".

In 2001, he and his wife Marcella Tresca acquired a farm in Dovadola (Ca' di Rico) on the Apennines between Romagna and Tuscany. "There were Cabernet and Sangiovese grape vines. I made the wine myself, convinced that my idea would be successful. I got vinegar. Since then I have relied on oenologists, while remaining faithful to my philosophy". He continues: "I want to make good, healthy wine without abandoning my belief: the less chemistry we use the better, in medicine and oenology. Chemistry must not take over the cellar, just as a doctor must be free from the dominion of chemistry when he makes his therapeutic decisions. Whoever makes good use of it – in medicine or in oenology – for the benefit of the patient or the wine is worthy of credit. Our purpose, we doctors and oenologists, is to have a healthy man and a healthy wine. Preventive medicine and advice are needed. This is where our discussion about nutrition comes back into the picture. When it is mistaken or not healthy, it is a major cause of many pathologies, as my practice confirms to me every day. The first point is that chemistry is harmful. Certainly, to make good wine we must exercise sustainable winegrowing, make incontestable oenological choices and maintain the highest ethical standards. We know that grape vines are weary plants, like small tribes that have been isolated for too long."

When told that the Institute of Genomics in Udine had developed ten fungus-resistant varieties so that treatments could be drastically reduced, Degenhardt opened his arms in a gesture of thanks and exclaimed: "At last! Science and research are essential for making wine without chemistry, the objective of many producers, not only organic winegrowers."

It is a fact that his Sangiovese, which follows the organic protocol and avoids systemic treatments, has more than three times the amount of resveratrol found in normal wines. In his words: "Resveratrol is a powerful anti-oxidant. This phenol provides protective action against cardiovascular pathologies, slows tumour diseases and reduces cell ageing. The plant uses it to defend itself from sunlight damage during the chlorophyll function. The concentration is greater in red wines, but if the mechanism is inhibited, by systemic treatment for example, the production of this substance drops off sharply. The analyses of my Sangiovese 2010, which won the Merano WineFestival 2013 and again in 2014, report the presence of 7.42 mg/l of resveratrol compared to 2 mg/l for a non-organic Sangiovese. It is no accident that resveratrol is present in many pharmaceutical formulas such as wrinkle creams, nasal allergy sprays, cholesterol capsules and tablets to prevent cell damage."

The farm brochure opens with a motto by Hippocrates: "Let your food be your medicine and your medicine be your food." In the spirit of Massimiliano Degenhardt.

The doctor's first harvest was in 2002. The farm covers 24 hectares, of which 4 organic vineyards of Sangiovese and Syrah for 20,000 bottles.

The estate makes three wines: Manano, from Sangiovese and Syrah; sparkling Rosa Batista, a brut rosé from Sangiovese and Bioni-Pezzòlo.

The latter, a Sangiovese Superiore di Romagna DOC from a vineyard of 4,000 plants/ha of fifteen years, is produced using a technique to retain the antioxidants in the grapes by means of a long, soft maceration on the lees at controlled temperature. It ages for approximately one year in oak casks. *W.F.*

New Disease-resistant Varieties

Variety and Terroir: *The Other Side of the Coin*

The combination of variety and *terroir* defines great wines produced in the right territories. This concept is well-known to the media and is held in high esteem by the wine world. It was not discovered by French winemakers as the French term for "territory" would seem to suggest. Pliny wrote in his *Naturalis Historia* that "some vines are so in love with their territory that they leave all the glory to the place and they cannot be transferred anywhere else without suffering poorer quality" (Pliny, III, 2–26).

In recent years, this culturally and biologically intriguing concept has led to recognition of outstanding wines and territories, the excellence of which is not challenged in any way. Maintaining these fortunate combinations is a tribute to culture and tradition, but it has a cost that even experts in the history of viticulture tend to underestimate.

For 10,000 to 12,000 years, vines cultivated in Europe and the Near East required no defence from pathogens and pests. The involuntary introduction of phylloxera, downy mildew and oidium from the Americas in the mid-nineteenth century has dramatically changed the scenario. It was necessary to introduce rootstocks and abandon the original non-grafted vines to control phylloxera. The fungi diseases (downy mildew and oidium) have led to systematic use of fungicides, and there is no end to it in sight. Today, European viticulture occupies 3% of agricultural land and employs 65% of the fungicides used in agriculture (Source: Eurostat 2007). This means 62,000 tonnes of pesticides that European winegrowers must purchase and distribute each year. This is a heavy burden for their wallets, the healthfulness of the product and the environment.

The Battle for Life

What is the reason for this apparently dead-end situation? Darwin, the father of the theory of evolution, explains it. In short, we can say that plants evolve together with the pathogens they host, developing resistance continuously. The microorganisms, for their part, must change and select strains that surpass the resistances in an unending struggle for survival. Darwin calls it the "Battle for Life" in his *The Varia-*

tion of Animals and Plants under Domestication, published in 1868.

Vitis riparia is a spontaneous wild grapevine of North America. If we should decide to undertake a courageous trekking in the eastern regions of North America, we would find plants of *Vitis riparia* that are resistant and others that are sensitive to downy mildew. If we then had the patience to collect and analyse the fungus as well, we would find strains that attack some *riparia* plants and not others. Couched in slightly more scientific terms, we would find populations of *Vitis riparia* characterised by plants sensitive to downy mildew as well resistant plants. Furthermore, the plants that are resistant to a given strain of the fungus are not resistant to all strains.

What is the reason for such a variety of vines and fungi strains? Because the co-evolution of the plant and the pathogen led the plant to develop resistances and the fungus to overcome them. Both with the objective to survive as long as possible.

European Vines and Diseases from the New World
When some American grapevine plants were transplanted in Europe in mid-nineteenth century for decorative purposes, downy mildew was inadvertently introduced. The cultivated vines in Europe and the Near East had no knowledge of this fungus, because they had had no previous contact. Consequently, during their evolution they had not developed resistance to this pathogen. They could develop it now, but we would have to let them reproduce and let time do the rest. Vines are not allowed to reproduce by seed, and the timing of evolution is incompatible with our haste.

So what is to be done? Until now, we have covered vines with fungicides. If we want to make a change, the simplest solution is to cross our vines with American or Asian ones that carry the resistance to the diseases and select, on the one hand, for wine quality, and on the other, for resistance. That is what European researchers have done for over one hundred years.

The first generation hybrids were not good. The American origin was too evident. With patience, researchers crossed the descendants of the first cross with the wine produced cing varieties. Today, in the sixth or seventh generation of re-crossing with the wine producing varieties, we have obtained varieties that are both resistant and interesting for their quality.

The Work at University of Udine
and the Institute of Applied Genomics
In 1998, researchers at University of Udine (UNIUD) began a programme of crosses between the best resistant selections to be found in the various research institutes in Germany, France, Austria, Hungary, Serbia and some vines of great quality.

In 2007, the Institute of Applied Genomics (IGA) joined in this research. In the meantime, it had successfully participated in the sequencing of the grapevine with an Italo-French group financed by both governments. IGA made its knowledge of the vine genome available to the project of the researchers in Udine and participated in the selection.

After fifteen years, the first results arrived. In late 2013, UNIUD and IGA submitted a request to the Ministry of Agricultural Policy to register ten varieties (five white berry and five red berry) resistant to downy mildew and oidium, with interesting oenological characteristics.

What Will the Future of Resistant Varieties Be?
Hard to predict. There are more than 200 disease resistant vine varieties in Europe. Some are already approved for cultivation in the European Union and have been registered for a few years in the national register of cultivatable vine varieties in Italy. Some regions have begun to authorise their cultivation.

Many of these varieties were selected in relatively cold environments, typical of central-eastern Europe (Germany, Hungary and Serbia). They are not well suited for Mediterranean cultivation zones with their long seasons and hot summers. From this point of view, the UNIUD varieties are of greater interest to countries such as Italy, France and Spain.

All of these varieties must, in any case, come to terms with the rigidity of the world of vines and wines, which does not love changes. Researchers believe that the rhythm with which thousands of new crosses are made each year will lead to obtaining varieties that are even better than those of today. It is just a matter of time and numbers. What frightens the world of wine is that the new varieties might lead to abandoning the traditional ones that made the wines of the great *terroirs* known around the world. On the other hand, when Merlot is crossed, it is not possible to reconstruct a resistant Merlot. The outcome is something else that cannot even be called Merlot.

Other Possibilities

There is an alternative for saving Merlot, Sangiovese, Primitivo and all the other illustrious companions: insert the genes of resistance recovered from wild vines by means of recombinant DNA technology. This, obviously, means opening the way to GMO. At this time, this path is barred by strong opposition from public opinion, strong enough to gravely influence the decisions of governments.

Researchers are willing to work in both directions and have no foregone conclusions. They are also interested in exploring other paths such as organic control of diseases, natural antagonists or other alternatives. A reasonable solution might be to leave the various actors of the chain of production free to explore different alternatives. In the end, the market will decree the success or failure of one initiative or another.

What cannot continue is that viticulture make such great use of pesticides as today. We must get out of this situation, because the countries that produce good wines throughout the world, but less bound to the religious conservation of European winemaking culture, could one day win over the market that continues to reward us for now. *R.T., M.Mo.*

Why a Paradigm Shift in Italian Viticulture Research Is Necessary

More than anything else, scientific innovations are a different way of thinking, of overcoming obstacles that at times appear to be insurmountable and which can be bypassed by taking unusual approaches. A shift in the scientific paradigm is represented by a new way of thinking, by switching from a mechanistic vision to a systemic vision that sees the grape vine as a computer network that must be regulated in a meticulous and physiological way.

An example of this new approach is offered by human medicine. Sickle cell anaemia or Mediterranean anaemia is an inherited genetic disease caused by a gene mutation that destroys red blood cells. Originally, this alteration was favourable to populations exposed to malaria, because the protozoan agent in the disease could not replicate in sickled red blood cells, although the cells transported oxygen less efficiently. This punctiform mutation in the hemoglobin gene is caused by the substitution of one base, adenine with thiamine, which makes the red blood cells function so ineffectively. With the technique of *genome editing*, a team of Australian researchers changed the defective gene, replacing the mutated gene in the base sequence, thus correcting the mutation which encodes for the protein that made the red blood cells sickled.

This technique can be transferred to the grapevine, to make our vines resistant to disease.

The European grapevine has a domain of numerous genes for disease resistance, but these genes are unable to encode for the proteins required to produce the substances to combat funguses. This inability is related to the evolutionary history of the European grapevines which, contrary to the case for American species, were unable to benefit from a long relationship over time with parasites, to highlight the individuals which by virtue of a mutation had been able to express genes capable of producing the antifungal substances.

By correcting the genome (which is considered one of the *new breeding technologies* and identified by the acronym *CRISPR/cas 9*), a kind of microsurgery with which to operate on the *susceptibility genes*, whose presence is necessary for it to manifest a disease, the inactivation of these genes produces a resistant plant. The best known example is the MLO genes (*Mildew Resistance locus O*) whose inactivation confers resistance to powdery mildew of the vine.

The operation is therefore comparable to a natural mutation, such as, for example, those that make white bunches appear suddenly on a vine that produces coloured bunches (Pinot Noir-Pinot Blanc).

Controlled pollination procedure required to create hybrids between resistant and sensitive varieties from which new varieties derive

Sporulation test for *Plasmopara viticola*, the causal agent of grapevine downy mildew.
The presence of spores as white powder indicates the ability of the mildew to infect and multiply.
On left: leaf discs from traditional varieties sensitive to *Peronospora*; on right: leaf discs from new resistant varieties

With this technique, which does not entail a transfer of genes (GMOs), it is possible to make our Italic varieties resistant to disease. It is not transgenesis (introduction of genes foreign to the species into the European vine's genome), but of cisgenesis, a modification of some bases of the genes present in our varieties. *A.S.*

The Edmund Mach Foundation of San Michele all'Adige

The Edmund Mach Foundation, which replaced the Istituto Agrario di San Michele all'Adige, is particularly distinguished for scientific excellence in the field of applied research in agriculture, with particular reference to viticulture and winemaking.

"We will have to double current agricultural production by 2030 to satisfy the nutritional demands of the population, which continues to expand in numbers and expectations. Only research will provide a response," predicts Francesco Salamini, who casts a dispassionate glance at the world, "today embellished with a romantic vision of mother earth. To the contrary, it will take a more rigorous and scientific method to find some of the answers" ("Sette" no. 25, supplement to *Corriera della Sera*, 20 June 2014).

Francesco Salamini is chairman of the Mach Foundation and former director of the Department of Crop Sciences at the Max-Planck-Institute in Cologne (Germany), who was then replaced by Andrea Segre from the University of Bologna.

The Foundation continues to carry out the purposes of the Institute of San Michele all'Adige, founded 12 January 1874. Edmund Mach was the first director and his philosophy was that "no wine of quality can be considered a fortuitous occurrence. To the contrary, it must be the outcome of a positive encounter between natural and human factors including, in any case, the predominant role of the grape vine variety". The Foundation unites 230 researchers plus approximately 100 post-graduate candidates. Of the latter, approximately 15% come from thirty-six different countries.

In addition to work in the field of viticulture, they have also sequenced the genome of *Drosophila suzukii*, a dangerous pest that attacks small fruits with a trend of rising economic damage. "The objective," emphasizes Roberto Viola, director of research, "is to comprehend how the plant functions so that we can improve the species and protect it. That is, by augmenting its resistance to disease and environmental aggression we will ultimately find new varieties. These control methods are intended to reduce use of chemicals to defend the cultivations". This is particularly important for grape vines, as the Institute of Genomics of the University of Udine explained to us. *W.F.*

A New Model between Research and Production, Universities and Businesses for the "M" Rootstocks

The worlds of university and production often remain very distant from each other, while they blame each other for their failure to apply the knowledge of the one to the needs of the other. The following short story demonstrates the great potential of close collaboration when an innovative project enters the field of production. In the late 1980s, University of Milan launched a genetic improvement project. The purpose was to produce new rootstock, capable of tolerating drought and withstanding high lime content.

It was not a new idea. When phylloxera arrived in Europe in the late nineteenth century, many rootstocks contributed to reconstruction of the viticulture. Since then, however, no new rootstocks had been created, while the changes that had occurred in viticulture were visible to all observers: diffusion in environments quite different from Europe, consumers' demand for higher quality and the stringent effects of climate change on plant development if irrigation is not activated.

The journey toward the valuation of agronomic characteristics significant enough to justify insertion of the new rootstocks in the domestic register of cultivatable vine varieties was very long. An important loan in 2010 instilled an important acceleration. The loan was floated by a consortium of bank foundations of the Ager project, which involved researchers at the universities of Milan, Padua, Turin and Piacenza, CRA-VIT of Conegliano and the Edmund Mach Foundation of San Michele all'Adige. At this point, there was only one missing link to reach the winegrower. It was created by constituting a new company, Winegraft, under the guidance of Marcello Lunelli (Ferrari), and the membership of nine leading wine producers in Italy: Ferrari, Zonin, Banfi, Armani, Due Palme, Magistravini, Bertani, Domains Castellare, Settesoli and Bioverde Trentino (an allied industry company) and the Cassa di Risparmio del Veneto bank. The commercial rights to this new rootstock are exercised by IpadLab, a spin-off of University of Milan, with facilities in the technological park of Lombardy in Lodi. It is responsible for monitoring the health and genetic correspondence of cuttings produced with these rootstocks. Vivai Cooperativi of Rauscedo was chosen to create fields of mother plants to supply the material. These nurseries have been entrusted with exclusive rights to multiplication and subsequent sales distribution in the whole world. The royalties from sales of cuttings will finance continuation of the genetic improvement project for the new rootstocks.

Four rootstocks have been selected, identified by the letter "M" for Milan:

– M1 (reduced vigour, high resistance to iron chlorosis and medium salt tolerance);

– M2 (medium vigour, good absorption of potassium and magnesium);

– M3 (medium-high vigour, good drought tolerance and very high nitrogen uptake efficiency);

– M4 (same vigour as M3, excellent drought and salt tolerance).

The Rauscedo nurseries are so convinced that they have programmed to plant 70 hectares of mother plants of these rootstocks, which will contribute four million cuttings to their production. In 2014, their production reached seventy million.

The vineyards that made the operation possible are ready to become the labs to test it out. "They are the most anxious to experiment and then plant new vineyards on 'M' rootstock," says Eugenio Sartori, director of Vivai Rauscedo.

This result deserves some consideration. The first concerns the significance of the initiative. This is the first example of project development that transfers concrete economic benefits from the Italian oenological industry to the university. Having revived attention for an aspect of viticulture that has been dormant for over a century is extraordinary. The second concerns Milan. This confirms its role as laboratory-city in the modern history of Italian wine. *A.S.*

The Way to Sustainable Viticulture

Italian viticulture has set off in two distinct directions, under the influence of the economic reality bridging the gap between the late twentieth and start of the twenty-first centuries.

The first is directed toward high quality wines linked to a specific territory and produced in particularly specialised environments with indigenous vine varieties. They are cultivated with refined techniques to produce wines of great spectrum targeted for less frequent consumption. The forms of cultivation are the most recent, but there are also cases where traditional cultivation is conserved (for example, arches in Valtellina, low pergolas in Valdaosta, bush vines in their original forms, double arches in Friuli, pergolas of Verona or Trentino, etc.), particularly suited to the microclimates and indigenous vines.

The second trend is fast-moving consumer goods. These are linked to their territory, but are produced in large zones with international vines. They are carefully produced to achieve a high quality level, but particular attention is directed to reducing production costs, because the target is more frequent use. Cultivation is based on more innovative forms that favour greater use of mechanical equipment. Until a few years ago, there was an overall inclination toward environmental protection and conservation, but it is only in the last few years that a genuine and concrete programme for defending our natural assets is being implemented. Probably this new mode of considering viticulture depends in part on the greater sensitivity of consumers to environmental issues. Their concerns are inevitably expressed to the producer through requests and demands for more detailed information.

Whatever the reason, it is in any case certain that the world of wine is again facing a critical crossroads where the options are both philosophical and concretely quantifiable. We are dedicating more energy to sustainable viticulture that plans for future generations. It considers future requirements in addition, not in alternative, to current issues. This leads to a profound change in the organisation of business activity. Respect for natural resources and conservation of the water, air and earth are primary concerns. In this new productive context, the primary objective of achieving quality and a healthy income statement is certainly not forgotten, but this goal is couched in a demand for sustainability that has completely convinced winegrowers and winemakers.

What does sustainable really mean and what are the first examples that come to mind?

Sustainable means taking action to ensure that winegrowing activities respect natural resources and the expectations of future generations: guaranteeing economic accessibility, social wellbeing and respect for the environment.

Thinking of the soil, the first reference is to the evident loss of organic substance on lands where vineyards stand and the possibility of integrating it by material recovered from the vineyard itself (compost of vine shoots, grape skins and stems). The wellbeing of the roots and their full functionality must be guaranteed by well-aired, non-compacted soil. The use of herbicides must be reduced and other strategies must be adopted (such as surface treatments and mulching materials), new mixtures, doses and timing of active components

Thinking of the vine itself, the quantities of mineral fertilizers must be reduced in consideration of the effective needs of the plant, when uptake effectively occurs and improved functionality of the roots growing in well-aired and well-drained soil. The vineyard must have a longer useful life.

Thinking of air, greater use will be made of subsurface drip irrigation, which saves a remarkable amount of product. The balance between the vineyard itself and the surrounding area will need reconsideration and may lead to reducing defensive measures against parasites.

Thinking of water, more and more on the decline, new subsurface irrigation systems will save up to 40% of water with confirmed qualitative improvement.

Studies and research of the last decade have made all of these real possibilities today, and make recourse to the principles of precision viticulture all the more practical and convincing. With these new techniques, the vineyard is broken down into small units (down to each single vine) and each unit is treated separately.

However, we believe that sustainable also means recovery of the plant's capacity to rely on its own self-defence mechanisms against pathogens and adverse weather conditions. For too long, we have been pursuing an excessively protected viticulture, sustained by almost daily actions. The vine has lost its capacity to adapt to the environment but, above all, has lost its relationship with its surroundings. Reduction of fertilizers and available water, less geometric and more physiological pruning (less aesthetics) with less vigorous buds leading to greater development will bring out the genetic characteristics of the plant once again.

In the end, even without changing the form of cultivation, the vineyards must be managed with a new mentality that tends to loosen its grip on the plants and make use of existing primary resources with greater attention.

Landscape is another important aspect, because it provides the most immediate image of the environment and can condition the consumer's choices and judgements. Sustainable viticulture will have to pay attention to this great resource that is demonstrating its power, but also its fragility. Type-approval of the forms of cultivation must not lead to type-approval of the landscape. This suggests dimensions of the cultivations in scale with the hedges, trees, conservation of rural buildings and less invasive management of the land.

All of these considerations are finding fertile room for growth and guaranteed success for the future through the professional competence of Italian winegrowers. *D.T.*

The Forum for Environmental Sustainability of Wine

At the start of the new millennium, the emerging areas of the market such as California, New Zealand, Australia and South Africa seemed to have a grip on a vision that integrated environmental themes with the production process to the point of characterising the marketing mix of their products, sustained by important investments along the chain of production and also by institutions. In South Africa, a programme that integrates certification of origin with respect for an environmental protection protocol, identified by a unique brand (today it is affixed to over 90% of wines in the country) was started in 1998.

The California Sustainable Winegrowing Alliance (CSWA) was born in 2001. This group has had great influence thanks to the economic power of the people it has attracted to date. These are undoubtedly innovative forces, perhaps dictated by the need to distinguish less qualified production on world markets, compared to those of the Old World. The decision to employ sustainability as a strategic driver in designing the processes and models of communications was dictated by two elements.

The first is that viticulture is perceived as an excellent and culturally sophisticated fruit of a territory, more so than any other agricultural product. The second derives from the fact that the world has decidedly opened the new millennium with considerable interest in the great environmental challenges.

Italy, quiet and clever, but gifted with an indescribable cultural legacy, has undertaken a parallel path, but today it resembles a perfect storm rolling in. It has missed none of the research and development experiences in the field of viticulture in general and sustainability in particular. To begin, the vineyards invested silently in organic and biodynamic experiences, improved energy efficiency and renewable sources, precision viticulture and finally the genetics of plants.

They were almost always supported by universities and research centres that embraced the force of innovation and social utility of the initiatives, at costs that were practically gratuitous. The terrain was particularly receptive for the birth of veritable programmes of sustainability that took their first steps at the end of the first decade, revealing the value of a vision that had more technical and scientific background than had been seen elsewhere.

In 2013, a total of fifteen national programmes were presented, proposing just as many models of analysis and management. The technical and scientific community realised it was necessary to conduct this creative chaos to a common denominator, given the evident similarity of the objectives. This led, in February 2013, to the birth in Rome at Città del

Gusto of the Forum for Environmental Sustainability of Wine, with the patronage of Gambero Rosso and the Italian Wine Union.

The initiative had been launched by Attilio Scienza, Michele Manelli and Marco Sabellico, "with the intention to promote the environmental sustainability of wine, an essential element of the qualitative excellence and competitiveness of our productions on the markets. It is based on the concept that the definition of a single system of environmental analysis, shared and comparable, is essential for the development of an economy for environmental improvement," as the constitutional statement declares.

Between 2013 and 2014 the Forum worked on the first *Report on the Sustainability of Wine*, published in October of the same year. This provided the sector with a snapshot of the situation and a constitutional proposal for continuing the journey. The Forum, with thirty-eight members including universities, research centres, associations and enterprise work groups, represents ten of the fifteen national programs for sustainability.

The approach of this movement to sustainability is based on a holistic vision of an enterprise in the context of society and the ecosystem, with ample and exhaustive social, economic and environmental objectives. Reading the interpretations of sustainability provided by the various members in the Forum, it is clear that basic cohesion in interpreting the foundations truly exists, albeit with varying degrees of intensity.

The indication of the potential (economical, among others) of this model for development depends on the fact that it is favoured by all types of enterprises, whatever their size.

The value of the work carried out also emerges in the technical proposal that resulted from examination of the fifteen programmes under consideration, which agreed to create models for approaching sustainable development of wine: Biodiversity Friend, CasaClima Wine, CCPB / Certiquality, ECO Prowine, Eko Cantina / Eko Wine, Gea Vite / Itaca, Magis, Montefalco 2015 / New Green Revolution, Salcheto Carbon Free, SosTain, Tergeo, Vino Libero, Vite.Net, V.I.V.A. and Vini 3S.

The Forum centres on three macro-indicators of environmental sustainability, interconnected and for integrated use among them:

– GHG emissions. Direct (for energy consumption) and indirect (linked to process and product) emissions of greenhouse gases;

– water. Consumption, direct and indirect water pollution;

– biodiversity. Maintenance and protection of biodiversity in the ecosystem.

In particular, the biodiversity macro-indicator emerges from the Italian panorama as a strong and innovative proposal from both the environmental and social points of view. There are also interesting connections with the agronomic management of the vineyards. The objective of this new interpretation is to unite best practices, putting the agronomic choices of the vineyards in direct relationship with maintenance of the effective levels of biodiversity in the soil, the air and the water of the agricultural enterprises and the surrounding ecosystems.

Finally, it is clear that Italian vineyards aim to intensify the relationship between the new expressions of sustainability and the classic elements of their marketing combination.

The report highlights the fact that the first five strategic factors for creating the added value of sustainability are linked to key words such as "landscape", "work", "safety" and "healthfulness" of the product. Among these drivers, the first and only typically environmental consideration – protection of biodiversity – stands out. Although indirect, through reduction of treatments, the vineyards actually consider this to be the first strategic factor for creating added value. Energy, GHG and water are considered to be important but on a second level, together with organic and biodynamic certifications, also considered less important.

It is a market demand: someone opened the way, applied research has been very successful and the system has acknowledged the necessity to join forces in a shared project. The objective seems to be within reach, and the vineyards clearly perceive that they can link sustainability to transversal elements of their processes and marketing combination, adding greater prestige to their products. The storm is ready. *M.M.*

Winegrowing and Oenological Training in Italy

Agrarian education in general and the branch of specialisation dedicated to wine and oenology have a short history in Italy, but also in Europe. In the nineteenth century, significant development of economic studies, usually as applied to the management of a farm, was not accompanied by a similarly decisive educational and analytical force in the disciplines related to productions, which were subject to traditional and empirical dogma.

In particular, the potential contribution that genetic improvement could make was completely ignored until at least the second half of the century.

The state, only recently united, perceived the need to create schools and experimental institutions after the arrival of phylloxera and downy mildew. The high institutes in Milan and Portici (Naples) were constituted in 1871–1872, followed by analogous initiatives in Pisa, Perugia and Bologna.

These became the first Schools of Agrarian Science in the first half of the twentieth century. During the same years, the most important oenological schools were founded, taking their inspiration from those in Klosterneuburg in Austria and its offshoot, the Istituto Agrario di San Michele all'Adige, founded in 1874. The schools of Conegliano (1876), Avellino (1879), Alba and Catania (1881) and Cagliari (1886) were founded in rapid succession.

These schools were under the control of the Ministry of Agriculture and, in the first half of the twentieth century, represented a system that was closely linked to the high institutes of experimentation. So-called itinerant professorships allowed many academics to develop training, research and diffusion to the territory concurrently and made Italy a leading nation in the field of winegrowing and oenology. New institutes specialised in winegrowing and oenology were not founded until the mid-twentieth century in Marsala, Locorotondo, Siena, Ascoli Piceno and Cividale. The academics who constituted these structures should be remembered: Edmund Mach in San Michele all'Adige, M. Carlucci in Avellino, Ottavi and Cavazza in Alba, Carpenè and Cerletti in Conegliano.

The necessity to reconstitute Italian viticulture imposed by the phylloxera contagion made it essential to proceed with systematic descriptions of many Italian vines, most of which were unknown to the world of research. This led, in the early years of the twentieth century, to the production of valuable grapevine monographs dedicated to the indigenous varieties of the Italian regions. The authors included Molon, Giovanni Dalmasso and, in particular, Italo Cosmo, director of the experimental station in Conegliano. From the 1930s, he laboured systematically to write the descriptions of Italian grapevines. This led to publication in 1965, by the Ministry of Agriculture, of a fundamental reference work in five volumes, *I principali vitigni da vino coltivati in Italia*.

An initiative of former students of the oenological school at the experimental institute of viticulture in Conegliano led, in 1948, to the foundation of the *Viticulture and Oenology Review* on the ashes of the *Annals* (first published in 1873). Unfortunately, the review ceased to issue its worthy publication in 2012.

Italy also made important contributions to the printing of books about viticulture and oenology. The first oenology textbook was written by Cantoni in 1867 followed, in 1882, by *L'Enologia teorico-pratica* by Ottavio Ottavi.

The schools of oenology were not definitively adjusted to the domestic regulations governing tertiary education until 1956 when the diploma of agrarian expert specialising in viticulture and oenology was recognised, although the profession of agrarian expert had been protected by a professional order since 1929. Dalmasso and Cavazza had a fundamental role in defending the education of oenotechnicians in the 1930s with the reform introduced by Gentile. It was only in the 1950s, with the introduction of the sixth year of study in the technical institutes for oenology, that the course acquired stability which lasted until the reforms introduced in the 1990s.

In 1990, education of oenologists was entrusted to the universities as elsewhere in Europe, initially via direct schools for special purpose specialising in Oenological Technique and subsequently via the so-called short, three-year degree.

In 1991, Law no. 129 instituted the title of oenologist, granted to holders of the three-year degree.

This educational cycle, for lack of appropriate structures, was first conducted at schools of oenology in collaboration with universities.

However, organisational difficulties and misunderstandings led to termination of the collaboration. Although deeply restructured, the course is still offered at the Edmund Mach Foundation in San Michele all'Adige, the oenological schools in Conegliano and Alba and the technical institute of agrarian science in Marsala. The teaching degree developed by some Italian universities has raised tertiary education in viticulture and oenology in Italy to the educational level of other European countries. *A.S.*

The Accademia Italiana della Vite e del Vino

The Accademia Italiana della Vite e del Vino (Italian Academy of the Vine and Wine) was founded in Siena, as proposed by the national viticulture committee on 30 July 1949. The objective was to create an association to promote viticultural progress in Italy. The event was praised and encouraged by eminent members of the government and illustrious Italian and foreign scholars.

It was founded, by decree of the President of the Republic with the signature of Luigi Einaudi on 25 July 1952, in the form of a non-profit organisation.

The objectives, as set out in art. 2 of the articles of association, are as follows:

– to promote studies, research and discussion of the major problems concerning grapevines and wine, including teaching at the various levels;

– to promote seminars and lectures conducted by academics or other persons invited by the Academic Board, concerning viticultural improvements and oenological development;

– to promote the constitution of observatories, laboratories and study commissions;

– to organise meetings to discuss the most vital technical, economic and judicial issues regarding viticulture directly and in relation to the agricultural and economic framework of the nation;

– to publish Academic acts, papers, surveys, monographs and collected works;

– to propose and encourage regional, national and international initiatives for vine and oenological expositions;

– to establish connections in the course of its work with similar Italian and foreign institutions;

– to administer foundations and contributions for conferral of awards to technical and scientific works and for actuation of specific studies, and for attributing special awards to distinguished personalities for special merits in the field of viticulture, in Italy and abroad;

– to promote the constitution of an association for the purpose of uniting all the persons who make diverse contributions to lauding the social, artistic and literary aspects of wines of noble origin;

– to collect in its own library, available to academics and the public, Italian and foreign publications concerning the scientific, technical, economic and judicial aspects of viticulture and oenology.

The Academy is subject to control by the state and operates only in the viticulture and winemaking sector for scientific, cultural and promotional purposes. Thus, it represents an original example of a specialised academy that is unique in the world in its category.

Its operations are regulated by the academic directors, nominated to office for terms of four years. The academics are chosen among persons who have distinguished themselves in studies and technique, viticultural activities, promoting noble products, agrarian sciences and related economic and judicial aspects.

Since its foundation, the Academy has acknowledged the special category of foreign correspondents among the academics. These represent the most important foreign scientific and technical personalities with an interest in grapevines and wine.

The number of academics is closed and cannot exceed the limits set by the articles of association for each category, except for honorary Italian and foreign members.

The official seat of the Academy has always been in Siena.

The Academy holds several sessions every year, also in other important viticultural centres, following upon their

requests. In this way, its activities are itinerant, which brings it into direct contact with various local issues. It has also constituted and regulated several work groups to acquire greater insight into special themes.

The sessions conducted abroad have aroused great interest because they make international activities more incisive, create useful contacts with academics and technicians in the countries where they visit through revealing exchanges of ideas and favour appropriate coordination of research.

The Academy publishes a volume of Acts every year, which includes all the papers presented and discussed at the various sessions.

Finally, the Academy has instituted three awards: the Arturo Marescalchi prize to honour the memory of its first honorary chairman; the international Giovanni Dalmasso viticulture prize to honour the memory of its founding chairman and the Pier Giovanni Garoglio prize to honour the memory of the academic who held the office of chairman for several years.

The prizes are awarded biennially and are assigned in alternate years by the Academic Board to candidates nominated by ordinary and honorary Italian and foreign academics. *A.C.*

Ottavio Missoni
In Osteria, "a Place that Becomes a Shop, School, Crossroads and Forum"

Noon, twelve chimes. To the tavern for an aperitif. A few Venus clams with a glass of white wine. "Try this *Traminer*. There's nothing better with clams." Other friends arrive. Another glass of wine. "How's life?" "Not bad." "Remember?" "It's good, this white wine." "A few more clams?" It was a holiday. All Souls Day.

One chime. A few friends go home. Others come and take their place. A bite to eat: ham, pickles, Istrian stew, meat with cabbage. We drink red wine, *Teran*. We finish with coffee and grappa. The good grappa from Istrian farmers.

Two chimes. Some get up to go to the cemetery, to pay their respects. Others arrive and take their place.

Three chimes. Another cup of coffee. Another shot of grappa. Someone who doesn't drink sticks with the wine, but asks to change it "because *Teran* doesn't satisfy him". We try *Refosco*, glasses for all. Talk about wine *it's all sophisticated now* and in the end everyone agrees that all wines fit in one of only two categories: *the good* and *the bad*.

Four chimes. There are seven of us to play cards. One missing to make two tables. There's the tavern keeper. Four for *scopa* and four for *briscola*.

Five chimes, six chimes, seven chimes. Losers pay up. Back to white wine. Not the wine for the clams. A wine that is a little drier. A little salt-cured ham. Also baked, like *Prague* ham. All sliced by hand. No pickles. They ruin the palate for wine. A taste of cheese perhaps. Talk about politics. Governments are always thieves. The guys are almost all free thinkers. Not much talk about football. Triestina in the B series. Memories of good days with Rocco, Valcareggi and Memo Trevisan. Two musicians among us. An artist painter and a poet. "Now Saba was a real poet." A fellow in insurance and one who works in the port. Means he doesn't work. "That is a pity. No one loading. No one unloading." Poor port and poor shipyard, too. "'Course, under Austria . . ."

Eight chimes. "It's very good, this white wine, isn't it from Istria? No this is *Tocai del Collio*." "Sir, bring two hard-boiled eggs. The best white wines are from Collio."

"Yes, but it varies from cellar to cellar." "Sir, have you got some beans with chicory?" "Ah, for me, too. But with a couple of leaves of rucola." "Well, good night to you, I'm going home, tonight there's my mother-in-law, too." "Wait, we'll come with you." In the meantime, the cemetery people are back, with their wives. "Missus, would you like some white wine?" "Thanks, with a Spritz and a hard-boiled egg, better not to drink on an empty stomach."

Nine chimes. Some come, some go. For dinner we are seven, nine with the wives. "Sir, what's for dinner?" "You ate the Istrian stew at lunch, I've got pasta with beans." "Well, stew for the ladies, we'll have a taste of the pasta with beans." "I made it with the ham rind and bone. I'll give you a good Friuli red wine, a *Merlot*, they say Julius Caesar's legionnaires drank it, too." "Missus, how's the stew?" "Good, just like what my mother made!" "My mother was good at making potato casserole." "We went fishing this morning." "What did you catch?" "We caught a cold." "You twat, why don't you use your arse for bait, you'll see how many fish you catch." "It's good, this red wine!" "To your health! Cheers."

Ten chimes. "Heard the latest? The one about the two deaf?" "Don't be a pain in the arse, tell those jokes to your insurance buddies tomorrow."

Eleven chimes. "Sir, let's have a round of grappa." Meantime, someone starts singing. "*Dove te ieri fino sta ora... iero in malora, iero a far l'amor...* [*Where have you been 'til now . . . I was in trouble, I was making love . . .*]". Not all together, everyone singing on their own, "*La mula de Parenzo, ga messo su botega... [The lass in Parenzo opened a shop . . .*]", a little better but still a lot off-key. With the choir voices, the best sentiments have emerged. Even if the voices of the last hurrahs are a little hoarse, it's a great sign. Tomorrow they'll be fresh again.

Midnight, twelve chimes. I've been sitting in the same place for more than twelve hours. Some are starting to leave. "Good night." "Say hello at home." "Tomorrow will be a good day, want to go fishing?" "Yes, as long as it's not windy." "Sir, goodnight."

*The Colours of Friuli Wines
Interpreted by Ottavio Missoni,
1987
Work donated to the Chamber of
Commerce of Udine and presented
on 6 April 1987 at the Galleria
Marconi in Milan*

I leave, too. "Be seeing you." I head for home, feeling the warmth of friendship, of gratitude. Yet, because every joy conceals a shadow of melancholy, as I walk I recall other identical evenings in Zadar with friends from there, identical to friends from here and the words we sang come back to mind:

"*Val più un bicer de dalmato, che l'amor mio,
che l'amor mio, mio proprio amor.
Non voglio amar più femmine perché son false,
perché son false nel fare l'amor...*

[*A glass of Dalmatian wine is worth more than
my love, my love, my own true love.
I don't want to love women anymore because they're
false, they're false in love . . .*]".

(The original Italian version was published in *Osterie d'Italia*, Arcigola Slow Food Editore, Bra, 1990, preface to Regione Friuli Venezia Giulia)

PART THREE

The Geography
of Italian Wine

Italian Viticulture and Landscape

Paolo Benvenuti, Rita Biasi, Walter Filiputti
with Umberto Gambino, Attilio Scienza

The Art of Observation and the Pleasure of Comprehension

Analysing a landscape is an inimitable undertaking. Each feature reveals traces of its origin, the mystifying transformations in successive geological eras and human presence expressed through daily work. With respect to the landscape as defined by geographers or anthropologists whose science is qualitative, because form is aesthetics and beauty, thus quality, for winegrowers the landscape is substance. They study the origins of soils, climatology and other factors of the viticultural model to transform the peculiarities of places into the originality of wines.

We perceive the landscape that we want to see. Many things remain invisible, because they fail to express the visual messages that fix perception. The problem is to comprehend how the visible and invisible elements of the landscape are perceived. The force of an iconeme is the image that remains in the memory. The towers of San Gimignano are not the place, but the part of it that allows for appropriation of a *momentum*, in the etymological sense of "something that remains in the memory".

The elusiveness of the landscape must be taken as a given, as a starting point for clarifying its general characteristics. Vineyards, in our culture, are seen as the image of a utopian Garden of Alcinous, narrated by Homer, representing a neutral point of equilibrium between the spontaneity of nature and the order of reason that organises spaces by balancing the tensions of beauty and utility.

In 1758, Rousseau wrote: "nature hides true delights from men when they are not sensitive enough to perceive them and they decay or disappear".

Wine captures the essence of a place through torturous cerebral paths that enable our minds to recognise a wine, distinguishable zone by zone, just as we recognise people by their traits, the sound of their voices or the way they move.

Neuromarketing, based on the application of cognitive sciences to the dynamics of buying, uses stories to stimulate synaesthesia.

The process involves a visual stimulus (the landscape with its iconemes) or a cultural evocation (the relation between medieval Vernaccia and the Via Francigena) that is associated with the sensory perception of wine and the desire to repeat the tasting experience.

In the collective imagination, the aesthetic and the sensory characteristics seem to be incompatible. What do they actually have in common? Historically, art and science have always been intertwined. Nevertheless, after the Renaissance their paths separated. Why is art less prestigious today and why has science become so inaccessible? The difficulty lies in allowing the two cultures, as they are perceived, to interact. Humanistic culture still commands greater respect although our world is technological.

Things are not miracles, fire was not a gift of Prometheus and science makes progress by means of intense application of theory and practice.

However, culture is still a thing of myths. Beauty, a fundamental value, can be taken as the point of contact between such diverse disciplines. "The art of observation and the pleasure of comprehension" must guide us. The instrument for applying this philosophy is viticultural zoning. The emotive reactions to vineyards in the context of the landscape, which form a synthesis of nature and culture, offer the indications to conserve their symbolic significance and environmental requirements, to adjust aesthetic expectations to economic reality and to respect the tensions of production and tourism simultaneously.

Let us start from an observation. The viticultural landscape we admire today, typical of sites with great aesthetic appeal, do not even vaguely resemble what our great-grandfathers saw one hundred years ago, and it is very likely that our grandchildren will also see agricultural and viticultural scenes that are quite different from those of today.

The arbiters of our landscape, in the exercise of their powers in their respective fields of competency, such as architects, planners, environmentalists of various sorts and a few enlightened politicians, are sensitive to the importance of models and theories in the laws regulating agriculture and the landscape, so as to avoid considering the vineyard exclusively as an aesthetic space, composed of light and shadow, line and contrast, horizon and perspective, while ignoring its biological characteristics, its structural iconemes and the nature of its materials.

Below
The Langhe

Following pages
Barolo country

In this renewed perspective, the concept of viticulture as a multidisciplinary enterprise demanding organic knowledge of the vine has opened new fields of research based on description, analysis and interpretation.

Modern analysis of the viticultural landscape goes to the heart of the vineyard to discover the distinguishing marks and make them available for consultation. This will enable a reader to virtually travel through the most ancient vineyards of Italy, back to the origins of Italian viticulture. The goal is to encourage a new mentality in all persons who have any relation with winegrowing and making, from producers to consumers, including local government officials, tourist operators and landscape architects. The ultimate purpose is to influence public opinion and create a movement to conserve the last feeble traces of two thousand years of viticultural history in Italy.

Within a few years, these sites only will remind our grandchildren of how their ancestors grew grapes and modelled the landscape.

There is no future without memory. *A.S.*

The First UNESCO Site Dedicated to Wine Speaks Italian

During the meeting, held 25 June 2014, of the World Heritage Committee in Doha (Qatar), UNESCO recognized the "Vineyard Landscape of Piedmont: Langhe-Roero and Monferrato" as a World Heritage Site. This is the fiftieth site that UNESCO has assigned to Italy out of a total number of 1,007, making Italy the nation with the greatest number of sites and the first in the world for an area dedicated entirely to wine.

The motivation states: "The cultural landscapes of the Piedmont vineyards provide outstanding living testimony of tra-

ditions that stem from a long history that have been continuously improved and adapted related to winemaking expertise".

Aldo Grasso, a journalist from the Langhe area, has written: "If a great treasure has resisted over time, the treasure of the Langhe, this is truly the merit of the local breed of winegrowers who succeeded in diffusing, refining and raising their wines to greatness . . . They were a rural aristocracy comprising winegrowers, oenologists, cellar masters and noble entrepreneurs who stubbornly aimed at the only things they should have aimed for: the wine and the best quality". Grasso goes on to say that Carlin Petrini, the inventor of Slow Food, also deserves thanks: "Following his lead, the Langhe area is thinking big again"!

Let us take a closer look at the zones authorised to display the UNESCO World Heritage emblem.

Not all of the Langhe and Monferrato are protected. The inscription regards six specific zones in twenty-nine different municipalities, in the provinces of Asti, Cuneo and Alessandria. The history, geography and wine production of these territories are particularly important and therefore deserve protection. The six zones, as below, have a surface area of over 10,000 hectares:

– Langa of Barolo (municipalities of Barolo, Serralunga d'Alba, Castiglione Falletto, La Morra, Monforte d'Alba, Novello and Diano d'Alba);

– Grinzane Cavour Castle (in the municipality of the same name);

– Hills of Barbaresco (municipalities of Barbaresco and Neive);

– Nizza Monferrato and Barbera (municipalities of Montegrosso, Mombercelli, Agliano, Castelnuovo Calcea, Vinchio, Vaglio Serra and Nizza Monferrato);

– Canelli and Asti spumante (municipalities of Santo Stefano Belbo, Calosso and Canelli);

– Monferrato of the *Infernot* (municipalities of Cella Monte, Ozzano Monferrato, Sala Monferrato, Rosignano Monferrato, Ottiglio, Olivola, Frassinello Monferrato, Camagna Monferrato and Vignale Monferrato).

Angelo Gaja, a member of the committee that promoted the nominations, has declared: "We will not let this go to our heads, we will remain the same with our heritage of the sacrifices and wisdom of our ancestors, the revered lessons of Cavour and Einaudi, and the perception of the spirit of these places that is so dear to us as narrated by Pavese and Fenoglio. I am confident we will succeed in doing well by thinking of the future generations, too." *W.F.*

Pantelleria

The UNESCO protection of Langhe-Roero and Monferrato refers to a viticultural area of great economic value that has always continued to grow.

Just a few months later, on 24 November 2014, the 161 UNESCO member states meeting in Paris unanimously granted inscription on the Representative List of the Intangible Cultural Heritage of Humanity for the traditional practice of cultivating head-trained bush vines (*vite ad alberello*) on the island of Pantelleria.

This was a welcome response to the complaints of winegrowers on the "black pearl of the Mediterranean", who feared they were forgotten. On the contrary, they received a hand that stirred hope and freed them from the burden of feeling useless and out-dated. Those 161 delegates had struck a bull's eye. There are times when modernity means conserving ancient traditions. These are the outcome of centuries of innovation that have reached their apex. In the words of the author: "Pantelleria without its bush vines would not be Pantelleria. This is not merely a type of grape vine cultivation; it is an iconeme that characterises the territory of the island. This is no commonplace bush vine, but the last remaining legacy of the Greek who allowed the vine to creep along the ground and rest the bunches on the earth so they would absorb the radiant heat and avoid the sharp and salty breezes that persistently buffet the Aegean islands [*as on Pantelleria*]. This bush vine offers no opportunity for adaptation to new demand for more economical management: it grows in a hol-

low in the ground to keep the vegetation low. The numbers tell the story: from grape production of 350,000 quintal [*100 kg*], it is now only slightly more than one-tenth of that amount [*35,000 quintal*]. Likewise, the cultivated surface has dropped from 4,000 hectares [*already down from the 5,000 hectares in the 1950s when the vineyards covered 48% of the island*] to the current 600."

"These numbers are bound to shrink further," predicts Diego Maggio, managing director of the local consortium uniting 300 to 400 winegrowers. "This is a continuous decline and I felt that the international community should take action. The vineyards need to be appreciated. What is happening? It happens that the father cultivates the vineyard and the children do not want to do it anymore".

Maggio, a lawyer, published a book in 1998 (*Una provincia DOC*) in which he bluntly asked UNESCO to protect the vineyards of Pantelleria. "Far-sighted? It will suffice to say that I have spent my adult life launching ideas," he responds. "As one who was not born here, I immediately perceived that these vineyards, once so florid and splendid, were losing their force all over the island". This recognition is also, in some way, a merit of his.

One thing is certain: on Pantelleria the vine depends exclusively on the work of man. There are 7,000 kilometres of dry mounted walls that surround and sustain the terracing! The vineyards are very steep. These are the reasons for calling viticulture a heroic undertaking on Pantelleria. The work that must be done during the year calls for a total number of man hours that is at least three times what is required to cultivate a normal vineyard on the mainland. The Black Pearl will save itself only if the income of the local winegrowers reaches a profitable level with respect to the hours invested.

The hope is that after this recognition the world will start to buy these magical wines and contribute to saving them, now that they belong to the world.

Before accompanying the reader to the description of Passito di Pantelleria, written by Umberto Gambino, consider that the most profound and concealed significance of this recognition is the restitution of credit to man's work. An unknown man, who speaks the language of the vines, cares for them and creates the conditions for them to produce their best fruit. Let

us dedicate UNESCO's fifty-first recognition of Italian heritage to the 400 wise men who grow vines on Pantelleria.

Luigi Veronelli wrote: "The farmer will cease to be when there is no more wine. Wine is immortal . . . Why is wine the song of the earth for the sky? Because the earth speaks through the vines to the listening sky."

Passito di Pantelleria

As Umberto Gambino wrote: "The name *Zibibbo* derives from the Arab *zabīb*, which means 'raisin' or 'wilted grape'. Phoenicians brought the grape vines for producing Zibibbo (or Moscato d'Alessandria) to Pantelleria, where the traditional method of cultivation, head-trained bush vines, is still in use.

Passito di Pantelleria is a sweet wine for dessert or meditation (as you wish) obtained from Zibibbo bunches. No more than 1.5 kilo are harvested from each bush after over-ripening. Bunches are laid out to dry on traditional trellises of wood called 'stinnituri' for twenty to thirty days. After drying, the grapes weigh 60% less than at the start. The Passito di Pantelleria DOC protocol was issued in 1971.

We cite three excellent examples of Passito among the numerous products.

Salvatore Murana, an authentic and 'indigenous' guru of Passito di Pantelleria, calls his oeno-creations 'heat wines'. His wines – Mueggen, Khamma and Martingana – named after the locations of the respective vineyards – inspire ecstatic emotions and are truly crus.

Bukkuram, by Marco De Bartoli of Marsala, is a brilliant example of a wine for celebrations with its notes of pannettone, Sicilian cannolo and walnuts.

Another wine that deserves a top position is the best-known Passito di Pantelleria beyond Sicily and the award-winner of recent years: Ben Ryé di Donnafugata. It has a fresh sweet taste that is never cloying, aromas of white raisin, hon-

ey, candied fruits and other delights: an authentic nectar of the gods!" *W.F.*

United Italy of Wine

I, the undersigned, born in Fruili in the town of Percoto, in the family trattoria in my father's name (da Germano), pleasantly infatuated by the *sommellerie* of the Italian sommelier association (AIS), in 1976 prepared a wine menu that united the best Italian crus of the time. I served them even by the glass, to accompany the dishes my mother prepared. For dessert (today we would say, pre-dessert), loyal to the philosophy of the sommeliers who had a mission to spread the best Italian wines, I suggested Tanit, a Moscato di Pantelleria by a forerunner of fine Sicilian wines, Ignazio Miceli, to accompany mountain cottage cheese with jams.

That is how even the people of Friuli contributed to introducing the jewel of Pantelleria to the world. *W.F.*

Viticultural Landscape: A Diverse yet Unique Asset

The Unique Relationship of Humans and Nature in the Viticultural Landscape

The vineyard is an archetype of the Mediterranean agricultural landscape. The history of the vineyard is primarily a history of grapevines. The domesticated grape (*Vitis vinifera sativa*) is an extraordinarily resilient plant with a great capacity to adapt to diverse environmental conditions. It has modelled the agrarian landscape by invading the plains, occupying the best slopes on the hills and even rugged spaces on the mountains. In Italy, it is also cultivated in fruit and decorative gardens in the cities.

The agrarian landscape is an anthropogenic landscape, the result of human impact on the natural environment.

With regard to grape cultivation, the Human to Nature relationship has unique characteristics related to the specific site. The winegrower is aware that the vine can produce unique grapes and wines as a result of his work in the vineyard, but also in relation to the micro-climate that cannot be reproduced elsewhere. The viticultural landscape is an expression of the winegrower's empathy with the vineyard. This materialises in the process of conserving the rootstock, purposeful soil management and personalised vinification techniques to enhance identification of the wines, the sites and their landscapes. The link of wine to its specific zone and landscape has become, more than for any other type of cultivation, the recognisable and competitive emblem of quality. Only the cultivation of olives and production of oil have recently developed a comparable situation.

In viticulture, the concept of a top-quality product has always been associated with distinctive character. The ancient history of wine and grapevines includes many references to exceptional wines of many places on the peninsula and the islands. Modern chronicles confirm the longevity of this perception in the affirmation of the "territory" concept. This has strengthened the link between wine and its cultivation environment and contributes to the coupling of wine with its landscape in promotional activities. Various parameters contribute to the uniqueness of a viticultural landscape. The viticultural landscapes in Italy are an integral part and expression of territories that are unequivocally distinguished by a particular conformation and a particular assortment of diverse cultivations. The diverse modes of approaching cultivation of the earth is, in some cases, so specific as to constitute the iconeme of a specific viticultural region and an element of distinction and value.

The vineyard is one of the most fascinating forms of botanical landscape architecture and represents its distinguishing characteristic. Vines trained onto arbours or trellises (canopy management), in rows, head-trained bush vines or vines trained to grow on trees: each is an unmistakeable landscape of a single place. Each is the emblem of the attempt to adapt the plant to an environment that may be hostile, requiring such particular or extreme solutions that persevering in the cultivation requires heroic determination.

Viticulture: A Different Way of Considering Agriculture?

The vine is one of the species of agrarian interest that is most susceptible to surface erosion and genotype characteristics. A vineyard is virtually a single-crop system that relies on intensive use of phytopharmaceuticals to check pathogens, parasites and weeds that compete with the rootstocks. Today, the vineyard is considered an excellent agricultural ecosystem

that can guarantee provision of ecosystem services in addition to quality products. Such services are essential for sustainable production. To achieve the goal of environmental sustainability in agriculture, cultivations must also contribute environmental benefits such as preservation of biodiversity, mitigation of climate change, carbon sequestration and soil fertility maintenance.

The structure and management of the vineyard can be organised to satisfy these requirements by designing new viticultural landscapes adjacent to the historical and traditional ones. The future viticultural landscape, representative of a competitive, productive and innovative viticulture, will continue to be the emblem of one of the typical agrarian traditions of Italy and will be capable of meeting the challenge of sustainability by simply accepting a few elementary principles of landscape ecology: complexity, connection and resilience.

Viticulture will also undergo changes as it dedicates greater attention to agricultural ecosystem services. As the ecological functions of the agricultural ecosystem become stronger, they will contribute to greater and improved production. The winegrowers' sensitivity to the multiple functionalities of the vineyard might favour replacement or recovery of vines instead of uprooting them. This would also revitalise their role as architects and custodians of a sustainable agrarian landscape. *R.B.*

"The Territory Gives Birth to the Wine, the Wine Grows the Territory"

Camilla Lunelli made this statement in 2006 at a Symbola meeting on the 20th anniversary of the methanol scandal.

She is one of the new-generation family members of the owners of Cantine Ferrari of Trent.

The city-states, the Renaissance, the Unification of Italy (Risorgimento) and the Resistance: the entire history of civilization in Italy was born and has developed in areas with a particular vocation for winemaking. The extraordinary agrarian landscape of these territories is the result of centuries of winegrowers' work, the growth of trade and diffusion of wine shops serving the city centres of ancient Italian cities. The rising value and prestige of many wines, and great wines, created a unique culture in the world. Each wine bears the thoughts of its maker and the character of the terrain where it is born. Each wine is also a powerful generator of landscapes.

It is no accident that viticulture and wine, an element of identity and unity of Europe as a whole, constitute one of the twenty-five European Cultural Routes, *Iter Vitis*. The viticultural landscape is considered a tangible and intangible asset of the community. It is an essential component of the history of a territory. It leaves traces that others can read and live, it is an instrument of human knowledge and enriches the quality of life. Italy has a great wealth of places and routes linked to wine, with an extraordinary variety of panoramas, terracing, ancient grape vats, centenary plants, long slopes and small gardens, and exquisite mosaics of woods and fields, olive plantations and vineyards. Evidence of heroic viticulture, other than the sites consecrated by UNESCO in the Cinque Terre

(1997), Langhe-Roero and Monferrato and Pantelleria, is to be found in the terracing throughout Liguria, in Valtellina, Valle d'Aosta, Valle di Cembra, Carso, Lamole in Chianti, the islands of Tuscany, the Amalfi coast, on Etna and the Aeolian islands. Historical vines, still cultivated inside ancient city walls, are typical of cities such as Siena, Brescia and Rome. In Irpinia, Pompeii and the Valley of the Temples in Agrigento, the recovery of ancient plants and grapevines has fostered the creation of variety archives and viticultural gardens open to visitors like open-air museums. The story of the virtuous transformations of agrarian landscapes by the work of man is evident at a multitude of sites in Italy (Giglio island, Pietragalla [Potenza], Ardauli [central Sardinia], Ferruzzano [Reggio Calabria], etc.) where vats were excavated in the rock or tufa to press the grapes (*palmenti*) and ferment the must from protohistoric times to today. The hills of Vallagarina are dotted with castles and vineyards. The landscape reveals how the care dedicated to the production of Marzemino, accompanied by a strong sense of respect for the environment, revitalised the significance and appreciation of the entire landscape. Isera is the only example in Europe of a model municipality for quality production of renewable and sustainable energy. The sandy soils of the island of Sant'Antioco (Carbonia-Iglesias) host centenary vines, even in proximity to the sea. These indigenous vines are cultivated on their own (phylloxera-resistant) rootstocks as bush vines in the form called "alberello latino", a practice handed down from generation to generation. *P.B.*

Wines of the Volcanoes

"Volcanic Wines" is the name of a volunteer association promoted a few years ago by the Soave consortium for the purpose of joining forces and improving communication among the viticultural volcanic territories that range from Veneto to Sicily. Italy is the country with the greatest viticultural surface area planted on terrain of volcanic origin. More importantly, it has the greatest variety of physical and chemical composition of the geological matrices and the greatest number of ancient vines cultivated on such lands.

The ancient civilisations of the Mediterranean developed around volcanoes. The earliest emporia of the colonists from Eubea (an Aegean island) on Naxos and Ischia, and the Mi-

noan settlement on Santorini are just a few examples of such settlements. The proximity of humans to volcanoes in ancient times did not mean that they had exorcised their fear and believed they were protected by the gods. Rather, the fertile soil and the fine, abundant waters rising from the depths attracted them.

The "earth machine", as Anglo-Saxon scientists have defined the volcano, perfectly expresses the role that volcanoes played in the primordial formation of the planet. In the late eighteenth century, the volcano was seen, perhaps for the first time, "as a creative rather than destructive force, like an immense plough that nature uses to overturn the innards of the earth".

The word "volcano" usually calls to mind the image of a cone-shaped mountain, bereft of vegetation with a snow-covered peak and a plume of smoke.

Although this typology is very frequent, there are many diverse types of eruptive activity that form volcanic edifices of very different shapes. When land is generically identified as volcanic, the extreme heterogeneity of its physical and chemical composition is not considered analytically and thus the influence of soil composition on the qualitative expression of wines is also ignored.

Volcanic soils differ in their physical structure and their pH factor. Physically, soil structures range from the lightest, pumice of the island of Salina, to the heavy clay soils of Lessini and Soave vineyards, the tufa of Montefiascone and the sands of Frascati. With regard to the pH factor, there are alkaline soils deriving from degradation of basalts, neutral and sub acid soils consisting of porphyry or granite (Terlano and Gallura, respectively), and at the acidic end of the scale, the morainic soils of Etna and the volcanic ash of the vineyards of Vesuvius. Differences in the chemical composition are very important, particularly as regards the presence of potassium and microelements. No other soils derived from limestone, moraines or metamorphic rock have a comparable wealth of minerals.

To a consumer's way of thinking, wines such as Soave, Castelli Romani, Vulture, Gallura or the Cembra valley are not volcanic wines. However, the evidence of extinct volcanic activity in such soils prevails over that attributable to active volcanoes. Volcanic soils normally derive from very slow degradation of lava or pyroclastic material (volcanic ash, lapilli, etc.). In the case of lava, the soil often has a holocrystalline structure similar to porphyritic rock or granite. Volcanic ash, on the other hand, is found in deposits that may have imposing dimensions where the layers, of different colours, identify the various phases of eruption. There are some less-known exceptions. These are soils derived from forgotten volcanoes.

The volcanic phenomena that gave birth to these soils are usually more recent, in terms of geological eras, and took place underneath deposits of seabed sediments or in direct contact with seawater.

The presence of limestone and/or seawater led to the formation of solidified magma with very particular structural and compositional characteristics that are unique in the context of volcanic activity in Italy. For the sake of simplicity, there are two main aspects that produce an important influence on the organoleptic quality of wines: the presence of clay

Vineyards on the slopes of
the Vesuvius

and active lime. The clay content, usually higher than in soils deriving from volcanic accumulation, confers structure and longevity to wines, especially white wines. The presence of active lime, normally absent in other volcanic soils, confers finesse and elegance.

Volcanic wines have been famous for their quality in every epoch, as reiterated in the numerous references to their alcoholic content and keeping quality, which enabled them to withstand long journeys.

Volcano slopes are often very difficult to cultivate because of hard rock or the steep inclination. The viticulture they host is often the outcome of centuries of work, with impressive terracing modelling the surface, making such landscapes true masterpieces of art.

What are the physiological consequences for the plant and thus the effect on the wine? The colour of the soil, its physical structure, the sequence of soil horizons and its depth determine the soil climate. Similar to the aerial part of the plant, the soil climate conditions the development of the root apparatus via the temperature, the percentage of air and the quantity of water.

Among the metabolic compounds of the plant, those that produce the greatest discrimination among different zones are the carotenoids, the norisoprenoids (in particular, damascenone, responsible for the notes of tropical fruit) and TDN (trimethyl-dihydronaphthalene, for bottle mature aromas of kerosene and flint or minerals). Volcanic wines, in the anthropological model of cyclical history, reiterate the myths of origin and restore the ancient yearning to ingratiate Mother Earth and become the founders of a viticulture that will unite the originality of the sites, the vines and the humans to oppose the standardisation of flavours. *A.S.*

The Excellence of Italian Wine from the 1960s to Today

Introduction to the Work

In this chapter, we will be talking about approximately 200 of the finest wineries to add value to the modern history of Italian wine.

The chapter is divided into decades. The wine producers were not reviewed according to the year in which they were established, but the period in which they made their most innovative product; the product that made them take off, generating a positive impact on the area they came from and strengthening the image of Italian wine as a whole.

To make the reading and research easier, the winemakers are grouped by region.

The producers that contributed the most to the modern history of Italian wine, therefore, complement those described in the section "The Renaissance of Italian Wine. The People Who Changed History".

The decade of 2010, instead, takes into account a small number of wine producers that were established or emerging in this period. These are producers that are not well-known but that are, however, deemed capable of bringing new ideas and lifeblood to the evolution of Italian wine.

The difficulty in preparing this chapter arose from the fact that, due to limited space, we could not include just as many fine winemakers.

The book is dedicated "to all Italian vintners" and also to those who are not mentioned. To those of you not mentioned, we ask you to please be understanding.

Collaboration on drafting the winegrowers' stories:
- Valle D'Aosta: Riccardo Modesti
- Piedmont: Piera Genta, Mario Busso and Roger Sesto
- Lombardy: Riccardo Modesti, Roger Sesto and Walter Filiputti
- Trentino-Alto Adige: Angelo Carrillo and Walter Filiputti
- Veneto: Bernardo Pasquali, Paolo Ianna and Mario Busso
- Friuli Venezia Giulia: Walter Filiputti and Angelo Solci
- Emilia-Romagna: Daniele Bartolozzi
- Liguria: Daniele Bartolozzi
- Tuscany: Guido Ricciarelli and Daniele Bartolozzi
- Umbria: Daniele Bartolozzi and Guido Ricciarelli
- Lazio: Umberto Gambino
- The Marches: Umberto Gambino and Guido Ricciarelli
- Abruzzo: Franco Santini
- Molise: Franco Santini
- Campania: Umberto Gambino
- Puglia: Franco Santini
- Basilicata: Umberto Gambino
- Calabria: Umberto Gambino
- Sicily: Alma Torretta, Umberto Gambino and Walter Filiputti
- Sardinia: Gilberto Arru
- "Emerging": Guido Ricciarelli, Umberto Gambino and Walter Filiputti

The 1960s

The DOCs and the Abolition of Sharecropping

The 1960s were a period in which winemakers abandoned a purely peasant form of management to become more entrepreneurial. There were two monumental steps: first, the promulgation of the DOC of 12 July 1963. This law displeased many people, in particular **Luigi Veronelli**, and in fact, he became the standard-bearer for the appeals of the small-scale winemakers and of all those who wanted a more courageous set of laws to defend quality. Paradoxically, the limits of the law resulted in the first reaction of many producers who had guessed what the new trends would be, to the point of repudiating the law itself with "table wines". In hindsight, and thanks to the commitment and vision of our winemakers, the law on DOCs remains in any event a milestone in the process of the "renaissance of Italian wine".

The second was the abolition of sharecropping, which took place on 15 September 1964. In Italian law, sharecropping (a term derived from the late Latin *mediator*, or intermediary), was an agrarian contract of association with which a landowner and a farmer (sharecropper) shared the products and profits of a farm. This was possibly a much more important and influential revolution than that of the DOCs, because it involved the socioeconomic system of Italian agriculture as a whole.

On the one hand we witnessed the abandonment of the countryside by the sharecroppers – called the "great transformation" – which caused a break with centuries of tradition, the loss of many varieties, not only of grapevines (and, fortunately, part of these have been recovered), the urbanization of many farmers and the separation between city and countryside. On the other hand, for the first time in our history, many former sharecroppers managed to become modern farmers. Many entrepreneurs joined them from other sectors, people who had decided to invest in wine and who brought with them the managerial culture that was the foundation of the sector's future success.

INSTITUT AGRICOLE RÉGIONAL (IAR)

Wine Training

VALLE D'AOSTA

www.iaraosta.it

For viticulture in winemaking in the Valle d'Aosta, a key role in the transition from a purely local phenomenon to a wider dimension was undoubtedly played by the Institut Agricole Régional of Aosta (IAR, Regional Agricultural Institute).

The history of the IAR begins with the establishment of the École pratique d'agriculture (School of Agricultural Practices), in 1951, set up to give both theoretical and practical training to future farmers. The École had two directors: one was the region of Valle d'Aosta, the other the canons of the Casa Ospitaliera of Gran San Bernardo. This coupling was to prove invaluable in the history of the School, first and foremost for the IAR, then: the canons of Gran San Bernardo, long led by the charismatic Joseph Vaudan, were to play a formidable role in agricultural education and the students' human development, as well as serve as an authoritative interface between the region and the IAR.

The training course for winemaking was perfectly adapted to the needs: classroom theory was followed by hands-on experience in the five vineyards around Aosta and in the cellars of the school. This is the forge that turned so many young hopefuls into entrepreneurial farmers over the years.

Furthermore, the IAR, from its small but very well cared-for vineyards, produced a range of wines that were highly representative of middle Aosta Valley winemaking, adding to the very special local indigenous product other highly successful products made with international varieties.

It is strange but true that the wine considered to be the flagship wine is neither native nor international: it is the Petite Arvine, a wine made from white grapes whose origin is disputed between the Swiss Valais and the Aosta Valley. The wine label says everything there is to know about the vineyard, the cellar and consumption.

INSTITUT AGRICOLE RÉGIONAL /AOSTE

PETITE ARVINE 2012

ZONA DI PRODUZIONE · IL VIGNETO È SITUATO SULLA COLLINA DI AOSTA IN LOCALITÀ COSSAN AD UNA ALTITUDINE DI 620 M S.L.M. CON ESPOSIZIONE SUD. L'APPEZZAMENTO SISTEMATO A RITTOCHINO HA UNA PENDENZA MEDIA DEL 35% ED UN TERRENO RICCO IN SCHELETRO A TESSITURA FRANCO-SABBIOSA.
LE VITI ALLEVATE A GUYOT SEMPLICE CON UNA DENSITÀ DI IMPIANTO DI 10.000 CEPPI/ETTARO GODONO DI UN CLIMA ENDOALPINO ASCIUTTO E VENTILATO CHE NE FAVORISCE LA COLTIVAZIONE.
UVE: ARVINE 100%.

DALL'UVA AL VINO · LE UVE VENDEMMIATE NELLA SECONDA DECADE DI SETTEMBRE A SEGUITO DELLA DIRASPATURA SONO STATE CRIOMACERATE E PRESSATE AL RIPARO DALL'OSSIGENO. IL MOSTO OTTENUTO, RESO LIMPIDO PER FLOTTAZIONE, HA FERMENTATO LENTAMENTE A TEMPERATURA E OSSIGENAZIONE CONTROLLATA. IL VINO È STATO QUINDI CONSERVATO PER 5 MESI SULLE FECCE DI FERMENTAZIONE ED AFFINATO PER ALMENO UN MESE IN BOTTIGLIA.
PRODUZIONE: 2.600 BOTTIGLIE.

CARATTERISTICHE DEL VINO ED ABBINAMENTI · COLORE GIALLO PAGLIERINO TENDENTE AL VERDOGNOLO. IN EVIDENZA SENTORI DOLCI, AGRUMATI, MINERALI E FLOREALI, PERCEPIBILI SIA AL NASO CHE AL RETROGUSTO. LA BUONA STRUTTURA ED IL SAPORE FRESCO E SAPIDO LO RENDONO INDICATO PER ACCOMPAGNARE LA FONTINA D'ALPEGGIO D.O.P. O LA PASTA ALLA CARBONARA.
TEMPERATURA DI SERVIZIO: 10-12°C.

BERSANO

The New Way for Barbera Wine

PIEDMONT

www.bersano.it

At the end of the nineteenth century, in Nizza Monferrato, the first Bersano nucleus was established, but the turning point came in 1935 under the leadership of **Arturo Bersano**, a lawyer by profession, but winemaker by passion. He was a man of great intuition, modern and innovative enough to anticipate tastes and trends. He is considered to be the father of Barbera and the pioneer of sparkling Brachetto. "If you want to drink well, buy yourself a vineyard". This statement summarizes the thinking and working philosophy of the Bersano of yesterday and today, and respects the tradition of the *terroir*, now owned by the **Soave** and **Massimelli** families.

The Bersano adventure began in 1912 with the acquisition of the Cascina Cremosina, the ancient palace of the Counts of Cremosina, with 12 hectares of vineyards in the heart of the area known as the cradle of production for Barbera d'Asti. Later came the vineyards of Langa (Cascina Badarina in Serralunga), the expansion of the favourite (Cascina La Generala, Vigneto Monteolivo, Cascina Buccelli, Cascina Prata) and prestigious estates that grew Moscato (Cascina San Michele), Brachetto (Cascina Castelgaro) and last in order of time, Ruchè and Grignolino (Cascina San Pietro). These ten estates are equal to 230 hectares and produce 1.8 million bottles. In the 1960s, Barbera Cremosina, a generous cru, came into being, and was aged in the traditional way in large oak casks. The Barbera Superiore Generala, from the vineyards located in the municipality of Agliano Terme, also came into being that same year, 1996, from 5 acres with an arc of exposure to the south and east, and an award-winning, elegant, full-bodied and very balanced wine. In addition to the Barbera, the winery produces all of the most important wines in Piedmont.

The spirit of Arturo Bersano lives on in two museums: that of Contadinerie e della Cultura materiale, in Pino Torinese – which boasts a unique collection of farming tools and equipment, including presses from the 1700s and old ploughs – and the museum of prints, in Nizza Monferrato, which preserves the *Pomona* by Giorgio Gallesio, a rare volume from 1817 considered to be the first database of Italian grapevines.

FONTANAFREDDA

The Story Continues

PIEDMONT
www.fontanafredda.it

"After Marquis Falletti, the person who helped bring fame to Barolo was Count Cavour . . . Later the Count of Mirafiori also entered the race, producing Barolo on his Fontanafredda estate. He took it from the private sphere where it was deemed a luxury wine to the common market by selling it very commercially". In these few lines, taken from *Il Paese del Barolo* by Domenico Massè (1924), we can easily trace the history of this winery, which takes in Barolo history.

The Tenuta di Fontanafredda (estate) in fact became part of the heritage of King Vittorio Emanuele II in 1858. It was then handed over to Rosa Vercellana, the "bela Rusin", first the lover and then the morganatic wife of the king, then Countess of Mirafiore and Fontanafredda. Historical reminiscences and popular suggestions follow one after another and unite. Here, the king who "made Italy" let himself become involved, become carried away by his amorous passions and built the country house dedicated to his fiery lover here.

From this love, two sons were born. One, Count Emanuele, decided to cultivate a vineyard on these lands, to have cellars dug and to found the Mirafiori-Vini Italiani, currently the Tenimenti di Barolo e Fontanafredda (then simply Fontanafredda). He gave it a great boost nationally, but even more, the boost for the Barolo market internationally, followed by the work of Count Gastone, his son, involved in politics and economics.

Wartime and economic strife in the early twentieth century sanctioned the collapse of the Mirafiori. In 1931, it was taken over by the bank, Monte dei Paschi di Siena, which appointed the winemaker Bressano as manager to replant the vineyards and revive the cellars. In recent years, the property passed to another visionary, **Oscar Farinetti**, who revitalized its sales and the commercial image of this brand which today, with its 90 hectares and concessions, produces about 7.5 million bottles.

PIO CESARE

The Epic Moment Is Still Topical

PIEDMONT
www.piocesare.it

Langa and Barolo are the languages spoken by this winery founded in 1881 by **Pio Cesare**, great-grandfather of the current owners. Its cellars speak of history, cellars built on the foundations of Roman and medieval walls, because it is the only one left in the centre of Alba. Its label speaks of history, that of Barolo, with the coat-of-arms of the city of Alba granted by the City Council and stylized gold medals, symbols of numerous awards: first prize in Asti, then in Turin in 1902, in Brussels in 1910 and Cetinje, and then in far off Montenegro, home of Queen Elena.

Pio Cesare believed in the potential of the Nebbiolo grape, especially in wines like Barolo and Barbaresco: at the beginning of the last century, his winery was ready to take on the European market, becoming one of the first wine exporters in Alba. Today as yesterday, this family offers the style of its Barolo with the pursuit of excellence, maintaining limited quantities and carefully managing all the phases of the grapes from vineyard to cellar. The 50 hectare property is located in some very advantageous positions.

In the Barolo area in Serralunga d'Alba (Cascine Ornate and Colombaro), in Grinzane Cavour (Cascina Gustava) in La Morra (Roncaglie vineyard), in Novello (Ravera vineyard). In Barbaresco a Treiso (Cascine Il Bricco and San Stefanetto), Sinio, Diano d'Alba and Trezzo Tinella. In addition, grapes with some historical attributes are used, from Castiglione Falletto, Monforte and Serralunga.

The style of Pio Cesare's Barolo, exported to more than forty countries, comes down to the fact that the Nebbiolo grapes from the different vineyards are blended, in appropriate percentages in fermentation, to bring out all the features of the different *terroirs* of DOCG.

PRUNOTTO

The Selections that Make a Winery Great

PIEDMONT

www.prunotto.it

Today, Prunotto is part of the Marchesi Antinori group, a family that has reached its twenty-sixth generation, and, as **Piero Antinori** likes to say, counts the vintages of its wine in centuries. The history of Prunotto began, however, in 1923 when **Alfredo Prunotto** took over the cooperative winery Ai Vini delle Langhe, founded in Alba in 1904, and gave it his own name, making it a popular winery through sale of its wines abroad, especially in Argentina. The Prunotto did not own vineyards, but selected and vinified the best grapes from the vineyards of the Langhe, the Alba and Monferrato areas, the properties of vintners bound by cooperative relationships based on the same vision and philosophy of production. In 1956, Prunotto left it in the hands of the Colla brothers who, from the early 1960s, began the selection of the most suitable vineyards to produce cru, like Barolo Bussia or Barbera d'Alba Pian Romualdo. In 1989, Antinori began working with the winery, first handing with the wine distribution, and then taking the helm in 1994, when the Colla brothers retired.

It was Marquis Piero's first-born, Albiera, who looked after the development of the estate. They purchased important vineyards, such as cru Bussia, an amphitheatre of just over 7 hectares in Monforte, one of the most renowned in the area of Barolo, Costamiole in Agliano for the production of Barbera d'Asti, Bric Turot in the Barbaresco area and Treiso for the production of

Moscato, amounting to an area of 50 hectares with an annual production of about 800,000 bottles, mostly reds and, to a lesser degree, Moscato Bianco and Arneis.

ISTITUTO AGRARIO DI SAN MICHELE ALL'ADIGE

No Quality Wine Can Be the Product of Chance

TRENTINO

www.fmach.it

The history of the agrarian institute has a certain starting date: 12 January 1874, when the Tyrolean Regional Diet of Innsbruck decided to open, in San Michele, the southernmost part of the Empire, an agrarian school with an experimental station attached. The credit goes to the first director, **Edmund Mach**, for having prepared the ground on which he then went about defining the current complex. Mach's philosophy – incidentally, Mach had married the daughter of the inventor of the saccharimeter, the Hungarian Babo – was that no quality wine can be considered the product of chance; it must be, instead, the result of a fortuitous encounter between natural and human factors, of which the vine always has the predominant part.

Today, the farm covers an area of nearly 200 hectares, of which only a few dozen are

vineyard. Six of them are dedicated to the harvesting of about 2,500 different genotypes of vines. The grapes produced are all vinified in the cellar, which was expanded and streamlined in 1994, with an admirable combination of ancient and modern. The part where the wine is aged preserves inlaid barrels that remind one of various directors of the Institute or particular historical events.

In 1957, the Association of Former Students of the Institute organized a study trip to Bordeaux. With them was Professor Defrancesco, then director of laboratory analysis and research, as recalled by his friend Leonello Letrari. That trip was to result in the birth of two important wines, true forerunners of the great modern Italian *Bordolesi* or Bordeaux blends: Castel San Michele and the Fojaneghe, the latter produced by Letrari at Bossi Fedrigotti, where he worked.

TENUTA SAN LEONARDO

Bordeaux Love

TRENTINO
www.sanleonardo.it

In 1724, the Tenuta San Leonardo was founded. It has always belonged to the same family, and is now owned by the direct descendant, the Marquis **Carlo Guerrieri Gonzaga**. The splendid farm, located in Vallagarina, to the extreme south of Trentino, includes around 300 hectares of which 25 are devoted to vineyards: there grow the rows of Cabernet Sauvignon, Carmenere, Cabernet Franc and Merlot vines, some of which were already growing in the late 1800s. The Guerrieri Gonzagas have always been ambitious in their aim to produce distinguished wines. A pioneering role was played by the Guerrieri Gonzagas, especially in the line of *bordolesi* or Bordeaux wines. Since the 1970s, they have been at the forefront of production in Italy. The winemaker's true development took place with Carlo Gonzaga, who studied oenology in Lausanne and fell in love with the vineyards and wines of Bordeaux. The vineyards are between 150 and 200 metres above sea level, mainly sandy soils and rich in sedimentary pebbles. Some fifteen years ago he discovered that what was believed to be a Franc, is actually just a Carménère. The similarity with the great reds like the Bordeaux or Sassicaia did not end there, inasmuch as Carlo, in 1984, took on Giacomo Tachis, who was a consultant until 1999. In 2000, Tachis was replaced by Carlo Ferrini, who in 2008 was awarded best oenologist in the world by *Wine Enthusiast Magazine*. The company produces a total of about 300,000 bottles, more than half of which are destined for the foreign market, thanks to major and forward-looking investments, such as the new cellar for aging wine. Made with an imposing structure (also impressive to look at) it is only dimly lit, so as to give the visitor the feeling of being in a place of worship. In the large wine shop in front of the winery are all the vintages produced from the 1960s to today.

ABBAZIA DI NOVACELLA

900 Years in a Convent

ALTO ADIGE
www.abbazianovacella.it

The Novacella Abbey near Varna is the largest convent in the Tyrol. Founded in 1142, from the beginning it was conceived as a large independent institution, dedicated to various activities. While long ago it was also a hospice for pilgrims, today many businesses, all economically autonomous, are linked to the monastery, from agriculture to viticulture, the herbal medicine shop, the winery, the power plant, and the culture and education centre. Viticulture in particular has given a special lustre to the Abbey in recent decades. Consider that here we are in the most northerly part of Italy with regard to the cultivation of the vine. The last vineyard in the Italian territory is located just behind the mighty wall of the convent, which collects the accumulated heat from the stone and gives back ripe and fragrant grapes. Like all of the Isarco Valley, the wine cellar of Novacella or Neustift has been increasingly distinguished by the production of white wines, especially those of Germanic derivation. Sylvaner, Kerner, Gewürztraminer and Veltliner are the most important varieties. Entrusted to the capable winemaker **Celestino Lucin**, the Abbey makes wine from grapes grown in about 50 hectares by 400 associates on the sunny slopes around Neustift, ideal for whites rich in minerals. Succulent products arrive from the deep cellars of Neustift. The soil rich in minerals, on partially steep slopes, and the warm daytime temperatures and cool nights give the grapes unmistakable aromas. Modern winemaking techniques, traditional methods, the delicate relationship with the raw materials and, finally, centuries of experience, all do their part. It is no coincidence that the white wines from the cellars of the Abbey are always considered the best at national and international tastings and receive the highest awards.

BERTANI

A Great Family in the History of Italian Wine

VENETO
www.bertani.net

In Quinto di Valpantena, the brothers **Giovan Battista** and **Gaetano Bertani** founded one of the most successful Italian wineries in 1857. It profoundly marked the history of Italian wine and its international prestige. They were the precursors of bottled wine in Italy already at the end of the nineteenth century, and exported to the United States. Gaetano's passion led him to revolutionize the production style thanks to agronomy studies carried out by Professor Guyot in France. In 1957, the Bertani acquired the beautiful villa Novare in the Valpolicella Classica, a Venetian villa with 220 hectares of property. It was in the wineries of this villa that Adelino Lucchese, in 1938, pronounced for the first time the epithet "Amarone". The word became the name of the great Italian red wine. Bertani was one of the first to try to make the ancient Recioto della Valpolicella "bitter". The family remained owner of the business until 2014. "From January 1, 2014," says the President **Emilio Pedron**, "the Tenimenti Angelini branch of the business with agricultural activities in the Marches and viticulture in Tuscany was granted to Cav. G.B. Bertani. Now its name is Bertani Domains, and it maintains the head office in Grezzana. The values of a brand that is so important and prestigious for the entire Italian winemaking sector will not be lost, on the contrary . . . Never having renounced the origins, while remaining intimately linked to the winemaking territory, without indulging in easy fashions and trends, they have made Cav. G.B. Bertani a brand with a very good reputation and recognisability, where identity is the stronger appeal for markets around the world. Bertani is an example of a historic wine brand in which, in addition to the quality of the product, there is a series of evocative values linked to a business, to a territory, to a vineyard. An example of an extremely important model on which to build a successful path for the future as well".

BOLLA

The Carter and the Key

VENETO
www.bolla.it

"Ready-to-eat tripe and Soave white" is the main attraction of the ancient stop at the Osteria Del Gambero, which was run by *siora* Giulia who, in the late nineteenth century, married a handsome young man who loved life. He was called Abele and was the son of a butcher. From their union seven children were born. The first-born, Alberto, stayed on to help his mother. He liked to be in the cellar of the house fiddling around with wine. He found it to be so good that, one day in 1883, he loaded the first 50 litre *bigoncia* onto his shoulders and

started selling it to the families of Soave. Thanks to this, the **Fratelli Bolla** was born. From families, he went on to propose changes to the taverns of Soave and, finally, every night, with a gig pulled by a horse, he carried two 5 hl barrels into the city, one to Verona and then one to Venice. They called him *il carrettiere* (the carter). In 1901, the adventure of the Calice in Venice began, an inn that was later expanded with the Della Posta tavern. In 1918, the winery in Soave was built, but Alberto was one who could see into the future and understood well that Valpolicella had enormous potential; so, in 1931, the adventure began in Pedemonte, still the base of Bolla today. While Alberto was the founder, his son Giorgio was the driving force behind this great Italian wine business. His innovation was a lesson: from 1935, wine was increasingly sold in the bottle. In 1940, he acquired the Valdo cellars in Valdobbiadene, having realized that Prosecco bubbles would be the new great wine market. With Giorgio, Bolla became a strong brand; with him began the exports to the United States and Europe. After his death, Bolla experienced difficult times and was bought out by the American company, Brown-Forman. Since 2008, finally, Bolla has become an Italian brand under the aegis of the Italian Wine Group.

TEDESCHI

Pioneers of the Land on a Quest for the "Perfect Wine"

VENETO

www.tedeschiwines.com

Renzo Tedeschi's story is about pioneering, in terms of his relationship with the land and his ability to interpret wine. Bearing witness to this, in 1964 was the vinification of grapes from a single vineyard, the cru that made the history of the business and represented a landmark for the entire area, Monte Olmi. The Tedeschi family consists of generations in confrontation, and today there are the impassioned children of Renzo: Antonietta, Sabrina and Riccardo. A collection of experiences and stories that share the enthusiasm of the quest for the soul of the land suggested by their father. The vineyards on the property are wonderfully scenic. They cling to the marl fossil outcrops of Maternigo, or the white clay of Fabriseria. These pristine lands are a clear sign of the business's production style and emphasize the power of interpretation, decidedly autochthonous, bound to the typical grapes of Valpolicella: Corvina, Corvinone, Rondinella and other local cultivars such as Oseleta, Dindarella, Negrara, Rossignola and Forselina. Vines that touch the sky to a height of 400 metres, where the fresh breeze of the Lessini Mountains preserves the integrity of the plant and the purity of the fruit. Innovation in the care and management of the vineyard, looking for modern solutions that maintain the basic nature of the tradition in the cellars are the company's foundations, combined with a great capacity to penetrate markets. Today the Tedeschi family is committed, with the "Amarone Families", to a major project to protect the value of this great wine in the world.

FATTORIA PARADISO

Mario Pezzi, the Talent Scout of Forgotten Grapes

EMILIA-ROMAGNA

www.fattoriaparadiso.it

Mario Pezzi is linked to a large part of the history of viticulture in Romagna. We are on the hills of Bertinoro, in view of the Roccca (fortress) which was the fine residence of Emperor Frederick, known as Barbarossa (Redbeard), at the time of the Holy Roman Empire. Mario started to become familiar with the vineyards in the early 1950s, bringing order to the old family rows, purchased by his grandfather and virtually untouched over the years.

In 1955, almost by accident, he identified an unknown vine, perhaps an old complementary vine "to the Romagnola" of Sangiovese. With a name from myth and legend, he called it Barbarossa, as proud and vigorous as a Roman emperor. The Pagadebit and Cagnina met the same fate, finding redemption beyond their humble blazon.

However, Mario Pezzi focused his attention on the Sangiovese grape. From a special vineyard where hares run, a reserve was born, and destined to age well. Luigi Veronelli praised it, often electing it as a touchstone for the reds of the era. President Pertini poured Vigna delle Lepri into Ronald Reagan's glass when he was visiting Rome. The Holy See stores it in their sacred cellars and the University of Bologna celebrated nine centuries of history with it. Although the wines of Fattoria Paradiso began their pilgrimage to the tables of the world, their soul remains deeply that of Romagna. Bearing witness to this are the labels designed by Tonino Guerra, the names that pay tribute to Federico Fellini, their talkative and breezy spirit. Even today, with daughter Graziella and grandson Jacopo, who took over the winery after his father's death, the hares run happily between the rows of grapevines in the shadow of the Ugarte Castle, home of the cellar and guest rooms.

Friuli Venezia Giulia

Before the arrival of the great oenological innovator in Friuli, Mario Schiopetto, between the end of the 1960s and the early 1970s, several wineries in Friuli Venezia Giulia had accepted the challenge of the great marketplace and decided to bottle their wine.

One of the most fascinating among these is **Rocca Bernarda** (built in 1567) in Ipplis, in the Colli Orientali zone. Its story is forever linked to the recovery of Picolit, merit of the Antonini Perusini family, who bought the estate in 1905.

Picolit owes its fame – in the second half of the eighteenth century it was on the tables of all the European courts – to Fabio Asquini of Fagagna. After his death, in 1818, Picolit was eclipsed. **Gaetano Perusini**, a highly learned man, decided to put the wine in a bottle in 1958. His early production of Picolit (recovery of vineyards which had been started by his father Giacomo) followed the dictates of the Asquini: the grapes were left to wither, then de-stemmed and left overnight in the skins. They were poured into barrels to be fermented and then the fermentation was blocked by filtration bags. After 1968, Gaetano introduced pressing without maceration, while the withering process and aging in wood remained the same. The Picolit was simply divine!

Professor Gaetano also deserves the credit of having intuitively understood how high-quality wine should be supported by history and culture through, for example, the publication of brochures and books, such as *Mangiare e Ber Friulano* from 1962, written by his mother Giuseppina, who lived to be almost 101 years old. This book is still vital for historical research on Friulian cuisine.

In 1977, Gaetano passed away and left the business to the Order of Malta which, since 2006, has run it through the Società Agricola Vitivinicola Italiana (Italian Agricultural Wine Society).

Not far from Ipplis, at Buttrio, another winery decided to face the market: that of **Count d'Attimis-Maniago** who began bottling in 1932. "In an empirical way," as Count Gianfranco d'Attimis-Maniago himself remembers, "just to participate in the trade fairs in Buttrio and Cividale". After the war he was one of the first to follow the dictates of the new wine, with advice from Marcello Pillon, an oenologist from Trieste, who worked at the winery from 1955 to 1965. In 1957, his bottles were sold in Turin, Bologna, Padua and Trieste. Three years later, he was also selling in Asiago, Treviso, Rome, Venice, Aosta, Milan, Rome and Siena. Now the winery – founded in 1585 – belongs to Alberto d'Attimis-Maniago, who brought it to 400,000 bottles with 86 hectares of vineyards, all in the DOC Friuli Colli Orientali (eastern hills). After Pillon, in 1968, another oenologist arrived with a forward-looking vision, Antonino Spitaleri. In 2002, his son Francesco, as talented as his father, replaced him.

In the area that was once Austrian Friuli, namely the Goriška, the **Tenuta Villanova** – founded in 1499 – was the first winery to make bottled wine its productive and commercial strategy. In August 1898, the then owner Alberto Levi opened a store to sell their wines in Paris. In 1869, he had already hosted Pasteur, to carry out studies on grapevine diseases. Always looking to the future, Tenuta Villanova, in the late 1920s and first in Friuli, added a production line of sparkling wine, using the Martinotti-Charmat method.

Now the company – 27 hectares in the DOC Collio and 100 in Isonzo, for 500,000 bottles – belongs to **Giuseppina Grossi Bennati**, who carried out an exemplary restoration and entrusted the leadership to her grandson, **Alberto Grossi**. The original distillery of 1797 was restored to perfection and is still used in the business; it boasts a Habsburg license.

In Cormòns, in the Isonzo plain, the Tenuta di Angoris has been in existence since far-off 1648. In the early 1950s, the **Miani Counts**, the then owners, called on **Giovan Battista Turcotti**, a Piedmontese oenologist who remained there until 1965. The oenological innovation was radical and the results were evident. His wines received coveted awards. In 1963, at the IX Fair in Ljubljana, his Pinot Grigio and Tocai were awarded the gold medal, while his Traminer and Merlot received silver, all 1959 vintages. In 1966, at the Fourth World Selection in Brussels, he won the bronze with his Pinot Grigio 1962 and silver in 1962 with his Merlot. In Paris in 1967 (V World Selection of Wines, Spirits and Liqueurs) he won the gold with Pinot Grigio, while his Tocai and Merlot were awarded silver, all 1964 vintages.

In 1968, the estate was purchased by the **Locatelli family**, who still owns the property.

Another turning point came in 1969 with the arrival in the cellar of oenologist Luigi Soini (who worked there until 1978). For the white wines, he applied the teachings of the Istituto Agrario di San Michele all'Adige, which drew inspiration from German oenology and then influenced all the producers of the Friuli Venezia Giulia region and beyond. Angoris bought the first two horizontal Willmes presses in the region which were, together with those of Cavit of Trento, the first sold in Italy. The innovative techniques were soft pressing, cold settling of must, fermentation temperature control, cold sterile bottling thanks to Seitz technology.

Luigi Soini, in 1971, started the first production in Friuli Venezia Giulia of sparkling wine – called Modolet – produced with both the Charmat and the Champenoise methods.

In 1973, Angoris reached one million bottles, and the workers, to commemorate the event, gave Locatelli a bottle with a silver collar.

The winery – which has an area of 620 hectares, of which 120 are vineyards in the DOC Colli Orientali, the Collio and Isonzo – currently produces about 750,000 bottles a year.

RUFFINO

Drinking Chianti throughout the World

TUSCANY
www.ruffino.com

Let's talk about one of the "major" Italian wines. The company was founded in 1877 by the cousins **Ilario** and **Leopoldo Ruffino,** in Pontassieve, where the headquarters are still located. Already by the end of the nineteenth century, they were working on the selection of grapes and vineyards. In 1913, the winery was taken over by another great wine family, the Folonari. In 1947, Chianti Classico Riserva Ducale Oro was born, today the symbol of "drinking Ruffino". Meanwhile the business expanded, acquiring new estates in Tuscany that today amount to 600 hectares of vineyards owned by the winery, for an annual production of nearly 15 million bottles. In 2011, it took another historic step: Ruffino is the first Italian wine to be part of Constellation Brands. This was a new phase for Ruffino, one that had to combine a Tuscan soul with the international market. Poggio Casciano, Montemasso, Santedame, La Solatia, Gretole and Greppone Mazzi make up the highest quality groups. Labels such as Romitorio di Santedame, Modus, Brunello di Montalcino and Greppone Mazzi, along with the previously mentioned Riserva Ducale Oro, represent the "great classic Tuscans". In a world that demands more and more "territory", the challenge now is to increasingly enhance the local nature of each productive area. Like the 2008 vintage, with its credible Chianti ancestry in its cherry and undergrowth flavours. An evenly distributed tannin in the wine's structure stimulates the properties and takes them from one sip to the next. Like the most austere and rigorous wine, typical of the Montalcino slopes, we find it in Brunello Greppone Mazzi 2008, which in its notes of orange peel and tobacco hints at its potential evolution. And finally, faced with a more casual glass of Nuovo Fiasco Chianti Superiore, it comes automatically to recite the slogan "The future belongs to those who began it".

LEONE DE CASTRIS

From Salento . . . to the Whole World

PUGLIA
www.leonedecastris.com

It was 1925 when the marriage between **Piero Francesco Leone** and **Anna Luisa Filippa de Castris** joined the vast land holdings of two of the most important families in the province of Lecce. Over 2,000 hectares on the hills between Salice Salentino, Guagnano, Campi, San Pancrazio and San Donaci. These fertile lands are caressed by the wind and kissed by the sun. The same year Piero, who, though very young, had already dedicated himself to wine production long before, bottled the first wine from Puglia. And since then, the producer of this wine that combines tradition and modernity has made great inroads in the exportation of "Made in Salento" to the rest of the world.

Another historic year was 1943. This is when the first rosé wine bottled in Italy was born: the renowned Five Roses. "My grandfather," says **Piernicola Leone**, "who headed the company for a decade, at the end of the last war, received a large order for rosé wine from General Charles Poletti, Commissioner for Procurement of the Allied Forces. They, however, wanted a wine with an English name and so, taking inspiration from a family district named Cinque Rose for the fact that for generations the de Castris had had five children, Five Roses was born. Since the northern glassworks were in German hands, for the first bottlings they used beer bottles recycled by American troops in Brindisi."

Today, Five Roses, produced with the classic blend of Salento, Negroamaro and Malvasia Nera, is one of the best known rosé wines in Italy and is marketed in three versions: the classic, the anniversary and the very recent version of Classic method sparkling wine. The trip back in time then stops in 1954. That year, Salice Salentino Rosso was born, thanks to Salvatore Leone, and in 1976 received the DOC.

DUCA DI SALAPARUTA

A "Degree" for the Nero d'Avola

SICILY

www.duca.it

Illva di Saronno, famous for the production of Amaretto, brings together three historic Sicilian brands: Corvo, Duca di Salaparuta and Florio (we have dedicated a separate entry to this last brand).
Augusto Reina, the patron of Illva, acquired Corvo in 2001 from the Sicilian Region, which in turn had taken it over from the family of the Duke of Salaparuta. The Region put in place a very innovative model whose flagship is Duca Enrico, the first Nero d'Avola of Sicily. The idea came from the then technical director, the Piedmontese oenologist **Franco Giacosa**, with the vintage of 1984. So it was that Nero d'Avola proved that it could compete on world markets. The company was founded in 1824 by **Giuseppe Alliatas**, Prince of Villafranca and Duke of Salaparuta, who started making wine and bottling it from grapes from his property in Contrada Corvo in Casteldaccia, in the province of Palermo. The business was continued by his son Eduardo, reaching a production of 100,000 bottles a year and exporting them to Europe and America under the brand Duca di Salaparuta. Its wines were different from most Sicilian wines at the time, with a smooth fruity taste and light body. The business continued in the twentieth century led by Duke Enrico Alliata, connoisseur of French winemaking techniques, which he introduced in Sicily. In 1959, Topazia Alliata, daughter of Enrico, sold the business to the Region.

Augusto Reina immediately entrusted the direction to Carlo Casavecchia. They revived the historic labels, but the turning point was the choice of new properties. Now there was the Tenuta Suor Marchesa, in Butera – the place of provenance for Nero d'Avola grapes – Risignolo in Salemi, Vajasindi on the slopes of Etna, where he focused on Pinot Noir. There were almost 120 hectares of properties. Around Duke Enrico, other wines were born, like the Bianco di Valguarnera, the Lavico di Vajasindi, the blend of Nero d'Avola and Merlot Triskele.

ATTILIO CONTINI

Protecting Ancient Vines

SARDINIA

www.vinicontini.com

Standing out in the chaotic wine scene of the 1960s was **Attilio Contini**'s winery in Cabras, one of the oldest, founded in the late nineteenth century. "We followed in the footsteps of our grandfather, Salvatore, who since the beginning of the twentieth century, was able to bring Vernaccia and Nieddera [*then called Vino Nero or Black Wine*] into the regions of Northern Italy and abroad". This is how **Paolo Contini**, current president of the winery, remembers the founder. He continues: "In the 1960s, we focused all our efforts on also protecting other local vineyards such as Muristellu and Caddiu, which were in danger of being abandoned". The interest of many companies had turned to two continental vines, Trebbiano and Sangiovese, which had arrived on the island a few decades earlier, when the wetlands of Oristano were reclaimed. The Contini, on the other hand, believed in Vernaccia, the princely wine of the island, and one with great character. At the end of the nineteenth century the author of *Vini d'Italia* (Buenos Aires, 1895), Pompeo Trentin, wrote: "It is a wine that is an exception to the rule, and one that wants to know absolutely nothing about the oenological rules". Compared by many to the great Xeres, in the 1960s, its fame increased for its wealth of aromas and especially for its extraordinary longevity, which in particular vintages can even go beyond a century, improving.
Given the great potential and versatility of the

grape, the winery began to plan for the future, thinking of new types of wines based on the Vernaccia grape, both on its own and in a blend, without sacrificing its traditional qualities. The tenacity of such courageous producers as the Contini helped in its obtaining the first DOC in Sardinia, a few years later, in 1971.

The 1970s

The Decade of Oenology

At the time, while the work between the rows deserved an excellent rating, in the cellar the rating was negative. Modern oenology – as a science capable of explaining the processes to transform grapes into wine and manage them wisely – found its first spaces at the beginning of this decade.

Until then it was the wine of the alchemist. What we call oenology today was, in fact, a true dispensation of chemicals with which we ran all the production processes, at very low costs.

It was in the early 1970s that we saw the beginning of the long process that would lead knowledgeable oenology to drive that chemistry away from the temple. It was also the beginning of sustainable oenology that, thanks to research applied to technology – primarily, controlling the temperatures of fermentation and hygiene – would bring Italy, in a very short time, to become a world leader in the production of wine-making machinery.

This radical transformation, which took place between 1968 and 1970, had a dual origin. Tuscany, which pointed the way for red wines thanks to **Piero Antinori**, with his Sassicaia (then) and Tignanello. He took advantage of **Émile Peynaud**'s school of Bordeaux and **Giacomo Tachis**'s skill. Piero Antinori's thinking can be summarized as follows: "Modern technology simply allows us to express our full potential".

Then Friuli, with **Mario Schiopetto**, dictated the style of modern white wines, primarily had German technology as its oenological model.

In the Rauscedo in Pordenone, a system was developed to guarantee the quality of nursery clones for the new vineyards.

Again from Friuli, thanks to the Premio Nonino Risit d'Âur (Barbatella d'oro), and at the wishes of the Nonino distillery along with Luigi Veronelli, the cultural movement for the recovery and preservation of local varieties in danger of extinction was launched. A long-term vision. If we can now boast the largest world heritage of indigenous varieties, we owe it to Risit d'Âur.

PRODUTTORI DEL BARBARESCO

The Vindication of Cooperation

PIEDMONT

www.produttoridelbarbaresco.com

The light beige label is unmistakable, and has not changed since the 1960s: it shows the imposing medieval tower of Barbaresco, a symbol of the town, and a coin from the Roman period displaying Emperor Publius Helvius Pertinax, who was born precisely in the area of Barbaresco di Pertinace.

The wine is that of the Produttori del Barbaresco, a cooperative winery founded in 1958 by father **Fiorino Marengo** to give dignity to a depressed area and to keep people in the town and in the vineyards during a period of heavy migration to the city, especially after World War II. In 1958, the story that began in the nineteenth century was taken up once again, when Domizio Cavazza, director of the Royal Oenological School of Alba, founded the Cooperative Winery of Barbaresco, to make wine under the name of Barbaresco with the grapes of nine local growers.

Today there are 51 members, 105 hectares of vineyards, and 9 cru: Rabajà, Asili, Montestefano, Pora, Ovello, Rio Sordo, Montefico, Moccagatta and Pajè. They represent just under 20% of all the DOCs. Each member is obliged to give all the Barbaresco Nebbiolo that it produces, and is not allowed to sell the grapes to third parties or make their own wine. This cellar is considered one of the best cooperatives in Europe.

The range of wines has always been focused on Barbaresco. Today's version of the "basic" wine has existed since 1958, while 1967 was the first vintage with the vineyard indicated on the label. Since 1975, they have been producing a Langhe Nebbiolo, a pure Nebbiolo from grapes which meet the parameters of the specification for Barbaresco DOCG. Since 1986, the oenologist Gianni Testa has managed the cellars and they produce about 450,000 bottles, 50% of which are sold in Italy.

BARONE DE CLES

The Affirmation of Campo Rotaliano

TRENTINO-ALTO ADIGE

www.baronedecles.it

The story of the prince of Trentino wines, Teroldego, is inextricably tied to the land and sinks into the mists of time, even if it is from the 1950s that the wines from this area started to experience a revival. It was in 1943 that the Barons de Cles come into possession of the heritage of the extinct family **Scari di Cronhof**, who had cultivated Teroldego grapes on their farms in Campo Rotaliano since the late seventeenth century. Their cellar in the historic centre of Mezzolombardo already existed in 1759. In 1833, the Scari added to their old possessions a vast rocky moorland – then located along the bed of the Noce stream, diverted in 1852 into today's river bed – that they, with labour that cost them decades of sacrifice, reclaimed and planted. And right there, in the heart of Campo Rotaliano, there arose a beautiful vineyard: the Maso Scari, perhaps the best known Teroldego cru. This legacy reinforced the tradition of de Cles, who already in the fourteenth century possessed vineyards on the slopes around Castel Cles, the *ab immemorabili* fiefdom still owned by them. Bernardo de Cles, the most famous of the dynasty, was born there in 1485. He became Prince Bishop of Trento and Bressanone and Supreme Chancellor to King Ferdinand of Austria. He was a true gentleman of the Renaissance.

It was in the 1960s that the estate became a proper business, and began bottling its best wines in 1964. Under the guidance of **Michele de Cles**, the winery soon focused on a late harvest, to the point that at Maso Scari, the harvest rarely began before 25 October. In this way, the wine takes on that body and structure that makes it one of the difficult to achieve champions of Teroldego.

FORADORI

Copernican Revolution

TRENTINO-ALTO ADIGE
www.elisabettaforadori.com

One of the first and most authentic women in wine, **Elisabetta Foradori** is one of the pioneers of viticulture in Trentino and throughout Italy. Her father, Roberto, was one of the most significant producers of Teroldego in Piana Rotaliana. After his death, in 1985, together with her mother Gabriella, she took over management of the business, bringing it to the point of creating a small Copernican revolution. Her union in life, as well as in the field, with the brilliant oenology professor **Rainer Zierock**, definitely influenced the beginnings that led to removing the Trentino pergolas and replacing them with Guyot systems, giving lower yields, but in exchange giving a greater assurance of quality. When produced this way, Teroldego began to show its true nature: from a mortified wine with huge yields to a sumptuous red with a spectrum that is almost impenetrable and fleshy fruity aromas. The diligent use of small oak barrels gave it the elegance necessary to tackle the international market, which has led to significant recognition. These memorable wines, such as some of the vintages of Granato, are real touchstones. Then Elisabetta sought something more, a system that was more appropriate. She reconsidered her role, that of plants and that of the territory, as parts that could no longer be separate, but that formed a single whole. It was "a mental and personal leap", taking her to a different level, in a profound and creative interaction with her

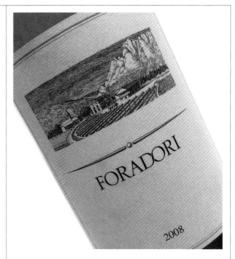

vineyards. From 2002, she has been practising biodynamic cultivation, a choice embraced with passion and conviction. Then she adopted the amphorae. The quest for natural wines has once again revolutionized the image of the symbol of this land where Regina Elisabetta (Queen Elizabeth) reigns.

CA' RUGATE

The Golden Garganega and its Volcano

VENETO
www.carugate.it

Amedeo Tessari, in the early years of the twentieth century, bought a small inn on the Verona plains, at Presina. He used it to sell his product. He was called to serve in the Army during the Great War. Towards the end of the conflict, he became seriously ill at the front, returned home and, ironically, died on Armistice Day. These were difficult years. His young son **Fulvio** was filled with great hope. He would eventually run the business and give it the dynamic strength that still sets it apart. He bought one of the most prestigious vineyards on the Rugate hillside, in Monteforte d'Alpone, and began to deal in his own grapes and wine. The success of the product was suddenly "explosive". For this reason, in the early 1950s, Fulvio bought the first vineyards on Mount Fiorentine. The land was not yet prized for its vineyards. It is ancient, hot, and today continues to produce one of the most prestigious cru of Soave. In the 1970s, the winery owned 10 hectares of vineyards and Fulvio decided to turn it into a real company, calling it Azienda Agricola Tessari Fulvio. Since 1986, the winery has been called Ca' Rugate, in honour of the hill and the birthplace of the Tessari family, which is still located there. Next to join the company was his son Fulvio, called Amedeo like his grandfather, and the nationwide marketing of wine began. All of this still took place in the fossil basalts of Brognoligo, the ancient village of Monteforte. But, in 2001, Amedeo's son Michele joined the company, and was a

volcano of ideas that completely changed communication strategies, and the definitive investment for the new business along the Val d'Alpone was launched. In the same year, the project Campo Lavèi came into being, the first Valpolicella for the Tessari family. Today Ca' Rugate is one of the most noble and enterprising wineries in the area east of Verona, with a surface area of 60 hectares and a market that extends to over 34 countries.

PIEROPAN

The Simple and Revolutionary Soul of Soave

VENETO
www.pieropan.it

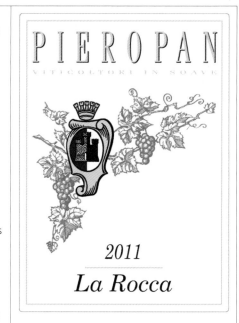

Leonildo Pieropan does not think twice: "I'm fine when I'm in the vineyard. It's my world and I feel particularly close to it, as I always have!" The story of this great winemaker of Soave lies in the simplicity and passion that every gesture expresses. Teresita, his wife, lovingly calls him a nineteenth-century man. His journey began in 1967 when, just having graduated in Conegliano, he decided to take over the vineyard of his father Fausto. The vineyard, Calvarino, is just over 4 hectares, and was bought in 1901 by his grandfather Leonildo, who had the same name and was born just a century before him. Leonildo is a young visionary with a strong sense of perfection. He has *his* vineyard and *his* wine in mind. He knows that he must revolutionize a world that is still teetering on outdated practices and farming systems. With him, viticulture and the Soave grape have changed their look. He was the first to plant espaliered vineyards in 1969 and, subsequently, to reduce the buds from 50 to 10 in the pergolas of Garganega. He was the first to adopt green pruning methods, removing undesired clusters of grapes. He was the first to use the horizontal Vaslin press, bought in 1968, which was to completely change the characteristics of Soave. Finally, he was also the first to restore the value of Recioto as a wine and a historical identity. In 1970, with the blind tastings, his wines came to be considered extraordinary. That evolved technique makes them more fragrant, finer, more pleasant: these were the Soave wines that were to inspire everyone.

Leonildo unwittingly became a reference point in the oenology of Soave between the 1970s and 1980s. In 1971, he produced the Soave Calvarino, and in 1978, Soave La Rocca, aged in wood, another revolution for his territory.

The First Crus – Subzones – of Friuli Venezia Giulia

"I solved the problems of the re-fermentation of my Ramandolo when Giuseppe Lipari invented the mobile bottling centre, Centro Mobile d'imbottigliamento [*today Centro di Riferimento Enologico*]". The speaker is **Giovanni Dri**, the first winemaker in the small, but important, area of Ramandolo to have walked the path of enhancement with this great sweet white wine, made from withered yellow Verduzzo grapes. He produced his first 600 bottles in 1968, but many of them had a tendency to re-ferment. This issue was finally resolved in 1976, when he was able to access the Mobile bottling service. However, he owes the launch of this wine onto the Italian stage to the Milanese **Angelo Solci**, oenologist. Together with his brother Piero, he ran the family wine shop, for which he created a selection that was made by Filippon, a local winemaker.

The Ramandolo from the Enoteca Solci was the wine that – combined with Neapolitan pastries – gave the victory to Claudio Boni, who became Italian champion of sommeliers during the national congress which was held in Naples in 1970. The wine had such a vast audience that Veronelli included it – the vintage was 1969 – in his *Catalogo Bolaffi dei vini del mondo* of 1973.

The great rebellion provoked by **Giannola** and **Benito Nonino** together with **Luigi Veronelli** with the Nonino Risit d'Âur award (Barbatella d'oro), to save the native varieties, influenced many winemakers. The first edition of the Risit prize was awarded to Dina and Paolo Rapuzzi for also planting, at the **Ronchi di Cialla**, Schioppettino, a variety in danger of extinction. The writer had, then, the wine consulting and sales activities and introduced for the first time in Friuli – it was 1977 – aging in the barrel. Schioppettino (but also the company's other indigenous varieties such as Picolit, Verduzzo and Refosco) found, in this interpretation, a new, exciting dimension.

The consultant's clear desire was to produce wines of high lineage that spoke a new language, also subverting the coded criteria of taste. A new way forward was opened, even if it provoked a deep rift among producers. The following years eventually determined who was right. Even the detractors, and there were many of them, converted to the new teaching. If Ronchi di Cialla was the first interpreter of the modern Schioppettino, its salvation was thanks to the Nonino.

LINI 910

The Art of Lambrusco – Classic Method

EMILIA-ROMAGNA
www.lini910.it

That number, standing out clearly on the Lini labels, has a precise meaning. It recalls the founding year (1910 to be precise) of this winery, one of the many success stories on the Italian boot that here, along the Via Emilia, includes no small number of addresses. Founded by three partners, **Oreste Lini** along with **Fratelli Massari**, it began as a winery that made wine from Reggiano grapes, the chosen homeland of Lambrusco. Immediately after the war, when wine was more of a food than a source of pleasure, Lini had some success related to the production of sparkling Lambrusco and musts that even at the time began to have value on the most important international markets. Despite a thousand vicissitudes, Lini stoically endured and in the early 1950s decided it was time to start again. With the Massari brothers leaving the company due to their age, the whole Lini family took on the burden of relaunching the company. This initiative did not take long to achieve initial success, thanks to the new generation (Anita, Fabio and Massimo) who did not skimp on investments to make the company grow. It is therefore no coincidence that, in 1957, with the beginnings of the economic boom, the winery installed a very modern plant for the sparkling wine process, at the time the only one in Emilia and one of the first in Italy, for the Charmat. This brings us to the early 1970s, when the Lini's bottled Lambrusco decided to take the American route. In 1975, they tried the Classic method, perhaps a heresy at the time, but actually a test of vision and ability to read the future. The results were to prove them absolutely right.

Today, it is the cousins Alberto and Alicia who hold the company banner high. The new generation is following old traditions; Lambrusco continues to lead the way in both the Charmat method (rosé and red) as well as Classic (an excellent Gran Cuvée).

VIGNETO DELLE TERRE ROSSE

A Winemaking Land

EMILIA-ROMAGNA
www.terrerosse.com

The amphitheatre of the Terre Rosse has optimal exposure for the vine, to the point that when **Enrico Vallania,** at the beginning of the 1960s, commissioned an agronomic land study, the answer was clear: this was winemaking land. In fact, the vineyard on the hills of Bologna was already there, as the many old vines of Cabernet Sauvignon Riesling, Malvasia Bianca di Zola and "Reno" (nickname for Sauvignon) bear witness. Enrico was a doctor by profession, but the countryside, by family tradition, was close to his heart. With the scientific rigor of his professional background, he carried out endless tests and experiments in the vineyard and in the winery, where he preferred the cleanliness of steel to wooden tones. Clonal selection, denser planting patterns, thinning clusters, selected harvesting and divided times for ripening were some of the novel ideas that this doctor from Bologna with the fixation of wine gave the agronomists and oenologists of the future Italian renaissance.

Luigi Veronelli included the Cuvée Enrico Vallania, a pure Cabernet Sauvignon, in the *Top Wines* of his catalogue of 1970. Enrico passed away in the mid-1980s, but fortunately had a large family. His children grew up smelling the fermentation of must. Giovanni – Professor of Dentistry at the University of Bologna – and Elisabetta – with a literature degree and specialization in America – could not resist the urge to make wine along the hills of Bologna. Today, the company is in the hands of the new generation, the grandson Enrico, Jr, with careful supervision from Aunt Elisabetta, proud of the Vallania name, written in gold letters in the book of Italian viticulture for the last half century.

CANTINE LUNAE

Polo Bosoni: The Lord of the Vermentino dei Colli di Luni

LIGURIA

cantinelunae.it

25 September 1946: a vineyard of Vermentino in full harvest, a woman bent over the vine-shoots intent on harvesting the fruit despite the fact she is expecting. Here begins the story of **Paolo Bosoni**, born between the rows of those grapes that made him famous. We are in Castelunuovo Magra, a remote corner of Liguria that already smells like Tuscany. The Bosoni family is a farming family. Paolo's father owns a few acres of land on which he grows a mix of crops. At the time, *contadino* or farmer, was synonymous with extreme poverty, certainly not a good match for the young women of the town who were aiming high. First Paolo tried a career in uniform, then as a clerk in a military factory, but the land left him no choice. The family vineyards demanded manpower, then he realized that it was his turn. To hell with the "peasant poverty!"

Early 1970s: the honeymoon, with the car full of bottles, was a double honeymoon. With his wife and the wine, he made a pilgrimage through the most renowned wineries in France and Spain. After returning, his ideas were clear; it was time to give lustre to the vineyards of the Colli di Luni. The rise was unstoppable and the Vermentino di Lunae was the protagonist. Thanks also to his brother Lucio, Paolo began to bottle and sell his labels in every part of Italy. Paolo was a generous man and never hesitated when the mayor of the town asked him to take charge of the grapes of small farmers in the

area, who were unable to keep up. He did not hesitate to take big financial risks, suddenly doubling production. The time was ripe for the leap. Today Ca' Lunae is the fine parlour where the Bosoni host the many admirers. There you will find Diego and Debora, the children following in Paolo's footsteps, aware that they could not have had a better teacher.

CAPEZZANA

From Trips in France to the Future

TUSCANY

www.capezzana.it

Many families have had this property, up to the current **Contini Bonacossi family**. The baton once held by Count Ugo, a true Tuscan wine gentleman who passed away in 2012, was picked up by Vittorio and his children, with Serena, Beatrice and their brothers. Vittorio traces the winemaking decades on which this story is structured: "The 1960s: what comes to mind are the carts pulled by donkeys and oxen queuing to unload the grapes in the fermentation room, almost always a mixed fermentation, white and red; the only monochrome exception were the grapes grown directly and managed by the winery, those that were used in Villa di Capezzana [*still Carmignano par excellence today*]. The 1970s were years of great transformation, with long trips to France. It is no coincidence that some of our wood that was then re-grafted came from Château Lafite. This is how Ghiaie della Furba was born, a blend of Cabernet Sauvignon, Franc and Merlot. It was 1979, a year when a 'vineyard' wine was produced, Trefiano. The 1980s saw the arrival of technology in the cellar, stainless steel, the first *barriques*; hygiene and white coats replaced a more patchy and intuitive way of working, more method and more cleanliness. The 1990s placed importance on research into clones of the highest quality to achieve the perfect wine of our dreams [*a utopia*]. The results can be clearly seen today, clonal selections, variety, different pruning and growing systems, density of the hectares. Today,

we have reached a point of obsessive attention to the land, terrified of potentially polluting what we have been given. The task of passing on to our children and grandchildren a rich clean land is an enormous concern".

CASE BASSE SOLDERA

The Paladine of Brunello

TUSCANY
www.soldera.it

At Case Basse, there is a "before" and an "after". The "before" is a path full of successes that span more than twenty years of great wines, according to the many tastings experienced by the writer. It starts with the Brunello Riserva 1983 that is branded on my mind as one of the highest levels of quality achieved in my memory of a Sangiovese. The legend of the Brunello of **Gianfranco Soldera**, who arrived in Montalcino from Milan in 1972 and inspired by the advice of Giulio Gambelli, immediately went on the international markets, powered by a certain detachment from his creator, a former insurance broker, not prone to the limelight. He was a solitary researcher, whose last frontiers involved measuring the vigour of the individual vines. He was a staunch defender of traditional Brunello notes, and was not moved from his credo one iota by the siren call of international style that led astray more than one producer of Montalcino. He chose isolation, focusing on the management of his nearly 10 hectares of vines, tended like gardens and located in the villages of Case Basse and Institieti. The last two wines that I tasted are absolute masterpieces (Riserva 2004 and Riserva 2005). The Riserva 2004 leaves you breathless for the way it manages to be seductive in structure yet innervated by flashes of freshness. Tannin and acidity enliven a sparkling drink in which perfectly ripe cherry dances with liquorice, cumin, thyme and wild berry notes.

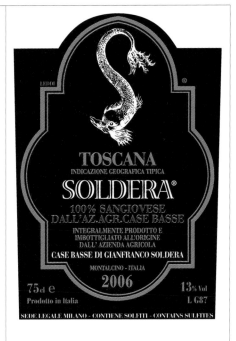

The Riserva 2005 is visceral earthiness, almost suspended between a floral note of rose, a more discreet fruitiness and a shimmering, elusive spiciness. Then sabotage, in December 2012, carried out by a former worker, with the loss of 600 hectoliters of Brunello.
Now comes the "after".

CASTELL'IN VILLA

The Riserva Enters the Gotha

TUSCANY
www.castellinvilla.com

Castell'in Villa identified itself in **Coralìa Ghertsos** (the "princess" for everyone), but also in the volcanic figure of **Massimo Maccianti**, a type of Brand Ambassador who worked alongside the owner for a long time, in wine distribution. In reality, the decision to buy the estate was made in 1967 by Coralia's husband, Riccardo Pignatelli della Leonessa, of noble Neapolitan origin and Ambassador of the Republic. Castell'in Villa is a true hamlet in Castelnuovo Berardenga, and its size (nearly 300

hectares) required a large-scale project. From the 1 hectare of vineyard to over 50 today, with Coralia at the helm for three decades, after the untimely death of her husband, the winery has been focusing on Sangiovese.
The legend of Castell'in Villa has its roots in the 1970s and some of its reserves immediately became part of the Gotha of Chianti Classico (of all of them, the 1971 and 1977, extremely good even today). Not at all worried about riding the wave of the Super Tuscans – the only distraction for the company was Santacroce, a blend of Cabernet Sauvignon and Sangiovese that has an unmistakable Chianti stamp – the Princess continued to turn out wines with a strong territorial impact (such as the extraordinary Riserva 1985). In the decade that followed, Riserva 1995 stood out, masterful with its pulp and momentum in a vintage that in terms of longevity has had its Achilles heel. The new millennium, where styles in international taste and the rediscovery of the finest and best wines has made perceptions foggy, once again strongly proposes Castell'in Villa in the canon of the Chianti Classico, with wines of haunting beauty.

CASA D'AMBRA

Ancient Origins and a Modern Heart

CAMPANIA
www.dambravini.com

If you say D'Ambra, it means that you want to talk about the history of wine on the island of Ischia. In fact, D'Ambra Vini has ancient origins and a modern heart. It was born in 1888 on the initiative of **Francesco D'Ambra**, who already delivered wine to the most famous Neapolitan families, even though the wine of Ischia was already known in the sixteenth century, when it tells of a D'Ambra who brought thousands of hectoliters of wine from the island to the harbour in Naples, to then export it to England. In 1955 came the turning point: D'Ambra became a bottler. **Mario**, **Michele** and

Salvatore D'Ambra perfected the separate vinification of the three wines Biancolella, Forastera and Per' 'e Palummo, the names of the grapes from which they are made.
In 1966, the DOC came to Ischia. Then it was the turn of the new cellars of Forio, in a unique viticultural landscape. In those years D'Ambra was grappling with the difficult cohabitation with the Americans of Winefood, who were also trying to close the cellars on the island. To fight the legal battle, there was Mario D'Ambra, who in November 1984 took over ownership of all the shares and started to produce. On the death of Mario (in September 1988), the grandchildren Corrado and Andrea continued the wine business, starting with a greater selection of vineyards.
In September 1999, Andrea, oenologist, bought out Corrado's shares, thus becoming the sole owner, continuing to recount the unique area of Ischia, enhancing the pure quality of the grapes, the soil and microclimates that each of the approximately 4,000 farmers on the island has known well for millennia.

TENUTA RAPITALÀ

A Breton in Belice

SICILY
www.rapitala.it

The great earthquake of 1968 in Belice not only brought death and destruction, but also led a young couple to devote their passions to rebuilding the wine cellars of her family from Palermo: **Luigia**, known as Gigi, **Guarrasi**, daughter of one of the then most powerful men in Sicily, the lawyer Vito Guarrasi. That year she married **Hugues Bernard, Count de la Gatinais**, a Breton from Saint-Malo, a naval officer with a father, who in turn, was a wine producer. The couple decided to rebuild the property the "French" way. Besides the typical varieties of the area, they planted Chardonnay, Cabernet Sauvignon and then, Pinot Noir and so on. In the cellar, the finest winemaking techniques from beyond the Alps arrived. The name chosen, Rapitalà, is a reminder of Sicily as a complex land of ancient history: the name is, in fact, from the Arabic *Rabidh-Allah*, which means "river of God" and is the name of the stream that runs through the property's vineyards, a unique, large plot that from the hills of Camporeale extends down to the sea of Alcamo. The first bottle signed by Hugues de la Gatinais was in 1977, while in 1990 came the great Rapitalà cru, a Chardonnay that represents the union of France and Sicily, and became the winery's symbol. In 1999, business was good, but they felt they were at a crossroads: should they stay small or merge with a larger producer? The decision was made to sell a majority stake to the Italian Wine Group. So, from 500,000 bottles in 2000, they have reached 3 million

today. The family is still involved in the business; in fact, Laurent, one of Hugues and Gigi's two sons, has been the president since 2007.

The 1980s

Italian Wine Appears on World Markets

The conquest – or rather, the mastery of oenological science – put us in a position to tackle global markets, along with the courage and entrepreneurial vision of thousands and thousands of producers. In this pioneering phase of market acquisition, winemakers received an enormous amount of help from Italian restaurants spread throughout the world, a factor that could be called strategic and which still continues today. These are the years in which the United States, in particular, after Germany and Switzerland, were starting to become the reference market, which would then prove decisive for global expansion, thanks to the media interest of the stature of *The Wine Advocate* by **Robert Parker** and *The Wine Spectator*.

The 1980s was also the decade of methanol (1986), a tragedy that dramatically put an end to cheap wine. "The most important reason for definitively putting the lid on the ugly methanol story," says Ampelio Bucci, "is that this dramatic episode had nothing to do with the world of winemakers, the people who grow the grapes in the vineyards, transform them into wine in the cellar, and then bottle and sell it with their own name. It related instead to sordid dealings between unscrupulous dealers and distributors interested only in making money. We winemakers had nothing to do with it."

The Italian producers, however, did not start suddenly, after 1986, making quality wines; In fact, the history of the renaissance was born almost twenty years ago. This tragedy was in danger, if anything, of compromising its progress.

It was not like that!

Since then research, by foreign importers in particular, turned to producers who had behind them a real history, a project supported by their own vineyards (it was always the first verification that they asked for then), an identity, a moral ethic in their work. They found that Italy was morally sound and made up of such people.

A last but fundamental contribution came from the Ministry of Agriculture, which took a number of initiatives both in terms of communication, especially in foreign markets, and of controls, with the reorganization of the Fraud Service and by introducing magnetic resonance imaging in the controls, equipment that was installed for the first time at the Istituto Agrario di San Michele. Both actions had the immediate effect of restoring confidence to Italian wines.

CAVE DU VIN BLANC DE MORGEX ET DE LA SALLE

New Mountain Viticulture

VALLE D'AOSTA

cavemontblanc.com

Take a sample of individuals who like to drink wine and ask this question: What is the highest altitude in Europe where grape vines grow? Very few of them will answer that this place is Morgex, in Valle d'Aosta, at an altitude of between 1,000 and 1,200 metres above sea level. Therefore, it is an Italian primacy that Italians can be proud of. It does not end here: it is a special place and a unique wine. At that altitude it can be cold until spring and the temperatures begin to drop as early as late autumn. Moreover, in Morgex and the surroundings, it is inevitable that it often snows in winter. Since the climate is so important to viticulture, it takes a slightly special vine for this seemingly hostile environment. There is a vine and it is called Prié Blanc, an autochthonous

white grape, for the short growing season and also a bit difficult to grow, because it has a thin skin and is therefore vulnerable to some adverse weather conditions. Over time the pergola was then chosen, adapted to the climate though and the vine, much lower than normal, so uncomfortable to handle. Here, too, the reasons are sensible: since in the winter it snows heavily, it is necessary to prevent the pergola from collapsing on itself; if the grape is fairly close to the ground it can benefit from the nocturnal release of heat accumulated from it during the day. If we also consider that this type of cultivation does not use grafting and that some vineyards are very close to Mont Blanc, we can draw some very significant conclusions. At this point, the wine, if we take into account some indispensable quality parameters, represents nothing other than the closing of the circle. Established in 1980, the Cave du Vin Blanc de Morgex et de La Salle, which is a wine cooperative (82 members), produces about 150,000 bottles from Prié Blanc alone, divided between still wines, sparkling wines and even a Classic method Eiswein.

LA CROTTA DI VEGNERON

Heroic Viticulture

VALLE D'AOSTA

www.lacrotta.it

Chambave is a quiet village, where there beats a winemaking heart which deserves to be more famous than it is for its originality and quality. This is where Crotta di Vegneron operates. It is the most significant winery in the area, and also a cooperative. Established in 1980, it went from twenty-five members to eighty in five years. It now has around a hundred members that produce about three hundred thousand bottles. In the last thirty years, the cooperative has played a major role in the local community: it is

guaranteed economic remuneration for the work of grape producers; it has contributed, as a secondary effect, to maintaining mountain grapevine *terroirs*, fascinating but fragile; over the years, through a gradual process, it has built a quality winemaking proposition which is also wide and varied, with a judicious mix of grape varieties, local and international. The Crotta di Vegneron project focuses mainly on the wealth of local autochthonous vines such as Petit Rouge, Fumin, Vien de Nus, Muscat de Chambave and Nus Malvoisie, which give wines a lightness, a pleasurable quality and personality. The best-known of these is Chambave, which uses the Moscato Bianco, a variety that adapts well to the *terroir,* and is the basis of a dry wine and a sweet wine. The flagship wine of the Crotta di Vegneron is in fact the dry Chambave Muscat, which is made with a short cold maceration, a vinification and aging on the lees for a few months. This wine has a strong personality, captivating scents and has an extraordinarily pleasant mouthfeel. This wine is only the tip of the iceberg of what Crotta di Vegneron is capable of producing.

High Piedmont

This territory stretches from the Alps to Lake Maggiore with Monte Rosa in the background, a mountain that determines the microclimate. Of the 40,000 hectares of vines that grew there a century and a half ago, just under 400 remain.

Gattinara is a wine with ancient origins whose vineyards were planted by the Romans in the second century BC. Its base is Nebbiolo, called Spanna by the locals, and can be aged for a very long time. It must be aged in wood for two years, and for the Riserva, three years.

Ghemme, less known than Gattinara, is named after the town in the province of Novara, also a child of the Nebbiolo grape. Already known in the nineteenth century, it was celebrated by Fogazzaro in *Piccolo mondo antico*. Count Camillo Benso di Cavour tasted it on his way back from the Plombières meeting with Napoleon III.

Bramaterra, the ancient "wine of Masserano", is produced in the territory of seven villages in the hills above the Vercelli Baragge.

The name Bramaterra appeared for the first time in a document of 1447 and apparently means the agricultural affinity and vocation of this area.

Fara is a wine that was highly appreciated by abbots, bishops and lords who, in medieval times, were devoted to its production for liturgical purposes. It is produced from a blend of Nebbiolo, Vespolina and Uva Rara or Bonarda Novarese.

Sizzano was already appreciated in the nineteenth century by Cavour, who considered it to be the equal of the great French wines. Its area of cultivation is very small.

Boca became famous for being the "wine of the Popes", because it was so highly appreciated by the Roman Curia, supplied by the Finazzi counts, once owners of vineyards in the area. It is very special due to the composition of the soil, rich in minerals, and is one of the historical DOCs of Novara.

MICHELE CHIARLO

The Barbera of La Court

PIEDMONT
www.michelechiarlo.it

Michele Chiarlo, an oenologist, founded his winery in 1956 starting with a paternal farm property of only 5 hectares, in Calamandrana in Monferrato. This exciting journey led him to become one of the protagonists of change in the philosophy of Barbera, which from a low-profile wine became the standard-bearer of the territory. The cru of La Court, Nizza, which is from one of the best vineyards in the area of Nizza Monferrato in Castelnuovo Calcea, is an important wine that is exported to over sixty countries worldwide. In May 2001, this label conquered, along with only three other bottles, the cover of the American magazine *The Wine Spectator*.

Chiarlo immediately decided to expand his borders, and also acquired vineyards in Langa. The first Barolo came just two years after the company's inception. Now he owns 60 hectares of his own and rents 50, located in three areas of Piedmont: Langhe, Monferrato and Gavi, with vineyards of the first magnitude, including the historical Cerequio and Cannubi vineyards, in the area of Barolo. The Cannubi parcel, purchased in 1989 with a gradient of nearly 50%, was the first vineyard in Langa to be terraced with no masonry support, with the help of **François Murisier**, Swiss professor of Viticulture.

Michele Chiarlo was the inspiring force behind the project for Albarossa, an ancient red grape vine, a cross between the Nebbiolo di Dronero and Barbera, obtained over thirty years by professor Dalmasso. These 4 hectares on the Serra di Montaldo Scarampi estate are behind the extraordinary Montald.

On the estate Tenuta Aluffi, purchased in 1995, the heart of La Court and Cipressi vineyards, in 2003, the art park Orme su La Court was founded, an open-air museum with striking installations by various artists dedicated to the four elements: air, fire, water and earth.

CHIONETTI E PECCHENINO

The Two Faces of Dolcetto

PIEDMONT

chionettiquinto.com

www.pecchenino.com

Dogliani, a few kilometres from Monforte d'Alba and the southern boundary of Barolo, is historically a land of Dolcetto, second only to Barbera in terms of regional distribution. Here the vine occupies the hills and the best exposure. Dolcetto for some refers to the dialect *duset* – small bump or hill – while for many instead it indicates the sweetness of the flesh, characteristic of this grape, also used as an eating grape. It is a typically Piedmontese wine, not widespread outside its territory and with a wide sprinkling of designations – a good eleven DOCs – and with the 2005 vintage, it received the Dogliani DOCG label without the name of the grape variety.

In Dogliani, we find one of the wine patriarchs, **Quinto Chionetti**, born in 1925, a small Veronelli-style producer who carries on the tradition of the area. His winery was founded in 1912 by his grandfather Giuseppe. He has 18 hectares, with just over 85,000 bottles. He produces only two cru: the San Luigi, a wine that is drunk young, and Briccolero, the vineyard above the wine cellar where the aged wine is made. He also makes Dolcetto without using wood during the aging, and they are sold almost a year later than the wines of other producers in the area.

While Quinto Chionetti is conservative, **Orlando Pecchenino** was the leader of the reformists of the denomination. Not everyone likes his wines, but with time they changed style setting aside

the concentration that characterized them. The company, founded in the early 1900s with grandfather Attilio, numbered just over 8 hectares, and now number 25, 70% dedicated to Dolcetto. In 1986, the true winery was founded and run by brothers Attilio (agronomist) and Orlando Pecchenino (oenologist). Starting with this difficult variety, they create the most elegant wines. Their Dolcetti are San Luigi, Sirì d'Jermu (the best known) and the Bricco Botti made from grapes from a single vineyard, vinified like a Barolo, with a long maceration and aged in medium sized wood barrels for two years.

CONTERNO FANTINO

The Courage to Innovate, without Uprooting

PIEDMONT

www.conternofantino.it

The winery owned by **Claudio Conterno** and **Guido Fantino**, who both have peasant origins, was founded in 1982 and is one of the few in which two distinguished Piedmont families have formed a long-lasting successful entrepreneurial partnership in the winemaking business. The important decade was the 1980s, and Conterno considered it to be a crucial historical period for wine in the Langhe area: "The 1960s summarize the decline of agriculture; those who abandoned it and those who let themselves be seduced by chemistry, believing it to be a panacea. But twenty years later, the chickens came home to roost. We rolled up our sleeves. We pruned heavily in the winter to contain the buds and we thinned in the summer. We drastically reduced the use of chemicals, and took the utmost care of the vineyards". What Conterno means to say with this is not that tradition has nothing to offer, but simply that it is necessary to pick out the most positive aspects of tradition and separate them from the unwanted ones, with the maximum respect for the work carried out by one's predecessors, but also the desire to improve and question things. Speaking of barrels, which in Langa have created a stir and caused rifts, Conterno Fantino's approach is pragmatic: right from the start it was considered merely an oenological instrument to be employed only when useful. After the experiments of 1983–1984, the conclusion is that it is not needed for the Dolcetto, while for the Barbera, it is almost essential, and for the Nebbiolo, it should

2009

BAROLO

DENOMINAZIONE DI ORIGINE CONTROLLATA E GARANTITA

SORÌ GINESTRA®

I filari di una vigna folta sono schierati - verdi o rossicci o gialli - come le onde di un mare, e contengono a gorghi la ricchezza di un mare. Frescura, stupore, tesori celati.

Di questo vino sono state prodotte n. 14.904 bottiglie.

PRODUCT OF ITALY
RED WINE

Estate bottled by
Imbottigliato all'origine dall'azienda agricola

CONTERNO FANTINO

MONFORTE D'ALBA - ITALIA

750 ML ℮   L 05/12   ALC. 14.5 % BY VOL.

be used with caution. For the refining of Barolo, they opted for a twelve-month aging in carat, so as to stabilize the colours and concentrate the fruitiness, followed by a one-year aging in barrels of 25 hectolitres, useful for harmonising and stabilizing the wine. "We believe we are artisans, more mathematical than philosophical, but above all, we owe so much to the earth, our true capital. Also for this reason, since 2011 we have been certified organic. Finally, speaking of the cru, we think it is useful to enhance the identity of the individual vineyards, then all of our wines are from single vineyards – *monovigneto*".

COPPO

Underground Cathedrals

PIEDMONT

www.coppo.it

The winery is one of four "underground cathedrals" (the others are Bosca-Cora, Contratto and Gancia), in other words, the historic wineries involved at the start of the project to nominate the winegrowing areas of Piedmont as a World Heritage Site.

When one surpasses a hundred years, every occasion is a reason to celebrate: if we are also talking about a winery, it is even easier to uncork bottles, and this helps to understand the meaning of life under the banner of oenology. The **Coppo family**, originally from Canelli, passed that milestone and decided to compare their wines in their different vintages, examining their strengths and weaknesses. In the area, known for vines that were completely different from the Nebbiolo, it seemed that the thing to do was clearly to produce the famous "everyday wines", those with a good quality/price ratio – small wines, to sum it up – in other words, a product that would be of little interest to the passionate connoisseur. Instead, the four Coppo brothers – Piero, Gianni, Paolo and Roberto, grandsons of the founder Piero – assisted today by the latest generation of sons, Massimiliano and Edoardo, accepted the challenge and took two directions: international varieties such as Chardonnay and Cabernet Sauvignon, and Pinot Noir used for making sparkling wine, but also a new way of producing Freisa and Barbera, capable of withstanding aging over time in an unusual way. They decided to produce Barolo and also sparkling wine, Gavi, in the Oltrepò Pavese area, but what characterizes them is precisely the decision to work with something unusual.

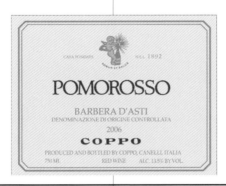

VIGNETI MASSA

The Discovery of Timorasso

PIEDMONT

vignetimassa@libero.it

To those who ask him why he does not make DOC wines, he answers that he prefers to make good wines which require three ingredients: grapes, time and common sense. "Since 1978, when I joined the winery to represent the fourth generation, we gradually moved toward the bottle," says **Walter Massa**. "In the last few years, all of the product has been sold in bottles and, when these begin to run low, instead of buying grapes or wine to meet the demand, I prefer to raise the prices". Massa is considered a vintner who applies "reasoned" agriculture, without communicating through certifications (organic, biodynamic . . .), in regard to environment and the earth, to protect both those who come after him to run his vineyards and the customer-consumer who must "drink and enjoy". His communication showcase consists of the vineyards, his customer must walk the lands of Monleale and smell their aroma: "I don't want to take him for a ride by going around the world. By dint of hearing so many lies, I cast off my shyness by being a 'wine commentator' and the 'Mass (a)-media' for my territory".

"Born in the midst of thousands of hectares of Barbera and not seeing – as a teenager – wines that expressed my territory, I set out to 'do justice' through the creation of a great Barbera. Today, I produce it calling it strictly by the name of its town of origin, Monleale, and it is distributed worldwide. To achieve this I had an exceptional sales manager: Timorasso, a grape that in recent decades had almost disappeared. A fantastic native white grape that, since 1987, has made my life less exhausting, bringing those who care most about the hills of Tortona closer".

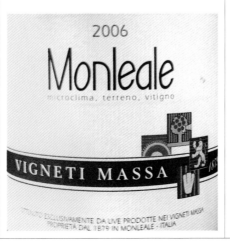

MONSUPELLO

An Avant-garde Oltrepò for Four Generations

LOMBARDY
www.monsupello.it

Despite its certain vocation, the history of wines in the Oltrepò Pavese area is one the most tormented, and the area still feels this today. The spearhead of this highly varied world is the winery Monsupello in Torricella Verzate. Its history has been written by the last four generations of the Boatti family since 1893, the year in which they purchased the first vineyards in the town of Oliva Gessi.

The man who turned things around was definitely **Carlo Boatti**, of the third generation, who dedicated his life not only to the business, but also the fate of major projects, such as the Classese and the Oltrepò Pavese Consortium, of which he was president. Unfortunately, he passed away in 2010. Not only was he an enlightened man, but also absolutely ahead of the times. Already in the early 1980s, in fact, he introduced manual harvesting in crates, the use of presses with a pneumatic lung for white wines and sparkling wines, bottling total production, aging in barrels, with Pinot Noir at the centre of the project, produced in its various forms, but particularly as a sparkling wine. The company's flagship wine is just that, a sparkling wine made with the Classic method, Nature has been produced since 1981 from Pinot Noir grapes, with a small amount of Chardonnay, and thirty month-old yeasts. It is a refined, well-structured spumante with great class. Today, the winery – with 50 hectares of vineyard – is run by the fourth generation of Boatti, the children

Laura and Pierangelo, as well as their mother, **Carla Dallera**, who has always been an important reference point for everyone.

SOLCI'S

From Wine Shop to Spumante Vineyard

LOMBARDY
www.solci1938.com

In 1938, in Milan, in Piazza Cinque Giornate, **Angelo** and **Piero Solci**'s parents began to sell wines which they bottled, and that came in demijohns from Piedmont and the Oltrepò Pavese. In the 1960s, they began to offer the first Italian DOCs and more established French wines, including Champagne, to a clientele that was wealthier and more demanding because of the "economic boom".

Already in the 1970s, Piero and Angelo selected and imported Champagne from small producers, RM (*Récoltant Manipulant*), purloining their small or big secrets. So it was only natural that they would make their own Classic method spumante, "their Champagne".

This is how Solci's spumante was born in 1981 with a single product, Brut Chardonnay.

Angelo and Piero then embarked on a joint venture with the brothers **Marco** and **Roberto Maggi** from Stradella – owners of a winery equipped to make Classic method sparkling wines – working with the grapes from their farm in Valle Versa, made mostly from a spumante base of Pinot Noir, a variety which has an ideal habitat in these areas.

As long as the Solci's Wine Bar on Via Morosini, 19 in Milan was open – and it became an "institution" – the Solci's Classic method could only be found in those wine bars. Today, it is sold directly to private customers and abroad. In 1985, Solci perfected a rosé made from a Pinot Noir of noble lineage, which has been gradually improving thanks to the experience acquired by Angelo over twenty years of consulting for Rosa Del Golfo in Puglia. Now it is without a doubt one of the best in Italy, to the extent that in a blind tasting between co-producers of great Italian Classic method rosé wines, it earned first place, to everyone's surprise. The company provides a service for producing Private Label spumante.

The range has been expanded with Light Perlage, an increasingly appreciated low pressure spumante that always does extraordinarily well in a rosé. The company produces about 30,000 bottles with the Solci's label.

Cooperative in Trentino

Most of the vineyards and wine production in Trentino-Alto Adige are cooperative wineries.

After the giant Cavit di Ravina, in Trentino there is **Mezza-corona**, whose history is over a century old, having been founded in 1911. The Group became structured as an actual holding, with the production and marketing of Rotari spumante and a number of companies, including one that deals with the marketing of their wines in the United States. The vintners number 1,300, owners of 2,600 hectares of vineyards that provide about 29% of the total wine production in Trentino. The beautiful **Cantina Rotari** has a production capacity of 5 million bottles of Classic method spumante and is part of the Cittadella del Vino, a complex that includes, in addition to a major winemaking centre, a business centre and a multipurpose auditorium with 1,200 seats. The vineyards of the contributing shareholders are subjected to quality controls and cultivated with the use of integrated pest management systems.

In 2001, the winery launched the Sicilia (Sicily) project, with the acquisition of two farms in Feudo Arancio and Villa Albius, for a total of about 1,000 hectares of agricultural land of which 650 hectares were already planted with vines.

La-Vis was founded in 1948 and has been equipped with a technical assistance office since 1956. In the spirit of innovation, its flagship project is called Zoning – summed up in the slogan "the right variety in the right place" – launched in 1980 with the school of San Michele, then directed by **Attilio Scienza**. It was an Italian pilot project that also became an example for Europe.

It made it possible for the agronomists and winemakers of La-Vis to isolate and identify some vineyards of excellence that then, over time, would become part of their Autoctoni, Ritratti and Bio product lines, which represent the best product the winemaker has to offer.

The Autoctoni line addresses the need to bring in the Trentino region with the highest vocation. This is the case of the mild Nosiola Sette Fontane, the subtle Schiava Piaggi, the strong Teroldego Rover, the surprising Incrocio Manzoni, the Altro Manzoni Maso Franch, the elegant Lagrein Greggi, or the "highly mineral" Müller Thurgau Cadrobbi.

The Ritratti line identified the most prestigious sites for international grapes, proposing the fine Chardonnay Del Diaol, the fragrant Gewürztraminer Maso Clinga, the aromatic Sauvignon Maso Tratta, rather than the intense Cabernet Sauvignon, the enveloping Pinot Noir or the Pinot Grigio with its great freshness.

POJER E SANDRI

"Leaving it to Chance Is Not Always the Best Way"

TRENTINO
www.pojeresandri.it

For viticulture in Trentino, **Mario Pojer** and his partner from the beginning, **Fiorentino Sandri**, represent a small tornado. In thirty-five years, they built a business from nothing into one of the most important wineries in the region. Mario Pojer is one of Italy's most famous winemakers, pioneer of the movement of the winegrowers from Trentino, always one of the first to experiment with new farming and winemaking systems. With his moustache like that of a Hun, or a Burgundian winemaker, and his outspoken personality, he has been a driving force for the

winery since the beginning. He was the one to understand that the land which extends from South Tyrol up to these hills has a unique volcanic origin and that it is well suited to the cultivation of important vines, even international ones like the Pinot Noir.

It might have been ignorance, but things immediately went well. A beautiful label, but especially an innovative Müller Thurgau (first vintage 1975) demanded the attention of the market. This was followed by a Chardonnay and a more native Nosiola and after a few years, their wines were in New York restaurants. Mario Pojer's desire to experiment never ceased: "To preserve the freshness of the wines you have to have perfect musts, without oxidation" – a belief that led him to test new systems for pressing grapes. From the historic grape-washing machine and the international Bucher Inertys patent for processing musts in hyper-reduction, preserving the primary aromas, with the use of small doses of sulphur; or again, the balloon for nitrogen. "Leaving it to chance is not always the best way" is Pojer's motto. He supports a natural approach managed by people. Then there is the distillery, the *pupitres* for his sparkling wines, and wines like his Merlino, the first fortified wine in the region: a red liqueur like chocolate.

Cooperative in Alto Adige

The cooperative winery of San Michele Appiano is located between Bolzano and Lake Caldaro, the largest and most important wine area in South Tyrol. Here, in the 1980s, perhaps one of the most important chapters of the wine renaissance in South Tyrol was written. This is thanks to two wineries and two extremely strong and innovative personalities in the form of *Kellermeister*. We are talking about **Hans Terzer** from the San Michele winery and **Luis Raifer**, the "lord" of the **Producers of Colterenzio**.

San Michele Appiano is the largest winery in South Tyrol, with its more than 2 million bottles produced each year and 350 grower members. It was established in 1907 in the wake of the Austrian boom of late nineteenth-century cooperatives. The architecture of the San Michele winery – the impressive Jugendstil building of 1909 with its deep vaulted cellars, refurbished in 2001 – bears witness to its important history. But it was *Kellermeister* Terzer who renovated its outward appearance and profile. He introduced the Sanct Valentin line and new concepts in quality, first in the vineyard, where thinning and strict quality controls led to success in recent years. Pinot Grigio, but primarily Sauvignon Blanc and Gewürztraminer, conquered the critics and the market with a success that is still ongoing.

In the Cantina Colterenzio, Luis Raifer (now replaced by his son Wolfgang) has taken the same road as San Michele, but in the field of red wines. Particularly in the case of Bordeaux, he and a few other South Tyrol producers find that choice woods and meticulous care of the vineyard produce Cabernet Sauvignon and Merlot grapes of the highest quality. And of course Pinot Noir and Lagrein, whose best grapes come together in the prestigious Lafòa line. The result of 28 small winemakers joining forces in 1960, the winery now has 300 passionate winemakers who cultivate just as many hectares, or slightly more, of vineyards in the hills above San Michele Appiano. Among other innovations, they are experimenting with developing a new energy concept.

The **Cantina Girlan** is another important winery that has been producing since the 1950s. In the last decade, it has been returning to the forefront thanks to the talented oenologist **Gerhard Kofler**. In the homonymous, ancient village vineyard above Appiano, the winery was founded in 1923 by 23 growers, though there are now 200, in the village of Girlan/Cornaiano, in a historic sixteenth-century farm. The vines are located in a cultivated area of 220 hectares. In the 1970s, Cornaiano prevailed for its excellent selection of wines with a base of the typical Schiava, including the famous Schiava Fass n. 9 (barrel 9).

TIEFENBRUNNER

The Famous Castel Blend

ALTO ADIGE

www.tiefenbrunner.com

The historic home of Niclara, in the municipality of Kurtatsch, was documented for the first time in 1225. The Linticlar estate is often mentioned in the late medieval chronicles of Trento's cathedral. However, it was in 1537 that the first traces of the name Turmhof appeared in the documents, a name that was then changed to Thurner Hof. From 1675, the farm belonged to the family of the current owners. But it was in 1848 that the commercial winery was launched and has gradually taken on an increasingly important role both for the family and for Oltradige agriculture. In addition to their own grapes, the winery bought the raw materials from the winemakers in the area. The wines were then sold in casks to customers throughout the Tyrol. So it has been for over a century, but it was with the launch of the famous and still-functioning blending at Castel Turmhof that **Hilde** and **Herbert Tiefenbrunner** took the first step in 1968 towards a new era. They had intended to sell the wines, but began bottling them. New domestic and foreign markets quickly opened up, and the number of bottles produced continued to increase. Since 1983, their son Christof has been managing the farm and, with his wife Sabine, making a worthy contribution to this long tradition of wine, in the strength and passion for the continuous quest for quality. The flagship wine is the Feldmarschall von Fenner, a Müller Thurgau originating in the high Favogna plateau, a ward of Margreid found at over 1,000 metres above sea level, protected from the north winds and characterized by a special microclimate.

TIEFENBRUNNER

PINOT GRIGIO

——— 2010 ———

ALLEGRINI

Fruit Philosophy

VENETO
www.allegrini.it

Allegrini means passion, elegance, courage and sacrifice. This is how we could summarize the long history of this family in the hills of Fumane. With the Allegrini family, Valpolicella takes the form of art, of a lifestyle where the beauty and light of Italy shine through wine. Already in the first half of the seventeenth century, Allegrini was the largest landowner in the Fumane area. The champion of the prestige acquired to date is definitely **Giovanni Allegrini**, a true innovator. In the early 1960s, he was the spokesperson for a new winemaking philosophy, fully aimed at preserving and enhancing the fruit from the vine to the bottle. By introducing the Guyot planting technique, he changed agricultural and production habits and chose an inimitable style of pleasure, elegance and freshness in the wines. He left his beloved Fumane hills in 1983, when he was still young. Everything passed into the hands of his three children, Walter, Franco and Marilisa. Walter continued to be the innovative force behind the vineyard but, once again, the Allegrini family was tested by fate. Walter passed away in 2003 and left a significant gap, uniting the family even more. Marilisa, with her charm, proved to be another driving force, able to convey the elegance of her land and her favourite wine, Amarone. It was an ongoing adventure that enhanced their image in the world. Today, thanks to the new generations, Silvia, Caterina and Francesco, the winery has become a consolidated group which also produces in Tuscany, Bolgheri and Montalcino, and is passionately dedicated to the appreciation of art in all its forms, within the splendid rooms of the eighteenth-century Palazzo della Torre in Fumane.

ANSELMI

The *enfant terrible* of Soave

VENETO
www.anselmi.eu

"Being from outside the pack is good for the pack." **Roberto Anselmi**, a visionary but practical man, turned a territory into something international, Soave, with a new concept of global quality. He was born in 1948 in the ancient lands of Monteforte and breathed the world of wine thanks to his father, a *négociant* who took him around Italy and taught him the art of selling. Up to 1979, he bought grapes from select winemakers, and in 1980 bought his first small vineyard that he made famous with the name Capitel Foscarino.
Roberto's life changed when he was running through Milan with a bottle in hand, so that he could let a great journalist taste it, a journalist who was revolutionizing the concept of quality wine. It was Luigi Veronelli, and he told him: "Bravo Roberto. It's a good dignified wine! A wine that smells of warm earth . . ." That meeting changed his life, and Roberto Anselmi was forever grateful to Veronelli, to the point that up until 2013 he was chairman of the Luigi Veronelli Seminar. Another important date is 1988, the international consecration, when a Recioto di Soave – I Capitelli 86 – managed to rank fourth in the wine competition in Bordeaux, winning over thirty Sauternes. Roberto's life is a constant quest for truth and absolute quality for this territory that he loves so deeply. "I'm not capable of being the diplomat; you can't build anything if you don't go to the bone and keep your feet on the ground. It's one of the qualities required for anyone who wants to succeed in life." This sentiment forced him to make some hard choices in 2000 when he definitively left the Soave name and wrote a testament that he called *Caro Soave*. "I wanted more from men who come from an area that deserves so much. Maybe I was not understood, but I could not compromise".

CESARI

The Dynamism and Modernity of a Family

VENETO

www.cesariverona.it

There is a pleasant coincidence in the history of the Cesari winery that shares the spirit of the founding father **Gerardo** and his son **Franco**, still at the helm of the group: 1936 is the year in which the winery was established and it is also Franco Cesari's birthday. This fate has accompanied Franco throughout his life and still makes Amarone and its territory a globetrotter today, in the five continents where it can be found. This history of achievements and successes has turned a family business into a "family group", as Franco likes to say, also made up of **Rinaldo Corvi** and **Annibale Materossi**. The winery's headquarters are located in the beautiful scenery overlooking Lake Garda in the Cavaion Veronese and the property is 100 hectares, located in the most important vineyards of the main names in Verona. In the early 1970s, the wines were sold in Canada, Germany, England and the United States where, in 1975, the first hundred cases of Amarone were unloaded. "I believed from the very beginning in the potential of the Valpolicella and its wines. The commitment and a little luck, as in all things, did the rest," Franco recalls. Cavaion Veronese has developed an important network of controls for the environment, to the point of being one of the top five Italian wineries to be awarded ISO 14001 environmental certification. This goal entails research and means developing techniques for using alternative energy sources, with a lower environmental impact and carbon footprint. Franco cares a great deal about this. "The Gerardo Cesari has really been an ongoing project since 1936. The future requires us to produce wine but avoid waste, and on this front we were able to reduce our energy consumption by about 100 kWh. We do it for our children with respect for a product, the wine, which continues to be the natural nectar of our land".

DAL FORNO ROMANO

Strength, Elegance, Style and Territory

VENETO

www.dalfornoromano.it

While Amarone is one of the most famous and desired wines in the world, it also owes its existence to the farmer of Cellore of Illasi, **Romano Dal Forno**, born in 1957, in Capovilla. "My father had set out to have me do another job, because at that time, being a farmer meant staying poor. Except that nothing could give me more satisfaction than the vineyards," he says. At twenty-two he married Loretta, an important figure who accompanied him in all his choices. "Together we shared the challenge of taking over the vineyard that my father had partly abandoned". The thing that inspired him came after he stumbled on a bottle of Amarone di Quintarelli. "For quite a while I didn't sleep at night, thinking about that wine. I felt small and helpless. I wanted to meet Bepi and from that meeting I saw my dream again". To achieve the levels of quality in the wine, Romano decided to radically change his approach in the winery and in the vineyard, planting high-density raised vines using the Guyot technique. So they turned to green pruning and thinning. The practice of withering the grape become scientific. Oenology was avant-garde. He used very thick stainless steel, inert gases to remedy any oxidation and precious woods for aging made of French oak. His first Amarone Vigneto Monte Lodoleta came in 1983. It was revolutionary: power and elegance, style and terroir. The big American magazines, *The Wine Advocate* and *The Wine Spectator*, placed it alongside the world's best wines. The 1994 and 1995 vintages received

98 points from Parker. Those of 1996 and 1997 received 99, again from Parker. In 2004, the family jewel, the Serè, which comes onto the market after five years, earned another 98 points (Parker).

In 1990, the new winery in Cellore was inaugurated. Today, he continues his extraordinary adventure with his wife Loretta and the help of his children Marco, Luca and Michele.

GRUPPO ITALIANO VINI

The Strength of a United Italy

VENETO

www.gruppoitalianovini.com

The Gruppo Italiano Vini (Italian Wine Group, IWG) is the largest Italian group of this type and one of the first in the world to produce and market wines. It is made up of fifteen historical Italian cellars. Everything began on 31 July 1986 with the acquisition from Crédit Suisse of all the shares of the Italian Wine Group by eight Italian wine cooperatives. The historical Italian Wine Group consisted of Santi and Lamberti in Veneto, Nino Negri in Lombardy, Melini and Conti Serristori in Tuscany, Bigi in Umbria, Fontana Candida in Lazio and Calissano in Piedmont. The first president was Dr. **Selleri** with Dr. **Chiossi** as vice president. The group's headquarters moved from Milan to Calmasino, in the charming Villa Belvedere. The goal was to give the group a national presence that included the most important wines on the peninsula, to launch a cutting-edge service for customers, while ensuring a commercial organization specialized for each sales channel, with integrated logistics services. The historical brands expanded. In 1996, IWG found Conti Formentini in San Floriano del Collio, then Ca' Bianca in Monferrato; between 1999 and 2001, there came Tenute Rapitalà in Sicily, Castello Monaci in Puglia and Terre degli Svevi in Basilicata. In 2008, it acquired Bolla from the American Brown-Forman winery, completing the acquisition of the brand in 2010. From 21 April 2010, IWG began distributing Carpenè Malvolti in Italy. The most recent transaction (January

2011) involved Cavicchioli in San Prospero, in the province of Modena. Over the years, it managed to create major international distribution structures. In 1987, it acquired Carniato in Paris, and six years later, Frederick Wildman & Sons. In addition, the group completed its action bringing the number of its subsidiaries and/or controlled companies to ten. The IWG leaves its wineries enough independence to maintain a strong identity. "Our mission is to control the supply chain and offer the highest quality and support at the highest level. At the same time we feel very strongly about the territories of origin, keeping alive these differences in order to exalt them in the wine," says the director and oenologist of the group, **Christian Scrinzi**. It has 1,340 hectares of property and the work that the IWG does to train individual grape producers is painstaking. Bearing witness to this is the launching of the pruning school of the Friuli Simonit & Sirch, held at the Bolla cellars in Pedemonte in Valpolicella, open to all farmers in the area.

ZENATO

"Never Give Up And Listen Carefully!"

VENETO

www.zenato.it

There is a corner of the sky that is reflected in the green of the vineyards and the blue of the lake. An enchanted place where Zenato chose his Valpolicella. Costalunga is a vineyard facing east towards Peschiera del Garda, and the site of the historic seat of the family. These are two aspects of this strong and courageous human journey, visionary and sometimes unexpected but, still, a story that is emblematic of the Italian oenological scene. **Sergio Zenato** founded his winery in the clay lands of San Benedetto di Lugana in 1960 and his first bottles were Lugana 1967. "Back then wine didn't have the consideration that it has today. Outside Italy, no one knew grapes like Trebbiano di Lugana and even Amarone was also given little consideration".

Together with his wife Carla and two children Alberto and Nadia, he consolidated an important winemaking patrimony. He saw far

ahead of the times and knew the market. Ripasso wine was the result of a conversation between him and his wife during a trip to the United States; it became one of the most innovative products of the Valpolicella of the 1990s. The Lugana wines become international when Sergio, driven by his tenacity and the fact of his being a dreamer with his feet firmly on the ground, decided that such a good wine had to be able to compete with the great white wines worldwide. Thus the idea of the Riserva Sergio Zenato Lugana was born, with 1993 being the first vintage. The story of Amarone was the family's other great challenge. The bright vineyard of Costalunga was the dream that made the will to produce great Valpolicella wines a reality. From those grapes came the success of Ripasso and Amarone. Sergio bottled his first Riserva in 1980. His wines were aiming toward the future. The Cresasso is another example. An extraordinary Corvina that exalts the value of the Valpolicella is another. Today Alberto and Nadia run the winery with their mother Carla, who has the same dynamism as their father had in everything she does.

EDI KEBER

Calling a Wine with the DOC Name

FRIULI VENEZIA GIULIA
www.edikeber.it

The **Keber family** has been in this place for a good 300 years. Edi has help running the family business from his wife Silvana and his son Kristian, an oenologist, who also handles the marketing.

Edi is a tireless promoter of the territory, but went down in the history of Collio in 1987 when he chose a path that opened an important road to success in terms of the wine-territory equation, producing just one type of white wine, Collio.

He explains his decision:

"It's my *ponca* [*marl or limestone soil*], together with this microclimate, which give my wines their character. And this is why we decided to name our most important wine by its place of origin, Collio . . . It was very tough. I also lost quite a few customers. So on 12 hectares we had 5 varieties of white and 2 reds. The names of the vine are, rightly, the same as everyone else's. But the Collio – and its *ponca* – no, those are just ours! I had a problem that then revealed itself in all its heaviness: after the first decades of success of our wines by grape variety, we found ourselves on the market with a vast number of Pinot Grigio, Chardonnay and Sauvignon . . . How could we tell one apart from another? I became well aware of the importance of dealing with the new markets that were opening up, of having a sufficient critical mass to meet their needs. The solution was to produce only one white wine. But what variety? The answer was found in tradition: our ancestors did it with Tocai [*now a Friuli wine*], combined with Ribolla Gialla and Malvasia, the ultimate expression of these vineyards. So I did the same . . . In the vineyards, the times coincide with the generations: they have long life and you have to look far. In fact, the idea of 1987 was completed twenty years later, with the 2008 vintage, the first year that my winery produced only one white, Collio, alongside the one red, Merlot".

KANTE

Stone, Work, Wine

FRIULI VENEZIA GIULIA
www.kante.it

Edi Kante is immortalized in a photo with his friends from the Group of Oslavia: Josko Gravner, the inspiring force of the society, is the only one sitting, in the middle. Beside him, from the right, are Niko Bensa, Edi Kante, Jordi Bensa and Stanko Radikon. The five men identified a common way to enter the market, but also the style of the wines produced. It was the mid-1980s, then the group broke up and Edi changed direction, giving a free interpretation to his vineyards, his territory, his wines.

There are three words that define his commitment as a vintner: "Stone, work, wine".

He describes his land: "The Karst is an environment with a rough beauty, a land without soil, where the vines are struggling to survive in the stone, so much stone. The limestone formations are shaped by the atmosphere, the sea, the wind and minerals. The Karst is a world suspended between the Adriatic Sea, the Balkans, the Alps and the Po Valley".

The vineyards are intensely planted (between 7,000 and 8,000 plants per hectare) and there is a charming cellar which also becomes a place to be admired, excavated in two different periods: 1988 and 1993.

Its wines play like the Bora – which lends its name to one of the white wines – between the houses: they try every kind of experimentation, as if Edi were looking for a wine that still had to materialize in his mind.

This is how we find the autochthonous varieties. The white and Vitovska and red Terrano, marketed both as young wines and in the selection that calls for a long aging before going onto the market. The quest for a wine that recounts time, condensing it, and the variables of the grape harvest, is Opera Viva, for which the best barrels are bottled, the best vintages of red wines produced within ten years.

The labels are as strong and pictorial as the colours of his Karst in autumn. Or as rigorous and basic as the one for Opera Viva.

LIVON

Intuition for Innovation

FRIULI VENEZIA GIULIA

www.livon.it

We are looking at one of the oldest renaissance wineries in the history of Friuli wine.

Dorino Livon, an entrepreneur of wood with peasant origins, more than fifty years ago – fifty years that were celebrated on 6 September 2014 – sensed that the Collio had great potential. At the time, he purchased land in the best spots in Ruttars. Everyone thought he was crazy, but instead he was right. His children Valneo and Tonino continued to invest in the choice he had made, leading the winery into world markets with nearly 190 hectares of vineyards in three different DOC regions: Collio, the eastern hills of Friuli and Friuli Grave. The vineyards of Ruttars, in particular, are truly spectacular, true masterpieces of agrarian restoration. The TiareBlù, the great red wine of Livon, was born next to the castle of Trussio. However the Braide Alte, the winery's top white, grows on the highest point of the hill 200 metres above sea level, with stunning views, and terminating at what was once the border of Slovenia until 19 December 2007. Many years before, the Iron Curtain passed below it!

"Our pride," says Tonino, "are the vineyards and their density per hectare [*we have 7,500 strains*]. These hills are beautiful to look at, but very difficult to prepare and then to work. First of all they must be respected and we did that, leaving the earth intact, earth which is only 60 cm deep. When you're on the tractor, some of the slopes are terrifying if you don't know what you're doing". At Chiopris-Viscone, in 2008, they

opened a resort in the eighteenth-century Villa Chiopris, with nine very comfortable rooms and three apartments, as well as rooms for conferences and meetings. The villa is surrounded by 100 hectares of vineyards in the Grave area. The Livon family also owns a winery with 15 hectares of vineyards in the Chianti Classico area (Borgo Salcetino) and one in Umbria (farm Colsanto di Montefalco) with 20 hectares of vineyard, where they produce exclusively red wines.

VENICA & VENICA

The Magic of Ronco delle Mele Sauvignon

FRIULI VENEZIA GIULIA

www.venica.it

The siblings **Venica, Gianni** (General Manager) and **Giorgio** (cellar master) have essentially built their brand around one wine: Ronco delle Mele Sauvignon. Several factors have contributed to its success: the research and the skill of the siblings, the ability of Gianni's wife Ornella in communication and relationships and the youthful input of Giampaolo, young oenologist who represents the fourth generation.

Ronco delle Mele is the result of constant research in the cellar and careful vineyard management. Alongside the first vines of Sauvignon on the northwest side of Cerò – now Ronco delle Mele – others were planted from 1984 onward, but in different areas, to find the best positions for this variety. In the cellar, the grapes from each vineyard were vinified separately. The wine of this Ronco was distinguished by its character. Ornella recounts that "in 1995, we began to bottle it alone and took the name of the plot of land, Ronco delle Mele, in fact. While the Ronco del Cerò comes from the other Sauvignon vineyards with different exposures and locations".

Ronco delle Mele is an exuberant wine whose scents have a long finish, an agile mouthfeel and have vigour and a measured alcohol content. The latest developments in winemaking – grapes removed from the stem, cold maceration of the must and aged in large wooden barrels – give it a noble silky quality, without affecting the varietal timbre and freshness.

Those vineyards are nearly thirty-five years old now and are expressing their maximum potential, ensuring a constant improvement in the quality of the wine.

Of course, all the other wines are excellent, from the Ribolla Gialla L'Adelchi – father of Gianni and Giorgio – to the Perilla, a great Merlot that is made for aging.

VILLA RUSSIZ

Wine at the Service of Children in Need

FRIULI VENEZIA GIULIA
www.villarussiz.it

Before discussing the winery, which belongs to the group that nurtured modern oenology in the region, it must be noted that today Villa Russiz (one of its labels shows the medals won in Vienna in 1873 and it was one of the first to return to the business of bottled wine after the war, in 1959) is a Foundation owned by the Friuli Venezia Giulia Region. Business revenues make it possible to pursue the original objective, that is, assistance to needy children.

Yes, the history of Villa Russiz began in 1868 when it was founded by the French Count **Theodor de La Tour**. His wife, the Austrian Countess **Elvine Ritter von Zahony**, opened a charity for poor, orphaned and abandoned children when her husband died. The work of the charity was carried on by **Adele Cerruti**, a member of the aristocracy.

In the words of a great chef in Udine, Massimiliano Sabinot of the Vitello d'oro: "Seeing that every bottle we sell helps these children is a great pleasure."

Many of their wines have attracted attention and important acknowledgements on the markets around the world. One of these is Sauvignon de La Tour, with a powerful structure but at the same time, it is harmonious and offers many fresh and finely amalgamated bouquets. The two vineyards that produce the de La Tour were selected after a long and detailed search conducted inside the 40 hectares of the estate. This wine (first year of production: 1988) is the

ancestor of the grands crus of the winery. Only later did the others follow: in 1993, Merlot Graf de la Tour and, in 1999, the Chardonnay Gräfin de La Tour. Finally, the Cabernet Sauvignon Défi (challenge) de La Tour, with the first year of production in 2007, on the market from mid-2011. Except for the first, they are all aged in wood in the historic cellars of the castle.

LUPI

Grand Wine Ambition Takes Shape

LIGURIA
www.casalupi.it

It was the early 1960s and **Tommaso Lupi** found himself working as a taster, able to select good lots of wine to offer to his numerous customers. The step from there to producing wine was short. In 1965, in Pieve di Teco, a small village in western Liguria, with his brother **Angelo**, Eno Valle d'Arroscia was born, a small garage where they made wine with grapes purchased from trusted local farmers. The choice of venue was not accidental. The town was in fact a symbolic hub between the two most important wine valleys that run down from the hinterland to the sea. One was Imperia, the other Albenga.

At a certain point, the Ormeasco, Pigato, Vermentino and Rossese were no longer enough. With suitcase in hand, packed with bottles, Tommaso Lupi began to travel around Italy in search of new types of wine to "exchange" with his. It was the early 1970s, the era of Giacomo Bologna and Mario Schiopetto, friends that Tommaso could talk to and compare wines with. Professor **Lanati** had always backed him and was still an indispensable advisor. The ambition of the great wine took shape in 1988 when, from an older vineyard, Vignamare was born, a Pigato that was one of the first in Italy to measure itself against the wines in small barrels. The name, and it is no coincidence, has several interpretations: "*vigna a mare* – vineyard by the sea", which is glimpsed in the distance, but also "*vigne da amare* – the vineyard to love", to emphasize the family passion. Finally, the "*vigne*

amare – bitter vineyards"; to never forget the sacrifice that working these rugged lands requires. With about 20 hectares, some of them rented, some in concession, the running of the winery passed to Massimo, Tommaso's son who studied oenology in Alba, someone with great passion and great expertise.

TERRE BIANCHE

The Charm of Vineyards

LIGURIA

terrebianche.com

Filippo Rondelli, slightly emotionally, tells us about his father **Claudio** and when they went down along the rugged road to the village of Dolceacqua, a market place for products of his land, as miserly as it was enchanting. "My father, along the way, used to stop at Arcagna to admire the Rossese vineyard, which was breathtakingly beautiful. With an entirely Ligurian perseverance and determination, that patch of land soon became Rondelli land; first rented and then owned". The father's intuition, supported by brother **Paolo** and assisted by the strong hands of **Franco Laconi**, underlies the unstoppable progress that led Terre Bianche to play a leading role in Italian viticulture in the last decades. The standard-bearer, together with a handful of small wineries, which includes Testalonga and Macarius, one of the great treasures of Italy: Rossese grapes.

"Nothing happens by chance," warns Filippo. The peculiarities of the Terre Bianche in this strip of Liguria, between the sea and the Alps near the French border, were already known to the Romans and the Benedictine monks who for centuries cultivated it. Soon, on these plots of land, vines of great vocation were being rediscovered and then came the first experiments in the mid-1980s, confirming the excellence of the Rossese planted here. There was such enthusiasm that in 1988 he decided to make wine from the grapes on the plot individually, with today's first unofficially

celebrated vintage being the cru Bricco Arcagna. When, a little later, in the late 1990s, it was young Filippo's turn to replace his father Claudio, alongside his Uncle Paolo and Franco Laconi, nothing changed. Rossese remains the driving force behind the winery, ably supported by the white varieties more typical of the region, such as Vermentino and Pigato.

FATTORIA ZERBINA

The New Albana Queen

EMILIA-ROMAGNA

www.zerbina.com

Maria Cristina Geminiani, the granddaughter of Vincenzo – who founded Zerbina in 1966 – came into the business in 1987 with a lot of passion and a degree in agricultural sciences, to which she added a degree in oenology over time, and a large number of prestigious master degrees. In the course of a few vintages, she "thoroughly overhauled" her grandfather's farm. She took the nobility of this land, the homeland of Sangiovese (the same one that is

famous beyond the Apennines) and the much maligned Albana, and resurrected it to a new life with the withering process. Of course, in the following decades, it needed a conductor who could tune the instruments, but the talent was already in the DNA of the rows of Marzeno, a stone's throw away from Faenza. New vineyards (also saplings, according to an old local tradition), a clonal selection that was the envy of nearby Tuscany were two features that brought the Pietramora, Sangiovese and Marzieno, with the balance of international varieties, to the attention of the critics.

The year was 1987. At a table in the dining room of a great Italian restaurant (La Frasca, Gianfranco Bolognesi's place) were guests Cristina and an acclaimed oenologist, Vittorio Fiore, who insistently haunted the woman from Romagna. The discussion revolved around how to reinterpret the Albana grape that grew on the valley floor, which had been enslaved by an unhealthy situation. They had the idea of exploiting the humidity and frequent fog, followed by warm sunny afternoons, to "stimulate" the attack of noble mildew that was recklessly left on the vine. Checkmate! (or, *Scacco matto*, which became the name of this wine). The first trial, in November of that year, proved the neo-Queen of Albana to be right. In the years that followed, not always, but often, Cristina won the match.

MEDICI ERMETE

Lambrusco, from Sparkling Drink to Top Italian Wine

EMILIA-ROMAGNA
www.medici.it

For once we are not starting from the beginning, but the end: the present. We begin our story of Medici Ermete from the shelves of department stores in the heart of the City of London, the menus of the many multi-starred restaurants abroad, the most exclusive lounge bars across the world where what we like to call "an Emiliano-style happy hour" (made up of cured meats, cheeses and other delicacies) now has a worthy companion to pour into glasses: Lambrusco. Up until a few years ago, this wine was called (and not always wrongly) "Italian Coca-Cola", but has now become one of the "Made in Italy" labels, showing that Lambrusco, if respected, can fill an irreplaceable role on tables every day, not only on tables in *grassa* (fat) Emilia.

We return to the beginning. It was the early 1960s when **Ermete Medici**, assignee of the vineyards of the father Remigio, developed an all-new project for Lambrusco, treating it like the other more important grapes (lower yields, strict selection during the harvest, appropriate winemaking techniques). Sons Valter and Giorgio then joined the winery and we were already in the 1980s, and they did not change their father's project one iota. The winery expressed itself "in music" (we must not forget that the Reggiano area is home to great musicians and composers): thus came Concerto in 1993 and Solo in 2003. The quality grew with each year, but the prices remained affordable.

The consecration to the success came, as so often happens, in the pages of an American magazine that "gave customs clearance" to the humble Lambrusco. The national press was lining up and re-launching. The critics were singing a whole new tune and awards were raining down. The era of the "Lambrusco renaissance", as the Americans dubbed it, had just begun.

BADIA A COLTIBUONO

Territorial Brand of Wine

TUSCANY
www.coltibuono.com

What explains a "simple" Chianti Classico in a gallery of "stellar" wines like the ones described in this publication? And to think that in Badia a Coltibuono as well, they produce such a well-reputed Super Tuscan as Sangioveto, acclaimed by critics and the public, with a strong history dating back to 1980. Yet, knowing how to read it, it is actually with the Chianti Classico vintage that the Abbey of the Buon Raccolto (Good Harvest) not only gave a new impetus to its long history, but a real impetus to the so-called movement of "natural wine" in a district that, even in the 1990s, appeared to be snoozing. Important inroads were made by a larger-scale Chianti winery with a long tradition, for years now certified organic, a winery capable of giving a basic wine all the unique, fine, complex, reserved and scintillating character of an authentic territorial Sangiovese. In Coltibuono, the viticulture became less and less invasive, the cellar practices more discrete, with the declared intention of rediscovering the strengths that have made Tuscan wines so well-known and appreciated: elegance, drinkability, digestibility and a capacity for pairing with foods. The revitalization of all the winemaking mechanisms resulted in a clear focus, playing on the natural qualities of the fruit, but also the more austere and mineral undertones that can result in a finer and more flavourful, vibrant and balanced palate. In the surrounding area, called the Sangioveto, is an extensive range with labels that are no less distinguished by the necessary territorial footholds. Normally, the Chianti Classico Cultus Boni has a feminine voice, with seductive floral traces and hints of berry. The Chianti Classico Riserva has more masculine accents, and is highly recommended for those who prefer wine with a subtly evolving flavour.

BOSCARELLI

"Nobile" Wine of Quality
in the Town of Poliziano

TUSCANY
www.poderiboscarelli.com

It was the early 1960s. Italian wine "of quality", as we know it today, was still far away. Even in Montepulciano, a land dedicated to Prugnolo Gentile (one of the many nicknames given to Sangiovese in the Tuscany of a thousand bell towers), the situation was languishing.

With the foresight of those who make history, **Egidio Corradi** convinced his daughter **Paola** and son-in-law **Ippolito De Ferrari** to invest in wine in the shadow of the towers of the city of Montepulciano. Confirming his instinct, he bought land in the small hamlet of Cervognano where the farmers of the area say that the best grapes in the municipality are harvested.

The year was 1967, and five years after the purchase of the farm came the first handful of bottles branded Boscarelli. From then on, recalls Paola, it was all a crescendo. The result of major investments increased the hectares of vineyards, that then were 15, and the number of bottles, which today number 100,000 units. In the mid-1980s, Paola was joined by her two sons, Luca and Nicolò, who immediately became involved in the project, taking on the oenological and agricultural management of the winery. The lucky star never abandoned Boscarelli, from the collaboration with oenologist **Maurizio Castelli**, starting in 1984 and still flourishing, to the purchase in 1989 of an old vineyard called in the local peasant dialect "del Nocio" for the presence of a big walnut tree on its fringes. It is at this last farm, just over 3 hectares planted in

1972 with Prugnolo gentile, that the winery's success was consecrated. In the cellar, they quickly realized that the grapes had something extra, so much so that in 1991 they decided to make wine individually. The name of the wine was already written: thus Nocio dei Boscarelli came into existence.

CASTELLO DEI RAMPOLLA

Story of the Earth

TUSCANY
www.castellodeirampolla.it

"As for our history, there are no special decades. Our history unfolds slowly, according to the events that happen to us. We do not make big plans, because nature doesn't make them, but year after year fulfills its task with great seriousness and discernment. So Luca and I try to do the same. To make wines that reflect our personality and the earth in which they grow. For us the land has great importance, and everything is a consequence of it. Our family has always tried not to forget that. If we love the earth, the earth loves us accordingly and gives great results. A great book about wines must talk about the earth and not people". These are the words of **Maurizia di Napoli** who summarizes her thoughts on Castello dei Rampolla, the result of an intuition of **Alceo di Napoli**, one of the architects, in Panzano in Chianti, of the oenological renaissance that swept through Tuscany in the 1980s. The cultivars which conditioned the project were Cabernet Sauvignon, from one of the legendary places in Bordeaux (Château Lafite-Rothschild). It was through a Sangiovese blend that Sammarco was born, one of the first Super Tuscans. Success on the domestic and international markets came immediately. The earthly parable of Alceo di Napoli ended here, and Maurizia and Luca devoted La Vigna d'Alceo (now simply renamed D'Alceo) to his memory. It began with the 1996 vintage and a prevalence of Cabernet Sauvignon balanced by Petit Verdot. A debut with a bang: it was classified as the red of the

year by Gambero Rosso, and today it still has extraordinary class and power. With the first ones, the nose might make you mistake it for a great Pauillac, but the palate speaks Chianti dialect. And every year the derby between Sammarco and D'Alceo returns with dizzying results.

CASTELLO DI AMA

A Story about Firsts

TUSCANY
www.castellodiama.com

On thinking about Castello di Ama's story, it is one about firsts, and it began in 1976. This is where, in 1978, the concept of cru was introduced for the first time in Chianti in the Bellavista vineyards, followed, in 1982 by the San Lorenzo vineyard, in 1985 by the Casuccia vineyard and in 1988 by the Bertinga vineyard. In 1979, the fermentation cellar was completed (the first thermo-conditioned) with cutting-edge criteria. The turning point began with the arrival of **Marco Pallanti**. In 1982, **Lorenza Sebasti** entrusted him with the technical management of the winery. A long period of study that lasted for a decade accurately discerned the potential of the area to the point of understanding that the surface area where Sangiovese was planted, and that the DOC attributed to the winery, was too extensive. The boundaries had to be rethought – namely reduced! In 1983, they were the first to transform a vineyard, using a lyre system and replanting it with Merlot. In 1984, they were the first to experiment with high-density planting (8,800 plants per hectare) in Chianti. In 1991, in Switzerland, the Académie internationale du vin, during a blind tasting dedicated to Merlot around the world, awarded L'Apparita 1987 as best wine, over all French wines. The 1988 and 1990 were the best vintages for the Chianti Classico Bellavista. It was the beginning of a decade of successes (the legendary 1992 vintage, for L'Apparita). The new millennium was no exception and there

was an astounding Chianti Classico Casuccia 2004 and the "simple" Chianti Classico 2006, a true delight. And in 2006, Marco Pallanti became the ambassador of the Chianti Classico, serving for two three-year terms as president of the Consortium, a position that falls under the banner of quality, innovation and continuity.

CERBAIONA

The Technique of Non-technological Vinification

TUSCANY
cerbaiona@alice.it

Cerbaiona is still a reference winery in the Ilcinese district and consequently, a national reference point. It was precisely in 1980 that **Diego Molinari** produced his first Brunello after moving to Montalcino in 1976. The commander (for his past as a pilot on Alitalia intercontinental routes) found himself about 15 hectares, a good half of which was forest where for the most part gardens and olive groves grew. Of vineyards there was little or nothing, just a few Moscadello and Sangiovese grapes. He began to

gather information. He planted Sangiovese. The soil, very stony, is a mix of marl and limestone, with clay intrusions. He mainly used the spur-pruned cordon method (inspired by Biondi Santi). By himself and without the support of special oenological expertise, Diego then decided to opt for a vinification using very little technology. From fermenting in cement vats to decanting into steel tanks, the Brunello ages in barrels of 30 hl for at least three years. He uses no selected yeasts, no fining agents or filtration. Following that, it is aged in the bottle and put on the market according to the product regulations. This simple formula for wines rapidly gained public attention. Of those famous 1980s, today there is still a memorable version of the 1988, a splendid blend of cherries, dried flowers, herbal tea and liquorice. The body is extraordinarily full and it has a fascinating airiness. Of the 1990s, there is an overestimated vintage such as 1997: the first of many hot years that we would later come to know, here is shored up with skill. It has a nice mineral and persistent note fading into a trail of liquorice. The 2001 is extraordinary, perhaps the most complete ever, for its complexity and finesse. In late 2015, the company was acquired by the American Gary Rieschel.

COL D'ORCIA

Affirmation of the Cru

TUSCANY
www.coldorcia.it

The flagship wine of this winery (Brunello di Montalcino Riserva Poggio al Vento) came into being with the 1982 vintage. It was a choice that marked a break with the Tuscan traditions of the time, sometimes favouring a cut of the best selections from various vineyards with blends that more or less hit the mark, instead of a separate bottling of individual crus. This direction definitely proved to be a driving force for the territory of Montalcino, as **Edoardo Virano**, director of the estate since 1977, recalls. "In the years going from 1979 to 1982, we continually verified in the periodic tastings that the Brunello from the Poggio al Vento vineyard always proved to be superior to others. With the harvest of 1982, we decided to allocate it to a special Reserve". The vineyard, just over 5 hectares, is located on a thoroughfare south of Sant'Angelo in Colle and has special characteristics compared to other parcels of property (a single unit of 540 hectares, of which 90 are vineyards). The sand content, significantly higher compared to all the winery's other vineyards, promotes the permeability of the soil; the altitude, located between 320 and 370 metres above sea level, plays an essential role, since this is probably one of the hottest and driest slopes of the appellation. The constant ventilation (hence the name of the vineyard) is favourable for the vegetative stages for the plant, avoiding any stress from heat and safeguarding the health of

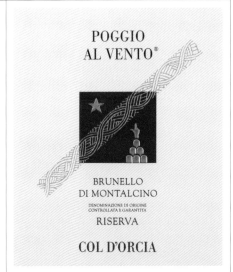

the grapes with clear benefits for the final accumulation of sugars and aromatic precursors that here manage to combine intensity and depth with true grace. Special attention is paid to the harvest, to avoid over-ripening, because here one wants to favour elegance rather than an excessive concentration. The aging is in barrels of 25 and 50 hectolitres for four years and a long aging in the bottle. Only the great vintages are put on the market.

ISOLE E OLENA

A Piedmontese Who Interpreted Tuscany

TUSCANY
www.isoleolena.it

Established in 1956, Isole e Olena quickly carved out a leading role in the arena of Chianti and, consequently, Tuscany and the rest of the country. From 50 hectares located in the town of Barberino Val d'Elsa, owned by **Paolo De Marchi**, Piedmontese by birth but Tuscan by adoption, came wines with strong territorial characteristics, from whatever cultivar was available. With rare exceptions he preferred mono-varietal wines. Around one of these – the Cepparello, a Sangiovese – he built his legend. Also exploring the other labels, there is a Chardonnay that is one of the greatest heights of Tuscan white wine production. Among the reds made with international varieties, in the vote within the so-called Private Collection, we choose the Syrah, which in a hot year like 2007 shows similarities in flavour, starting with a solid fruitiness (blackberry and black cherry) and opening into hints of chocolate, licorice and tobacco. Balms and spices characterize the long finish. Isole e Olena also has one of the best Vin Santos in circulation, with the quintessential quality in its sensual hints of dried fruits, barley and enamel tones. Proper space should be made for Cepparello, that accompanied us in our tastings throughout the 1980s. Those that shone for me because of their elegance on the palate were the 1982 and 1983 vintages. Then come the more "muscular" 1985 and 1988 vintages, absolute masterpieces that still move me. However, the 1990 is the winner for its breadth and depth, still leaving room for the

interim vintages. Then there is the famous 1997, today a little tired, and the 1999, still bursting with energy. Worth mentioning for the new millennium is the 2006, one of the best ever for Paolo De Marchi.

VALLOCAIA

Rudi Bindella's Vino Nobile

TUSCANY

www.bindella.it

BINDELLA

VALLOCAIA

*terra
vite
vita*

"Terra Vite Vita", the winery's motto on all the bottles produced in Vallocaia, Montepulciano, is the summary of the guiding philosophy for the management of **Rudi Bindella**'s winery, which he bought in 1984. From the beginning, he followed an approach to viticulture and to crops in general, driven by deep respect for the land and the environment, which immediately led him to apply the basic criteria of sustainability of agricultural systems.

When he purchased the land there were only 2.5 hectares of vineyard – but these now number 40, out of a total of 130 (the rest was arable land, olive groves and forest). Vallocaia is the realization of a dream: to produce his own wine in a pristine area, from the ancient tradition of winemaking and in Italy, a country that Rudi Bindella loves.

The reigning variety is Sangiovese, which in Montepulciano is called Prugnolo Gentile. It accounts for 65% of the planted area and is used to make three Montepulciano DOCG wines, each different expressions of the same Sangiovese.

So the Vino Nobile di Montepulciano Bindella, from Sangiovese di Vallocaia, blended with Colorino, Canaiolo nero and Mammolo, expresses the fine and elegant quality of the sands; while the Vino Nobile di Montepulciano I Quadri, pure Sangiovese, makes a powerful and concentrated wine that is a product of the clays; finally, the Riserva di Vino Nobile di Montepulciano Vallocaia, produced with Sangiovese from higher vineyards and a small percentage of Colorino, combines finesse, complexity, concentration and elegance and is the perfect expression of the terroir of Vallocaia. Among the international wines, the most cultivated is the Sauvignon Blanc, of which Gemella is one of the first in Tuscany, with a strongly varietal character. It now accounts for about 20% of the winery's production. Also worth mentioning is the small-scale, but valuable few hundred bottles a year of Vin Santo Occhio di Pernice Dolce Sinfonia, made from grapes left to wither for four or five months and whose name could not be more appropriate.

VOLPAIA

The Fortress of Chianti

TUSCANY

www.volpaia.com

Volpaia, even before being one of the most famous Tuscan names, is a place, a destination. The castle is located in a strip of Chianti that boasts extreme natural beauty. The **Mascheroni Stianti family** is to be given credit for preserving the old structures of this fortified village between the eternal rivals, Florence and Siena. Fermenting rooms, cellars, wineries, rooms for making vinsanto, crushers, urn rooms and vinegar rooms are still housed in the various buildings and connected by underground tunnels that directly or indirectly involve the inhabitants in the rural business of making wine and oil. The visitors and tourists are all convinced, making this place a must-see for every wine tour worthy of the name. There are now 50 hectares of organically grown vineyards. We come to our history. I was taking the first steps of my journey and there were not many tasters of Chianti Classico who aroused my curiosity when I was young. The labels of the bottles were covered and at the end the labels were revealed, and the verdict was quietly marked in a notebook, regardless of the importance of the wines. Well, Volpaia expressed that continuity and that common thread between vintage Chianti Classico and Chianti Classico Riserva that was really the preserve of a few winemakers in the late 1970s. In the early 1980s, Volpaia went through the epic moment of those wines that Frank J. Prial, for years the wine columnist for *The New York Times*, called, with an apt neologism, the "Super Tuscans", launching Coltassala (which was back with Chianti Classico) and Balifico, one of those deemed part of the "renaissance of Tuscan wines" that precisely in Chianti Classico found its greatest impetus. Since then Volpaia has safely sailed the stormy seas of fashion and trends.

BARBERANI

Quality Beyond History

UMBRIA
www.barberani.it

You find yourself in the early evening sitting in front of the cathedral of Orvieto, with the last rays of sunlight illuminating the rose window in its grand facade, the fourteenth-century masterpiece by Andrea Orcagna. You turn around, almost dazzled by so much beauty and see the smiling face of **Luigi Barberani** in the historic wine bar on the square, whose windows frame the church. Barberani, winemakers since 1961, recites the winery brochure. In fact, it was his father Vittorio, in the early 1960s, who decided to take on wine, stimulated by the idea of being able to offer a good glass of Orvieto in the three bars owned by the family. Luigi became a lawyer. The meeting with Giovanna changed his life: together – in the mid-1970s – they decided to take the helm of his father's winery. The former lawyer threw himself headlong into his new profession, so much so that even on his wedding day, subverting the unwritten rules, they had to wait for him to reach the altar because of a cargo of wine that needed to be shipped to the US.

The deserved success came in the late 1980s when a Vinitaly Luigi Veronelli introduced himself at a Barberani stand to taste what they told him were the Italian Sauternes. The taste came as a shock. A few years before, in fact, Luigi Barberani developed the idea of exploiting the humidity of the neighboring Lake Corbara to cause an attack of noble mildew on the classic Orvieto grapes. With the harvest in 1986 came the first bottles of what in the next thirty years was to become one of the biggest sweet wines in Italy and the world: the Calcaia Muffa Nobile. The testimonial is now in the hands of the third generation of Barberani. Luigi and Giovanna look proudly to their two sons, Bernardo and Nicolò, masterful interpreters of the most current business needs (the first son) and the productive needs (the second son) of the winery.

CASALE DEL GIGLIO

The Lack of Tradition that Stimulates Innovation

LAZIO
www.casaledelgiglio.it

The origin of Casale del Giglio dates back to 1967, when **Dino Santarelli**, fascinated by Agro Pontino, established the winery.

His son **Antonio** understood that those reclaimed lands could be a very interesting area in terms of wine, but they were still unexplored. With his father he carried out intensive research and experimentation, with the collaboration of the oenologist **Paolo Tiefenthaler**, from Trentino. The decisive stimulus toward the highest degree of innovative freedom was the complete absence of a winemaking past in the chosen area. Since that time nearly sixty different experimental varieties have been planted, selected according to the cultivation standards practiced in Bordeaux, Australia and California, areas exposed to the influence of the sea like Agro Pontino.

This adventure was rewarded by the first major results with red grapes (Syrah and Petit Verdot) and white grapes (Sauvignon, Viognier and Petit Manseng), from which were created different labels from a single grape or a blend. The winery's flagship product is the Mater Matuta, a blend of Syrah (85%) and Petit Verdot (15%). Made in collaboration with the leading researchers in the field of university experimentation, the project Casale del Giglio was authorized by the Department of Agriculture of the Lazio Region and still sees the collaboration of many leading experts. The European Union has endorsed the results of this research by authorizing, from 1990, the cultivation of new recommended varieties in the province of Latina: Chardonnay, Sauvignon Blanc, Cabernet Sauvignon and Merlot.

To date Antonio has converted all of his 160 hectares of vineyards to rows and introduced new varieties characterized by the high degree of qualitative interaction with the territory.

GAROFOLI

The Oldest Winery in the Marches

THE MARCHES
www.garofolivini.it

It calls itself the oldest winery in the Marches. It was founded, in fact, in 1871 by **Antonio Garofoli** who began to produce and sell typical regional wines.

Then the generations followed him right up to our times. Its inclusion in the great movement of change in Italian wine took place thanks to the two brothers, sons of Franco Garofoli: **Carlo**, who studied agronomy and oenology, and **Gianfranco**, who had a degree in business administration. Both joined the winery in 1973. Their real revolution began in the 1980s when, while the whole area of Verdicchio was still offering the usual easy-to-drink wine, associated with the classic image of the amphora-shaped bottle, the Garofoli began to reduce yields in the vineyard, picking only the most perfectly ripe grapes: the result is a Verdicchio with greater body, in line with new consumer tastes, presented in a Bordeaux bottle. For the time, there was a Verdicchio that really went counter to the trends, the Macrina, called "the other Verdicchio", followed in 1984 by the Serra Fiorese, the first Verdicchio aged for at least two years (between wood and bottle). Then came Le Brume, the first Verdicchio Passito, demonstrating the versatility of the grape. The 1992 vintage saw the birth of Verdicchio Podium, a wine that is sold after a year of aging in steel and in the bottle. It is the faithful interpreter of this *terroir* because it expresses balance, breadth and aromatic finesse,

combined with ability to last over time (as much as ten years).

In September 2005, the fifth generation of the Garofoli family joined the winery: Caterina and Gianluca (children of Gianfranco) and Beatrice (daughter of Carlo). The Garofoli family story is, therefore, the story of a winery (the word "*casa* [home]" is not accidental) that continues to be innovative in the name of tradition.

UMANI RONCHI

Not Only Verdicchio

THE MARCHES
www.umanironchi.com

Established by **Gino Umani Ronchi** in 1957 in Cupramontana, in the heart of the production area of Verdicchio Classico, the turning point for the farm came in the mid-1970s when **Massimo Bernetti**, son of Umani Ronchi, took the helm. A man of great foresight, Massimo realized that the wine scene was dominated by Marches Verdicchios, which overshadowed the other wines from the Marches and Abruzzo, in particular Rosso Conero and the Montepulciano d'Abruzzo, which Umani Ronchi was also producing, and which, since then, he decided to promote. It turned out to be a good choice. In fact, in the 1980s Rosso Conero made its name: the first vintage of San Lorenzo came in 1983, and in 1985 came the Cumaro. Without neglecting the role of Verdicchio, they began to make cru and Reserves that were capable of competing with the best Italian white wines: among these the most famous is the Casal di Serra that has been produced since 1983, followed by Villa Bianchi. In the 1990s, Massimo Bernetti was joined by his son Michele, with whom he decided to invest in the neighbouring Abruzzo as well, in the DOCG area of the Teramo Hills. The Umani Ronchi galaxy was now able to count on two different winemaking centers with a good 230 hectares of vineyards. There are twelve crus in total, which respect and enhance the *terroir* and vines. Michele Bernetti is a tireless traveler, spokesman for their winery and the Marches in the world.

It is thanks to him that Umani Ronchi has

focused strongly on further innovation to increase quality. Of the many successful labels worth mentioning there is Campo San Giorgio, a Conero Riserva DOCG whose label incorporates a Conero wine of the late 1960s. The vineyard is near Osimo. After some targeted experimentation with harvests, it has been distinguished for its expressiveness and uniqueness of character. An elegant wine with a great territorial quality.

VELENOSI

The Marathon Runner of Wine

THE MARCHES

www.velenosivini.com

The beautiful and charming **Angela (Angiolina) Piotti Velenosi**, for the last thirty years, has been the protagonist in the world of wines from the Marches and Piceno. She also has a passion for the marathon (she has run ten of them, including New York, Berlin and London) and never stops. Her parallel course between vineyards and cellars began when she was very young, in her late teens, when she decided to embark on a double adventure: producing quality wines in the Marches, where only cooperative wineries and bulk wine reigned, and make her way in a man's world, oenology. The Velenosi Ercole Vini winery was founded in 1984, in Ascoli Piceno, by Angela and her husband Ercole, starting from only 5 hectares which produced Falerio and Rosso Piceno. Immediately the young Velenosi couple began to pursue the production of DOC quality wines. While Ercole mainly worked in the vineyard and winery, Angela was in charge of the corporate image, the true ambassador of Piceno wines worldwide. And in three decades, she has covered so much road: today the vineyards cover 105 hectares; they produce 2.5 million bottles, of which a large share is exported to five different continents.

With the choice to enhance the local and regional DOCs, Angela and Ercole were the first to understand the potential of some native vines: Passerina and Pecorino first of all, but also Lacrima di Morro d'Alba, the three jewels of regional winemaking.

In the wide range of Velenosi wines, the ones that stand out are the Roggio del Filare, Rosso Piceno Superiore DOC, a blend of Montepulciano and Sangiovese in which the skillful use of oak barrels is appreciated, with notes of ripe dark fruit and a spicy background, smooth and charismatic. It is a real jewel of Piceno winemaking, thanks to the care of the oenologists Attilio Pagli and Katia Gabrielli.

EMIDIO PEPE

Wines That Do Not Fear Time

ABRUZZO

www.emidiopepe.com

At age eighty-two, **Emidio Pepe** celebrated his first fifty vintages on the Stock Exchange in New York, where his Montepulciano d'Abruzzo was auctioned off for charity with a bottle that earned 4,100 Dollars.

After all, if there is a winery that more than any other is identified with the traditional red wine of Abruzzo, this is Pepe's. His cellar preserves almost all the vintages from that distant 1964, when Emidio, "the Don Quixote of the vineyards", began planning to produce a red Abruzzo for aging. His wines did not need to fear time, but rather make it their best ally. So he began to stockpile bottles, often mocked for this crazy initiative of his. He travelled throughout Italy and abroad, especially to the United States. Driven by an unwavering strength and a great belief in the inalienable value of life, he never abandoned his old and slightly _naïf_ way of making wine: even today his white Trebbiano is pressed by foot and bottled by hand! All this he explained and taught to the younger generation of the family – his daughters Sofia and Daniela and his granddaughter Chiara – who, under his still watchful eye, runs the winery today.

Pepe's wines may throw you off at first glance, but if you have the patience to listen to them, they will tell their original story. The wine of reference is obviously the red: true, animalesque, with notes of dark fruit and leather, its best expression comes a few years after the harvest. This wine is democratic, equally at ease in the most remote tavern in Abruzzo or the many-starred tables in Tokyo or New York, where it can be found on the wine lists of the eight 3-star restaurants.

QUINTODECIMO

Few Wines but Greatly Tied to the Land

CAMPANIA

www.quintodecimo.it

Quintodecimo is a name given in honour of the ancient history of Mirabella Eclano, a town in Irpinia 500 metres above sea level, in the area of the Taurasi DOCGs.

Aeclanum is the name of the original settlement in the valley of the river Calore, dating from the fifth century BC. In the second century AD, it became a Roman colony, but with the advent of the Lombards was annexed to the Duchy of Benevento. In 663, Aeclanum was destroyed by the Greek army and was called Quintum Decimum, because it was exactly 15 miles from Benevento. This is where Professor **Luigi Moio** created the winery where he grows his vines with love, along with his wife **Laura Di Marzio**, biologist and oenologist. "The wines of Quintodecimo were born," says Moio, "in an ancient territory, with whom we entered into a sort of covenant marriage and an absolute commitment to the production of great wines". After spending most of his career as an oenologist to make the wines of so many cellars great, in 2001 the professor decided to buy an estate for himself. "Quintodecimo for me is freedom," he explains. "I need the freedom to do what I want".

Luigi Moio was born and raised in a family from the area of Falerno (Caserta) that had been making wine for centuries. He was a researcher in Dijon, France, then Professor of Oenology at the University of Naples. "Wine has conditioned my whole life: I am the son of Michele Moio, historic producer who relaunched Falerno del Massico. From an early age I breathed in the scents of the barrels in the cellar".

Quintodecimo, thanks to its unique location, enjoys a special microclimate: the vines benefit from cool nights and mild summers, tolerating winter snow well and cold spells in spring. The goal is to produce a few wines that have a strong bond with the land.

D'ANGELO

Wines Marked by Volcanoes

BASILICATA

www.dangelowine.com

The D'Angelo winery is the history of the Aglianico del Vulture in Basilicata. It was established around the 1930s, founded by **Rocco D'Angelo**, grandfather of the current owners, **Erminia** and **Rocco D'Angelo**, children of **Lucio**.

In the early days of the business, they exported fresh Aglianico grapes to Northern Italy, grapes that were used to "cut" wines with little body or colour. In 1971, with the awarding of the DOC, the D'Angelo winery – like other Lucan winemakers – began to market using their own identity. The winery is located in the most classic production area of Aglianico del Vulture, between Rionero, Barile, Rapolla and Ripacandida, and produces 400,000 bottles of different types. There are two wineries: one for the processing and the other for the aging in barrels and *barriques*.

"Aglianico," explains Rocco D'Angelo, "is a grape that was cultivated in Southern Italy in ancient times, and especially in Basilicata and Campania. The grape was introduced by the ancient Greeks. It prefers hilly terrain of volcanic origin, clay and limestone. It buds and ripens late." This apparently rough and angular vine has found a well-defined identity in the last three decades, thanks to modern winemaking techniques and new farming methods. In the inland areas of Basilicata, the harvesting is done between the last week of October and the first of November.

Oro del Vulture (named after the ancient extinct volcano) or simply the Vulture, as they call it locally, is a great asset to this area of Lucania. D'Angelo has a strong regional imprint, class and character. Two of the winery's best interpretations are the Caselle Reserva and the Valle del Noce, both aged in large Slavonian oak casks.

IPPOLITO 1845

The Essence of Cirò

CALABRIA
www.ippolito1845.it

The story of the Ippolito family began in 1845, when **Vincenzo Ippolito** had his initials engraved on the country house in the marina of Cirò between vineyards, olive and orange groves. Another Vincenzo, after World War I, created the first modern winery of Cirò with underground tanks. The years 1969 brought the first DOC regulations that identified Gaglioppo and Greco Bianco to obtain the Cirò Rosso, Rosé and Bianco.

Vincenzo Ippolito's Cirò is first spoken of in a letter by the Calabrian poet and writer Leonida Repaci.

An important date was 1989, when the first Calabria cru was made, the Cirò Rosso Classico Superiore Riserva Colli del Mancuso. This wine goes on the market three years after the harvest and is the very essence of Cirò Rosso. But the "beloved wine" for the winery is the Ripe del Falco, a Cirò Riserva whose first vintage was 1956. In those years, the Cirò was a bulk wine intended to reinforce the alcohol and structure of prestigious Piedmont wines. Vincenzo Ippolito was the first to decide, with pride, to bottle it, choosing just one asymmetrical Piedmont bottle. By 1991, he decided to give a greater identity to the wine, giving it the strongly evocative name of the vineyard of origin: Ripe del Falco. Deliberately, the wine is bottled after at least ten years from the harvest to demonstrate the incredible potential of Gaglioppo in terms of elegance, power and longevity. A timeless wine,

in fact. Running the winery today are the brothers Gianluca and Vincenzo Ippolito, who divide the tasks equally: the first is responsible for marketing, while the second handles sales. For them it is a big responsibility to be at the helm of the oldest winery in Calabria.

BENANTI

Etna Viticulture

SICILY
www.vinicolabenanti.it

Sicily discovers her winemaking jewel: Mount Etna, which can attract the attention of enthusiasts around the world. **Giuseppe Benanti** is the Knight of Etna, the man to whom we owe in large part the revival of viticulture on the slopes of the volcano. Another Giuseppe Benanti, the grandfather of the Knight, in the nineteenth century began to produce wine in Viagrande, on the southeast slope of Etna. From that villa with a millstone,

business started up again in 1988 with the Knight, together with the oenologist **Salvo Foti**. His passion is divided just as successfully with a pharmaceutical business.

Foti started out to rediscover viticulture on Etna, the most suitable terrrains, the most interesting clones of native vines. The old sapling vines were re-evaluated. The Cavaliere or Knight was convinced of the great potential of Nerello Mascalese, the red grape variety typical of Etna, and he wanted to show them to the world. The cru like Serra della Contessa and Rovittello were created, with a small percentage of Nerello Cappuccio, as was the tradition with the old vines up there. But it was a white, Pietramarina, that immediately became a legend. It was made of purely Carricante, also indigenous. This wine needed at least four to five years to begin to give its best, but then became a winner for its unique personality.

In the wake of Giuseppe Benanti many other local producers, the rest of Sicily and Italy, but also many foreigners, in recent decades have discovered or rediscovered Etna as a privileged place to make wines with a distinct personality. Antonio and Salvino, the two sons of the Cavaliere, have been running the business alongside their father for some years now.

DONNAFUGATA

Business Nature Culture

SICILY
www.donnafugata.it

In 1983, **Giacomo Rallo** created Donnafugata. Until then he had managed the cellar in Marsala, founded in 1851 by Diego Rallo. In California, he had seen how cold technology made it possible to produce excellent white wines, fresh and fruity as the market wanted them, even in in hot climates. Starting with the historic family winery, which he had inherited, and the land of Contessa Entellina, part of the dowry from his wife **Gabriella Anca**, he created the new winery, immediately oriented toward the market and communication. "Impresa Natura Cultura (Business Nature Culture)": producing quality wines while respecting the environment and promoting the territory. From this came some of the activities in support of archaeological research on the site of the fortress, Rocca di Entella Elimo, carried out with the University of Pisa. Between them, they organized the successful communication campaign, Vendemmia Notturna (Harvest by Night), seen in Australia and tested for the first time at Contessa Entellina in August 1998, making headlines throughout the world.

José, his daughter, soon showed herself to be a formidable communicator. Furthermore, "the voice" of the winery is also a talented jazz singer and the many initiatives that combine wine and music have helped give the winery a particularly brilliant, young, passionate and modern image. If success was achieved initially with the whites produced at Contessa Entellina, at Pantelleria Donnafugata there is another production site of choice. Passito Ben Ryé, whose first vintage was 1989, soon joined some the most famous award-winning sweet wines in the world. Today there are three wineries, in addition to the historic atmosphere of Marsala, in the Contrada Duchessa at Contessa Entellina (1990s), and at Khamma in Pantelleria (2000s) where the ancient Zibibbo vines are valued as true monuments of nature.

FAZIO

From Müller Thurgau to the Erice DOC

SICILY
www.casavinicolafazio.it

The north wind and the constant sea breezes that characterize the slopes of Mount Erice cool the vineyards, mitigating the hot Sicilian summer. In addition to the most modern techniques applied, this explains how the Fazio family of Trapani was able to make wine, for the first time in Sicily – 500 metres above sea level – and with good results, a Müller Thurgau, with a vine of the North. The first vintage was 1998. It introduced the winery and made it part of the history of the wine of the island. That same year the brothers **Girolamo** and **Vincenzo Fazio** established Fazio Wines, a new brand to relaunch a business that had been in the family for four generations. Together with the oenologist **Giacomo Alsaldi**, they set about drastically restructuring the winery, first in the vineyard and then in the product line and cellar. While they experimented with international cultivars, they also worked at constantly improving local varieties, both white and red. Among the latter was Nero d'Avola. Fazio was one of the main promoters of Erice DOC (since 2005). The winery always focused on the connection to the territory, eliminating the word "wines" in the brand and at the same time adding graphics, the medieval arch of Erice. Lilly, Girolamo's wife, handled communication, while Girolamo handled marketing and exports.

The protagonist of the winery's last development was again Müller Thurgau, this time harvested early and made into a sparkling wine with the short Charmat method, ideal as an aperitif, designed for young people. This innovation was made possible by the fact that the Fazio family already made, in the autoclave, a sparkling Petali Moscato and Petali Brut from Chardonnay grapes.

FIRRIATO

From International to Autochthonous

SICILY

www.firriato.it

The islands of Sicily were full of grapevines. Then the migration of populations led to drastically reducing production. At Favignana, after a century of disuse, 5 hectares were replanted thanks to the vision of **Salvatore Di Gaetano.** Within a few years, he made Firriato one of the most important wineries on the island. Certainly Di Gaetano's choice – the first harvest was in 2011 – was of the highest socio-economic value. There were 5 hectares of

sapling vines on tufaceous and red sand soil, where he experimented with different Sicilian vines.

Back to the story of Firriato, whose first bottles were of 1983. The most important strategic decision was made in 1994, when Di Gaetano chose to focus on the overseas market, relying on a team of Australian oenologists, thus helping to publicize Sicily througout the world thanks to the production of wines from international varieties, such as Camelot, a Bordeaux cutting of Cabernet Sauvignon and Merlot.

Once he had fulfilled his aim to be present on the markets, the winery began to use traditional island vines. The Australians went away. Wines like Perricone Ribeca were created, a wine that almost no one vinified in purity, and Nero d'Avola Harmonium. The number of bottles produced went from 400,000 in 1994 to 4,000,000 in 2004, and more!

The face and the author of a such remarkable success is the beautiful wife of Di Gaetano, **Vinzia Novara**, who since 1998 has been engaged full-time in running the winery and becoming the witness to this success.

Soon there were not enough grapes, and this prompted Di Gaetano to buy several properties in Trapani, as well as on Mount Etna, in 2007, with the estate Tenuta Cavanera in Castiglione di Sicilia.

MURGO

Bubbly Etna

SICILY

www.murgo.it

The Murgo were some of the first to relaunch the potential of the Nerello Mascalese as a base for spumante (it had already been mentioned in the second half of the nineteenth century), a native red grape variety par excellence from Etna. They led the way, along with Benanti and the Baron of Villagrande, in reviving the viticulture on Etna. The first sparkling wine was the Classic method of Murgo Brut 1989, aged two years on the lees. This was followed, in 2001, by the Extra Brut, with an aging on the lees for at least forty-eight months. The year 2004 was the birth of the fragrant rosé. It was immediately successful. It was a prize for the renewal work started in 1981 on the estate of San Michele by Baron **Emanuele Scammacca del Murgo** who, despite the many commitments in his diplomatic career – he was Italian Ambassador to the Holy See, in Brussels, in Moscow, as well as Secretary of State for Foreign Affairs – also found time to supervise the modernization of the vineyards and cellars of the family farm where already in the mid-nineteenth century Nerello Mascalese was grown. A vine in which the Murgo enhanced the strong organoleptic connection to Pinot Noir, which in France was used to make the great Champagnes. Nerello Mascalese in fact, like Pinot Noir, has a low concentration of tannins and high acidity. As with the Champagnes, on Etna, too, there is a territory with unique characteristics, although very different, due to the special mineral notes of the volcanic territory

that are added, exalting them, to the typical aromas of sparkling wine aged for long periods on the lees. Today the winery is run by brothers Michele – who is in charge of wine production – and Pietro – who instead manages the holiday guest farm on the estate.

PUPILLO

The Rebirth of the Moscato di Siracusa

SICILY

www.pupillowines.com

If we can still enjoy the Moscato di Siracusa, it is thanks to Baron **Antonio Pupillo** who, at the end of the 1970s, fought to prevent the disappearance of a such an old and special wine. A battle that can now be considered as won: Moscato di Siracusa is recognized and appreciated as one of the best wines of Sicily, both in the dry and the sweet version, and there are almost ten producers making it now. This relaunching is bringing back the viticulture in the area. Moscato di Siracusa is the descendant of Pollio wine, made from the Biblia (from Biblos, a Phonecian city), brought to Siracusa by Pollio, king of Thrace, who was in Sicily and became tyrant of Siracusa. If this is true, its origins date back to the eighth–seventh century BC. The Pupillo family winery, founded in 1908, still occupies a large part of the extension which once constituted the largest fief of Targia, famous for the beautiful castle of Frederick II and for an equally impressive historical garden with rare plants. It was recently restored and can be visited along with the winery. So, in the 1970s, Antonio Pupillo began his defense action and to replant the vines. The delicious wine is moderately sweet and very floral and in 1973, received the DOC for Moscato di Siracusa. It was a long process: the original plants had to be retrieved, propagated, the vineyards replanted and a modern cellar built. In 1994, finally, the first two sweet labels of Moscato di Siracusa from the Pupillo winery went on the market, the elegant and complex Pollio, made with slightly withered grapes, and the Solacium, made exclusively with overripened grapes on the vine. In 2000, it was the turn of the Moscato Secco Cyane. Moscato di Siracusa was saved.

CANTINA DI SANTADI

The Other Great Sardinian Red

SARDINIA

www.cantinadisantadi.it

The Cantina di Santadi relaunched Carignano del Sulcis which, together with Cannonau, is the other great Sardinian red. A colourful, rich, powerful red, and for these reasons was the basis of trade in blending wines between Sardinia and France. This was the cause behind the so-called "war of wine" – and Sicilian reds were also "involved", due to the rebellion of the *vignerons* of the Midi who attacked the trucks and tankers of Italian wine.

Returning to Carignano, in the Sulcis, one can still find vineyards on *piede franco*, in other words, vines that became acclimatized there millennia before and have not necessarily been grafted. The Cantina di Santadi, which has always played a leading role in the whole area, in the 1980s began to promote a new winemaking philosophy, entrusting the technical management to **Giacomo Tachis**, who was then joined by the young **Angelo Angioi**, a *rossista*, red wine expert who began working on the selection of vineyards and grapes, diversifying production. This is how the Terre Brune was born in the mid-1980s, with Carignano grapes and a small percentage of Bovaleddu, from vineyards using the *alberello* or sapling style of cultivation. A wine with a new style, without adulteration, soon became the spearhead of the winery. **Antonello Pilloni**, the much-esteemed president, ran the winery for nearly four decades. He wanted to give a special *imprimatur* to Terre Brune, labels that were numbered and guaranteed by the notarized stamp and signature. This was a wine with great personality, first aged in barrels and then in the bottle, with a perfect blend of the *terroir's* expression and an international character. The versatility of the variety lends itself to diversity in the product range, which is enriched with other reds such as Rocca Rubia, Grotta Rossa and Araja. Today, the Carignano Sulcis is exported to every continent.

The 1990s

Rediscovering the Importance of Vineyards and Definitive International Success

We have advanced from the terrible wines of the 1960s, which had no technical input, to the first wines to benefit from oenological know-how, taking their first steps to being competitive on world markets. A new sensitivity suggested that where technical know-how was adequate, the only way to give wines their own personality was to go back to the vineyard. It was the right choice as time has revealed. The ancient cultural sedimentation of Italy revealed a simple concept: the vineyard itself was the source of better quality.

Of course, without initial oenological input, there would have been no earnings to invest in improving the vineyards. In short, the conditions for developing oenological excellence had been established. The vineyard was the foundation, with all the variations that territory and microclimates would allow. Italy has unique assets in this respect. They must be recognised and appreciated. The world of Italian viticulture is now dedicated to this. The style of Italian wine emerged from this process and began to mature in the 1990s.

Viticulture took its place again at the centre of the wine system. Applied research became decisive. Zoning was no longer an exception. Many wineries undertook the task independently and the DOC consortia worked in the same direction. Vineyard investments were conspicuous. Precision viticulture, implemented by applying greater phenological knowledge of the plant, microclimates and the terrain, was born. All choices depend on the final product to be obtained.

The 1990s were also, and above all, the years when Italian wines definitively conquered world markets. Brunello di Montalcino became a symbol of this extraordinary success, but it was not alone. The wines of Southern Italy were in the spotlight, and took their places on the market very quickly. There was undoubtedly a renaissance within the renaissance, because Italy could not do without the noble wines such as the South has demonstrated, from the 1990s, to be able to produce. The wines of Southern Italy exited definitively from the spiral of distillation and blending support to the wines of the North and acquired a place for themselves among quality products.

LES CRÊTES

Celebration of *Terroir* in the Aosta Valley

VALLE D'AOSTA

www.lescretes.it

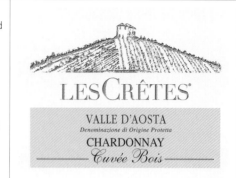

There is a tunnel called *Les Crêtes* near the Aosta toll booth on the road between Aosta and Turin. In the vicinity, there is a small pyramidal hill with a little house at the top. It is an unmistakeable landmark for anyone passing through. A man lives there who appears to be perfectly ordinary. One day, when viticulture in the Valle d'Aosta was still a strictly local matter, he began to dream about producing a wine and selling it all around the world.

Les Crêtes is also the name of the winery directed by this man, **Costantino Charrère**. The aforementioned hill is, first of all, a significant cru and secondly, a symbol of the winery that is reproduced on every label. This is the town of Aymavilles. It was here in the 1980s that Charrère, together with other partners, began to think of starting a viticultural activity, because he perceived potential worth developing. The idea was simple, but powerful: enhance the unique qualities of the *terroir* in Valle d'Aosta.

Les Crêtes actually became a winery with the first harvest in 1993, which was processed in the family wine cellar. They made two wines: Torrette, based on a traditional mix of indigenous grape vines, and a Chardonnay, an international variety. The start was encouraging and the wines worked well. However, despite its international origin, the Chardonnay was marked by the *terroir*. This fact inspired Charrère to develop the decisive idea that led to Cuvée

Bois, the wine that revealed Valle d'Aosta to the whole world, which he carried forward while also pursuing other projects and expanding the types of wines in production.

LA SPINETTA

Icon of Modern Wine Cellars

PIEDMONT

www.la-spinetta.com

Founded in 1977 in Castagnole Lanze by **Giuseppe** and **Lidia Rivetti**, La Spinetta was one of the first wineries to cite the location of the vineyards on the label instead of the producer's name. The breakthrough came in the early 1980s when they began to produce Bricco Quaglia, a high-quality, selected Moscato d'Asti. The three brothers – Bruno, Carlo and Giorgio (the last was also one of the *Barolo Boys*) – grew La Spinetta with the acquisition of vineyards in excellent locations, choosing exclusively indigenous vine varieties. They have also been present in Tuscany since 2000, between Pisa and Volterra. In 2011, they bought La Contratto, which represents 200 years of spumante history in Piedmont, situated in the heart of Canelli (Asti).

In 1985, they came out with their first red wine, Barbera d'Asti Ca' di Pian, followed in 1989 by Pin, a grape mixture of Nebbiolo and Barbera, dedicated to their father who had founded the winery. In the mid-1990s, they offered Barbaresco and in 2000, Barolo. The latter gave new vitality to the sub-zone of Grinzane Cavour. It had a surface area of 8 hectares and was biodynamic for 75% (they worked the vineyard with two horses, no tractors). The winery has 165 hectares of which 100 in Piedmont and 65 in Tuscany for an annual production of about 450,000 bottles of which: 4% Barolo, 8% Barbaresco, 20% Sangiovese, 8% Pin, 20% Barbera, 30% Moscato, 8% Vermentino and 2% Chardonnay/Sauvignon.

Considered an icon of the modern winery, the distinctive mark on almost all of their labels is the rhinoceros. This choice descends from the great admiration that Giorgio Rivetti, the volcanic oenologist of the company, has for the German artist Albrecht Dürer. Dürer had done a woodcut print to celebrate the arrival of this rare animal in Europe at the court of the King of Portugal. The lion is another exotic animal, which appears on the Barolo Campè label, again inspired by Dürer and a pencil drawing of his.

In 2009, they launched the One Litre Club to introduce the larger bottles, absent from the market for years.

The New Frontier of Lugana

Lugana is a white wine produced from Trebbiano di Lugana (Turbiana) vines. The production zone spreads through five towns south of Lake Garda in the provinces of Brescia and Verona. It is prevalently flat terrain with clay soil. Although local sources are full of references to the presence of grape vines in the past, it seems that viticulture became a specialised activity only from the start of the twentieth century, but its renown is growing exponentially. Current statistics indicate that Lugana vineyards occupy about 1,200 hectares and are continuing to expand. There are 130 bottling companies producing about 12 million bottles annually of the five types of wine included in the current Lugana DOC protocol, first introduced in 1967. Refined, elegant, mineral and gifted with explosive aroma: these characteristics synthesize the wines produced by **Ottella** in Peschiera del Garda, with its crus situated in San Benedetto di Lugana. Owned by the **Montresor family**, the names on the labels of these surprising yet satisfying wines are Le Creete and Molceo.

The products of the Ca' Lojera winery in Peschiera del Garda are very traditional interpretations of Lugana, originating in Sirmione at the heart of the Lugana zone. It is a real jewel of a family business carried forward impeccably by the **Tiraboschi family**. The quality of these products is very solid and reliable, year after year. The wines have an important structure that allows them to age gracefully. Basic Lugana never disappoints, Lugana Superiore unites stylistic clarity with fine drinking and Lugana del Lupo is favoured by austerity lovers.

Ca' dei Frati, located in Sirmione and managed by the **Dal Cero family**, is perhaps the first name that comes to mind when approaching Lugana. The Dal Cero family came here in 1939 from nearby Veneto. Their Brolettino is a very successful expression of Lugana, characterised by structure and aromatic complexity, as well as long life. I Frati is simpler, but no less reliable. It offers guaranteed value year after year and is perfect for approaching this type of wine.

Provenza, a wine producer in the town of Desenzano sul Garda, is managed by the **Contato family** with great entrepreneurship. The heart of their activities centres on Cà Maiol, a site that dates back to 1710, and base of the Contato family since 1967 when they started their business. We mention only three of the Lugana wines they produce. The first is Prestige, a simple wine that is faithful to its link with the vine. Molin, the second, has a sapid and appealing character that sparks enthusiasm. Finally, Fabio Contato is a wine offering the profound rotundity of the grapes themselves after a brief but intense passage in *barrique*.

ARPEPE

Or Rather, Arturo Pelizzatti Perego

LOMBARDY
www.arpepe.com

The story of ARPEPE, an historic reality in the Valtellina, is similar to that of the territory itself: many difficulties, but also much beauty. **Arturo Pelizzatti Perego**, fourth generation of a family that began cultivating vines and producing wine in 1860, has characterised recent history.

In 1973, Guido Pelizzati died. Since it was he who guided the business, it was sold. The 50 hectares of vineyards were allotted to relatives, including a share for Arturo who rented them back to the new owners while he bided his time. Better times came in 1983 when he reacquired the vineyards and processed his grapes in a small family wine cellar in Sondrio.

That was when Rocce Rosse was born, first offered to the public in 1990. The concept today is still the same. It is the product of traditional vinification and long ageing in wood and bottle to recreate an historic wine of the Valtellina. Arturo was unswervingly faithful to this oenological credo until his death in 2004.

The fifth generation, his children Isabella, Emanuele and Guido, are completely dedicated to the same belief as their father. They have, therefore, continued to produce Riserva only when the year is propitious and direct their efforts to capturing the great finesse, delicate balance and subtleties that Nebbiolo of the Valtellina can offer. Today, the winery produces about 70,000 bottles annually.

We mentioned Rocce Rosse (red rocks), their emblem. It is produced only in worthy years from a single vineyard near Sassella and is the archetype of traditional wine of Valtellina. The skins macerate for weeks in the vat with spontaneous fermentation. The wine ages for four years in large casks and then three years in the bottle.

COSTARIPA

The One-Night Wine

LOMBARDY

www.costaripa.it

Mattia Vezzola is one of the very few oenological technicians who deserve recognition for having taken the Italian spumante Classic method to the heights of quality and image. It is sufficient to cite Bellavista, the outcome of a visionary intuition of Vittorio Moretti. Mattia made a decisive contribution to its success by seeking an expression that was detached from champagne, to arrive at a truly Italian style.

His winery, founded by his grandfather Mattia in 1936, is near Moniga del Garda. He has continued to invest in the vineyards from 1973 – his 50 hectares of direct cultivation – as well as research and wine cellar technology.

He brought nobility to a widely diffused wine of the territory, Chiaretto del Garda, based on Groppello, the indigenous vine of the Valtènesi, "a fine nursery for still rosé wines", bringing it to its essence in RosaMara, "the one-night wine", as the creator defines it. It is the result of so-called teardrop vinification, that is by collecting the static dripping of the pure juice exuded without pressure (one night). Then 50% ferments and evolves in pièces (barrels) for about six months. The blend includes Marzemino, Sangiovese and Barbera, in addition to Groppello.

RosaMara – a classy wine, a pale rose petal pink – is included among the twenty-four best rosé wines "not to miss". It is also the winery's leading product, with 150,000 bottles of the total 450,000.

Of course, spumante, Mattia's oenological true love, could not be absent. The Brut Rosé Metodo Classico, a blend of Chardonnay (80%) and Pinot Nero (20%), is quite charming. The Pinot Nero is vinified in part with maceration for rosé and in part for red. Then 35% ferments in used pièces.

The Valtènesi Campostarne, with prevalence of Groppello Gentile grapes, originally developed with the collaboration of the great South African heart surgeon, Christian Barnard, is today defined a "metabolic wine". Mattia himself explains the reason: "To contribute to the realization of a social project that involves sixty countries of the world, conceived by Chef Luca Barbieri and Professor Macca [*nutritionist*], to create a diet dedicated to specific pathologies that would reverse the axiom of diet equals sacrifice, gloom and depression, into diet equals wellness of the taste buds and health. The choice is attributable to this land where the characteristics exist to transform a high quality red wine into the therapeutic nectar that Professor Macca hopes for".

CANTINA TRAMIN

Grand Interpreters of Wines from Alto Adige

ALTO ADIGE

www.cantinatramin.it

TRAMIN

Founded in 1898 by Father **Christian Schrott**, today the Tramin wine cellar has almost 300 associates cultivating vineyards for a total of about 245 hectares in the area of the towns of Termeno, Egna, Montagna and Ora. This wine cellar has not had an easy life, especially between the two world wars when it was entrusted to a fascist commissioner. United with the winery of the town of Egna in 1971, it did not immediately find its vocation. Today, it has become one of the cult wineries on the Italian scene thanks to Gewürztraminer, an ancient and aromatic vine that has always been associated with Termeno. It was a young cellar master or *kellermeister*, **Willi Stürz**, who singled it out and made it known to the market. He perceived and was able to ride the wave of the growing passion for the white wines of Trentino-Alto Adige in Italy. Termeno is, however, not only Gewürztraminer. While the production of Schiava continues to diminish, the wine cellar has not completely abandoned its red tradition: Pinot Nero, Lagrein and Schiava have excellent champions in Termeno. A carefully studied vineyard requalification campaign has also produced noteworthy results among the whites, too. Although not the largest, there are vineyards of associates in important zones such as Sella where Nussbaumer, the best-known Gewürztraminer, is grown. The slopes, ranging from 350 to 500 metres in elevation, with south/southwest exposition have a soil composition with strong clay and lime components.

Valpolicella: The Ancients Are Contemporaries

The oldest traces of grape vines in the territory of Valpolicella were discovered in archaeological excavations at Archi di Castelrotto, with origins in the fifth century BC, where numerous seeds of *Vitis vinifera sativa* and of *Vitis vinifera sylvestris* or *selvatica* were found. Ambrosan is another very important site. Here excavations revealed *apothecae*, rooms or cellars where wine matured, and spaces for grape pressing known as *torcolarium*. The origin of the word "Valpolicella" itself is contradictory, and some trace it back to the name *Vallis polis cellae*, meaning the "valley of many cellars". The idea is fascinating, but has no certified historical value. The provenance is more scientifically demonstrated from the name *Val Polesela*, found in documents of the city of Verona of 1177. The term *Pol* referred to large mounds of sand and gravel deriving from flooding along the bends of the Adige River. Today, there is still a place known as Pol in the southernmost part of the Valpolicella.

This great land of wines has always practised the characteristic technique of over-ripening and drying the grapes as documented in the writings of Flavius Magnus Aurelius Cassiodorus, a senator and prefect of the Praetorium at the court of King Theodoric in Ravenna. In a document dated approximately 500 AD, he describes a wine produced from such wilted grapes that he calls *acinaticum*, for which he also explains the drying technique, not very different from that used today. In medieval times, official documents already distinguish production between *vinum de plano* and *vinum de monte*, the latter accredited with greater quality and commercial value. The true story of the red wine of Valpolicella thus winds its way through sweet wine or as it used to be called, *vino santo* (holy wine). Once it had been known as *acinaticum* and later as *recioto*. This term was spontaneously adopted into the language of the farmers and came from a Venetian word *recie*, which meant the "ears" of the grape bunch, that is, the sections that were selected for drying. All the remaining history of the wines of these lands is an unending effort to make something bitter of something sweet. This attitude appeared in the salons of the nobility in Verona at the end of the eighteenth century. One of its most determined protagonists was Scipione Maffei, a playwright and man of letters. He detested serving sweet wine at the table and was the first the mention the existence in Valpolicella of a "wine called Santo that is sweet, but not sweet and has the property of not going bad no matter where it is kept". These were the first manifestations of Amarone, a wine that is gleaning great success around the world.

Valpolicella is a complex system of territories and people, but it is a complete system that took energy from the consolidation in 1968 when the DOC protocol became effective and extended the denomination to the eastern valleys toward Verona: Mezzane, Illasi and Tramigna. The decision did not convince the most strenuous supporters of Valpolicella Classica but today, after forty-five years, it does confirm the force of the territory and the capacity of those eastern lands to maintain the faith in the value of quality with a gust of innovation and, at the same time, create a place of work for many young people in love with their territory. There has been a long escalation since 1968 that is unique on the Italian oenological panorama. The force of raisin wines decreed the success of Amarone for twenty years, from 1990 to 2010, and continues today with its cousin, Ripasso.

TOMMASI

A Family Epic in Valpolicella Style

VENETO

www.tommasiwine.it

The extraordinary adventure of this great family of Verona covers more than a century of history. The Tommasi family is truly a miracle of Veneto. It was 1902 when **Giacomo Battista**, called "Titti", married Augusta who owned a few vineyards in the hamlet of Torbe. It was a little spark of love for the grape vine and the intuition that wine would become the agricultural success of the twentieth century. In jest, Giacomo was also called "il palanca" from the name of the ancient coins of Venice of the eighteenth century and for his great business instinct. In 1919, he was entrusted with management of Corte Masua, and from 1921, of all the vineyards of the noble family Campostrini. What followed is the story of a great family. It was a very close family that had its meals together at

a single table for years, where Giacomo's dream came true. His nine children are all in wine and restaurants, a peculiarity that continues today with the ownership of the Park Hotel Villa Quaranta, Caffè Dante in the heart of the city and Albergo Mazzanti in Verona. The first Amarone came out in 1959. The need to appear on the international market with high-quality products became a reality when the first orders arrived from the United States after the contract in 1972 with Rolar of New York. Today they reach sixty countries around the world. The foresight of the Tommasi family was to stake out their original territory and, at the same time, to choose new territories where they could produce distinguished Italian wines.
They launched the "1997 Project" that set the dimensions for the winery at Pedemonte. By late 2004 they owned 135 hectares of vineyards in the province of Verona. In 1997, they bought 66 hectares in Tuscany in the splendid zone of Pitigliano, between Poggio al Tufo and Doganella. Today, they have become 150 hectares with the acquisition of other vineyards near Scansano. Later they bought Tenuta Filodora in Prosecco and then near Manduria in Puglia, Masseria Surani. Dario Tommasi is also a founding member of the "Amarone Families" group.

BASTIANICH

An American Friulano

FRIULI VENEZIA GIULIA

www.bastianich.com

The **Bastianich family** bought its first 12 hectares of vineyards in the eastern Fruili-Colli Orientali DOC in 1997. The main objective was to produce a white wine that could compete with the great wines of the world. It was Vespa, which hit the bull's-eye right from the first harvest in 1998. It had accumulated the points needed for a 3-glass classification at the Gambero Rosso tasting, but it was not possible to consign the award, because regulations banned assignment of this level to a newly created wine. The white Vespa blend is composed of Chardonnay and Sauvignon in equal parts, with 10% Picolit. Later it would win 4 glasses. A very fine wine!
It would become the ancestor of the premium wines such as Plus, from Friulano 100%, with a part of the grapes left to dry, the red Vespa (Merlot 50%, with Refosco 30% and Cabernet Sauvignon/Franc) and Calabrone (Refosco and Schioppettino, with a part of the grapes left to dry), Merlot and Pignolo.
In 2006, the Bastianich family acquired another 10 hectares of the same DOC protocol in the town of Cividale del Friuli. Here they built their wine cellar and extended their proposals with the addition of young wines: Friulano, Sauvignon, Pinot Grigio, Ribolla Gialla and Refosco.
The oenologist of the firm is Emilio Del Medico, and the PR/marketing man is Wayne Young, an American who worked for a long time as sommelier In the first restaurant that Joe

Bastianich opened right in New York, the Becco. A country house, right across from the wine cellar, was refurbished and today houses Orsone, a restaurant and tavern with four guest rooms. A top-of-the-line restaurant with an elegant classic style and an open kitchen. It proposes the delicious Italian-American dishes of Lidia (Joe's mother). Instead, the tavern offers typical American specialities, from hamburgers to Caesar salads. There is a good selection of wines, in addition to those of the house.
The Gagliano estate, with 35 hectares of vineyards (including property and leased), produces about 260,000 bottles.
The family also owns La Mozza near Scansano in Tuscany, 35 hectares acquired in 2000. There are only two wines here: I Perazzi, a Morellino di Scansano DOCG; and Aragone, 40% Sangiovese, 25% Alicante, 25% Syrah and 10% Carignan.
Maurizio Castelli is the excellent oenologist consultant for both wineries. His name is a guarantee.

CASTELLO DI SPESSA

Management View of Wine

FRIULI VENEZIA GIULIA

www.castellodispessa.it

Castello di Spessa is a textbook example of what it means to link sales of high-quality wines with refined country tourism provided with all comforts.

Loretto Pali, an entrepreneur of wooden furnishings who manufactures and exports baby cribs to the whole world, began to invest in this project in 1979 with La Boatina estate near Cormòns.

He bought Castello di Spessa in 1988. The origins of the castle date back to the thirteenth century, but the structure visible there today was built in 1881. He did an intelligent refurbishment, transforming the castle, surrounded by its ancient park, into one of the most fascinating resorts in the region. There is an 18-hole golf course set in among the 25 hectares of vineyards. A military bunker from 1939 was transformed into the wine ageing cellar, 18 metres below the surface. It is now connected to the castle by a long stairway and guarantees the wine ageing. From 2003, he has relied on one of the most illustrious Italian oenologists, Gianni Menotti. La Tavernetta al Castello, the top-of-the-line restaurant with ten guest rooms located at the foot of the castle hill, and the Hosteria del Castello propose a local menu. There are also five guest rooms at La Boatina estate, which has 55 hectares of Isonzo DOC vineyards. The two crus, Collio and Isonzo, are bottled with the Castello di Spessa label.

Loretto Pali represents that group of entrepreneurs who have invested in wine, not only in Friuli, and introduced a managerial attitude that was missing from the agricultural world.

"Alas, I am no oenologist," he says deprecatingly. "My task is to sketch the general project and identify the strategies to achieve the objectives. The selection of wines and the techniques follow the history of these lands influenced by Austrian and French culture. Thus, the Pinot Nero is dedicated to Casanova who stayed in the castle for a long period. Our wines are the continuation of this history of ours."

ERMACORA

The Success of Not Having Given in to Fashion

FRIULI VENEZIA GIULIA

www.ermacora.it

Dario and **Luciano Ermacora** produce one of the best Picolit, the historic meditation wine of Friuli. The colour is a dense antique gold, bewitching with its tones of wildflower honey, brushstrokes of ripe apricots and fresh custard. It is broad and supple to the palate where the sweetness becomes a sensual caress. One of the great wines!

Dario and Luciano took over the family business in 1982. From the start, they chose to focus on indigenous vines. Now the winery owns 47 hectares of vineyards, with 65% dedicated to

white wines. Indigenous varieties account for 60% of the red wines and 20% of the whites, which will increase in the replanting programmes. These include: Ipplis, Buttrio, Montsclapade.

The stylistic interpretation they have applied to their wines has been instrumental to their success. They have never given in to the fashion of overly alcoholic wines. On the contrary, they have listened to and exalted the tones that these terrains and microclimates can offer: elegance, finesse, minerality, accessibility, harmony and longevity of white wines. Pinot Bianco is the wine that can represent all the others.

Among the red wines, the decision to favour indigenous vines was even more drastic. They are moving toward production of indigenous vines only: Pignolo, of noble descent; Schioppettino and Refosco dal peduncolo rosso. As Dario says: "Our decisions have been coherent over time. Now, the market is rewarding us. There is undoubtedly an evolution of taste preferences. However, it is one thing to evolve, quite another to alter our style completely. Abandoning it would be a marketing error in addition to a cultural non-sense. If we leave all behind to mimic the others, how can we distinguish ourselves? We must defend our recognition. This is a crucial step toward freedom of movement in the future".

FORCHIR

A Marketing Model

FRIULI VENEZIA GIULIA
www.forchir.it

Founded over a century ago in 1900, the Forchir estate was fortunate enough to encounter **Gianfranco Bianchini**, oenologist, and Enzo Deana, accountant. It was 1984 when they acquired the estate, bringing the force of radical renovation with them.

Now, with the harvest of 2014, the whole property belongs to Gianfranco, whose daughter Giulia is his right arm. The winery has vineyards in the Grave zone of Friuli distributed between the provinces of Pordenone and Udine.

Its rapid success depended on their marketing strategy – producing fine wines at competitive prices – a few steps ahead of the rest of the market. As early as 1998, their Pinot Grigio Forchir was a prize-winner in the United States when the *Wall Street Journal* named it the wine with the best quality to price ratio.

The winery has 230 hectares of vineyards, all with high density, low yield per vine, punctilious and timely management interventions and a well-trained work force, which guarantee an average annual production of one million bottles. As Bianchini explains: "We manage our vineyards in accordance with the rules of low environmental impact viticulture by rationally coordinating all production factors, so recourse to methods that are negative for the environment or consumer health are reduced to a minimum. We use products of natural origin to implement an integral fight against parasites".

In 2014, this philosophy led Gianfranco and Giulia to build a futuristic wine cellar amidst the vineyards at Camino al Tagliamento near Casali Bianchini. The form and the substance of the cellar are both futuristic, because the structure is totally carbon-free and makes use of solar energy only.

They also produce an excellent Pinot Grigio from the Spilimbergo vineyards where the combination of climate and terrain is ideal. The Sauvignon (vineyards at Camino al Tagliamento) and Ribolla Gialla are also top quality. Among the red wines, Refosco dal Peduncolo Rosso is noteworthy.

LIS NERIS

The Austrian-German Culture of Alvaro Pecorari

FRIULI VENEZIA GIULIA
www.lisneris.it

As **Alvaro Pecorari** puts it: "My generation was in the right place at the right time. I was eighteen in 1978 when I was given responsibilities in the business and a profound modification of white wines was underway, as only Mario Schiopetto had comprehended. In place of the flat, mediocre wines of the day, we were proposing rotundity, depth, minerality and inviting aromas. I was convinced that our viticultural heritage descended from the Austrians and the Germans, which meant naming the wines after the vine varieties. This decision was our winning finesse and I felt it should not be abandoned. The vine is still at the centre of my project today. Especially, one in particular: Pinot Grigio. Fifty percent of the 70 hectares we own of Isonzo DOC is, in fact, planted with Pinot Grigio".

In 2001, his daughter Francesca (who has passed away) presented it with these words at a tasting in New York: "My father says this is the wine close to his heart".

"We propose it as a single vine variety and in blends. Pinot Grigio 100% is the base line – inviting, fresh and easy – and the selected wine from old vines, with ageing in second-use *tonneaux* is 'Gris'. For blends: 'Lis' – Pinot Grigio, Chardonnay and Sauvignon, aged in second-use *tonneaux*; 'Confini' – Pinot Grigio, Gewürztraminer and Riesling Renano, steel and *tonneaux*".

It is curious to note that the estate was named for a red wine of Merlot (80%) and Cabernet Sauvignon; the first year was 1989. They called it Lis Neris. It became the label of the winery. And the vineyards are managed to perfection. "At the start, the vineyard was just work. Then it was transformed into a project, quality and sustainability. It takes years to achieve these objectives. For this purpose, collaboration with Simonit and Sirch, the 'Preparatori d'uva', was fundamental. Among other things, they taught us how to work the vines so they can live well and for a long time".

VISTORTA

Wine Identifies Property

FRIULI VENEZIA GIULIA
www.vistorta.it

The Vistorta winery has been directed since the late 1980s by **Count Brandino Brandolini d'Adda**, son of Brando Brandolini d'Adda and Cristiana Agnelli. It was founded in the nineteenth century by Guido Brandolini d'Adda. Brandino's first project was to produce an important red wine. He adopted the cru concept of Bordeaux, that is, identification of the wine with the name of the estate, where the family owned Château Greysac. As Brandolini puts it: "We might say that Vistorta is the result of a well-thought osmosis between two cultures, the Bordeaux way and the Friuli way. In fact, the cellar is directed by Alex Ongaro, a man of Friuli, under the supervision of monsieur George Pauli, a great oenologist from France, and Samuel Tinon, the oenologist who produces Tokay in Hungary [*which Vistorta distributes in Italy*]". Brandino has chosen to set aside a conspicuous number of bottles of reserve for each harvest. The Vistorta price list proposes at least ten vintage years on the European market, while all years of production, including the first, are still present in the cellar. Excellent years begin with 1990 (the first harvest of Merlot only), followed by 1997, 1999, 2004, 2009, 2011, 2012 and 2013.

Another important decision was made in 2005 when the vineyard was converted to organic management and the first certified harvest was made in 2010. This decision also led to a reduction in production. In fact, since the change the annual average is about 40,000 bottles.

As Alec Ongaro explains with satisfaction: "Since 2008, when the vines had already converted to the organic method and had reached an average age of twenty years, the grapes have acquired such a superiority and extraordinary flavour. It is worth noting that we still have 270 Merlot vines planted just after World War I, 1915–1918. Now there are two vineyard descendants from those mother vines almost one hundred years old".

BARONE RICASOLI

Ancient Coat-of-Arms and Contemporaneity

TUSCANY
www.ricasoli.it

1141. The history of the **Ricasoli barons** covers almost a thousand years now. It is one of the most ancient of aristocratic Italian families and has owned the lands in Gaiole in Chianti from its origins, where the heart of the production is still rooted today. The latest descendent, Baron Francesco Ricasoli, cannot limit his activity to defence of the ancient coat-of-arms, but must stay apace with contemporary taste that is always in evolution. In the past, it was from here that casks first departed to aristocratic Anglo-Saxon families. Still today, having redefined the production standards with the proper input in terms of innovation, the winery turns out 2 million bottles a year, shipped to all corners of the world. A place of pilgrimage, as becomes one of the few true castles, Brolio is as fascinating as ever for visitors. Here pilgrims can slake their thirst at the Enoteca and satisfy their appetites at the Osteria, a full immersion in the authenticity of Chianti. The wines are once again acquiring qualitative merits after a period of levelling off to more mundane international standards. The Chianti Classico Gran Selezione Colledilà 2011 provides a typical example. It was first produced in 2007. It is capable of translating the local dialect into the language of globalisation: ineffably precise and clean, supple, toasty in the long after-taste and perfectly balanced with ample and copious fruit. Convincingly alluring.

FATTORIA LE PUPILLE

The Queen of Morellino di Scansano

TUSCANY
www.fattorialepupille.it

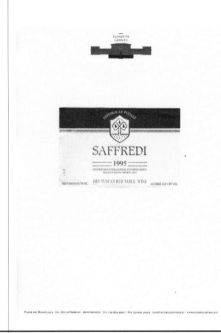

It is only natural to name **Elisabetta Geppetti** as one of the women who traced the rising parabola of Tuscan wine. In the midst of a life lived very intensely, five children, a sequence of commitments to the Morellino consortium, she also led her winery, Le Pupille, through exponential growth to surpass the threshold of half a million bottles. Born in Rome but settled in Maremma, she is a distinguished lady with charm, nerve and personality who landed in this far corner of Tuscany for love. She was studying art history and spent her summers in Pereta, the medieval settlement where the farm houses of Le Pupille are also located. Her father-in-law's family had been harvesting a few rows of Sangiovese for about twenty years. Then this simple Rosso di Pereta became one of the first Morellino di Scansano when the DOC protocol was introduced in 1978. The year 1985 was the turning point of her life. Her father-in-law died at just over fifty years of age and Elisabetta was suddenly catapulted from the languid halls of Roman academe to the toughest Tuscan countryside.

The beginning was anything but simple for a young woman starting out in viticulture as a guest in Maremma, a land given to a certain dose of machismo. But she had no fear and was simply spurred to do her best. With the support of people of the calibre of Giacomo Tachis, she was successful almost immediately. Saffredi, a pure Cabernet Sauvignon at the time, came out with the 1987 harvest and critics around the world called it a miracle. She consolidated her position and then launched a new challenge. In the mid-1990s, she bought a parcel registered as Morellino called Poggio Valente – *nomen est omen*. This was the birth of the "wine of wisdom" as she called her personal interpretation of Morellino and Sangiovese of Maremma.

The new generation is making its appearance at the helm, with her first-born, Clara.

PETROLO

Painting amidst the Vines

TUSCANY
www.petrolo.it

In this book, you will find other stories where producers' destinies are entwined with the mythical **Giulio Gambelli**, one of the best known experts about Sangiovese. But not everyone knows that the master taster suggested the introduction of a new variety to Lucia Sanjust as early as 1992. It was Merlot and it was better adapted to a particular portion of the terrain at Tenuta di Petrolo. In 1994, bottled separately, it became a symbol of the estate: Galatrona. Lucia bought out the family shares from her sisters and developed Petrolo with her son Luca. He was a painter and a devotee of art and the other beautiful and good things in life. Their acceleration involved renewal of the vineyards, changing their marketing (distribution in Italy and export) and introduction of fresh forces in the oenological sphere. Having moved from Rome, Luca made Petrolo and relations with the world of wine the centre of his own world. Exchanging opinions with people like Sergio Manetti, Alceo di Napoli and Nicolò Incisa and sales guidance, first by Silvano Formigli, then by Cesare Turrini, were crucial steps in Luca's career as a producer, in relation to his family history. We may have lost a good painter, but we certainly gained a great wine producer. In 1997, Galatrona revealed its greatness with daring comparisons to the most majestic and historical Tuscan Merlots. The heat of the year was softened by acidity in a setting where notes of ripening emerge against a fresh background. Alcohol, structure and tannins were perfectly balanced for a drinking pleasure that is still bewitching today. 1999 was another fine year and no less successful, with a surplus of taste verve that made it terse and vibrant.

TENUTA DI TRINORO

New Replanting in the Vineyards

TUSCANY
www.tenutaditrinoro.it

The story of Trinoro has something that is intrinsically unique and unrepeatable. In 1990, **Andrea Franchetti** made a decisive choice regarding his life mission. After returning from New York, he imagined the wine that wasn't there in the wildest area of Val d'Orcia, an area of Tuscany with no pedigree. He withdrew in isolation for six months and thought about what to make of a completely abandoned estate. His inspiration matured during long visits to the Bordeaux area. The first planting was done in 1992, for the most part of Cabernet Franc. At the cadence of 3 hectares a year, the mosaic was completed in 1999 with Merlot, Cabernet Sauvignon and Petit Verdot. The planting density was at the absolute limit, approaching 10,000 vines per hectare in double Guyot array, although later bush vine training was introduced. Bunches were drastically thinned to leave only 300 gm of grapes on each plant. In 1995, the goal of the first harvest was to comprehend the potential of these terrains, parcel by parcel. Blending was done after eighteen months of ageing in *barrique* and the wine was bottled with Le Cupole label. After 1999, this name was given to the second wine of Trinoro. The 1997 harvest introduced the first "Tenuta di Trinoro" with the superior quality difference that was expected. This was the turning point. At Bordeaux, the wine won a blind tasting challenge against the most prestigious *Château* of the same year. Placement

by *négociants* rapidly positioned it as a cult wine and the price shot up from the initial 12,500 Lire to 200,000 Lire for the year 2000. It was a wine with an unmistakeable stage presence. It had an opulence that descended from the light, but was inclined to expressive delight and, at times, to balsamic refreshment of the velvety fruitiness. The year 2001 was quite extraordinary in this regard, but 2009 is a very close runner-up. In 1981, Andrea Franchetti and his cousin **Gelasio Lovatelli** had opened a wine import company in New York called River Wine. That was the beginning of a very important period of six years for them, but above all for fine Italian wine. They chose a marketing policy that apparently had never been attempted before at a national level, that is, to select and distribute only the very best of small independent wine growers. "We weren't businessmen at the time," says Andrea, "but we learned a lot". River Wine closed in 1986. Their contacts were at the highest levels, difficult to attain for anyone. Their work made the fortune of the selected wineries, which took up strategic positions in the most important restaurants.

FALESCO

The Cotarella Siblings

UMBRIA
www.falesco.it

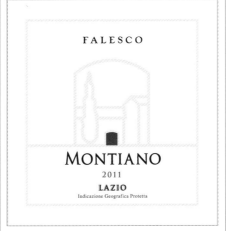

The Falesco wine estate extends from Umbria (in the town of Montecchio) to Lazio (in the town of Montefiascone). The vineyards embrace the splendid territories Orvieto and the Bolsena Lake. It was founded in 1979 by the oenologist brothers **Riccardo** and **Renzo Cotarella**. One of their first objectives was to recover the ancient, abandoned vines of the area. At the same time, Riccardo and Renzo identified the areas with the best viticultural characteristics to guarantee wines of excellent quality.
They began to produce Est! Est!! Est!!! only in 1989. Poggio dei Gelsi, the vineyard planted with Roscietto, Trebbiano and Malvasia, succeeded in restoring the fame of a territory

and a wine that had been unjustly forgotten. Then it was the turn of a particular clone of Merlot, known as Montiano (first harvest in 1993). It was immediately considered one of the most outstanding and innovative Italian red wines: extremely elegant, with refined aromatic assets and great concentration. With the harvest of 2001, they introduced Pomele, obtained from indigenous Aleatico vines in the Bolsena lake area. In recent years, Falesco has increased its assets by acquisition of the Marciliano farm of about 260 hectares, situated on the wonderful hill south of Orvieto in the towns of Montecchio and Baschi. These vineyards provide Merlot, Cabernet and Sangiovese grapes for production of Vitiano and Merlot d'Umbria; also Vermentino and Verdicchio grapes for Vitiano Bianco. The best vineyard of the estate produces the Cabernet Sauvignon bunches for production of the namesake wine of the estate, Marciliano.

CASTEL DE PAOLIS

Tradition Meets Innovation

LAZIO

www.casteldepaolis.it

Castel de Paolis immediately set out on the road to profound renewal of the family vineyard near Grottaferrata in the Castelli Romani area at 270 metres above sea level. It is an area of antique volcanic origins. As such, these terrains are particularly favourable for viticulture. These assets were at risk after the launch of the Frascati DOC in 1965 because the objective was quantity.

Giulio Santarelli decided to challenge this approach and turned to Professor Attilio Scienza for advice. Already familiar with the quality of the volcanic terrains of Grottaferrata, he suggested planting an experimental vineyard. His advice was to accompany the traditional varieties with international varieties Sauvignon Blanc, Chardonnay, Semillon, Viognier, Shiraz, Cabernet Sauvignon, Merlot, Petit Verdot and even Moscato Rosa, a typical variety of Trentino-Alto Adige. Since then Castel De Paolis produces mainly IGT wines of Lazio with the aim of quality above all.

Right from 1993, the first harvest of the experimental vineyards planted in 1990, the results were noteworthy. Castel de Paolis produces white, red and dessert wines that are well received by Italian and foreign markets. They also attracted the attention of Veronelli, who dedicated a whole page of *L'Espresso* magazine to the wines of Castel de Paolis in 1995, with this eloquent title: "Miracles in the Hills", where he claims that "great wines were produced in the Castelli Romani zone in ancient times and they are going back into production". Among many fine labels, the leading wine is Donna Adriana, dedicated by Santarelli to his wife. It is a white IGT of Lazio consisting of Viognier (60%), Malvasia Puntinata (30%) and Sauvignon (10%).

COLLE PICCHIONI

The Lazio Jewel in the Crown

LAZIO

www.collepicchioni.it

At the end of the 1960s, **Paola Simonelli** (known to the wine world by her married name as Paola Di Mauro) decided to buy a villa with a small plot of land near Rome so she could spend some weekends out of doors. The owner of that terrain near Fratocchie di Marino was a French woman who had planted vineyards of the classic varieties of her home territory on 3 hectares of her land.

After several (unsuccessful) attempts by the farmer to create a wine that was at least dignified, Paola realised what the potential of the terrain, volcanic and sandy, would be and decided to invest in it. She put the problem in the hands of a fine winemaker, Riccardo Cotarella, but not without studying everything she could about oenology at that time. Paola dedicated so much energy to it that what seemed to be a hobby rapidly became her primary occupation. Cotarella immediately accepted to accompany her, step by step, in her adventure in the world of wine.

That is how Colle Picchioni became the jewel in the crown on the viticultural scene of Lazio. "The most important wine is undoubtedly Vassallo, formerly Vigna del Vassallo. It was created at the beginning of the 1980s from a simple but inspired idea: select the best of everything, the grapes, the oldest vines, the best vats and *barriques*. That is how, just when we thought we had made a good wine, we realised that we could actually make an excellent wine. Even today, we still do things in the same way". Vassallo is a Bordeaux blend with 60% Merlot, 30% Cabernet Sauvignon and 10% Cabernet Franc. It is a Lazio red that ages in *barrique* for eighteen months, gifted with great elegance and personality.

SERGIO MOTTURA

A Man from Piedmont Discovers Grechetto

LAZIO

www.sergiomottura.com

The man who rediscovered Grechetto, the historical indigenous vine cultivated in Upper Tuscia (the area of Viterbo) and throughout Umbria and made it a must, **Sergio Mottura**, comes from Piedmont. The estate is located in a zone with many natural resources, bordered on the west by the hills and clayey gullies of Civitella d'Agliano, and to the east by the Umbrian plain of the Tiber, close to the border between Umbria and Tuscany.

1999 was the first year for Latour a Civitella from Grechetto grapes. In 2001, it was the first white wine in the history of Lazio to be awarded 3 glasses by Gambero Rosso. The best grapes of the five Grechetto vineyards are selected for the final assembly. The clone, Poggio della Costa, replanted in several parcels, provides the greatest volume from an historical point of view.

Louis-Fabrice Latour is a famous wine dealer in Burgundy, who gave this good advice to Sergio Mottura after tasting his Poggio della Costa Grechetto of 1992: "Why don't you trying ageing in wood"? he asked. The Frenchman himself provided the first *barriques* that were appropriate for white wines and, above all, the know-how to make use of them. That took place in 1992. 1994 marked the début of Latour a Civitella, an homage to the good friend from France. This is the story that Sergio Mottura has told to all the guests who visit his farm holiday, L'Istrice.

Among the other wines, Muffo is certainly worthy of mention. It is a straw wine of grapes from relatively low positions, subjected to the mists from nearby Lake Alviano that favour noble rot. Some of the indigenous varieties that Mottura cultivates include Procanico, Verdello and Drupeggio. The farm is fully organic and the wine cellar has very low environmental impact.

IL POLLENZA

An All-Italian Château

THE MARCHES

www.ilpollenza.it

In the midst of the softly rolling hills of the countryside near Macerata, Il Pollenza appears unexpectedly. It is unexpected not only because it is a beautiful property with an important, historical building, but also because it is an authentic château surrounded by perfectly drafted vineyards and a park with perfect geometric lines that conceals the villa, built to the design of Sangallo in the sixteenth century. **Count Aldo Brachetti** took his inspiration from French châteaux in his choice of vine varieties for his vineyards, which are mainly Cabernet Sauvignon and Cabernet Franc, Merlot, Petit Verdot, Syrah and Pinot Nero. Consequently, his banner wine labelled with the name of the estate and Bordeaux varieties interprets this role perfectly. This all occurs as the result of disastrous snowfall that destroyed the existing vines on the property and made replanting a necessity. After thorough study of the terrains, international varieties were preferred to indigenous ones. The vineyards occupy about 70 hectares between 100 and 150 metres above sea level on rocky flood plains with much crumbly clay. Even if the main activity of the family is in the field of petroleum and energy, the estate includes the private dwelling of Aldo Brachetti Peretti and is managed with great care by an extremely well-trained and committed professional staff. The wine cellar is technologically advanced and has an immense *barrique* cellar. The progress achieved in little more than a decade is impressive. It is the

leading wine of the estate (Il Pollenza) that marks the measure. It has been a crescendo leading up to the latest version (2010) so it is no surprise that it has attracted awards from Italian guide books.

CANTINE ANTONIO CAGGIANO

The Great Red Wine of the Region

CAMPANIA
www.cantinecaggiano.it

A professional photographer for many years, then a surveyor, **Antonio Caggiano** (born 1937) began to leave his mark on viticulture in the Campania region in the 1990s.

His first harvest was in 1994 with a Taurasi DOCG, Vigna Macchia dei Goti, one of the best red wines in the Campania region. Antonio Caggiano works side by side with his son Giuseppe, while professor Luigi Moio has been their illustrious consultant from the earliest years of the Taurasi wines. The best idea was to have

understood that Aglianico di Taurasi was and should continue to be a wine for long ageing, for drinking even after twenty or thirty years. The construction of the wine cellars, at Contrada Sala di Taurasi in the Irpinia, emerged in part as an amusement and in part as a gamble, but also as a personal challenge for Antonio. "I wanted to rediscover the flavours and perfumes that had disappeared from my territory. To do it, I had to create a museum of the farmers' life," he says. Built to modern technical standards and antique aesthetic style, a visitor will find an atmosphere of mystery in the wine cellars. The entrance suggests a hidden underground world, with walls of massive stones, arches and vaults overhead.

In accordance with the intentions of Luigi Moio and the owner, every year 500 bottles of Vigna Macchia dei Goti are set aside for the purpose of studying their evolution over time.

Today, the Caggiano wine cellars are a veritable wine temple. Antonio Caggiano produces three red wines with Aglianico di Taurasi grapes only: Taurasi DOCG Vigna Macchia dei Goti, Salae Domini DOC and Taurì DOC. He also produces four white wines from Fiano and Greco di Tufo grapes. Fiagre is the interesting and perhaps unique wine made from the grapes of Fiano (70%) and Greco di Tufo (30%), processed in steel.

GALARDI

A Prophet in the Land of Labour

CAMPANIA
www.galardi.net

One label, one wine and a success that has continued for twenty years: the Galardi estate is on the slopes of Roccamonfina, an extinct volcano in the province of Caserta, and is managed personally by the owners. Terra di Lavoro was first harvested in 1994 from vineyards at about 400 metres above sea level, amidst groves of chestnuts and olives on the mountainside sloping down toward the gulf of Gaeta.

From the beginning, Riccardo Cotarella made a decisive contribution to Terra di Lavoro, enabling this splendid red wine of the South to reach the highest levels of quality with such an evidently unique character.

The project for the production of high-quality olive oil and red wine, carried forward by the four owners – **Maria Luisa Murena**, **Francesco Catello**, **Arturo** and **Dora Celentano** – got started in 1991. The first intervention was to recover the old vineyards. The next step was to create new plantings. From the first year of production, Terra di Lavoro received the praises of numerous international critics.

Today, they produce 33,000 bottles of IGT Roccamonfina Terra di Lavoro. It is a blend of Aglianico with small percentages of Piedirosso, with its unmistakeable bouquet of smoky and volcanic aromas. Well-structured and aged in *barrique*, when poured into the glass and drunk the essence of the South is present in the air. The label name, Terra di Lavoro, derives from the name of the province of Caserta, during the

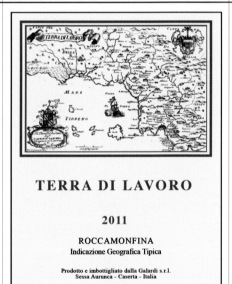

Kingdom of the Two Sicilies. From 1997, the winery has adopted the European regulations for organic farming.

MARISA CUOMO

The Sea and Stone in Wines

CAMPANIA
www.marisacuomo.com

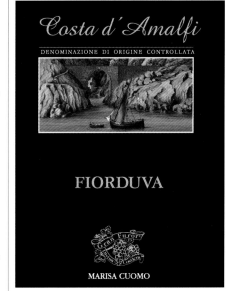

"A passionate wine that tastes of stone and the sea, without a hint of sweetness". This is what the unforgettable Gino Veronelli wrote about the best-known wine on the Amalfi coast, the Gran Furor Divina Costiera Bianco by **Marisa Cuomo**. These are the grapes and the wine stripped from the rocks of the Lattari mountains, the cliffs rising up to 500 metres above the sea. The wines from the cellar of **Andrea Ferraioli** and his enchanting wife Marisa are unique. The vineyards cover 10 hectares of territory cleared by hand on the hills of the splendid wild coastline. Founded in 1980, the intent from the start was to aim only for quality. The objective has been achieved with great satisfaction, thanks also to the contribution of oenologist Luigi Moio. The vineyard strips are generally no more than five metres wide. The terracing has an irregular profile as imposed by the anarchy of the rocks and contain four rows of vines cultivated on pergolas. The vines are as indigenous as can be found and are typical only of this area of Amalfi: Fenile, Ginestra, Ripoli, Pepella and Tronto.

The best-known wine is the white wine Fiorduva. Defining this wine as extreme is an understatement: the notes of exotic fruits emerge, while the taste is soft and dense, with agreeable after-tastes of raisins and candied fruit. This wine has a bold taste that includes all the typical elements of the natural surroundings, the sea and the rocks, but also the sun and the wind. The tenacity and courage of Andrea and Marisa, today with the collaboration of their children Dorotea and Raffaele, have prevailed and created authentic jewels of oenology. The very fine Ravello Bianco, from Falanghina and Biancolella, or the intriguing and refined Furore Rosso Riserva from Aglianico and Piedirosso in equal parts are wines of great aroma and emotion.

MONTEVETRANO

The Tide of Women

CAMPANIA
www.montevetrano.it

Silvia Imparato, a beautiful woman of the South, is strong, dynamic and far-sighted. She is the heart and soul of Montevetrano, the innovative winery in the province of Salerno. The turning point for her in the world of wine was an apparently random event in 1983. At that time, she and her sisters were the owners of Montevetrano, an estate that their grandparents had bought in the 1940s. She lived in Rome, worked as a photographer and had a studio specialising in portraits. In 1980, a customer of hers who was a wine enthusiast invited her to participate in an evening at a wine shop in the centre of Rome. As Silvia recalls: "It was certainly 1983 when, after a special tasting of Bordeaux wines in Rome, I claimed that in my part of the South [*near Salerno*] we would have no difficulty in producing a prestigious wine. At least we could try!" The decisive contribution came from oenologist Riccardo Cotarella. It was his merit that, in 1991, Montevetrano was first harvested. It is a red IGT composed of Cabernet Sauvignon (60%), Merlot (30%) and Aglianico (10%). With the exception of Aglianico, already present in the vineyards, the other varieties were grafted onto existing rootstocks. The first marketed harvest was 1993, which came out in 1995. "It gave me an incredible boost of enthusiasm," Silvia says. "I even sent three bottles to Robert Parker, to find out what he thought of it. A ground-shaking article in his *The Wine Advocate*, calling it the Sassicaia of the South, was the answer". This experience radically changed Silvia's life.

Montevetrano is a wine with a complex style that is intense, concentrated and very recognisable.

"Ours is a wine of the territory, because its excellent quality speaks of it," Silvia says with great conviction. "Born in the terrain of Montevetrano, under that sky, in that climate, no one can copy it! There is no recipe for this wine". Montevetrano produces 30,000 bottles a year, sold all over the world in small quantities.

SALVATORE MOLETTIERI

Renewal in Four Generations

CAMPANIA

www.salvatoremolettieri.com

The business of **Salvatore Molettieri** was founded in 1983, conferring entrepreneurial dignity to a farming experience of at least four generations. In 1983, as head of the business activity Salvatore made the decision not to sell his grapes to third parties any more. He obtained important successes from the first year, when he won first place at the annual wine fair in Montemarano, his birthplace. He also won first place each year from 1985 to 1988, the year when he began to bottle his product as Taurasi DOCG Riserva 1988. The vineyards cover more than 13 hectares at an elevation of about 500–600 metres on the hillsides of Montemarano, one of the seventeen municipalities that fall in the area of the Taurasi DOCG protocol. The territory has clay/lime soils and is particularly appropriate for viticulture. Production of all the DOC and DOCG protocols of the Irpinia is allowed for red and white wines, including Fiano and Greco di Tufo.

Quality in every phase of work: this is the business philosophy that inspires Salvatore Molettieri. It is really a distinguishing characteristic that Salvatore, his four children (Giovanni, Giuseppe, Luigi and Paolo) and his wife Angela are never completely satisfied. The business has evolved significantly thanks also to son Giovanni, an oenologist. One of Salvatore's original goals has been reached: to carry the name of Montemarano outside of Irpinia and to link it to top-quality production.

The cru vineyard is Cinque Querce, which has surpassed twenty years of DOCG harvests. Some vine rootstocks are older than the phylloxera epidemic. In the Renonno vineyard, there are Aglianico plants over seventy years of age.

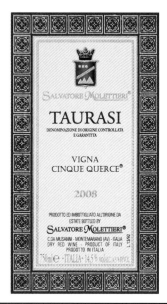

TERREDORA

Discovering Ancient Vines

CAMPANIA

www.terredora.com

Walter Mastroberardino and his children **Paolo**, **Lucio** and **Daniela** founded Terredora as a winegrowing estate in 1978. From the start, they concentrated their efforts on the rediscovery of ancient indigenous varieties of Campania, contributing to the viticultural renaissance of this region with their interest in Aglianico, Fiano, Greco and Falanghina.

In 1994, following the division from his brother Antonio, Walter Mastroberardino and his children began to process the grapes from their own vineyards directly and to bottle the wine with the name of their estate, Terredora.

Terredora is many things at once: the story of strong, persistent men and women committed to their territory by an ancestral passion for the vines. It is an ongoing project that puts the land and its values at the centre of its activities.

It began with the family patriarch, Walter, who led the business he so ardently desired from 1994, together with his children. Lucio died prematurely in January 2013 after a long illness, during his term in office as the president of the Italian Wine Union. The fate of Terredora is now in the hands of his brother Paolo, oenologist, and sister Daniela, managing director and chief of communication.

The vineyards are located in Irpinia. This is the land of Taurasi, but also of extraordinary white wine DOCG protocols. Their full-bodied Greco di Tufo, Loggia della Serra, has notes of ripe fruit, hawthorn blossoms and citrus. Their Fiano di Avellino, Terre di Dora, is rich and complex, well-structured and aromatic, and evolves well as it ages. The vineyards are in different zones, among the best in Irpinia. Terredora cultivates indigenous vines only.

CANTINE DEL NOTAIO

A Volcano Awakens

BASILICATA
www.cantinedelnotaio.it

Gerardo Giuratrabocchetti is the man who created Cantine del Notaio, the most important oenological company in the Basilicata region. He remembers that when he was seven, his grandfather promised him that one day the vineyards would be his, because he, too, when he was seven, was called Gerardo. Giuratrabocchetti recalls: "Today I smile when I think of him, considering how I have so proudly rediscovered my roots by accepting this inheritance from my grandfather and deciding to make it the centre of my life".

Gerardo got a degree in agrarian science. To continue the family tradition, in 1998, he and his wife Marcella decided to found Cantine del Notaio with the precise goal of promoting Aglianico del Vulture. At the end of the 1990s, they planted the same clones of Aglianico del Vulture on the same rootstocks with the same system of cultivation in new terrains. The "new" vineyards are situated in five different municipalities, among the most typical and famous of the Vulture area. They have different soils, including pozzolanic, sandy, firm soils and clay, but they all have volcanic tuff in depth, which collects water in the winter providing the indispensable water reserve during the summer period. "We study Aglianico del Vulture in its natural environment," Gerardo says. "Together with professor Luigi Moio we have demonstrated that this vine is very eclectic and has enormous potential". Just consider that

Cantine del Notaio creates nine different wines from a single type of grape: traditional method spumante, white wine, rosé wine and four incrementally concentrated red wines (L'Atto, Il Repertorio, La Firma and Il Sigillo). The choice of names? They all refer to the duties of a notary (*notaio* in Italian) and are all original and unique interpretations of this extraordinary vine.

ACCADEMIA DEI RACEMI

Seeking, Discovering and Sharing Success

PUGLIA
www.racemi.it

In ancient Greece, the academy was a place to exchange ideas and share experiences. Starting from this concept, **Gregory Perrucci**, born in Manduria and a graduate of Bocconi University in Milan, started his Accademia dei Racemi project to relaunch Primitivo di Manduria, the indigenous vine of his birthplace.

"It has been an exalting and fascinating task," says Perrucci. "It was dedicated to rediscovering some varieties that were already extinct [*Fiano Minutolo, Ottavianello and Sussumaniello*] and reinterpreting others that are widely diffused but used mainly for the wholesale market. That experience has left traces such as Castel di Salve in the Salento zone, De Filippo near Trani, Torre Guaceto near Brindisi and Paolo Petrilli's estate near Lucera. And, of course, La Felline, the

Perrucci family estate near Manduria, which has inherited the assets of information and knowledge linked to the first zoning conducted in the territory of Primitivo. The direct result of those years of intense activity was the identification of the Primitivo crus: Felline in red earth, Sinfarosa in black earth and Dunico in sandy soil".

Aside from Primitivo, the most representative vine of Accademia dei Racemi is Sussumaniello. "It had completely disappeared and I had found it in an old book that was published during the Kingdom of Naples," continues Perrucci. "After three years of searching, we identified a few rows in an old vineyard near Brindisi. After a few micro vinifications, we launched a mass selection and planted a new intensive vineyard on the Torre Guaceto estate. That was the birth of Sum, the first pure Sussumaniello".

CANTINE DUE PALME

Joining Forces!

PUGLIA
www.cantineduepalme.it

Cantine Due Palme is a demonstration of the fact that cooperative wineries can, if well managed, earn recognition in the guidebooks and oenological competitions. The arbiter of this success, with a numerous squad of valid assistants, was **Angelo Maci**, the oenologist and chairman of the cooperative.

"My family has been linked to the world of wine for generations. Today, Cantine Due Palme represents about 2,400 hectares of vineyards, of which 150 belong to my family. We have over 1,000 members who produce 200,000 quintals of grapes, the vast majority of which are black-skinned. We have reached the threshold of 7 million bottles. Our goal is to always strive for improvement along the whole chain of production. We do cultivate the international varieties such as Merlot, Cabernet Sauvignon, Syrah and Chardonnay, but we have always favoured the indigenous vines, Negroamaro and Primitivo, above all".

The leading wine of the cooperative is undoubtedly Selvarossa. It is produced in two versions. Riserva, obtained from Negroamaro and Malvasia Nera, is a profoundly Mediterranean red wine with a dense and imposing impact on the palate. Selvarossa Riserva Speciale is made from highly selected grapes and is subsequently aged in *barrique*. Due Palme is also conducting an important project to conserve bush vine cultivation. The goal is to block the members' abandonment of

it due to the higher costs and the greater commitment involved. Attilio Scienza has commented: "Unlike the bush vine of Pantelleria, which cannot be changed, the other versions of this type of cultivation, suffering a very drastic contraction in Southern Italy, in the province of Trapani, in southwestern Sardinia and the Salento zone of Puglia, just to name a few of the zones where the bush vine is still in widespread use, can be transformed without losing the qualitative advantages for improved mechanisation. The initiative undertaken by Cantine Due Palme is certainly far-sighted because it is intended to protect extraordinary qualities. While developing the project, they called on the Simonit-Sirch 'Preparatori d'uva' duo and they are transforming what was cultivation of a volume structure into cultivation of a wall structure. Working with machines in cultivation operations is complex, because it must respect the structure of the form of cultivation over many years without mutilating cuts, to avoid desiccation cones that could threaten the vitality of the plants. This is an intervention that must be implemented in the course of multiple years, intervening only on the younger parts of the plant".

ODOARDI

Germans in Calabria

CALABRIA
www.cantineodoardi.it

The Odoardi family descends from an ancient family of Germanic origin that settled in Calabria in 1480, in the territory near what is now Nocera Terinese in the province of Catanzaro. The members of the family quickly revealed an innovative land-owner's mentality, linked to the territory and its development. The ample estate of over 270 hectares stretches from the Savuto River to Falerna, with its central operations centre in Nocera Terinese. The farm produces olive oil, wines from single vine varieties and also

cultivates the vines for Savuto DOC (in the municipality of Nocera Terinese) and Scavigna DOC (municipality of Falerna). The hilly terrains face the Tyrrhenian Sea and the spectacular natural backdrop of the Aeolian islands. The cultivations are at different elevations, from sea level up to 600 metres. **Gregorio Lillo Odoardi** and his wife **Barbara Spalletta** represent the latest generation of the Odoardi family.

GB is the leading wine of the house, created to celebrate 500 years of Odoardi family history in Calabria. A red meditation wine, the family wished to honour Giovanni Battista Odoardi, a physician and winegrower who continues to be a guide and point of reference for Gregorio, for his wife Barbara (an oenologist, married in 2000) and for their two children, Anna Gaia and Giovan Battista (nicknamed G.B.). The wine first came out in 2009. It is a blend of Gaglioppo, Magliocco, Nerello Cappuccio and Greco Nero with ageing in *barrique* for twelve months and refinement in the bottle for another six months. GB Odoardi 2011 was ranked the best red wine of Southern Italy at the Oenological Competition for the wines of Southern Italy held at Camigliatello Silano. Fifty percent of the Odoardi viticultural production is directed to foreign markets.

CANTINE FLORIO

The Marsala Wineries

SICILY
www.duca.it/cantineflorio/

Despite its history and renown – one of the oldest and most famous wineries of Italy – its true renaissance was accomplished relatively recently. Founded by **Vincenzo Florio**, an entrepreneur of Palermo in 1833, the property passed through various hands until **Augusto Reina**, the owner of Illva di Saronno and producer of the famous Amaretto, bought it in 1998.

Looking back at the history of the winery, Vincenzo Florio's family came from Calabria. He was the first Italian to produce Marsala, which had been invented by the English.

Marsala, one of the best known Italian wines in the world, received a DOC protocol in 1969. The company building overlooking the sea in Marsala was built by Vincenzo Florio, with an intriguing arcade of pointed arches, built of tuff, the ideal material to maintain a constant temperature for the wine ageing in oak casks. It is a majestic construction of 20,000 square metres and has an enormous 60,000 litre cask placed at the southern entrance. It was made for the universal exposition held in San Francisco in 1894.

At the beginning of the 1920s, Cinzano bought out Florio, but the real change arrived with Augusto Reina who already held 50% in 1987. The production, directed by oenologist Carlo Casavecchio, made a fundamental contribution to the rebirth of Florio and restored the qualitative image of Marsala in general. Casavecchia led the way to the creation of Donna Franca, Marsala Superiore Riserva, a wine with over fifteen years of ageing and an homage to Donna Franca Florio, Vincenzo's wife. Now the Florio brand also produces a Passito di Pantelleria, a Malvasia delle Lipari and Morsi di Luce, all from zibibbo grapes, and a sweet spumante. These all represent the best Sicilian traditions of dessert wines.

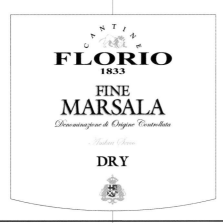

CARLO PELLEGRINO

Two Towers between Past and Future

SICILY
www.carlopellegrino.it

There are very few Sicilian wine production enterprises that have both a long history and the capacity for renewal while remaining the property of the founding family. This production house was founded in 1880 by **Carlo Pellegrino**, a notary, to produce Marsala. Pellegrino has progressively expanded its variety of wines and has acquired various properties in western Sicily through the years. Today it is the third-ranking wine business in Sicily. While continuing with Marsala, it also produces with the Duca di Castelmonte label. With an eye to the future, it invested in Pantelleria by building a second wine cellar there in 1992, becoming the leading wine producer on that island. The 1990s were the years of the most visible innovations, symbolised, in Marsala, by the recovery of two old wine silos from the 1950s, over 25 metres high. Known as Le Torri, they are now the heart of the business with a professional kitchen, a tasting room and a spectacular view of the Egadi islands, Stagnone and Mothia. This is where the "Pellegrino Cooking Festival" has been held every year since 2004. It was one of the first grand events in Italy with chefs as protagonists. It is a competition not only among dishes, but among ideas about food and wine. 2004 was also the year when the new cellar in Cardilla was inaugurated. It is in the suburbs of Marsala and its capacity was doubled after only two years. Pellegrino sponsored recovery of the famous Punic ship found at Mothia, now on display in the regional archaeological museum of Marsala.

A copy of the ship is on view inside the Cantine, where visitors can also browse through the 110 rare volumes of the commercial correspondence archives of Ingham-Whitaker and admire a collection of Sicilian carts.

COS

Architects with Amphorae

SICILY
www.cosvittoria.it

They make their wine in amphorae as people did thousands of years ago, yet **Giusto Occhipinti and Giambattista (Titta) Cilia** are among the best-educated and avant-garde wine growers in all of Sicily. The contradiction is only apparent, because they simply wish to return to wines that are as natural and authentic as possible. This has led them to rediscover ancient techniques of vinification and to adopt the procedures of biodynamics.

The Cos estate was found in 1980 by three young friends. Cirino Strano was one of the three, but he soon preferred to withdraw from the undertaking. The acronym of their three names (Cilia-Occhipinti-Strano) became the name of the winery. They rented the old family wine cellar from Giuseppe Cilia (Titta's father), together with the adjacent vineyard, cultivated with bush vines, in Contrada Bastonaca, municipality of Vittoria, and harvested their first year of Cos wines in that same year. Their project was to produce the typical wines of the zone, Frappato and Cerasuolo di Vittoria (a blend of Nero d'Avola and Frappato), which now has a fine reputation thanks to them. However, they meant to do it without giving in to market demand, which at the time meant hyper concentrated wines.

In 1991, they bought Villa Fontane, a property of 9 hectares. In 2005, they bought 20 hectares adjacent to Villa Fontane with a nineteenth-century wine cellar on the property. After

restoration, it became the new Cos wine cellar, inaugurated in 2007 with 150 amphorae of 400 litres each. The first amphorae had arrived from Spain as early as 2000. The material does not add any characteristic aroma. This was perfectly aligned with their intention to make wine that expressed the profound character of its own terrains. Pithos, a Cerasuolo di Vittoria, was born in this way, with natural yeast fermentation entirely in the amphorae, a revolution that was widely applauded. From 2007, they also produce white Pithos, from Grecanico grapes.

MORGANTE

The Champions of Nero d'Avola

SICILY
www.morgantevini.it

Father Antonio with his sons Carmelo and Giovanni: three men of the South, a little old-fashioned, but very down to earth, so results came quickly. It was 1994 when the **Morgante family** decided to take the big step and produce wines on their own with their own grapes, knowing how difficult it would be. Before their exploit, few had ever heard of Grotte, in the hills of the back lands near Agrigento. Once the sulphur mines had been a source of work, but the mines were exhausted. They had to overcome difficulties in logistics, natural circumstances and mentality to demonstrate that it was not necessary to emigrate, that it was possible to do business in Sicily, and do it well. The turning point came in 1997, with an almost casual encounter with oenologist Riccardo Cotarella and definition of the project to produce a great Nero d'Avola wine. The following year Don Antonio was presented. It was intense, complex, elegant and, occasionally, pleasingly rough and authentic, with a precise and unmistakeable personality. The great success spurred them to introduce profound modernisation in the vineyard and wine cellar. Management was not simple with over 200 hectares of vineyards divided into many small plots spread among the hills in a range of 30 kilometres. The plots included almond groves and arable land, in addition to vineyards. The Morgante family began to dedicate more time to communication and presentation of their territory. It seemed to be so apparently remote,

but is actually only 25 kilometres from the Valley of the Temples in Agrigento. The basic Nero d'Avola and the banner wine, Don Antonio, were joined by other wines over the years. One was a lighter version of Nero d'Avola, perfect for the summer or to accompany fish dishes, the Scinthilì. The latest addition is Bianco di Morgante from Nero d'Avola, of course! All the wines are at the top of their categories.

PALARI

The Elegance of Faro

SICILY

www.palari.it

If Faro wine, known since Roman times, has not disappeared, it is the accomplishment of the Geraci brothers, **Salvatore** and **Giampiero Geraci**. In the early 1990s, they decided to relaunch production of this wine starting from the family vineyard with the collaboration of oenologist Donato Lanati, from Piedmont.
It was a success in the making, first announced by Luigi Veronelli, who perceived the potential of those old vines overlooking the Messina Strait that papa Geraci used to make wine for family and friends. It was a wine quite different from the heavy red wines of Sicily, with a pale colour, unusually light-bodied and elegant. The great Veronelli convinced Salvatore Geraci, an architect with a passion for fine food, fine wine and writing, that he should begin to market it.

The first bottles of Faro Palari, produced in 1990, were offered for sale only in 1995. Through the years, production has remained more or less at the same level. The vineyards are composed of vines almost 100 years old, growing at an elevation of about 500 metres on small terracing with slopes up to 70%. The vines are cultivated as low bushes in sandy soil with very low yield, less than one kilo of grapes per plant. The grape varieties are Nerello Mascalese e Cappuccio, Nocera and other indigenous varieties that were disappearing such as Tignolino, Acitana, Core 'e Pallumma and Galatena. Faro Palari has notes of dark red fruit with a hint of sea salt. It has body, but remains fresh; it is dry, but soft, persistent and long-lived: in a word, a great wine. Vinification is done in the eighteenth-century villa of the family, Villa Geraci, where it ages in *barrique* for eighteen months and then three more years in the bottle.

PLANETA

Marketing and Communication Strategy

SICILY

www.planeta.it

Diego Planeta accomplished taking the wines of Settesoli to the markets of the whole world. He created his masterpiece by the company that bears the family name: Planeta. He entrusted it to the cousins Alessio, Francesca (Diego's daughter) and Santi. He remains their guide, indicating their path. They came out officially in 1995 on the shores of Lake Arancio, in Sambuca in Sicily, with the inauguration of the Cantina dell'Ulmo and the desire to demonstrate that Sicilian wine could compete with the best in the world. They had an oenologist from Piedmont at their side. The enterprise was supported by a well-studied marketing and communication strategy. The first great success was Chardonnay aged in *barrique*. Powerful and elegant, this wine contributed to changing the image of Sicilian wine in the world. The first year was 1994.

The Planeta cousins love to say that their business is like a "trip in Sicily", a journey to find the best terrains and the wines that represent them. In 1996, the first great Fiano of Sicily with a unique personality came from the Contrada Dispensa vineyard near Menfi. The second wine cellar was built in Dispensa in 2001. Among the traditional vines of Agrigento, they favour Grecanico. In 1997, in Vittoria on a plot that already belonged to the family, they planted Frappato di Vittoria and Nero d'Avola to produce the Planeta interpretation of Cerasuolo di Vittoria. Another stage of their journey. In 1998, the Planeta family bought vineyards of about 50 hectares near Noto where they built the third wine cellar. From the harvest of 2003 they began to produce Nero d'Avola in its home territory, Santa Cecilia, and Moscato di Noto. In 2008, they ascended Etna. First they arranged the vineyards and then built the wine cellar. A new challenge has already appeared on the horizon: rediscover the viticulture of the Nebrodi and relaunch Mamertino, the vine that Julius Caesar preferred. The vineyard is near Capo Milazzo, where Nero d'Avola and Nocera are cultivated, but other antique varieties of the area are also grown experimentally.

CANTINA GALLURA

The Courage to Change

SARDINIA
www.cantinagallura.net

Most of the cooperative wineries of Sardinia have failed to contribute to creating a good image of Sardinian wine because, incapable of renewing themselves, they think only of producing great quantities of wine, without taking any interest in image and marketing. Cantina Gallura in Tempio Pausania was in a similar situation when the arrival of oenologist director **Dino Addis** announced important changes. The project that Addis proposed to all the conferring members was clear: focus on the indigenous vines without giving in to the fashion for planting international varieties. That is how, in the 1990s, Vermentino di Gallura (its preferred homeland, although it probably arrived from nearby Corsica) became the most qualitatively and quantitatively representative white wine of Sardinia. It is cultivated on difficult terrains, originated from granite erosion, at various elevations and expositions. These elements stimulated the curiosity of Addis who

studied it until he discovered the viticultural and oenological potential of the vine. It was not easy to convince the members of a large cooperative to lower yield from 150 to 90 quintals, while reconverting the cultivation from arbours to short Guyot. For most of them it meant an immediate loss of income. Results confirm that it was a winning decision that was necessary in order to take on important markets. In addition, it was the first time that a cooperative winery created its own cadastre, mapping all the vineyards. This will be essential for diversifying production. On the basis of these givens, Addis set to work to rewrite the protocols and obtained the DOCG in 1996, the first and still the only one in Sardinia.

First Decade of 2000

Sustainability, a Model to Follow

The dialogue between Human and Nature on the issue of sustainability has also become an instrument of marketing and a mark of distinction. Viticulture, thanks to the intentions of the great majority of producers and scientific research, has definitively opted for environmental respect. Simonit and Sirch, the "Preparatori d'uva", are an example of restoring the ancient dialogue between Human and the Vine, recovering the manual dexterity of hand pruning, with the objective of improving quality and leading the vineyard through a long life.

The wine tourism movement became an important reality that stimulated millions of visitors. Famous architects designed inspiring wine cellars and transformed them from simple production sites into showrooms for wine. The cellar had become more communicative than advertising. It incorporated all the intrinsic aspects of wine and had the function of a three-dimensional label representing the brand.

The true touch of genius was to make this the subject of an interdisciplinary debate in which the wine cellar is perceived as a sort of Pandora's vase that can diffuse all aspects of wine culture and associate it with beauty. The cellar has become a meeting place for social exchange and aggregation, where the applied arts contribute to illustrating the specific technological culture of a community.

The modern wine cellar represents globalisation in the best sense of the word. Wine is, in fact, a global product that facilitates cohesion among persons but, above all, it expresses concentrated individual local cultural phenomena. Ampelio Bucci has disarmingly suggested that the "think global, act local" concept should be reversed because it does not fit Italian artisans very well. Bucci claims that "think local, act global" would be much more congenial for Italians because this – the place – cannot be exported, even if we act with our eyes focused on the world.

Reclaiming and Rediscovering. The Soave System

The power of Italy lies in the distinction of its vines and the great number of indigenous grape varieties. They are an evocative vehicle of culture and territories. Each variety is an ambassador of rarity, peculiarity and uniqueness. These are precisely the incisive elements of marketing programmes today because it is no longer sufficient to produce fine wines. In fact, the market is no longer a place of products, but of values. In this context, wines from indigenous vines can make the difference. Such wines are endowed with added value deriving from their identification and specificity linked to their land of origin. Soave provides one of the best interpretations of this role. Over the past ten years, it has been able to tell the story of one of the most significant moments of Italian oenological history. The producers discovered that Garganega is a noble vine that should not be vexed with absurd yields. Present in the area for over two thousand years, it covers some 13,000 hectares of vineyards and produces one of the best-positioned wines in recent times on the markets of the world. Led by the Soave consortium, producers and co-operative wineries realised that a wine considered the oenological emblem of Italian white wine for so many years, easy to drink and reasonably priced, could appear on all the tables of the world, but it was necessary to rethink everything from the start. Following a series of courageous and intelligent actions guided by the Consortium, today the Soave system represents a fine example of how a DOC can go beyond simply guaranteeing the origin of a wine and its quality. The Consortium also interacted with the markets, orienting promotion toward the new objectives, which marketing frontiers demand of Italian wine. The Soave system, created by the Consortium and the producers by focusing on the Garganega vine, succeeds in offering added value to the wine, an operation that has yet to be accomplished by all in Italy. The Consortium also succeeded, with great difficulty, in settling the useless conflicts between large and small producers. They understood that it was necessary to identify and develop synergy among the various types of products so that they could interact in harmony. If, on the one hand, the apex of the qualitative pyramid plays an essential role in image-making, the large companies with their superior production, financial and distribution capacities, contribute to extending the market and, in the end, to increasing the consumption. Often they are the bridgeheads to opening and growing a market. The niche producers can follow in their wake. At the same time, the Soave consortium aimed at quality improvement and development of the territory. The producers were capable of obtaining wines from Garganega that express and transmit, through their different styles, microclimates and production processes, the emotions of their territory of origin.

The Custoza System

Custoza is known as the site of a famous Risorgimento battle won by the Austrians, but it is also a beautiful vineyard clinging gently to the morainic hills formed during the glaciation of the Garda Lake basin and one of the historical denominations in the area of Verona. The denomination has suffered alternate fortunes, but has recently recovered its own space. The Custoza system depends on a typical usage around Verona, that is, the use of grape blends rather than single varieties for vinification. Custoza seems to represent the epitome of this typical practice in the area. In addition to the indigenous vines present from the end of the nineteenth century, such as Garganega, Trebbianello (a local biotype of Tocai from Friuli) and Bianca Fernanda (a local clone of Cortese), the production protocol also allows for other vines such as Trebbiano, Malvasia, Riesling italico, Pinot Bianco, Chardonnay and Manzoni. There is also a Custoza Superiore denomination and it has a fresh, tasty character, elegant aromas and attractive notes of fruit. It has always been the white wine for an aperitif in Verona. Today, thanks to wineries with international standing, it has consolidated distant and heretofore unexplored markets. Custoza has become a contemporary wine even in its style, thanks to its authenticity, which means a return to the values of simplicity and elegance and, above all, to the strong bond with its territory. The denomination was formalised in 1972, and today the vineyards cover 1,200 hectares. There are about seventy producers. Production totals about 12 million bottles. The municipalities included in the DOC protocol are represented mainly by Sommacampagna (of which Custoza is a part), Sona, Bussolengo, Castelnuovo del Garda, Lazise, Pastrengo, Peschiera del Garda, Valeggio sul Mincio and Villafranca.

Bardolino: Female Success

The history of grape cultivation around the Garda Lake is documented by many findings of amphorae, situla, ladles, drinking vessels and ceremonial vases. Catullus, the great poet who lived in this area with an ideal climate, praises the *raeticum* wine. It is a prosperous territory for olives as well as grapes. The history of these lands continued in the Middle Ages. Cultivation of grape vines kept being a source of significant commercial earnings during the epoch of the Republic of Venice and on into modern times. The definitive recognition came with the adoption of the DOC protocol in 1968. The Bardolino that makes use of the "Classico" denomination is produced in the municipalities of Bardolino, Garda, Lazise, Affi, Costermano and Cavaion Veronese. All together, the DOC includes sixteen municipalities, all on the eastern shore of Garda Lake. The main indigenous variety is Corvina, which can represent up to 80% of the blend, accompanied by Rondinella, Molinara and Corvinone grapes. The Bardolino DOC protocol also includes a rosé version known as Chiaretto and the Superiore DOCG. There are 3,000 hectares of vineyards and production of about 32 million bottles, of which 22 Bardolino and 10 Chiaretto. Forty percent of the production is in the "Classico" zone, the remaining 60% in the other areas of the DOC. There are 1,130 producers registered with the Consortium. From 2011, all bottles of Bardolino and Chiaretto have a government-issued tax band around the bottleneck to guarantee consumers against the risks of counterfeit labelling of wines that are not certified. Bardolino wine is attracting a lot of attention and is repositioning significantly on the marketplace. Its simple essence is a guarantee of elegance and easy drinking. Its ruby colour captures the luminosity of the territory where it is born, and its freshness is an unmistakeable characteristic of the Garda Lake.

CASTELLO DI BUTTRIO

Wine and the Charm of Hospitality

FRIULI VENEZIA GIULIA
www.castellodibuttrio.it

Alessandra Felluga is the youngest child of **Alba** and **Marco Felluga**. Her father is one of the great founders of the new regional oenology. Until 2005, she brought up her family, raising three splendid daughters. She lived in Treviso where her husband is a notary. In 2005, her father Marco decided to leave the family businesses in the hands of his three children. The Castello di Buttrio went to Alessandra. Her father had acquired it in 1994 and begun the viticultural restoration with the collaboration of Professor Attilio Scienza. That is

how Alessandra once again found herself inhaling the aroma of wine.

The project was ambitious and exacting. The intention was to make Castello di Buttrio (of the eleventh century, with successive interventions) a resort where the importance of the wine was equal to that of the hospitality (eight rooms plus halls and salons for events) with an inn offering traditional fare. The resort is truly a treasure of pure femininity and class.

In 2011, the Castello acquired a part of the vineyards and the Dorigo wine cellar bordering on its farmland. At this point, the size of the wine sector, a total of 27 hectares plus the new wine cellar is strategic. Castello di Buttrio became her abode. The eldest daughter, Maria Vittoria, took her degree in oenology in Milan. With that, wine immediately took back its leading role in the consideration of the entire family. The 27 hectares of vineyards include the parcels implanted in the 1940s. Father Marco implanted others, including Pignolo, between 1995 and 2000. The undertaking was completed recently. The vineyards will dictate the future. The foundation for obtaining fine wines is ready. In fact, the results are arriving and growth is constant.

COLUTTA

Courage on the Market

FRIULI VENEZIA GIULIA
www.colutta.it

The Colutta family are pharmacists in Udine. The winegrowing dates back to 1930, but they began to bottle their wine in the 1960s. In 1998, **Giorgio Colutta** became the owner. He, too, was a pharmacist, but with a passion for winegrowing. He introduced environmentally sustainable cultivation techniques such as mechanical weed control instead of herbicides, recycling rainwater for treatments with low environmental impact products, soft and respectful pruning (Simonit and Sirch method) and harvesting by hand. The wine cellar, situated in eighteenth-century rural architectural

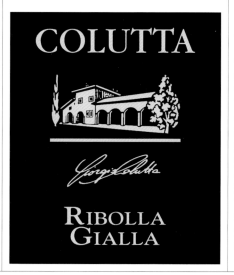

structures, is self-sufficient with regard to energy consumption.

Giorgio was one of the first among the small producers in the region to understand that it was necessary to take on new markets, particularly the Far East, while preserving the classic markets for our wine: United States and the European nations. He began to invest in Asia in 2004, in Vietnam and Singapore.

He played on two tables at the same time. He used Pinot Grigio as his passe-partout to introduce the indigenous varieties, not subject to competitive assessment, after consolidating the commercial relationship. He also offered his importers a sort of cultural assistance about Italian wines together with an efficient service to overcome bureaucratic hang-ups. These are all normal strategies for a large company, but not for one of his size. Paola (his very efficient employee) provided the only assistance he had for years.

That is how it passed in ten years, from 5% export (when it produced 70,000 bottles) to the level of 60%, calculated on the total of 140,000 bottles. The goal? To reach 80% export and production of 250,000–300,000 bottles quickly, while taking the opportunity to produce Prosecco in Friuli as well.

Today, the winery is present in Ireland, the Czech Republic, Estonia, Russia, Vietnam, Singapore, Hong Kong, Australia, South Africa and, of course, United States and Italy.

Ramandolo: The First DOCG in Friuli Venezia Giulia

Ramandolo was the first DOCG in Friuli Venezia Giulia (2001). More importantly, it was the first regional site to identify itself with the name of the production location, which is part of the Friuli Colli Orientali DOC protocol.

Ramandolo is a difficult jewel to find. This is one of the heroic viticultural undertakings: the hillsides have slopes up to 45%. Almost all the work is done by hand. The harvest begins after the middle of October and the grapes are set to dry in shared spaces equipped for the purpose. Pressing takes place between November and December, and then the must is set to ferment in wood, where it remains for at least twelve months. The wine is ready about one year after the harvest. Some producers propose selections of dried grapes from vines with particularly good exposition. Such wines go on the market after three to five years.

Ramandolo is a sweet, but clear wine that does not tire the palate and finds many combinations at the table. In addition to sweets – especially those based on walnuts and pine nuts such as the traditional *gubana* and *strucchi*, cornmeal cookies with almonds, apple strudel or the Neapolitan *pastiera* – it goes extremely well with cheeses (for example, Montasio aged at least eighteen months, or Formadi frant, the full-fat, sharp cheese of Carnia), with San Daniele Dok Dall'Ava 24 months and figs, baked ham in Dentesano bread, sweet pizza, or to accompany plum dumplings dressed with sugar and cinnamon, dumplings or ravioli of yellow squash, sweet *cjarsòn* from Carnia and duck paté.

It has a shiny antique amber colour with hints of orange. The bouquet opens with hints of apricot and prunes, followed by chestnut honey. It offers a lasting embrace in the mouth that is powerful and persistent.

DI LENARDO

A Calling for Export

FRIULI VENEZIA GIULIA

www.dilenardo.it

In 1998, **Massimo di Lenardo** took over management of the family wine business founded in 1878. He took action in three coordinated directions: new wine style, implementation of modern communication targeted at foreign markets and development of a satisfactory sales network.

The production areas are in Colli Orientali, Aquileia and Grave, Ontagnano and near Palmanova. Here, the administrative offices and the wine cellar are housed in the family villa, built in the second half of the eighteenth century, as Massimo explains: "We have retained the original architectural structure and intend to preserve it. We apply a precise policy in our interventions, of adding the modern without touching the antique. In fact, the construction conceals a highly technological wine cellar, equipped for modern vinification management and storage. That derives from our intention to give our wines a style that brings out the fruit and makes easy drinking. We want our wines to be fluid and carefree, but gifted with a clear personality. The business goal is export. Of the 700,000 bottles we produce each year on the average, about 70% are sent abroad to twenty countries. That is the reason for our choice of an international language. Naturally, we are in Friuli Venezia Giulia but, above all, we are citizens of the world".

What inspired you for Toh!, Friulano, Father's Eyes or Just Me?

"We had registered the name Toh! long before the use of the name Tocai 'was prohibited'.

It means [*as this exclamation in Italian suggests*], 'Surprised? Even if you have cancelled the name, the wine is just as surprising as ever!' In fact, it is our white wine bestseller. Father's Eyes, a Chardonnay with balanced ageing in wood, is a 'tender' wine, like the eyes of a father looking at his own children. Just Me means that we have dedicated our best efforts to this single-variety Merlot wine".

PETRUSSA

Newfound Youth of the Schioppettino di Prepotto

FRIULI VENEZIA GIULIA
www.petrussa.it

Prepotto is the historical birthplace of Schioppettino, where it remained safe from the wave of rejection that indigenous wines suffered for decades. It became an outlaw in spite of itself: bureaucratic folly! It was rehabilitated on 8 March 1978, thanks to the commitment of a few people including Giannola and Benito Nonino with their Risit d'Âur prize, Luigi Veronelli and the mayor at that time, Bruno Bernardo. At the suggestion of the author of these notes, the mayor convened the town council on 15 January 1977 to pass a resolution in defence of Schioppettino and certify disobedience to a senseless law.

Gianni and **Paolo Petrussa**, whose family has cultivated these terrains from the start of the twentieth century say: "Our work is finished when the wine interprets these particular plots faithfully". The Prepotto basin is a cool zone, so proper management of the vineyard at harvest time is essential. They interpret this territory with a light hand: delicate maceration, skilled use of wood and long ageing in the bottle. This produces a refined, but also vigorous red wine. It is modern, but has roots in the past and is capable of interpreting today's cuisine. It passes easily from substantial first courses, such as pasta with beans, to white meats, blue fish and fish soups with tomato.

In addition to Schioppettino, on their 9 hectares Gianni and Paolo produce white wines (Friulano, Sauvignon and Chardonnay) and Pensiero, a sweet white wine of dried Verduzzo grapes. Among the red wines, they do a Merlot that always gives excellent results. The goal is to increase Schioppettino in future replantings. Schioppettino di Prepotto is enjoying a second youth with the founding (on 16 October 2002) of the association of producers of Schioppettino di Prepotto, created by the will of thirty-three producers. On that day, they celebrated their first success: having obtained the status of the fifth sub-zone of the eastern hills. This led to a decisive revision of the protocol with the scope of high quality, meaning lower yield per hectare and ageing in wood.

Obviously, the most satisfactory victory of the Association was having coalesced the majority of local producers in support of the project, by stimulating their pride of belonging. Gianni and Paolo Petrussa participated in the initial phase of the movement.

SIRCH

New Knowledge of Ancient Culture

FRIULI VENEZIA GIULIA
www.sirchwine.com

Brothers **Pierpaolo** and **Luca Sirch** remodelled the family winery in 2000 starting from the vineyards. Together with Marco Simonit, Pierpaolo founded the "Preparatori d'uva". This may seem to be obvious, but actually it is not. Although vines are the "crib" of wine, they are also closely linked to the terrains and microclimates. In this part of the eastern hills, these factors have significantly varied parameters.

Thus the brothers bought and rented vineyards as a function of the sacred vine-terrain-microclimate relation, because the ideal vineyard for Friulano is not the same as the one for Sauvignon or Schioppettino. As a result the property was anything but united (simpler and less expensive to manage) and had vineyards in various areas of the DOC. The vineyards of Cladrecis were at the heart of this visionary project. Cladrecis is a tiny hamlet in the town of Prepotto, which rises to over 300 metres above sea level. It is an area of extraordinary natural beauty where the vineyards are set in among the forests. There are sharp temperature differences between night and day and rainfall is superior to other areas. This guarantees excellent vegetation for the vines even in periods of drought forecast. The Sirch wines recovered the style of the white wines of Friuli, which had made this region famous. The wines are aromatic, mineral and have an elegant structure that is anything but muscular. All the characteristics are quite distinct among them.

In addition to the Friulano, a selection of which is confirming the grandeur of what Tocai was, the Ribolla is frank and accessible, again confirming its value; and there is a very fine Sauvignon. The warmest vines at Prepotto provide the grapes for a very elegant Schioppettino, a red wine with an ancient history, and a Merlot blended with indigenous varieties, which has great expressive power and charm.

A modern and efficient wine cellar with the knowledge and ancient culture of the vine: that is the Sirch project.

ZIDARICH

A Passion for the Karst Plateau

FRIULI VENEZIA GIULIA

www.zidarich.it

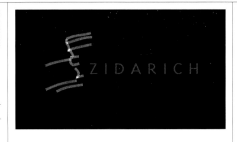

In 1998, **Beniamino Zidarich** and his wife **Nevenka**, inspired by his passion for viticulture, decided to begin producing traditional quality wines that would fully express the character of the Karst region, a unique territory and quite diverse. "To accomplish this, I apply natural methods in cultivation of the vineyard and in the wine cellar. I say no to chemical fertilisers, no to systematic treatments of the vineyard and yes to working the soil," he says. It was a rigorous productive vision that led him to prefer vinification of white wines with maceration on the pomace for two weeks without the addition of selected yeasts, followed by ageing in wood and bottling without filtration and clarification. In 2002, they began construction of the new winery, completed in 2009. It consists of five underground stories carved into the rock. It was an immense undertaking. Stairs, underground passages and walkways take visitors down 20 metres past stone columns and other structures made of the stone of the excavation.

"Our vines, considering the nature of the Karst terrain, never reach ample extensions, but rather develop in small parcels extracted as they are among so much limestone rock and some scarce red earth. A poor soil that offers products with rich qualities and a strong personality, above all. Extremely low yields depend in part on us and are partially dictated by Mother Nature. From our 8 hectares, hosting about 60,000 vines, we select an average of 25,000 bottles per year. Most of the wines are indigenous," Beniamino continues. "The whites include the Vitovska, for which we also select a reserve, Istrian Malvasia and the Prulke blend obtained from the first two combined with Sauvignon. The reds include Terrano, an ancient wine that belongs to the Refosco family and Ruje, a blend of Terrano and Merlot".

Sangiovese di Romagna: Technical Trials for Excellence

Unequalled king of the vines in Central Italy, the name of this variety refers to the blood of the god Jupiter (or Jove in archaic Latin): *Sanguis Jovis*. It prospers in two homelands. The first is, obviously, Tuscany where Sangiovese is the acknowledged leader, in the lands of classic wines from Montalcino to Montepulciano and the infinite universe of Chianti, and in the lands where viticulture is just emerging such as Maremma, Montecucco and so forth. The second, coming as no surprise, is assuredly Romagna.

For decades, the viticultural comparison between the two regions has been unfair. On the one hand, the blue-blooded Sangiovese of Tuscany; on the other, the popular character of the same variety cultivated just behind the noisy beaches of the Riviera. The link between Romagna and Sangiovese has always been profoundly sincere and it has roots in distant centuries. They say that *Sanzvés*, the name in dialect of this variety, represents the best of the character of the people in Romagna: frank, exuberant, forthright, sturdy and sociable; as rough and ready outside as thoughtful and sensitive inside.

The idea of quantity as an essential element of viticulture has been untouchable for decades throughout Romagna. This was true even in the 1980s when there was big change in the air and the Tuscan cousins focused their efforts on achieving fine quality. With very few exceptions, in Romagna attention focused on vineyards on the plains with a preference for international varieties, limiting Sangiovese to a secondary role. However, it was just a matter of time. A handful of producers, today in growing numbers and all impetuous, in reaction to rejection by the market of some international varieties, realized that the time had come to place their bets on this vine and to try to catch up with the progress made by their Tuscan cousins. The first step was to rehabilitate the terrains on the highest hills, often abandoned because they were considered expensive to manage and provided low yields. The next step was to reconsider the vineyard and to draw on the vast heritage of local clones to select the most appropriate varieties for quality. Sangiovese di Romagna in its various expressions was and continued to be planted in Tuscany with good results when not excellent. The results of this sudden acceleration, initiated with the new millennium, did not take long to appear. In short, thanks to some fine harvests, Sangiovese di Romagna, especially of the Superiore Riserva type, captured the attention of critics and appeared on worldwide markets as one of the most interesting innovations of the new millennium.

The new protocol, in force since 2011, introduced two important changes. The first concerns the name, changed to Romagna Sangiovese. The other was the institution of twelve different subzones: Bertinoro, Brisighella, Castrocaro-Terra del Sole, Cesena, Longiano, Meldola, Modigliana, Marzeno, Oriolo, Predappio, San Vicinio and Serra.

A Wonder from Romagna: The *Bursôn* of the Po River Delta

The history of Longanesi grapes began with an intuition of Antonio Longanesi, known to his fellow townsmen as *Bursôn*. Antonio was born in 1921, in the town of Bagnacavallo, in a small farmhouse. The eldest of three sons, from his youth he was destined to work the fields his grandfather had acquired before World War I. A hunter, he spent his autumn days in a cabin beside an oak tree covered by a centuries-old wild grape vine, the fruits of which attracted his game. It was an unfamiliar variety for him, but it aroused his curiosity because it was so sweet and had continued to resist adverse weather for so long. He gathered the fruit and made wine with it, a wine with rich colour and high alcoholic content, almost 14°. He did not yet know that he had recovered an extinct variety that would be named for him fifty years later.

The era was the mid-1950s and the Longanesi family was preparing to undertake modern viticulture. With the help of his brother Pietro, very capable as a grafter, that wild vine was multiplied and saved from oblivion. In 1956, they planted the first vineyard of Longanesi grapes. The fame of this wine reached the University of Bologna, where a young professor of oenology in the Agrarian School of Faenza, Sergio Ragazzini, studied and experimented with it according to the scientific method.

The creation of Bursôn wine, as it is known today, began in 1996 when Sergio Ragazzini and his winegrower friend Roberto Ercolani decided to use these grapes to create "a great red wine of the plains".

Sergio called on Antonio Longanesi and proposed to call the new wine Bursôn in his honour, with his dialect nickname as he was known to his family. With the first harvest, for a wager, they produced only 780 bottles, sold out immediately during the festivities for San Michele in Bagnacavallo. The next step was taken in April 1999 when, with the intent to amply promote the products of the territory, the Consortium of Bagnacavallo was formed. About fifteen producers joined immediately (now they number over thirty), convinced as they were of the potential of Bursôn. The consecration arrived in the year 2000 when, after the studies conducted by the Istituto di San Michele all'Adige, the grapes salvaged by Antonio were written in the National Registry of Varieties with his surname: Longanesi. The registered Bursôn mark was then granted to the Longanesi family gratuitously and to the Consortium, which is responsible for protecting its characteristics.

A wonder born of a unique territory, today Bursôn is produced in two versions: blue-label normal production and black-label Riserva. Normal production is the result of partial carbonic maceration for a wine with very pleasing notes of fruit. Riserva aims for a wine of great power and long life. Around half the bunches are dried before pressing and the wine is aged in wood for at least twenty months. The result is a red wine with a fine structure that surprises even the most experienced tasters.

CASANOVA DI NERI

At the Top of *The Wine Spectator* List

TUSCANY
www.casanovadineri.it

The story began in 1971 when **Giovanni Neri** bought an estate of 200 hectares near Montalcino. The DOC protocol had been issued a few years earlier (1966) and the protagonists on the stage in Montalcino were fewer than ten. The first harvest was in 1974, but the turning point came ten years later when son Giacomo entered the business. Together in 1985, father and son decided to buy a very special lot, Cerretalto, composed of volcanic rock and alluvial deposits. It is a sort of natural amphitheatre where harvesting lags up to three weeks behind the other vineyards of the winery. This circumstance, applied to a variety such as Sangiovese that is late by its own nature, means that no harvest can be taken for granted and consequently, this selection has so far come out only in the best years. The collaboration with Carlo Ferrini led, in 1987, to a new programme of investments that culminated with the acquisition of Tenuta Nuova, the grapes of

which are included in another selection of Brunello. This decision favours, on the one hand, emphasis on the characteristics of the diverse slopes in favourable years, and on the other, greater tranquillity in the years of poor harvests. An innovator with regard to wine styles (shorter maceration and ageing in *barrique*), this winery came to represent the archetype of the so-called international taste, in spite of itself. This is a superficial judgement, as our privileged, bird's-eye view of Brunello Cerretalto evolution will demonstrate. The audacity of a wine such as 1996, without any excess manifestation; the stratification of 1999, still young; the definition of 2001, monumental yet sapid; and the smoky grandeur of the latest three-year cycle (2006–2007–2008) are there to demonstrate it.

Casanova di Neri

BRUNELLO DI MONTALCINO
DENOMINAZIONE DI ORIGINE CONTROLLATA E GARANTITA

COLLEMASSARI

Organic and Traditional

TUSCANY
www.collemassari.it

Claudio Tipa, an industrial entrepreneur of Rome with a fascination for great wine, began his career as a producer in a zone that was then completely unknown to the public. It was 1998, in Maremma at Cinigiano in Montecucco, a district known only to specialists for Leonardo Salustri's first exploits. The project was noteworthy from the start given the impressive investments which included restoration of the fourteenth-century castle, ColleMassari, preparing a technologically advanced wine cellar by building an important structure of bio-

architecture on four levels, and raking in the best terrains, making this winery the point of reference for the entire zone with over 80 hectares of vineyards. The decision to go organic and produce quality wines, with a preference for traditional vines, gave something of a shock to the denomination and, in the meantime, Tipa had become the president of the Consortium. Considering the successive development of the expansive strategy of this group, with acquisitions first in Bolgheri (Grattamacco) and then in Montalcino (Poggio di Sotto), today it might seem that Montecucco is the least interesting of the settlements. We are firmly convinced of the contrary. Poggio di Sotto and Grattamacco have given many demonstrations of their standard of excellence. However, the challenge of an environment without a pedigree is much more fascinating. For a few years now, in addition to the overall solidity of the labels of the house, numerous but not abundant, an important wine is emerging here – Montecucco Sangiovese Lombrone Riserva – with a well-defined physiognomy. In 2009, the modern imprint at the start seems to serve a design that privileges aromatic fragrance and lively taste, all to the advantage of the natural aromatic fragrance.

GUADO AL MELO

Cellar with Library and *Viticetum*

TUSCANY
www.guadoalmelo.it

I have seen cellars with collections of painting or antique autos, with museums of tools for agriculture and winemaking. But I have never before found a library of 20,000 books in the heart of the wine cellar. The estate also has a *viticetum* of 1 hectare called Giardino where many varieties from many winegrowing regions of Europe have been planted.
This is Guado al Melo, in the Bolgheri DOC area and founded by Caterina and Attilio Scienza and run by their son Michele (oenologist). Annalisa, Michele's wife, organises the cultural events related to wine that they offer periodically.
The library and *viticetum* were created by Attilio, a passionate bibliophile and one of the major scholars and experts in the world of viticulture. He teaches at the University of Milan. The library contains about 5,000 volumes on viticultural and oenological subjects, with particular attention to ampelography. About 200 volumes are nineteenth-century editions. The collection includes about 300 theses written by students of **Attilio Scienza** under his guidance. Attilio explains the Giardino: "The motivations are didactic and experimental, in order to have material for my students' theses and to identify the diverse varieties, like monitoring maturation, micro vinification using a variety of techniques such as in amphora, comparison of clones, between grafts of different buds or rootstocks, research on hydroponics and minerals, and so forth".

There are also 60 varieties set out in 31 rows to evaluate which of them are best adapted to the terrain and microclimate of Bolgheri. They come from France (also many cross-breeds), Spain, Portugal, Italy and Croatia, of both white and red varieties. There is also a collection of red and white fruit vines from Georgia.
The red fruits are harvested at different times, depending on their maturation, vinified separately and then blended. This is the origin of Jassarte, 3,000 bottles that go to market after two years in *barrique* and two in the bottle. A remarkable, endearing and very personal wine.
Michele, who earned his diploma in oenology at San Michele all'Adige in 1990 and his university degree in biological sciences in 1995, has directed the winery from the first harvest in 2002. At that time there were 30 hectares, planted in 1999 and 2003, of which 29 were dedicated to the grapes of the Bolgheri DOC: Cabernet Sauvignon, Cabernet Franc, Merlot, Syrah and Petit Verdot. Petit Manseng is also present. Among the local whites, Vermentino, which contributes 70% to Guado al Melo white together with Incrocio Manzoni white.

MASTROJANNI

A Matrimony of Passions: Coffee and Wine

TUSCANY

www.mastrojanni.com

Gabriele Mastrojanni, a lawyer, bought a farm near Montalcino in 1975, in the area of Castelnuovo dell'Abate. However, it was the arrival of Andrea Machetti in 1992 that marked the decisive turn of the wines toward excellence. Machetti had a background of important professional experiences, such as Villa Banfi, then collaboration with Castiglion del Bosco together with his inseparable friend Maurizio Castelli, one of the great technicians operating in Tuscany from the 1970s.

Machetti is a Brunello purist. This means 100% Sangiovese, maniacal care for the vineyard and ageing in casks, never in *barriques*.

The **Illy family** bought the winery in 2008. When Mastrojanni died in 2005, his children did not wish to continue and Francesco Illy, older brother of Andrea and Riccardo, who guide the Illy Group together with him, had owned a farm (initially without vineyards) adjacent to Mastrojanni for many years. When he learned that it was for sale he decided, with his family, to buy it and insert it in the high range of their agricultural products, which already included Agrimontana for preserves, Domori for chocolate and Dammann Frères for tea.

Among the brothers, Riccardo was the first who entered into the world of Italian wine: "I entered the business in 1977. In the expansion programme for coffee, we had identified Italian wine makers as our first allies. I made friends with many of them. Wine became a passion. In fact, I was chairman of the Veronelli Seminary for years".

With the arrival of the Illys, Machetti became the managing director and Maurizio Castelli was responsible for technical assistance. They launched a plan of investments to favour qualitative growth and increased production by acquiring vineyards. Machetti clarified: "We could reach about 34 hectares of which 16 for Brunello and the remainder for Rosso di Montalcino, Rosso di Sant'Antimo and Moscadello".

Ernesto, architect and son of Francesco, chairman of the company, designed the new cask cellar according to the canons of green building. Since 2008, sales have increased by 72%, while investments, including those of 2015, amount to 3.9 million Euro. Today the winery produces about 100,000 bottles annually, with the objective of reaching 150,000.

Riccardo Illy defines their Brunello as "Elegance and Tradition". Machetti adds: "We need to give verticality to the Brunello. This is not a wine for tasting, but for dining, so acidity is fundamental".

In the Mastrojanni Brunello, the mark of Montalcino is clearly recognizable. There are two crus: Vigna Schiena d'Asino (the name coined by Gualtiero Marchesi) and Vigna Loreto.

PETRA

Franciacorta in Tuscany

TUSCANY

www.petrawine.it

Exiting from the Rosignano-Rome highway at Venturino-Piombino, an architectural marvel by Mario Botta begins to appear in the landscape. Founded in 1997 as the Tuscan branch of the Terra Moretti group (the Bellavista and Contadi Castaldi brands) from Franciacorta, it was entrusted to **Francesca Moretti**, who had taken a stand in favour of the project and succeeded in convincing her father Vittorio to set out on this adventure. After many, many photographic reports on the container, interest has finally turned to the contents. Looking at the estate as a whole, the total of about 100 hectares is divided into three distinct nuclei. The highest, at an elevation of 400 metres with mineral rich soils, pebbles and galestro, is reserved for Sangiovese. The terrain surrounding the winery is more compact and clayey, ideal for Merlot, where the oldest rootstocks are planted. The third area is in the Potenti zone, above the hills of Riotorto where the Cabernet Sauvignon grapes grow. The prestigious oenological consulting of Pascal Chattonet has accompanied Petra from the start of its development and the range has taken on a precise physiognomy as it developed. There are three single variety labels: Potenti (100% Cabernet Sauvignon), Quercegobbe (100% Merlot) and Alto (only Sangiovese). The blends are Ebo, a *second vin* produced in consistent quantities from the assembly of Cabernet Sauvignon, Merlot and Sangiovese, and the *grand vin*, Petra, a classic Bordeaux, prevalence of Cabernet Sauvignon with Merlot in the balance. This has grown over time as is only natural for a wine deriving from recently planted vineyards. The year 2008 was emblematic: juice, juice and more juice of raspberries and blackberries, a whiff of Mediterranean wild bush and refreshing mint; a long and complex after-taste with toasted return and mineral persistence. A success.

PODERE POGGIO SCALETTE

On the Field

TUSCANY
www.poggioscalette.it

At the beginning of the 1990s, **Vittorio Fiore** had already made a decisive contribution to the Tuscan and Italian oenological renaissance by overseeing the creation of many wines that would become the points of reference for the entire new wave of the moment. The desire to take part personally in the historic enterprise and the desire to live in Tuscany led him to take the big step. He succeeded, together with his wife **Adriana Assjé di Marcorà**, in acquiring some lots of land and a farmhouse on Ruffoli hill in the town of Greve in Chianti. The name, Poggio Scalette, evokes those slopes marked and shaped by the dry-stack walls, which climb the hill like a little stairway. New acquisitions in 1996 and 1999 followed that first step and completed the mosaic surrounding the main building and the wine cellar. When his son Jurij entered the business after returning from university at Beaune, company ambitions exploded exponentially. The winery had a portion dedicated to Piantonaia, a single-variety Merlot, assigned exclusively to Enoteca Pinchiorri, but the project, based essentially on Sangiovese, originated with a vineyard over sixty years of age, planted at the end of World War I. The name of the wine, Carbonaione, originated from the old vines on the edge of the woods where the farmers used to produce their wood charcoal. Those same vines, together with the more recently planted vineyards at elevations ranging from 300 to 500 metres, on soils of

sand and galestro with low clay content and southwest exposition, produce a red wine that corresponds to the stylistic archetype of the producer. In fact, the label reads "The wine of Vittorio Fiore" with the autograph of the author.

POGGIO DI SOTTO

The Elegance of Sobriety

TUSCANY
www.collemassari.it

Today, Poggio di Sotto represents one of the top-ranking names in qualitative oenology in Italy. Montalcino is a result achieved in very few years of history and a context among the most competitive on the Italian peninsula. Drinking the red wines that used to belong to Piero Palmucci, and from September 2011 belong to the ColleMassari group led by Claudio Tipa, it is hard to believe that this ascent began only in the early 1990s. Without any intention on his part, Piero was a pioneer of the reawakening of interest for a fresher and more natural type of

wine that today has been massively adopted in the Brunello zone, with a choral representation of many voices that represents the best guarantee of the prospects for the denomination. Viticulture without impositions, a traditional approach to winemaking and a listening phase consisting of continued tasting: first with the advice of master taster Giulio Gambelli, today with that of the no less gifted Federico Staderini, all to decide what to dedicate, of the various vineyards, to Red, Brunello and Brunello Riserva. A passionate defender of the purity of Rosso di Montalcino, Piero Palmucci could hardly mask his delusion when Brunello or Brunello Riserva was requested during tastings, ignoring the wine that made him proudest. He presented, almost every year, the best red in circulation. Another wine for which he cared particularly was Il Decennale 2001, a pure Sangiovese of "blinding" truth. Claudio Tipa received these "divine" wines as part of the assets. They had that "serene force" that so many try to rediscover today. Riserva 2006 and Riserva 2007 represent the most brilliant duo of Brunello I have ever encountered.

ROCCA DI FRASSINELLO

Joint Venture in Maremma of Castellare and Lafite Rothschild

TUSCANY
www.castellare.it/eng/introFrassinello.html

Paolo Panerai acquired the Castellare estate in Castellina in 1980. It is an historic estate in Chianti Classico with wines such as the famous I Sodi di San Nicolò, which was twice consecutively included in *The Wine Spectator*'s Top 100. The 30 hectares of vineyards produce about 200,000 bottles.

In 2000, Castellare created Rocca di Frassinello with the intention to find other terrains in Maremma, as qualified as Bolgheri or even better. This led to the choice of a cru in the town of Gavorrano near the ancient settlement of Giuncarico, where the first – and until now the only – Italo-French joint venture winemaking project was born. Here the terrain is a sort of geological extension with characteristics as found in Chianti and Montalcino, but with a substantial difference: average temperatures 4–5°C higher and more extensive temperature variation between day and night, a perfect premise for producing great wines.

In two years time, five farms were united to form the 500 hectare estate of Rocca di Frassinello, of which almost 90 are vineyards. The wine cellar was designed by one of the great architects in the world: Renzo Piano. The first Rocca di Frassinello harvest was in 2004, under the guidance of the oenologists for the two houses: Alessandro Cellai and Christian Le Sommer. They produced about 130,000 bottles, divided as in Bordeaux, in three wines: Poggio alla Guarda, the third label; Le Sughere di Frassinello, the second label. And, of course, the first label, le grand vin: Rocca di Frassinello, a blend of Sangiovese 60%, Cabernet Sauvignon 20% and Merlot. The peak is shared by Baffonero, a single variety Merlot, rated 94/100 by Robert Parker after only a few harvests, and Le Sughere di Frassinello (Sangiovese 50%, Cabernet Sauvignon 25% and Merlot), classified among the top 100 wines of the world according to *The Wine Spectator*.

Pecorino: The Most Appreciated Indigenous Vine of Central Italy

Pecorino is the indigenous vine of Central Italy that has achieved the greatest commercial success. The rapid success also led to a boom of cultivation. Today, there is no winery in Abruzzo that has not included it in its line of products.

A grapevine with white fruits found prevalently in the Marches and Abruzzo, the origins of Pecorino are uncertain. It seems that the first written references date to the pen of Cato the Elder (second century BC), who classified it among the Aminea, a group of vines including Greco di Tufo, Grechetto and Pignoletto, brought into Italy during the migration of the Greek Aminei people.

The name seems to be linked to the seasonal movements of shepherds and their flocks, the famous transhumance between summer and winter pastures. It seems the sheep devoured these grapes voraciously because, maturing earlier than other regional varieties, they were already quite sweet when the flocks passed in autumn.

However, low yield induced producers to abandon it in favour of other more prolific varieties, and by the end of the 1980s Pecorino had practically disappeared.

The principal merits for its rediscovery must be attributed to **Guido Cocci Grifoni**, a producer in the Marches who discovered a tiny mountain vineyard in the mid-1980s, to the precious advice of master sommelier Teodoro Bugari, and to the experiments conducted by the Institute for Viticulture of Conegliano Veneto and the Agrarian Institute of Ascoli Piceno.

In 1996, in Abruzzo, Luigi Cataldi Madonna bottled the first wine with the name Pecorino on the label. It was only in 2001 that the Marches created the Offida DOC protocol. Pecorino is one of the three types of the denomination, the other two being Passerina and Rosso. In Abruzzo, Pecorino today is still one of the basic vines of diverse IGT wines, including Alto Tirino, Terre di Chieti, Colline Pescaresi, Colline Teatine, among others and the recent DOC Abruzzo.

It prefers high, cool hill terrain with strong day/night temperature variations. In these conditions, it expresses the best of its aromatic character with notes found also in vines such as Riesling and Sauvignon.

CANTINA TOLLO

Where Quantity Rhymes with Quality

ABRUZZO

www.cantinatollo.it

With almost 13 million bottles on the market, 840 members and 3,200 hectares cultivated, Cantina Tollo is one of the most important Italian enterprises in the wine sector. It began as an agricultural cooperative in 1960, at a time when farmer battles for assignment of land and recognition of more dignified working conditions made associations a natural point of aggregation. Today, there are over forty cooperative wineries in Abruzzo, representing a fundamental pilaster of the regional economy. Management, in the persons of chairman **Tonino Verna** and general director **Gianfranco Di Ruscio**, is proud to emphasize the great development of the company during the past fifteen years:

"At the end of the 1990s, a crucial decade began for the company characterised by a common awareness at all levels that attention had to focus on the market and its evolution. Innovation was concentrated on qualitative improvement of the conferral process. Cantina Tollo is in fact a first level cooperative and one of its strong points is the capacity to intervene directly in the selection of the vineyards, in the conviction that good wine is born on the vine. The concrete demonstration of this commitment is the 'advanced vineyard' project, which introduced retribution to members based on the hectares worked instead of the old standard based on quintals produced, bringing the culture of quality into the vineyard. This radically changed the productive philosophy of everyone and led to obtaining quality consistency never seen before. Every member has thus become an essential element inside the winery.

The pride of being Cantina Tollo is thus the pride of an entire country, a community that faces difficult times with courageous determination and acts to favour the development of a whole territory."

In conclusion, a curious little-known fact: Cantina Tollo is one of the largest Italian producers of organic wines in Italy.

The cooperative has implemented conversion policies from the start of the 1990s and today organic production concerns 237 hectares, with potential grape yield of 45–50 thousand quintals.

CATALDI MADONNA

A Restless Philosopher Winegrower

ABRUZZO

www.cataldimadonna.com

A philosopher and a winegrower, **Luigi Cataldi Madonna** divides his time between academic commitments and the family estate, which called him back to the land almost thirty years ago.

The first bottling year was 1988. "At that time, I had no intention to enter the farming world. I was an intellectual and thought that peasants were peasants. I made my first wine, Tonì, as an homage to my father using *barriques* I had bought secretly. It was a wine made with much enthusiasm, but little technique. However, it helped me to understand the great power of the Ofena territory".

The rebirth of this very beautiful territory of the interior near L'Aquila is undoubtedly an accomplishment of this estate. "At the beginning, I was alone. Now we are six winemakers and new investments continue to arrive. To explain the unique character of this place, I always use the metaphor of an oven under a refrigerator. This is the only place I know where a sunny valley, that can easily exceed 40°C in the summer, is under the southernmost of perennial glaciers, the Gran Sasso".

The winery has never lost sight of the social importance and hedonistic character of wine. "One of the problems with wine is the excessive halo of importance and sobriety that has been created around it. For me, wine has always been a drink, the best in the world. It must entertain us, help us to express our emotions and enjoy the company of others. Above all, it must be popular and accessible to all".

Wishing to select the two most representative wines, the difficult choice is between Cerasuolo Piè delle Vigne, a rosé based on Montepulciano that stands above competitors for its quality and character, and Pecorino, the most fashionable white wine in central Italy, which owes much of its rediscovery to Cataldi Madonna.

Tintilia, the Great Protagonist in Molise

Tintilia is the only indigenous vine of Molise. Some years ago, thanks to the efforts of an unswerving handful of producers, it made its way back from oblivion as the most interesting viticultural product of this small region.

The history of this vine is controversial. For a long time, it was considered a close relative of the Sardinian vine Bovale. In fact, the two were considered synonyms in the National Registry of Vines. Recent genetic analyses have excluded any form of relationship between them. Now, the most accredited hypothesis is a Spanish origin, with introduction into Italy during the Bourbon dynasty in the eighteenth century. This thesis is reinforced by the fact that the Spanish adjective *tinto* means red, so the name *tintilia* is supposed to refer to the particular chromatic force of the fruits of this vine, capable of generating wines with a particularly intense colour.

The first documented references to Tintilia in Molise date to 1800, when the census at the end of the century reported that it was the most cultivated vine in the region, particularly in the province of Campobasso. The real crisis arrived in the 1960s when it was abandoned in favour of more generous varieties, thus sharing the sad fate of many other indigenous vines with low yields.

The wine produced by these grapes, in addition to the aforementioned bright red colour, has an ample and enticing olfactory profile, dominated by flowers and very intense red fruits, with a characteristic spicy note of pepper. The best expressions are those from the hills where day-night temperature variations and sunshine amplify the aromatic assets of the genes and make it quite recognisable. The best interpretations are produced by **Cantine Cipressi**, **Di Majo Norante**, **Angelo d'Uva**, **Borgo di Colloredo**, **Cantine Salvatore** and **Terre Sacre**.

TERRE DEL PRINCIPE

Enhancement of the Ancient Vines of Caserta

CAMPANIA

www.terredelprincipe.com

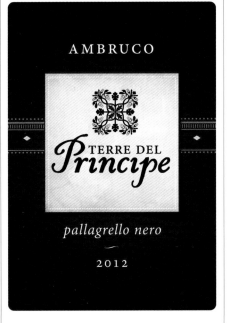

Terre del Principe was founded in 2003 by **Peppe Mancini** and **Manuela Piancastelli**, husband and wife united in destiny by vines and wine. It is the only estate in Campania working exclusively with Pallagrello Bianco, Pallagrello Nero and Casavecchia.

Peppe Mancini left his work as a lawyer to dedicate himself to this. "I am a lucky man, because I have lived two lives in one, the life of a lawyer and the life of a winegrower. I am proud to have been the pioneer of a territory and the father of these grapes".

His wife Manuela Piancastelli, formerly a journalist of the Neapolitan daily *Il Mattino*, adds: "My choice was guided by my passion for wine and my love for my husband. These grapes changed our existence, but we transformed their destiny".

Together with professor Luigi Moio, they brought their grapes – planted on 11 hectares of vineyards – to the attention of the world. Peppe is a reserved and generous man. He has given shoots to dozens of winegrowers, while Manuela handles marketing, hospitality and communications given her sunny personality. There are at least three banner wines at Terre del Principe: Le Sèrole of Pallagrello Bianco, Ambruco of Pallagrello Nero and Centomoggia of Casavecchia.

Le Sèrola has an Alsatian style, with brief fermentation in *barrique* and one year ageing in the bottle. The two red wines, Ambruco and Centomoggia, are completely different from each other. Ambruco, a single variety Pallagrello Nero, is refined, never blatant and very rich in spicy aromas. Centomoggia, a single variety Casavecchia (including the grapes of a small historic vineyard about 150 years old) has domineering fruit and silky tannins.

VITICOLTORI DE CONCILIIS

Loyalty to the Earth

CAMPANIA
www.viticoltorideconciliis.it

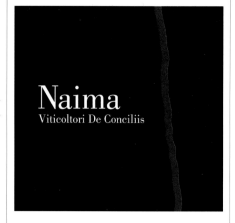

Twenty years of work in Prignano, in the heart of the Cilento area, by the De Conciliis siblings **Bruno**, **Luigi** and **Paola De Conciliis**, and Paola's husband, **Giovanni Canu**, have carried forward the labour that their father Alessandro (who died in 2007) had begun.

The three siblings and brother-in-law divided up their tasks: Bruno, after studying at DAMS, the university institute for the performing arts in Bologna, rejuvenated the company image by defining himself, his brothers and sister, and the staff as a full-fledged rock bank where each person plays and acts his part. Luigi is in charge of the vineyards, Paolo handles the administration and her husband Giovanni is the cellar master. Bruno does a bit of all things and coordinates the work of the company.

De Conciliis began to make wine in the mid-1990s. "Then off we were, with no delays," Bruno says, "burning our bridges behind us so there was no turning back. The decision was made. The rich family breeding farm disappeared and vineyards became its fulcrum". The Cilento has space, is enjoying an extraordinary tourist boom thanks to the outstanding cultural and environmental attractions and offers an infinity of opportunities. The largest national park in Italy is here, there are old and new vineyards, old and new vines of the territory. "We have a responsibility to represent the home of the Mediterranean diet in the world," is the De Conciliis philosophy, "there's an unwritten contract with consumers for a wine that will never fail to be true to its land, its vine and the intelligence of those who drink it and those who make it".

The vineyards are in the valley facing the sea at Agropoli. They cultivate Aglianico and Fiano in particular.

The leading wine is the austere Aglianico Naima, from the name of a piece by jazz saxophone player John Coltrane, first produced in 1997.

ELENA FUCCI

The Hermit Who Transmits the Vulture

BASILICATA
www.elenafuccivini.com

Very young (born 1981), **Elena Fucci** is already a typical example of the modern multitasking woman. She's the jack-of-all-trades of a small and dynamic company in Barile in the Basilicata region. Her grandfather Generoso bought the vineyards in the 1960s, by selecting the highest parts of the farms in the Contrada Solagna del Titolo settlement at the foot of Mount Vulture, the ancient and now extinct volcano. During the years, the grapes were sold to other producers. When the idea of selling the land leaked out "there was no lack of interested buyers," as Elena recalls, "but at the last minute, my heart refused. I could not stand the idea that someone could slip the vineyards out of my view and that another name could do something grandiose with the oldest vineyards on Mount Vulture. Most of them are 55 to 60 years old, a part are 70 years old. So I decided, courageously and a little recklessly, to change the entire programme of my life and my family, by investing in the territory".

That was in the year 2000. Elena Fucci decided to study oenology and to take care of the family vineyards. Another strong decision was to aim for a single wine. The first harvest was in 2000. For the first four years, Elena had the assistance of a professional consultant. After that, she took over management in the vineyard and the wine cellar on her own. Titolo is the only label produced, a "first-class wine" as she loves to say. It leaves its mark and is fully recognisable. This is true because the vineyards are in an inner

mountain zone at an elevation of 600 metres. The soil is volcanic, highly mineral, with a dark colour in which the history of the ancient Vulture, and all its eruptive phases, are clearly legible.

CANTELE

How to Express Wine and Territory

PUGLIA
www.cantele.it

This winery was born from a story of reverse emigration, from North to South instead of the opposite, romantic and a slightly crazy. **Giovanni Battista Cantele**, originally from the Veneto region, was a wine broker. He travelled all over Italy selecting bulk wines in the South for sale in the rich markets of the North. During one of these stages, his wife Teresa Manara fell helplessly in love with Lecce. That is how the Cantele couple began their adventure in Salento, a real frontier land in the 1950s. Actually, the first wines labelled Cantele appeared only a few decades later at the end of the 1990s, before Teresa's still vigil eyes. Today, the third generation of the Cantele family runs the business and one of them, Paolo, takes on the role of spokesman for the project. "Together with my brother and my cousins, we suddenly realized that the story of our family, its wines and its lands deserved the best possible narration. We were among the first to approach communication in a modern way, coordinated

and logical in every detail. The web and then the blog that has become a diary about the Salento and its endless attractions". Borrowing from digital annotation, we might call Cantele "a 2.0 winegrower company", looking toward the future, but still anchored in tradition. It follows that the leading wine can only bear the name of the matriarch, Teresa Manara. It is a Negroamaro cru, an elegant full-bodied wine, full of vitality like the woman who inspired it (there is also the Chardonnay version in her name). Another confirmation of the special relationship between this vine and the Salento.

TERESAMANARA

NEGROAMARO

Luce pura irradiò il paesaggio, lei lo immaginò senza alcuno sforzo. Il mare, le sue onde azzurre trasformarsi nella terra che l'avrebbe accolta

CANTELE

GIANFRANCO FINO VITICOLTORE

Instinct, Perseverance and Passion at the Heart of Success

PUGLIA
www.gianfrancofino.it

Gianfranco Fino's adventure began only in 2004. After about twenty years of experience in the field of oenology and agronomy and having entered his forties, he decided to buy a small vineyard with old Primitivo vines. The success with critics and the public was immediate. His fame has gone far beyond national borders. "At that time I often accompanied the great Veronelli around Puglia to discover new extra virgin olive oils, his great passion late in life," says Fino. "Gino frequently advised me to realise my ideas and philosophy about wine in a project of my own. It was just after one of those trips when I discovered a fifty-year-old vineyard of Primitivo. I fell in love with it immediately and quickly concluded the deal. I had always nurtured the idea that it was possible to produce a very great wine in my home territory that would be capable of competing at the top level of markets around the world. So I began to refine the agronomic details and cellar factors with maniac devotion, immediately adopting strict temperature control. This may seem obvious elsewhere, but ten years ago it was still a very uncommon practice here in our area. Then I aimed straight at the use of the *barrique*. To my mind, they were fundamental to exalt the characteristics of Primitivo. The old bush vines and the fantastic *terroir* where they live did all the rest".

The results prove him right. ES – pure Primitivo, the name itself recalls the instinct and the boundless passion of Freudian memory – is

today one of the most celebrated prize-winning wines of Italy. While maintaining a full-bodied structure, it also has an aromatic focus and taste impact for which comparison is difficult to find.

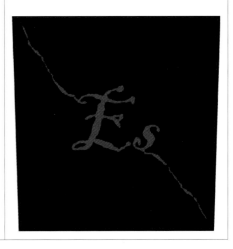

CERAUDO

Myths and Future Visions

CALABRIA
www.dattilo.it

The presence of Magna Grecia is evident in the wines and the entire estate of **Roberto Ceraudo**, who is fortunate to have the support of his three children, collaborating in all the activities: Giuseppe in the wine cellar and amidst the vineyards; Caterina, the young chef of the successful restaurant Dattilo, one of the best in the South; and Susy, very active in the work of marketing and communication. A united family of people who all pull together and never back down in the face of difficulties. Those are never missing in the land of Calabria.

Roberto Ceraudo bet on himself when he began in 1973. His terrains occupy 60 hectares in the area of Crotone, only a few kilometres from the Ionian Sea. The entire estate has been certified organic since 1992.

All the names of the Ceraudo wines are linked to history and mythology. Dattilo, for example, was the name of a Greek god. Petelia was the name of Strongoli as a settlement of Magna Grecia. *Grayasusi* means "lady Susi" in *arbereshe*, the local language that fuses Albanese and Greek, dedicated to his eldest daughter Susy. *Imyr* means good. From the start of 2000, the entire range of Ceraudo wines has taken on the current characteristics of absolute quality. The two Grayasusi rosés are particularly worthy of note. Both are 100% Gaglioppo: copper and silver label. A note on the latter: the silver label is the lead wine of the winery. It is a fascinating example of a rosé fermented in stainless steel tanks, then aged four months in *barrique*. The focus on indigenous vines must be mentioned: Grisara, a white wine from Pecorella grapes and the red wine, Dattilo, of 100% Gaglioppo, aged 18 months in oak casks. Very elegant and complex wines. The pride of the Ceraudo house is, however, the Dattilo restaurant. Opened in 2003 and directed by Caterina, the youngest starred chef in the South.

Moscato Passito di Saracena: History Dictates the Future

Among the many delicious straw wines made in Italy, there is one in the South that has very particular characteristics and history, Moscato Passito di Saracena. Saracena is a town in the province of Cosenza perched on a hill at an elevation of 600 metres, south of the Pollino national park. This wine risked extinction, but ten years ago a handful of producers in Saracena took it upon themselves to recover the vineyards and the antique method of vinification. Today, there are less than a dozen winegrowers who are dedicated to production of this spectacular sweet wine. The key personality in recovery of this precious nectar is Luigi Viola (Cantine Viola), an elementary school teacher for thirty-five years. With a passion for agriculture, in 1999 he began to market the first 180 bottles of Moscato di Saracena.

Another leading producer is Roberto Bisconte, of Feudo dei Sanseverino, who has created other wines that are just as rich and refined. In addition to the Moscato Passito, the "al Governo" di Saracena version is also very interesting.

This sweet wine was already requested by popes in the sixteenth century. Cardinal Sirleto had whole cases shipped from the port of Scalea for Pope Pius IV. Centuries later, English writer Norman Douglas (1915) described it enthusiastically in his book *Old Calabria*: "Near at hand, too, lies the prosperous village of Saracena, celebrated of old for its Muscat wines. They are made from the grape which the Saracens brought over from Maskat".

In fact, the first Moscato vines were planted by the ancient Saracens (as the Arab peoples were then known) in 900 AD. The wine-making procedure is quite singular. This is how it is done. The Moscato di Saracena (also known as Moscatello) vine is the base for this straw wine and it grows only in the territory of this small town in Calabria. There is no formal evidence of any genetic relationship with other more widely diffused Moscato vines such as those of Alessandria or Hamburg. The other grapes in the blend are Guarnaccia and Malvasia Bianca. Some producers add a minimal part of Odoacra, another indigenous vine that confers a more aromatic halo. "Moscato is harvested in September before the start of the general harvest. The other grapes are gathered in October," explains Luigi Viola. "The Moscato bunches are hung up one by one to dry in the cellar for about three weeks. The dehydrated berries are then selected and pressed one by one to obtain the must. The procedure for the Guarnaccia and Malvasia Bianca grapes is different. After a soft pressing, the must is concentrated by boiling down to one third volume in steel vats. This is the most delicate phase of the entire production cycle. The concentrated must is left to cool for some time in barrels".

The second phase is very delicate. "The must of the dried Moscato grapes," continues Viola, "is then thrown into the other must [*previously boiled down*]. At this point, a very slow natural fermentation begins. The skins macerate for six months in the cask. Then the wine obtained ages in steel. Finally, it is bottled. This is the same winemaking method as was used in 1500".

It is the only sweet wine in the world that can do without the addition of sulphur dioxide.

CENTOPASSI

Vineyards Liberated from the Mafia

SICILY

www.centopassisicilia.it

Demonstrating that agriculture can offer a life without suffering extortion and abuse is one way of suppressing the mafia even in the Sicilian countryside, historically one of the areas most tainted by organised crime. Centopassi is the viticultural heart of the cooperatives that cultivate the lands confiscated from the mafia in Sicily, in the name of Libera Terra. The great challenge is to produce wines of quality from the 90 hectares farmed organically (a part of the over 400 hectares assigned to them), with the assistance of the "Preparatori d'uva" **Marco Simonit** and **Pierpaolo Sirch**. It is an historic undertaking. Since then, the Centopassi wines are often expected to represent to the world the will of Sicilian agriculture to free itself of the mafia. In addition to wine, the cooperative also produces pasta, legumes and conserves.
The first harvest was in 2006. The wine cellar in San Ciprianello was inaugurated in 2009 and was built in a structure confiscated from the mafia, with the funds of the national safety programme distributed by the Ministry of the Interior. The wine cellar stands in the Don Tommaso cru. It includes a tasting station.
The most important wines are the Tendoni di Trebbiano (vinification in steel, aged 8 months in *tonneaux*); Catarrato Terre Rosse di Giabbascio; and Grillo Rocce di Pietra Longa (vinification completely in steel). And finally, Argille Di Tagghia Via, a single-variety Nero d'Avola. The name of the winery refers to the 100 strides

that separated the house of Peppino Impastato, the young journalist of Cinisi killed by the mafia, from the house of Tano Badalamenti, a mafia boss. It is also the title of the film dedicated to Impastato in 2003 by director Marco Tullio Giordana. Some Centopassi labels – beautiful and striking – are dedicated to politicians and trade union officials killed by Cosa Nostra, namely Pio La Torre and Nicolò Azoti.

CUSUMANO

Walk through the Vineyards of Sicily

SICILY

cusumano.it

The **Cusumano** story is the story of an extraordinary commercial success, built systematically from sale of bulk wines to the production of over two and a half million bottles of quality wines distributed in thirty-five countries. It is also the story of a return to the land, of the search for the zones of Sicily best suited to propose area wines from indigenous vines. The Cusumano success story depends on the capacity to intercept changes of taste and fashion at the critical moment, to be quick and dynamic, to have the right intuitions and to know how to work in the right perspective. Today, they are among market leaders, in addition to being the proprietors of over 400

hectares of vineyards in the provinces of Palermo, Trapani, Caltanissetta, Siracusa and most recently, on Etna as well. The new company was founded in 2001 by father Francesco, from Partinico. His brilliant, well-educated and handsome sons, Alberto and Diego, are by his side. They built a modern wine cellar in minimalist style, with low environmental impact, in a rural nineteenth-century walled yard. It is really thanks to the Cusumano family if the reputation of Partinico is changing in the collective imagination of the world of wine. Their marketing project intends to satisfy all tastes and all expectations. This is the origin of two lines of wine. The first is single variety, the second includes more complex wines, the names of which recall ancient territorial denominations. In 2007, they began to produce a new Moscato dello Zucco, thus completing their proposals with a sweet wine and a fascinating history. "There's a piece of the land and the history of Sicily in each one of our labels," as the Cusumanos say.

PASSOPISCIARO

Andrea Franchetti, a Celebration of Hamlets

SICILY

www.passopisciaro.com

Since the first few years after 2000, **Andrea Franchetti** of Rome, who was already the proprietor of the Trinoro estate in Tuscany, decided to buy an estate on the north slope of Etna near Passopisciaro in the town of Castiglione di Sicilia, to recover and replant the vines, both indigenous and international varieties, restore the villa and grape processing structures and refurbish the wine cellar. In the late nineteenth century, when Catania was the province with more vines than any other in Sicily and the wine trade was the main source of traffic in the port of Riposto, every winery on Etna had its own stone vat where the must fermented into wine.

Franchetti understood that the each location, each hamlet or *contrada* in the local dialect, made a difference on Etna, because they were positioned on different lava flows, at different heights, of different eras and from different depths of the volcano. The grapes that grow on these terrains have different flavours, even if only a few metres apart. Thus, after his first label dedicated to the indigenous Etna red wine of excellence, Nerello Mascalese, all grapes from Passopisciaro in the first year 2005, he added a series of crus expressing the other *contrada* of origin: Chiappemacine, Porcaria, Rampante, Sciaranuova and Guardiola, all presented for the first time with the 2008 harvest.

More importantly, he organised an event, "Contrade dell'Etna" with the first edition in 2007, where he invited all the producers to intervene and share their points of view.

The wineries were all in favour of the *contrada* so the miracle occurred. Even the smallest wine cellars, reluctant to participate in fairs or tasting events, were present with Franchetti. Year after year, the event became an indispensable appointment to discover what was happening on Etna and to taste all the production. It is a great festivity. Franchetti hosts the other wineries in his wine cellar, offers an abundant barbecue to participants and journalists from around the world. It is a private initiative that has done much more than so many public efforts to make the wines of the volcano known and appreciated and to unite, even if only for two days, all the producers.

In Contrada Guardiola, at elevations between 800 and 1000 metres, on 8 hectares of the steepest terracing, Franchetti has planted international vines such as Chardonnay and Petit Verdot, but also Cesanese d'Affile, a typical vine of Lazio. With the latter two red vines, he has been producing his Franchetti since 2005.

TENUTA DELLE TERRE NERE

Searching for Lost Vineyards

SICILY

www.tenutaterrenere.com

His masterpiece is the Etna Rosso Prephylloxera-La Vigna di Don Peppino, obtained from an old vine of Nerello Mascalese that survived the phylloxera epidemic. **Marc de Grazia**, a Florentine, is an importer of Italian wines in the United States. The search for the best vines in the world brought him to Etna where he found what he was looking for: vines capable of wines of great harmony, depth, grace and elegance. In 2000, de Grazia was among the first to buy, together with his brother Sebastian, old abandoned vineyards and bring them back to life. That was the birth of the wine cellar in Contrada Calderara Sottana near Randazzo. The oenological critics and the market soon gave their approval to his work,

making him the pioneer of wines from Etna. The Prephylloxera was presented in 2006 from vines that were 130–140 years old on non-grafted rootstocks, although the first production year, organic from the start, was 2002. The back label calls Etna the "Burgundy of the Mediterranean". It may seem to be a far-fetched comparison, but repeated by others because, in reality, the great complexity and variety of pedoclimatic conditions that are characteristic of Burgundy are to be found all over Etna, albeit in different ways. The vineyards start at an elevation of 400 metres and go upward to 1,000 metres, with temperature variations between day and night that can reach an extension of 30°C in the summer. The volcanic soils were formed by lava over millions of years. Each flow has a mineral composition of its own, and exposition ranges from straight south to straight north. Average rainfall is six to ten times superior to the average for Sicily. These climatic conditions make the harvest one of the latest in Europe.

In addition to the Prephylloxera-La Vigna di Don Peppino, de Grazia produces other Nerello Mascalese crus that are labelled with their vineyard locations. Guardiola, Feudo di Mezzo, Calderara Sottana and Santo Spirito. In 2005, he produced the first Etna white wine from a blend of indigenous vines: Carricante (prevailing), Catarratto, Inzolia, Grecanico and Minnella.

Baptism of the Vineyard, to Save Malvasia di Bosa

It is undoubtedly one of the most extraordinary wines of Sardinian and Italian oenology, but unknown to the public. The production zone defined in the protocol is ample, but the greatest concentration is in the Magomadas, Modolo, Tresnuraghes and Bosa valleys. The total vineyard surface of this Malvasia is less than 100 hectares, of which only about 20 for production and bottling. Many of the vineyards are limited to micro vinification for individual families. The first production protocol issued in 1972 provided for at least two years ageing in wood. However, in the local tradition Malvasia wine was sold from the spring after the harvest. With the variations introduced in 2011, the protocol now provides for production of amabile and sweet spumante, Riserva and straw wine types. This completes a range much closer to the tradition, particularly with regard to the amabile and sweet versions. The dry type has few enthusiasts and as it ages, the organoleptic characteristics are very similar to Vernaccia di Oristano. It apparently came from Greece and has been present on the island since the fifth century AD. The farmers care for their vines like gardens and are true to traditions. Even today, the vine is baptised by dampening the winemaker's head, and the terrain where the first vine is planted, with the same wine he intends to produce. This is a fertility rite to wish good production to the vine and prosperity to the producer. Today, production is in the hands of very few growers with very scattered areas of vines that total no more than 7–8 hectares in all.

The producers are: **Angelo Angioi** in Magomadas, **F.lli Porcu** in Modolo and **Zarelli Vini** in Magomadas.

The vineyards are distributed as follows: in the Magomadas, Modolo, Tresnuraghes and Bosa valleys, in Oristano province. Soils are mainly calcareous and dry, with vines cultivated at various elevations between 30 and 250 metres, close to the sea.

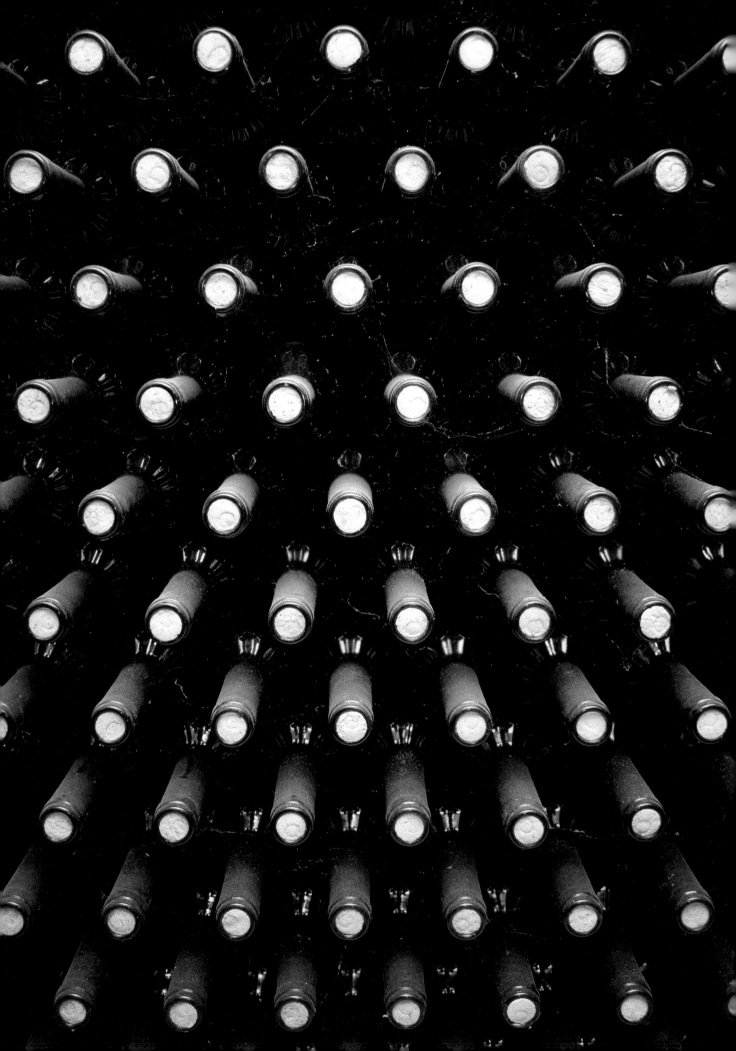

The Current Decade

Up-and-coming: Ideas for the Future, while Italian Cuisine Is the World's Favourite

The most advanced agricultural enterprises focus on marketing and communication: intrinsic value represents one-third of a product; the remaining two-thirds consist of marketing and strategy.

Vinitaly 2014 introduced Vinitalybio, transforming niche wines into trend wines. They understood that oenological expertise and techniques can only help to achieve the objectives without hindering, or worse, denying them. The proof is that many oenologists assist organic vineyards, a welcome sign that the wars of credos based on ideologies are over. These factors represent added value to the appeal of Italian wines on the market.

The fortieth anniversary of the Italian wine renaissance, which still has an enormous untapped potential in its unique heritage of indigenous vines, demonstrated that the vineyards and wine cellars needed new ideas and not ideological infighting.

Italian cuisine was a universal success and was expanding exponentially even in countries where Italians were not present. The cuisine and food specialities continued to be strategic references for Italian wines in the conquest of new markets.

Unlike other countries, the Italian wine sector has the greatest presence of women in the world. This ensures that young people stay in the business and guarantee its future. The presence of women also continues to turn out ideas and oenological projects linked to quality tourism, another true resource for Italy.

The family business, so heartily condemned and derided by superficial economists, has demonstrated that it is the most congenial business model for producing quality wines where long-term vision, sustained by solid assets, are essential. This has allowed for intense appreciation even of the small estates that form the productive backbone of Italian viticulture.

"Large and small producers have always gotten along together and they have even integrated their efforts. The small wineries make up for the deficits in the proposals of larger enterprises. More importantly, small businesses stimulate important impulses. They lead the way in tourism and promote innovation. For example, organic and biodynamic wines were the result of small producers who needed to distinguish themselves," as Angelo Gaja said.

Below, twenty-one testimonials about the Italian wine renaissance, as it continues. *W.F.*

Profile of Young Winemakers

According to Nomisma Wine Monitor and Agia-Cia (the young entrepreneurs association of the Italian confederation of farmers), there are about 24,000 young Italian winemakers and the businesses of these young entrepreneurs are growing, in proportion, twice as much as those of seniors and with half the credit. They use the web and social media to promote their bottles inside and outside the national borders and they study marketing.

These new winemakers are facilitating a generational switch that is not making much headway in Italy and even in Europe, where only 7.5% of the producers are under-35. Thus, even though Italy can boast of leadership results in the sector (second-ranked producer and first-ranked exporter in terms of volume, in the world), and has over 385,000 farms with vineyards and 63,000 vinification companies, only 3–4% of company owners are under-40.

The profile of young winemakers? They are between 25 and 36 years of age and have a medium/high level of education (75% have a secondary school diploma, 15% a university degree). They speak English and over 90% have excellent familiarity with the web. In eight out of ten cases, they connect to the Internet daily. In five of ten cases, they use the web to promote their products, enabling them to meet their customers and expand their clientele. Furthermore, they can use social networks to conduct market surveys in order to understand and anticipate the tastes and needs of buyers, to orient their offers accordingly. Sixty percent acquired the family business, while more than half conduct multifunctional business activities. *M.B.*

OTTIN

Culture of Mountain Wines

VALLE D'AOSTA
www.ottinvini.it

Elio Ottin left his job as a public servant, a technician for the regional institutions in Val d'Aosta, to become a winegrower in 2007. His mountain man culture resounds in every glass and every bottle reflects the fatigue of heroic viticulture. He calls his care for the vines "the true tradition" that depends on copper, sulphur and alga treatments to stimulate defences. On the shields, in a battle of wines that deserves complete tastings in any case, Petite Arvine (perhaps the winegrower's favourite vine) of 2012 engenders voluptuous drinking with its notes of alpine grasses and citrus fruits. The taste is fresh, harmonious and balanced. Torrette Superiore of 2011 is just as successful: above a base of extraordinarily refined tannins, an olfactory veil of spices and underbrush. A beautiful acidic verve on the palate that expands and lingers. Fumin and Pinot Noir are also very fine.

LA RAIA

Steiner in Gavi

PIEDMONT
www.la-raia.it

The **Rossi Cairo family** developed a full-fledged project when, in 2003, they created a way of thinking based on the principles of Steiner's philosophy for a classic farm enclosure near Alessandria, even before developing their winegrowing activity. Of the 180 contiguous hectares comprising the estate, only slightly more than 30 are vineyards. They also grow vegetables and grains, and dedicate space to animals and a nursery. Piero Ballario and Lorenzo Castelli provide the technical consulting to preserve fruit integrity. The Pisè 2011 is splendid with its admirable fusion of grassy notes, citrus aromas and sea breezes. Extensive progression on the palate, lingering with notes of bergamot. A wine that grows, as the greatest do, when the bottle is open. A good reason for a stop at Monterotondo di Novi Ligure.

VIGNE MARINA COPPI

Champions beyond Bikes

PIEDMONT
www.vignemarinacoppi.com

This young enterprise was founded in 2003 in Castellania, a town near Tortona where Fausto Coppi was born. It is named for **Marina**, the first child of the cycling champion, but the manager is his grandson **Francesco**. He took a degree in law, but has a great passion for country life. They have a few hectares on the hills characterised by marl stone such as that found in the Langhe of Barolo at Sant'Agata Fossili. That is why there is also a small Nebbiolo vineyard. Most of the terrains are dedicated to indigenous vines of lower Piedmont such as Barbera, Croatina, Favorita, Freisa and Timorasso. Their work ethic is respectful of nature; the artisan production is all linked to the family history. Fausto, a single-variety wine obtained from Timorasso, has great personality. The Barbera, from the fresher Sant'Andrea to the more complex Castellania, are interesting. Finally, the I Grop cru is produced with the grapes of an old vineyard and the wine ages in oak casks.

DIRUPI

Chiavennasca by Choice

LOMBARDY
www.dirupi.com

Dirupi is decidedly a rising star on the Italian viticultural panorama.

It is a young and dynamic company, hardly surprising given the young age of the owners, graduates of the University of Milan. The wine cellar is in Ponte in Valtellina in a fascinating and historical building.

As might be expected, Dirupi processes mostly the Nebbiolo vine, known locally as Chiavennasca, with which they create a range of very characteristic local wines, like the colours on a painter's palette.

There are fifteen vineyard lots from which the farm obtains the grapes destined for wine making. In particular, the organic vineyard in the territory of the town Tresivio, is used to produce their banner wine, Sforzato di Valtellina, with admirable expertise.

MAMETE PREVOSTINI

Home, Climate, Wine

LOMBARDY
www.mameteprevostini.com

Mamete Prevostini was one of the promoters of the Valtellina renaissance. This is the third generation dedicated to agriculture that had even acquired a *crotto*, a typical cellar for conservation of agricultural products, successively transformed by Mamete into a restaurant.

In 1996, he acquired the first vineyard, Sommarovina, in the Sassella zone. In 2012, the winery obtained the first "Casa Clima Wine" certification in Lombardy.

When possible, the vineyards have been replanted to follow the hill contour lines where high value added Nebbiolo clones were planted.

The estate owns 10 hectares and processes the grapes from another 15 managed by conferrers under his guidance, which allows him to produce about 160,000 bottles a year.

The first label of Prevostini can only be Sassella Sommarovina, produced principally on the vine and monitored year by year in the cellar depending on the quality of the harvest.

PERLA DEL GARDA

The Versions of Lugana

LOMBARDY
www.perladelgarda.it

Giovanna and **Ettore Prandini** launched their gauntlet to Lonato del Garda in 2006, building a wine cellar with an important architectural character and challenging themselves to raise the level of quality with respect to the district of Lugana where the family has its roots.

The Brescia shore of the Benaco and Trebbiano di Lugana (or Turbiana) has today acquired renewed fame for a range of wines from still to sparkling. The Lugana Madre Perla 2011 is tantalising, not to be missed with its rich orange aromas. Also citron, grapefruit peel and hints of sugared almonds to soften the wine as it surrounds the palate. Other wines also growing by leaps and bounds.

HARTMANN DONÀ

Technique and Love

ALTO ADIGE
www.hartmanndona.it

A famous oenologist, with long experience at the Cantina di Terlano, **Hartmann Donà** began to make wine from his own grapes in 2000. The fundamentals, which he studied at the University of Geisenheim in Germany, are not used to produce mechanically perfect wines, but are

integrated with an agricultural approach to sustainability and very low environmental impact. From his wine cellar in Cerme he sends out wines with proud personalities and character, of incontestable expressive purity. The minerality of the available soils is enhanced by the hand of the interpreter who faithfully reflects the characteristics. Among the more recent presentations, note of merit for the Alto Adige Pinot Bianco 2012, discrete and elegant as it has developed. Attention always to the Pinot Noir for its charming exposition.

VILLA PARENS

Doctor no!

FRIULI VENEZIA GIULIA
www.villaparens.com

Vittorio Puiatti was one of the founders of oenology in Friuli Venezia Giulia. His son **Giovanni** is also an oenologist and has followed in his father's footsteps.

Although the opportunity of the moment led him successively to transfer the company to the Andelini group, the call and passion for wine have always been a part of his DNA. So it was in 2013 that together with his sister Elisabetta he founded Villa Parens near Farra d'Isonzo with 6 hectares of vineyards near Ruttars in the Collio zone (*parens*, in Latin means "parents").

The brand motto describes the project: "There is no future without the past," as Giovanni says. This continues and develops his father's philosophy, enhancing its peculiarity.

Giovanni is a purist, but in a different way than the purists of white grape maceration. He combats ageing in wood and drafted his own code, which he called the "Puiatti Method. Doctor no", where he set down the principles of

his oenological choices: no maceration on the skins for white wines, no ageing on the lees, no malolactic fermentation for white wines, no use of wood for all wines, no sugar residues, no to alcohol content of more than 12.5°C.

Giovanni says: "Man is the protagonist, but without technology the master's work would remain unfinished". His wines are essential, refined and elegant but with simplicity "as nature makes them".

The wines of reference are Blanc de Noir Brut Millesimato, Sauvignon Ruttars and Pinot Nero Ruttars.

PODERE LE BONCIE

At the Head of Naturals

TUSCANY
www.leboncie.it

Giovanna Morganti dedicates little of her time to participation in the flamboyant wine circus. Instead, she is always interested in the search for the most natural expression of Sangiovese in Chianti near San Felice in the town of Castelnuovo Berardenga. She learned the first rudiments from master taster Giulio Gambelli. Vinification in small open vats led her Chianti Classico Le Trame to guide the Tuscan fleet of the so-called natural wines.

TERENZI

The Morellino Man

TUSCANY
www.terenzi.eu

The **Terenzi siblings** (Francesca Romana, Balbino and Federico, children of founder Florio) wasted no time when they took action in the land considered the "promised land" of Tuscany (meaning Maremma), in the inebriating atmosphere at the end of the previous

millennium. The property is almost 60 hectares, sloping down from Scansano toward Talamone. Their consultant is the well-prepared Giuseppe Caviola. Morellino di Scansano Riserva Madrechiesa, with its extraordinarily juicy fruity structure of strawberries and blueberries, is the winery's first label. Dynamic and unleashed to the palate, it lingers with a lovely after-taste of sage and laurel. Easy to drink and far from the muscular stereotypes that have misled many a producer in the vicinity of Grosseto. A fine example of how delicate and attractive a Sangiovese can be even at this latitude: meritorious rigour with regard to the type and variety.

TENUTA LA STAFFA

New Voices in the White Wine World

THE MARCHES
www.lastaffa.com

The Castelli di Jesi district, as polyphonic as can be found but famous for the virtues of one of the most interesting Italian white cultivars

(Verdicchio, obviously), proposes new and intriguing voices. **Riccardo Baldi**'s well-grooved La Staffa vineyards are easy to identify along the road that unites Staffolo to Cupramontana near Contrada Castellaretta. La Rincrocca Superiore, a wine aged in cement, is a Verdicchio with noteworthy tasting tension.

TREBOTTI

Sustainability Is Science

LAZIO
www.trebotti.it

Francesco Maria Botti, a lawyer in Roma, his wife **Giulia** and their three children just over thirty (Bernardo, Clarissa and Ludovico Maria) acquired the vineyards above Oasi d'Alviano. That was in the year 2003. The winery would be called Trebotti (three barrels) in honour of the

three children (Botti by birth). Their mother had noble viticultural origins, considering that her uncle was Luigi Manzoni, creator of the Manzoni 6.0.13 breed. Ludovico, the younger son, got a degree in agrarian science. The winery focuses on organic farming and sustainable processes. The wine cellar is underground to reduce impact on the landscape and for internal conditioning. It is situated at the top of the hill to take advantage of gravity during grape processing.
Almost indigenous wines: Violone, Sangiovese and Aleatico (the Bludom Passito is excellent). Grechetto and Trebbiano for white wines. A single exception: the 3S Manzoni Bianco (Pinot bianco and Riesling Renano), without sulphites. The total production total is about 20,000 bottles.

CIRO PICARIELLO

Natural Style

CAMPANIA
www.ciropicariello.com

Ciro Picariello and Rita Guerriero, with the assistance of their children, deserve mention for their contribution to consolidating the fame of one of the most important Italian white wines,

Fiano di Avellino. Montefredane and Summonte (where the wine cellar is located), with their terrains at an elevation of almost 600 metres, have turned out to be particularly adapted for this variety. With a completely natural approach (meaning low environmental impact, essential vinification processing with elevation in steel and malolactics reduced to a minimum), their Fiano di Avellino expresses a strong and unmistakeable character. The 2011 harvest came after a difficult year, but offers the usual profile of smoky and nutty notes that are the imprint of this wine. Creamy and persistent, it suggests that it has a great potential for ageing. It is accompanied along the way by a Greco di Tufo that acquires personality year after year.

NANNI COPÈ

The Sabbia di Sopra and Critics

CAMPANIA
nannicope.it

Nanni (born Giovanni Ascione), whose underground wine cellar is just across the way from his home, shook the whole world of critics with his first and only wine in production, Sabbie di Sopra Il Bosco. This was just about the 2008 harvest. The name refers to the geological and pedoclimatic conditions of the so-called Caiazzo sandstone where the lot of the property is located. It was planted with Pallagrello Nero and a few vines of Aglianico, trained for modified arbours, about thirty years ago. Casavecchia, the remainder completing the blend, comes from the Scarrupata a Pontelatone vineyard. Grace and taste go arm-in-arm in a wine that has taken a step back from the super-extraction mentality that characterised the super wines of the debut. The year 2012 is astonishing by definition, with great agility and juice. Lavender, pink pepper and earthy tones mingle in a harmonious dance.

CERATTI

Precious Wine with Ancient Methods

CALABRIA
www.agriturismoceratti.com

The Greco di Bianco DOC is a tiny and exclusive protocol (a few thousand bottles) for a vine that came with the Greeks in the eighth century BC. Pasquale and Umberto Ceratti (father and son) have their vineyards along the Ionian

coastline of Calabria. Their Greco has flashes of amber yellow with notes of orange blossoms, citrus and tropical fruits. A velvety taste that is sweet, but never cloying. The grapes are cultivated on lime-rich mudstone or marl. Umberto, today director of this estate with its attractive farm holiday accommodations, follows antique methods. The grapes harvested between mid-September and mid-October are dried in the sun on racks to a weight loss of about 50%. After delicate mechanical pressing, the must ferments in the barrels for twenty-four months before bottling. He also produces Greco di Bianco Passito, aged four months in *barrique* and Mantonico Locride Passito.

POLVANERA

The Exploit of Primitivo

PUGLIA
www.cantinepolvanera.it

If the Primitivo of Gioia del Colle today is enjoying a season of great notoriety, it is undoubtedly thanks to this estate and its exploits, the fruit of **Filippo Cassano**'s

meticulous work. On the 70 hectares constituting the vineyard park, old bush vines cohabit with new plantings on 30 of these hectares. Cassano's ability consists of wedding alcoholic content and the inborn power of his wines with heretofore unknown zest and sapidity. Taste it to believe it: Primitivo 17 (speaking of percentage) 2010. It has a typical blanket of dark fruit that is justly in contrast with the gusts of Mediterranean bush that uplift it. A glass of knock-me-down beauty, the result of very low yield. Coming in the near future, Fiano Minutolo, a white wine with juicy aromas of tropical fruit.

VESPA VIGNAIOLI PER PASSIONE – FUTURA 14

Winery Door to Door

PUGLIA
www.vespavignaioli.it

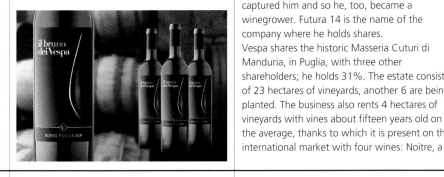

Bruno Vespa, the famous television journalist (on the show *Porta a Porta*, which means "Door to Door") and tireless author of bestsellers, also writes a regular column about wine in *Panorama*, which used to be Veronelli's, the same from which he took his inspiration forty years earlier. Evidently, he is not simply an unequalled television master of ceremonies, but also a refined connoisseur of excellent wines. In 2011, the enchantment of producing wines captured him and so he, too, became a winegrower. Futura 14 is the name of the company where he holds shares.
Vespa shares the historic Masseria Cuturi di Manduria, in Puglia, with three other shareholders; he holds 31%. The estate consists of 23 hectares of vineyards, another 6 are being planted. The business also rents 4 hectares of vineyards with vines about fifteen years old on the average, thanks to which it is present on the international market with four wines: Noitre, a

Classic method spumante rosé (three years on the yeasts) from pure Negroamaro grapes; Bruno dei Vespa 2013, a blend of indigenous vines based on Primitivo; Rosso del Vespa 2013 (Primitivo Salento) from pure Primitivo grapes; and Raccontami 2012 (Primitivo di Manduria Riserva), from pure Primitivo grapes. In spring 2015, another wine was added to the offering: Bianco dei Vespa 2014, from pure Fiano.
A famous name such as Bruno Vespa will certainly contribute to the take-off of Puglia, a region that must still express its enormous viticultural potential.
The wines are curated by the sure and steady hand of Riccardo Cotarella, who has succeeded in his intent to make wines with such a high alcoholic content so easy to drink. The first Futura 14 bottles tasted confirm the expectations.

GRACI

Exploring Etna

SICILY
www.graci.eu

The reference is to Etna, and we begin with a protagonist we might call a rediscovery rather than a newcomer. **Alberto Aiello Graci**, although very young, has climbed rapidly to the top in this extremely competitive corner of the world. White or red, it makes no difference to him, having already demonstrated that he knows what to do regardless of the field of practice. The most surprising force of communication in the last round of tasting was

the Etna Bianco Arcuria 2011, a Carricante with overflowing minerality, where the pulp of the fruit, in its citrus fullness, restricts and integrates the acid blade of the wine to perfection. Inspires great enthusiasm with its freshness and intensity. Those who prefer red will find joy in the Etna Contrada Arcuria Quota 600 2011, an exquisitely refined single-variety Nerello Mascalese.

OCCHIPINTI

Female Way to Natural

SICILY

www.agricolaocchipinti.it

When she was just over thirty, she rose quickly to international notoriety as the protagonist of a documentary and a book. Today, **Arianna Occhipinti** is a real star in the world of "natural wine". This experience began only in 2004 after she completed her studies in oenology in Milan, arousing great curiosity among the wisest consumers in Vittoria and the rest of Ragusa. Good agriculture and minimal intervention in the cellar bring light to every label in production. No accident that today her Frappato is on the wine lists at the worldliest tables of Parisian neo-bistrots. The 2011 is almost overwhelming with its blossom analogies, herbs and red fruits. Energy and lithe grace expressed in wine. The right concentration, bright but fresh. There are new projects on the horizon, with the acquisition of new property.

PALA

"Slow" Emergent

SARDINIA

www.pala.it

Calling this winery, founded in 1950, a "rising star" should not be taken for a mistake. It is rather an exemplary story of what might be a good way to develop Italian viticulture. Today, the grapes that **Salvatore Pala** cultivated and then sold to others are vinified directly by **Mario**

and children **Elisabetta**, **Maria Antonietta** and **Massimiliano**. They reinforced their decision by recently acquiring a vineyard of 37 hectares in Sernobi. It will join forces with the historical nucleus in the fine territory of Serdiana. Their Cannonau Riserva 2011, at a price that is accessible to all, turns out to be a wine that can teach how to rediscover tastes with an antique allure while being extremely up to date. It ages in large barrels, announces fresh firm fruit (blackberries), coats the palate without saturating it and lingers on very elegant notes of mild tobacco. Do not bypass the whites, capable like the banner wine Entemari, to age for a long time. It is a variegated selection, where structure and the taste project go together perfectly.

The New System of Wine

Paolo Benvenuti, Mario Busso, Walter Filiputti
with Magda Antonioli, Roger Sesto

In the early 1970s, the organoleptic quality of wine represented 95% of its value, and so a bottle of wine was virtually full. Today, the bottle is 70% empty.

Quality, which modern consumers take for granted, represents only 30% of the value. The rest consists of image, communication, language, brand, market positioning and sales policy, relationships, distribution, culture, territory, hospitality and more.

It is surprising that the new wines of Italy have spawned so many related activities and profoundly resuscitated others that already existed. The language of wine, wine tourism and the concept of territory are typical examples.

Many of these positive contaminations have already been studied. There are others that deserve attention and, together with the former, constitute the universe with wine at its centre.

Wine Guides in Italy

Italy is probably the country in the world where wine guides have played the most important role in spreading the image of wine. Naturally, oenological yearbooks also exist elsewhere. However, in the Anglo-Saxon world, such reviews appear prevalently in specialised periodicals. These include *The Wine Spectator*, *The Wine Advocate* and *Wine Enthusiast* in the United States, *Decanter* in Great Britain and *La Revue de Vin de France* in France.

The phenomenon of the guides appeared in Italy in the 1970s following the lead of Luigi Veronelli, the first true critic of oenology and gastronomy in the *Belpaese*. His books, *I Vini di Veronelli* in the late 1980s and *Vini d'Italia* published by Gambero Rosso and Slow Food, were the reference books for the Italian peninsula for a long time. In the second half of the 1990s, when the wine trend was most intense, many other wine yearbooks began to appear. They were, in chronological order: *L'Annuario dei Migliori Vini Italiani* (LM Editore), *I Vini d'Italia* (Gruppo Editoriale L'Espresso), *Bibenda* (Bibenda Editore, in collaboration with AIS) and *Slow Wine* (Slow Food Editore). Each had its own philosophy and a distinct approach to the interpretation of viticulture and tasting, although not always explicit and occasionally too subtle. There were also specialised guidebooks on specific themes. The leading example

was *Vinibuoni d'Italia* (Touring Editore), which focused on the evaluation of the wines produced from indigenous Italian vines.

Such an ample variety of publications could not fail to impact diffusion of Italian oenology. In the years of transition to the new millennium when wine became a fashion, not to say a fad, but information channels were still inadequate and Internet was not yet available to all, the guidebooks were almost the only means of orientation in a complex world. Myriad of denominations, sub-zones, typologies, producers, price ranges and distributive channels was inherently confusing. The classifications conferred by the different yearbooks, in particular the "3 glasses" of Gambero Rosso, became true reference points. Wine tourists from Italy and from abroad visited the wineries with the guides in hand, searching for prize-winning wines or the best quality-to-price ratio.

Today, with the diffusion of numerous online publications and the wine blogger phenomenon, the informative role of guidebooks has changed. They are no longer the one and only point of reference for neophytes and enthusiasts, but rather an accessory and a starting point for greater insight into themes of personal interest via other immediately accessible media sources. They are no less central, but the reader makes different use of them. The reader is no longer assuaged by the fact that a wine has won many awards. Today, attention is directed to smaller, emerging wineries in less well-known territories that offer attractive prices. Environmental compatibility, organic and biodynamic farming attract attention because they have a social function that goes beyond production. Wine seekers want to know where they can purchase specific labels and which have the best quality-to-price ratio. Today, competitions for the mere purpose of awarding prizes have no role any longer, and they are no longer the focal point of modern guidebooks. The reader is searching for other information. *R.S.*

Slow Food

Founded as a local association, only a few years were necessary to transform Carlo Petrini's organisation into a worldwide phenomenon. It had taken on a complex and daring challenge: to promote sustainable agricultural models adapted to each specific local reality all around the world.

Together with Luigi Veronelli and Gambero Rosso, Slow Food is the institution that has probably made the greatest contribution to renewing Italian viticulture. It has also promoted and protected gastronomic heritage and conserved agrarian assets in Italy (later also internationally).

Carlo Petrini founded the Arcigola association in Bra in 1986 and organised its first congress in Siena in 1988. The first edition of *Vini d'Italia* was published in the same year and it went on to become the best-selling oenological guide in Italy. In 1990, the International Slow Food movement was founded in Paris and drafted the statement of its mission. The first congress met the same year in Venice and the publication of *Osterie d'Italia* marked the debut of the Slow Food publishing house. The association began its international expansion in 1992. In 1994, the group organised "Milano Golosa", a trial run for what was to become the "Salone del Gusto di Torino". Many of the fundamental initiatives soon followed: launching the *Slow* magazine, the *Arca del Gusto* project, the start of educational activities with the "Dire fare gustare, Cheese" conference.

In 1999, Slow Food launched a public petition in defence of Italian oenological and gastronomic heritage, requesting a revision of the European HACCP regulation. In 2000, the "Presidi" project was launched. The Slow Food Prize was constituted to defend biodiversity. In 2001, the association launched the "No GMO Wine" campaign against sale in Europe of genetically modified vines. In 2004, FAO acknowledged Slow Food as a non-profit organisation with which to establish a relationship of collaboration. After renovation, the Pollenza agency (where the first University of Gastronomic Sciences has its seat) was inaugurated. *Slow Fish*, a review dedicated to sustainable fishing, was founded. The first edition of "Terra Madre" was held during the fifth edition of "Salone del Gusto di Torino". In 2007, Slow Food joined the Italy Europe GMO-free Coalition. The first edition of "Vignerons d'Europe", a meeting for all the winegrowers on the continent, was organised in Montpellier. In 2008, the first Slow Food on Film international festival of cinema and food was held in Bologna. As the Terra Madre project quickly developed, Slow Food and the Slow Food Foundation for Biodiversity (a non-profit organisation) inaugurated "Earth Markets", an international network of farmer markets, in the city of Montevarchi. The first edition of "Eurogusto" was held in 2009, and on 10 December of the same year, "Mother Earth Day" made its international debut. The second "Mother Earth Day", held 10 December 2010, celebrated over 1,100 events in 160 countries with the goal of collecting funds to create 1,000 gardens in Africa.

Slow Food and Wine: The Oenological Presidia
With specific reference to the wine sector, the Slow Food oenological Presidia, whose members belong to the Vignerons d'Europe network, exemplify winemaking dedicated to protection of agricultural territories that suffer particular threats and/or are difficult to manage, in order to safeguard the heritage represented by the vineyards. The biodiversity of vines must be maintained while rejecting monoculture and focusing on all the natural and traditional elements of the zone including trees, animals and typical cultivations. Wine production must enter and adapt to the original agrarian environment and conserve the footprint of traditional agriculture by applying the systems of cultivation, the layout and the plant forms of the territory. Production must be conducted on sites with a history of viticulture and only on appropriate parcels. The vines for cultivation must be identified with the territory. Defending the biodiversity of the vines and indigenous varieties is an objective of the Presidia project. *R.S.*

Women and Wine
After years in the background, today women have important roles in the viticultural chain of production in Italy. The data is surprising, because women now occupy key roles of responsibility and are recognised for their management and leadership in a sector that was controlled almost exclusively by men until the 1980s.

The point of no return was the foundation of the Italian association of the women of wine (Associazione Nazionale Le Donne del Vino) by Tuscan producer Elisabetta Tognana in 1988. The role and presence of women is greater today as a result of the work of the association. Women are more conscious of their entrepreneurial and technical capacities. The number of women qualified as agronomists, oenologists, oenotechnicians, sommeliers and wine shop managers continues to grow.

The data is emblematic. In Italy, women manage one in four of all wine production enterprises. This is the best result on the continent: 25% against 10% in the rest of Europe. Women also manage communication in 80% of the companies, and 92% are responsible for farmhouse hospitality. Reception in the wine cellar is a key moment in the narration of wine and the fascination it engenders. Women of wine have also interpreted it through their ability to develop new forms of relationships with consumers and marketing initiatives.

Their sensitivity leads women to focus their efforts on concepts and objectives that can be decisive. These include developing a new agriculture that is closely linked to the territory, protecting the environment, favouring quality production and resolving social issues. These women have moved from the fields and vineyards to the market, bringing their creativity and new ideas to bear, but without losing sight of their origins.

These are the clearly scientific conclusions drawn by Andrea Rea in his book, *Scenari di Marketing del vino. Una prospettiva al femminile* (Franco Angeli, Milan 2009). The testimony of many of the protagonists supports his analysis in the book.

While they all refer to the difficulties of competing on the marketplace given the unfavourable economic context of recent years, they also mention some strong potential levers for growth, such as identification with the territory. The most interesting aspect is the protection and growth of diversity, which becomes added value in communication. All agree on the need to preserve this element by drawing on tradition. Identity must have a new mode of presentation that will catalyse fertile interaction among the past, present and future.

As a whole, some extremely interesting data sustains these precepts. The wines and foods of Italy rank second among the reasons for travel to this country and first among the reasons for satisfaction of tourists who do visit Italy. Data is even more positive if the whole sector of Italian wines and gastronomy is considered. Italy is the only country in the world offering almost 200 products of protected origin (DOP or IGP) and around 500 wines classified DOC, DOCG or IGT. There are al-

so around 4500 traditional food products (PAT). In summer 2008, a decree specifically acknowledged this heritage as an expression of Italian cultural heritage. Almost two-thirds of the Italian population (63%) consider food, wine and good cooking the true symbol of "Made in Italy", far ahead of culture and art (24%), fashion (8%), technology (3%) and sport (2%). Consumers are expressing a strong desire to know the origins, production sites, history, traditions, and the contributions of handiwork and personality in a wine, cheese, salt-cured meats or sweet conserves that make their way to the dining table. In response to this demand, women in wine have succeeded in creating an unequalled synergistic system of wineries and food artisans. Almost all wine enterprises managed by women have hospitality structures to satisfy tourists' expectations, thus consolidating the cultural integration between the territory and the wine and gastronomical proposals. Wineries that open to the public obtain over 20% of their revenues from direct sales to tourists (with a strong upward trend) and this has an agreeable effect on cash flow, too. Approximately 50% of wineries with a proven or potential vocation for wine tourism have invested in improving their hospitality structures by introducing refreshment points, tasting rooms, museums, incoming services and tourist information points. Finally, another important fact is that almost half of the revenues in Italy from wine sales are produced by the part of the market managed by women. *M.B.*

The Wine Tourism Movement

The wine tourism movement was founded in 1993 thanks to the intuition of Donatella Cinelli Colombini, winegrower in Montalcino and first chairman of the association she guided until 2011. This non-profit organisation unites approximately one thousand wineries.

Promotion of wine culture through visits to wine production sites is its primary objective. It also sustains growth of tourism flows to all areas of Italy with strong viticultural character, and strives to expand the image and economic perspectives, including job opportunities, in wine territories.

Its most important and historical landmark event is "Cantine aperte", celebrated on the last Sunday of May every year since 1993. The idea of Colombini not only added value to

wine and food tourism, but also radically modified the role of the wine cellar. The first to perceive this change were the producers themselves who had considered it off-limits to strangers, a sort of catacomb where the secret rites of wine took place, a situation that left space for suspicion and fears of mysterious concoctions.

"Cantine aperte" was a declaration of maturity and the intention to collaborate, which united and led the sector to exponential growth. Subsequently, intelligent recovery of many agrarian homes lent new splendour to country hamlets and attracted the attention of tourists to the surrounding territories, undoubtedly among the most fascinating and best preserved of Italy.

Today Colombini declares: "Wine tourism produces an annual turnover of between 3 and 5 billion Euro [*depending on how the turnover of allied industries is calculated*]. It encourages foreigners to consider wine and food among the principal reasons for visiting Italy. It involves 21,000 wine cellars that make direct sales to visitors . . . The sector of wine and food artisans has enormous growth potential and is already the second ranked motive of satisfaction for foreign tourists who make return visits to Italy. Considering revenues, the combination of wine and food accounts for 11% of foreign tourists' expenditures, approximately eight billion Euro per year."

A comment by Attilio Scienza deserves attention on this point because it helps to broaden the scope of analysis with regard to wine and its territory.

"Two new expressions have now entered the vocabulary of today's cultivators: environmental compatibility and multiple functionality. The first identifies a viticulture capable of producing healthy grapes of high quality, including cultural biodiversity and the landscape. Multiple functionality defines the role of environmentally compatible viticulture in the economic and social context of the territory, in integration with other productive activities. To achieve this, it is necessary for local institutions, the extended chain of supply of the wine industry, and research and training for protection and development of the environment to identify an approach that they can all share . . . Thus, the presentation of the producer must accompany presentation of the product, revealing how the

product is formed. The primary intangible element of interest to the consumer is the credibility and trustworthiness of the winegrower. A new strategy of identifying the producer is necessary, one that will encompass cultural dominions where the landscape is an integral part of the emotional content of a wine, together with its historical background, forming a unique expression of the territory that is circumscribed and recognisable. To think that wines are born and continue to live for centuries with the benefit of local, ongoing procedures has a very reassuring effect on consumers."

Magda Antonioli, associate professor of economy and co-ordinator of the masters degree in the economy of tourism at Bocconi University in Milan, expands the view of wine (and food) tourism with these considerations: "The appeal of Italian resources and the excellence of the Italian wine and food heritage, with one of the richest varieties in the world, represents a very strong force of attraction for international demand. This accounts for its progressive growth over time. Today, there are about 6 million foodies [*data 2013*] on the move in and toward Italy who wish to enter into a state of communion with the territory by means of its typical and traditional wine and food products . . . Several studies indicate that visitors are progressively abandoning traditional models of tourism that tend to express a practice of one-upmanship [*big city destinations, busy and fashionable resorts at the sea or in the mountains*] and are searching for modalities of tourism that consist of experiences to live in the first person. Tourism becomes an opportunity for acquiring knowledge, insight and encounters. The combination of such lifestyles in the context of new forms of luxury, and the attitudes toward viticultural productions and traditional foods of fine quality, have contributed to the development of wine and food tourism in terms of direct motivation to travel and in connection with other forms of tourism. The quality of the product is no longer associated exclusively with its origin, but, above all, with the context of production for these new, cultural tourists to all effects. Wine and typical products, together with the local cooking itself, thus constitute elements of socialisation and evidence of traditions, culture, lifestyle and 'Made in Italy' for consumers from abroad. These factors are of particular importance on new and potential marketplaces and for top spender consumers. The return, in terms of promotion and knowledge, on purchases made after return to their lands of origin, is very high. Wine and food tourism is one of the most promising forms of cultural tourism on the Italian and international tourism marketplaces. It has the support of strong media communication [*guidebooks, magazines, columnists, fairs, events, etc.*], a vast territorial system of reference [*Italian localities, hamlets, farm holidays, resorts, agrarian homes, B&B, cine-tourism, etc.*] and a new consumer culture oriented to the purchase of wines and fine food. The orientation of the food and agriculture sector is perfectly synchronised with the rest of Europe. The scope is to educate consumers about quality without overlooking the supply chain [*traceability*] and communication . . . Wine and food products, tourist reception and the overall quality of the area constitute distinct levels of quality that will reveal the roots of a product to the visitor and offer a living experience of the environment, not merely the tasting of a speciality dish. In short, a vacation or an excursion will become an experience to remember and not just a buying spree! It is important to remember that this is all depends on the quality of the products, and protection of the territory and its people. These fundamental values sustain the attraction of our lands and regions." *W.F.*

The Cities of Wine

"Città del Vino", or Cities of Wine, was founded in Siena on 21 March 1987. It was the answer of thirty-nine mayors and the supply chain on the territory to the crisis that had crushed the sector. A series of events in the previous twenty years had introduced the ferment that later favoured the birth of new phenomena: introduction of DOC protocols in 1963, abolition of sharecropping in 1964 and the methanol scandal in 1986. The new phenomena accompanied greater attention for the environment, recovery of rural culture and the culture of wine, attention to health and physical wellbeing and the quality of life. The association has gone through a quarter of a century since then, has spoken on behalf of a network of small municipalities and has expanded to include over 150 members. It has sustained the importance of good government for the territories, has represented an ideal tourist and cultural jour-

ney through rural Italy and has been an extraordinary institutional and political experience.

Belonging to the association has always meant an inclination to undertake improvements, and to promote and protect the productive system in harmony with environmental and social sustainability. The new articles of association drafted in 2012 have definitively codified this principle. The municipalities have undertaken a commitment to the Quality Charter of the Cities of Wine and confirmed the validity of the policies implemented by the association through the years. These include the introduction of town planning with territorial planning methodologies, joint city planning policies that are coherent with the territory and community life; the foundation of *Iter Vitis*, the international body that promotes the European Cultural Route of the same name, dedicated to the discovery of the agricultural landscape linked to wine production; organisation of events to promote the culture of wine and rural traditions such as "La Selezione del Sindaco" oenological competition, "Calici di Stelle" events, the "Palio Nazionale delle Botti" and publishing activities; conducting studies and research on crucial themes of the viticulture world, such as indigenous vines and biodiversity, the phenomena of wine and food tourism, road traffic safety, health and diet, archaeology of vines and wines, transmission of know-how and flavours to coming generations, the green economy and many others.

The need to enter new markets, such as the Far East and other emerging areas, has led to the formation of various groups of producers to save on costs and reach critical mass on markets where penetration is still limited. Two of these include some of the most important figures in Italian oenology. *P.B.*

Federazione Italiana dei Vignaioli Indipendenti (FIVI)

The FIVI (Italian Federation of Independent Winegrowers) was founded in 2008 by a few Italian winegrowers encouraged by their French colleagues, already united in a European federation of independent winegrowers (CEVI, Confédération Européenne des Vignerons Indépendants) for many years. National federations were also founded in other European nations. They all depended on the CEVI.

An independent winegrower cultivates his vines, bottles his own wine and sells it under his own responsibility with his name and his own label. He is independent precisely because he personally handles the whole chain, from the vine to the consumer.

The scope of FIVI and CEVI is to represent winegrowers in relations with national and European institutions, protecting their interests and promoting the quality and authenticity of their wines linked to their territories of origin. CEVI participates in vine development policies at the European level and proposes economic measures and legislation in the interests of all European winegrowers.

At the national level in Italy, FIVI achieved legal status in 2002 and is written in the roll of legal persons of domestic importance. The Ministry of Agriculture has also accredited it as a participant in consultations concerning the wine chain of supply and production.

Among the initiatives promoted by FIVI in recent years, those intended to reduce bureaucratic complications of current procedures to reduce the barriers that still exist inside the European common market are particularly important.

It submitted a complete and detailed study of the complex bureaucracy that hinders winegrowers, entitled "Dossier Bureaucracy", with precise proposals to improve the situation. The paper was translated into English and distributed in Europe to all the CEVI member states. The practical solutions for simplification that it contains have inspired the elaboration of a Vine and Wine Act, currently on the agenda of the Agriculture Commission of the Italian Chamber of Deputies.

For several years now, FIVI has also been organising the Independent Winegrowers Market to favour encounters between winegrowers and end consumers. The market takes place at the Piacenza fair and is enjoying increasing success. *W.F.*

Istituto del Vino Italiano di Qualità Grandi Marchi

Alois Lageder, Argiolas, Biondi Santi - Tenuta Greppo, Ca' del Bosco, Carpenè Malvolti, Donnafugata, Gaja, Jermann, Lungarotti, Masi, Marchesi Antinori, Mastroberardino, Michele Chiarlo, Pio Cesare, Rivera, Tasca d'Almerita, Ambrogio e Giovanni Folonari Tenute, Tenuta San Guido and Umani Ronchi:

these nineteen enterprises have written some of the most important pages in the history of the modern oenological renaissance. They are all family-run businesses. A typically Italian choice, it has proven to be quite modern and strong enough to survive the challenges encountered on global markets. These enterprises also share a strong sense of belonging to their territories, the ongoing capacity to renew themselves and to communicate, the maintenance of stringent quality standards and the ability to create and impose a brand. Given these very solid foundations, these businesses decided to found the Istituto del Vino Italiano di Qualità Grandi Marchi (institute of major brand quality Italian wine) in 2004. The desire for collaboration stemmed from the need to be stronger and more incisive in promotional activities, education and marketing of Italian quality wines on worldwide markets. It is therefore not surprising that during its first ten years of activity, members of the institute travelled almost 800,000 kilometres to promote and present Italian wines to the world. In 2014, there were 248 international missions in 18 target nations, almost 50,000 targeted meetings with an equivalent number of operators, buyers and journalists, in addition to hundreds of walk-around tastings, seminars, gala dinners, news conferences, marketing activities and more. Some of the countries touched by these Grandi Marchi initiatives include Russia, India, China, Hong Kong, Taiwan, Korea, Japan, Singapore, Australia, Brazil, Mexico, United States and Canada; and Germany, England and Poland in Europe. The institute makes significant investments in education, as evidenced by collaboration with the prestigious Institute of Masters of Wine of London. In 2009, a programme was launched to grant Italian students access to the difficult course of studies to obtain the Master of Wine title. At the same time, courses and master classes about Italian wines, together with visits to several production areas, were reserved for international students and Masters of Wine who wished to know more about Italian wine. This collaboration was crowned by the organisation of the VII Masters of Wine Symposium held in Florence from 15 to 18 May 2014. Over 400 Masters of Wine, experts and international journalists participated. Piero Antinori, chairman of Grandi Marchi, then followed by Piero Mastroberardino, declared: "We are very honoured that our enterprises and the entire top of the market segment of our typical regional wines has had the opportunity to present itself and the abundance of its territories to the Masters of Wine symposium, organised once every four years and held for the first time in Italy. This is the coronation of the first ten years of activity of the institute and, at the same time, opens new horizons for the future". *W.F.*

Comitato Grandi Cru d'Italia

The Comitato Grandi Cru d'Italia (committee for grand crus of Italy) was founded in 2005 when a group of friends and leading producers, including Paolo Panerai, Piero Antinori and Vittorio Frescobaldi, decided to unite the Italian producers with the highest and most stable levels of quality in a committee. The objective is to protect and augment the prestige of wine producers that have been making wines with the highest ratings for at least twenty years.

The founding members are: Allegrini, Antinori, Argiolas, Arnaldo Caprai, Barone Ricasoli, Bellavista, Bertani, Braida, Ca' del Bosco, Castello d'Albola Zonin, Castello di Volpaia, Col d'Orcia, Conti Zecca, Domini Castellare di Castellina, Donnafugata, Ferrari, Feudi di San Gregorio, Fontodi, Franz Haas, Jacopo Biondi Santi, Leone de Castris, Livio Felluga, Lungarotti, Maculan, Marchesi de' Frescobaldi, Marchesi di Grésy, Marco Felluga, Masciarelli, Mastroberardino, Michele Chiarlo, Pio Cesare, Planeta, San Felice, Tasca d'Almerita, Tenuta San Guido, Tenuta San Leonardo, Tenute di Ambrogio e Giovanni Folonari, and Umani Ronchi.

Of the founding members, the following are promoting members: Domini Castellare di Castellina, Bellavista, Tenute di Ambrogio e Giovanni Folonari, Antinori, Biondi Santi, Tasca d'Almerita, Marchesi de' Frescobaldi, Castello d'Albola Zonin, Castello di Volpaia and Marco Felluga.

An Italian cru is defined as a wine produced on Italian soil, obtained from vinification of indigenous Italian or international grape varieties that the most authoritative Italian and foreign publications and guidebooks have classified at the highest levels of excellence.

Producer members were selected following strict quality criteria, in consideration of the history and tradition of each one in the sector to ensure that they have demonstrated a high degree of reliability over time in the production of the highest quality wines. The concrete implementation of the committee purpose involves some fundamental points of the programme. First of all, public diffusion and adequate knowledge of the specific identity of grand cru producers, by publishing books, organising events and creating a website illustrating the particular characteristics of each one is an essential necessity.

The most glamorous appointment is the dinner gala at Vinitaly where the awards for the best authors and publications in Italy and aboard are assigned. The prize itself emblematically represents a grapevine leaf in silver. Great Italian chefs are called upon to prepare the menu to exalt the grand crus served at the gala.

In 2008, the Committee published *Grandi Cru d'Italia. La storia, i volti, le cantine, le vigne dei migliori vini italiani* with the Electa publishing house in Milan. For its integrity and elegance, this work received the prestigious Prix Gourmand at the book fair in Paris in the category of books about wine. *W.F.*

Auteur Bottles and Labels

Angela De Marco, Maurizio Di Robilant, Walter Filiputti

From Labels to Expressing Talent

The modern history of Italian wine labels dates from 1971 when Silvio Coppola designed the label for Tignanello. Analysis of this milestone label offers the occasion to sketch a bird's-eye view of the factors that contributed to the new and autonomous influence of Italian design on the world of wine.

Although created for a noble family of ancient ancestry, the label had little to do with the dominant castle motif as expressed in France. Instead, it proposed a decidedly new type of language. Great simplicity and refined formal balance represent the canons of a new elegance that is subdued and meticulous. Its essentiality leaves the greatest space for the heart of the message, which was the overwhelming innovation of the production process and the product itself (the introduction of *barriques* for Sangiovese and Bordolese wine blending . . .). This innovation would reveal new qualitative standards and open the way, with other courageous wines, to the "renaissance of Italian wine".

The link between the radical product transformation and its authors reveals other significant factors. The relationship between the two pioneers, Silvio Coppola and Piero Antinori for example, represents an important characteristic of how Italians handle projects. The best examples of "Made in Italy", from fashion to industrial design, stem from the successful encounters and productive interactions between designer and producer, creative genius and enlightened entrepreneur inclined to experiment.

Another interesting and distinctive aspect of many Italian projects, whether for labels or not, is the curriculum of the designer. Silvio Coppola, an architect and designer, had worked side by side with Adriano Olivetti, an entrepreneur and a humanist, and encountered the label project in a casual way. He brought a transdisciplinary approach to the problem: spatial awareness, aesthetic sobriety, technical conscience, artistic sensibility and technological competence. This approach enveloped the business entirely and treated the label as an element of a greater three-dimensional representation. This explains his reticence about being considered "the wine label architect" and his unwillingness to design others. The involvement of Luigi Veronelli enabled him to overcome these inhibitions for Russiz Superiore by Marco Felluga

Among the many trades of Silvio Coppola, he was also the exclusive book cover designer for Giangiacomo Feltrinelli. Veronelli himself says he distracted Coppola from that trade because of his ability to "represent, in a single image from the start, the climax of texts uniting commitment and culture". As Veronelli wrote: "Nothing is more like a book than a wine". And we add, nothing is more like a publishing house than a winery.

The experience of Tignanello, or the other Super Tuscans (just to mention the most famous heroes), not only ferried Italy into its own oenological revolution, but traced the evolutionary line for the image of Italian wines, in advance of other European countries, especially France. In the 1980s and 1990s, the thrust of the so-called "new world" of wine – California wines and Southern hemisphere wines, respectively – gave the European producers a profound shake-up with their high-impact labels and calm savvy use of marketing and communications. The sequence of revolutionary domestic projects followed by the initiatives of transoceanic wine producers consolidated recourse to "designer labels" as a means of differentiation.

From an aesthetic point of view, the lesson of 1971 was immediately an expression of sophistication and accompanied wines with a new, typically Italian elegance. The other components of the same lesson, meaning the virtuous interaction among designer, entrepreneur and product, together with the relationship between the winery and its visual expressions, were more slowly absorbed.

The contents of wine labels in the decades that followed dipped into consolidated oenological themes such as the territory, collaboration with the world of art . . . These were not necessarily representative of the specific identity of a winery.

Only a few exemplary cases treated these themes in a systematic and specific manner. Alois Lageder, with the objective of coherence and profound collaboration between the artists and the enterprise, invited artists to stay on the estate to facilitate their interaction with the place and its wines. In this sense, it was a very rare and significant episode. The results, with full respect for the individuality of the author, in narrating a distinctive and unitary history.

The awareness of the need for a unitary image of a winery helped to identify new themes in some cases. These launched fragments of the winery history onto the new labels such as new architectural design (Cantina Petra), specific vineyard conformation (Nino Negri) or the natural approach (Villa Sparina).

Only recently, and actually only virtuous minority has acquired a deep sense of the radical and systematic change in a project of wine image. The label, or rather the system of products and the labels that identify them, and the set of points of contact between wine producers and consumers, have a common denominator in the essence of the enterprise: what according to the RobilantAssociati consultants is usually called talent. This approach implicates a process based on the Socratic method. It will begin with a detailed examination of the enterprise and the people who participate in it, its products, its particular cultivation and vinification processes, its culture, history and aspirations. From these it will distil an essence that goes beyond each of these individual components while providing the spark to illuminate the story of each one.

This is the specific vocation that each winery has, distinguishing it organically from every other without any need for purely aesthetic design efforts that shout a message of diversity by juxtaposition. A vocation clearly expressed by examples like Donnafugata, where the sinuous dream-like female figures on the label tell a special feminine version of Sicily, with all the passion and shivers of intense emotion. The same is evident in the literary evenings and jazz concerts, the joyous hospitality it offers and the impassioned presentations of its tireless ambassadress José Rallo.

At the other end of the peninsula, vocation transforms a cooperative winery such as Tramin into a "composer of refined olfactory symphonies". It creates elegant wines such as Nussbaumer with the punctiliousness of South Tyrol. It uses the sense of smell as a gate to the other senses and applies labels that seem to release the aromas. This composer offers aroma-savouring sessions and has made its architecture into an embrace for all the scents of the territory.

Another quite different example of vocation separates Ferrari from the territorial codes of spumante and justifies its capacity to represent the whole nation. Such representation at

the national level and its links to "Made in Italy" in general form the basis of an original language. Its presence at the key moments of community life and the celebration of Italian successes with the Ferrari prize are worthy of an Italian fashion brand that presents its spumante wines with the same carefree elegance as its lounges.

Respect for and discovery of this vocation that is the unique talent of each winery represents the foundation for an image design that is an authentic interpretation of the Italian project process. It is a transdisciplinary culture based on empathy, beauty and relationships.

This is the only way that a label can really be the cover for the history published by the winery, creating value over time. We hope that the future history of the image of Italian wines will be full of examples like these. *M.D.R., A.D.M., W.F.*

Master Printers

The wine renaissance has stimulated the maturation of other related sectors. Just as the quality of Italian wine fostered the Italian industry of oenological equipment and machines, the world leader today, so design and labels opened the way for many master printers, somewhat reduced in numbers in the digital era.

Tonutti Tecniche Grafiche of Fagagna in Friuli is one of the leading printers in Europe, ranking third for turnover on

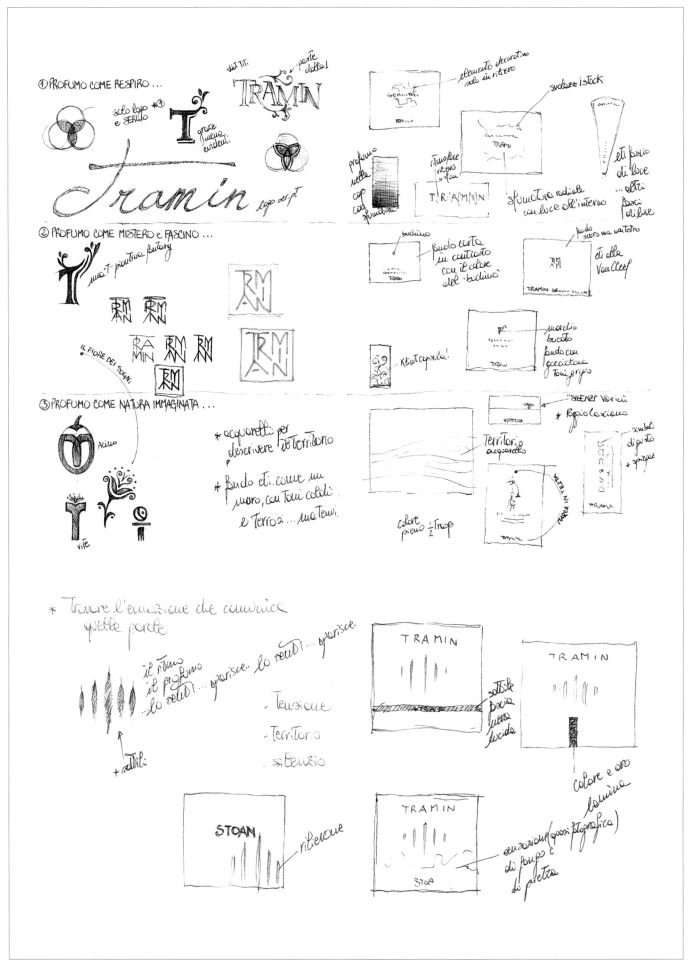

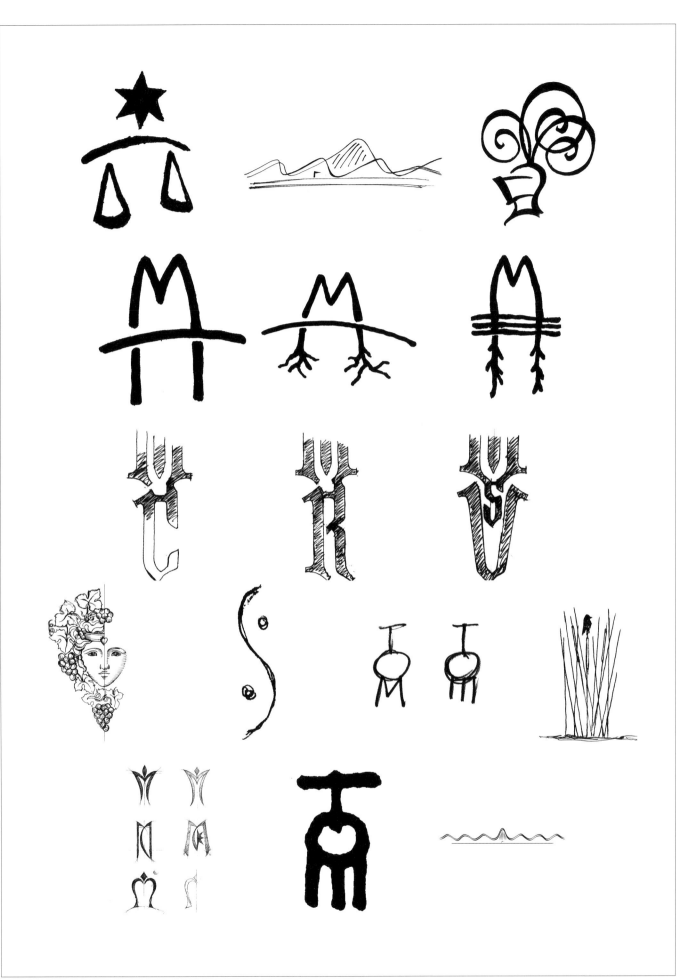

Manlio Tonutti and his children
Maria Teresa and Marco

Below
Label for the "Vino della Pace"
by Walter Valentini

Facing page
RobilantAssociati for Cantine
Ferrari. Studies for the "Cavaliere"

Below
Studies by Silvio Coppola for the
Russiz Superiore label of Marco
Felluga

the continent. Manlio Tonutti inherited the know-how from his father Pietro Maria and is passing it on to his daughter Maria Teresa and his son Marco. He reflects on the rapid evolution of this sector: "Printing has undergone very rapid changes. If I just think that when my father began in 1945, he was the first to use true fine art lithographic technique on stone and printed with a screw press. Methods and equipment evolved very quickly after that. Today, our company has cutting-edge machines and knowledge so we are able to resolve the requirements of the most demanding customers. Our slogan is 'The label made to measure'. We can propose materials for all labelling systems, whether applied traditionally [*pa-*

per+glue or adhesive paper] or the innovative sleeve type. We are one of the few companies in the world to utilize all printing technologies contemporaneously."

If you look closely, you will observe absolute precision in the lines, backgrounds, silhouettes, glossy and opaque surfaces, just like the label that Silvio Coppola had Tonutti print for Russiz Superiore by Marco Felluga. In fact, quite a few wine labels of the world, not to mention famous brands of liqueurs and beverages, speak the Fruilian dialect of Fagagna.

In Manlio's words: "We have recovered the ancient techniques of silk-screen printing, now applied to industrial systems. The structure is industrial, but the spirit is that of artisans, heirs to the grand tradition of those who transformed lithographic prints into works of art that were always printed in the presence of the artist. I believe that the apex of this art and creativity is condensed in the 'Vino della Pace' [*Wine of Peace*] labels that we have been printing every year since the harvest of 1985 for the Produttori di Cormòns winery. They reproduce the paintings of artists who have contributed to creating this marvellous gallery of labels." *W.F.*

SOGNO DI UNA NOTTE DI MEZZA ESTATE
LO SPAZIO BOLLICINE APRE A PORTO CERVO

2012: THE PARTY
FERRARI TI INVITA AL BRINDISI DI FINE ANNO

FERRARI

FERRARI

FERRARI

"TRE SOMMELIER A CONFRONTO"
UN INCONTRO FERRARI CON GLI ESPERTI DELLA DEGUSTAZIONE ITALIANA

SOGNO DI UNA NOTTE DI MEZZA ESTATE
LO SPAZIO BOLLICINE APRE A PORTO CERVO

L'ARTE DELLE BOLLICINE
FERRARI TI INVITA ALLA PRESENTAZIONE DEL PREMIO FERRARI

FERRARI

FERRARI

FERRARI

RUSSIZ SUPERIORE

2002

Da uve Tocai Friulano del Collio, V.Q.P.R.D., ossia vino di qualità prodotto in una regione determinata, ottenuto esclusivamente dalle uve dei vigneti di Russiz Superiore ed imbottigliato all'origine dalla Soc. Agricola Russiz Superiore s.s. in Capriva del Friuli
Il contenuto di questa bottiglia è di centilitri

75 e 13,5%vol

COLLIO

Denominazione di origine controllata

TOCAI FRIULANO

NON DISPERDERE IL VETRO NELL'AMBIENTE

Azienda Agricola Russiz Superiore s.s. - I - Capriva del Friuli - Italia

Wineries. New Architecture

Attilio Scienza, Luca Pedrotti

Wineries, a Metaphoric Stroll through Memory

Like the patrons of the Renaissance who called on the most famous artists of their time to build palaces and churches, many men of our time, in an attempt to unite beauty and efficiency, have commissioned the best architects to design wine cellars that will enchant the consumer and the curious, while also being capable of producing good wines.

The cellar is, therefore, no longer the place where no stranger can enter, but has become a display window or a mirror of the production philosophy of the company, a place to meet and taste wines, to present cultural events and art exhibitions.

Following the example of wine villages in California, the most important communication spaces are near to the wine production spaces. The cellar itself often has an unconventional form. Its volume, the perspectives and the play of light have become a bewitching call for a visit, to inspire speaking about that wine and writing about that territory.

The cellars designed by star architects, although they refer to very different styles and make use of the most unexpected materials, all represent a concept that can be expressed as a "metaphoric stroll through memory". It passes through all the winegrowing zones in Italy to capture the culture in the air, always original and never repetitive. It is a sort of renaissance reconciliation between man and nature, according to the *praxis* of *homo faber*. In the past, Italian wines received their cultural nobility from the arts. There are famous paintings from every epoch depicting sumptuous banqueting with wine on the tables, vineyards in the landscape, and still lifes of grape clusters, not to mention literature and music. Until now, architecture had never had the role of dramatizing viticulture and its territories, creating logos and company identity in the modern sense of corporate identity, the equivalent of *genius loci* in the landscape. In an epoch when the loss of cultural identity becomes the collective amnesia of the population regarding its own artistic traditions, adoption of an international style is a means to surpass the rhetoric of local supremacy. The artists who designed these wineries and the men who commissioned and financed them deserve our appreciation and admiration. *A.S.*

The Modern Winery: A 3D Label

There is a strong link between the structural solutions of modern wineries and the climatic, historic and social conditions of wine production in their specific geographical zones.

Modern wine cellars are probably one of the very few architectural categories that do not fit into a well-defined scheme, because each project is tailored to specific wine production requirements, transforming the patron once again into the protagonist.

One of the pioneers of modern rationalism in architecture in the United States, Louis Sullivan (Frank Lloyd Wright's mentor) based all of his work at the end of the nineteenth century on the motto "Form follows function". Over the decades, the context and the intention of this motto have been misinterpreted, creating a great distance between architects and the requirements of their clients. Modern architecture inspired by wine is one of the few trends of recent decades to swing the balance back toward the client and away from designers' theories. This explains why the wine cellar has automatically become the primary expression of the product that it hosts. Like a sort of 3D label, the cellar seems to be more communicative than advertising. It incorporates all the intrinsic aspects of wine.

The expedient of transforming a production site into an "open cellar" makes the genesis of wine comprehensible inside fascinating spaces instead of mediocre places. In a true touch of genius, this has become the subject of an interdisciplinary debate. The wine cellar is perceived as a sort of Pandora's vase that can diffuse all aspects of wine culture and associate it with beauty. It has become a meeting place for social exchange and aggregation, where the applied arts contribute to illustrating the specific technological culture of a community.

The modern wine cellar represents globalisation in the best sense of the word. Wine is, in fact, a global product that facilitates cohesion among persons but, above all, it expresses concentrated individual local cultural phenomena. A perfect example of the word "glocal", the wine cellar focuses on the specificity and uniqueness of the culture that spawned it in a global context.

The technological evolution of vinification is stimulating profound architectural reflections, just as the invention of the lift made it possible to develop skyscrapers.

All last-generation wine cellars share the relationship with land morphology. The architecture must come to terms with the place, evolving from the concept of a construction into an integral element of the environment. This all leads to innovative solutions, aligned with the latest trends of contemporary architecture. The protagonists are demonstrating how the wine cellar represents the apex of the sustainability transformation of agricultural territory.

The modern cellar can therefore be considered, in all of its variants, an expression of ecological and bio-climactic architecture with the scope (beyond respectful insertion into the territory) of achieving the greatest possible natural energy supply for a building that will rely on its architectural design to exploit all of the favourable external factors and obtain the best possible internal habitat. If we add to this, the search for an aesthetic connotation of the spaces, the cycle is complete.

These essential aspects have encouraged designers to harmonise with the territory in various modes, classified in three major categories. *L.P.*

Mimetic, Partially underground Wineries Identified by aboveground Architectural Elements
Luca Pedrotti

Manincor

Design: Walter Angonese, Rainer Koberl and Silvia Boday, architects
Owner: Count Michael Goëss-Enzenberg
Production area: Caldaro, Bolzano – Trentino-Alto Adige

The expansion of the wine cellar at Manincor of Caldaro designed by architect Walter Angonese is a wonderful example of the co-existence of antiquity and modernity. The dialogue between the topography and the type of cellar lead to the dimension that is part of the context and relates with history. This modern underground cellar had to be built of reinforced concrete. Gravel from the enormous excavation became the aggregate in the concrete, to make it indigenous too. The power and modernity of concrete is balanced by the weightless aspect of COR-TEN steel, the oxidised (rusty) surface of which is treated and conserved with the very ancient technique of boiled linseed oil. Building a wine cellar of this type means dedicating a unique, functional and technological shelter to a closely supervised product. The designer's task was to make simple things a little more complex and complex things a little simpler.

Cascina Adelaide

Design: Archicura studio – Paolo and Ugo Dellapiana, Francesco Bermond des Ambrois, architects
Owner: Amabile Drocco
Production area: Barolo, Cuneo – Piedmont

Archicura Studio designed this expansion for Cascina Adelaide under a blanket of green, as gentile as the surrounding landscape. Under a layer of earth between the heavens and the vineyards, this new wine cellar takes shape by following the natural traces of the metamorphosis that transforms grapes into wine. Perspicacious research and respect for the surrounding hills suggested a volume covered completely by grassy earth near Barolo. It has a very reserved demeanour, but the force of a new and contemporary architecture. The building adds another small ridge among the other hills without modifying the surroundings, elaborating it from the inside through the essential metamorphosis of grapes into wine.

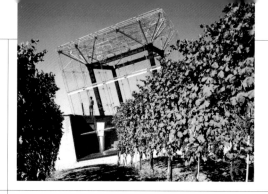

Cantina Bricco Rocche

Design: Luca and Marina Deabate, architects
Owner: the Ceretto family
Production area: Castiglione Falletto, Cuneo – Piedmont

On a site with a splendid panorama at the geographical centre of the Langhe area, the new wings of the Ceretto wine cellar at Castiglione Falletto are mainly underground and culminate in a welcoming/tasting pavilion. For the designers, the intention was to create a landmark for the whole zone near Alba, in spite of somewhat limited dimensions.

This small edifice, shaped like a cube, set askew atop a hillock, hovering above the surrounding vineyards, perfectly transparent, offers a sublimely unique view of the great and famous vineyards all around. Have adopted a building technology that is unusual for the zone, it should be interpreted as the projection of the enlightened and well-informed company image that the owners have cultivated for years.

Antinori nel Chianti Classico

Design: Studio Archea Associati – Marco Casamonti and Laura Andreini, architects
Owner: Marchesi Antinori
Production area: Bargino, Florence – Tuscany

Marchese Piero Antinori has defined his new winery on the estate in Bargino as "a sophisticated but unobtrusive earth palace; new but made of ancient materials, as harmonious as a Renaissance dome but also efficient . . . a magnificent place to make great wines".

The Archea Associati studio of Florence transformed their vision into reality by setting this construction, so unique in size and concept, into the Chianti hills. It is an introspective wine cellar, perceived like a great slash in the terrain, "powerful but discrete". Window walls reflect the landscape during the day; at night, they reveal the structure inside.

A great irregular winding staircase, like a corkscrew opening a prestigious wine, accompanies the visitor through the different levels of the cellar, up to its hilltop roof marked by rows of vines and great circular openings that illuminate its technological heart. Traditional materials delineate a very modern building. State-of-the-art construction techniques leave room for traditional vinification methods so there is no need for cooling systems to conserve and age the wine inside this "temple of *barriques*".

The new cellar is a modern renaissance factory, as antique as a cathedral and as modern as a poly-functional centre, but reserved for the exclusive service of its master: the wine.

Ca' Marcanda

Design: Giovanni Bo, architect
Owner: Angelo Gaja
Production area: Bolgheri, Livorno – Tuscany

The winery that architect Giovanni Bo has conceived for Angelo Gaja on the Ca' Marcanda estate near Bolgheri in Tuscany is set in an untouchable landscape. It is a perfect combination of contemporary architecture and the *genius loci*, where historical research meets the requirements of the patron. They call for functionality, precision, parsimony and the absence of formal opulence.

The functional mesh that cradles the appurtenances of the entire cellar disappears underground, forming two levels il-luminated and ventilated by horizontal and vertical cuts in the various surfaces.

The perception of the volumes disappears. Some solids designated for offices, tasting and pressing emerge. Their stonewall fabric and the geometry of their forms are remembrances of local construction trends.

Vegetation enfolds the entire building, revealing only limited portions.

The very canopies, with their interwoven metallic structure and copper roofing, will enter into the play of greens as it ages.

Tenuta Castelbuono

Design: Arnaldo Pomodoro
Construction: Giorgio and Luca Pedrotti, architects with Studio Pomodoro
Owner: Tenute Lunelli, the Lunelli family
Production area: Bevagna, Perugia – Umbria

The *Carapace* at the Tenuta Castelbuono in the hills between Bevagna and Montefalco is the first sculpture in the world where people live and work making excellent wines. It was commissioned by the Lunelli family and born of the visionary creativity of Arnaldo Pomodoro; it was made possible by considerable group work and by the professional experience of architects Giorgio and Luca Pedrotti.

A red dart marks the place where the winery erupts from the ground encircling it, revealing the elliptical form of the copper dome scored by cracks and the deep marks typical of the artist's sculpting language. The majestic interior calls to mind the anatomy of a primordial creature, custodian of "beauty" and "virtue", which over the years has become the leitmotif of the Lunelli company. The furnishings, as red as Sagrantino leaves in October and set under the centre of the great vault, invite the visitor to descend into the bowels of the *Carapace* by following the seductive winding staircase down into the heart of the *barrique* cellar, the treasure trove of production. The peculiarity of the materials selected for the realisation of each detail, balancing art, sculpture and architecture, makes this work as ancient as Umbria despite its original contemporary form.

Aboveground Wineries with Evident Ties to Tradition and Territory

Luca Pedrotti

Cantina Jermann di Ruttars

Design: Adriano Zuppel, architect and Alberto Padovan, surveyor
Owner: Società agricola Jermann
Production area: Frazione Ruttars, Dolegna del Collio, Gorizia – Friuli Venezia Giulia

The Jermann cellar stands where the foothills of Collio meet the plain of Friuli, in the hamlet of Ruttars. The project by Adriano Zuppel and Alberto Padovan, which unites houses, courtyards, porticoes, a tower and underground cellars to create a *dorf*, accumulated elements with the aspect of a settlement, but actually structured to meet precise demands for wine production and discrete appearance in the hilly landscape.

The cellar rests on the natural ledges of the terrain among the surrounding vineyards with the ambition to be, inherently, an environmentally sustainable "home for wine". The respect for the quality of the landscape accompanies the use of local materials, accurate management of earth, water and sunshine resources for energy recovery and innovative system solutions.

La Brunella

Design: Guido Boroli, architect
Owner: the Boroli family
Production area: Castiglione Falletto, Cuneo – Piedmont

The new La Brunella winery at Castiglione Falletto, designed by architect Guido Boroli, proposes a modern interpretation with local details of a volume faced with the solid oak staves of dismantled *barriques* to obtain a strong characterisation of the territory. The roofing represents a restyling of the geometry of adjacent traditional constructions: a simple two-pitch gable with no eaves. A window-walled volume for the tasting room, with a view of the vineyards, characterises the com-

plex. The stairway down to the underground level reproduces the company's patented wine bottle coffer. Descending the stairs, the visitor enters an environment where silence, darkness and the unmistakeable aromas of ageing Barolo and prized woods mingle all together.

Petra

Design: Mario Botta, architect
Owner: Vittorio Moretti
Production area: Suvereto, Livorno – Tuscany

A temple of wine stands at the foot of a sun-lit hillock in Tuscany, near Suvereto in Maremma. Its monumental forms of stone and concrete successfully mimic the colours and forms of the hill. It harbours the initiation ritual of the wine in the heart of the land that produces it.

This is how Mario Botta built one of the first monuments to wine in Italy for Vittorio Moretti, by interpreting the ancestral nature of the wine itself in an edifice that is "manifestly integrated" with its natural surroundings. The colonnaded porticoes on each side are a citation of Palladian villas and contain the functions that rotate around the central cylinder, sectioned parallel to the hill by a stairway that symbolically leads to an altar in heaven and in dichotomy with the rest of the cellar that slips under the hill. For the architect, Moretti relied on modern technology to create pre-fabricated concrete elements that form a monument to wine with an antique flavour. These lead the way from the open light of the hillside down into the intimate obscurity of the earth.

Cantina Podernuovo

Design: Studio Alvisi Kirimoto + Partners – Massimo Alvisi and Junko Kirimoto, architects
Owner: Giovanni and Paolo Bulgari
Production area: San Casciano dei Bagni, Siena – Tuscany

In the new winery project by Alvisi Kirimoto + Partners for Giovanni and Paolo Bulgari at Podernuovo near San Casciano dei Bagni, four partition walls of reinforced concrete set along the lay of the land enclose the major processes of the phases of production. A central corridor divides and organises all the spaces and reveals how the wine cellar is linked to the terrain. The perviousness of the building and the multiple points of transparency put the entire structure on display. The whole project stems from the concept that nature is not merely decorative, but actually completes it. The rhythm of the trees enveloping the winery seems to break down encountering the walls, but unexpectedly continues as the glance passes from the interior to the exterior. Reinforced concrete is an element of counterpoint to this landscape. The violence of the line and the materials disappear in the sienna-coloured earth and the subdued acceptance of the natural surroundings.

Cantina Icario

Design: Studio Valle Progettazioni – Tommaso Valle, Cesare Valle, Gianluca Valle and Gianluigi Valle with Giuseppe Mura, Stefano Rosa and Paolo Vacatello, architects
Owner: Azienda Agricola Icario
Production area: Montepulciano, Siena – Tuscany

The stone masonry used to construct Cantina Icario near Fucile di Montepulciano, designed by Studio Valle, interprets a non-invasive concept of architecture. With the simple and austere geometry of its four emerging volumes, it is a reinterpretation of the characteristics of rural construction in Tuscany.

The project aims for a visible combination with tradition in the spaces delineated by the geometry of metal tube trusses and the distribution of glazed surfaces. Consistent enclosures are artfully arranged near to glazed volumes, in a rhythm of solids and voids. Unusual openings in intermediate floor slabs allow zenith sunlight to enter and reveal interior perspectives that range from the museum-meeting room to the *tonneaux* hall. This introspective architecture refuses to glance outside of its enclosure and focuses on its interior.

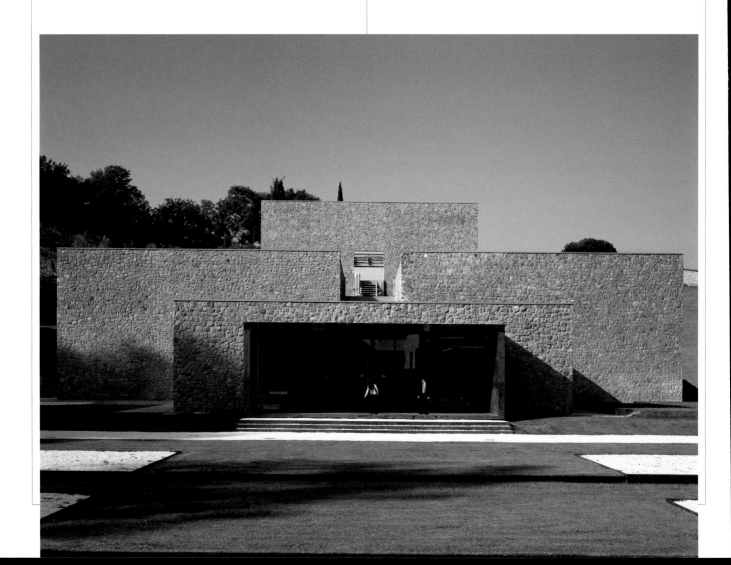

Badia a Coltibuono

Design: Piero Sartogo and Nathalie Grenon, architects
Owner: Badia a Coltibuono
Production area: Monti in Chianti, Gaiole in Chianti, Siena
– Tuscany

The winning strategy of architects Piero Sartogo and Nathalie
Grenon for one of the first architectural projects in the wine
sector, the new Badia a Coltibuono winery near Monti in Chianti, was to introduce a functional separation of the volumetric
elements characterising the different process phases: grape
gathering, pressing, fermentation and ageing.

In this regard, the decision to insert the body of the largest
volume into the foot of the wooded hill was the catalyst for
gravity flow vinification, as proposed by the most advanced
oenological theories. It also produced a protected in-scape
with significant energy-saving characteristics.

The configuration is that of a bastion, similar to military
earthworks fitted with ramps, stairs, passages and terracing,
both inside and out. Such pathways are necessary not only for
proper functioning of the oenological machine, but also for
visitors.

In the Renaissance, military engineer Francesco di Giorgio used this layout at several sites. It was later revived in civil structures in and around Siena. In this project, it compacts
the dimensions of the complex so that the structure is in scale
with the nearby hamlet.

Fattoria delle Ripalte

Design: Tobia Scarpa, architect
Owner: Fattoria delle Ripalte Società Agricola
Production area: Capoliveri, Isola d'Elba, Livorno –
Tuscany

Near Capoliveri on Elba island, set into the hillside of Colle di Gianni, Tobia Scarpa designed the new winery at Fattoria delle Ripalte. A close-knit mesh of pilasters clad with Calamita stone from nearby quarries marks the regular rhythm of the parallelepiped overlooking the surrounding vineyards and the island coastline, offering a breath-taking panorama.

The design-conscious choice of a dry-mounted, local stone facing and the simplicity of the forms creates an ongoing dialogue between the winery and the surrounding landscape, transforming a building that is clearly a centre for production into an integral element of the territory where it stands.

The simplicity of the facades is also evident in the functional clarity of the internal spaces. All the production processes benefit from gravity descent, from the terraced roof for sundrying the grapes down to the ground floor storerooms. Tobia Scarpa, with just few simple gestures, has succeeded in grafting a sort of factory into a sensitive area. The complete absence of formal virtuosity transforms the qualities of this splendid landscape in the Tuscan archipelago into architecture itself.

Taverna

Design: Onsitestudio – Angelo Lunati, Luca Varesi and Laura Quatela, architects
Owner: Azienda Agricola Taverna
Production area: Nova Siri, Matera – Basilicata

The new building designed by the architects of Onsitestudio near Nova Siri in the province of Matera is an expansion of the existing productive nucleus at Azienda Agricola Taverna. It is organised around a series of stopping places that function as nodes for the paths and flows that originate from an open patio, which offers different views of the surrounding landscape and the interior of the building. A bright, minimalist courtyard forms the entry to the winery. It is higher than the surrounding countryside and is accessible from an ample square adjacent to the Regio Tratturo. The play of the roof pitches and the white plaster facades are an inseparable link of this project to the tradition of the territory where it has been introduced.

Feudo di Mezzo

Design: Santi Albanese and Gaetano Gulino, architects
Owner: Aziende Agricole Planeta
Production area: Castiglione di Sicilia, Catania – Sicily

The new Feudo di Mezzo winery on the Planeta estate near Castiglione di Sicilia, designed by architects Santi Albanese and Gaetano Gulino, stands on a clearing levelled out in the middle of a lava flow on the slopes of Etna. It overlooks a splendid and luxuriant landscape. The project proposes essential volumes in a contemporary architectural language and materials that are solidly linked to the territory and its traditions.

The continuous relations with the volcano generate finite spaces between the lava flow and the buildings that are capable of encompassing paths and production areas without losing contact with their rural surroundings.

The building appears to be a monolith covered with volcanic rock, cut and dry mounted with the traditional technique used in stone fields of Etna. It is also an accessible roof covered with gravel. On this unique terrace, the visitor is entitled to feel perfect harmony with his environmental surroundings.

Cantina Khamma

Design: Gabriella Giuntoli, architect
Owner: Donnafugata
Production area: Isola di Pantelleria, Trapani – Sicily

The project for the new Donnafugata winery on Pantelleria island, designed by architect Gabriella Giuntoli, stands at the centre of a splendid and ample amphitheatre that has been terraced for centuries. This position minimises the volumes of the winery itself and focuses attention on a gracious construction that lends its character to the whole basin. To transform hospitality and tasting into an art, these functions are found in this *palazzotto*. The volumes harmonise with those housing the production. The centre of gravity of the whole complex is a great courtyard, often the stage for many cultural events.

The project has given the owner the opportunity to give full expression to the profound commitment to respect for the environment and the traditions of the area of production.

Technological aboveground Wineries

Luca Pedrotti

Cantina Nals Margreid

Design: Markus Scherer, architect
Owner: Cantina Nals Margreid
Production area: Nalles, Bolzano – Trentino-Alto Adige

The new Nals Margried winery near Nalles, the work of architect Markus Scherer, presents a new edifice encompassing a tower at the head of the complex. A spacious underground cellar connects to the existing cellar and a monumental, cantilevered flat roof covers the volumes and the central access square. The new building is made of insulation cement, pigmented to a reddish brown colour. Next to the other natural materials employed, it forms a chromatic and material unity that is in harmony with the context. The underside of the roof slab traces the lines of force and forms a stylised surface like an origami, to protect access to the complex. The scope of the whole project is to provide a concrete demonstration of the process of making wine, far from the static concept of a shop window-boutique sort of winery.

Here the wine production process is the generator of the architecture and the focal point of the visitor's attention.

Cantina Colterenzio

Design: bergmeisterwolf architekten – Gerd Bergmeister and Michaela Wolf, architects
Owner: Consorzio produttori Cantina Colterenzio
Production area: Cornaiano, Bolzano – Trentino-Alto Adige

The project by studio Bergmeisterwolf for Cantina Colterenzio near Cornaiano is: an expansion, a community process, a materialisation of distances and gaps, an addition and a subtraction; changing and enriching with substance, nature and colours; the creation of layers, the completion of a working process by creating a unity.

It is a splendid example of industrial recycling and technological adaptation of an existing winery. On the one hand, a facade of oak, like wooden casks; on the other, a facade of steel, like the stainless-steel tanks. The presence of courtyards favours the new element. The playful composition with the staves of differing thicknesses, the openings and the colours results in a vivacious and contemporary facade that retains the original form and structure.

The triptych form of the wooden facade runs on into a metal structure with climbing vegetation that ends in the adjacent courtyard.

Cantina Tramin

Design: Werner Tscholl, architect with Andreas Sagmeister
Owner: Cantina sociale Tramin
Production area: Termeno, Bolzano – Trentino-Alto Adige

The vine and its forms and function in the territory were the inspiration for the expansion project of Cantina Tramin by architect Werner Tscholl with Andreas Sagmeister, in the Tramin (Termeno) settlement. It is a symbol rising from the terrain, created by the knowledgeable hands of the cultivators and creates, in the case of the winery, an enclosure all around the building that houses it. The structure has thus become a sculpture, a work that identifies the presence and the mission of the winery. The iconographic impact of its environmental integration and, at the same time, of differentiation in its union of metal, cement and glass, make the construction into a sort of landmark Termeno, like a city gate.

Cittadella del Vino

Design: Alberto Cecchetto, architect
Owner: Cantine Mezzacorona – Nosio spa
Production area: Mezzocorona, Trento – Trentino-Alto Adige

The Cittadella del Vino di Mezzocorona, designed by architect Alberto Cecchetto, is the largest winemaking complex in Europe.

The project, which has no pretensions of monumental rhetoric, demonstrates how a large-scale industrial complex can be constructed in symbiosis with the surrounding landscape. Built in three stages, today the Cittadella is not only a place for production and marketing of wine, but also a programme for modern architecture.

In this project of grand dimensions, the productive activities accompany leisure time, fairs, cultural events and organisation of meetings and conferences. A new and complex urban reality.

This project demonstrates that fine architecture attracts public interest and can be built at industrial costs.

Cantina di Bianchini

Design: Silvio Cicuto, architect

Owner: Azienda Forchir, of Bianchini G. & C. S.A.S. –
Le vigne dei Bianchini

Production area: Camino al Tagliamento, Udine, and
Spilimbergo, Barbeano village, Pordenone – Friuli Venezia
Giulia

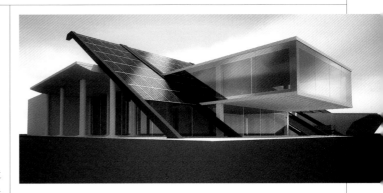

At Camino al Tagliamento, in the province of Udine, architect
Silvio Cicuto has designed a new winery that is quite distant
from the traditional agricultural style. The project combines
lines, forms, materials and colours not merely for a self-serv-
ing principle, but because they are contemporary, functional
improvements that are optimal and in harmony among them.

Starting from the production processes and their consequences, the technologies and the surface areas they require,
the architect extrapolated the form composed of malleable
structures that can adjust to time, space and requirements.
The building has a modern technological style and production from renewable sources makes it completely self-sufficient for its energy requirements. *Carbon-free*.

Rocca di Frassinello

Design: Renzo Piano Building Workshop, architects
Owner: Paolo Panerai – La Rocca di Frassinello s.r.l.
Production area: Gavorrano, Grosseto – Tuscany

In an amphitheatre in the heart of a hill, the spectacle of transforming grapes into wine has become the representation, by means of modern technologies, of an ancient art. At Gavorrano, Renzo Piano has created a new concept of wine cellar for Paolo Panerai. Underneath a grand, almost sacred, terracotta yard dotted with a series of inlet covers where the grapes are deposited, all the production processes are wound around a spectacular *barrique* cellar organised on wide steps. Above this theatre where the *barriques* participate in silence as the wine spectacle proceeds, at the highest point of the complex a steel and glass pavilion rotates around the great panoramic tower (sign and symbol of the project) in a 360° embrace of the territory. This is indestructibly linked to the *barrique* cellar by a device that illuminates its heart through the eye above centre stage.

The red colour of the complex and the tower of medieval memories reveal the force of a modern fortress to the visitor. It is the technological interpretation of a trade as old as the earth.

L'Ammiraglia

Design: Piero Sartogo and Nathalie Grenon, architects
Owner: Marchesi de' Frescobaldi
Production area: Magliano, Grosseto – Tuscany

The new winery of the Marchesi de' Frescobaldi near Magliano in Maremma was designed by architects Piero Sartogo and Nathalie Grenon. The lines of the building respond to precise criteria of style and environmental compatibility. They also respond to the needs of 150 hectares of vineyards of the Santa Maria estate. The harmony between the building and the surrounding natural environment is particularly significant. So is the use of industrial building solutions, subjected to the canons of aesthetics and functionality of the wine cellar.

A raised strip of earth opens a long narrow burrow in the natural slope of the land. This mark has a curved profile, a curve that follows the contour lines and thus is a replica of the natural slopes. This essential gesture catalyses the architectural configuration as it appears in the context of the rolling hills all around it. It is like a simple surface, slit along the slope that has scrupulously maintained its integrity so that the marks of artifice will merge with those of nature.

Cantina ColleMassari

Design: Edoardo Milesi e Archos s.r.l., architect
Owner: Maria Iris and Claudio Tipa
Production area: Cinigiano, Grosseto – Tuscany

The new winery at ColleMassari near Cinigiano, designed by architect Edoardo Milesi for the Tipa family, is a big box of wood. The storerooms, technical rooms and garage for agricultural vehicles have been excavated in the hillside. The only element that emerges above the hill is a white veil. It organises and reorders the exterior spaces for manoeuvring vehicles. The desire to design spaces rather than a building is even more evident in the wing that emerges beyond the wooden box and towers over its southeastern corner. A cage of wide-ly spaced narrow pilasters and beams of white cement, like a pergola, stems from the vineyard and rests, as if only temporarily, above the underground edifice. It is a white mesh that captures the surrounding landscape like a net, slowly filling with the events of wine production and marketing that it captures, together with promotion of the territory. It is an opposite but complementary space with respect to the solid belly built into the hill, which transforms and jealously protects its precious product. It is a space that pulses with activities linked to knowledge of wine, tasting and its scientific and convivial connotations. The great wooden box of Cantina ColleMassari alternates solids and voids along the internal-external axis that follows the functional track of production in the building in a precise reconstruction of the phases of the oenological process.

Cantina Pieve Vecchia

Design: Cini Boeri and Enrico Sartori, architects
Owner: Società agricola Pieve Vecchia – Vincenzo and Marco Monaci
Production area: Campagnatico, Grosseto – Tuscany

The new Cantina Pieve Vecchia winery is located in the Ombrone river valley among the hills of Maremma. Architect Cini Boeri designed the areas for receiving the public, while the production facilities were designed by architect Enrico Sartori. The site is near the little town of Campagnatico. The wine production facilities are housed in underground spaces. The restaurant, bar and offices are situated in the upper, aboveground storey.

Although she has never been a wine drinker, architect Boeri dedicated her respectful attention to an interesting topic although it was new for her. From the street, the building has the appearance of a lightweight metallic strip. It is divided into two parts, each covered by great sails that set off the profile as they disappear into the natural slope of the hills.

Most of the aboveground part of the building consists of window walls. At night, it illuminates the surrounding spaces like a lamp.

The project satisfies the owner's need for a place, adjacent to the facilities for producing and ageing wine, to offer visitors and customers a tasting room and restaurant with a view of the marvellous landscape of the surroundings.

Feudi di San Gregorio

Design: Hikaru Mori and Maurizio Zito, architects
Owner: Feudi di San Gregorio
Production area: Sorbo Serpico, Avellino – Campania

The restructuring project for the Feudi di San Gregorio winery near Sorbo Serbico in the province of Avellino was designed by Hikaru Mori and Maurizio Zito. The goal was to give the existing winery architectural unity and to confer the image of a modern and technological enterprise operating in a traditional sector.

The clean line of the single steel roof encompasses and marks the architecture of the winery, which reproduces the linear profile of the ridge where the building stands. Various volumes and forms made of different materials (glass, steel, titanium zinc, cement and stone) characterise the profile, which nonetheless proposes harmony. The result is a comprehensive intervention that is well integrated with the territory and the landscape. Most of the structure, for the functions and activities it comprises, consists of underground spaces. No signs of environmental impact disturb its integration with the landscape and surrounding terrain.

The intervention responds to the ambitious goal of Feudi di San Gregorio: to transform the winery into a meeting place for forums, exchange, friendship, meditation and a laboratory of ideas and culture. It is something of a fortress to protect its precious product, while revealing its secrets and the quality of its world.

Bibliography

G. Acerbi, *Delle Viti italiane*. Milan: Silvestri, 1825.

M.A. Amerine, V.L. Singleton, *Wine. An Introduction for Americans*. Berkeley: University of California Press, 1975.

B. Anderson, *Vino. The Wines and Winemakers of Italy*. New York: Little, Brown and Company, 1980.

B. Anderson, *The Mitchell Beazley Pocket Guide to Italian Wines*. London: Mitchell Beazley, 1982.

B. Anderson, *Wine of Italy An Adventure in Taste*. New York: Italian Trade Center, 1986.

B. Anderson, *Vino. The Wines and Winemakers of Italy*. Boston: Little, Brown and Company, 1987.

B. Anderson, *Guida ai vini d'Italia*. MIlan: Mediolanum Editori Associati, 1988.

B. Anderson, *The Wine Atlas of Italy*. London: Mitchell Beazley, 1990.

B. Anderson, *Vino. Italian Wines. The Quality of Life,* New York: The Italian Trade Commission, 1992.

B. Anderson, *Burton Anderson's Best Italian Wines*. New York: Little, Brown and Company, 2001.

L. Andreini, *Archea Associati Cantina Antinori. Cronistoria della costruzione di un nuovo paesaggio*. Poggibonsi: Forma, 2012.

P. Antinori, *Il Profumo del Chianti. Storia di una famiglia di vinattieri*. Milan: Mondadori, 2011.

C.M. Antonioli, R. Baggio, *Internet & Turismo 2.0*. Milan: Egea, 2011.

A. Bacci, *De naturali vinorum historia, de vinis Italiae et de conuiuiis antiquorum libri septem*. Rome: Nicholai Mutij, 1596.

D.N. Basile, *New Menu Italia. La rivoluzione che ha cambiato la tavola degli italiani*. Milan: Baldini Castaldi Dalai, 2009.

D.N. Basile, *Olio & Vino. Eccellenze d'Italia prima e dopo la crisi*. Milan: Dalai, 2011.

J. Bastianich, D. Lynch, *Vino italiano. The Regional Wines of Italy*. New York: Clarkson Potter, 2002.

L. Bastianich, *Lidia's Italian-American Kitchen*. New York: Alfred A. Knopf, 2001.

L. Bastianich, *Lidia Cooks from the Heart of Italy*. New York: Alfred A. Knopf, 2009.

L. Bastianich, J. Jacobs, *La cucina di Lidia. Distinctive Regional Cuisine from the North of Italy*. New York: Doubleday, 1990.

N. Belfrage, *Barolo to Valpolicella - The Wines of Northern Italy*. London: Faber & Faber, 1999.

N. Belfrage, *Brunello to Zibibbo - The Wines of Tuscany, Central and Southern Italy*. London: Faber & Faber, 2001.

N. Belfrage, *The Finest Wines of Tuscany and Central Italy*. Los Angeles: Aurum Press and University of California Press, 2009.

N. Belfrage, J. Robinson, *Life beyond Lambrusco. Understanding Italian Fine Wine*. London: Sidgwick & Jackson, 1985.

A. Bespaloff, *The Signet Book of Wine*. New York: New American Library, 1971.

Z. Bocci, *L'evoluzione del settore vitivinicolo negli ultimi trent'anni. Selezione da 2000 articoli per 34 testate*. Verona: Gruppo italiano vini, 1997.

C. Bolognesi, *Manuale del turismo enogastronomico culturale. Come fare sistema territoriale tra operatori pubblici, privati ed associazioni*. Verona: Ci.Vin, s.l. 2010.

M. Broadbent, *The Great Vintage Wine Book*. New York: Alfred A. Knopf, 1983.

F. Chiorino, *Architettura e vino. Nuove cantine e il culto del vino*. Milan: Electa, 2008.

F. Chiorino, *Cantine del XXI secolo* (texts by Ampelio Bucci and Carlo Tosco). Milan: Electa, 2011.

R. Cipresso, G. Negri, *Vinosofia. Una dichiarazione d'amore in 38 bicchieri*. Casale Monferrato: Piemme, 2010.

Z. Ciuffoletti, *I Pionieri del Risorgimento vitivinicolo italiano*. Florence: Polistampa, 2006.

F. Colombo, *Prosecco Perché? Le nobili origini di un vino triestino*. Trieste: Luglio Editore, 2012.

I. Cosmo, *Vitigni ammessi alla coltura*. Conegliano Veneto: Istituto Sperimentale Per La Viticoltura, 1974.

D. Darrow, T. Maresca, *The Seasons of the Italian Kitchen*. New York: Atlantic Monthly Press, 1994.

A. Del Conte, *Gastronomy of Italy*. New York: Prentice Hall, 1987.

F. Del Zan, O. Failla, A. Scienza, *La vite e l'uomo. Dal rompicapo delle origini al salvataggio delle reliquie*, II edizione. Gorizia: ERSA, 2009.

L. Di Lello, *Viaggio nel mondo del vino. I protagonisti, i territori, lo stile*. Rome: Lithos Editore, 1997.

G.A. Di Ricaldone, *La collezione ampelografica del Marchese Leopoldo Incisa della Rocchetta (1792-1871)*. Asti: Camera di Commercio, 1974.

G. Di Rovasenda, *Saggio di ampelografia universale*. Turin: Stefano Marino, 1877.

J. Dickie, *Con Gusto. Storia degli italiani a tavola*. Bari-Rome: Laterza, 2007.

R. Dogliotti, *Christie's World Encyclopedia of Champagne & Sparkling Wine*. New York: Absolute Press, 2013.

H. Dohm, *Flaschenpost aus Italien*. Munich: Keysersche Verlagsbuchhandlung, 1988.

H. Dohm, *L'Italia in bottiglia*. Florence: Cantini Editore, 1988.

G.P. Fabris, *Societing. Il marketing nella società postmoderna*. Milan: Egea, 2008.

O. Farinetti, S. Hayashi, *Storie di coraggio*. Milan: Mondadori, 2013.

L. Ferraro, L. Gardini, *Vignaioli e Vini d'Italia 2013. Guida a 200 produttori d'eccellenza*. Milan: RCS Mediagroup, 2013.

W. Filiputti, *Il sommelier e la sua funzione di educazione enologica del consumatore*, degree thesis, Universita di Trieste, 1972–1973.

W. Filiputti, *Terre vigne e vini del Friuli-Venezia Giulia*. Udine: Gianfranco Angelico Benvenuto Editore, 1983.

W. Filiputti, *L'Abbazia di Rosazzo e i suoi vigneti. Storia del restauro agrario del Monasterium Rosarum*. Udine: Tecniche Grafiche di M. Tonutti, Fagagna, 1986.

W. Filiputti, *I grandi vini del Friuli Venezia Giulia. Storie di Uomini e vigneti*. Tavagnacco: Arti Grafiche Editore, 1997.

W. Filiputti, *I grandi vini del Veneto e Friuli Venezia Giulia*. Rimini: Idea Libri, 2000.

W. Filiputti, *Collio. I volti di una terra*. Milan: Gribaudo Editore, 2005.

W. Filiputti, *Una terra, il Collio, un uomo, Marco Felluga*. Milan: Gustosì biblioteca Editore, 2007.

W. Filiputti, *Un friulano da amare. Monografie golose*. Udine: Friuli Venezia Giulia Via dei Sapori Editore, 2008.

M. Fini, *Sassicaia. The Original Super Tuscan*. Florence: Centro Di, 2000.

Franciacorta, un vino, una terra. Milan: Swan Group, 2010.

"Le frontiere nascoste della cultura del vino", symposium acts, G. Forni, G. Kezich, A. Scienza (eds.), in *Annali di San Michele*, San Michele all'Adige, no. 25, 2014.

G. Gaetani D'Aragona, *A Spasso con il vino. Fra terre, suoni e vignaioli*. Milan: Gribaudo Editore, 2013.

L. Gardini, *I migliori 100 vini del mondo*. Milan: RCS MediaGroup, 2013.

D. Gleave, *The Wines of Italy*. New York: HP Books, 1989.

D. Gleave, *Wines of Tuscany*. New York: Ebury Press, 1999.

D. Gleave, *Wine Renaissance in Tuscany*. London: Century, 1999.

A. Gosetti della Salda, *Le ricette regionali italiane*. Milan: Solares Editore, 2005.

Grandi Cru d'Italia. Milan: Electa, 2008.

N. Innocente, *Le globalizzazioni nella storia: esempi di sana contaminazione enogastronomica*. Udine: Forum, 2011.

Italian Wine Guide. New York: Italian Wine Center, 1982.

H. Johnson, *Hugh Johnson's Pocket Wine Book*. London: Mitchell Beazley, 1977.

H. Johnson, *Une histoire mondiale du vin*. Paris: Hachette, 1990.

H. Johnson, *Pocket Encyclopedia of Wine 1990*. New York: Simon & Schuster, 1990.

H. Johnson, *The Story of Wine*. London: Mitchell Beazley, 1990.

H. Johnson, *Wine Companion Third Edition. The Encyclopedia of Wines*. London: Mitchell Beazley, 1991.

H. Johnson, J. Robinson, *The World Atlas of Wine: A Complete Guide to the Wines & Spirits of the World*. London: Mitchell Beazley, 1971.

H. Johnson, J. Robinson, *Vintage: The Story of Wine*. New York: Simon & Schuster, 1989.

A. Jullien, *Topographie de tous les vignobles connus*. Paris: L. Mathias, 1832.

M. Kramer, *Making Sense of Italian Wine*. Philadelphia: Running Press, 2006.

G. Leone, *Gualtiero Marchesi e la grande cucina italiana*. Erbusco: La Marchesiana, 2010.

S. Maccioni, P. Elliot, *Sirio. The Story of My Life and Le Cirque*. Boston: Houghton Mifflin Harcourt, 2004.

D. Maghradze A. Scienza et al., *Caucasus and Northern Black Sea Region Ampelography*. Siebeldingen: JKI Julius Kuhn Institut, 2012.

A. Maniglio Calcagno, *Architettura del paesaggio*. Bologna: Calderini, 1983.

G. Marchesi, *La cucina regionale italiana*. Milan: Mondadori, 1989.

G. Marchesi, *Sapere di sapori!*. Erbusco: La Marchesiana, 2004.

F.T. Marchi et al., *L'anima del vino. Dispensa del degustatore*. Rome: Ais Editore, 1976.

A. Marescalchi, G. Dalmasso, *Storia della vite e del vino in Italia*, vol. I, II, III. Milan: Unione Italiana Vini Editore, 1979.

M. Mariani, *Bruno e Marcello Ceretto*. Curnasco di Treviolo: Veronelli, 2007.

Masi Gruppo Tecnico, *Atti di venticinque anni di seminari al Vinitaly*, 1989–2013.

S. Micelli, *Futuro Artigiano*. Venice: Marsilio, 2011.

M. Millon, K. Millon, *The Wine Roads of Europe*. London: Nicholson, 1983.

Ministero dell'Agricoltura e Foreste - Istituto Sperimentale per la Viticoltura Conegliano, *Catalogo nazionale delle varietà di viti*, Conegliano 1988.

Ministero dell'Agricoltura e Foreste Roma, *Principali vitigni da vino coltivati in Italia*, vol. I (1960), II (1962), III (1964), IV (1965), V, indexes edited by I. Cosmo (1966). Treviso: Arti Grafiche Longo & Zoppelli, 1960–1966.

S. Mondini, *I vitigni stranieri da vino coltivati in Italia*. Florence: G. Barbera Ed.,1903.

M. Montanari, *La cultura del vino in Italia*. Milan: Skira, 2013.

M.E. Mulligan, *Let's Throw an Italian Wine Tasting!*. New York: Italian Wine Center, 1981.

G. Navarini, *I mondi del vino*. Bologna: Il Mulino, 2015.

G. Negri, E. Petrini, *Roma caput vini. La sorprendente scoperta che cambia il mondo del vino*. Milan: Mondadori, 2011.

The New Italian Wine Guide. New York: Italian Wine Center, 1984.

G. Nonino, *Lectio "Storia di una passione"*. Udine: Università degli Studi, 2006.

A. Occhipinti, *Natural Woman. La mia Sicilia, il mio vino, la mia passione*. Rome: Fandango Libri, 2013.

A.P. Odart, *Traité des cépages les plus estimés: dans tous les vignobles de quelque renom*. Paris: Ed. Ducasq, 1849.

D. Paolini (ed.), *Arte di vino. Rossi e bianchi d'eccellenza*. Verona-Genoa: Banco Popolare Gruppo Bancario-Sagep, 2012.

R. Parker, *Wine Buyer's Guide*. New York: Simon & Schuster, 1987.

F. Pedrolli, P. Sola, *Vias Wines*. Roverè della Luna: Alvin Service, 1994.

F. Pedrolli, *Conoscere il vino*. Roverè della Luna: Alvin Service, 2001.

G. Perusini, *Il Piccolit*. Udine: Tipografia Giuseppe Seitz, 1906.

A. Piccinardi, G. Sassi (eds.), *Berealto. I cento vini italiani scelta da la gola*. Milan: Mondadori, 1986.

A. Piccinardi, G. Sassi (eds.), *Il libro degli Spiriti. Cocktail, liquori e altro. Scelti per la gola*. Milan: Mondadori, 1987.

A. Piccinardi, G. Sassi, *Champagne & Spumanti 100 Champenois scelti per la gola*. Milan: Mondadori, 1988.

F. Plotkin, *Italy for the Gourmet Traveller*. New York: Little, Brown and Company, 1996.

F. Plotkin, *La Terra Fortunata. The Splendid Food and Wine of Friuli-Venezia Giulia*. New York: Broadway Books, 2001.

G. Poggi, *Atlante Ampelografico*. Pordenone: Arti Grafiche, 1939.

A. Pomodoro, *Carapace. The Tenuta Castelbuono Winery*. Bologna: Compositori, 2012.

J. Priewe, *Italiens grosse Weine*. Stuttgart: Busse Seewald, 1987.

J. Priewe, *Wein. Die Neue Grosse Schule*. Munich: Zabert Sandman, 1997.

V. Rendu, *Ampelographie française*, vol. V. Paris: Masson, 1807.

C. Rischert, *Die Weinmacher. Begegnungen in Europa*. Munich: Zaber Sandmann, 1989.

E. Rivella, *Io e Brunello*. Milan: Baldini Castoldi Dalai, 2008.

T. Robard, *Terry Robard's, New Book of Wine*. New York: G.P. Putnam's Sons, 1984.

J. Robinson, *Vines, Grapes and Wines*. New York: Alfred A. Knopf, 1986.

J. Robinson, *Le livre des cépages*. Paris: Hachette, 1988.

J. Robinson, *The Oxford Companion to Wine*. Cambridge: Oxford University Press, 1994.

G.A. Rota, N. Stefi, *Luigi Veronelli. La vita è troppo corta per bere vini cattivi*. Florence-Bra: Giunti Editore-Slow Food Editore, 2012.

G. Santarelli, *La viticoltura a Roma e nei castelli romani. Origini, sviluppo, declino, idee per la rinascita*. Rome: Pieraldo, 2013.

S.G. Scarso, *Il vino in Italia. Regione per regione guida narrata al turismo del vino*. Rome: Castelvecchi Editore, 2011.

J. Scheidegger, *Friaul Julisch-Venetien. Seine Weine und Weinmacher*. Lucerne: Edizioni Enolibri, 1992.

A. Scienza, *Oltrepò Pavese. Aspetti viticoli, enologici ed economici*. Pavia: Amministrazione Provinciale di Pavia, Logos International, 1988.

A. Scienza, "Origine del Teroldego: un'ipotesi antropologica", in *Mezzolombardo nel Campo Rotaliano, contributi, documenti per la storia antica del territorio*, M. Di Stenico, M. Welber (eds.), Rovereto 2004.

A. Scienza, *Per una storia della viticoltura umbra dalle origini all'età moderna. Da Terni ad Orvieto un territorio ed i suoi vini*. Terni: Camera di Commercio, 2004.

A. Scienza, *Atlante dei vini passiti italiani*. Savigliano: Gribaudo, 2006.

A. Scienza, *Oseleta, paradigma della viticoltura delle Venezie. Analisi storico-ampelografica e risultati sperimentali*. Verona: Fondazione MASI, 2006.

A. Scienza, *Vitigni tradizionali ed antichi italiani*. Siena: Città del vino Editore, 2006.

A. Scienza, *Cosa è la tradizione? Il vino italiano tra*

innovazione e tradizione. Vent'anni attraverso le guide delle Città del Vino. Siena: Ci.Vin, 2007.

A. Scienza, La vite ed il vino. Bologna: BCS, Art Editori, 2007.

A. Scienza, Tradizione ed innovazione per valorizzare l'originalità della viticoltura italiana, atti della conferenza internazionale delle produzioni mediterranee. Parma: UNASA, 2008.

A. Scienza, "Per una viticoltura competitiva e sostenibile", in La difesa antiperonosporica per uve di qualità. Verona: Edizioni L'Informatore Agrario, 2009.

A. Scienza, L'origine del germoplasma viticolo atesino tra eventi climatici e vicende economiche. Antichi vitigni del Trentino di Stefanini M. e Tomasi T. San Michele all'Adige: Fondazione Edmund Mach, 2010.

A. Scienza, Interesse ed attualità della vite selvatica nello studio dell'origine dei vitigni coltivati, in Origini della viticoltura, conference acts, B. Biagini (ed.). Castiglione d'Orcia: Podere Forte, 2011.

A. Scienza, "La storia delle civiltà europea raccontata attraverso l'origine dei suoi vitigni", in G. Negri, E. Petrini (eds.), Roma caput vini. La sorprendente scoperta che cambia il mondo del vino. Milan: Mondadori, 2011.

A. Scienza, "Come leggere la storia di un territorio attraverso un vitigno: la Vallagarina ed il Marzemino", in Il Marzemino trentino ad Isera. Storia e cultura di un vino e del suo territorio, A. Biondi Bartolini (ed.). Mori: La Grafica, 2012.

A. Scienza, "La cultura dell'innovazione nella produzione del vino, un processo continuo nella storia della civiltà europea", in Vino, territorio, mercato, nuove prospettive per la Valtellina, F. Di Capita, R. Pastore (eds.). Sondrio: Amministrazione Provinciale, 2012.

A. Scienza, "La nascita e lo sviluppo della viticoltura moderna in Trentino. I confini nascosti delle viticolture del Trentino: l'origine delle diversità", in Storia Regionale della Vite e del Vino in Italia, AIVV. San Michele all'Adige: Fondazione Edmund Mach, 2012.

A. Scienza, "Sweet Wines: The Essence of European Civilization", in Sweet, Reinforced and Fortified Wines. Grape Biochemistry, Technology and Vinification, F. Mencarelli, P. Tonutti (eds.). Oxford: Wiley-Blackwell, 2013.

A. Scienza, Il Grappello Ruberti nella storia della viticoltura mantovana, Quaderno 11. Mantua: Amministrazione Provinciale, 2014.

A. Scienza, "La storia della civiltà del vino in Europa raccontata attraverso il DNA dei suoi vitigni", in Le frontiere nascoste della cultura del vino, symposium acts, G. Forni, G. Kezich, A. Scienza (eds.), in "Annali di San Michele", San Michele all'Adige, no. 25, 2014.

A. Scienza et al., Dizionario dei vitigni antichi minori italiani. Siena: Ci.Vin, 2004.

A. Scienza et al., "Il Progetto Vinum: metodi di analisi del genoma e primi risultati", in Archeologia della vite e del vino in Toscana e nel Lazio, A. Cacci, P. Rendini, A. Zifferero (eds.), Quaderni del Dipartimento Archeologia e storia delle arti. Siena: Università di Siena, 2012.

A. Scienza, D. Antonacci, L'uva da tavola. Bologna: BCS, Art Editori, 2010.

A. Scienza, P. Balsari, Forme di allevamento della vite e modalità di distribuzione dei fitofarmaci. Verona: BCS, L'Informatore Agrario Editore, 2003.

A. Scienza, F. Del Zan, O. Failla, La vite e l'uomo, dal rompicapo delle origini al salvataggio delle reliquie. Gorizia: ERSA, 2004.

A. Scienza, O. Failla, "La circolazione dei vitigni in ambito padano-veneto ed atesino: le fonti storico-letterarie e l'approccio biologico-molecolare", in 2500 anni di cultura della vite nell'ambito alpino e cisalpino, G. Forni, A. Scienza (eds.). Trento: Confraternita della Vite e del Vino, 1996.

A. Scienza, O. Failla, Alla scoperta del mondo del vino per un consumo consapevole,Naples: Merqurio, 2009.

A. Scienza, O. Failla, M. Labra, "Circolazione varietale antica in ambito culturale adriatico", in L'avventura del vino nel bacino del Mediteraneo, international symposium, D. Tomasi, C. Cremonesi (eds.). Conegliano: Istituto Sperimentale per la viticoltura, 1998.

A. Scienza, S. Imazio, L'origine del Teroldego, un'ipotesi antropologica in Teroldego, un autoctono esemplare, CS Mezzolombardo 2005.

A. Scienza, S. Miele, La ricerca dell'eccellenza. Montalcino: Banfi Editore, 2007.

A. Scienza, R. Pastore, Lo Chardonnay, storia, cultura e vocazione di un nobile vitigno nel Trentino e nel mondo. Trento: Cantina La-Vis, Lavis, 2004.

A. Scienza, D. Tomasi, A. Garlato, Le Venezie: le diversità di terroir riflesse nel bicchiere. Verona: Fondazione Masi, 2011.

A. Scienza, L. Valenti, Vitigni antichi della Lombardia. Pavia: Amministrazione Provinciale, 1999.

S. Sebastiani, Mangiamo. The Sebastiani Family Cookbook. New York: Lyle Stuart Inc., 1970.

R. Sennet, The Craftsman. New Haven: Yale U Press, 2008.

L. Simonetti, Contro la decrescita. Perché rallentare non è la soluzione, Milan: Longanesi, 2014.

M. Simonit, Manuale di potatura della vite Guyot. Verona: L'Informatore agrario, 2014.

K. Singleton, Mister Amarone. The Making of an Italian Wine Phenomenon. San Francisco: Board and Bench Publishing, 2012.

Le Soste. Grandi Ristoranti e Grandi Chef. Locali d'Eccellenza Cucina d'Autore. Florence: Giunti, 2012.

E. Steinberg, The Vines of San Lorenzo. The Making of a Great Wine in the New Tradition. New York: Ecco Press, 1992.

E. Steinberg, The Making of a Great Wine. Gaja and Sori San Lorenzo. New York: Ecco Press, 1992.

T. Stevenson, Sotheby's World Wine Encyclopedia. New York: Little, Brown and Company, 1988.

T. Stevenson, Sotheby's World Wine Encyclopedia, new revised edition. London: Dorling Kindersley Limited, 1991.

T. Stevenson, World Encyclopedia of Champagne & Sparkling Wine, third edition. London: Christie's, 2013.

T. Unwin, Wine and the Vine. An Historical Geography of Viticulture and the Wine Trade. London: Routledge, 1991.

L. Veronelli, Catalogo Bolaffi dei vini del mondo, n. 1. Turin: Giulio Bolaffi Editore, 1968.

L. Veronelli, Catalogo Bolaffi dei vini d'Italia, n. 2. Turin: Giulio Bolaffi Editore, 1972.

L. Veronelli, Catalogo Bolaffi dei vini d'Italia, n. 3. Turin: Giulio Bolaffi Editore, 1974.

L. Veronelli, Catalogo Bolaffi dei vini d'Italia, n. 4. Turin: Giulio Bolaffi Editore, 1974.

L. Veronelli, Catalogo Bolaffi dei vini rossi d'Italia. Turin: Giulio Bolaffi Editore, 1980.

L. Veronelli, Catalogo dei vini del mondo. Milan: Mondadori, 1982.

L. Veronelli, Guide Veronelli all'Italia piacevole. Milan: Garzanti, 1968.

L. Veronelli, I vignaioli storici, vol. I. Milan: Mediolanum Editori Associati, 1986.

L. Veronelli, I vignaioli storici, vol. II. Milan: Mediolanum Editori Associati, 1987.

L. Veronelli, I vignaioli storici, vol. IV. Milan: Mediolanum Editori Associati, 1989.

L. Veronelli, I vini d'Italia. Rome: Canesi Editore, 1961.

P. Viala, V. Vermorel, Ampelographie, vols. I, II, III, IV, V, VI, VII. Paris: Masson, 1909.

M. Vidoudez et al., Great Wines of the World. New York: Crescent Books, 1982.

G.C. Villafranchi, Oenologia toscana o sia memoria sopra i vini ed in specie toscani. Florence: Gaetano Cambiagi Stamp. Granducale, 1773.

S. and P. Wasserman, Italy's Noble Red Wines. New York: Sun Designs, 1987.

Wines of Italy. Rome: Italian Institute for Foreign Commerce, 2005.

Index of Winemakers

Index of Names

Photo Credits

The publisher would like to thank for their contribution
Arnaldo Caprai Società Agricola
Eugenio Collavini Viticoltori
Ferrari F.lli Lunelli
Azienda Agricola Conte Loredan Gasparini
Fernando Pighin & Figli
Conte Tasca d'Almerita
Tonutti Tecniche Grafiche